How to Manage
Project Opportunity and Risk

How to Manage Project Opportunity and Risk

Why *uncertainty* management can be a *much* better approach than *risk* management

The updated and re-titled 3rd edition of *Project Risk Management: Processes, Insights and Techniques*

Chris Chapman and Stephen Ward
University of Southampton
School of Management

A John Wiley and Sons, Ltd, Publication

Library of Congress Cataloging-in-Publication Data

Chapman, C. B.
    How to manage project opportunity and risk: why uncertainty management can be a much better approach than risk management/Chris Chapman and Stephen Ward.—3rd ed.
        p. cm.
    Rev. ed. of : Project risk management, c 2003.
    Summary: "Based on a sound conceptual foundation yet developed to meet practical concerns, Project Risk Management has become recognized as a standard work on its subject"—Provided by publisher.
    ISBN 978-0-470-68649-2 (hardback)
        1. Project management. 2. Risk management. I. Ward, Stephen (Stephen C.) II. Chapman, C. B., Project risk management. III. Title.
    T56.8.C52 2012
    658.4′04—dc23

                                                                                    2011035194

A catalogue record for this book is available from the British Library.

ISBN 978-0-470-68649-2 (hbk) ISBN 978-1-119-96263-2 (ebk)
ISBN 978-1-119-96666-1 (ebk) ISBN 978-1-119-96665-4 (ebk)

Set in 9/13pt Kuenstler by MPS Limited, a Macmillan Company, Chennai, India
Printed and bound by CPI Group (UK) Ltd., Croydon, CRO 4YY

For pessimists who want to release their inner optimist,
optimists who want to fully exploit their inner pessimist,
analysts who want to keep in touch with their common sense,
decision makers who want to understand their advisors.

Contents

Foreword to this edition

I am surely in a large majority in welcoming this new and substantially revised edition of the 1997 classic on risk management by Chris Chapman and Stephen Ward, two eminent authorities on the subject.

As mentioned in the book, Chris Chapman and I have worked together on a number of strategic consulting assignments and with Stephen Ward and others have collaborated in the development of RAMP and other risk management initiatives. From this I have gained a high degree of respect for Chris and Stephen's deep and wide understanding of risk management in all its forms.

Like the earlier editions, this book is wide ranging and thorough in its treatment of all aspects of the subject, particularly in regard to project risk management. It responds to the need for an update to reflect this fast developing field of risk management.

I am delighted to see that the focus has moved on to management of opportunities as well as risks, and that the book emphasises the crucial importance of uncertainty. Chris and I may differ on the precise definition of 'uncertainty' (which I describe as 'incomplete or imperfect knowledge' —i.e. lack of required information for decision making), but we are at one in believing that to date risk management has unduly and prematurely concentrated on identifying and analysing risk events. A much better return from the effort involved is first to assess systematically the information needed for decisions in pursuit of objectives; and only after this has been done to move on to evaluating risk events. The book makes a valuable contribution by putting management of uncertainty at the core of the recommended approach to risk management.

I am also pleased the book refers to the value of range estimating (based on confidence intervals) rather than spot estimates, which we recommended and helped to implement in the Highways Agency. This can help to avoid creating false expectations about the out-turn costs of projects when they are at an early stage where there is a high degree of uncertainty about their final scope and hence any single cost estimate is likely to be unreliable.

Three other points made which I particularly applaud are:

- decomposing all relevant uncertainty in a structured way which can avoid relying on optimism bias with its crude adjustment factors;
- the erroneous idea held by many that a defined or common approach in risk management is sufficient, when frequently it is neither best nor even good practice;
- increased reference to 'risk efficiency', and its extension to cover 'opportunity efficiency' and 'clarity efficiency'.

For these and other reasons too numerous to mention, I am very pleased to commend this book to readers whatever their levels of expertise in the management of risk.

Mike Nichols
Chairman & Chief Executive, The Nichols Group
Chairman, Association for Project Management
Board Member, Major Projects Association
Chairman, British Standards Institution Standards Policy and Strategy Committee

Foreword to the second edition

The analysis of risk and the development of risk management processes have come a long way over the last ten years, even since the late 1990s. Hence the need for a second edition of Chapman and Ward's *Project Risk Management*, first published in 1997.

They not only continue to push back the boundaries, Chapman has also been involved in the development of work aimed at practitioners – PRAM (Association for Project Management) and RAMP (Institution of Civil Engineers and Faculty/Institute of Actuaries). They importantly make comparisons between their work and both PRAM and RAMP, as well as with the Project Management Institute's PMBOK 2000. They have developed and named the generic framework SHAMPU (Shape, Harness, and Manage Project Uncertainty) process and compare it with PRAM, RAMP and PMBOK 2000. I suggest that the authors of these three will want to use SHAMPU as a challenge to their own further thinking.

Chapman and Ward say that their book is largely about how to achieve effective and efficient risk management in the context of a single project. Determining what can be simplified, and what it is appropriate to simplify, is not a simple matter! In their final chapter they adopt a corporate perspective on project risk management processes. Thus they mirror the work already under way by the ICE/Actuaries team who have embarked on the development of STRATrisk, designed to enable prime decision makers to deal more systematically with the most important opportunities and threats to their business.

They quote Walsham who has suggested a management framework which views organizational change as a jointly analytical, educational and political process where important interacting dimensions are the context, content and process of the change. They conclude by stating that 'most project risk is generated by the way different people perceive issues and react to them'. Those of us who have driven such projects as the Hong Kong Mass Railway (very successfully) and the Channel Tunnel (less so) will say 'hear, hear' to all of that.

Professor Tony M. Ridley
Imperial College London
Past President, Institution of Civil Engineers

Update to the foreword to the second edition

Since I wrote the Foreword for the second edition of this book, risk management processes have become much more widely used, but controversy about what should be done and how best to do it has grown. In this third edition Chapman and Ward clarify the nature of this controversy, explain why common practices fail, and offer practical solutions. They reshape successful perspectives, widely used in practice, with new simplifications that have worked, guided by deeper background understanding. This will inform the appropriate application of RAMP and PRAM processes, and how ERM needs to be developed.

Managing risk is a risky business. Chapman and Ward provide an in-depth explanation of why it is important to understand and manage underlying uncertainty in all its forms, in order to realize opportunities more fully and enhance corporate performance. They show what best practice should look like. The implications go well beyond the conventional wisdom of project risk management, providing an enlightening new perspective.

Professor Tony M. Ridley
Imperial College London
Past President, Institution of Civil Engineers

Foreword to the first edition

All projects involve risk – the zero risk project is not worth pursuing. This is not purely intuitive but also a recognition that acceptance of some risk is likely to yield a more desirable and appropriate level of benefit in return for the resources committed to the venture. Risk involves both threat and opportunity. Organizations that better understand the nature of risks and can manage them more effectively cannot only avoid unforeseen disasters but can work with tighter margins and less contingency, freeing resources for other endeavours, and seizing opportunities for advantageous investment that might otherwise be rejected as 'too risky'.

Risk is present in every aspect of our lives; thus risk management is universal but in most circumstances an unstructured activity, based on common sense, relevant knowledge, experience and instinct. Project management has evolved over recent years into a fully-fledged professional discipline characterized by a formalized body of knowledge and the definition of systematic processes for the execution of a project. Yet project risk management has, until recently, generally been considered as an 'add-on' instead of being integral to the effective practice of project management.

This book provides the framework for integrating risk management into the management of projects. It explains how to do this through the definition of generic risk management processes and shows how these processes can be mapped onto the stages of the project lifecycle. As the disciplines of formal project management are being applied ever more widely (e.g., to the management of change within organizations) so the generic project risk management processes set out here will readily find use in diverse areas of application.

The main emphasis is on processes rather than analytical techniques, which are already well documented. The danger in formalized processes is that they can become orthodox, bureaucratic, burdened with procedures, so that the practitioner loses sight of the real aims. This book provides the reader with a fundamental understanding of project risk management processes but avoids being over prescriptive in the description of the execution of these processes. Instead, there is positive encouragement to use these generic processes as a starting point for elaboration and adaptation to suit the circumstances of a particular application, to innovate and experiment, to simplify and streamline the practical implementation of the generic processes to achieve cost effective and efficient risk management.

The notion of risk efficiency is central to the theme. All risk management processes consume valuable resources and can themselves constitute a risk to the project that must be effectively managed. The level of investment in risk management within projects must be challenged and justified on the level of expected benefit to the overall project. Chris Chapman and Steve Ward document numerous examples drawn from real project experience to substantiate the benefits of a formal process-oriented approach. Ultimately, project risk management is about people making decisions to try to optimize the outcome, being proactive in evaluating risk and the possible responses, using this information to best effect, demonstrating the need for changes in project plans, taking the necessary action and monitoring the effects. Balancing risk and expectation is one of the most challenging aspects of project management. It can also be exciting and offer great satisfaction, provided the project manager is able to operate in a climate of understanding and openness about project risk. The cultural change required in organizations to achieve this can be difficult and lengthy, but there is no doubt that it will be easier to accomplish if risk management processes are better understood and integrated into the practice of project management.

This book is a welcome and timely addition to the literature on risk management and will be of interest to all involved in project management as well as offering new insights to the project risk analyst.

Peter Wakeling
Director of Procurement Policy (Project Management)
Ministry of Defence (Procurement Executive)

Preface and overview by the authors

Projects are about the planning and delivery of beneficial change. This beneficial change may involve the creation of a desired physical asset or some less tangible organizational change. In either case, the pursuit of opportunities is an inherent central concern. Throughout any project what can be achieved is subject to uncertainty and risk, both of which require careful management alongside an ongoing search for opportunities to improve performance. This book explains how and why uncertainty management should be employed in all projects to pursue all opportunities in the face of uncertainty and risk. This approach goes well beyond what can be achieved with most risk management practice.

The target readership for this book includes two groups of experienced professionals. One group is director level senior managers who would like to broaden the scope and effectiveness of their organization's current 'risk management' process capability for projects, operations and corporate strategy contexts – what some refer to as enterprise risk management (ERM). The second group is those involved in implementing that capability in a projects context. Aspiring members of both these groups are also target readers. This is a very broad target audience, beyond the scope of all 'project risk management' books.

In part the wide target readership is driven by the wide scope of the 'project' concept which we believe needs to be addressed. In broad terms a corporate view of 'projects' includes projects of all types and sizes, from the small and simple to the large and complex, including programmes and portfolios of programmes, fully integrated with associated corporate operations and corporate strategy. This book uses 'project' in this broad sense, with a direct concern for the whole lifecycle of projects and the associated deliverable asset or organizational change, from conception to termination. In all cases links between projects, operations and corporate strategy are part of the corporate perspective, and enhancing corporate performance is the basic concern. This goes well beyond the scope of common project risk management practice – one component of 'the bigger picture' this book addresses.

In part the very wide target audience for this book is also driven by a belief that whether experienced or not, board members or aspiring project management team members, all managers need a clear understanding of what an effective and efficient uncertainty management process for clarifying opportunity and risk can achieve, and in broad terms how and where it can be used. This kind of 'uncertainty management' approach goes well beyond the scope of common practice 'risk management' in any context. *All* managers *at all levels* also need to understand why much common practice risk management is seriously limited in comparison, and why a change of approach is warranted.

In our view much common practice 'risk management' – often misleadingly treated as 'best practice' because it is common practice and seems compliant with guides and standards – is riddled with bad practice features, attempting inappropriate tasks using inadequate concepts and tools. Limitations include insufficient scope, inappropriate working assumptions, and limited objectives in terms of pursuing opportunities to improve performance. Typically project risk management is regarded as a process for 'keeping things on track' by identifying potentially adverse 'risk events' or threats to performance, and aspiring to neutralize them. Most current guides and standards acknowledge the potential for favourable events or opportunities, and addressing uncertainty is now firmly on the agenda of all the guides we are involved with. However, common practice project risk management does not provide a convincing basis for understanding all relevant aspects of uncertainty and exploring all feasible opportunities to enhance corporate performance. The underlying basis for this understanding goes well beyond project risk management and involves a number of 'bigger picture' concerns. Comprehensive treatment of uncertainty beyond the scope of guides and standards is essential to transform common practice.

In addition to planning and implementation processes, governance processes also should be informed by the understanding an uncertainty management approach can bring. Such governance goes well beyond simply looking for an approach that is compliant with guides or standards. Setting aside uncertainty management issues which really matter as 'too difficult', because they are not readily addressed by existing risk management processes, is unprofessional and unacceptable in our view. This is especially so in a governance context. Effective governance of investment decisions and projects is a very important further 'bigger picture' concern.

Risk needs to be seen in terms of downside implications of any sources of uncertainty when commitments are made. Shaping plans to achieve a minimum level of risk for any given level of expected performance for all relevant objectives at any given stage of the project lifecycle should be a core concern. Opportunity needs a broad interpretation that embraces all ways to improve performance, including creative and lateral thinking in formulating plans, exploitation of favourable circumstances, and seeking better tradeoffs between all objectives. This includes objectives which are not measurable. It also includes process considerations. In particular, it includes exploiting improvements in practice that make decisions easier to make and easier to defend whatever the eventual outcome.

Effective management of corporate performance in any context requires an appreciation of the sources of uncertainty that can have a significant effect on future performance at a level of decomposition which reflects their importance and corporate capability to do something about them. 'Risk events' in projects, that may or may not occur, need to be seen as just part of a broad view of uncertainty that also includes sources of ambiguity, inherent variability and systemic uncertainty. Recognised lack of certainty has to include 'the unknowable', but sometimes uncertainty is usefully viewed as 'incomplete knowledge' which can be reduced at a cost or by the unfolding of the project lifecycle. Determining how the lifecycle should unfold has to consider these relationships from a different angle. All sources of uncertainty require attention, at an appropriate level of decomposition for the lifecycle position and process objectives. 'Risk events' are often the least important uncertainties.

In this book, 'best practice' is given a systematic basis using three component 'efficiency' concepts: risk efficiency, clarity efficiency, and opportunity efficiency.

'Risk efficiency' is the lowest level of risk for any given level of expected performance. Risk efficiency can be demonstrated graphically for all measurable performance criteria. It should be sought for all non-measurable criteria that matter as well as for all measurable criteria that matter. Risk efficiency matters because less risk for more expected reward is an opportunity that matters.

'Clarity efficiency' is the lowest level of effort for any given level of insight about upside and downside aspects of uncertainty which can be communicated to relevant parties. Clarity efficiency matters because less effort for more reward matters. Clarity efficiency is a function of the concepts and processes used to shape plans and decisions.

'Opportunity efficiency' requires risk efficiency and clarity efficiency, plus appropriate tradeoffs between risk and expected outcomes for all objectives, plus appropriate tradeoffs between all objectives. Opportunity efficiency matters because better tradeoffs between risk and expected outcomes and better tradeoffs between all objectives matters.

A key feature of this book is using plain English and common colloquial interpretations of key words like 'risk', 'opportunity' and 'uncertainty'. We shape perceptions about how these words are used by a limited number of explicit working assumptions, like our definitions of risk efficiency, clarity efficiency and opportunity efficiency. We explicitly go beyond the long legacy of conflicting and limiting technical definitions of terms like 'risk' which cripple current common practice.

An opportunity can still be seen in a colloquial sense as a situation where doing something desirable is easier than usual, and colloquial interpretations of other terms are still part of the language available. However, these three efficiency concepts collectively clarify why 'best' practice is very different from what many argue is 'good' practice, and why best practice involves a revolution relative to common practice.

All the central concepts and tools in this book have been used in successful practice since the 1970s, but they are more clearly explained in this book than in earlier publications by the authors, using simpler language and particularly simple but very effective recent applications, including a successful 2007 re-estimation exercise of a £20 billion portfolio of major road projects undertaken with the UK Highways Agency.

The way we choose to look at things matters. The concepts and words used to analyse situations and communicate our insights matter. They are part of the scope for opportunities that matter addressed in this book. Although all the words used in this book have plain English meanings, interpretations are carefully shaped using explicit working assumptions, as part of avoiding the implicit framing assumptions which plague common practice. This is part of 'keeping it simple systematically', a redefinition of the KISS acronym, 'keep it simple, stupid', which can lead to simplistic approaches which limit opportunities. It is also part of 'the big picture'.

We believe it is *very* important to think in terms of 'uncertainty' management while continuing to talk to everybody involved in whatever 'risk' management terms they are comfortable with. 'Legacy' issues are very important, in many ways. We understand that managers and consultants with an emotional, intellectual or financial investment in 'risk management' may not rush to embrace the replacement of a risk management perspective. However, it is important to appreciate that some obvious truths from an uncertainty management perspective are very difficult to communicate in the language of risk management. This is one of the inherent flaws in a risk management approach.

One of our very helpful informal reviewers has suggested that common practice risk management is a bankrupt concept which this book replaces. This may be putting it a bit too strongly. Some aspects of common practice can be reinterpreted in a broader framework and used very effectively. But most common practice starts in the wrong place with an inappropriate destination and inadequate tools. This book is not about marginal enhancements to current common practice thinking. It is about significant revisions to current orthodoxy. The fact that most of the key ideas have been used successfully in practice for more than a quarter century is evidence of a difficulty we now see as a clear opportunity, and we urge our readers to take the same view. Organizations that successfully adopt an uncertainty management perspective will have a significant advantage over those that do not.

This change in perspective is essential to capture all the benefits of seeing opportunity from a corporate perspective as the reason we undertake most projects. Uncertainty of all kinds needs to be regarded as a significant challenge for many projects, beginning with the first estimate of cost. Risk is sometimes important, but sometimes it is incidental, provided it is managed effectively and efficiently. Everyone involved in projects needs to start moving towards a plain English interpretation of all basic terms, avoiding restrictive technical definitions which limit and distort thinking. And everyone involved in projects needs to accept that repeated failure to deliver what others are expecting is just not good enough. This includes those at director level responsible for the governance of projects. Debate about how this is best done is futile if basic terms at a plain English level are not employed, coupled to explicit working assumptions which can be discussed and tested, avoiding the implicit framing assumptions built into most current guides and standards.

While the focus of this book is uncertainty management in a project context, many of the core issues are wider, and the wider applicability of the approach adopted here is important. Organizations need to speak the same language and use the same basic concepts when addressing opportunity, uncertainty and risk in any part of the organization. The implications of this for operations management, corporate level strategic management and what some see as enterprise risk management are not addressed directly until Parts III and IV, but this generality is a core aspect of our approach.

The foundations of a bigger picture view of uncertainty management for operations, corporate strategy and enterprises as a whole should be clear by the end of Chapter 16, but the focus of this book is projects.

What this book is about

This book is about transforming *corporate* performance by significantly improving *project* performance in terms of all relevant objectives. The basis for this transformation is clarifying opportunity and risk using effective project uncertainty management processes. By 'clarifying' we mean developing insight which can be shared with appropriate parties, and for this to occur, effective communication is essential. This book argues that effective formal uncertainty management processes for projects are an essential component of effective formal approaches to project management and to overall corporate management. It also suggests that the same uncertainty and project management principles are an essential part of effective informal approaches. This book is about asking the right questions, and shaping thinking effectively and efficiently, with a focus on process issues and underlying concepts.

The focus of this book is generic 'performance uncertainty management processes' (PUMPs), designed to clarify uncertainty, opportunity and risk in all kinds of projects and organizations. The emphasis is the strategy-shaping stages of the project lifecycle, in particular shaping the development of project execution and delivery strategy plans. However, a fully integrated approach to the whole lifecycle is addressed, using a 'PUMP pack' – a set of related PUMPs for all relevant lifecycle stages, from project conception through to termination. The project lifecycle structure described in Chapter 1 defines the PUMP pack structure. A key feature of the PUMP approach is attention to lifecycle issues.

Treating project management and project uncertainty management as closely coupled processes is central to the approach taken in this book. In practice, some separation is usually essential, because different people and different organizations may be involved, and because most people are most effective if they focus on one task at a time. However, the separability should be limited, to avoid working with inappropriate assumptions about independence between project management and uncertainty management processes that can prove very expensive. Effective use of separability is a key aspect of any practical approach to complex situations, and it should be a feature of all integrated and holistic approaches.

A key message in this book is the need to start to understand project uncertainty management by understanding processes. The details of models or techniques or computer software are important, but they are not of direct concern here.

One important characteristic of all effective processes is flexibility in different application contexts, avoiding a simplistic 'one size fits all' approach. This flexibility needs to accommodate the transition from formal to informal processes. It also needs to span projects which are as diverse as those interested in projects want to make them.

Most organizations will want PUMPs which are 'specific', in the sense that generic processes have been adapted to the kind of projects they usually deal with. This tailoring to specific corporate needs can be seen as the first step in a process of tailoring each application of any PUMP to the project being addressed. A key feature of both specific and generic PUMPs is a built-in adaptation of the process to what matters in each individual project context, adjusted each time the process is applied over that project's lifecycle. The rationale for such adaptations is the achievement of 'clarity efficiency', which involves delivering an appropriate form and level of clarity at the least cost in terms of immediate effort and other background or overhead costs. Understanding the available process choices and the potential cost of inappropriate project and process decisions are central issues. Clarifying how very simple, low effort PUMPs can deliver appropriate clarity in a variety of project contexts is a key feature of this book.

The layout of this book

This book is in four parts. Part I sets the scene and introduces basic uncertainty management concepts, including PUMPs. Part II explores the nature of PUMPs in detail, with a focus on one particular project lifecycle stage – the execution and delivery strategy development stage, when this aspect of plans at a strategic level is shaped. Part III generalizes the deployment of PUMPs to all other project lifecycle stages. Part IV explores key corporate implications.

Part I: Setting the scene (Chapters 1–4)

Chapter 1 introduces a broadly defined 'project' concept as part of a wider context involving an organization's strategy, operations and asset portfolios. It then explores the wide range of sources of uncertainty that can affect project performance. Two fundamental frameworks are discussed – a 12-stage project or asset/change lifecycle, and the seven-Ws framework: the who (parties involved), why (motives), what (design of the product of the project), whichway (plans for relationships and contracts, business case purposes, operations and activities), wherewithal (resources for operations and activities), when (integration of all timing questions) and where (the location of the project and wider context issues). These two frameworks are used throughout the book to clarify the context in which uncertainty management operates and the range of uncertainty management issues that need to be addressed. A third framework distinguishes uncertainty associated with events, inherent variability, systemic relationships and ambiguity – linking this to the idea that we generally deal with composites of all four, decomposing these composites as appropriate. Chapter 1 also introduces a basis for distinguishing uncertainty viewed for performance management purposes and uncertainty viewed for all other knowledge acquisition purposes.

Chapter 2 uses a 'minimum clarity' approach to quantifying uncertainty about future performance when this is useful. Opportunity and risk implications are distinguished. Relatively simple forms of quantification are used to illustrate key issues in effective and efficient quantification and evaluation of uncertainty. The importance of uncertainty which is not usefully quantified is explored briefly. The severe limitations of a risk event perspective using probability-impact grids are also discussed.

Chapter 3 describes the key motives for formal uncertainty management processes. These include developing and sustaining trust between key parties, and communicating an understanding of uncertainty via the use of 'clarity efficient' processes. Clarity efficiency and risk efficiency are parts of the opportunity efficiency view of best practice considered in this chapter. Other key motives discussed are the benefits of documentation, the value of quantitative analysis which facilitates distinguishing between targets, expectations and commitments, and related culture changes.

Chapter 4 outlines the basic seven-phase generic project uncertainty management process (PUMP) framework and the related PUMP pack. This framework is compared with a number of other published frameworks, as a basis for understanding the transferable nature of the concepts developed in the rest of this book for users of alternative process frameworks.

Part II: The generic process in one key lifecycle stage (Chapters 5–11)

Part II elaborates the basic seven-phase generic process of Chapter 4, one chapter per phase. The elaborations are a distillation of processes we have found effective and efficient in practice. This is 'theory grounded in practice', in the sense that it is an attempt to provide a systematic and structured description of what has to be done, and in what order, to achieve the deliverables each phase should produce. It is a model of an idealized process, intended to provide an understanding of the nature of uncertainty management processes. This model needs to be adapted to the specific terrain of specific studies to be useful. Examples are provided to help to link the idealized process back to the practice they are based on, to facilitate their application in practice.

Much of what most experienced professional analysts do is craft, based on craft skills learned the hard way by experience. Part II is an attempt to explain systematically as much as we can in a particular generic process context, indicating along the way areas where craft skills are particularly important. Some specific technique is also provided, but technique in terms of the 'nuts and bolts' or mechanics of processes is not the focus of this book.

Part III: The generic process in all lifecycle stages (Chapters 12 and 13)

Part II assumes a focus on one key project lifecycle stage to describe the basic seven-phase generic PUMP framework outlined in Chapter 4 of Part I. Part III relaxes this assumption to address the use of a PUMP in all other stages of the lifecycle.

Chapter 12 explores the implications of using a PUMP in all strategy development stages of the project lifecycle – all the stages prior to a watershed when strategy development ends (in principle) and strategy implementation begins. The primary concern is strategy shaping, continuing with the Part II focus. Strategy shaping is decomposed into three parts in the Chapter 1 lifecycle structure: concept strategy shaping; design, operation and termination strategy shaping; execution and delivery strategy shaping. Separate gateway processes involving consolidation and governance for each of these three strategy-shaping stages are also addressed.

Chapter 13 explores the implications of using PUMPs in the strategy implementation stages of the project lifecycle. In practice, strategy implementation may have to revisit strategy formation, reshaping strategic plans as detailed plans evolve and execution and delivery progress.

Part IV: Key corporate implications (Chapters 14–16)

Chapter 14 takes a corporate perspective and considers what is involved in establishing and sustaining an organization's project uncertainty management capability.

Chapter 15 addresses uncertainty and risk ownership issues in corporate terms, considering a contractor's perspective, and the need to align client and contractor motivation. Similar behavioural issues arise with intra-organizational relationships and governance.

Chapter 16 considers the implications of a PUMP approach for developing corporate capability to manage uncertainty beyond common practice enterprise risk management. Implications include the need to develop corporate capabilities in respect of organizational learning, an appropriate organizational culture, appropriate human resource capability, and decision support for addressing uncertainty.

Changes for the third edition

This book is a much extended and updated edition of *Project Risk Management* (Chapman and Ward, 1997 and 2003). *All* readers of previous editions will find it worth treating this third edition as a new book, to assimilate the full implications of the new perspective in the intended holistic terms. Readers of the first two editions who still believe that common practice approaches involve no fundamental problems, and that common practice approaches can be used as a basis for more sophisticated approaches like those outlined in earlier editions of this book, need to take this advice particularly seriously.

The mindset this book provides is consistent with earlier editions, but this edition clarifies ambiguities in earlier thinking and explanations. An uncertainty management perspective was implicit in the 1970s applications which underpinned the early risk management thinking developed by the authors. This uncertainty management perspective was explicit by the late 1990s, but the first edition of this book was still couched in conventional 'risk management' terms. By the 2003 second edition 'risks' had become 'sources of uncertainty' – a partial move away from risk management terminology. This movement has been very enlightening for the authors and our recent clients, especially when higher than anticipated levels of insight and clarity have been important and deliverable for low levels of effort. But this edition is our first book to fully embrace and exploit an uncertainty management perspective, suggesting that all readers embrace the idea of thinking in uncertainty management terms, even though they may have to speak the risk management language of those they need to converse with. Some clients took our advice to do this in the late 1990s, and it worked for them. We understand the risk of moving too quickly, but think the time is now right for an 'enlightened gamble' on our part. Whether or not the reader fully follows this lead, we think the new insights provided by thinking in uncertainty management terms, to fully clarify opportunity and risk, are well worth the mindset shift involved.

The structure of this book is similar to the second edition. However, the second edition Part II has been split into two parts, there has been some rearrangement of material between chapters, and the text has been substantially revised throughout. There are some important changes in basic definitions, which start in Chapter 1. The purpose is greater clarity, reflecting the evolution of our thinking within the spirit of earlier definitions. An important aspect of revisions has been to clarify the scope and significance of an uncertainty management perspective which addresses opportunity as a key priority and uncertainty associated with ambiguity in a wide variety of forms.

Several chapters contain new material and additional examples. In particular, Chapters 1–4, and 12–16 have been significantly revised in scope with new material.

An extended Chapter 1 now combines material from chapters 1 and 2 of the previous edition with new material contextualizing projects in corporate strategy and operations and clarifying the nature of project uncertainty. The project lifecycle has been elaborated to distinguish more clearly between strategy, tactics, associated gateways, and the asset utilization phase of the lifecycle. The relationships which link performance uncertainty to plans have been clarified. The composite nature of sources of uncertainty is explored. Discussion in all following chapters has been revised to reflect these changes.

Chapter 2 is a new chapter. Its focus is clarifying the difference between uncertainty, risk and opportunity, and some common sources of confusion about these terms. It also provides an introduction to some other key concepts and tools with a focus on very simple examples.

Chapter 3 provides more complex examples and completes the explanation of clarity, risk and opportunity efficiency.

Chapter 4 has been updated to reflect recent developments. It begins with new material concerning generic features of process frameworks and associated professional guidance. The basic PUMP process described here is a truncated version of the SHAMPU process of the second edition.

Chapters 5–11, Part II, integrate discussion of high and low clarity approaches to each of the seven basic PUMP phases, drawing on the previous edition chapter 15 material. Otherwise these chapters are relatively unchanged. Those who want a quick understanding of what is new in this third edition could skim read or skip Part II on a first pass.

Chapters 12 and 13, Part III, are a recasting of chapters 12–14 in the previous edition, with a significant increase in scope and clarity because of earlier revisions.

Chapter 14, the first Part IV chapter, is a revised version of chapter 17 in the previous edition.

Chapter 15, on contracts and relationship management, is a revised version of chapter 16 in the previous edition, with additional new material on multidimension incentive contracts and intra-organizational relationships and governance.

Chapter 16 is a new chapter for this edition, with all new material. It sets project uncertainty management in the context of overall corporate performance.

Acknowledgements

The foundation of all the concepts developed in this book is the authors' work with clients via a number of consulting firms on particular issues for specific projects over more than 30 years. This practical experience was shaped in part by working with both clients and professional bodies on generic processes. This grounding fed a research process concerned with synthesizing the authors' hands-on practical experience, its distillation in publications including synthesis with the broader literature, and feeding new insights back into practice in an ongoing iterative process.

The first process that the authors were involved in directly contained most of the key features of the PUMPs described in this book. The process was developed with BP (British Petroleum at that time) for their offshore North Sea projects by Acres International Management Services, beginning in 1976. It was successfully implemented on the Magnus project, then mandated world wide for all large or sensitive BP projects. It was referred to as SCERT (Synergistic Contingency Evaluation and Review Technique) for publication purposes (Chapman, 1979), to reflect its evolution from PERT (Program Evaluation and Review Technique) and PERT's numerous derivatives (Moder and Philips, 1970). It provides useful examples of some 'high clarity' PUMP features, drawn on throughout this book.

BP's attractiveness as an exemplar client was severely damaged by the April 2010 Deepwater Horizon accident in the Gulf of Mexico. However, effective use of SCERT would have avoided the Deepwater Horizon scenario, and useful lessons can be learned from failures as well as successes. Barriers to developing *and maintaining* corporate capability are addressed in Part IV.

An IBM culture change programme started in 1990, to which both authors contributed, laid the foundations for a number of 'minimum clarity' (easy to use) concepts developed in this book.

An important recent contribution to our thinking was two consulting assignments Chris Chapman undertook with Mike Nichols and The Nichols Group for the Highways Agency (Nichols, 2007; Hopkinson et al., 2008). These assignments led to useful illustrations of several important PUMP features, including 'low effort' approaches to unbiased estimates of project cost and significantly clarifying the role of all uncertainty beyond the event-based risk on which common practice is focused.

Preparing two recent publications (Chapman, 2008; Chapman and Harwood, 2011) and the underlying work for the former also contributed to our thinking about minimum clarity approaches.

The development of the process chapter in the Association for Project Management (APM) PRAM (Project Risk Analysis and Management) Guide (APM, 1997, 2004) significantly influenced

PUMP, to the extent that the chapter structure of the first edition of this book was changed more than half way through writing it to reflect the agreed PRAM process description. The slightly different processes described in the first two editions of this book can be interpreted as elaborations of this PRAM process. The PUMP pack of this edition can be interpreted as a synthesis of earlier edition processes, the RAMP (Risk Analysis and Management of Projects) process developed by the Institution of Civil Engineers (ICE) and the Actuarial Profession (ICE & AP, 1998, 2005), and other more recent developments.

The basis of the project lifecycle material in Chapter 1 is the *International Journal of Project Management*, Volume 13, S.C. Ward and C.B. Chapman, 'A risk management perspective on the project life cycle', pages 145–149, copyright 1995, with kind permission from Elsevier, PO Box 800, Oxford OX5 1GB, UK.

Chapter 15 uses material reprinted from the *International Journal of Project Management*, Volume 12, S.C. Ward and C.B. Chapman, 'Choosing contractor payment terms', pages 216–221, copyright 1994; Volume 9, S.C. Ward, C.B. Chapman and B. Curtis, 'On the allocation of risk in construction projects', pages 140–147, copyright 1991; and Volume 9, S.C. Ward and C.B. Chapman, 'Extending the use of risk analysis in project management', pages 117–123, copyright 1991; with kind permission from Elsevier, Oxford OX5 1GB, UK.

Chapters 14 and 16 includes some extracts from Stephen Ward *Risk Management Organisation and Context*, copyright 2005, with permission from the Institute of Risk Management, 6 Lloyd's avenue, London, EC3N 3AX, and Witherby & Co. Ltd, London .

Figures 8.2, 11.5 and 11.6 are reproduced from C.B. Chapman, D.F. Cooper and M.J. Page, *Management for Engineers*, John Wiley & Sons Ltd; Figures 8.3 and 14.1 are reproduced by permission of the Operational Research Society, Seymour House, 12 Edward Street, Birmingham B1 2RX, UK.

The authors would like to acknowledge the contributions of a large number of colleagues we have worked for and with over a number of years, and the seminar participants and students who have taught us important lessons. It would be inappropriate to list them and their contributions, but we would like to express our gratitude. Five people who were generous with their time reviewing this edition to good effect do need a mention: Matthew Leitch, Stephen Cresswell, Martin Hopkinson, John Gierlach and Michael Annon. Any errors or omissions are entirely our own.

Part I

Setting the scene

Part I sets the scene, introducing key concepts used throughout the rest of the book in Chapters 1–4.

Chapter 1 considers the nature of uncertainty in and around projects. It begins by considering the nature of projects, and the relationship between project management, strategic management and operations management. It then considers the implications of the project lifecycle, using a nominal 12-stage framework which can be adapted to any organization's preferred structure. This helps to clarify the context in which project uncertainty management operates and a range of project management issues that uncertainty management needs to address. For example, the nature of the process used to manage project uncertainty should be driven by when in the lifecycle it is used. Within this project lifecycle structure, the seven Ws are considered: 'who' (parties involved), 'why' (motives), 'what' (design of the product of the project), 'whichway' (plans for relationships and contracts, business case purposes, operations and activities), 'wherewithal' (resources for operations and activities), 'when' (integration of all timing questions) and 'where' (the location of the project and wider context issues). The role of inherent variability, ambiguity and systemic relationships in addition to events is then explored briefly, followed by an introduction to the use of a 'performance lens' and a 'knowledge lens' to view uncertainty for different purposes, and a final linking conceptual framework to prepare for Chapter 2.

Chapter 2 uses all the basic definitions and linking conceptual frameworks from Chapter 1 to explore the nature of uncertainty in terms of its relationship with opportunity and risk. It first introduces a 'minimum clarity' approach to quantifying uncertainty. This practical tool is also an important conceptual framework. It is used to explain the distinction between targets, expected outcomes and commitments. The linked 'opportunity/risk datum' concept is then introduced and its subjective and ambiguous nature is explored. In this framework a 'clarity efficiency' concept is introduced, concerned with maximizing insight which can be communicated for any given level of analysis effort and cost, and choosing an appropriate level of clarity. This framework is then used to consider a generalization of Markowitz's 'risk efficiency' concept, the conceptual basis of 'risk' used in this book. A linked 'opportunity efficiency' concept is also introduced, a key conceptual framework.

Chapter 3 describes the key motives for formal 'performance uncertainty management processes' (PUMPs). These include the benefits of documentation, the value of quantitative analysis which facilitates distinguishing between targets, expectations and commitments, the pursuit of risk efficient ways of carrying out a project, generalization of risk efficiency to 'opportunity efficiency', and related culture changes. Effective exploitation of opportunity efficiency implies proactive uncertainty management which takes an integrated and holistic approach to opportunity and threat management with respect to all seven Ws in all relevant stages of the project lifecycle for all projects in an organization's portfolio of projects.

Chapter 4 outlines the basic PUMP – a seven-phase generic framework central to this book. This basic PUMP framework plus associated processes defining a 'PUMP pack' is compared with a number of other published frameworks, as a basis for understanding the transferable nature of the concepts developed in the rest of this book for users of alternative frameworks, and as a basis for understanding the choices available when developing uncertainty, opportunity and risk management frameworks for particular organizations.

Chapter 1

Uncertainty in and around projects

I keep six honest serving men, they taught me all I knew; their names are what and why and when and how and where and who.

—Rudyard Kipling

Uncertainty management as addressed in this book is concerned with clarifying *all* relevant aspects of opportunity, uncertainty and risk in *all* projects. In a plain English sense at a basic level:

'*uncertainty*' means '*lack of certainty*',
'*risk*' means '*possible unfavourable outcomes*',
'*opportunity*' means '*possible favourable outcomes*'.

These three definitions are both basic and general, in the sense that they are consistent with *all* definitions in widely used dictionaries (Oxford Concise, 1995, for example). They are *nominal definitions* in the sense that readers can use their own comparable plain English alternatives if they wish – we do not want to open a book with counterintuitive definitions that inhibit colloquial use of words. More specifically, we do not want to inhibit richer or more specific colloquial interpretations, such as 'an opportunity is usefully seen as an occasion when it is relatively easy to achieve what you want', and 'risk is usually associated with problems and danger'. However, it is crucial to avoid the morass soon encountered if simple common practice technical definitions are used. The three definitions provided above are *basic default definitions*, in the sense that they will serve if the reader is unclear about an unrestrictive basic plain English interpretation.

These nominal/default definitions, or any comparable alternatives the reader may prefer, provide sufficient clarity for our purposes without the need for more restrictive formal definitions. This is because we will introduce explicit working assumptions as needed.

Managing opportunity is our top priority, and the identification and pursuit of opportunity are usually the starting points in terms of enhancing corporate performance. Risk may not be tangible assets – such as incremental improvements in operating systems, new ways of working, new knowledge acquisition or a new image creation – that have value beyond the delivery of tangible changes. Further, the acquisition of both tangible and intangible assets may be usefully viewed as changes for some purposes. The term 'asset/change' is sometimes a useful reminder that:

- projects may involve the creation of a physical asset, but it may be useful to view them in terms of the change to the organization or system in which the asset operates; projects may involve changing organizational processes, but it may be useful to view these changes in asset creation terms;
- most projects benefit from both perspectives – simple traditional asset creation terms are convenient sometimes, but management of change terms can be more relevant at other times.

A flexible approach to all terminology can be useful, adapting to the context. For example, a culture change project may be approached in change management terms for most purposes, but the initial concept evaluation of that project needs to value the culture change as an asset to justify the effort and expenditure involved. A new electricity generation power station project may be approached in asset creation terms for most purposes, but the initial concept evaluation of the project needs to value the power station in terms of all related changes to the electric utility's portfolio of assets, cost of capital, operating costs, reliability, plus other changes in terms of all relevant objectives, such as a green (environmentally friendly) image. Table 1.1 lists a sample

Table 1.1   Examples of projects and associated asset/change

Project examples	*Examples of the asset/change created*
The design and construction of new built environment facilities	New office buildings, housing, hospitals, schools, prisons
The design and construction of new production facilities	New power plants, factories, processing plants, production lines, storage facilities, computer facilities
The design and construction of new infrastructure assets	New roads, railways, airports, pipelines, power transmission networks, tunnels, bridges, operational infrastructure, communication networks, leisure facilities
The formulation and implementation of organizational process change	New processes for future working or more efficient and effective arrangements for carrying out operations including new procedures
The acquisition of specified data and its analysis	Additional knowledge/information to inform future decision making and actions
The design and creation of new tools, techniques or decision support systems	New software for data processing, data retrieval or data analysis
The modification of existing assets to improve their utilization and operating performance	Refurbished, upgraded or augmented plant or service facilities
The completion of maintenance work while minimising disruption to operations	Serviced or repaired assets with future operating performance assured or enhanced and extended service life.
The organization of a conference or away day for a management team	Enhanced knowledge for participants, development of relationships with work colleagues, suppliers, contractors, customers via networking and discussions
The change of an organizational culture or organizational reputation	Enhanced effectiveness or enhanced perceived effectiveness or both

of example projects in conjunction with the asset/change delivered to illustrate the variety of organizational changes and assets that may be associated with projects.

Turner's definition highlights the change-inducing nature of projects requiring formal management, the need to organize a variety of resources under significant constraints, and the central role of the objectives to be achieved. It also suggests inherent uncertainty related to a novel organization and a unique scope of work. In our plain English terms this uncertainty may imply risk, but it may not. In our terms this uncertainty always implies potential opportunity – projects without possible 'beneficial change' should be rejected, if 'beneficial change' is sensibly defined. As a central part of effective project management, all relevant uncertainty requires attention to clarify opportunity and risk, and enhance performance.

Much good basic project management practice might be thought of as uncertainty resolution by clarifying what can be done, deciding what has to be done, and ensuring that it gets done. For example, good practice in planning, coordination, setting milestones, and change control procedures seeks to progressively resolve and reduce uncertainty as a project progresses. However, uncertainty management is not just about uncertainty reduction – increasing project uncertainty and risk to seize opportunities or to reduce corporate bankruptcy risk may sometimes be the only rational option – and increasing uncertainty and risk when the rewards are worth it is always important. Uncertainty management as discussed in this book is about recognizing uncertainty wherever it matters, and taking appropriate, timely, decisions in the face of this uncertainty. Most texts on project management or project risk management do not take a sufficiently wide view of project related uncertainty, and most do not explore what a coordinated approach to proactive and reactive uncertainty management can achieve in terms of improved performance from a corporate perspective for the project owner.

Part of understanding where uncertainty matters involves appreciating the context within which a project takes place, and the extent to which this context both affects and is affected by the project. The relevant organizational and environmental contexts and the extent of interactions with a project will obviously vary substantially depending on the nature of a project and its scope of work. Sometimes projects can be viewed in very simple terms as largely independent operations. However, sometimes very complex interactions need attention. To deal with all possibilities we must have a sophisticated view which can be simplified in the most appropriate manner for each practical situation.

Operations, corporate and project-related uncertainty

To put projects and project management in context it is useful to consider the overall task of managing organizations in terms of three basic aspects:

- operations management – managing for 'business as usual';
- corporate management – deciding what changes to make at a corporate strategy level, providing appropriate resources and corporate capability, and ensuring appropriate governance;
- project management – designing and creating specific changes or assets.

In common with other ways of characterizing the task of managing, these three aspects should be seen as intimately related – not as separate 'silos'. Corporate management decisions are influenced by current and desired future operational capability; project management is driven by corporate decisions; and future operations are facilitated by project management that maintains or enhances operational capability. All three aspects involve uncertainty and associated challenges of complexity and novelty. In particular, all three aspects are influenced and affected in related ways by the wider environmental conditions prevailing, and by perceptions about the future operating environment.

Operations management

Operations management – managing existing assets for 'business as usual' – is sometimes seen as a relatively low level of management involving limited novelty. However, depending on the organization, high levels of complexity can be involved because of the need to manage the day-to-day behaviour of operating systems in great detail. Operations issues can be a major driver of strategic change, and major opportunities are often first identified by the people 'at the coal face' in operations management terms. 'Intelligent control' (Leitch, 2008) and intelligent organization and careful deployment of assets are usually crucial. Uncertainty, and the extent of its consequences, is typically minimized by frequent or continuous adjustments to operating processes in a control sense. Necessary or efficient specialization encourages a silo approach to various sources of operational uncertainty often involving a number of specialist functions focused on different aspects of control. However, the implications often ripple through the whole organization – as with approaches to health and safety, for example.

Sources of uncertainty can be internal to an operation, associated with the behaviour of employees and other assets, and their interactions, including communications and the provision and use of information. External sources of uncertainty are virtually infinite, but those that can materially affect operational performance are usually the only issues of interest. Further narrowing of attention is possible if only a short-term view of the future operating environment is taken. However, the choice of an appropriate operating horizon depends upon perspective and capability, shaped by the responsibility for making desirable adjustments. At a low level of operations management, horizons may be very short, even hours or minutes, and processes are largely routine, based on extensive experience and perhaps trial and error adjustments. At higher levels of operations management attention is on progressively more aggregated operations, which involves a wider set of contextual factors and related uncertainties, and usually longer planning horizons.

In most organizations, operational interdependencies between assets are significant. Shared objectives, shared supporting resources and common sources of uncertainty may be involved. Further, creating new assets may impact other assets, with goodwill and important relationships being particularly exposed if such effects are overlooked. Consequently, at almost any level in an operations hierarchy, concerns about managing uncertainty can have wider implications for other parts of the organization or strategic implications for the organization as a whole. These strategic implications might relate to the capability of current operational capacity and assets, and their ability to perform into the future. Any strategy formulation process needs to understand this capability, and the nature of all the major sources of uncertainty that can impact on future operational performance, whether these sources are internal or external to the organization. Operational uncertainty, be it short or long term, should be a key driver of strategy.

Corporate management

The uncertainty that must be addressed as part of corporate strategy management includes all significant sources related to operations just discussed. It also includes all significant uncertainty related to necessary resources and corporate capability. Further, it includes all significant uncertainty about the ambitions and aspirations of senior management and key stakeholders, and in relation to the interpretation of the organization's mission and key objectives. The scope of possible future ventures may be very uncertain, their desirability may be uncertain, and the extent to which these ventures need to be related to existing operations and assets may also be unclear. Part of the challenge of strategic management is to identify potential investment options that are suitable, feasible and acceptable in a very uncertain environment (Johnson et al., 2005). Strategy formulation involves developing a coherent and effective set of future investment options that will deliver specified benefits over some future time period. Part of the context is an existing portfolio of assets, current operations, future plans and commitments. Another part of the context is an uncertain environment.

In a top-down approach, long-term corporate strategy leads to the development of a hierarchy of projects reflecting long, medium and short-term planning. Long-term strategy is implemented via a programme of medium-term projects. These in turn may be achieved by a programme of linked, short-term projects, potentially constrained by short-term operations. Scope for managing sources of uncertainty exists at each level, reflecting the corresponding key issues at each level. However, management at each level also needs to be aware of potential impacts from adjacent levels. In particular, managers of medium-term projects need to take into account the potential impacts on their projects from both short-term and long-term issues.

Project management

It can also be important to appreciate and manage how a given project relates to other concurrent projects. For example, a project may be one part of a larger project, part of a portfolio of largely separate projects, part of a sequence of projects, or may itself be managed as a set of sub-projects. Figure 1.1 illustrates three basic interconnected project structures: the chain configuration, the parallel configuration and the project hierarchy.

In the chain configuration a sequence of component projects follows one another over time to complete a 'primary project' which overarches 'component projects', which are 'secondary'. In the parallel configuration a number of component projects run simultaneously, perhaps with interdependencies, to complete an overarching, primary project. In a project hierarchy the primary project is broken down by management into a hierarchy of component projects. The project hierarchy shown in Figure 1.1(c) is a simple example with embedded parallel and chain configurations. Much more complex configurations involving a combination of these three configuration types are employed in most organizations. In slightly different language, one person's project may be an activity in someone else's higher level project – different levels of decomposition may serve the needs of different levels of management.

Large engineering or construction projects are invariably managed as project hierarchies. Large projects may be managed as a set of component projects running in parallel, with each parallel

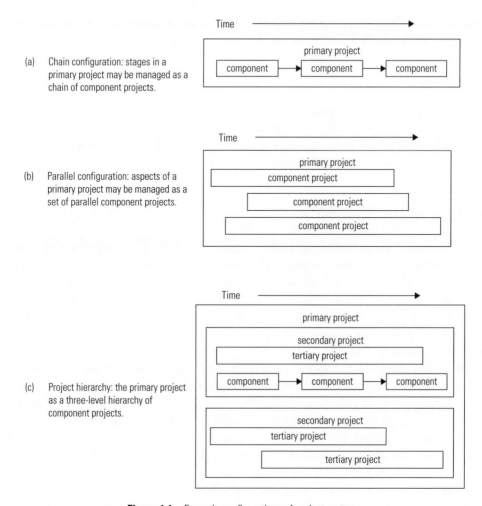

Figure 1.1   Example configurations of project systems

component comprising a hierarchy of component projects. Management of the 'primary project' can be tackled as a complex version of project management and is typically managed at a more senior level than management of the component projects. As a practical matter, managers of primary projects may not be interested in the 'nuts and bolts' of individual component projects, but they will have to understand them well enough to ensure that the component projects fit together as a whole.

The primary project may be thought of by senior management in terms which go beyond that associated with individual component projects – that is, as a strategy or long-term programme, using 'programme' in a 'portfolio of projects' sense, with links between the component projects defined by shared objectives, resources or other factors. For some purposes 'programmes' and 'portfolios' can be usefully distinguished from each other and from 'projects', but this book uses 'projects' in a generic sense which includes programmes and portfolios. It follows that we have to address a spectrum of project complexity, from very strategic projects that are usefully seen as portfolios of programmes for some purposes, to very tactical projects that are usefully seen as single activities or tasks for some purposes.

We shall not engage directly with alternative approaches to 'complexity' or alternative views of 'project', 'programme' or 'portfolio' distinctions, but we will address common concerns from an uncertainty management perspective using an inclusive 'project' concept. Readers may interpret what we are saying in 'programme' or 'other portfolio of projects' terms when such distinctions are appropriate. This issue is revisited briefly at the end of Chapter 12.

The following example illustrates some of the interconnectedness between the management of uncertainty in corporate, operations and portfolio/programme/project management.

Ontario Hydro example

At the beginning of the 1990s Ontario Hydro in Canada developed a 25-year strategic plan which included ten new nuclear power stations. They sought Ontario government permission to proceed with the whole plan. The approval process involved official 'interveners' making a case to receive funding from Ontario Hydro to challenge the basis of the plans. The Independent Power Producers Society of Ontario (IPPSO), representing all non-government power producers, received funding for a critical report on Ontario Hydro's approach to strategic planning prepared by Chris Chapman (1992a).

The report's argument was in two parts. First, confidence bands on Ontario Hydro's load forecast should have been several times wider; other uncertainties were similarly underestimated and, as a consequence of these uncertainties, the Ontario Hydro approach to strategic decision making was not fit for the intended purpose. Second, a very different planning approach, outlined in some detail, was needed. The mathematical optimization approach adopted by Ontario Hydro was flawed because the optimization did not consider uncertainty. But the common practice of addressing uncertainty via scenario robustness tests was not 'risk efficient' in a basic 'portfolio theory' sense, and Ontario Hydro's search for optimality was sound in principle if not in practice.

The applied research funded by the report writing exercise was an opportunity to integrate the thinking underlying this book's advocated approach to project uncertainty management with strategic uncertainty management and operations uncertainty management. About two weeks before Chris Chapman was to appear as an expert witness, demand fell outside Ontario Hydro's confidence band, and the strategic plan was withdrawn. This was clearly *very* lucky for IPPSO. The first part of Chris Chapman's report was validated in traditional empirical terms. The second part remains debatable, but the basic approach to integrating strategy, operations and projects outlined in Chapman (1992a) and developed in Chapman and Ward (2002, chapter 11) illustrates how to approach the management of the interdependencies between operations, strategy and 'projects' defined to include programmes and portfolios of projects.

We will return to this example in Part III, and draw on it occasionally in the interim. Of immediate interest are two points. First, an approach to corporate and operations management compatible with this book's approach to project uncertainty management was needed as a starting point for operational development. Second, the way a utility such as Ontario Hydro has to approach the operations–corporate–projects spectrum illustrates the nature of these interdependences when a top-down strategic perspective is adopted.

Viewing Ontario Hydro's uncertainty structure might start with a corporate level assessment of annual profit, P_t, equal to annual revenue, R_t, less annual costs, C_t, for $t = 1, 2, \ldots, n$, up to the chosen long-term planning horizon, $n = 25$ years, for example.

Revenue is a key source of uncertainty, worthy of a major uncertainty management effort. Forecast demand will be central here, in terms of consumer demand and industrial demand, with considerable underlying complexity and interactions in both cases. Also important are existing competing utilities, possible new competitors, market regulators, and political players concerned with relevant conservation and environmental issues.

Cost is also important. At the corporate level, cost is driven by long-term strategic planning decisions: What mix of sources of power should be aimed for 25 years hence? What proportion of nuclear, gas-fired, coal-fired units should be planned for? and so on. Through-life costs will be important, including fuel costs, the effects of environmental legislation or technology development, and liability for pollution or accidents.

At a basic operational level, management is concerned with cost effective day-to-day utilization of existing units. At an intermediate level, an important management concern is the timing of decisions to start building new power-generating units. Such decisions may be coupled to both short-term operational issues and longer-term strategic issues. The sudden failure of an existing unit may trigger a need to bring plans forward. Political events may significantly alter the need for a planned unit; or perhaps even eliminate the need for a unit; possibly doing so when construction of the unit is already underway.

The project manager for the construction of such a unit clearly needs to manage the project in a way that deals effectively with the sources of uncertainty for which he or she is responsible, and ensure that the sources of uncertainty for which other members of the organization are responsible are managed in a supportive manner. The director to whom the project manager reports, and all the directors responsible for the way the project fits into the corporate portfolio of projects, also need to understand and manage all important relationships across the operations–corporate–projects spectrum.

Most project managers have comparable concerns, but the relationship between their project and the rest of the organization may be more ambiguous, and a source of uncertainty needing attention. Most directors of organizations with a direct interest in projects also have comparable concerns, often with greater complexity and ambiguity.

Ontario Hydro had a lot of uncertainty to deal with. It is a useful example for the present purposes because its structure is intuitively obvious to most people, and an approach flexible enough to deal with all relevant uncertainty for this kind of utility can be adapted by most other organizations. At the same time, its uncertainty is easily structured by comparison to some organizations. It has only one product – electricity – and the assets are tangible and relatively inflexible. It will also be a useful example to build on later, especially in Part III.

Operations, project and corporate aspects of a single asset

All projects should originate from some level of corporate strategy formulation in the project sponsoring organization. This is usually the case for projects involving substantial investment in the delivery of an asset involving significant corporate change, but it may not be so apparent with projects involving smaller levels of investment or corporate change. Similarly, all projects, whatever their size or impact, ought to involve consideration of any relevant sources of uncertainty that affect both the creation of an asset and its subsequent operational performance, and any corporate change implications. This consideration should include the complete set of corporate sources of uncertainty that impact on an individual project and may require responses from the project manager or other parties. Motivation to undertake this uncertainty analysis in a top-down strategic manner needs to come from the organization's board level managers. Ideally this will be undertaken using an approach comparable to a suitable adaptation of that outlined for Ontario Hydro in Chapman (1992a), its generalization in Chapman and Ward (2002, ch. 11) and its brief treatment in Part III. However, even if a project manager's organization chooses to ignore such issues completely, a competent manager of project uncertainty should not do so.

The focus of this section is projects associated with a single asset. Putting aside the issues noted in the preceding paragraph, linkages between operations, corporate and project management perspectives also exist within the context of a single (primary) project and the associated asset/change lifecycle. Table 1.2 portrays a traditional view of the relationship between the three basic aspects of management and a generic asset lifecycle characterized as four basic stages: conceptualization, planning, execution and delivery, and utilization.

The conceptualization stage encapsulates concept development and the development of a business case for investing in the asset concept. It may be initiated bottom-up to meet operations needs, or top-down to meet corporate level strategic needs, but corporate management considerations usually dominate the end of the conceptualization stage and the beginning of the planning stage. The planning stage encapsulates a complex and potentially lengthy process that begins at a strategic level and progressively refines the design of the asset, an understanding of intended benefits from the asset, how it will be used, how it will be created, what resources will be needed, and when and how it is to be delivered. The execution and delivery stage encapsulates the implementation of plans for the creation and delivery of the asset, with project management preparing for this during much of the planning stage. The utilization stage encapsulates the operation of the asset throughout its operating life to eventual termination of use, with operations staff building on their earlier contribution to the planning stage, assuming they were involved earlier.

This portrayal of the lifecycle uses the term 'stage' rather than the common alternative 'phase' to reserve 'phase' for discussions on related processes. A range of labels similar to those used for Table 1.2 stages may be found in the literature behind this simple four-stage structure, along with alternative views of why such a structure is useful. The asset lifecycle is a convenient way of conceptualizing the generic structure of projects over time for a wide range of purposes. An

Table 1.2   A traditional four stage view of the asset lifecycle and dominant management aspects

Basic lifecycle stages	Dominant management aspect
Conceptualization	Operations or corporate management initially, then corporate management
Planning	Corporate management initially, then project management
Execution and delivery	Project management
Utilization	Operations management

alternative terminology example is 'formation', 'build-up', 'main programme' and 'phase-out' (Thamhain and Wileman, 1975), but the underlying structure is essentially the same. Whatever the stage terminology, these stages are commonly described in terms of the extent to which they differ in the level of resources employed (Adams and Barndt, 1988), the degree of definition, the level of conflict (Thamhain and Wileman, 1975), the rate of expenditure, and so on. This can help to show how management attention to the factor being considered needs to vary over the lifecycle. More recent references in the project lifecycle literature include Tummala and Burchett (1999), and Bonnai et al. (2002).

The way the traditional dominant management aspect pattern portrayed in Table 1.2 changes over time, and the lack of real separability between these management aspects, encourages a wide range of different and more detailed project lifecycle structures in different project contexts to ensure that who does what, when and how, in an orderly manner, is clearly defined. For example, the UK rail industry has developed an eight-stage investment lifecycle as part of its GRIP (Guide to Railway Investment Projects) process (Network Rail, 2007) which is widely cited.

Looking at Table 1.2 from an uncertainty management perspective, responsibility for each stage in the lifecycle is clearly important, but the dominant issue is ensuring that all uncertainty associated with different stages of the lifecycle receives appropriate and timely attention. Maximizing the opportunities presented by the creation of proposed assets warrants careful attention to all stages of the asset lifecycle, taken together as a whole, as well as attention to the role the asset will play in the context of the asset owner's other investments and operations.

Taking a traditional corporate management perspective, the basic form, timing, cost and envisaged benefits from the proposed asset are a central concern. From this perspective the prospective asset owner will be considering the need for the proposed investment and the opportunity it represents in the context of an existing portfolio of assets, current operations and the future shape of both. Deliberations can be challenging due to high levels of uncertainty about what is desirable, possible and affordable, future operating conditions, and how the proposed asset will perform as part of a portfolio of existing and future assets. This warrants early consideration of later stages in the asset lifecycle. For example, in projects that involve the large-scale use of new and untried technology, design and future operating issues can be a very early focus in preparing a business case.

With a conventional project management perspective, the central concern is determining how to create the proposed asset once conceptualization and planning have reached a sufficiently well-defined point. Project management in these terms often begins with more detailed design planning and working to create and deliver the required asset at a detailed planning level. Approaches to project management have become increasingly sophisticated, particularly in respect of the design and construction of large physical assets such as infrastructure, buildings, processing plants, transport vehicles, etc. This has led to the development and formalization of the processes involved. Such formalization has encouraged the 'projectification' of all kinds of organizational initiatives in the hope or expectation that the application of project management techniques will bring about a more timely, beneficial and cost effective delivery of initiatives in an organization.

However, critics of conventional project management argue that the focus of project management has been much too narrow, with an overemphasis on execution and delivery of given asset specifications. Conventional project management techniques may help to deliver efficiently well-defined prespecified assets within a well-defined, relatively stable environment, but, critics argue, where asset design and construction is more fluid or uncertain, a wider perspective of associated uncertainty is needed. Further, in some contexts conditioning on (assuming fixed) cost and time, and treating performance as variable, may be more practical than conditioning on performance and treating time and cost as variables. In addition, critics argue that project management should encompass the 'front end' project definition phase – that is both the conceptualization and planning stages in Table 1.2 – and in particular that project management should include a concern for the operational benefits to be derived from a created asset, not just performance of execution and delivery. Morris (2009, p. 60) puts the argument as follows:

> . . . shaping and delivering projects requires that directions be established, value optimized and opportunities created. Projects need to produce business value as well as deliver predictable outcomes. Both are needed. But whereas most project managers are happy to see themselves as efficient execution tacticians, the prize is for project managers to begin thinking about how the project, as it is developed, can enhance the value of the sponsor's strategic position.

When considering the management of uncertainty from an asset lifecycle perspective, this wider view of projects and project management seems entirely appropriate, and even essential. In this sense the discipline and techniques of common practice project management may be considered of limited use in managing strategy or programmes, leading to excessive separation of strategy (primary project or programme) management and project management of the component projects. This separation may be formalized by organizational structures, and may increase the chances of the uncertainty management of component projects being treated separately from the consideration of strategic uncertainty, risk and opportunity. An obvious example is a contracting organization where the ongoing business involves tendering for individual contracts. Each contract won is treated as a project, and these contracts form a mixture of the chain and parallel configurations in Figure 1.1. Interdependencies exist between contracts to the extent that they utilize common corporate knowledge, skills and other resources. An important task for senior management is to manage the (often implicit) primary project – the organization's short and long-term strategy. Unless this is managed explicitly at 'the top', strategy is likely to emerge *ad hoc* and 'bottom-up' in an unintended rather than deliberate manner (Mintzberg, 1978).

A lifecycle stage structure with a 'purpose' focus

Characterization of the asset lifecycle as four sequential stages starts to indicate the scope of the basic tasks involved from operations, corporate and project management perspectives and the associated scope of uncertainty that warrants attention. However, a more detailed consideration of the four basic stages of conceptualization, planning, execution and delivery, and utilization with a purpose focus as portrayed by Table 1.3 provides deeper insight into the scope of decisions involved in different parts of the lifecycle: the goals being addressed; the identity of the main players; and the extent and nature of the uncertainty involved. In particular, elaborating Table 1.2 as Table 1.3, suggests three areas of concern.

Table 1.3 A 12-stage *nominal* project (asset/change) lifecycle with a purpose focus

Four basic stages	Stage purposes	Steps	Labels
Conceptualization	Concept, project objectives and business case development in corporate strategy terms	Trigger event Concept capture Clarification of project purpose Concept elaboration Business case development Concept, objectives and business case evaluation in corporate strategy terms	**Concept shaping**
	Governance	Consolidate plans and confirm deliverables	**Concept gateway**
Planning	Design, operations and termination (DOT) strategy development from a design and operations management perspective	Design and operations strategy capture from corporate strategy Development of lifecycle performance criteria Integrated development of design, operations and termination strategy Integrated evaluation of design, operations and termination strategy	**DOT shaping**
	Governance	Consolidate plans and confirm deliverables	**DOT gateway**
	Execution and delivery (E&D) strategy development from a project management perspective	Activity and related resource use capture from corporate strategy and design strategy Development of timing targets and milestones Strategic plan development for execution and delivery Evaluation of execution and delivery strategy	**E&D shaping**
	Governance	Consolidate plans and confirm deliverables	**Strategy gateway**
	Detailed design and planning for execution, delivery, operation and termination purposes	Shifting the perspective to implementation Development of detailed design and planning criteria for implementation purposes Development of detail designs and plans Development of resource allocation and contracting criteria Detailed design and plan evaluation	**Tactics shaping**
	Governance	Consolidate plans and confirm deliverables	**Tactics gateways**
Execution and delivery	Execution	Implementation of actions plans Coordinate, control and monitor progress Modification of all targets, commitments and resource allocations as needed Ongoing execution evaluation	**Execution**
	Delivery	Undertake delivery Deliverable modification Manage stakeholder expectations about delivery and operational performance Delivery evaluation	**Delivery**
Utilization	Operation and support (O&S)	Operational utilization of asset Ongoing development of operations & support criteria Ongoing development of operations & support Ongoing operations & support evaluation	**O&S**
	Termination	Development of detailed plans for transfer of ownership or replacement or decommissioning Termination execution Termination evaluation	**Termination**

First, it is important to distinguish between strategic planning for operations, project execution and corporate strategy purposes. They are related but involve different purposes – a different 'why' in Kipling's terms, with implications for the 'who'.

Second, it is important to distinguish between strategic and tactical planning for all purposes, and to ensure that all strategic planning precedes all tactical planning. Strategic and tactical planning also serve different purposes and often involve different people. In our terms 'strategic planning' must include detailed design and detailed planning to test strategy when appropriate, but detailed design and planning for execution, delivery, operations and termination purposes is associate with 'tactical planning'. It is often useful to recognize an important boundary after the strategy gateway stage, when 'strategy shaping' ends and strategy implementation begins with 'tactics shaping', especially if a contractor responsible for execution and delivery is also given responsibility for detailed planning for execution and delivery purposes. Separating detailed planning to test strategy when appropriate, and detailed planning to implement strategy, helps to facilitate clarity about this boundary.

Third, it is important to understand the difference between 'evaluation' for corporate governance approval purposes and 'evaluation' for internal control of a management process designed to be iterative – again a different 'why' and 'who' are involved.

The second column of Table 1.3 breaks down the basic four-stage characterization of the asset lifecycle. It uses eight stages with traditional lifecycle stage functions. It also uses four 'gateway' processes involving consolidation of plans to date and associated governance, usefully treated as if they were stages. This makes 12 stages in total. It does so in a way that explains the key objectives or 'purpose' of these 12 component stages – the 'why'. The reason more divisions than the traditional basic four are useful is that greater clarity about the purpose of each stage leads to simpler and more effective processes. *Simple and effective processes* are goals that matter.

For simplicity we will often refer to 'the project lifecycle' or just 'the lifecycle', with the default meaning 'the project (asset/change) lifecycle of Figure 1.3' – all 12 notional stages or some comparable equivalent. However, sometimes we will use 'asset lifecycle' to emphasize that we are talking about the whole lifecycle from a client's corporate perspective. Further, sometimes it is important to recognize that some people may use a 'project lifecycle' that starts much later and ends much sooner – for example, a contractor hired to complete a task within one or two stages of a broader client's perspective of 'the project' is working with different lifecycle and project concepts.

The third column of Table 1.3 breaks each stage into 'steps'. The breakdown into stages goes some way towards highlighting important sources of uncertainty and facilitating their management as well as clarifying different purposes. However, the more detailed description of the lifecycle provided by the steps in Table 1.3 is useful to underline where particular sources of uncertainty arise in the lifecycle and how uncertainty management might be most effective. In the early lifecycle stages these steps imply a process of gradually increasing detail and a focus on the nature of the deliverable asset. Later steps focus on delivery and operation of the asset followed by termination in the sense of decommissioning or selling an asset.

For reference purposes the column two 'stage purpose' descriptions are abbreviated to lifecycle stage 'labels' in column four. There is a good argument for adding the word 'strategic' to all the labels for the first five stages – they are all focused on strategy, and a constant reminder can be useful in some contexts. There is also a good case for using *overall* strategy gateway' as the label for the sixth stage. Further, the design and operations management perspective of the DOT-shaping stage versus the more traditional project management perspective of the E&D-shaping stage may need emphasis sometimes. Finally, the DOT label does not have its common USA interpretation 'Department of Transportation' – an illustration of the virtually impossible task of always using uniquely identified acronyms. However, the labels adopted here are as simple as possible while avoiding obvious ambiguity. They are *nominal* in the sense that if additional words or alternative labels will make communication clearer, such adaptation is clearly desirable and should be used. This notion applies to much of our recommended terminology – there is no need to be dogmatic about terminology *provided everyone understands what is being said – it is the concepts that really matter.* Using minimal labels when the meaning is clear, but adding additional words for clarity whenever this might be useful, is a policy adopted throughout this book. It is also a policy which is highly recommended as a corporate strategy. In our experience simple 'handles' are a form of jargon practitioners need for efficient communication when they all understand each other, but such jargon can seriously impede effective communication when they do not, and effectiveness can be the key.

The lifecycle structure of Table 1.3 is also *nominal* in the sense that alternatives can be used whenever appropriate, but effective uncertainty management should not oversimplify any of the distinctions that matter.

Any organization adopting the uncertainty management approach advocated in this book may wish to preserve features of lifecycle structure variants from Table 1.3 for a range of corporate reasons which go beyond the purposes of project uncertainty management. However, this book assumes that the features of the Table 1.3 *nominal* structure will be preserved, in the sense that compatible expansion of the components may be involved for other purposes, but not a collapse of components which would lead to confusion. An agreed synthesis of Table 1.3 or equivalents, with appropriate simple labels for all stages, is an essential aspect of full integration of project uncertainty management with all other aspects of project management, including integration with operations and strategic concerns. Table 1.3 is a *nominal* framework because it may need simplification or elaboration according to the context in which it is used.

Concept shaping

The concept shaping stage involves strategic planning from a corporate perspective, although it may be initiated top-down or bottom-up. Top-down is often assumed, but bottom-up is often a more important source of strategic initiatives – a marketing department sees new market opportunities, a research and development department sees new product opportunities, a production department sees new manufacturing process possibilities, and so on. This stage involves identifying a deliverable asset to be produced by a project and the benefits expected from the deliverable. In essence, this involves an innovation process that begins with a 'trigger event' (Lyles, 1981), when a member of an initiating organization perceives an opportunity or need for a new asset or an organizational change. At this point the project deliverable may be only a vague idea, and some initial development may be associated with the 'concept capture' step. 'Clarification of purpose of the possible asset' should involve the identification of operational performance objectives and their relative importance to relevant stakeholders, and associated design and delivery criteria. This step may be problematic to the extent that different views about the appropriate objectives are held by influential stakeholders who try to negotiate mutually acceptable objectives. At this stage objectives are likely to be ill-defined or developed as aspirations expressed as constraints (for example: latest completion date, minimum levels of functionality, maximum capital cost, and so on).

Before the concept can be developed further, in 'concept elaboration' and 'business case development' steps, sufficient political support for the idea must be obtained and resources allocated to allow the idea to be refined and made more explicit. Other individuals, organizations or potential stakeholders may become involved. At this stage support from stakeholders may be passive, merely allowing conceptualization to proceed, rather than an expression of positive approval of the project.

Eventually an evaluation of the asset concept, objectives and business case, as defined to date, becomes necessary. The last step for the concept shaping stage is an internal evaluation by the team responsible for concept shaping at this point. It purpose is iteration control. Evaluation for iteration control purposes here (and in later stages) is not simply a 'yes/no' or 'go/no-go' decision – a 'maybe' possibility is very likely and should be anticipated for early iterations, when a 'maybe' decision involves a *planned* iteration through one or more previous steps. For reasons explored later, it is not cost effective to manage uncertainty using a single-pass process. Early passes are about sizing uncertainty, asking 'Does it matter?' Later passes are about 'Where it matters most, what would be the best way to approach managing it?' A 'go' decision takes the process on to the next stage. A 'no-go' decision causes further investment in the project to stop, possibly subject to governance confirmation, or possibly a pause in the project's evolution rather than its elimination.

Concept gateway

It is useful to separate the concept gateway stage because it serves a very different purpose from concept shaping. The parties initiating and controlling the concept shaping stage should be taking a corporate perspective, but they are likely to have views of what matters most which are rooted in particular parts of the organization. The concept gateway is about consolidating the plans as shaped in the first stage for communication outside the concept stage team followed by appropriate governance – ensuring that a balanced overall corporate perspective decides whether more money and effort should be invested in developing plans for the asset or not. A 'maybe' decision is a possibility, but a resulting iteration is *unplanned* and usually unwelcome. A 'no-go' decision may be the appropriate choice, and no loss of reputation for anyone involved may be appropriate. A 'go' decision takes the lifecycle on to the next stage.

Design, operations and termination (DOT) shaping

DOT shaping initiates design, operations and termination strategy formulation, beginning with design and operations strategy capture from the corporate strategy of the concept shaping stage. This usually requires a step increase in the effort and resources involved. The sequence of the words 'design' and 'operations' reflects the usual precedence ordering, but future operation of the proposed asset or corporate changes might be addressed before design to emphasize the importance of future operations at this stage in the lifecycle, with step titles indicating that design is operations-led in practice.

'Development of lifecycle performance criteria' builds on the basic design and operations objectives from the first stage. For many projects this involves refining such objectives, but it may involve the identification of additional objectives and further negotiation where pluralistic views persist among relevant stakeholders. This step influences an 'integrated *development* of design, operations and termination' that leads to 'integrated *evaluation* of design, operations and termination' using the developed performance criteria to assess the current asset design in 'go/no-go/maybe' terms.

As in the concept stage, a 'no-go' evaluation should kill the project or put it on hold. A 'maybe' evaluation is most likely to lead to iteration through one or more development steps, and such loops should be expected *planned* iterations, because this is the most effective way to manage uncertainty. If fundamental difficulties that were not anticipated in the concept stage are encountered, the concept stage may be revisited, but this is an *unplanned* iteration. A 'go' decision takes the lifecycle on to the next governance gateway stage.

Building any relevant termination considerations into the design and operations strategy needs attention in this stage if this was not addressed earlier.

Design, operations and termination (DOT) gateway

The DOT gateway is a consolidation process followed by a governance process with the same role as the concept gateway – deciding whether more money and effort should be spent on proceeding to planning for execution and delivery from a balanced perspective considering overall corporate strategy. A 'maybe' decision is a possibility, but a resulting iteration is *unplanned* and usually unwelcome. A 'no-go' decision may be the appropriate choice, with possible loss of reputation issues if the first gateway 'go' was a clear mistake. A 'go' decision takes the lifecycle on to the next stage.

Execution and delivery (E&D) shaping

The E&D shaping stage initiates formal capture and development of activity and resource use plans at a strategic level, indicating how the asset design will be executed and delivered, and the resources that will be required by these activities in broad terms. 'Development of delivery targets and milestones' involves reconciling how long execution and delivery should take and how long various parties would like it to take. Even more individuals and organizations may become involved. 'Strategic plan development for execution and delivery' follows. This leads to 'evaluation of execution and delivery strategy' in 'go/no-go/maybe' terms.

A 'maybe' decision may require further development of strategic plans, including targets and milestones within the E&D-shaping stage, as part of a process planned to be iterative because this is the most effective way to manage uncertainty. More fundamental difficulties may take the process back to asset design and operations strategy development, or even to concept development, but this would be an *unplanned* iteration. A 'no-go' decision kills the project or puts it on hold, usually subject to gateway approval. A 'go' decision takes the lifecycle on to the next gateway stage.

Strategy gateway

The strategy gateway is a consolidation process followed by a governance process with the same role as the earlier gateways – deciding whether more money and effort should be spent on the project from a balanced perspective considering overall corporate strategy. However, this time the 'overall strategy gateway' can be a useful label extension because *all relevant aspects of strategy* are involved. This includes E&D strategy as shaped by the preceding stage plus updates to asset design, operations and termination strategy as defined at the DOT gateway. It also includes updates to the overall concept and business case strategy as initially defined at the concept gateway and possibly updated at the DOT gateway. Further, the *overall* strategy gateway is a significant 'watershed', a stage where turning around later means significant extra effort, because expenditure on the project grows at an increasing rate from now on if it progresses. A 'maybe' decision is a possibility, but a resulting iteration is *unplanned* and unwelcome. A 'no-go' decision may be the appropriate choice, with possible loss of reputation issues if either of the first two gateway 'go' decisions were a clear mistake. A 'go' decision takes the lifecycle on to the next stage, but later 'no-go' or 'maybe' decisions could be severely 'career limiting'.

Tactics shaping

Tactics shaping involves an important shift in perspective – to the implementation of a strategy which is assumed to be robust and viable. 'Shifting the perspective to implementation' is a useful first step to ensure that everyone involved appreciates this transition.

Separate tactics shaping is needed for asset design, execution, delivery, operations and support, then termination – in that order of priority. Operations tactics shaping might be delayed for some time – provided the design strategy does not need to be revisited – and does not need to be completed until the O&S stage is about to begin. Termination tactics shaping can be deferred until needed for the termination phase. A detailed allocation of resources and contracts to achieve the design and implement the execution activities is part of the initial priorities. But it is useful to begin with the 'development of detailed design and plan criteria'. This includes issues such as clarifying the level of detail needed, and the extent to which those executing the project can be left to 'plan as they go' as part of execution. Subsequent 'detailed plan development' has to build on this basis.

The tactics shaping stage is a significant task involving decisions about execution and delivery organization, identification of appropriate participants and allocation of tasks between them. Resource allocation and associated contracting with a view to project execution requires much more detail than earlier stages.

Either implicitly or explicitly, the tactics shaping stage involves the allocation of execution uncertainty and associated risk and opportunity between participants unless this has been done earlier. Risk and opportunity allocation is an important source of project uncertainty because it can significantly influence the behaviour of participants and hence impact on project performance – and how best to do it is itself often very uncertain. In particular, allocation of execution and later stage uncertainty influences the extent and manner in which such uncertainty is managed. This warrants careful consideration of the basis for allocating tasks, uncertainty, risk and opportunity in the 'development of resource allocation and contracting criteria' step.

'Detailed plan development' necessarily involves revising detailed design and planning in order to allocate tasks unless this whole stage is contracted out along with the balance of the project. Contract and subcontract structures may require development. Indeed, in some cases 'tactics shaping *including contracting*' would be a better label for this stage, unless contracting was addressed earlier – as in design and build or design, build and operate contracts (with or without a 'transfer' stage), which should be addressed initially in the concept-shaping stage.

The nature of the issues changes with the change of stage as with all earlier stage transitions, and the level of effort escalates as noted earlier.

As in the earlier lifecycle stages, development during this stage is followed by a 'detailed design and plan evaluation'. A 'maybe' decision which requires revisions to aspects of detailed designs or plans should be seen as part of the iterative process of shaping details effectively and efficiently – a *planned* iteration. A 'maybe' decision which involves changes at a strategic level to execution and delivery plans, design and operations strategy, or concept strategy, is usually extremely unwelcome, and a 'no-go' decision will be seen as a serious disaster in many cases. If the 'devil is in the detail', earlier shaping and governance evaluation steps will be seen to have failed unless the environment in which the organization operates has changed to an extent that even risk efficient and robust planning could not have anticipated.

Tactics gateways and a start of execution gateway

Tactics gateways for various aspects of detailed designs and plans provide a pre-execution consolidation of plans and a governance check on internal evaluations used initially for iteration control. They have to assess detail in the context of corporate, operations and project strategy when appropriate. A 'start of execution' gateway can be a useful summary concept for all details gateways relevant to a 'start of execution' decision – a recommended enhancement of the *nominal* Table 1.3 structure.

Separation of consolidation and governance in the four gateway stages

Separation of the four gateway stages from the shaping processes leading to them has benefits which will become clear when the details are considered later, if they are not clear now. One key benefit is distinguishing between *planned* iterations, which are an inherent aspect of effective uncertainty management, and *unplanned* iterations due to earlier shaping and governance evaluation failures. Other aspects include distinguishing the responsible party and the purpose of the exercise, the processes used, and the outcomes of the processes. There is a growing concern about the effectiveness of common practice governance processes. One key issue worth noting now is that governance should test the validity of all plans and associated decisions as well as the processes used to develop the plans and make the decisions. Put slightly differently, it should consider *all* relevant assumptions – working assumptions and framing assumptions.

Separation of three aspects of strategic planning and all tactical planning

The decomposition of the Table 1.2 'planning stage' into six stages helps to distinguish the very different management purposes and attendant issues in all eight of the stages considered above. A possible argument against this decomposition is the interdependent nature of the eight stages, and the need to iterate between them. However, the importance of this dependence, and the process threats and opportunities it generates, is highlighted by their separation. Each stage involves quite different tasks, different goals and end products, different levels of detail in some cases, and different sources of process uncertainty. The importance of decisions to move from each stage to the next increases with each successive stage, because the costs of going back a stage or more escalates. This makes it important to treat the planning stages as separable, while recognizing important interdependencies between them.

There is a very strong case for a clear boundary between the overall strategy gateway and tactics shaping, *provided* strategy is effectively tested by detailed planning on a selective basis when appropriate. Given this proviso, there is a good case for allowing tactics shaping and associated gateways to overlap execution in those areas where this will not lead to delay. For example, shaping tactical plans for the operations stage or the termination stage can wait until they are needed, and some areas of detailed design or tactics shaping for execution may overlap the execution stage.

Assuming a strict boundary can simplify the nominal lifecycle structure. Its relaxation may be important in practice, but the resulting risk needs to be understood.

Execution

The start of the execution stage initiates the main work of the project from the project manager's perspective. The start of this stage signals the start of order-of-magnitude increases in effort and expenditure. The planning is over, the action begins. The four individual steps in this stage are obviously basic project management; they are not worth detailed development here, other than noting that all plan revisions can be supported by a variant of the steps used earlier.

During execution, the essential process threat is that coordination and control procedures prove inadequate. A common perceived threat in the execute stage is the introduction of design changes, but these may be the result of earlier sources of uncertainty, including opportunities that should have been noticed earlier to take full advantage of them. Consequent adjustments to production plans, costs and payments to affected contractors ought to be based on an assessment of how execution, delivery, and future operations performance is affected by the changes and the extent to which revised plans are needed.

For most projects, repeated iteration will be necessary through the steps within the execution stage. Exceptionally, revisiting earlier lifecycle stages may be necessary. Big surprises, including major opportunities missed earlier, could take some aspects of the project back to the concept shaping stage, or lead to project abortion.

Delivery

The delivery stage involves commissioning and handover of the project deliverable. Again the management issues may vary from previous stages because the purpose of the delivery stage is different. In certain respects the delivery stage is a 'gateway' for all earlier effort; however, it is more than that, with a transfer of ownership at its heart. The 'basic deliverable verification' step involves verifying what the delivered asset will do in practice – that is, its actual operational performance as distinct from its designed performance. An important threat is that the delivered asset fails to meet expected operational performance criteria. Modification of operational performance may be achievable, but modification of performance criteria or stakeholder expectations and perceptions may be necessary. Such shortfalls in performance may be a realization of unmanaged sources of uncertainty in earlier stages of the lifecycle. 'Delivery evaluation' focuses on the need for quality assessment and possible revisiting of earlier steps, including compensating for unanticipated weaknesses by developing unanticipated strengths. In principle, revisiting the concept stage or a project abort decision is still possible.

Operation and support (O&S)

The O&S stage involves living with the delivered asset, the ongoing legacy of apparent project 'completion' from a conventional project management perspective, possibly in a passive 'endure' mode, until the asset is replaced, decommissioned or otherwise disposed of. 'Basic operations and support verification' is the starting point once delivery is complete, noting that handover may be an internal matter in a single organization. 'Development of operations and support criteria' informs 'operations and support development' and subsequent 'operations and support evaluation'. These three steps may be repeated periodically, or perhaps many times over the operational life of the asset. The focus of operation and support evaluation is likely to be a within-stage return to development of perceptions, or revisiting aspects of the delivery stage. Exceptionally, the outcome could be unplanned asset withdrawal or other explicit withdrawal of support for the asset as in product recalls, or computer software products. This could result from developments or surprises in the operating environment, or from inadequate management of operational uncertainties earlier in the asset lifecycle.

Termination

Termination may involve simple withdrawal of the asset requiring little prior planning, but it clearly needs corporate approval if not initiation, and the purpose of the termination stage is very different from that for earlier stages. Major infrastructure benefits from decommissioning considerations that are built into the initial business case and design of the asset, as with, for example, nuclear power stations and offshore oil platforms. A speculative office block might have to be sold when there is a market surplus of similar accommodation, so designing a more flexible use into the structure before construction may be a considerable advantage. Most of the detailed planning in most terminations can wait until termination approaches. When it is important to consider strategy at the outset, the costs associated with not doing so can be substantial.

Simplifications and elaborations for the nominal lifecycle

The 12-stage structure of Table 1.3 provides a useful basis for understanding the asset lifecycle, but some projects might warrant a simplified version. As noted earlier, various possible simplifications are one reason for the 'nominal' nature of the 12-stage structure. However, despite the number of stages and steps in Table 1.3, planned iterations within stages, and the possibility of unplanned iteration, this 12-stage description of the lifecycle is still a simple one by comparison with the complexities of some projects. It can be built upon in various ways, illustrated by the following example elaborations.

Separable project dimensions

In practice, some projects are planned and executed in several dimensions that are separable to some extent: physical scope, functionality, technology, location, timing, economics, financing, environmental, and so on. This means that each step in Table 1.3 could be viewed as multi-dimensional, with each step considering each dimension in parallel, or in an iterative sequence. In this latter case, the lifecycle might be visualized as a spiral of activities moving forward through time, where each completed circle of the spiral represents one completed stage in Table 1.3, and each spiral represents sequential consideration of the various dimensions. Charette (1993) uses similar notions in a related context.

Parallel components

Many projects, especially large ones, may be managed as a set of component projects running in parallel. The stages in Table 1.3 can still be used to describe the progress of each component project, although there is no necessity for the component lifecycles to remain in phase at all times. 'Fast tracking' in construction is a simple example of this, where completion of the parent project deliverable can be expedited by overlapping the planning and execution stages for different components. This implies that some components of the parent project deliverable can be designed and planned, and execution commenced for these components, before designing and planning is complete for other components. As is widely recognized, such staggered execution is only low risk to the extent that the design of components first executed is not dependent on the design of subsequent components. Plans that involve an element of 'fast tracking' should be supported by an appropriate uncertainty management process, with a focus on feedback from more advanced components into the lifecycle steps of following components.

Contracting

When allocation of tasks in the tactics shaping stage involves the employment of contractors, the tendering and subsequent production work of the contractor can be regarded as a component project in its own right. For the contractor, all the steps in Table 1.3 are passed through on becoming involved in the parent project. What the client regards as the tactics shaping stage may be regarded by the contractor as a compressed version of the first eight stages. In the case where the contractor has a major responsibility for design (as in turnkey or 'design and build' contracts), the client will move more quickly through the first four stages, perhaps considering these stages only as a general outline. The contractor then carries out more detailed work corresponding to these stages. For the contractor's project, the initiating 'trigger' event involves both a need and an opportunity to tender for work, usually managed at a high level in the contracting organization. The concept shaping stage corresponds to a preliminary assessment of the bidding opportunity and a decision to tender or not (Ward and Chapman, 1988). This is followed by costing design specifications and plans provided in more or less detail by the client, perhaps some additional design and plan development, evaluation of the tendering opportunity, price setting and submission of a bid. For the contractor's project, the tactics shaping stage involves further allocation of tasks, perhaps via subcontracting, more detailed design work, and production scheduling, as indicated above.

Objectives not easily defined

For many projects, delivery objectives and operational performance objectives for the delivered asset can be refined progressively through the first eight stages of the lifecycle. However, in some projects – for example, information systems or software development projects – it may not be practicable to ensure that all performance criteria and related objectives are well defined or crystallized prior to the execution stage. This becomes apparent in earlier stages, where 'go' decisions acknowledge the situation as part of the 'fit for purpose' nature of the governance evaluation. In this scenario, an 'execution evaluation', which is undertaken each time a milestone is achieved, ought to include a 'configuration review' (Turner and Cochrane, 1993; Turner, 1992) of objectives currently achievable with the project. If these are unsatisfactory, further stages of design and planning may be necessary.

Incomplete definition of methods

In some projects, such as product development, it may not be practicable to define completely the nature or sequence of activities required prior to commencing the execution stage (Turner and Cochrane, 1993). In such cases management expects DOT shaping through to execution stages to take place alternately on a rolling basis, with achievement of one milestone triggering DOT shaping to execution of the next part of the project deliverable. In this scenario, previous 'go' decisions within a DOT shaping to execution sequence are made on the understanding that subsequent execution evaluation steps will send the process through further sequences as necessary when the appropriate milestone has been achieved. In effect, the stages from DOT shaping to execution are managed as a sequence of component projects.

Prototyping is a special case of this scenario, and a natural approach where the intention is to mass produce a product, but the product involves novel designs or new technology. For the production project, the first two lifecycle stages are managed as a prototype project (with its own lifecycle). On completion of the prototype, the production lifecycle proceeds from the execution and delivery strategy stage through to the termination stage in Table 1.3.

Projects involving high uncertainty

Some projects involve speculative product development, the application of novel technology to create new types of asset, new methods of construction, large investment, and/or high levels of organizational and technological complexity. Such high uncertainty contexts warrant careful, early attention to project management strategy, starting with the design of an appropriate life-cycle structure that does not necessarily follow a simple sequential progression through the lifecycle stages in Table 1.3. For example, in addition to variations to address initially ill-defined objectives or an incomplete definition of methods as noted above, novel projects might warrant processes that involve parallel trials and iterative trial-and-error cycles within the basic Table 1.3 structure (Lenfle and Loch, 2010).

The seven Ws framework

In the authors' experience the initial motivation for applying formal risk and uncertainty management often arises because of concerns about design and logistics issues in major projects which involve the large-scale use of new and untried technology. Sometimes shortages of key resources are the issue, including finance. Sometimes communication and trust concerns dominate. Sometimes conservation, pollution potential or political imperatives drive the need to understand the issues. However, in all sizes and kinds of project, and at any stage of the lifecycle, the most important issues requiring management – the underlying drivers of uncertainty giving rise to really significant opportunity and risk – are often related to uncertainty about performance objectives and relationships between project parties. For example, a common and sometimes persistent issue is: 'Do we know what we are trying to achieve in clearly defined terms that link objectives to plans?' It is important to understand why such concerns arise, and to respond effectively, in *any* project context at *any* stage in the lifecycle.

A valuable framework for considering uncertainty around objectives, stakeholders and other parties during the basic project definition process is the set of seven basic questions shown in Table 1.4.

As observed by Kipling in the opening quote for this chapter, there are some very basic questions that can be usefully applied to almost any situation or proposed activity. Table 1.4 just adapts these questions to a project uncertainty management context with Table 1.3 in mind. The underlying structures of Tables 1.3 and 1.4 are closely linked. Stephen Ward initiated a six-Ws foundation for this concept during the development of the first edition of this book, and its role and evolution have been central to the journey of both author in developing understanding about the uncertainty–opportunity–risk relationships since the mid-1990s.

For convenience we refer to the key questions in the middle column of Table 1.4 as 'the seven Ws', using the left-hand column 'W labels' in **bold** as a short form when appropriate. Also, for clarity when appropriate, we use the *italic* designations in the right-hand column of Table 1.4. While somewhat contrived, this terminology helps to remind us of the need to consider all seven of these aspects of a project, their multiple components in some cases, their basic interdependence, and the basis for their links with the lifecycle stages in Table 1.3.

relevant provided it is understood and acceptable. However, uncertainty needs to be understood and managed to clarify both opportunity and risk, and that is why exploring the scope for uncertainty in and around projects is a useful place to start to understand how effective uncertainty management can enhance corporate performance.

An appreciation of the potential for uncertainty management in projects has to be informed by three somewhat different views of 'projects'. One is projects as those concerned with 'operations management' see them. A second is projects as those concerned with 'project management' see them. A third is projects as those concerned with 'corporate management' see them. All three perspectives need a common framework and language for communication.

This three-part perspective requires a clear understanding of the scope of decision making involved in project management and the nature of linked concepts. One key concept is the project lifecycle which forms part of the lifecycle of the asset or change created by a project. This lifecycle is a natural framework for examining decisions and associated uncertainty. A structured view of this lifecycle is also important to provide a framework for looking ahead for sources of uncertainty that can be seeded by decisions in earlier stages of the lifecycle. Further, a structured view of this lifecycle is central to understanding how the 'performance uncertainty management processes' (PUMPs) of central interest in this book ought to change as the lifecycle of the project unfolds and the priorities of associated project management objectives change.

An appreciation of uncertainty also has to draw on Kipling's 'six honest serving men' as identified in the opening quote for this chapter – plus a linked 'resources' concept – for convenience referred to as the seven Ws: 'who', 'why', 'what', 'whichway' (how), 'wherewithal' (using what resources), 'when; and 'where'. That is, to clarify in more detail where and how we need to look for uncertainty that needs managing, project uncertainty management has to be informed by seven basic questions associated with these seven Ws.

Exploring the lifecycle structure and the seven Ws is the central task of this chapter. However, our focus on performance uncertainty management needs to be linked to other aspects of uncertainty management, and it has to ensure that *all* aspects of uncertainty are addressed in a holistic manner. Such concerns are addressed in an introductory manner at the end of this chapter.

Begin by considering a standard definition of a 'project' and the 'asset/change' concepts that underlie it.

Projects and the associated 'asset/change' concepts

Turner (1992) provides a useful illustrative definition of a project:

> *an endeavour in which human, material and financial resources are organized in a novel way, to undertake a unique scope of work of given specification, within constraints of cost and time, so as to achieve unitary, beneficial change, through the delivery of quantified and qualitative objectives.*

Turner's definition covers a very wide variety of projects where the 'beneficial change' to be delivered is a tangible asset of some kind that will subsequently be made use of in an operating mode – such as a building, aeroplane or computer system. It also includes the creation of less

Table 1.4 Key questions in the basic project definition process – the seven Ws

1. who	who are the parties involved?	*parties*
2. why	what do the parties want to achieve?	*motives*
3. what	what is the deliverable product that the parties are interested in?	*design*
4. whichway	how will all relevant plans in each lifecycle stage deliver what is needed?	*plans for: relationships and contracts, business case purposes, operations, activities*
5. wherewithal	what key resources are required to achieve execution of these plans?	*resource plans for: operations, activities*
6. when	when do all relevant events have to take place?	*integration of all plan-based timetables*
7. where	where will the project take place? (in location and all other context terms)	*context*

Figure 1.2 uses the Table 1.4 *italic* designations as well as the **bold** W labels, showing a set of relationships that elaborate how Table 1.3 purposes can be pursued.

In the concept shaping stage the plans for business case purposes should become the central concern before too long. A cash flow model at the heart of the business case may act as the axle of the wheel, while the plans for business case purposes act as the hub.

The 'hub' status of plans for business case purposes is emphasized by bolder lines for its box. The bold lines of the overall box signify the wheel rim. The other boxes are analogous to spokes. Those worried about square wheels and hubs might use circles instead of boxes – we have stuck to boxes as a more convenient shape for most purposes of interest – all analogies can produce problems if taken too far, and the 'spokes' notion is useful but not a perfect analogy.

The 'who' is a good place to begin considering the spokes of the wheel that circles this hub. The 'who' includes 'project initiators' and a much wider set of 'project parties ultimately involved'. Project initiators kick the whole process off in the concept shaping stage of the lifecycle. If a client perspective is the concern, the client is obviously the key party, but contractors, customers, shareholders, other investors, regulators and competitors may also need attention.

The client's objectives should dominate the 'why', but aligning client, shareholder, contractor, and regulator concerns may not be straightforward, and competitor responses may be critical. One or more project initiators first identify the basic purpose of the project, or intended benefit from it, the 'why' or motives for the project. These motives will usually include profit, involving revenue and cost, along with 'other motives'. Initially the nature of these motives may or may not be defined, and they will not necessarily be quantified as objectives. That is, in terms of a mission–goals–objectives hierarchy often used to move from an overall mission statement to quantified objectives, the initial focus of the 'why' may be on mission and broadly defined goals rather than specific performance objectives.

The initial 'what', an outline design, is driven by the initial 'why', the initial conception of the project's purpose. The design should be driven by competing agendas that have been aligned in the client's interests as far as possible, with appropriate concessions to other parties. This implies initial attention to relationship plans and contracts *before* getting too deeply into design, and is usefully seen as early attention to the 'why–who–whichway' (plans for relationships and

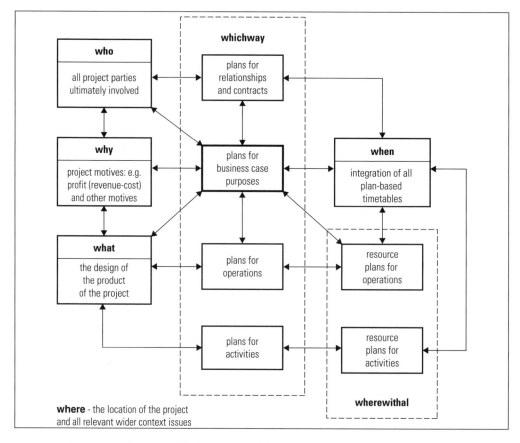

Figure 1.2   The basic project definition process – the seven Ws

contracts) trio as an integrated set. For example, an oil company developing oil wells in a sensitive area may do its best to minimize the intrusive characteristics of all new facilities as well as provide 'planning gain' such as new local jobs plus social and recreational facilities for *all* local residents. All these features can be designed into the facility and the project management process from the start, to plan and manage local resistance in a constructive and transparent manner before anyone is aware of the possibility of such a project.

This outline design, be it of a physical facility such as a building, a less tangible asset such as a service, or a relatively intangible organizational change, drives an initial strategy for operation, the 'whichway' (plans for operation). The plans for operation need to be considered in conjunction with the design from the start, as may the 'wherewithal' (resource plans for operation), and the timing of all these aspects.

The 'who–why–what' trio also drive the 'whichway' (plans for activities) and 'wherewithal' (resource plans for activities) with timing implications, but in the concept-shaping stage the plans for activities and associated resources may be driven by business case considerations from both ends – capital cost and delivery time for a very high level design concept may be all that is required. How the project's asset would be produced is relevant only insofar as its cost, duration and 'quality' impact and interact with the business case.

The 'who–why–whichway' (plans for relationships and contracts) initial development may be driven later by the 'when' and the business case as a whole. The initial pass around the hub may be largely clockwise, feeding the business case through the spokes, with feedback shaping in reverse directions.

In the DOT shaping stage the focus shifts to the way the 'who–why–what' and the business case and overall timetable drives the plans for operations and associated resources from a design and operations strategy perspective instead of a corporate strategy perspective, with feedback as appropriate. The purpose of the exercise and the team of people involved usually change significantly. Involving operations staff or ultimate users and linked stakeholders as well as design staff at this point in the project definition process usually has significant benefits, particularly in terms of building in 'operability' and 'user-friendly' opportunities via feed-forward and feedback between the 'what' and the 'whichway' (plans for operation). This may lead to feedback to modify the 'why' or 'who'. This stage also provides a refined quantification of operating cost, possibly linked to refined revenue feedback, and 'why' in terms of a more developed, measured definition of performance objectives.

In the E&D shaping stage the purpose of the exercise and the team of people involved usually change again significantly. The focus shifts to the way the 'who–why–what' trio drives the execution and delivery strategy shaping from a project perspective, with feedback as appropriate. When execution stage strategic plans are fully developed, delivery stage strategic plans can receive similar consideration. Design development drives the execution plans, associated resource-use plans, and the delivery timetable. But as execution and delivery plans are developed from a project strategy perspective as distinct from a corporate strategy perspective, there is significant feed-forward and feedback between 'whichway' (plans for activities), 'wherewithal' (resource plans for activities) and 'when'. Some 'buildability' opportunity for feedback to the 'what–whichway' (plans for operation) may also prove useful.

As the three strategic planning stages progress, it may be appropriate to bring in other stakeholders, enlarging the 'who' (for example, to banks for resource reasons). It may also become appropriate to consider other interested parties who are not direct players (regulators, or local authorities, for example).

Other lifecycle stages will not be considered now, but later the role of the seven Ws will be explored for each stage. They are of interest when identifying and managing uncertainty throughout the lifecycle.

The 'context 'where' aspect is an obvious influencing factor on the project, and a potentially major influence on most if not all the other six Ws. The physical location of the project execution activity and of the delivered asset in operation are obvious fundamental influences of the context 'where'. However, other aspects of context can also be very important, including:

- the position of a project in relation to a wider set of projects or portfolio of assets operated by the project sponsor;
- the broader economic, political, environmental or technological context;
- the organizational infrastructure provided by key project participants, within which project activities must take place and draw on for support.

Taken together, the seven Ws are key aspects of any projects that need to be explicitly recognized and appropriately managed. They are central to each stage of the lifecycle, although the emphasis and focus vary as the lifecycle unfolds. They should be addressed initially in the context of project definition during the concept-shaping stage, developed and used as appropriate in all subsequent stages.

This brief description of the project definition process in terms of the seven Ws involved is an oversimplification for many projects, but it is sufficiently complex to highlight the nature of important roots of uncertainty in projects. It also helps to make more tangible the nature of the issues involved in the well-known cost–time–quality triad. The limited perspective inherent in the simple cost–time–quality triad characterization of project performance is then apparent. Further, Figure 1.2 provides a useful operational basis for addressing cost–time–quality tradeoffs.

Clearly, significant uncertainty in relation to any of the seven Ws will have major implications for the management of any project. As Figure 1.2 shows, if all of its network of connecting arrows are interpreted as 'the roots of uncertainty', these roots may extend back to the basic purpose of the project and the associated deliverable asset, and even the identity of relevant parties who are not stakeholders in the usual sense. Any uncertainty associated with each aspect earlier in the cycles portrayed by the diagram can be of fundamental concern later because of the potential for significant knock-on effects. A central concern in uncertainty management is ensuring that these interdependencies are understood at an appropriate level of clarity and that they are managed effectively.

Uncertainty associated with project parties

The 'whichway' (plans for relationships and contracts) aspect of Figure 1.2 emphasizes the need to formally address both formal contractual relationships and other important relationships. The involvement of multiple parties in a project introduces uncertainty about important issues that can give rise to massive uncertainty with significant risk and opportunity implications. For example:

- perceptions of influence, roles and responsibilities;
- specification of responsibilities;
- communication between parties;
- capabilities of different parties;
- formal contractual conditions and their effects;
- informal understandings on top of, or instead of, formal contracts;
- mechanisms for coordination and control.

Basic project management processes aim to reduce uncertainty and ambiguity from these areas, but recognizing and managing ambiguity about roles and responsibilities for bearing and managing project-related uncertainty can be crucial. This ambiguity ought to be systematically addressed in any project, not just in those involving formal contracts between different organizations. Informal understandings between different parts of the same client organization or client–regulator relationships can be *very* important. Contractor organizations are often more aware of this source of ambiguity than their clients, although the full scope of the threats and opportunities that this ambiguity generates for each party in any contract (via claims, for example) may not always be fully appreciated until much later. For example, interpretations of risk apportionment implied by standard contract clauses may differ between contracting parties (Hartman and Snelgrove, 1996; Hartman, Snelgrove and Ashfrati, 1997). The nature of assumptions about contractual relationships and associated uncertainty may drive uncertainty about objectives and priorities with further knock-on effects. If a 'fair weather partnership' cracks when the going gets tough, everything else comes apart, and lost opportunities may be the biggest casualty. This is another important part of integrating project uncertainty management and other aspects of basic project management.

Uncertainty about objectives and priorities

The 'who–why–what' trio emphasizes the importance of uncertainty about appropriate tradeoffs between appropriate objectives. Major difficulties arise in projects if there is uncertainty about project objectives, the relative priorities between objectives, and acceptable tradeoffs. These difficulties are compounded if this uncertainty extends to the motives and objectives of the different project parties, and the tradeoffs parties are prepared to make between their objectives. A key issue is: 'Do all parties understand their responsibilities and the expectations of other parties in clearly defined terms which link objectives to planned activities?' The emergence of 'Value Management' (Kelly and Male, 1993; Green, 2001) to address this issue is perhaps indicative of a perceived failure of common practice risk management to address such matters. However they are approached, uncertainty, risk, opportunity and value management need joint integration into project management, and this needs careful, explicit management as part of the definition of project objectives and tradeoffs.

Uncertainty about design and operation and resources for operation

In the process of project definition, the nature of the process deliverable and the process for operating it – with revenue and cost implications – are fundamental uncertainties. In principle, much of this uncertainty is removed in pre-execution stages of the project lifecycle by attempting to specify what is to be done, how, when, and by whom, at what cost. In practice, a significant amount of this uncertainty may remain unresolved even when execution commences. The nature of design and operations assumptions and associated uncertainty may drive a significant portion of the uncertainty about the basis of planning estimates in the early lifecycle stages. This uncertainty needs careful explicit management in two separate modes. One mode is knowledge management as part of the basic project management process – ensuring that knowledge needed later in the lifecycle is generated in a timely manner. The other mode is part of an uncertainty management approach to dealing with incomplete information – assessing ambiguity uncertainty or defining appropriate conditions to achieve unbiased estimates before the first mode has been completed. This is an important part of integrating project uncertainty management with other aspects of basic project management.

Uncertainty about design, execution, delivery and termination logistics

In the process of project definition the nature of the project deliverable and the process for producing it are also fundamental uncertainties. Again, in principle, much of this uncertainty is removed in the pre-execution stages of the project lifecycle by attempting to specify what is to be done, how, when, and by whom, and at what cost. In practice, a significant amount of this uncertainty may remain unresolved even when execution commences.

Sources of uncertainty as both components and composites

Together, the nominal lifecycle and seven Ws frameworks indicate a wide range of sources of uncertainty that ought to be considered in any project uncertainty management process, providing a structure for effective and efficient search processes. They define what might be called 'the roots of uncertainty' in the sense that they are part of complementary generic frameworks. However, 'sources of uncertainty' in this sense do not have a natural or inherent 'base level' of detail for practical analysis purposes. In most contexts, all identified sources of uncertainty may be further broken down or decomposed to provide a more detailed picture, and if we have not yet decomposed them, their composition is uncertain. Alternatively, identified sources of uncertainty may be regarded as components of a higher level, less detailed, composite source that has been decomposed to clarify this composite.

Overall total cost or duration uncertainty for a project is clearly a high level composite of many lower level sources of uncertainty. However, even the most decomposed structures that are viable still involve low-level composites. Further decomposition to clarify a source may be possible, but in practice the limits to decomposition will be defined by what is useful. Further, the most effective and efficient decomposition structure is a matter of choice, which is necessarily dependent upon the process objectives.

Most common practice risk management does not recognize the principle involved in the above paragraph, let alone use it effectively and efficiently. Accepting the last paragraph as a framing assumption provides a different mindset, and explaining its implications is central to this book.

The absolute minimal level of decomposition for total project cost and total project duration is a single source of uncertainty for both – one cost item and a single activity portrayal of a project, with perfectly correlated uncertainty driven by one common source. This is a very special case. If a very modest level of decomposition is involved, the most decomposed sources of uncertainty might equate directly to item cost or activity duration and comparable composites. The nature of any desirable further decomposition will depend upon the goals of the analysis.

However uncertainty is decomposed, identified response options are part of the identified source of uncertainty structure. These response options may be proactive and preventative or reactive and selected after a problem arises. An important implication is that *unidentified* option choices which might be used are an inherent part of the uncertainty involved. Identified option choices that have not been made are also part of the uncertainty involved.

In seeking to identify and manage all sources of uncertainty at an appropriate level of detail, two very different planning processes need to be integrated in an iterative framework: 'top-down' and 'bottom-up'. Most traditional project planning is 'bottom-up'. For example, PERT (Program Evaluation and Review Technique) starts by defining a project activity structure, and individual activity durations are then estimated. The precedence relationships defined by the activity network diagram are then used to compute the project duration. Such bottom-up processes are iterative, in the sense that in a PERT analysis any surprises or difficulties with resources and other issues not considered at the first pass are addressed on a feedback basis. The level of decomposition used initially is usually assumed to be 'fit for purpose' in terms of planning objectives that do not explicitly include understanding uncertainty, and assumptions about the level of decomposition adopted may not be revisited.

An iterative top-down process for planning and costing uncertainty was pioneered by Lichtenberg (2000) in the 1960s. In simple terms, a top-down process might begin with a direct estimate of overall project duration or cost in terms of probability distribution. Two to six of the greatest sources of uncertainty are then identified, and the largest of these sources of uncertainty is decomposed further in the same way. This 'successive' decomposition continues until the structure is considered to be 'fit for purpose'.

The uncertainty management processes explored in this book use an iterative approach to a synthesis of both top-down and bottom-up analysis, specifically avoiding further decomposition in the successive estimation sense unless the insight provided is worth the effort. There is an important synergy between iterative processes, integrating top-down and bottom-up processes, and a flexible approach to composition and decomposition.

Four different types of uncertainty component

In seeking to understand and then manage sources of uncertainty, a further aspect of decomposition is the need to recognize four different forms that uncertainty associated with these sources can take. At a very basic or highly decomposed micro level, 'uncertainty' in the plain English 'lack of certainty' sense can involve four very different types of component: ambiguity, inherent variability, event uncertainty and systemic uncertainty.

1. **'Ambiguity uncertainty'** involves lack of complete/perfect knowledge for various reasons including: a lack of definition of project objectives in the early lifecycle stages, lack of agreed contracts and the unpredictable behaviour of relevant project players, lack of specification of what has to be done in design or planning terms, lack of clarity about proactive or reactive responses if plans do not work, lack of data, lack of detail, lack of structure to consider issues, known and unknown sources of bias, and ignorance about how much effort it is worth expending to clarify the situation. 'Ambiguity uncertainty' or just 'ambiguity' is usefully distinguished because, unlike inherent variability, event uncertainty or systemic uncertainty, ambiguity uncertainty can be reduced by resolving the ambiguity, and the ambiguity may reduce over time without direct action as a consequence of progress with basic project management.

2. **'Inherent variability'** involves the equivalent of events that always happen – it is always a question of degree – like inflation rate variations (referred to as 'issues' by some people, although others use 'issues' to refer to risk events which have been realized already). 'Inherent variability' or 'inherent variability uncertainty' is usefully distinguished from event uncertainty because of its implications for conceptual frameworks and tools that are

limited to dealing with events. It includes the implications of specified or unspecified specific responses – like a client insisting that a contractor takes responsibility for inflation.

3. **'Event uncertainty'** involves events, conditions, circumstances or scenarios that may or may not happen plus associated specific responses – like a particular important piece of equipment failing (or not) in a particular way and being repaired/replaced or not (referred to as 'risks' by many people).

4. **'Systemic uncertainty'** involves simple forms of dependence or complex feedback and feed-forward relationships, including general or systemic responses (often referred to as 'systemic risk') between sources that have been decomposed. A simple example is dependence between all materials and labour prices when markets strengthen modestly or seriously overheat. An effective general response can be early buying and contracting in market lulls. A more complex example is knock-on relationships like a 20% delay in one activity leads to a 30% cost increase but a comparable 20% delay in five related activities leads to a 500% cost increase. An effective general response may be starting the whole project early and proactively managing good luck in early activities to balance later possible bad luck.

In the early stages of the asset lifecycle, ambiguity is the dominant component of all sources of uncertainty. When projects go very badly wrong, systemic uncertainty is usually the dominant component. However, all four types of component are important throughout the lifecycle of most projects.

In operational terms, uncertainty generally has to be considered as an ambiguously defined composite of two or more of these four types of component at various levels of analysis. For example, even a simple event uncertainty source associated with the failure of important equipment usually involves a composite of the many different ways it might fail, including unknown failure modes, plus ambiguity about data, and systemic uncertainty relationships, such as the way three or four minor faults at the same time can lead to total system failure, and systemic uncertainty about the best way to eliminate, transfer or otherwise manage this source of uncertainty. 'Pure event uncertainty' – with no associated ambiguity or systemic uncertainty – is not a practical proposition for analysis purposes. The same is true of inherent variability and systemic uncertainty, because ambiguity uncertainty is ubiquitous – to be found everywhere. We have to get used to the idea that we are normally dealing with ambiguously defined composites of all four kinds of uncertainty even at low levels of composition, without losing sight of the nature of the dominant types of particular interest. The way we choose to structure all relevant uncertainty as suitable composites is the basis of both quantitative and qualitative analysis of uncertainty – it is not practical to attempt full decomposition, and some approaches to partial decomposition are better than others.

The term 'ambiguity' has its critics, for reasons we understand. 'Ambiguity' has the basic dictionary meaning 'capable of more than one meaning', but 'ambiguous' can mean 'of uncertain issue', and 'ambiguity' is the best term we could suggest to capture the idea of uncertainty generated by incomplete knowledge which, in principle, could be completed and agreed. One useful rationalization is the idea that people tend to form hypotheses about everything uncertain; but these hypotheses tend to be different for different people for all uncertainty which involves ambiguity, as distinct from uncertainty which involves accepted explanations – what some people might call 'aleatoric' uncertainty or risk (predictable variability or randomness).

These four categories and their labels involve working assumptions, and alternatives may be preferred. For example, 'ambiguity' might be formally defined as 'incomplete knowledge which could be completed', and given some alternative label. However, some people may prefer seeing all uncertainty as 'incomplete knowledge', which is knowable in principle if not in practice, and others may prefer further decomposition of 'ambiguity' with a variety of labels. Further, some people like the label 'epistemic' when lack of knowledge or lack of predictability is involved, or 'aleatoric' when predictable randomness is involved. In practice what seems important is:

- a reasonably simple and memorable basic structure and terminology;
- an approach that explicitly includes *all* uncertainty;
- recognizing that quite different modelling approaches to events, variability and systemic relationships may *all* be needed;
- recognizing that some uncertainty (such as lack of clarity about objectives) cannot be fully modelled with any of these approaches;
- recognizing that 'fuzzy', 'chaos' or 'complexity' concepts may have a useful role;
- recognizing that an 'incomplete knowledge' view of uncertainty lets us view all processes concerned with knowledge acquisition as potentially relevant;
- recognizing that some uncertainty is about things which are inherently unknowable or unpredictable in the relevant planning period;
- understanding that effective and efficient knowledge acquisition focused on decomposing the uncertainty composites that really matter in any given context is crucial to performance uncertainty management as addressed by PUMPs.

There are other 'type of uncertainty' structures that may also prove useful for some purposes. For example, it can be useful to order the importance of sources of project uncertainty using the list:

1. variability associated with estimates via common practice risk measurement;
2. uncertainty about the basis of estimates;
3. uncertainty about design and logistics;
4. uncertainty about objectives and priorities;
5. uncertainty about fundamental relationships between project parties.

The farther down this list we go, the more important the uncertainty becomes, in terms of risk and opportunity implications. In principle, project manager responsibility may be associated with 1–3, and more senior management responsibility may be associated with 4 and 5. In practice all parties need to be clear about all five: their relationships and their relative importance.

A 'performance lens' and a 'knowledge lens' for uncertainty

The focus of this book is the use of a conceptual 'performance lens' to consider uncertainty. It is always important to be clear when we make working assumptions, and this 'lens' concept is just a way of flagging an important assumption. The central concern of this book is managing performance uncertainty using *'performance* uncertainty management processes' (PUMPs) because we want to shape strategy in the first six stages of the project lifecycle, then shape tactics, then update the shaping of both when execution begins. 'Shaping' in this sense involves making decisions about how best to proceed in terms of project and process objectives – addressing all aspects of uncertainty in performance terms. *'Uncertainty about the achievement of objectives'* is what we see when we look through our *'performance* lens', using all the concepts introduced in this chapter as working assumptions.

We employ this performance lens to answer such questions as 'how much will this project cost?' 'how long will it take?' and 'to what extent will it deliver the intended benefits?' We also need this performance lens to make all decisions that involve tradeoffs between all relevant objectives, using the opportunity and risk concepts discussed in Chapters 2 and 3. Further, we need this performance lens to clarify the relationship between base plans plus contingency plans and performance, to optimize performance by optimizing plans. Effective and efficient use of a performance lens is the basis of the rest of this book.

It can also be useful to use a *'knowledge* lens' to consider uncertainty in the form of incomplete or imperfect knowledge that is beyond the direct focus of PUMPs. Managing uncertainty as incomplete knowledge in our knowledge lens sense is about 'what do we need to *know* to get to the next stage in the project lifecycle beyond what the performance lens perspective will tell us directly?'

'What do we need to know to get to the next lifecycle stage?' is very close to 'What do we need to *do* to get to the next stage?' What we need to *know* and what we need to *do* are so closely coupled, using a *knowledge* lens with associated *'knowledge* uncertainty management processes' (KUMPs) is usefully seen as addressing an important part of the glue between project uncertainty management in performance terms and all other aspects of project management involving uncertainty.

This book will limit its interests in KUMPs to their role when interfacing with PUMPs, but a more general interest in KUMPs could prove fruitful. As a simple example of their recent use in practice in the context of road system planning, Nichols (2007) drew up a list of sources of uncertainty facing a new major road project in the concept shaping stage with two purposes in mind. One purpose was to assess appropriate timing for design development in strategic and then detailed terms – land purchase, ground condition assessments, contracting and other key project lifecycle decisions, which is arguably a *very* important KUMP for basic project planning purposes. The other purpose was to use this list to guide concept shaping cost assessments, when lack of a design, final route, knowledge of ground conditions and contracting approach are key sources of uncertainty. Whether or not we choose to decompose cost uncertainty using these categories raises separate questions, as discussed in Chapters 2 and 7. Viewing uncertainty as incomplete knowledge is the key to recognizing these dual purposes and a very helpful perspective for both PUMPs and KUMPs, a notion we attribute to Mike Nichols.

Viewing uncertainty through a performance lens involves a generalization of a modern decision analysis view of uncertainty in 'decision making' mode. Standard textbook decision trees provide a framework for considering successive decision choices with variable outcomes in terms of all relevant measurable attributes. However, we do not want to make any of the restrictive framing assumptions usually associated with decision analysis – such as discrete value outcomes, or attribute measurability, or the attribute 'utility' functions used to maximize 'expected utility'. Nor do we want to build in the kind of restrictive market-based assumptions used for 'real options' (Trigeorgis, 1997) and other approaches built on a decision analysis basis. The reasons should be clear by the end of this book and, for those interested, further exploration can start with Chapman and Ward (2002, ch. 9).

Viewing uncertainty through a knowledge lens might be associated with a generalization of a modern decision analysis view of uncertainty in 'value of information mode'. Standard textbook decision trees provide a framework for evaluating decision choices under conditions of both 'perfect information' and 'imperfect information' about alternative outcome possibilities. However, knowledge is a much more general concept than information, and incomplete knowledge is the concern of PUMPs as well as KUMPs. We do not want to make restrictive assumptions about what we know, what we do not know, and what we need to know – ambiguity is at the heart of the reality we need to cope with – and managing uncertainty has to cope with all aspects of ambiguity. The key aspects of KUMPs and PUMPs addressed in this book do not address the value of knowledge – they just address 'what do we need to know?' for specific PUMP purposes and related specific basic project planning purposes.

Figure 1.3 portrays some key features of this 'two lens perspective' on uncertainty.

Figure 1.3 clearly puts uncertainty at the centre of deciding whether or not we want to continue to develop a project and, if we do, what needs to be done to get to the next lifecycle stage. In this sense project uncertainty management is central to project management, and PUMPs and KUMPs are complementary key components of our recommended perspective.

Our two-lens view of uncertainty could be elaborated to multilevel compound lens perspectives. For example, we could use a 'trust' lens on top of a 'behaviour' lens on top of our 'performance' lens to focus on uncertainty about trust between key parties in terms of behaviour that has implications for project performance. A trust/behaviour/knowledge lens combination would provide a different perspective, but both may be relevant. Zaghloul and Hartman (2003) provide an example of what these kinds of lens combinations can reveal.

Criteria–plan and knowledge–plan relationship structures

When we look at uncertainty through a performance lens for PUMP purposes, to see uncertainty about the achievement of objectives, we have to use 'criteria-plan relationship structures', part of the integrated seven Ws and project lifecycle structure that defines the roots of uncertainty. For example, project capital cost is central to plans for business case purposes. When considering uncertainty about project capital cost, a capital cost item structure is the obvious starting position for sources of uncertainty. Direct estimation of item cost uncertainty may be an appropriate basic source of uncertainty structure for some capital cost items purchased directly – a specific plot of land currently for sale to be used for a new building, for example. Other capital cost items may involve an uncertain quantity that has to be multiplied by an uncertain cost per quantity unit – the amount of steel needed to build a new oil refinery and the cost per ton of steel, for example. Further items may involve resources with an uncertain cost per unit time and an uncertain duration for the activity defining when they are needed – for example, the cost per unit time of a barge for laying offshore pipelines and how long it will take to lay the pipe. This involves

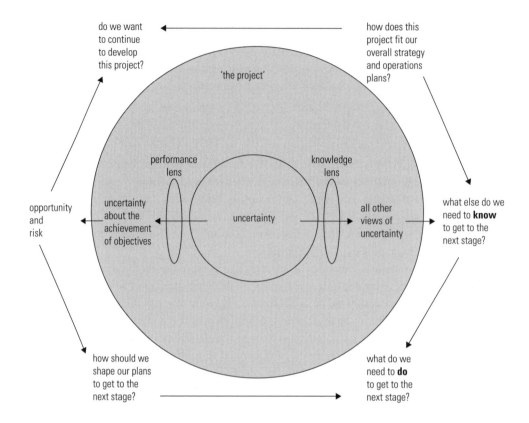

Figure 1.3   The role of the performance lens and the knowledge lens to visualize uncertainty

links between plans for resources and plans for activities. If inflation is a concern, uncertainty about inflation rates needs to be integrated with these planning frameworks, and contractual structures may have important implications. If the cost of the capital tied up during construction is a concern, this depends upon a cost of capital interest rate per unit time, expenditure to date at the end of each relevant time period, the total duration of the construction period, and associated contractual arrangements. A high clarity assessment of capital cost involving components that are duration dependent may have to start by assuming that the primary criterion is duration, and then build on a clear understanding of all relevant capital cost–duration relationships. Capital cost–design and operating cost–design relationships are further examples of criteria–plan relationship structures that may need to be understood. A direct capital cost estimate that leaves these considerations ambiguous may be appropriate at the concept shaping stage of a project, but associated uncertainty should not be overlooked. All relevant plans as defined by the integrated seven Ws and lifecycle structure and all relevant criteria have relationships that need to be understood at a suitable level of clarity.

Shaping project strategy, then shaping project tactics, involves refining base plans and contingency plans. We have to understand the relationships between plans and performance to understand how to shape a project. The criteria–plan relationship structure is a basis for understanding uncertainty in PUMP terms.

When we look at uncertainty through a knowledge lens for KUMP purposes, we use a 'knowledge–plan relationship structure', and what we see may be relevant for PUMP purposes. For example, detailed design for a new highway may have to be done by the prime contractor for its construction, and this may require detailed ground condition surveys, which may not be feasible until the land has been purchased. Planning and executing associated activities is part of the 'what do we need to know?' and 'what do we need to do?' coordination that is a necessary part of basic project planning. Lack of information about ground conditions and detailed design and their relationship with contracting choices is an example of part of the uncertainty that also has to be accommodated in all PUMP analyses early in the lifecycle, whether or not we actually realize it. Failing to see this kind of complexity does not make it go away.

Knowledge–plan relationship structures are also part of the integrated seven Ws and project lifecycle structure, and the way both KUMPs and PUMPs use them needs to be understood at an appropriate level of clarity, acknowledging any ambiguity implied by the chosen level of detail.

Conclusion

Any designated project is a particular reference point in a larger system, affected by the wider system, and with the potential to affect the wider system in turn. Essentially, strategic decisions driven by perceived mismatches between management expectations about future needs and current operational capabilities give rise to project management activity that creates organizational changes, and new or modified assets that in turn have implications for future operational capability and performance. In addition, operational management, corporate management and project management are each influenced by the wider environmental conditions prevailing, and by views about the future operating environment.

Taking a corporate view of enhanced performance, it is important to recognize the extent to which projects are part of a programme of interconnected projects, driven by operations and strategic goals, each requiring management. The desirability of an approach to uncertainty management that addresses the overall system increases dramatically as the interdependency between projects increases.

As well as recognizing the role of a project as part of a larger, corporate picture, it is also important to look inwards, at the detailed internal structure of individual project lifecycles. The management of uncertainty should be an integral part of project management at each stage of the lifecycle, designed to address the pertinent issues at each stage, but cognizant of implications for the following stages of the lifecycle. Many different aspects of uncertainty are involved, from making incomplete knowledge more complete, to getting things done that must be done in order to proceed to the next stage of the project., The scope of the uncertainty that needs to be addressed is at its greatest at the outset, but the depth of analysis should increase as the project progresses towards the execute stage. Prior to each stage, a preliminary analysis of uncertainty, opportunity and risk should guide the first step, but as more details and options are considered in subsequent steps, further analysis should be performed with increasing detail and precision to continuously guide and inform the project management process. Table 1.3 provides a fairly detailed generic lifecycle stage-step framework for doing this.

The value of a *nominal* lifecycle structure at this level of detail might be questioned on three grounds:

- the steps and stages will be difficult to distinguish cleanly in practice;
- in practice some of the steps may not be necessary;
- this level of detail adds complexity, when what is required to be useful in practice is simplification.

For example, it might be argued that some of the later evaluation steps may be regarded as non-existent in practice because the decision to proceed is not usually an issue beyond a certain point. However, it is worth while identifying such steps beforehand, given their potential significance in managing sources of process uncertainty, because many serious sources of project uncertainty are late realizations of unmanaged uncertainty from earlier lifecycle stages, and many organizations spend too much money advancing projects beyond their budget capabilities, often leading to inappropriate project choices. In many projects there is a failure to give sufficient attention to 'go/no-go/maybe' decisions, and to distinguish between efficient *planned* iteration associated with evaluation by the people directly involved, and more debatable *unplanned* iteration which governance evaluation should help to control. Such 'go/no-go/maybe' decisions should involve careful evaluation of uncertainty, both to appreciate the sources of uncertainty inherent in a 'go' decision and the rewards forgone in a 'no-go' decision. Equally important is the need to recognize when a 'maybe' choice should be on the agenda. Many projects appear to involve just one 'go/no-go' decision – at the end of the concept-shaping stage. Yet the large number of projects that run into major problems of cost escalation, time overruns and quality compromises suggests that explicit 'go/no-go/maybe' decision points in later stages would often have been worth while.

A further reason for specifying a detailed step structure for the project lifecycle is to highlight the process of objectives formation. As we will see, the formation and modification of objectives has great significance for uncertainty management, and vice versa. In the early stages of the project lifecycle, objectives and performance criteria are often initially vague for good reasons, but they must be progressively clarified and refined prior to the execution stage. This process needs to be recognized and the implications understood. A situation in which the objectives of a project change imprecisely during the project without proper recognition of the implications of the new situation is particularly risky. From an uncertainty management viewpoint, any changes in objectives and performance criteria at any stage of the lifecycle need to be carefully evaluated for knock-on implications.

The fundamental importance of performance objectives when managing uncertainty warrants careful and detailed consideration of:

- the scope of a project's objectives, including the intended operational performance of the associated asset;
- stakeholders who play a part in shaping these objectives;
- other 'parties' not usually seen as stakeholders who might thwart project objectives (competitors or terrorists for example);
- how different tradeoffs between objectives might be aligned for different parties;
- implemented tradeoffs between these objectives; and
- how all these considerations influence the root sources of uncertainty in any project.

This leads naturally to a need to understand the uncertainty related to the seven Ws and, in particular, the knock-on effects between each of the seven Ws as a project progresses. Consideration of these issues also clarifies some aspects of the 12 stages of the asset lifecycle.

As with the detailed lifecycle structure, the detailed framework provided by the seven Ws framework in Figure 1.2 can be criticized on similar grounds, but defended on comparable grounds. For example, planning relationships and contracts from an early stage in a project can pay huge dividends. Such opportunities are often available but seldom seized effectively because the interaction between parties, contract structures, the rest of the lifecycle, and the rest of the organization, are not clearly understood.

The importance of the four components view of uncertainty (ambiguity, inherent variability, event uncertainty, and systemic uncertainty), and the need to deal with composites of all four at many different levels of composition, may not be immediately apparent, but should become more evident in later chapters.

Similar comments apply to the importance of the performance and knowledge lens views of uncertainty, the implied generalizations of a decision analysis view of uncertainty and the role of criteria–plan and knowledge–plan relationship structures.

All the structures and concepts introduced in this chapter are working assumptions that lay a foundation for the rest of this book. The authors' purpose is not a definition of the best way to view projects and all associated uncertainty, but guidance at a level of detail that avoids, as far as possible, simplifications that might obscure important aspects of the understanding needed in practice, even if very simple approaches are employed.

Chapter 2

Uncertainty, risk and opportunity

An optimist sees the opportunity in every difficulty, a pessimist sees the difficulty in every opportunity.

—Sir Winston Churchill

This chapter explores the implications of distinguishing between risk and opportunity from an uncertainty management perspective, building on the Chapter 1 view of uncertainty in and around projects. This chapter's starting point is contexts when quantification of uncertainty using probability distributions facilitates an effective appreciation and treatment of both risk and opportunity in relation to underlying uncertainty – but objectives that do not lend themselves to quantification are considered later.

Chapter 1 began with very simple definitions for uncertainty, risk and opportunity:

'uncertainty' is 'lack of certainty',
'risk' is 'possible unfavourable outcomes',
'opportunity' is 'possible favourable outcomes'.

As noted in Chapter 1, these are nominal/default definitions, and are as simple and unrestrictive as we could make them. With these definitions, it might be expected that the relative attention paid to 'risk management' or 'opportunity management' in a project context would depend on the degree of pessimism or optimism exhibited by project managers. However, much depends on how possible unfavourable outcomes are distinguished from possible favourable outcomes – and from whose perspective – as well as the extent to which possible responses to risk are treated as opportunities to enhance performance, and vice versa.

The scope for opportunities that matter should be extended via lateral thinking and creativity with a spirit of both optimism and pessimism in Churchill's sense. The search for opportunities should also include looking for improvements in planning and decision-making practice that enable decisions to be more easily made and easier to defend whatever the eventual outcome. Our recommended uncertainty management perspective involves perceiving, in terms of opportunity, all sources of uncertainty that matter which have both 'positive thinking' and clarity of thinking benefits that are significant. There are alternative uncertainty management perspectives, and the reader's understanding of what 'uncertainty management' means may need to be adjusted.

Opportunity, uncertainty and risk are a 'tricky trio', in the sense that they are linked concepts and any attempt to formally restrict the definition of one of these three words can cripple the practical interpretation and pursuit of all of them, and impose a significant handicap on project management as a whole.

One example of confusion with terminology arises from meanings for the terms 'uncertainty' and 'risk' usually attributed to Frank Knight, an influential economist of the early 20th century. A century later they still form a common basis for confusion.

Knight (1921) proposed that the term 'risk' should be applied to situations where probabilities of possible outcomes can be measured, and the term 'uncertainty' should be applied to situations where probabilities cannot be specified. The key implicit assumption was that subjective probabilities were not appropriate. When Knight argued this position, most people took the view that probabilities had to be objective – subjective probabilities were not 'proper' or 'acceptable'. At this time 'decision analysis' was in its 'classic' (pre-1960s) form. It discussed 'decision taking under risk' (when probabilities were available) and 'decision taking under uncertainty' (when probabilities were not available) as two separate paradigms. 'Modern' (post-1960s) decision analysis (Raiffa, 1968, for example) which firmly established the ubiquitous nature of subjective probabilities, should have eliminated this distinction, but surprisingly it persists in many circles, with a legacy of considerable unnecessary confusion. Adding to this confusion, many people interpreted the basic lessons of modern decision analysis to mean that it was no longer necessary to distinguish between 'risk' and 'uncertainty', and the two words were interchangeable. Using safety management paradigms that see 'risk' from a zero incident baseline – with no clear role for opportunity by definition – makes a bad situation worse when opportunities are important. In *The Failure of Risk Management*, Hubbard (2009) points out that Knight's distinction was (and is) inconsistent with the prevailing common language use of the term uncertainty – as when referring to 'quantifying uncertainty' – and with the term 'risk' meaning 'possible unfavourable outcomes'. Hubbard calls Knight's terminology 'a blunder' – 'it was ill-conceived and didn't clarify anything'.

To consider the relationship between uncertainty, risk and opportunity with more precision, a useful place to start is recognizing the desirability of quantifying uncertainty about the achievement of relevant performance attributes – to quantify uncertainty about performance as seen through a performance lens. This implies estimating the range of possible uncertain outcomes for the performance attribute of interest, with some point in the range defining the boundary between what are regarded as favourable or unfavourable possible outcomes. We call this point the 'opportunity/risk datum'. This datum point might correspond to some designated performance target for management purposes, but an expected value is our presumed default interpretation.

Assuming a performance measure with negative consequences such as cost, management might define a lowest (most desirable) possible cost L, and highest (least desirable) possible cost H, a most likely cost ML, and use simple rules of thumb based on a Beta or triangular distribution approximation to define an expected value E, a target T and a budget B, with the risk/opportunity datum defined by E, T or B. This approach is seriously flawed by the ambiguity associated with the use of absolute minimum and maximum values, as discovered early in the application of PERT (Program Evaluation and Review Technique) approaches and explained by Moder and Philips (1970).

The simplest way of avoiding these difficulties involves the use of 'plausible minimum' and 'plausible maximum' values defined as suitable percentile values, usually P5–P95 or P10–P90 percentile values. We recommend the P10–P90 approach for simplicity, as a default assumption, and use of P10 to P90 range estimates.

A P10 to P90 range estimate could be associated with a Beta or triangular distribution. However, a simpler and more general approach involves two components: a model using a uniform density function assumption (implying a linear cumulative distribution) as portrayed by Figure 2.1, plus a general interpretation of the underlying reality like Figure 2.2. Figure 2.2 shows only the density form, which is very convenient to illustrate the model–reality relationship involved, but the usual transformation from a density form to a cumulative form (as illustrated by Figure 2.1) could be used.

The examples of Figures 2.1–2.2 use P10 = 6 and P90 = 14. In Figure 2.1 this means an absolute minimum of L = 5 and an absolute maximum of H = 15, with a convenient P0–P100 range of 10. However, Figure 2.2 should make it clear why asking for estimates of L and H in these terms is not a good idea. In essence the tails could meet the axis anywhere, and the exact point does not matter.

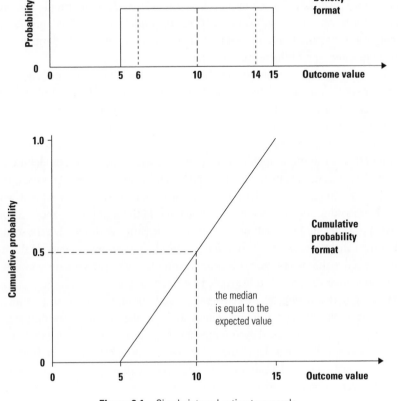

Figure 2.1   Simple interval estimate example

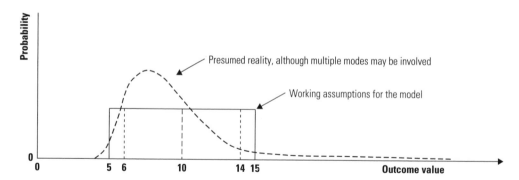

Figure 2.2   An illustration of the approximation involved

Figures 2.1–2.2 should make it clear that E = 10 is a precise estimate in terms of the Figure 2.1 model, and a robust approximation in terms of the Figure 2.2 model, without any limiting distribution assumptions associated with Figure 2.2. Similar comments apply to the P10 = 6 and P90 = 14 estimates.

T = 6 might then be an acceptable stretch target cost (with a P10 interpretation in terms of Figure 2.1) and B = 13 might be an acceptable commitment budget (with a P80 interpretation in terms of Figure 2.1). This might imply a 'provision' estimate defined by E − T of 10 − 6 = 4, and a 'contingency' estimate defined by B − E of 13 − 10 = 3. Some people use other terms, like *'management reserve'* for 'contingency' and *'contingency'* for 'provision', providing a routine source of confusion. As noted earlier, what matters is that everyone involved must be clear about the intended interpretation of the terms adopted.

These Figure 2.1–2.2 interpretations should make it clear that someone who is working to a target T = 6 may see outcome values above 6 as realized risk, but budget holders working to a B = 13 may only see outcome values above 13 as a risk, while others concerned with E = 10 may see 10 as the opportunity/risk datum. The difference clearly matters. Agreeing to use a common opportunity/risk datum for all communication purposes is clearly good practice.

The Figure 2.1–2.2 interpretations involve subjective assessments and modelling approximations with attendant issues about the quality and reliability of estimates. However, these are all explicit working assumptions, which can be assessed for robustness and refined when this is appropriate. Not making such explicit assumptions makes them implicit – they do not go away.

A similar approach could be used for performance measures with positive consequences, like revenue, but the mirror image transformations involved are usefully avoided for the moment. A performance objective that is not quantified can be interpreted in the same framework, but again the complications involved are usefully avoided for the moment.

Distinguishing between targets, expected values and commitments is important in a direct sense – they are typically very different values and are defined for very different purposes. Confusing them is a typical source of dysfunctional behaviour in organizations that only use point estimates. Employing probability distributions to describe possible future levels of performance forces people to clarify the distinction between 'provisions' (E − T, in cost terms the additional cost needed on average) and 'contingency allowances' (B − E, in cost terms, an additional cost allowance to provide an acceptably low probability of failing to meet commitments defined by budgets, more generally linked to any suitable commitment). This clarification produces further insight when ownership of provisions and contingencies is addressed. All measurable objectives can be associated with comparable provisions and contingencies, and these issues should be a central concern for most organizations. However, many organizations with a long history of formal project risk management still do not appear to understand these distinctions.

A minimum clarity approach to quantifying uncertainty

In practice, there may be limited data on which to base estimates of probability distributions for sources of uncertainty that can affect performance in relation to one or more performance criteria of concern. However, in terms of clarifying key uncertainty management issues, even very simple forms of probability distribution are preferable to one-dimensional point estimates or risk assessments based on subjective ratings (for a general critique of risk ratings, see Hubbard, 2009).

This book uses a 'minimum clarity' approach to quantifying uncertainty as both a basic conceptual device and a basic operational tool, as set out in Table 2.1 This 'minimum clarity' approach to the quantification of uncertainty provides the minimum acceptable level of clarity for the lowest feasible level of effort. More clarity provided in an efficient fashion is always an option, but less clarity is a major and fundamental problem in the authors' view. The motive for adopting this minimum clarity base for quantifying uncertainty is clear communication about key issues.

Some people prefer the alternative term 'minimum effort' approach, and it can be very useful to emphasize this positive feature. However, it is also important to remember that the minimum acceptable level of clarity is involved, as well as the minimum level of effort required to deliver this level of clarity.

Table 2.1   A minimum clarity approach to quantifying uncertainty

Associated with possible outcomes for an easily measured attribute with negative consequences like cost, the 'minimum clarity' approach to quantifying uncertainty involves a range-based approach to estimating with the following characteristics.

1. A 'plausible minimum' value, interpreted as a *nominal* ten percentile (P10) value in order of magnitude terms, is estimated on a suitable precision scale.
2. A 'plausible maximum' value, interpreted as a *nominal* ninety percentile (P90) value in order of magnitude terms, is estimated on the same scale.
3. If the plausible maximum and the plausible minimum are equal at the level of precision selected in step 1, a point estimate is acknowledged. This would be a very unusual special case. In any case the scale of uncertainty as defined by the range is acknowledged, and the possible relevance of the following steps is considered.
4. The mid-point of the P10 and P90 estimates is interpreted as a *nominal* fifty percentile value (P50), and assumed equal to the *nominal* expected value.
5. If a 'stretch target' value is relevant, its default value is the plausible minimum. If an alternative value is more appropriate, it should be chosen, usually in the P10 to P50 range.
6. The difference between the stretch target and the expected value (expected value less stretch target value) is 'provision' by definition.
7. If a 'commitment value' is relevant, the expected value is its default value. If an alternative value is more appropriate, it should be chosen, usually in the P50 to P90 range.
8. The difference between the commitment value and the expected value (commitment value less expected value) is 'contingency' by definition.
9. A suitable 'opportunity/risk datum' defines the boundary between risk and opportunity for this particular source of uncertainty.
10. Everyone involved understands all relevant words, concepts and assumptions to a suitable level of clarity.

To interpret this minimum clarity approach in probability distribution terms, the simplest model involves a uniform probability distribution density function, implying a linear cumulative probability distribution. Figure 2.1 provides an example, assuming a plausible minimum P10 value of 6 and a plausible maximum P90 value of 14. This very simple model can be associated with a more complex underlying reality, as illustrated by Figure 2.2. Suppose the distribution in Figure 2.1 represented an estimate of the total capital cost for a proposed project. For budget-setting purposes, when an organization is committing to a project's execution, a commitment value like P80 = 13 might be selected, implying a contingency of 13 − 10 = 3 defined by the P80 − P50, and a 20% chance that cost will exceed this commitment value. The rationale for such a 'commitment value' is that the organization does not want more than one in five projects to exceed their budgets, because there is what economists call 'an asymmetry in the penalty function' – any overestimation or underestimation involves costs, but assuming that they are effectively managed, overestimates, on average, cost less than underestimates. The basis may be additional governance costs when a budget is exceeded, as well as financial costs associated with under- and overestimates.

In principle, estimates associated with components of a project's costs should be stripped of all contingencies to ensure that contingencies are only added once, and not double counted.

At all levels, who owns contingency and provision is an important issue. In principle, the project manager could own both, and there are good arguments for this position. Those at the 'sharp end' (the 'coal-face' or other labels implying 'directly responsible for meeting targets') could manage and be managed to suitable stretch targets set between P10 and P50 values of 6 and 10 (warranting a provision between 4 and zero). This implies that most of the time those at the sharp end will not make their targets, and extra time and money or other performance relaxations will be necessary, drawing on provision and contingency.

If the opportunity/risk distinction is of interest at this level of cost estimation, then the P50 = 10 expected value associated with the currently assumed approach to the project could be adopted as the opportunity/risk datum, where outcomes above 10 will involve realized risk, and outcomes below 10 will involve realized opportunities. In terms of a common understanding of risk and opportunity in projects, this is a reasonable default position with respect to cost and duration.

A project manager might reasonably regard a P80 value used to set his or her budget as the opportunity/risk datum, and a shrewd project manager will usually endeavour to maximize scope for opportunity and minimize scope for risk in relation to how they will be judged. Similarly, a project team member at the sharp end might reasonably seek a P80 for his or her stretch target, unless the management of provision plus contingency explicitly discourages this view. Such behaviour will be more likely if it is felt that earlier cost estimates have been systematically optimistic. For example, at the concept shaping stage of the lifecycle, an estimator who is not likely to be involved in project delivery, and who is under pressure from various quarters to reduce cost estimates, may respond accordingly, unless governance processes discourage all conscious or unconscious bias. More generally, the opportunity/risk datum may be personal or corporate, contingencies and provisions may be explicit and managed at a corporate level, or implicit and managed by all parties involved in their own interests – resulting in considerable dysfunctional behaviour.

If the opportunity/risk datum is agreed at a corporate level, it may be useful to shade the area above and below this datum differently on diagrams like Figures 2.1 and 2.2, and clarify all provisions, contingencies and their ownership at the same time. If safety is a performance criterion using a metric like 'equivalent fatalities', then a zero opportunity/risk datum may be appropriate, and 'searching for opportunities' can be visualized in terms of seeking to reduce levels of risk relative to current expectations.

Confusing targets, expectations and commitments can be part of important failures to manage expectations. Such confusion is of particularly obvious importance in safety contexts, but is always seriously dysfunctional. The key to effective management is clarity about the status of targets, provisions and contingencies.

It is important to understand that Figures 2.1 and 2.2 quantify uncertainty, opportunity and risk in graphical terms, as a two-dimensional shaped area in the density format, as a two-dimensional shaped curve in the cumulative format. Any attempt at one-dimensional consideration involves assumptions that can obscure what is involved.

Clearly organizations that use point estimates have no conceptual basis or tools for recognizing and managing any of these issues.

The probability-impact grid (PIG) – a tool that needs scrapping

A very common tool in risk management practice for projects and other contexts is the 'risk matrix' or 'probability-impact grid' (PIG) or 'probability-impact graph'. The matrix or grid graph comprises cells defined by categories of likelihood or probability, and severity or impact. Identified possible adverse events or 'risks' are assigned to a particular cell in the grid according to the estimated level of probability and impact of the possible event. Proponents and users of PIGs often refer to them as 'probability-impact matrices' (PIMs) or other variants, but we will use the PIGs terminology favoured by the growing band that dislike PIGs or find that PIGs better suits their sense of humour.

PIGs suffer from major inherent limitations (Cox, 2008; Hubbard, 2009), and require a simplistic characterization of risk and uncertainty that falls well short of a minimum clarity requirement. As Cox (2008) concludes, 'the meaning of a risk matrix may be far from transparent, despite its simple appearance', but worse, their evidently attractive simplicity can discourage efforts to produce a more meaningful and useful analysis of uncertainty and risk. Their continued use involves a classic 'tail wagging the dog' illustration of much poor 'risk management' practice, and their use should now be scrapped in all contexts, along with *all* definitions of risk, opportunity or uncertainty designed to accommodate them.

The basic rationale for PIGs is a *very* simplistic definition of 'risk' – limited to potential adverse events, and measured by the product of an event's' probability times its impact. The use of this definition for risk and associated PIGs emerged in pre-1960s safety, reliability or maintainability management/engineering contexts – where events were the concern, little data was available, and subjective probabilities were not acceptable. Consider how a safety manager concerned about the operation of a dangerous facility like a chemical plant might have employed an example PIG, like that in Figure 2.3, in the 1950s.

'Risk' would have been defined in terms of 'possible unfavourable outcomes' using a 'zero accidents' risk/opportunity datum. This would have been consistent with our basic definition and our risk manager's common sense.

'Risk' was formally defined and measured for safety purposes in terms of probability times impact, a single metric equal to the expected outcome (what should happen on average). Risk assessment

the tick. The i_1 value can be interpreted as a P10 value, and the i_2 as a P90 value of any possible impact, given that an impact occurs. Similarly, the p_1 value can be interpreted as a P10 value, and the p_2 as a P90 value, for the uncertain probability of the 'risk' occurring (whatever its uncertain impact), a subjective assessment of the probability uncertainty. A tick in the medium probability–medium impact box has no other plausible minimum clarity interpretation, although a more sophisticated interpretation is feasible.

If the same is done for the rest of the PIG pad, our project manager or other interested person might then wish to assess the combined effect of all these 'risks'. Unfortunately the PIG entries permit only a crude approach to computing the combined effect. A common practice approach involves assuming that each plotted 'risk' corresponds to midpoint values of the relevant cell allowing an expected impact to be calculated from each 'risk'. Summing these individual expected impacts gives an overall expected impact for all 'risks' provided all the 'risks' are independent – and this is invariably assumed to be the case. What does this approach reveal? In brief:

1. A PIG-based approach is not 'qualitative analysis'; it is *weak quantitative* analysis, because it ignores the obvious minimum clarity subjective probability interpretation of ticks in PIG boxes.
2. Any identified 'risk' must be categorized into one of the nine cells (sometimes 16 cells with a 4 by 4 grid). This is the limit of precision involved in delineating estimates of probability of any impact, and the size of the impact assuming an impact occurs.
3. A focus on 'risks' in the common practice 'event uncertainty' sense means that *most* ambiguity, inherent variability and systemic uncertainty usually get ignored – some insightful analysts will force-fit some of it into pseudo events, but this is not easy and is often frowned upon.
4. Using the word 'risks' means that opportunities get ignored.

If the p_k and i_k values, where $k = 0, 1, 2$ or 3, were to be interpreted as P10 and P90 values for the size of impact and the probability of some impact occurring, then there is actually no need to predesignate particular standard cell boundaries. There is no need to force-fit identified sources of event uncertainty into pre-prepared cells which they may not fit – each source can have subjective P10 and P90 values for probability and impact which suit the context. Some probabilities may be very uncertain in conjunction with impacts which are relatively certain, and vice versa. However, this does not resolve points 1, 3 and 4 above.

In terms of point 4, Hillson extended PIGs to embrace favourable events (Hillson, 2002b) – now included in various guides (APM, 2004 and PMI, 2008, for example) – a step in the right direction, but this does not resolve points 1, 2 and 3 above. The term 'project *risk* management' is often held to mean PIG-based approaches; it often involves inadequate attention to opportunities beyond event uncertainty, and it invariably sends the wrong messages about the interconnected roles of uncertainty, opportunity and risk. These are *some* of the basic reasons for the authors abandoning '*risk* management' as a 'brand name' for what we have been attempting to do since the 1970s, replacing it with '*uncertainty* management'. Underlying confusion about what 'risk' means is fuelled by those who have an emotional or commercial investment in PIGs, and by those who are keen to retain the 'risk management' label for similar reasons. To make sense of the resulting literature and related common practices it is important to understand some of the different views that dominate the literature, starting with some basic definitions of 'risk'.

Getting beyond the limitations of a focus on risk

Common usages of the word 'risk' often assume a PIG-based approach. Even if PIGs are not involved, common usage of the word 'risk' often reflects the standard, dictionary definition as: *hazard, chance of bad consequences, loss, exposure to chance of injury or loss*. When the intention is addressing opportunity too, 'risk management' is somewhat unhelpful. Clarity is not enhanced by the ambiguous use of the term 'risk' as a synonym for probability or chance in relation to an event or outcome, the nature of an outcome, or the cause of an effect on performance. Moreover, there is always at least the suspicion that risk assessments and evaluations will be affected by psychological differences in considering potential losses rather than potential gains. In an entertaining and well referenced paper, involving a discussion with Humpty Dumpty, Dowie (1999) argues persuasively for abandoning use of the term 'risk' altogether: *'it is simply not needed'*. Dowie (1999) argues that the term 'risk' is

> *'an obstacle to improved decision and policy making. Its multiple and ambiguous usages persistently jeopardize the separation of the tasks of identifying and evaluating relevant evidence on the one hand, and eliciting and processing necessary value judgements on the other.'*
>
> *'[The term] "risk" contaminates all discussions of probability because of the implicit value judgements that the term always brings with it, just as it contaminates all discussions of value assessment because of the implicit probability judgements that it contains.'*

Dowie's argument is appealing, and it might be coupled with a modern decision analysis perspective to attempt to accommodate risk evaluation via expected utility functions. However, most people would have difficulties if they abandoned the use of the term 'risk' completely. We see no reason to try to forgo all colloquial use of 'risk', and we see good reasons for using the term 'risk efficiency', introduced shortly. In our view ambiguity about the term 'risk' is best avoided by the use of terminology that clearly distinguishes between probability in relation to an event or outcome, the cause of an effect on performance, and the uncertain effect on one or more performance attributes. Use of the word 'risk' to refer to any of these inter-changeably is not helpful and can be a source of confusion. In particular, it is essential to distinguish clearly between 'risk' as the uncertain effect on one or more performance attributes, and common usage of the terms 'a risk' or 'risks' to refer to causes of uncertainty about the achievement of objectives. As an illustration that care is needed with terminology, consider the definitions of 'project risk' offered by the USA-based (but with worldwide reach) Project Management Institute (PMI) and the UK-based Association for Project Management (APM).

The PMI defines 'project risk' as 'an uncertain event or condition that, if it occurs, has a positive or negative effect on a project's objective' (PMI, 2009, p. 9; PMI, 2008).

The APM PRAM guide refers similarly to 'an uncertain event or set of circumstances that, should it occur, will have an effect on achievement of one or more of the project's objectives', but calls this a 'risk event' rather than a 'project risk' (APM, 2004, p. 17). The APM PRAM guide reserves the term 'project risk' to describe the joint effect of risk events and other sources of uncertainty, defining project risk as 'the exposure of stakeholders to the consequences of variation in outcome'. This definition is similar to the ISO 31000 definition of risk as 'the effect of uncertainty on objectives' (International Standard, 2009). This latter definition is a considerable improvement on earlier ISO definitions and most common practice, but in our view, this is a better definition of 'performance uncertainty', the basis of 'performance uncertainty management' – uncertainty as it is seen through a performance lens. This indicates a direct alignment of our perspective and an ISO 31000 approach in principle, but in practice the terminology differences are important.

Notwithstanding the somewhat different terminology in relation to cause and effect, we have two concerns with the PMI and APM definitions. First, defining risk in terms of 'events' ('conditions' or 'circumstances') does not facilitate consideration of potential variability in performance that is driven by underlying ambiguity or limited knowledge. As noted in Chapter 1, sources of ambiguity related to the quality of estimates, gaps in plans, the nature of objectives, and working relationships between different project participants, can have major implications for performance. Further, event-based definitions of risk also obscure the often crucial role of inherent variability and systemic uncertainty affecting project performance.

Second, both the PMI and APM definitions of risk include the potential for both upside and downside effects on performance objectives (as does the ISO 31000 definition among others). Such definitions recognize the desirability of seeking to manage both upside as well as downside possibilities. However, they fail to clarify associated opportunity/risk datum setting issues. For a given performance measure, the opportunity/risk datum chosen is significant, and the associated management issues matter, including different people having different perceptions of what constitutes an adverse or favourable outcome. These issues require careful management, and this demands appropriate visualization and terminology. For this reason 'risk' is more usefully defined in terms of 'possible unfavourable outcomes with respect to an opportunity/risk datum for all relevant objectives'. 'Opportunity' is usefully defined as the flip side of risk, as possible favourable outcomes with respect to the same opportunity/risk datum points. Any directly comparable alternative definitions that the reader may prefer are not an issue – these definitions are nominal/default definitions, as indicated at the outset of this chapter. As far as possible we want to use unrestrictive plain English. However, restrictive simplifications are not helpful.

For those concerned to broaden the scope of the 'risk management' brand beyond potential adverse outcomes, defining 'risk' to include possible favourable outcomes as well as possible unfavourable outcomes may not produce the desired result. The problem is overcoming the near universal tendency for people to associate the term 'risk' with 'hazard' or 'loss'. One consequence of this is that risk management guidance that employs upside–downside inclusive definitions of risk tends to be subverted, or at least biased, in implementation, to activity focused on reducing, or at best neutralizing, the potential adverse consequences of 'threats' – sources of uncertainty that can only impair performance. Event-based definitions of risk are likely to encourage this tendency. Such a focus on threat reduction can mean that potential opportunities to enhance performance, even by merely creatively managing threats, are never even looked for, let alone evaluated. At the very least, threat-focused risk management should not only consider ways of reducing adverse consequences, but also consider ways of managing threats to create benefits. Courses of action are often available which reduce or neutralize potential threats while simultaneously offering opportunities for positive improvements in performance. This is the idea of 'making a virtue out of a vice', or 'turning a weakness into a strength'. Consider two examples which illustrate this point.

Capturing the benefits of 'fair weather' in offshore North Sea projects

BP (British Petroleum at that time) successfully pioneered the use of SCERT (Synergistic Contingency Evaluation and Review Technique) for their offshore North Sea projects in the 1970s and 1980s (Chapman, 1979), a precursor of the performance uncertainty management process (PUMP) based approach advocated in this book. A key source of uncertainty addressed in this North Sea context was weather. Offshore pipe laying involves significant uncertainty associated with weather. Relative to expected (average) performance, long periods of bad weather can have a significant, sustained impact. Although it is important to recognize and deal with this 'threat', it is also important to recognize that the weather may be exceptionally kind, providing a counterbalancing opportunity. Making sure that supplies of pipe can cope with very rapid pipe laying is essential, for obvious reasons. Also important is the need to shift following activities forward, if possible, if the whole pipeline is finished early. If this is not done, 'swings and roundabouts' are just 'swings': the bad luck is accumulated, but the good luck is wasted, with a ratchet effect preserving unanticipated delay as a project progresses. Fair weather is an example of inherent variability uncertainty which can be treated as an opportunity event, but full and natural treatment as inherent variability uncertainty plus associated ambiguity and systemic uncertainty is much more effective. This approach was used successfully by BP in the 1970s and 1980s, and thereafter by clients of the authors with a wide range of application areas.

A threat resolved creates an opportunity in a National Power project

National Power successfully adapted SCERT for National Power projects in the 1980s, beginning with a combined cycle gas turbine electric power station used internally as a 'demonstration project'. The team responsible for this demonstration project were concerned about the threat to their project's completion time associated with various approvals processes which involved important novel issues. Gas was to be provided on a take-or-pay contract in which the gas supply would be guaranteed from an agreed date, but gas not required from that date would still have to be paid for. This made any delay relative to the commitment operating date very expensive, the cost of such unused gas being in effect a project cost. The only response identified was to move the whole project forward three months in time (planning to start the execution stage three months earlier and finish three months earlier), and arrange for standard British Gas supplies for testing purposes if the project actually finished three months early. Using British Gas supplies for testing was a non-trivial change, because its gas composition was different, requiring different testing procedures and gas turbine contract differences. This response would deal with planning delays, the motivation for first suggesting it, but it would also deal with any other reasons for delay, including those not identified, the 'unknown unknown'. Further, it provided a very high degree of confidence that the combined cycle gas turbine plant would be operational very shortly after the main gas supply initiation date. But of special importance here: this response made it practical to maintain the strategy of using British Gas supplies for testing, but move the whole project (this time including the main gas supply availability date) back (starting and finishing later) in order to time the take-or-pay contract date to coincide directly with the beginning of the peak winter demand period, improving the corporate cash flow position. The opportunity to improve the cash flow position in this way, while maintaining confidence with respect to the take-or-pay contract for gas, was deemed to be a key impact of the uncertainty management process. The search for a way to resolve a threat was extended to the identification of a related but separate opportunity involving a different objective which had custodians in a different part of the organization. Finding this opportunity was widely seen as the key benefit of the process, the key reason for rolling the process out to all other projects.

This is an example of an opportunity that involves resolving a 'mess' of related problems including (a) responses to an accumulation of ambiguity, inherent variability and systemic uncertainty as well as event uncertainty, plus (b) effective 'general' responses to all kinds of uncertainty, plus (c) clarity about communicating the scope for other objectives and agendas to be addressed jointly.

Towards a focus on uncertainty management

The BP example just discussed involves managing opportunities on a very local scale. The National Power example involves managing opportunities on a much broader scale. These two examples jointly illustrate the importance of opportunities as well as threats, the first in cost terms at an activity level, the second in cost and revenue terms at a project level. In the first example, if the implications of good luck are not seized, and only bad luck is captured, the accumulated effect is reasonably obvious once the mechanism is understood, and it should be clear that this applies to all activities in all projects. The second example illustrates the benefits of creative, positive thinking, with good communication of what is involved across the whole organization, looking beyond merely overcoming or neutralizing problems to associated opportunities. This aspect of problem solving is more subtle, and it is not widely understood, but it can be very important, in direct terms and from a morale point of view.

High morale is as central to good uncertainty, risk and opportunity management as it is to the management of teams in general. If a project team becomes immersed in nothing but attempting to neutralize threats, the ensuing doom and gloom can destroy the project. Systematic searches for opportunities, and a management team willing to respond to opportunities identified by those working for them at all levels (which may have implications well beyond the remit of the discoverer), can provide the basis for systematic building of morale.

Effective management of uncertainty, opportunity and risk in integrated terms – whatever it is called in brand name terms – requires a proactive approach that seeks to reduce the size and possibility of threats, and increase the size and possibility of opportunities. Potentially, these are separable activities, but it is not usually efficient or effective to treat them as such. Indeed, opportunities and threats are seldom independent. Just as it is inadvisable to pursue opportunities without regard for the associated threats, so it is rarely advisable to concentrate on reducing threats without considering associated opportunities. For this reason, use of the term 'uncertainty management' can be more helpful that the term 'risk management', because it implies exploring and understanding the origins of uncertainty before seeking to manage it, with no preconceptions about what is desirable or undesirable. This is a significant change in emphasis compared with most established risk management processes. BP and National Power did not use the term 'uncertainty management', but for some time the authors have suggested its use to clients, and Stat Oil successfully adopted an 'uncertainty management' label in the late 1990s (Jordanger, 1998). The authors believe the PUMP 'performance uncertainty management process' terminology will help all organizations to achieve all the goals sought earlier with greater ease, plus new goals.

More generally, replacing the word 'risk' with the word 'uncertainty' in all relevant standards and guides should significantly broaden thought processes. 'Risk identification' becomes *'uncertainty identification'*. A process involving *uncertainty* identification (rather than risk identification), should draw attention in a natural way to uncertainty about planning choices, uncertainty about objectives and priorities, and uncertainty about fundamental relationships between the organization and its stakeholders. Additionally, an *uncertainty* identification process should induce identification of a wider set of possibilities for managing a particular source of uncertainty. For example, a *risk* identification process focusing on potential threats might highlight 'unavailability of a key resource' as a risk, prompting possible responses such as 're-schedule activities' or 'obtain additional resource'. However, an exercise seeking to identify sources of *uncertainty* encourages a more neutral description of factors, which facilitates a less constrained consideration of response options. Instead of the risk 'unavailability of a key resource', an exercise identifying sources of uncertainty would express this as 'uncertainty about the availability of a key resource', prompting questions about all factors influencing availability, essential characteristics of the resource, and the possibility of excess as well as shortage of the resource. In particular, how to make good use of excess resource has to become an issue. After the simple substitution of 'uncertainty' for 'risk' in all terminology, a linked additional step would be to modify wording in risk management guidelines wherever this associates risk (uncertainty) with threat. For example, a 'mitigation' response option could be described as 'effect modification' rather than 'impact reduction', and the generic 'prevention' response could be described as 'changing the probability of occurrence'. Decisions about the transfer of risk would become decisions about sharing significant uncertainty, considering both upside and downside effects. Not only would this terminology induce a more considered view of the wisdom of risk (threat) transfer, it would also stimulate consideration of the wider implications of transfer strategies.

The authors recognize there are strong barriers to many people dropping current common practice 'risk management' terminology in favour of the 'uncertainty management' terminology used in this book. However, in our view it is essential to *think* in uncertainty management terms to get the full benefits of a PUMP approach, while being prepared to *speak* whatever local risk management language prevails whenever necessary. For reasons that will becomes clear later, a PUMP approach can embrace all common practice risk management approaches as special cases, but it is broader in scope, more efficient and more effective, and this makes some common practice features redundant. Probability-impact grids are just the obvious 'tip of the iceberg' in this respect.

A basic feature of uncertainty management as advocated by this book is managing *all* uncertainty using integrated quantitative (probabilistic) approaches and qualitative approaches. Quantification is not limited by the availability of objective data. However, quantification should not be attempted unless it looks potentially useful, and it needs to work from at least a 'minimum clarity' base. Lack of data should not be an excuse to settle for the limited perspective offered by simplistic probability-impact grids. The following example demonstrates what can be achieved taking an uncertainty management perspective and employing 'minimum clarity' quantification.

Quantification of uncertainty for the Highways Agency

Taken as a whole, the guide *Prioritising Project Risks*, published by the UK Association for Project Management (Hopkinson et al., 2008), can be reasonably interpreted as a fatal blow to the credibility of PIGs and event-based approaches more generally. It was prepared by a working party of the APM (Association for Project Management) in liaison with individuals influential in the development of PMI (Project Management Institute) risk management guidance. Part of the *Prioritising Project Risks* argument is based on a 2007 Highways Agency re-estimation study, summarized below. This case study illustrates:

- the practical role of a composite view of all uncertainty;
- the role of ambiguity, inherent variability and systemic uncertainty as well as event uncertainty ('risks' in common practice terms);
- the way a residual composite forces completeness; and
- the way both qualitative and quantitative approaches can be used together.

Review of Highways Agency's Major Roads Programme: Report to the Secretary of State for Transport (Nichols, 2007) is available on the Department for Transport (UK) website. It is a personal report by Mike Nichols, Chief Executive of the Nichols Group, with support from a small group of Nichols Group staff, including Chris Chapman. It was accepted by the Highways Agency (HA), and initial implementation involving a Nichols team, including Chris, was deemed a success by all concerned, including HM Treasury.

Of immediate interest, when considering the capital cost of a proposed new major road programme at the beginning of the concept shaping stage, the report made it clear that *all* uncertainty had to be addressed, starting top-down. Three component composites were worth identifying:

(1) uncertainty best owned and managed by the government (not the HA),
(2) uncertainty best owned and managed by the HA at a portfolio of projects level,
(3) uncertainty best owned and managed by the HA at an individual project level.

Uncertainty composite (1) included inflation, escalation of construction costs over and above general inflation because of economic cycles, and the impact of delays for government funding reasons with systemic uncertainty connections to inflation and escalation. *Complete (100%) qualitative treatment* was advised for component (1), *complete (100%) quantitative treatment for component (3), and a mix of the two for component (2)*. This meant that all concept shaping stage projects were estimated in 'present £' terms, 'money of the day', subject to timing and funding assumptions involving government decisions. Transfer of this uncertainty to contractors via the Highways Agency only made sense *after* contracts between the HA and contractors were signed *if such contracts transferred responsibility for inflation, escalation and delay to the contractor*. To the extent that government funding delays impacted costs after the start of construction, responsibility had to stay with the Government – part of the 'whichway' (planning relationships and contracts) aspect of Figure 1.2 best addressed at corporate level. There was no acceptable rational argument for the Department for Transport (DfT) not accepting this uncertainty on behalf of the government.

Uncertainty composite (2) included changes in cost linked to changes in road 'quality' driven by European Union (EU) regulations or HA decisions to improve 'quality' beyond EU minimums – for example, changes in design regulations about crash barriers. The HA needed to manage some uncertainty at a portfolio level because this was managerially efficient and effective.

Uncertainty composite (3) was, *by definition*, everything else, a residual of all uncertainty not explicitly part of (1) and (2). Before a project had a designated manager, all involved managers and project cost estimators needed clarity about what was explicitly excluded and their responsibility for the ambiguities – like crash barrier costs that go beyond EU minimums and standard additional HA provisions.

The initial implementation involved a re-estimation exercise. The HA wanted to re-estimate the cost of a portfolio of major road projects worth about £20 billion in about six weeks. A stratified sample of projects was taken, scaled up to size portfolio cost. To estimate uncertainty composite (3) for each project, a simple decomposition was used: construction cost, cost of land, and cost of traffic management are good examples of the half dozen components involved.

When considering a proposed new project at the beginning of the concept shaping stage, most of the uncertainty involved is ambiguity uncertainty involving incomplete knowledge. This uncertainty in respect of construction cost might have been estimated directly, asking the estimator originally involved for a direct estimate of P10 and P90 values in terms of Figures 2.1 and 2.2. However, given the history and context, a three-part approach was adopted. Construction cost was decomposed into three components: cost uncertainty the estimator had in mind when the original point value construction cost estimate was prepared; risk provisions calculated via common practice project risk management approaches; and everything else – a residual so that *all relevant uncertainty* was addressed in quantitative terms. The cost uncertainty that the estimator had in mind when the original point estimate was prepared included such ambiguities as no design as yet, no surveys as yet, no definitive route as yet, and no agreed contracting approach as yet – a list of major sources of ambiguity uncertainty that would be resolved before a contract was signed unless early contractor involvement forced HA commitment to build before these issues were resolved.

After a careful briefing to ensure that the estimator involved knew what was required, the estimator and a facilitator constructed a 'sensitivity diagram' (illustrated by Figure 2.4) that was used as a framework for the in-built integration of the three-component probability distribution estimation processes.

Figure 2.4 uses a 'normalized' scale, with 100% as a base estimate value, to avoid project specific information and portray the 'typical' outcome of interest here. The relative positions of lines 1 to 3 is typical for major road projects assessed at an early stage in their lifecycle, but it is not an accurate portrayal of particular projects.

The vertical dashed line is a 'line zero' – the original point value, base estimate value produced earlier by the estimators.

Four sources of uncertainty were identified and explained to the estimators responsible for the line zero estimates.

- Source 1 was 'base value estimating uncertainty' – all the uncertainty about working assumptions normally considered in qualitative terms by the estimator when producing the base estimate.
- Source 2 was 'uncertainty associated with previous risk registers'– the joint effect of all sources of uncertainty in the risk registers used previously.
- Source 3 was 'other uncertainty sources for which the HA is held accountable that have not been addressed at a portfolio level' – the joint effect of all other sources of uncertainty for

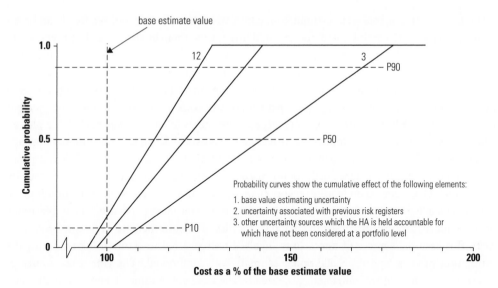

Figure 2.4   Sensitivity diagram: Highways Agency (HA) example

which a minister could reasonably hold the HA accountable, such as the impact of reasonably foreseeable changes in EU safety rules involving crash barriers with project-specific impacts not accounted for separately at a portfolio level.

- Source 4 was 'portfolio level sources' plus 'government level sources', separated out for collective treatment at portfolio and government communication levels as noted earlier, treated as non-quantified conditions defined by scope assumptions for construction cost estimation purposes.

Line 1 was defined by source 1, 'base value estimation uncertainty'. Line 1 would have passed through the line zero P50 if appropriate provision and zero contingency for estimating error had been built into the original estimate. Line 1 was estimated by asking the estimators to provide P10 and P90 values of uncertainty associated with their base estimate excluding sources 2, 3 and 4. This involved asking for a Figure 2.1–2.2 estimate with predefined conditions using the format of Figure 2.4 for estimation purposes.

Line 2 was line 1 plus source 2, 'uncertainty associated with previous risk registers'. The P50 for line 2 shifted to the right by an amount equal to the previous risk allowance point estimate if contingency and provision for risk register events was fully embodied. This line was estimated directly using Figure 2.4. It might have been produced by asking for a separate Figure 2.1–2.2 estimate for source 2, then adding it to source 1, assuming perfect positive correlation, with further options discussed later.

Line 3 was line 2 plus source 3, 'other uncertainty sources for which the HA is held accountable that have not been addressed at a portfolio or government level' – the joint effect of all other sources of uncertainty for which a minister could reasonably hold the HA accountable. This line was also estimated directly using Figure 2.4. Again it might have been produced by asking for a separate Figure 2.1–2.2 estimate for this source, then adding it to sources 1 plus 2 assuming perfect positive correlation, or alternatives discussed later.

Lines 1–3 components were estimated in cumulative form directly, not separately and then summed. That is, HA staff located line zero and line 1, then thought about the shift necessary to define line 2 directly, and also about the shift necessary to define line 3 directly. This implies a level of dependence less than perfect positive correlation could be assumed and estimated directly without losing the convenient simplicity of linear cumulative probability curves. Separate estimates in terms of Figures 2.1–2.2 plus a perfect positive correlation assumption is simpler, but more restrictive. A further simple option is separate estimates in terms of Figures 2.1–2.2 plus an addition using Monte Carlo simulation with a robust statistical dependence assumption, usually in the range 0.5 to 1.0 if a coefficient of correlation definition is used, and 50% to 100% dependence if a percentage dependence definition is used. An assumption of high dependence generally has a much closer correspondence to reality than an assumption of independence. To minimize bias it is usually better to begin with an assumption of significant dependence. The implications of these alternatives are discussed in Chapter 11 – they are not immediately relevant here.

In this case the sources of uncertainty involved were ordered to clarify thinking during the estimation process, and each additional estimate was conditional. The composite source of uncertainty addressed by component (2), sized by the gap between lines 1 and 2, was the total of all common practice event risks considered previously, plus the implications of dependence between them. In most individual projects, the composite sources of uncertainty addressed by component (2) proved to be much less important than components (1) and (3), as indicated by Figure 2.4. Because lines 1 and 3 were previously unmeasured, persistent underestimation bias was inevitable, of the order indicated by Figure 2.4. Previously this had been addressed unsuccessfully using an 'optimism bias' adjustment processes mandated by HM Treasury (2003a, 2003b). There are fundamental problems with most optimism bias adjustment processes which Chapter 11 addresses.

One key message here is that more refined and restructured treatment of source 2 is a waste of time compared to more refined and restructured treatment of sources 1 and 3. Another key message is frameworks that omit consideration of sources 1 and 3 are failing to address what really matters in any comparable context. Conventional project risk management does not address sources 1 and 3 directly – some skilled users will introduce aspects of sources 1 and 3 partially, but the conventional process framing assumptions do not cater for these components of uncertainty – predominantly inherent variability, systemic and ambiguity uncertainty. A further key message is that optimism bias needs to be addressed in an uncertainty management framework that addresses all components of uncertainty.

In the HA study, a separate estimate in Figure 2.4 form was then used for each sampled project's 'cost of land', 'cost of traffic management', and several other cost items of this kind.

At the next level up in the composition process, the contractor's construction cost for each project was added to such components as the cost of land and the cost of traffic management using coefficient of correlation assumptions in the 50–100% dependence range. The sensitivity diagram format of Figure 2.4 was used to clarify the relative importance of expected values and variability for all components at the project level, with lines 2, 3 and so on taking a curved shape because of the less than 100% dependence. The resulting sample project cost estimates were then scaled to provide a re-estimate for the project portfolio as a whole, excluding portfolio level uncertainty.

Separate estimates of portfolio level sources of uncertainty could have been quantified and then combined in the same way using the same diagram format. However, the treatment here becomes more complex. For example, much of the need for changes to HA projects is driven by government actions and HA responses to changes in world conditions which are portfolio level changes – an illustration of corporate strategy level changes driving related project changes. This needs systematic treatment in portfolio terms, with project level provisions for minor changes, plus clear qualitative treatment of relevant condition sets in scenario terms, plus clear ownership of all related issues – both financial and managerial.

For each sampled project, at each level of composition, the re-estimation displayed in the format of Figure 2.4 provided a first pass view of where the greatest sources of uncertainty lay relative to original point estimates. For example, Figure 2.4 shows that uncertainty related to previous risk registers (component (2)) are less significant than uncertainty related to other uncertainty sources (components (1) and (3)), which is usually the case.

A key assumption underlying an uncertainty management approach is that all sources of uncertainty relevant to any assessment of uncertainty should be considered in an optimal decomposition structure using an optimal approach to portraying what matters and other optimized working assumptions, even if a simple unbiased estimate is the only concern. This is a necessary deliverable of the PUMP approach developed in Chapter 4 and the rest of this book, as illustrated by this HA example.

Working assumptions associated with Figure 2.4 might have included perfect positive correlation between the three sources of uncertainty 1–3 had separate estimates for these sources been combined, but the conditional relationship embedded in the approach adopted avoids the assumption of any particular level of dependence, and there was no need to explore dependence in detail to achieve a first pass correction of earlier bias associated with overlooked sources of uncertainty at the project level involved in Figure 2.4.

The motives for uncertainty management served by the Figure 2.4 sensitivity diagram tool plus their linked nesting structures (and more sophisticated forms) include achieving clarity of understanding of uncertainty in terms of where it comes from and how it combines. Those responsible for a PUMP need the understanding provided by sensitivity diagrams to drive the process, building the structure in a bottom-up manner as the process proceeds. They also need to use sensitivity diagrams selectively in a top-down manner to explain their conclusions to all other relevant parties. What this involves is explored in more detail in Chapter 11, along with alternative approaches to sensitivity diagrams.

A key point of immediate relevance is that the HA example as discussed so far is about clarifying *uncertainty* with a view to eliminating bias. The wide variability depicted in Figure 2.4 should not be associated with *risk*, because during the concept shaping stage there is no commitment to build, and much of the uncertainty associated with components 1 and 3 would be reduced before a commitment to build – by completing surveys, designs and contractual arrangements.

There are, however, other important sources of risk the HA needs to manage. In particular, bias is important to the HA because persistent underestimation of costs (overestimation is not a problem) could damage the credibility of HA staff. Any organization that persists with estimating approaches that are significantly biased is likely to incur a reputation for not understanding what it is doing. Immediately obvious implications of such unaddressed bias include too many projects that get beyond the concept gateway and have too much money spent on them too early – money that may be wasted completely. But it is also a symptom of a much deeper problem: the failure to understand the 'opportunity efficiency' implications of uncertainty in more general terms.

Bias is a major risk with wide-ranging implications, and addressing bias is an important aspect of the PUMP approach. It is not an integral part of most common practice project *risk* management processes, which cannot deliver unbiased estimates because they do not explicitly address *all* sources of uncertainty, quantified or non-quantified, in an integrated manner.

Developing initial trust and sustaining trust between key parties

Highways Agency estimators of proposed possible road projects have a lot of knowledge about costs which gets lost in a traditional point estimation process. Figure 2.4 illustrates this in terms of the range covered by line 1 – uncertainty normally considered by an estimator when arriving at a point estimate. What may be less obvious is that asking an estimator for his or her estimate of a plausible minimum and maximum in clearly defined terms demonstrates trust by the facilitator involved, and this trust will usually be rewarded with an estimate that can be trusted. If processes based on such approaches are used by estimators and all other members of the organization, this trust becomes more general. There is significant evidence, dating back to such books as Moder and Philips (1970), that one of the biggest payoffs from interval estimates as introduced in early PERT applications is reducing both conscious and unconscious bias – getting estimates that can be trusted.

When an HA project manager takes responsibility for a project and inherits an early estimate of the project's cost and other performance parameters, trust in earlier analyses is important. So is trust between the project manager and the manager to whom he or she reports in terms of what uncertainty belongs to the project and what belongs to the organization – at portfolio level or corporate level, or to client organizations – that is, the government, in the HA example. So too, is trust between the HA overall and the responsible minister. When contractors become involved trust is again a central issue. An early detailed look at risk management in contractual terms by Curtis, Ward and Chapman (Curtis et al., 1991) produced a memorable quote by one of the participants: 'When the contract comes out of the drawer everybody is in trouble.' The lawyers are usually an exception, but no one else.

Trust involves an understanding of intent. It also involves an understanding that there is scope for good luck and bad luck. This means that there has to be scope for substantial variation in all performance estimates at the beginning of a project lifecycle which can only be reduced as more is known about 'what' has to be done, 'when', 'how' and 'why'.

Sustained trust is the lubricant that keeps the wheels on a project turning. Lack of bias in initial estimates, understanding the difference between bad luck and bad management, clarity about responsibilities, and clarity about professional competence, as well as intent, are all key ingredients.

A 'golden rule' of relationships management is 'unreasonable expectations are premeditated resentments'. Initial trust between key parties is important. At the outset of a project, building trust involves making sure that all key players have reasonable expectations of each other, , judging 'reasonable' from all perspectives, and communicating effectively about important gaps in perceptions that develop as the project evolves. A 'crisis of silence' (Grenny et al., 2007) needs to be avoided.

A simple approach to contracting risk

The Highways Agency case study discussed above involves risk in terms of bias from the perspective of a large client organization at the front end of large projects, in a portfolio of large projects addressed in parallel. This is a form of risk that is not part of a common practice project risk management agenda. Consider another example to demonstrate how the PUMP approach and its uncertainty–risk–opportunity language address in a simple manner those risks that are not on a common practice project risk management agenda – this time from the perspective of a very small contractor who undertakes a series of very small projects.

In 2005 Bruce Chapman Solutions (BCS) was founded – a domestic bathroom and kitchen refurbishment business. By 2007 it was clear that Bruce seemed to have found his vocation, but he was not making much money. His brother Andy, a programme management consultant, and his father Chris, offered to help by designing a practical approach to contracting risk based on a minimum clarity approach to cost estimating and two basic contract options. Chris simplified an approach to bidding originally developed for IBM UK, and Andy developed a spreadsheet package to make its implementation as simple as possible, as discussed in Chapman (2008). To illustrate the approach now working to Bruce's satisfaction, consider how Bruce initially approached a client called Sally, who just wanted a new floor covering in a bathroom.

When Bruce arrived to give Sally an estimate for a new floor covering she had three questions in mind, which Bruce understood without being told.

1. Would the cost be 'affordable' – or would the money be better spent on something else?
2. Would the cost be 'competitive' – or would someone else provide better value?
3. Could Bruce be trusted, in terms of honesty and competence?

After the usual social pleasantries and inspecting the site, Bruce started by indicating a plausible range for the cost of the floor covering material: £100 to £400 retail cost, depending upon the quality. He made the point that Sally would obviously want to make the choice herself. Bruce then said he had a trade account with several suppliers he could take her to, and he would give her his trade discount. First impressions matter. Bruce wanted to start building trust and a competitive position at the outset, and capture other opportunities discussed later.

Bruce then sat down with Sally and used his laptop computer with Andy's software to provide an estimate and basis for a contract. Table 2.2 shows an extract with the information of immediate concern.

Three data entry lines for three items are shown: one for removing the old floor covering and preparing the surface, one for laying the new flooring, and one a provision for cleanup and other time. Bruce had to enter the text for each task line, according to the job, but line 3 was a residual item for 'everything not included above' which Bruce uses for all contracts. Each of these three items has two estimates of the number of hours Bruce will need, input by Bruce, shown in bold: a 'target minimum' (plausible minimum) and a 'target maximum' (plausible maximum). As also shown in Table 2.2, the spreadsheet software calculated mid-point estimates, summed all three estimates, used Bruce's hourly rate (£30 per hour assumed) to convert duration to cost, and provided an 'estimated contract value' of £726. Bruce explained each row as he and his software produced it, based on the following.

Table 2.2 Extract from Sally's BCS cost estimate and contract

Item description	Target minimum	Target maximum	Target mid-point
Remove old floor covering and prepare surface	4	12	8
Lay new flooring	8	12	10
Provision for cleanup and other time	2	6	4
Total hours	14	30	22
Total cost	£ 420	£ 900	£ 660
Estimated value contract option basis is £ 660 + 10% = £ 726			

The 4-hour target minimum in the first data entry line is a 'no problems' minimum which is where Bruce intuitively starts, using 'target' in the stretch target sense to emphasize that this is what he will aim for and his targets are all ambitious – he works carefully but effectively. The 12-hour target maximum in this same line is a 'target' in the sense that it is the maximum Bruce is prepared to take responsibility for. He had to explain to Sally that there is considerable scope for variability associated with this task that he cannot predict until he starts work and takes the old floor covering off – a factor of 3 increase on his plausible minimum of 4 hours is a plausible outcome. Further, he had to make it clear to Sally that *much* more time would be needed if he discovers the floor underneath is rotten or otherwise damaged – possibly a factor of 5 or 10 increase on the 4 hours plausible minimum. He had to reassure Sally this did not look likely from his inspection, and unless she was planning to move soon it would need attention sooner or later in any case. He also had to convince Sally that it was not in Sally's interests for Bruce to guess at such possibilities and make proper allowance for this possible problem in his estimate. It was important for Bruce to convince Sally that this is a risk that Sally has to take – additional costs might be involved that was not covered by his estimate – or by the estimates of any competitors. If he did not do so it becomes his risk, or his problem, depending on your terminology preferences. He had to get Sally to understand this clearly for two reasons. First, his risk becomes Sally's risk, with no residual ambiguity leading to arguments later. Two, the clarification of the transfer becomes a realized opportunity – because any competitor who fails to address this issue will not be trusted by Sally.

The second line 8- and 12-hour entries involved comparatively little variability and no real risk for Sally or Bruce. The relatively small range helped to reassure Sally that Bruce knew what he was doing when significant inherent ambiguity uncertainty was not involved.

The third line was a provision for *all* problems and omissions not addressed earlier. It was presented as an opportunity as far as possible. Bruce wanted to emphasize that he will cleanup daily on a big job, with a discount if the client goes on holiday so this is not needed. He also wanted to make sure he gets paid for taking the client to choose her floor if she would prefer this, picking up materials if necessary, adding more time that is easily forgotten on a big job.

The calculated fourth line gave Sally a clear understanding of variability due to uncertainty addressed by the estimates, which she needs to understand if she opts for a 'time and materials' contract. The calculated fifth line converts this into cost, which gives her a plausible range for the labour aspect of a time and materials contract.

Sally could select a 'time and materials' contract option. The calculated sixth line gave Sally the basis for an 'estimated value' contract which Bruce explained was a second option Sally could select, adding a 10% 'contingency' to the mid-point labour cost estimate of £660. Bruce explained that this is what some contractors would call a 'fixed price' contract, but like Bruce they would exclude consideration of a rotten floor, possibly without pointing this out. In part the 10% increase is because Bruce would be taking 'the risk' of variations in the £660–900 range, not fully compensated by the opportunity associated with variations in the £420–660 range. However, the real risk for Bruce was arguments about marginal cases of responsibility when his target maximums are exceeded. He wants to encourage clients to trust him and save the 10% 'on average' – bearing in mind that they will be responsible for issues like rotten floors in any case. Sally opted to save £66 (on average, as explained by Bruce) because she now trusted Bruce and this made a time and materials contract an opportunity worth seizing from Sally's perspective.

The biggest risk for Bruce is clients he cannot trust. Bruce has refined his ability to pick up 'weak signals' that trust would be misplaced, via body language, tone of voice and casual remarks – his best defence is to decline to bid if he has any serious reservations. The bigger the potential contract, the more important it is for Bruce to avoid associated risks – non-payment being one, an unhappy client another.

Non-payment is a serious risk for Bruce. The contract deals with this by a 10% payment when a start date is agreed, a 40% advanced payment when the work starts, a further 40% half way through, and 10% on the day of completion. Giving the customer confidence to pay in advance (apart from the last 10%) is a key objective, to remove the risk that the client will default. If they are not prepared to trust him he is well advised not to trust them or waste any more time. Weeding out potential clients who are a waste of time has to start with the first conversation. And an estimate/contract has to be seen as the foundation of a relationship. The well-known 'golden rule' – 'do unto others as you would have them do unto you' – has a corollary for relationship management: 'Try to make it easy for others to do unto you as you would do unto them.' Insisting on prepayments is an example implementation of this rule.

An unhappy client is also a serious risk for Bruce. His business is based on reputation and recommendations. Clarity is a key objective, to minimize this risk. So is completing within his plausible maximum total. Adding all the plausible maximums with less than perfect positive correlation between items means that the nominal P90 interpretation of individual plausible maximums should rise to P95 or better, but he usually does not have to explore this sort of detail with clients. Bruce needs a deep understanding of the implications of uncertainty which his clients may not need.

Now consider further the opening offer to let Sally use Bruce's trade discount to purchase the flooring material. Offering Sally a sizeable discount on the materials from the start is an approach Bruce insisted on from the outset, which Chris initially interpreted as symptomatic of Bruce's very generous nature – 'generous to a fault' in figurative terms for sure, perhaps literally on this matter. Chris now sees it as a good example of managing 'systemic uncertainty'. It involves transforming a threat into an opportunity, comparable to the National Power example, albeit on a smaller scale.

- First, there is no doubt it is a very effective opening gambit, making a very good first impression.
- Second, any competitor who does not do the same will be seen by Sally as very uncompetitive, even if his labour charges are revealed and are much lower than Bruce's.
- Third, as a result of his competitive position, Bruce has a high success rate on his quotes. This reduces the amount of time he spends quoting, an aspect of his business he does not enjoy. He wants to minimize the risk of wasted time with potential clients who choose another contractor.
- Fourth, by taking all his clients to a selected set of suppliers to choose their materials – whole kitchens in some cases – he builds a good relationship with suppliers. Suppliers reciprocate by recommending Bruce when their direct customers ask who can install a potential purchase. Bruce does not advertise, and he has yet to run out of work. The risk of running out of work is a big concern.
- Fifth, if Bruce does not offer his discount in this way, clients may shop around to choose the material, and select suppliers who would not give Bruce a discount, or prove unreliable, or suggest other installers. These are all risks that are usefully avoided.

There is a cost tradeoff of course – the lost mark-up. Further, this approach means that an unhappy client who complains to suppliers about Bruce's competence because of misunderstandings is probably Bruce's most serious risk – illustrating the complex systemic uncertainties involved. However, with all these issues considered, it is worth while from Bruce's perspective, which is what matters, provided he understands the issues.

Andy and Chris would like Bruce to go a bit farther in terms of formal project management, with more formal planning of work execution for example. However, even with no formal planning beyond the simple spreadsheet estimate/contract document, which on signing indicates work start and payment dates, Bruce's business has been turned around by this limited but carefully designed project uncertainty management approach.

A key message this case illustrates is that very simple versions of the PUMPs that this book is about work in practice for very simple projects when no other formal project management processes are involved; but for effective practice, 'simple' does not mean 'simplistic', and the difference matters. Bruce's approach is simple to use, but it was very carefully designed for a very specific context and it has been polished by Bruce over time.

Evaluating risk for option choices

An important feature of the Table 1.3 lifecycle structure discussed in Chapter 1 is the inclusion of evaluation steps highlighting the desirability of explicit attention to go/no-go/maybe decisions at each stage of the lifecycle, from concept shaping through to termination. However, the scope of decision options in the project lifecycle goes beyond these go/no-go/maybe decisions; it also includes evaluation of choices of all kinds between alternative ways of proceeding, and alternative ways of addressing risk and opportunity in particular.

Most common practice risk management processes do not address the problem of choosing between alternative options whose outcomes are uncertain. Yet this is a key part of the process of moving from assessment of risk and uncertainty, identifying possible responses, and then taking appropriate action.

To illustrate some of the basic issues involved in choosing between alternative options, we consider a simple example. This example has been adapted from the paper defining 'Optimal risk-taking and risk-mitigation' in the *Encyclopaedia of Operations Research and Management Science* (Chapman and Harwood, 2011). It illustrates an approach initially developed for IBM UK for bidding purposes (Chapman et al., 2000). It also illustrates simple working assumptions within a general framework, and how more complex working assumptions can be addressed as necessary.

An office manager's photocopier decision

The single photocopier in a busy office failed terminally. The office manager had to replace it quickly, and justify the choice of replacement later. The office manager could obtain the same machine from the same supplier on a comparable contract. The contract cost for a minimum of five years was a rental charge per month plus a maintenance charge per copy. The only source of uncertainty associated with contract cost over the five years was the number of copies needed. This meant that the office manager did not need to decompose uncertainty along the lines used in Figure 2.4 or Table 2.2 – it was reasonably simple to think in terms of Figures 2.1 and 2.2 directly. The office manager used a direct Figure 2.1–2.2 approach to estimate uncertainty for three possible choices, putting all three on a single 'decision diagram' as illustrated by Figure 2.5.

Figure 2.5 was used to make and demonstrate the rationale for choosing option A. The option A line portrayed the office manager's estimate of the average contract cost per year if the same machine from the same supplier on a comparable contract was chosen. It assumed a linear cumulative probability distribution, corresponding to a uniform probability density function, and a direct approach to a Figure 2.1–2.2 estimation using P10 and P90 estimates of the average number of copies per year scaled by the cost per copy plus the cost per year. Figure 2.5 shows P10 and P90 dashed lines that were used for direct estimation purposes. The office manager recognized that the true option A curve would be non-linear and asymmetric, as illustrated by Figure 2.2, and pointed this out when explaining the option A line on Figure 2.5.

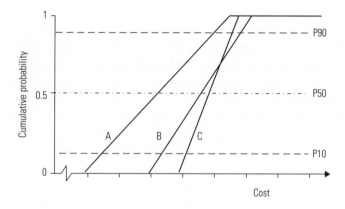

Figure 2.5   Decision diagram: comparison of approaches A, B and C.

Alternative suppliers offering comparable machines on the same contractual basis were evaluated using 10 and 90 percentile estimates based on the same estimates of the average number of copies per year. They are portrayed as lines B and C on Figure 2.5.

The P50 dotted line indicates expected outcomes for all three options reflecting the linear approximations involved. In expected value terms, A is the cheapest, followed by B then C, if the lines or curve generalizations are in approximately the right places. The expected value of option A is usefully seen as the opportunity/risk datum in this example *for all three options shown*, and it is worth remembering that maximizing expected payoff is always the long-term optimal strategy *provided* we can afford to take any associated risk.

The slopes of the option lines of Figure 2.5 indicated variability. The line for A had the lowest slope, indicating the highest variability because the cost per copy was the highest, with a lower cost per month than B or C. The line for C had the steepest slope, indicating the least variability because the cost per copy was the lowest, with a higher cost per month than A or B. However, variability on its own does not measure or indicate risk – risk also depends on the expected value. In this case if the opportunity/risk datum is defined by the expected value of option A, option C is riskier than A, as is B.

Assuming that minimizing the contract cost was the primary objective, and making this assumption clear, the office manager argued that A was the only 'risk efficient' choice in cost–risk terms. 'Risk efficiency' means the lowest level of risk for any given level of expected cost. Option A clearly has the lowest expected cost. Option A also has the lowest level of risk, because its cumulative probability distribution is entirely to the left of B and C, by a margin which is big enough to suggest that a more precise estimation producing non-linear cumulative distributions would lead to the same conclusion. There was no obvious need for more precision, and any 'overall optimality' concept which includes the cost of decision taking will keep it simple unless more effort pays.

As the option A machine was marginally faster than B or C, option A dominated when considering this secondary objective too. Had this not been the case, employee time lost waiting for copies might have been estimated and converted to an opportunity cost, followed by aggregation to a single cost attribute. Alternatively, any important secondary objectives might have been considered using separate graphs in Figure 2.5 form, or a simple judgement made about whether the gap between Figure 2.5 primary objective lines was large enough to more than counterbalance secondary considerations.

As the office manager knew that the colour and design style of the current supplier's products was consistent with the corporate consensuses of an optimal house style, this third-order objective was not an issue either. Had this not been the case, the gap between the curves would have to be evaluated by the relevant person or group in terms of tradeoffs between non-measurable objectives as well as measurable objectives. Any 'overall optimality' approach which addresses all relevant objectives uses simple dominance tests for additional objectives unless more sophisticated approaches look useful.

Had the option A machine been unavailable in a feasible time-frame, a choice between B and C might have been forced. Let us assume for the moment this is the case. Unlike option A, option B would not dominate C in cost terms, or vice versa. Both B and C are risk efficient given A is not available. B has a lower expected cost, but more risk, indicated by the way the lines cross. However, the lower expected cost of B justifies the marginal increase in rental cost risk – at a corporate level this kind of additional variation should be regarded as just 'noise'. This alternative starting position would also have to be tested in terms of additional objectives, measurable or non-measurable.

Had B or C seemed preferred choices because A was not available in a feasible time frame, reliability risk and risk associated with a new supplier who might not deal effectively with reliability or other issues would need care. Risk to the company and risk to the office manager might need separate consideration by the office manager, whose reputation might suffer from a highly visible mistake, perhaps costing his job if times were tough. Optimal mitigation of this risk might involve exploring more general working assumptions, like borrowing a copier from the existing supplier until A is available – a simple example of a reformulation of the choices available to deal with emerging concerns in a general framework.

More complex problem formulation and reformulation issues could be considered, but this example illustrates a flexible general framework that can address multiple attributes, some non-measurable, risk and opportunity which are not limited to variability of measured attributes, and risk and opportunity perceived differently by different parties. This approach assumes a multiple criteria approach to each attribute, involving expected outcome and risk. Risk is not measured by a single criterion like variance – it is depicted graphically by cumulative probability distributions. Comparing the B and C options graphically and choosing one implies an underlying decision function approximation to preference functions that addresses tradeoffs between expected outcome and associated risk exists, but it does not require specification of the decision function, or agreements between different relevant parties. Similarly, choices involving more than one attribute imply the existence of appropriate decision function approximations to preference functions which address tradeoffs between attributes, but they do not require their specification or agreement between relevant parties.

Non-measurable performance attributes, like optimal house style and the office manager's reputation, may also require consideration, as may attributes not worth measuring, like the reliability of other machines and suppliers. Distinguishing between risk to the organization and risk to the office manager is important. Links like the effect on the office manager's reputation of a commitment to a faulty machine and supplier are also important. Effective consideration of these tradeoffs involves utilizing the concept of risk efficient tradeoffs and generalization of this concept to the search for 'opportunity efficiency'. These concepts are considered in more detail in Chapter 3.

Judgements about value, value tradeoffs and associated uncertainty, including process as well as option issues, are core concerns explicitly illustrated by this example, via a flexible approach to working assumptions suitable for the context. Specifically, working assumptions in this analysis include no need to look beyond the minimum rental contract period of five years, or decompose average variability per annum within this period, or estimate Figure 2.5 using more sophisticated probability distributions. This kind of concern is central to an efficient and effective PUMP pack. No concerns of potential importance should be overlooked, even if they cannot be measured (like optimal house style or office manager's reputation) or measurement is not practical (like the reliability of a new supplier).

Conclusion

While 'uncertainty' is just 'lack of certainty', we can view uncertainty through a performance lens and see it as 'uncertainty about achievement of objectives'. When we represent this in quantitative terms, even in a simple format like Figures 2.1–2.2 or 2.5, identifying an 'opportunity/risk datum' lets us view performance uncertainty in opportunity and risk terms. Qualitative consideration can follow the same structure, in formal or intuitive terms, as can multiple objective versions. For example, National Power did not quantify the 'risk' they would get a less favourable cash flow had they not recognized the 'opportunity' provided by confidence that they could produce power shortly after the gas supply was available, but the benefit realized was clear to everyone involved. In the BCS example, Bruce and Sally also understood comparable risk and opportunity issues informally.

While 'risk' is just 'possible unfavourable outcomes', a performance lens clarifies what is involved even in a simple format like that of Figures 2.1–2.2, and portrayals of option choices using a decision diagram like Figure 2.5 begin to explain the role of 'risk efficiency' in choosing between alternatives. 'Risk efficiency' is developed further in the next chapter, as a central motive for uncertainty management.

Similarly, while 'opportunity' is just 'possible favourable outcomes', a performance lens clarifies what is involved even in a simple format like that of Figures 2.1–2.2, and the example on which Figure 2.5 is based, begins to explain the role of 'opportunity efficiency'. This idea is developed further in Chapter 3, which argues that opportunity efficiency is a useful term for the kind of overall optimality we need to seek – a practical optimality which involves stretching to do the best we can with limited time, knowledge and other resources – making the best of our circumstances. There are many other objectives uncertainty management *can* pursue, depending on the circumstances, as explained in Chapter 3.

Those who do not want to abandon the term 'project *risk* management' can define 'risk' as 'possible unfavourable or favourable outcomes' or equivalents like 'departures from expectations about objectives' which still imply a performance lens perspective and an opportunity/risk datum defined by expectations. With these redefinitions everything in this book is still directly relevant. All readers of this book will have to work with people who adopt this position, speaking their language. However, the authors believe the benefits of moving from an uncertainty driven view of '*risk* management' to '*uncertainty* management' is well worth while.

Common practice project risk management cannot address many of the concerns discussed in this book because it starts in the wrong place. Whether 'the wrong place' is inappropriate tools like PIGs or inappropriate definitions of 'risk', or an inappropriate brand name like 'risk management', is debatable. Both authors have been involved with numerous working groups for guides and standards addressing risk in projects, operations, strategy and 'enterprises' which have argued about these issues for more than a decade – with no resolution in sight. However, we believe the uncertainty–risk–opportunity relationships and definitions given in this book provide readers with a sound basis for thinking about all the relevant issues, communicating with people who may use any of a number of alternative frameworks, and understanding the literature. These are all prerequisites for effective practical implementation of the ideas involved in uncertainty management in projects and in associated operations and strategy.

Effective uncertainty management needs to address uncertainty in a broad sense. This means fully integrating the management of projects, operations and strategy, fully integrating quantitative and qualitative analysis, and fully integrating consideration of uncertainty, opportunity and risk, starting from a basis of 'minimum clarity' interval estimates in a way that a simple organization like BCS can fully implement, but which large organizations seldom fully understand. Risk management processes that focus on event-based threats will not address many of the sources of variability and ambiguity outlined in this chapter. Risk management processes concerned with both threats and opportunities will do better, but still tend to be focused on uncertain events or circumstances. A weakness in most current risk management processes is that they are not readily focused on all sources of uncertainty about all performance objectives of concern. This weakness is not limited to project risk management, but extends to operations, strategic and enterprise wide approaches to risk management.

Current confusion about what terms like 'risk' and 'uncertainty' mean are part of the problem, and this is a big problem. The credibility of professional organizations promoting unhelpful definitions is 'at risk', but this does not mean that early changes can be anticipated. In the meantime individuals and organizations are encouraged to think in the language adopted in this book, being prepared to discuss issues in whatever terms suit the context.

The key message of this chapter is: If the way project uncertainty, opportunity and risk are visualized does not facilitate looking for all the uncertainty that matters, and all the ways it can be managed, much of what matters, and most of what can be done about it, will probably be overlooked. To address opportunity and risk effectively, an explicit focus on uncertainty management is essential, including effective treatment of ambiguity uncertainty and systemic uncertainty. Uncertainty about anything which matters has to be the starting point for holistic and integrated project uncertainty management, considering all relevant parties, their motives, other Ws, and the whole of the project lifecycle, including the operations stage.

This implies deciding what knowledge – including but not limited to information – is needed by the end of each stage of a project's lifecycle in order to progress to following stages, in addition to making choices about proceeding, or not, without having this knowledge. It is about addressing 'ambiguity' associated with: lack of clarity due to the behaviour of relevant project players; lack of data; lack of detail; lack of structure to consider issues, working and framing assumptions being used to consider the issues; known and unknown sources of bias; and ignorance about how much effort it is worth expending to clarify the situation. A key concern is to understand where and why uncertainty is important in a given organizational context, and where it is not.

The simple linear format of the Figure 2.4 'sensitivity diagram' can be simplified to the spreadsheet tabular format of Table 2.2. It can also be generalized to non-linear curves as discussed in Chapter 3. The simple linear format of the Figure 2.5 'decision diagram' can be generalized to non-linear curves, as illustrated in Chapter 3. These two tools, for making decisions and associated sensitivity assessments, are central to managing uncertainty in the spirit of this book.

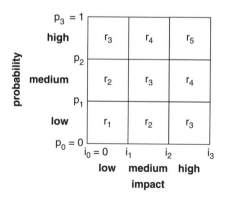

Figure 2.3   A basic probability-impact grid or graph (PIG)

was limited to identifying sources of 'event uncertainty' – ignoring the three other types of uncertainty identified in Chapter 1: ambiguity, inherent variability and systemic uncertainty. Casting risk in these terms naturally leads to a focus on low-level, specific sources of uncertainty – faults or events traditionally captured by event trees and fault trees (Fischoff et al., 1978) if complex models are used. This narrow focus would have worried some risk managers, but 'stopping bad things happening' was a reasonable interpretation of what had to be done as a first priority, and starting with a 'risk log/register/list' of bad things that might happen ('risks') might have seemed reasonable.

Our safety manager would have had very little data, making accurate objective probabilities unobtainable. However, he or she needed a way of prioritizing entries in risk logs, which might have run to a hundred or more adverse events or 'risks'. To resolve this problem, a PIG of Figure 2.3 format (or a variant with more than three classes and colour coding instead of a numeric 'risk index' like the r_i (i = 1, 2, . . . , 5) shown, was reasonable. Our safety manager could in effect, preprint a pad of PIGs, with 'high', 'medium' and 'low' probability boundaries defined by standard p_j values (j = 1, 2, 3), and a space to enter appropriate i_1, i_2 and i_3 values. He or she could use red colouring for the r_5 box, green colouring for the r_1 box, two shades of orange plus yellow in between. One PIG could be used for each risk, ticking one of the boxes. The reds would be the first priority, then dark orange, light orange, yellow and green.

The safety manager would understand that a low probability–high impact risk may have the same r_3 value and expected outcome (probability x impact) as a high probability–low impact risk, but would recognize that they are not even remotely comparable in a wide range of respects, and use his or her discretion when ordering them, perhaps even altering the colour coding.

The safety manager would also understand that adding up all the risk index values might look like an approximation to an expected outcome measure of plant safety if a common logarithmic impact scale is used for all 'risks', but that on its own this total is a meaningless metric.

Now consider how a modern day project manager, their managing director, or any other interested person within any organization might interpret a pad of our safety manager's PIGs complete with ticks for identified possible adverse events or 'risks', when impact is measured in cost terms and the 'risks' are sources of event uncertainty with a cost impact.

Assume that the first PIG in the pad involves a medium probability—medium impact risk. In terms of Figures 2.1 and 2.2, a subjective assessment of the impact uncertainty is implied by

Chapter 3

Key motives for uncertainty management

The Light of Lights looks always on the motive, not the deed, The Shadow of Shadows on the deed alone.

—William Butler Yeats

Chapters 1 and 2 argued for an uncertainty management perspective concerned with understanding where and why uncertainty is important and when it is not an issue. Proactive management of important uncertainty leads to benefits beyond improved control and neutralization of threats. It can facilitate enhanced project performance by influencing and guiding a project's objectives, parties, designs and plans. However, these benefits are not automatic – they depend very much on the scope and quality of the uncertainty management processes carried out. So much so that potential benefits should be identified up front, and proactively sought out by designing and employing uncertainty management processes accordingly. In this manner, *potential* benefits of proactive management should be used to clarify *appropriate* objectives for *each specific application* of uncertainty management, objectives which then need active pursuit.

The opportunities for uncertainty management during the lifecycle of any given project are considerable. Part of an effective understanding of this wide scope involves understanding how and why the objectives of uncertainty management applied at different stages in the project lifecycle can change significantly. The concerns at different stages vary. Further, what is known about the project changes, sometimes in profound ways. This warrants significant modifications and changes of emphasis in the application of an uncertainty management process over the lifecycle.

To begin to develop the necessary understanding of these issues, Table 3.1 gives examples of ways in which analysis of uncertainty and associated risk and opportunity could contribute to each stage of the lifecycle. The roles listed suggest that analysis could be usefully applied for specific purposes in each stage of the lifecycle without the necessity for uncertainty management in any previous or subsequent stages. Applied in this manner, the focus of analysis is likely to be on immediate project management concerns in the associated project stage. For example, uncertainty analysis might be undertaken as part of the tactics-shaping stage primarily to consider the feasibility and development of the work schedule for project execution. There might be no expectation that such analysis would or should influence the design, although it might be perceived as a potential influence on subsequent work allocation decisions. In practice, many 'risk' analyses are intentionally limited in scope, as in individual studies to determine the reliability of available equipment, and the likely outcome of a particular course of action, or to evaluate alternative decision options within a particular lifecycle stage. This can be unfortunate if it implies an *ad hoc*, 'limited view', 'bolted-on', 'optional extra' approach to uncertainty management, rather than undertaking it as an *integral*, 'wide view', 'built-in' part of project management. Wherever it is carried out in a project lifecycle, any 'risk' analysis needs to be regarded as a contribution to uncertainty management of the whole project. The opportunities for uncertainty management include looking forwards and backwards at any stage in the lifecycle, addressing all the issues indicated by Table 3.1 as appropriate. But this is just a starting point, a 'bolt-on' perspective as opposed to a 'built-in' perspective. The rest of this book will build on Table 3.1 to develop a fully integrated 'built-in' perspective.

Inspection of the roles listed in Table 3.1 suggests the following generic objectives for PUMPs applied at any stage in the project lifecycle:

1. Understand the project context of interest in sufficient detail.
2. Identify pertinent performance criteria.
3. Identify sources of uncertainty about performance with respect to these criteria.
4. Estimate the size of uncertainty due to various identified sources of uncertainty, and assess the significance of the various sources of uncertainty.
5. Control unconscious and conscious bias in estimates.
6. Allocate financial and managerial responsibility for sources of uncertainty.
7. Identify desirable options for modifying uncertainty and make provisional decisions.
8. Clarify related risk and opportunity with respect to the pertinent performance criteria.
9. Assess the effectiveness of each option and identify preferred options.
10. Adopt a 'clarity efficient' approach to seeking 'opportunity efficiency', decision-making concepts defined and elaborated in this chapter.

Objective 10 is the overall summary objective which defines best practice in our terms. Objectives 1 to 9 are specific components of best practice which can be linked to various approaches.

Experience of common practice risk management suggests that relatively few of the roles for uncertainty analysis listed in Table 3.1 are actively pursued, and that not all the generic objectives listed above are pursued as carefully as they might be. For example, a common practice risk management approach might focus on objectives 2 to 4 using simplistic methods to assess the relative importance of identified sources of uncertainty, typically in terms of potential adverse events or threats to a single performance criterion plotted on a probability-impact grid (PIG). Risk management processes that are truncated in this way severely limit the benefits that can be achieved. Later chapters in this book provide a detailed consideration of how all ten of the above objectives can be effectively pursued as a fully integrated set, built in to the rest of project management.

Table 3.1   Roles for uncertainty analysis in the project lifecycle from a 'bolt-on' perspective

Project lifecycle stages	*Roles for uncertainty analysis*
Concept shaping and concept gateway	Identifying stakeholders and their expectations Identifying appropriate performance objectives Providing unbiased initial estimates of business case outcomes Evaluating concepts and business cases in corporate strategy terms
DOT shaping (design, operations and termination strategy development) and DOT gateway	Developing lifecycle performance criteria Assessing the feasibility of design strategy Assessing the likely costs and benefits of design changes Evaluating operations and termination strategies Testing the reliability of designs and their operations effectiveness
E&D shaping (execution and delivery strategy development) and overall strategy gateway	Estimating resources required at a strategic level Identifying and allowing for regulatory constraints Assessing contracting strategy at an overview level Assessing the feasibility of plans Assessing the likely duration of execution Assessing the likely cost of execution and delivery Determining appropriate milestones Assessing the effect of changes to plans Determining appropriate levels of contingency funds
Tactics shaping and tactics gateways	Estimating resources required at a more detailed level Assessing contracting strategy at a more detailed level Evaluating alternative procurement strategies Defining contractual terms and conditions Determining appropriate risk sharing arrangements Assessing the implications of contract conditions Assessing and comparing competitive tenders Determining appropriate target costs and bid prices for contracts
Execution	Supporting execution Identifying remaining execution issues Assessing implications of changes to designs or plans Revising estimates of cost on completion or completion time Supporting responding to crises and disasters
Delivery	Supporting delivery Identifying issues impacting delivery Assessing the feasibility of a delivery schedule Assessing the feasibility of meeting performance criteria Assessing the availability of commissioning facilities Assessing the reliability of testing equipment Assessing resources needed to modify the delivered asset
O&S (operation and support)	Assessing the effectiveness of uncertainty management strategies Providing ongoing uncertainty management of all relevant concerns Updating assessments of asset performance Supporting the design and planning of maintenance Assessing the appropriate levels of resources required Supporting responding to crises and disasters
Termination	Assessing options for replacement, decommissioning, or transfer Identifying the extent of future liabilities Supporting termination

This chapter considers some fundamental motives for adopting formal performance uncertainty management processes (PUMPs). These motives underlie objective 10 but sometimes go well beyond objectives 1 to 9. All these potential motives are important because they underpin all the potential benefits achievable from formal PUMPs, and they need to be viewed as potential objectives when choosing or shaping an effective PUMP for any given context. They also need to be considered when shaping corporate capability for managing uncertainty and associated opportunity as well as risk.

Trust

It can be argued that establishing and maintaining well-founded trust should be a central objective for all formal uncertainty management processes at all stages in all project lifecycles, because well-founded trust is the lubricant that keeps the wheels turning, the basis of all other objectives. Its pursuit should start with unbiased estimates of performance from the outset of the concept stage. We developed a basis for this view in Chapter 2. It simply needs explicit reiteration here, plus observing that the role of trust may not be obvious when considering the list above. This observation is also true of some of the benefits discussed below.

Documentation

PUMPs that produce the benefits in the list above usually require a formal approach, integrated with other formal aspects of project management. Documentation is a key feature of a formal PUMP and indeed of all formal management processes. This documentation should be regarded as a key *deliverable* of any formal PUMP, but it is also a *tool* which facilitates the operation of the process, and it provides a means of assessing the performance of the process. All project managers are aware of the importance of documentation for effective project management. Formal PUMPs require appropriate documentation for similar basic reasons, but documentation is especially important because of the need to deal with uncertainty in terms of both variability and ambiguity. This can include information in a wide variety of forms: describing activities, sources of uncertainty, identified responses, identified trigger points, the rationale for decisions taken, and so on. Such documentation might be regarded as a by-product of project uncertainty management, rather than a central concern, but it serves a number of useful purposes which may be worth pursuing in their own right, a set of *motives* for uncertainty management documentation worth explicit attention if they are relevant in any given context.

1. *Clearer thinking*. A focus on documentation can clarify the initial thinking process. If people have to set down their thinking in writing, this forces clarification of what is involved.
2. *Clearer communication*. Documentation can provide an unambiguous vehicle for communication at any given point in time. If people explain what they mean in terms of designs and activities, sources of uncertainty and responses, in writing at a suitable level of detail, the scope for misunderstanding is significantly reduced. This can be particularly important in communication between different organizational units or in client–contractor situations. In such settings a number of questions concerning the PUMP effort need to be addressed. For example: who is responsible for which activities? who bears the financial

consequences of which sources of uncertainty? and who will respond to realization of shared sources? Clear documentation can also be an essential part of making all threats and opportunities and all key assumptions clearly visible to all interested parties. A key role for any formal analysis process is the collective use of team input to a joint decision, drawing on a range of expertise as appropriate. Communication is a vital aspect of this process.

3. *Familiarization.* Documentation can provide a record to assist new project team members to 'get up to speed' quickly. Staff turnover on a project can be a significant source of uncertainty, which documentation helps to mitigate. PUMP documentation is a very valuable training tool specific to the project to which new staff are attached.

4. *A record of decisions.* Documentation can provide a record which explains the rationale for key decisions. In some industries (and for some careers), such records may become very important if subsequently adverse outcomes due to bad luck are experienced, or hindsight suggest that some other decision might have produced a better outcome.

5. *A knowledge base.* Documentation can provide a record that captures corporate knowledge in a manner useful for subsequent similar project teams. If the kernel of the thinking behind one project is available in a readily accessible form for those doing the next project, the value of this information can be very significant. For contracting organizations this information can amount to a competitive advantage over rival firms. Such information can also provide the basis of ongoing training as well as an individual learning tool, and a basis for fundamental research.

6. *A framework for data acquisition.* When organizations first introduce a formal uncertainty management process, appropriate data is usually difficult to come by. However, the use of a formal process should clarify the nature of appropriate data, and lead to the systematic collection and appreciation of such data, as part of the documentation process. The importance of this development is difficult to understand for organizations that have not introduced formal processes of the kind described in this book, but it is recognized as a major benefit by those who have. It is important to ask whether this issue is relevant up-front, because a current lack of data that could be collected in the future should not distort the development of an approach which best serves long-term needs.

If clearer thinking is the only one of these six purposes that is of interest, limited documentation may be appropriate. However, the other purposes deserve careful prior attention, even if the design of the documentation has a fairly free format and it is appropriate to use a very low effort level of documentation. The key underlying purpose of documentation is to integrate the expertise of teams of people so that they can make effective, collective decisions based on clearly articulated and communicated premises. This obviously applies at a point in time when decisions need to be taken. It also applies over time, when later use of expertise and effort effectively captured via documentation can save a lot of money, and an effective audit trail can save reputations.

Developing a clarity efficient approach

Whenever in the lifecycle a formal project uncertainty management process is first introduced, it needs to be effective immediately, and it needs to evolve effectively as the lifecycle progresses. Efficiency is important, in terms of 'doing things right', but effectiveness is the key, in terms of 'doing the right things'.

An important overall objective is formal processes that are effective in this sense, because they are central to using everyone's time and effort effectively to make the right decisions. Such processes have to emphasize 'approximately correct answers to the right questions' – avoiding a common tendency to focus on 'precisely correct answers to the wrong questions'. One way to visualize what this means, which many people find helpful, is the concept of 'clarity efficiency'.

In this book the use of the word 'clarity' is consistent with most plain English meanings. However, it is useful to use the formal definitions

'clarity' is *'insight (understanding) which can be shared'*,
'a clarity efficient process' is *'the lowest cost (in terms of time and effort and other resources) process for achieving any given level of clarity'*.

Figure 3.1 is a standard two-criterion tradeoffs diagram used to portray efficient tradeoffs by economists in many contexts. In this case clarity is one criterion, and the cost of acquiring clarity the second criterion. Clarity/cost tradeoffs typically involve decisions about how much time and resource to devote to analysis, where to focus effort, and how much detail to go into. If too much time and resources are spent on gathering information and analysis that adds little to understanding, this is clearly an inefficient combination of cost and clarity. The clarity efficient boundary divides the feasible area and the non-feasible area. The slightly abstract conceptual basis provided by Figure 3.1 will become more practical as a working tool as we explore a variety of examples that can be visualized in the feasible solution region of Figure 3.1, but we have a few examples from Chapter 2 to get started.

Point *a* is the feasible process which delivers the maximum feasible level of clarity – the 'maximum clarity approach'. More effort would simply result in 'paralysis by analysis'.

Point *c* is the feasible process which delivers the lowest appropriate level of clarity for the least effort – the 'minimum clarity approach'. The BCS process in Chapter 2 was aimed at point *c*.

Point b_3 is an example of a feasible process intermediate between points *a* and *c* which delivers a modest level of clarity for the least effort. The Highways Agency re-estimation exercise was aiming for b_3. Future HA processes need to aim for a point like b_2.

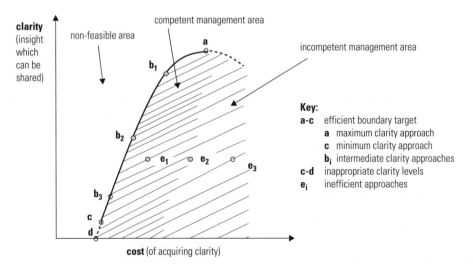

Figure 3.1   Clarity efficiency in an 'efficient frontier' portrayal

Choices about how to apply PUMPs that are clarity efficient will vary with the particular application contexts, and will depend on the knowledge, skills and motivation of the people involved.

The competent management part of the feasible area is where all organizations *should* be. All organizations should be seeking processes that involve further opportunities for improvement to get still closer to the clarity efficient boundary, but they should already be in the right region, within striking distance of their goal. Many are not.

Organizations in the incompetent management part of the feasible area need radical changes they are not usually able to make without help plus incentives ('carrots and sticks'). They often do not even recognize they have a problem. Because they are using inappropriate framing assumptions, conversations about the possible existence of a problem and how to do better, are very difficult.

Qualitative and quantitative analysis

An important driver of clarity efficiency is the manner in which qualitative and quantitative analysis is fully integrated in any given context. Some analysis processes focus on qualitative analysis, some on quantitative analysis, and some use both, using 'quantitative' in the common 'probabilistic quantification' sense. We argue for both qualitative and quantitative analyses, with the emphasis varying at different stages in the project lifecycle and at different points in a PUMP. What is crucial is understanding that at each stage in a project's lifecycle, an effective PUMP will necessarily be a largely qualitative, identifying and structuring process early on, and a more quantitative, evaluating and choosing process later. Whatever the application context, quantitative analysis is driven to an important extent by the quality of the preceding qualitative analysis and the joint interpretation of both. Many of the key motives for formal risk and uncertainty analysis may seem to be driven directly by quantitative analysis, but the underlying role of the qualitative analysis this depends upon should never be forgotten, and some of the key corporate learning motives are met by the qualitative aspects of the process. Further, both qualitative analysis and quantitative analysis on their own have severe limitations – it is their effective integration that provides the clarity and understanding needed for effective management. Achievement of this clarity and understanding is a key purpose of the whole tool set provided by a PUMP approach and associated deliverables.

Targets, expectations and commitments

As noted in Chapter 2, an important reason for quantifying uncertainty is that doing so helps to force all members of an organization's management to appreciate the significance of differences between 'targets' to which people can aspire, 'expected values' used to provide a predictor of outcomes, and 'commitments' that provide a suitable level of contingency allowance. Targets, expected values and commitments need to be distinguished in terms of cost, time and all other relevant measures of performance, and they all need to be free of bias. In this context 'bias' has a persistent tendency to be too low or too high. Bias is endemic in most estimates of targets, expected values and commitments.

Unbiased estimates of expected values should reflect the scope and likelihood of all possible upside and downside variations that are not explicitly excluded via documented 'conditions' which are sensible and understandable.

'Conditions' in this sense are assumptions we intend to treat in qualitative terms. Important scope assumptions are often best treated in this way. They apply to commitments and targets as well as to expected values.

In addition to the scope for departures from expectations, commitments should reflect 'asymmetric penalties' if they are not met or exceeded. This applies to costs, durations and other performance measures. For example, the implications of being over cost are typically worse than being under cost. Unbiased estimates of commitments require an unbiased understanding of these asymmetric penalties as well as unbiased estimates of the scope for upside and downside variability.

Targets in a 'stretch target' sense usually involve a 'no significant problems' assumption, to facilitate the management of good luck. Unbiased stretch targets require an unbiased understanding of what 'no significant problems' means. 'Targets' without a 'stretch' qualifier may be given a default 'stretch target' interpretation, but it is important to avoid confusion between stretch targets and contractual targets.

Targets in a 'contractual target' sense, when incentives and penalties are involved, are very different. Such targets should be viewed as 'commitments' on the contractor's part. It can be useful to refer to them as 'trigger values', because they trigger 'gain' and 'pain' payments, to avoid the potential confusion that a 'target value' label with two possible interpretations can cause.

In cost terms, expected values are our best estimate of what costs should be realized on average. Setting aside a contingency fund to meet costs that may arise in excess of the expected cost, and making a 'commitment' to deliver within the expected cost plus the contingency, involves a probability of being able to meet the commitment. Organizations may wish to standardize this probability in a context dependent manner to clarify what 'commitments' mean in various contexts. By definition, the contingency allowance provides uplift from the expected value which is not required on average if it is properly determined. Determining this level of commitment ought to involve an assessment of perceived threats and the extent to which these may be covered by a contingency fund, together with an assessment of the opportunities and the implications of both over- and under-achievement in relation to the commitment. High penalties associated with being over cost relative to the penalties associated with being under cost can justify setting commitment levels which have a much higher probability of being met than the 50–60% chance an expected value might provide. Setting commitment levels which have a 70–90% chance of not being exceeded is common among organizations that understand contingencies in the sense discussed here.

In cost terms, contractual targets should have a 60–90% chance of not being exceeded, so that both the contractor and the client have a reasonable chance of success, with other terms adjusted to reflect this presumption of success. To do otherwise is to build in failure.

In cost terms, stretch targets are set at a level below expected cost, with provisions accounting for the difference. Stretch targets need to reflect the opportunity aspect of uncertainty and the need for goals which stretch people. Targets explicitly referred to as 'stretch targets' clearly reflect this, and might be set at a level that has less than a 20% chance of being achieved. Targets need to be realistic to be credible, but they also need to be lean. If targets which are optimistic are not aimed for, expected costs will not be achieved on average, and contingency funds will be used more often than anticipated. If expected costs together with contingency funds are treated as targets, following a version of Parkinson's Law, work will expand to fill the time available for its completion, leaving insufficient margin for anything going wrong. Sometimes differences between targets, expectations and commitments are kept confidential, or left implicit. We argue that they need to be explicit, and a clear rationale for the difference needs to be understood by all, leading to an effective process of managing the evolution from targets to realized values. Ownership of provisions and contingencies is a central issue when making this work, and is a critical aspect of uncertainty and risk allocation between project participants.

It is important to recognize that organizations which do not quantify uncertainty in terms comparable to the minimum clarity range estimate approach associated with Figures 2.1–2.2 have no real basis for distinguishing stretch targets, contractual targets, expected values, and commitments. When single-value performance levels are employed to serve three or four separate purposes, the consequences can be disastrous, with costly and unnecessary dysfunctional organizational behaviours. 'The cost estimate', 'the completion date' or 'the promised performance' become less and less plausible; there is a crisis of confidence when the goal posts are moved, and then the process starts all over again. Several senior project managers involved when BP's version of SCERT was introduced in the 1970s stated that the avoidance of this cycle was the key benefit of the new process for them. In some organizations with a long history of processes that still do not deliver this insight, senior managers see its absence as their central problem. The ability to manage the gaps between targets, expected values and contingency levels, and the ability to set these values appropriately in the first place, is a fundamental motive for uncertainty management.

Understanding uncertainty and communicating understanding

Understanding the uncertainty being addressed in the application of a PUMP is crucial. Communicating that understanding as appropriate is part of building and sustaining trust. PUMPs are the key vehicles that organizations need to use to understand uncertainty and communicate that understanding.

One important tool already introduced in Chapter 2 is the minimum clarity portrayal of quantified uncertainty illustrated by Figures 2.1 and 2.2. The 'minimum clarity' label can be linked to point c in Figure 3.1, suggesting that higher clarity ways of portraying uncertainty ought to be sought if more clarity is worth while. The details will be left until Chapter 10, but the basis of higher clarity is a rectangular histogram portrayal of any shape, like the assumed underlying distribution curve of Figure 2.2 portrayed by a dotted line, using as many classes as necessary for appropriate precision. This avoids the need for restrictive assumptions associated with specific probability distribution functions, although such functions can be very useful as special case tools in appropriate contexts. Figure 2.1 is a special case rectangular histogram with only one class, but it provides a simple framework for understanding the difference between targets, expectations and commitments.

In Chapter 2 common practice PIGs were reinterpreted using a Figures 2.1–2.2 interpretation of both impact and probability uncertainty. That reinterpretation can clearly use higher clarity multiple-class rectangular histograms or appropriate specific distribution functions. PIGs should be dropped as a means of prioritizing sources of uncertainty limited to event uncertainty ('risks'). They should be replaced by a clarity efficient tool set that includes a sensitivity diagram portrayal of uncertainty that has been quantified in a nested structure that integrates consideration of all relevant uncertainty, but allows a focus on a digestible portion one bite at a time. Figure 2.4 is a simple example of this tool. Table 2.2 is a still simpler tabular equivalent example – a 'sensitivity table'. Consider a more sophisticated example that illustrates what may be appropriate when important uncertainty needs careful attention to shape strategy.

An offshore oil project layered portrayal of uncertainty

When BP employed Acres International Management Services to help to develop a new process for project planning and costing for offshore North Sea projects in 1976, the obvious motive was unbiased performance estimates. Projects were coming in late and over budget.

By the early 1980s objective statistical analysis had demonstrated that the new BP process achieved this 'unbiased estimates' objective. However, from the outset a much richer set of objectives was also addressed:

- understanding uncertainty in terms of all relevant sources at a suitable level of decomposition;
- understanding how best to manage that uncertainty source by source;
- understanding how uncertainty accumulated across sources;
- understanding how that accumulation process could be best managed; and
- demonstrating that understanding as and when necessary at all relevant levels of management.

Figure 3.2 illustrates one of the key tools used for this purpose in an early study of a jacket fabrication activity – a 'sensitivity diagram'. The relatively simple format of Figure 2.4 used to discuss the Highways Agency example in Chapter 2 is a linear version of this built-in sensitivity analysis approach to combining uncertainty components.

The 'jacket' is the steel structure which sits on the ocean floor and provides the basis of the 'platform'. It supports the 'modules' containing equipment, accommodation and so on to produce the oil. The tool illustrated by Figure 3.2 is a sensitivity diagram which shows successive contributions to an accumulating total of the quantified uncertainty at this level. This particular example is at an 'activity' (jacket fabrication) level. It uses smooth curves based on BP's multiple-class rectangular histogram software (Clark and Chapman, 1987), but Monte Carlo simulation and any smooth curve representations could be used to get directly comparable curves.

Figure 3.2 illustrates an activity level portrayal of completion date sources of uncertainty. Each source of uncertainty includes associated mitigation measures specific to that source within this activity. The term 'source' is sometimes a convenient short form for 'source of uncertainty'. The term 'source of uncertainty' is itself a convenient shorter form for a 'relevant source of uncertainty and associated response measures including any secondary implications specific to that source'. When BP and other organizations first used sensitivity diagrams like Figure 3.2, the term 'risks' was used instead of 'sources of uncertainty'. Further, the term 'layered risk diagram' and variants were used instead of 'sensitivity diagram'. The authors believe both changes are well worth while, in terms of overall clarity. The reasons were discussed earlier in terms of uncertainty – risk – opportunity terminology general implications. But searching for 'sources of uncertainty' including the 'good weather' used to illustrate opportunities in Chapter 2 is a simple basic example illustration of the difference a positive perspective makes. The consistent use of the 'sensitivity diagram' term emphasizes a key purpose of this tool.

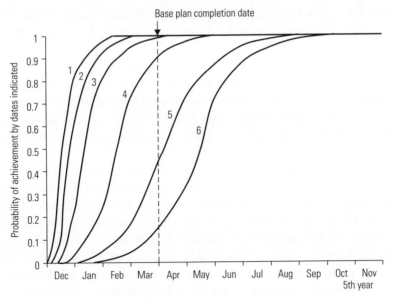

Probability curves show the cumulative effect of the following sources of uncertainty:

1. yard not available, or mobilisation delays
2. construction problems / adverse weather
3. subcontracted nodes delivery delays

4. material delivery delays
5. industrial disputes
6. delayed award of fabrication contract

Notes:
1. the curves assume a minimum fabrication period of 20 months
2. no work is transferred offsite to improve progress
3. no major fire, explosion or other damage

Figure 3.2   Sensitivity diagram: activity level offshore project example

Curve 1 in the Figure 3.2 sensitivity diagram is the cumulative probability distribution associated with source of uncertainty 1 given any specific mitigation measures for that source. Curves 2 to 6 successively add comparable cumulative probability distributions for sources 2 to 6. Curve 6 provides the overall total for the quantified uncertainty at this level, and curves 1 to 6 show the contribution of that component via the successive gaps – 5 is the biggest, 2 the smallest.

Looking at the gap between successive curves along P50 indicates the approximate contribution of each source in expected value terms – precise calculations can be used as an alternative, with nodes on the curves representing expected values to allow visual interpretation. Looking at the gap between successive curves along the P90 indicates the approximate contribution of each source in downside variability or risk terms – the shape of the gaps above the expected values is a more precise portrayal of additional risk. Looking at the gap between successive curves along P10 indicates the approximate contribution of each source in upside variability or opportunity terms – the shape of the gaps below the expected values is a more precise portrayal of additional opportunity.

To compute these curves using a standard Monte Carlo simulation package assuming independence between sources of uncertainty, X_1 to X_6 could define the outcomes of samples from each of the six source of uncertainty distributions, with $X_7 = X_1 + X_2$, $X_8 = X_7 + X_3$ and so on to

$X_{11} = X_{10} + X_9$. Then curve 1 is defined by X_1, curve 2 is defined by X_7, and so on, with curve 6 defined by X_{11}. That is, n sources require $n - 1$ composites instead of just one overall composite to provide all n curves.

Source 2 dependence can be defined in relation to source 1. Dependence specifications for sources 3 to 6 have to be defined in terms of preceding composite components. Independence is a very special case of the implied separability conditions. Discussing the details of dependence and computational issues will be deferred until Chapter 11, but it is important to understand that dependence can play an important role in Figure 3.2 format graphs, and other considerations relevant to ordering choices also need to be addressed.

When ordering the sources for the Highways Agency Figure 2.4 version of Figure 3.2, as indicated in Chapter 2 the ordering facilitated estimation. In the Figure 3.2 case the ordering of sources 5 and 6 reflects mitigation discussions for which this graph was initially prepared.

Source 6 could fairly simply be eliminated by senior management action, as the first mitigation measure discussed – early award of the fabrication contract. This still leaves an uncomfortable situation. Source 5 could be almost eliminated by more complex management action which might impact source 6. Source 5, industrial disputes, was initially sized subjectively, but its size led to later data analysis which suggested that industrial disputes were the result of a 'feast or famine' environment for platform constructors. The only viable mitigation identified was collaboration with other oil companies to smooth the flow of work to 'yards' used to construct jackets. This would lower contracted prices as well as the chance of industrial disputes – an example of an opportunity discovered while looking for effective responses to overall uncertainty. It is of note here that this was an insight that needed immediate attention at board level if it was to be used effectively. In this role Figure 3.2 was embedded in immediate communication to the board by the senior management involved.

If the uncertainty portrayed on Figure 3.2 for sources 5 and 6 is effectively eliminated by mitigation in this way, the total uncertainty previously portrayed by curve 6 is in effect redefined by curve 4, and uncertainty measured in probability distribution terms by curve 4 = 6 portrays an acceptable picture within this activity. Communicating this message to all relevant levels of management was an important role for this insight generation and communication tool.

The 'notes' indicate three key working assumptions, which involve sources of uncertainty that have not been quantified, treated as conditions. It is always important to understand *all* relevant uncertainty, but it is not always useful to quantify all identified sources, and some will be basic scoping assumptions that need clear identification and shared understanding for effective *qualitative* management. It is always useful to integrate qualitative and quantitative treatment of related sources at any given level of composition.

Curve 1 is itself a composite of two sources of uncertainty, both assessed in relation to mitigation measures prior to estimation of curve 1. For example, 'yard not available' might have arisen because another company's jacket is not finished by the contracted time to start BP's jacket, and the 'yard' (a dry dock) cannot float it out until it is finished. The first choice response was 'find an adjacent site and start stockpiling steel to cope with a short delay'. This involved a secondary source of uncertainty – 'a long delay may be involved', when mitigation shifts to 'find another yard'. The secondary source of uncertainty here is 'there may be none available'. 'Accept a long delay' then becomes the only available choice. Ambiguity uncertainty is also involved to the extent that underlying events or inherent variability (like weather) or systemic uncertainty (forms of dependence) or responses to uncertainty or secondary sources of uncertainty and responses have not been identified and appropriate data has not been available or analysed. This is true of all six sources shown on Figure 3.2, and all components of measured uncertainty more generally.

Figure 3.2 shows only six sources of uncertainty at this activity level because more than approximately six curves make these sensitivity diagrams too complex to read easily. However, each curve can involve a lower level structure, and each of these can be further decomposed. In the same way activity level uncertainty can be composed upward to define overall project uncertainty. A 'nested' structure can be used to decompose any overall uncertainty measure into as many components as we wish, with two to six a convenient number of components at each level.

The first source on an activity level graph is often 'delays caused by earlier activities', a composite built up by working through the activity network, capturing earlier knock-on effects. The second source is often a composite with a label like 'productivity problems' – 'construction problems/adverse weather' in Figure 3.2. This is an important composite of all sources of uncertainty not deemed worthy of separate analysis. Its use is central to treating all uncertainty to be quantified in terms of composites that are worth separation plus a residual source not worth decomposition. Judging how far to decompose uncertainty for a cost-effective understanding of both appropriate mitigation and unbiased estimates is the target of the PUMP used to manage these decisions, discussed later.

The sensitivity diagram portrayal of uncertainty illustrated by Figure 3.2 proved itself a key tool for other offshore and Arctic oil and gas projects assessed by BP, Gulf, PetroCanada and Stat Oil. More important, it proved to be a key tool for clients of the authors using PUMP variants in a wide range of other contexts, including the Highways Agency versions like Figure 2.4. In the authors' view sensitivity diagrams like Figures 2.4 and 3.2 are a key basic PUMP tool in all contexts, at a suitable level of clarity, and their absence in a formal probability based analysis suggests a possible failure to understand the role of sensitivity analysis in the nested decomposition of uncertainty which underlies any effective and efficient PUMP. Why this is the case will be discussed in Chapter 11.

For a 'high clarity' PUMP applied to a strategic level project plan for activities, each critical activity needs to be addressed in the manner illustrated by Figure 3.2. Managing mitigation specific to each source of uncertainty at a level of detail which provides a high level of insight for an appropriately skilled analyst is essential. So is communicating this insight to all relevant people. Further, 'general' mitigation measures which can address accumulated uncertainty from many sources, including knock-on effects, require careful consideration at a number of levels. Further still, at all levels, conditions (working assumptions about unmeasured uncertainty) like the three associated with 'notes' on Figure 3.2, need effective consideration.

For a 'low clarity' PUMP we may need a simpler version of this layered portrayal of sources of uncertainty, illustrated earlier by Figure 2.4 and Table 2.1. However, all the issues illustrated by Figure 3.2 will need to be addressed as part of the simplification process, and it can be very helpful to understand simple representations in terms of underlying more sophisticated portrayals. For example, a basic PERT (Program Evaluation and Review Technique) model (Moder and Philips, 1970) of activity duration in effect treats all uncertainty as 'productivity variations' – there is no decomposition. Further, it assumes independence between all activity distributions. Users of a PERT analysis who do not understand this invariably fail to understand how misleading the results can be.

Risk efficient choices and linked opportunity management

A central reason for employing formal uncertainty management should be the identification, evaluation and selection of desirable options for modifying uncertainty and related opportunity and risk – objectives (7)–(9) in our earlier list of generic objectives for any PUMP. A key tool in the pursuit of these objectives is the concept of risk efficient options, and how risk efficiency is portrayed will influence choices between alternative risky options. The office manager's photocopier decision discussed in Chapter 2 was a simple illustration of the basic issues involved.

In its basic form risk efficiency involves one attribute (like profit, or return) and a two-criteria view of a portfolio of risky investment opportunities. One criterion is the 'expected value' or 'mean value', an unbiased estimate of the outcome of the performance that can be expected, and the best measure of what should happen on average. The other criterion is 'risk', defined as 'possible unfavourable outcomes' for our purposes, requiring a two-dimensional graphical portrayal for each attribute, but traditionally measured by the variance or downside semi-variance of the distribution of possible levels of performance (Markowitz, 1959). The mean-variance approach to investment selection involves selecting alternative portfolios of investments on the basis of their expected performance and their risk as measured by variance in anticipated performance for a given expected value. The mean–variance decision rule says that if a portfolio B has both a preferable expected value for performance and lower variance than another portfolio A, then B should be preferred to A, and B is said to be 'risk efficient' with respect to A. Used in the context of portfolios of stocks and financial securities, Markowitz's approach to investment risk management has become one of the foundations of modern economics. For project uncertainty management purposes, we extend Markowitz's approach to more general choice decisions that arise in a project context. This generalization has been central to PUMP variants since the 1970s, and has been widely used by well-known organizations, but it is not fully exploited by most common practice.

The idea of risk efficiency is most easily pictured using a graph like Figure 3.3. The format of Figure 3.3 is identical to that of Figure 3.1 to aid interpretation – they are both two-criterion efficient frontier portrayals of choices involving efficient tradeoffs, but in this case one criterion is expected reward (return, profit or a more general composite of positive objectives) and the other criterion is risk (in terms of all relevant objectives).

Part of opportunity management is identifying alternative options that are close to or define a risk efficient boundary that is as far to the left as possible, and changing plans accordingly. In practice the risk efficient boundary will not be a smooth curve, it will not be feasible to identify the boundary directly – only a specific set of option points – and options like e_1 may represent worthwhile opportunities that are the best identified option available and reasonably near the unidentified boundary. Clearly there is a danger that some organizations habitually operate around points like e_3 because for various reasons they fail to seek out or identify more risk efficient opportunities. Most people and most organizations tend to be optimists about their abilities. Most organizations will wish to assume that their plans are in the risk efficient set. However, an assertion that an adopted plan is reasonably risk efficient is not good enough unless it has a demonstrable basis. Such an assertion needs to be tested. It can be tested by the organization itself, in terms of externally assisted assessment of the quality of the management processes used, which depends upon the quality of the concepts they rest on, the culture of the organization within which they operate, and the quality of

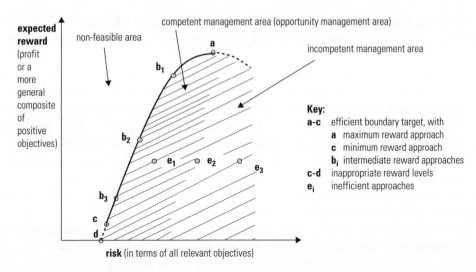

Figure 3.3   Risk efficient options in an 'efficient frontier' portrayal

the people. Or it may be tested by the stock market, relevant government watchdogs, other interested parties, or extreme scenarios/events. Sooner or later it will be tested by one or the other, and an ineffective or complacent internal test will lead to a negative external test. This 'test' in one form or another is as inevitable as death and taxes. This is a 'stick' incentive to understand and pursue more risk efficient opportunities, which governance needs to address. However, the 'carrot' incentive of improved project performance will be more profitable and more fun.

Point c in Figure 3.3 is the risk efficient feasible choice which delivers the minimum acceptable level of reward at a minimum feasible level of risk. The boundary from c to d also comprises risk efficient options, but it is of no interest because the expected reward level is too low. Point a is the risk efficient feasible choice which maximizes expected reward. On the risk efficient boundary, a scenario that yields a higher rate of expected reward can only be achieved, *ceteris paribus*, by accepting a higher level of risk. Likewise, to move to a scenario with a lower level of risk, a lower level of expected reward must be expected. Point a represents a maximum expected reward (or minimum expected cost) project plan, but with a high level of risk despite its risk efficiency. Point c represents a minimum risk project plan, but with a low level of expected reward despite its risk efficiency. If an organization can afford to take the risk, a is the preferred solution. If the risk associated with a is considered to be too great, it must be reduced by choosing an option further along the risk efficient boundary towards c. In general, successive movements to lower risk options will prove less and less cost effective, larger decreases in expected reward being required to achieve the same reduction in absolute or relative risk. In practice, an intermediate option like b_1 usually needs to be sought, providing an appropriate balance between risk and expected reward, the exact point depending upon the organization's ability to take risk.

The scale of a project relative to the organization is a key issue in terms of the attractiveness of alternative options like b_1, b_2 and b_3. If the project is one of hundreds, none of which could threaten the organization, b_1 may be a sensible choice. If the organization is a one-project organization, failure of the project probably leading to failure of the organization, a more prudent stance may seem to be appropriate, like b_2 or b_3.

Traditional portfolio theory discussions of alternative choices on the risk efficient boundary (Markowitz, 1959, for example) usually treat these decisions as a simple matter of preference: how much risk does the decision maker want to take? In the context of an ongoing portfolio of projects, choosing b_1, b_2 or b_3 is better viewed as a matter of corporate level risk. That is, corporate risk efficiency means never reducing risk for a project by decreasing expected return unless the risk involved threatens the organization as a whole. In these terms an aggressive approach to risk taking at a project level is part of a risk efficient approach to corporate level risk management. IBM UK developed project risk management with support from both authors of this book in the early 1990s to facilitate taking more risk, not less, to exploit this perception of corporate risk management. Its introduction was the centre piece of a two-day programme introduced by the CEO and run about 40 times to ensure that all relevant IBM UK managers understood the implications of the intended corporate culture change.

In principle, if an organization can afford not to worry about risk at the individual project level, then maximizing expected return (or minimizing expected cost) should be a standard decision rule for making all choices and managing all uncertainty within each project. This has the obvious very great merit of simplicity. At a project level risk management becomes redundant – but not opportunity management or uncertainty management. However, risk in terms of financial return on a project is only related to one objective. As the BCS example demonstrates, there are usually a wide range of other risks and rewards which need effective treatment – including dealing with other key parties who cannot be trusted, reputation risk, the long-term availability of business opportunities and the effort saved by ensuring clients are satisfied.

In terms of the management of individual projects, the pursuit of risk efficient options (and hence objectives (6) and (7) above) is a central reason why uncertainty management should not be seen as an 'add-on' activity , an overhead, with limited focus on questions like 'how much is this project (or project component) likely to cost?'. It is the central reason why uncertainty management in a PUMP sense should be seen as an integrated 'add-in', an improvement to the basic project planning process, which is always worth while.

Whether or not recognition of possible changes in plans by specific project team members is the result of a formal PUMP, demonstration of the need for changes is a separate and very important aspect of making changes. For a variety of reasons, if it is not possible to demonstrate clearly the need for changes to relevant project stakeholders, such changes may not be made, even if most of those involved acknowledge the need to make the changes. Obstacles include determined resistance to changes by those with vested interests, inertia, complacency, or the lack of a suitable conceptual basis to assess and compare alternative plans.

Application of the concept of risk efficiency and risk efficient tradeoffs between alternative options in project planning and uncertainty management can provide the means to demonstrate the need for changes in projects plans. The following example illustrates this in particularly clear terms.

Identifying a risk efficient alternative for an offshore oil project

The first BP project to use the SCERT process on a 'live' basis, the Magnus project, was about to seek board approval and release of funds to begin construction. SCERT analysis was undertaken to give the board confidence in the plan and its associated cost estimates. One activity involved a 'hook-up' operation – connecting a pipeline to a production platform. It had a target date in August. In the base plan a 1.6 m barge was specified, equipment which could work in waves up to a nominal 1.6 m height. The SCERT analysis demonstrated that August was an appropriate target date, and that use of a 1.6 metre barge was appropriate in August. However, this analysis also demonstrated that there was a significant chance that the hook-up would have to be attempted later, in November or December, because this operation was late in the overall project sequence and there was considerable scope for delays to preceding activities. Using a 1.6 m barge at this time of year would be time consuming and might mean that hook-up could not be completed until the following spring, with severe opportunity cost implications.

An alternative option was available in the form of a 3 metre wave height capability barge, costing more than twice as much per day as the 1.6 m barge. A revised SCERT analysis assuming use of the more capable 3 m barge virtually eliminated the risk of going into the next season, and an associated risk of a significant cost overrun. Employing the 3 m barge also reduced the expected cost of hook-up. Figure 3.4 illustrates the nature of the 'decision diagram' used to make this choice.

The cumulative probability distribution curves for the two barges cross above the P50 (50 percentile line), indicating that the 1.6 m choice will be cheaper most of the time. However, the 3.0 m barge distribution curve is much steeper, because the outcome is less uncertain. The 1.6 m barge distribution has a much longer tail to the right, because of the relatively low probability, but high cost, of a lost season. It is the long tail to the right that drags the expected cost of the 1.6 m barge option to the right of the expected cost for the 3 m barge option. Analysis indicated that the 1.6 m barge had a better than 50:50 chance of being cheaper, but the expected cost of using the 3 m barge was less than the expected cost of using the 1.6 m barge, by about £5 million.

Based on a discussion of Figure 3.4, the base plan was changed, and it was recognized at board level that this one change paid for the SCERT study many times over. The board approved the plan – successful despite some surprises – and the board also mandated the underlying process world wide for all large or sensitive projects because the board was convinced that the anticipated increases in project risk efficiency would more than pay for the process.

In the event, hook-up was actually completed in October in good weather conditions, and it was evident after-the-fact that the company could have got away with using a 1.6 m barge.

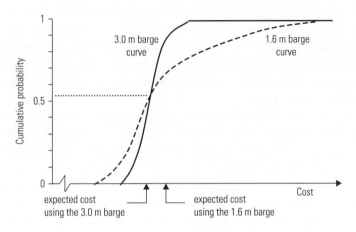

Figure 3.4   Decision diagram: one risk efficient choice example

The use of Figure 3.4 demonstrated that the project manager had done a good job as well as making the right barge choice, and BP had been lucky with the weather.

Figure 3.4 was not referred to as a 'decision diagram' at the time. Doing so now provides a simple common label for Figures 2.5 and 3.4 and all similar diagrams. This emphasizes the key role of decision diagrams, and it complements adopting the 'sensitivity diagram' label to clarify the role of two key complementary tools.

Wider use of the offshore oil project example

Cost and related cost risk was the focus of attention in the BP example using Figure 3.4. Risk efficiency was evident in the evaluation of an alternative option from the initial base plan option that simultaneously reduced risk and improved expected performance. The preferred option, use of the 3 m barge, was assessed to be superior to the use of the 1.6 m barge, both in terms of offering lower risk and a lower expected cost. The 1.6 m barge was not a risk efficient choice when compared with the 3 m barge option – there was only one risk efficient choice. In terms of Figure 3.3, the 1.6 m barge option corresponds to a point inside the shaded area like e_1, while the 3 m barge option corresponds to a point above and to left of e_1, hopefully a point on the risk efficient boundary, like b_2.

Pursuit of risk efficiency is also the basis of a number of other ways of pursuing objectives (7)–(10) above:

- Facilitate, demonstrate and encourage 'enlightened caution'.
- Facilitate, demonstrate and encourage 'enlightened gambles'.
- Explicit culture change programmes
- Achieve better tradeoffs between multiple objectives.

Facilitate, demonstrate and encourage enlightened caution

'Enlightened caution' is 'a willingness to commit resources which may not be needed, because in expected value terms (on average) it will be cost effective to commit them'.

Had problems in the earlier part of the project associated with Figure 3.4 caused the hook-up to take place in November or December, with seasonably bad weather, the change to a 3 m barge would have been clearly justified. The wisdom of enlightened caution associated with the choice of barge would have been verified empirically. However, given that the hook-up actually took place in October in good weather, it was a very important to be able to explain why the more expensive 3 m barge was deployed.

If a PUMP had not been followed, with the result that Figure 3.4 was not used to decide on a 3 m barge, and the decision was instead made on intuitive grounds by the project manager, his career might have looked much less promising when it became clear he could have got away with a 1.6 m barge. That is, the SCERT analysis made it clear that the project manager had done well to achieve hook-up by October, and that BP had been lucky with the weather. Without the Figure 3.4 analysis output, the project manager would have been accused of wasting money on the more expensive barge, overlooking completely his good management of the project (getting to the hook-up by October), and blighting his career. A worldly wise project manager would explicitly recognize this possibility, and might opt for the 1.6 m barge in the absence of a PUMP with these SCERT features, deliberately making a bad management decision from a corporate perspective because good luck with the weather would subsequently be confused with good management, and bad luck with the weather would subsequently just be interpreted as plain bad luck. If an organization cannot distinguish between good luck and good management, or between bad luck and bad management, individuals will manage risk and opportunity accordingly. Without PUMP support to demonstrate the rationale for their decisions, astute managers who are naturally and reasonably cautious with respect to their own careers will see risk efficient decisions comparable to choosing the 3 m barge in Figure 3.4 as unwise, potentially dangerous to their careers, and seeming to demonstrate a 'wimpish' uncalled-for caution whenever they actually manage the preceding work effectively. Very astute managers will avoid even looking for opportunities to increase risk efficiency in this way, and avoid the moral hazard of the obvious conflict of interests. More generally, if bad luck and bad management cannot be distinguished, such opportunities will not be looked for, and for the most part they will be passed over if they are stumbled upon.

An effectively supported PUMP can facilitate and demonstrate enlightened caution in particular instances, and by doing so encourage a more general culture change associated with circumstances that are not amenable to quantitative analysis.

If everyone involved understands the lesson of examples like that illustrated by Figure 3.4, the organizational culture can change as a consequence of everyone looking for and making changes which increase risk efficiency and linked opportunity capture through enlightened caution. This means that sometimes most people will spend money on 'insurance' – options that are not subsequently needed. However, any organization that never spends money on unnecessary 'insurance' is habitually 'under-insured'. Enlightened caution needs to be facilitated and demonstrated to overcome this widespread cultural phenomenon, the documentation of instances when the wisdom of enlightened caution was not empirically verified being of particular importance.

Facilitate, demonstrate and encourage enlightened gambles

While promoting enlightened caution, formal PUMPs can and should also encourage 'enlightened gambles', defined here as 'the selection of a high return option from a set of risk efficient options when relatively significant risk that comes with the high return is considered bearable'.

To illustrate what this involves, consider a fabricated alternative to Figure 3.4, developed for use in the culture change programme for IBM UK in the 1990s mentioned earlier in this chapter. Figure 3.5 is similar to Figure 3.4, but with the cumulative distribution for the 3 m barge shifted to the right; the £5 million expected cost advantage for the 3 m barge of Figure 3.4 then becomes a £5 million disadvantage in Figure 3.5. This is a fabricated example, but if the numbers in the real example had been different, this result might have been obtained.

The point where the curves cross now suggest that the 1.6 m barge has about an 80% chance of being cheaper, but crucially the ordering of the expected outcomes has been reversed – the expected cost of the 3 m barge is now about £5 million more than the expected cost of the 1.6 m barge. However, the long tail for the 1.6 m barge still implies much more risk, associated with a lost season, assumed for illustrative purposes to be comparable to a 10% chance of an extra £100 million in costs. The key question is: Should this extra risk be taken?

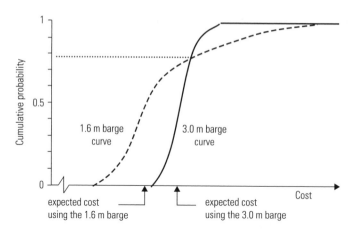

Figure 3.5 Decision diagram: two risk efficient choices example

A basic Markowitz approach implies both options are risk efficient – the 3 m barge option involves less risk but a higher expected cost, the 1.6 m barge involves more risk but at a lower expected cost. The choice of barge is therefore a matter of decision-maker preference – the board needs to make a decision based on corporate 'risk appetite' and corporate risk-taking capability, determined via a corporate view of risk efficiency for all projects and other corporate operations.

In the real example portrayed by Figure 3.4, BP's decision to change from a 1.6 m barge to a 3 m barge is comparable to moving in Figure 3.3 from point e_1 to point b_2. Had Figure 3.5 replaced Figure 3.4, the same change would have been comparable to moving in Figure 3.3 from point b_1 to b_2, when b_1 involved a level of risk within the organization's risk appetite and capability.

For oil majors involved in £1000 million projects in the 1970s and 1980s, potential losses much greater than £100–200 million were part of the territory. To enable them to live with these risks, joint ventures were common. Over ten such projects, taking the 1.6 m barge risk described by Figure 3.5 equates to an expected cost saving of £5 million times ten, or £50 million. Oil companies could not afford to pass up expected cost savings on this level in order to reduce risk which did not need to be reduced. Enlightened gambles were a key part of the culture. Organizations that do not take enlightened gambles and spend too much on reducing gambles, reduce their average profitability, and may eventually go out of business. Formal PUMPs can facilitate, demonstrate and encourage enlightened gambles as a basis for engineering-associated organization culture changes.

In the context of a choice like that portrayed in Figure 3.5, if the gamble paid off, the wisdom of the enlightened gamble would have been verified empirically. However, the occasional visible failure of such gambles is extremely important, because it demonstrates that good managers who take risk efficient gambles are sometimes unlucky. If no quantified uncertainty analysis were undertaken to demonstrate an expected cost saving associated with an enlightened gamble like that of Figure 3.5, this message would be lost, whatever the outcome. In the absence of a demonstrated expected cost benefit and of an organizational culture which promotes enlightened gambles, astute managers do not take such gambles, and very astute managers don't even look for them.

Option choice curves portrayed by decision diagrams like Figures 3.4 and 3.5 and simpler linear versions, are key tools for all PUMPs, at a suitable level of clarity. They are the basis for risk and opportunity efficient choices for all applications.

BP and the Deepwater Horizon accident in the Gulf of Mexico

The Gulf of Mexico oil spill disaster caused by the Macondo well 'blow-out' accident while Deepwater Horizon was drilling under contract to BP on 20 April 2010, caused major strategic damage to BP because of the environmental damage and linked knock-on impacts. The reasons why it happened will not be explored in this book, but it is important to note that mainstream press reports and more extensive studies (see, for example, Freudenburg and Gramling, 2010) suggest that 'an enlightened gamble' was not involved (the choices made were not risk efficient, nor was the level of risk taken appropriate), and an effective variant of the SCERT process developed for BP's North Sea projects was not being used. Since April 2010 the authors are very aware of the risks associated with using BP as an example, where a well-earned reputation for best practice developed in the 1970s and 80s can be lost. The authors think that although an organization that has a well-earned reputation for best practice can lose both its best practice and its reputation, it is better than hiding the BP use of SCERT and its role as part of the basis of the PUMP and associated ideas. Some implications of the transitory nature of best practice and reputations will be developed later.

A broad understanding of 'enlightened' decision making in the present context

PUMPs can facilitate a search for opportunities to take enlightened gambles, demonstrate whether such gambles are worth taking, and encourage a culture change where this mode of thinking and behaviour becomes the norm, even when formal risk analysis is not involved. Enlightened gambles mean that sometimes money will not be spent on proactive risk management when subsequent events will suggest it should have been. Enlightened caution means that sometimes money will be spent on proactive risk management which in the event proves unnecessary. The general cultural issue is distinguishing between good luck and good management, and between bad luck and bad management, in order to persuade people to take the right risks and avoid the wrong ones, in terms of risk efficiency and risk/expected performance tradeoffs.

In the context of gambles and caution, important aspects of a deep understanding of what 'enlightened' means are:

- the need for clear preventive and contingency planning when big gambles are involved;
- the need for clarity about the point at which big gambles are no longer enlightened because they put too much at stake;
- the need to understand the risk inefficiency of unenlightened caution; and
- the possible need to demonstrate why spending money on enlightened caution must be sustained when nothing goes wrong for a long period of time.

The pertinence of these aspects of enlightened risk taking should be clear by the end of this book. In the meantime three basic lessons can be drawn from BP's post-April 2010 situation which a 2010–11 client of the authors has found central to their decisions, and many other organizations could adapt.

First, running a serious risk which could be realized is not a good idea if effective uncertainty management has not been undertaken and its recommendations implemented.

Second, effective uncertainty management may involve significant costs which need effective justification if nothing goes wrong for an extended period of time, and effective culture management can be essential.

Third, choices often involve tradeoffs between money in direct cash terms (spent on uncertainty management and implementing associated preventative and contingency plans), and issues not easily translated into monetary equivalents (like environmental damage, loss of reputation and loss of life). A parametric approach developed into a marginal cost or 'shadow cost/price' concept like 'the value of an avoided fatality' can be crucial in such cases. For example, suppose 'option A' involves expected costs of £1 million more than 'option B' per annum. However, suppose option B involves 0.5 fatalities more than option A per annum in expected value terms, associated with low probability high impact events involving multiple fatalities – for example, 100 people killed in an accident with a 200-year return period (100 fatalities/200 years = 0.5 fatalities per annum on average). Then choosing option A implies a 'value of an avoided fatality' greater than £2 million (£1 million/0.5), and choosing option B implies a value of an avoided fatality less than £2 million. Choosing option A requires justifying a large annual expenditure to avoid low probability events. Choosing option B implies that Option B can be explained as a reasonable thing to have done when there are multiple fatalities. The £2 million figure is the expected cost of an avoided fatality defined by a decision 'flip-point', a parametric value based on actual costs and probabilities. It does not involve a 'value of life' concept in a direct valuation sense. But choosing options A or B implies a 'value of an avoided fatality' concept which is clearly very similar in some respects, whether or not the decision makers choose to admit it or reveal the implied value. The transport industry have recognized this kind of concept for many decades (see, for example, Chapman and Ward, 2002, ch. 7). Environmental and reputation issues can be addressed in comparable terms.

Part of the broad understanding required, which is also worth a brief note here, is the complex nature and competing explanations of low probability and high impact events. Some explanations focus on the inherently unpredictable aspects – like Taleb's (2007) 'black swans', normal accident theory (Sagan, 1993; Perrow, 1984, 1994), and the human error aspects of system failures (Reason, 1990). Both systemic uncertainty and ambiguity uncertainty, and their role in the 'unknown unknown', have to be a general aspect of any comprehensive attempt to explain such events.

Another part of the broad understanding required, and also worth a note here, is the way the office manager's photocopier choice example of Chapter 2 uses the decision diagram of Figure 2.5 – a simple version of Figures 3.4 and 3.5 combined – to make risk efficient choices and consider risk and reward tradeoffs. Very simple approaches like that discussed for BCS do not need decision diagrams like Figures 2.5, 3.4 or 3.5, but any analysis involving probability distributions and risk efficient choices needs some variant of these decision diagrams for clarity efficiency. In the authors' view these option choice diagrams for considering risk efficiency are a key basic PUMP tool in all contexts, at a suitable level of clarity, and their absence in a formal probabilistic analysis, suggests a possible failure to understand the need to address risk efficiency within the nested decomposition of uncertainty which underlies any effective and efficient PUMP. Why this is the case will be discussed in Chapter 11.

Explicit culture change programmes

Particularly at middle and lower levels of management, changing the culture to promote enlightened gambles can have a significant impact on organizational performance. 'Unenlightened gambles' (gambles which are not risk efficient) are an obvious concern, to be rooted out and avoided. Eliminating 'unenlightened caution' (risk reduction measures which are not risk efficient, or are risk efficient but not necessary) is arguably an even more important target for PUMPs and associated culture change. IBM UK was the first organization of which the authors are aware to recognize this and implement a major culture change programme based on it – but in our experience many other organizations would benefit from similar programmes. Opportunity management facilitated by an effective PUMP should be particularly concerned with enlightened gambles, but it should also address the need to understand the role of enlightened caution. The need to distinguish between bad management and bad luck, good management and good luck, is at the heart of it, with good uncertainty management at the heart of good management. This is a reminder that circumstances may present opportunity efficient choices involving significant risk exposure, and luck is then very important. 'Making your own luck' is part of 'enlightened planning' – but there is a residual 'in the hands of the Gods'. The Duke of Wellington is often attributed with the notion that 'being lucky' is a key characteristic of good commanders, but even lucky commanders in his terms could fail. There is nothing wrong with stretch targets that have little chance of success but are designed to manage good luck, provided they are backed up with realistic expectations and sensible commitments, and that associated uncertainty is fully understood and reflected in the project plans.

Culture change programmes can address other important culture issues at the same time or as separate exercises. Chapman and Ward (2002, ch. 12) discuss a number of culture issues, including 'a conspiracy of optimism' and 'irrational objectivity', two widespread and highly dysfunctional examples of 'blocks' or impediments to opportunity efficiency. Part IV addresses a number of culture-related issues.

Achieve better tradeoffs between multiple objectives

Risk efficient tradeoffs between expected cost and cost risk has direct analogies in terms of duration, quality and all other relevant performance criteria. Expected value and associated risk tradeoffs in terms of cost, duration, quality and other measures of performance need separate consideration, but also joint management. In particular, risk efficiency ought to be pursued via joint management of tradeoffs across all performance attributes of concern. The pursuit of risk efficiency and associated opportunity management in a multiple attribute context links project uncertainty management to project value management, project quality management, and so on – to project management *in toto*. The objective is jointly optimizing the design associated with a project, the duration of the project, its resource usage, its cost, and the quality of what is delivered, in terms of expected performance and associated risk, with appropriate tradeoffs on efficient frontiers. All seven Ws introduced in

Chapter 1 are involved, and their relationships. Much of the uncertainty to be managed is ambiguity about how best to manage these tradeoffs. What might go wrong (or better than expected) with a particular way of approaching a project is part of what a PUMP has to address, but it is a small part of a much bigger uncertainty management picture. PUMPs are about effectiveness as well as efficiency – doing the right things in every sense, as well as doing them the right way.

Tradeoffs between expected outcomes and associated risk may be quite different for different objectives. Issues like safety or quality when corporate image is involved may require an approach superficially 'out-of-character' with tradeoffs adopted in a financial risk context. For example, for a range of very sensible reasons, an aggressive approach to taking cost risk might be coupled to a very cautious approach to environmental risk or safety risk, and the 'value of an avoided fatality' approach discussed above can be used when very difficult tradeoffs are involved. The Chapter 2 BCS and office manager's photocopier choice examples illustrate other examples of the potential for better tradeoffs between different objectives.

The concept of 'opportunity efficiency' is at the core of the underlying framework adopted here and is basic to all PUMPs. A formal definition of *'opportunity efficiency'* is *'risk efficiency and suitable risk–reward tradeoffs for all relevant objectives with appropriate tradeoffs between all relevant objectives'*. By way of emphasis, there are three components:

- risk efficiency with respect to all relevant objectives;
- suitable risk–reward tradeoffs for all relevant objectives;
- appropriate tradeoffs between all relevant objectives.

The last includes being on efficient frontiers, generalising the first two. This is an 'overall optimality' concept if the reader's conceptual basis is grounded in mathematics, or an aspiration for 'best practice' concept if the readers perspective is implemented practice. Opportunity efficiency in this sense involves a minimum level of risk for any given level of expected outcome for any attribute of interest including non-measurable attributes. Further, it has to address all relevant attributes as a basis for optimal tradeoffs between them. A significant generalization of Markowitz's notion of risk efficiency is involved. One aspect of this generalization is recognising that measures of skew and other moments may be relevant, not just mean and variance, addressed by working directly with cumulative probability distributions. Another is considering all relevant attributes, using Figure 3.4, or simpler Figure 2.5 equivalents, for all measurable attributes. Non-measurable performance attributes, like optimal quality and reputation, may require consideration too, as may attributes not worth measuring, like the reliability of alternative options and associated suppliers. Distinguishing between risk to the organization and risk to individual decision makers is also important. Links like the effect on a decision maker's reputation of a commitment to a poor supplier are also important.

Those seeking a deeper understanding of this multi-criteria approach could start with Chapman and Ward (2002, chs 9 and 10).

It is worth adding here that clarity efficiency at an appropriate level of clarity is one of the multiple objective considerations that need to be seen as part of the opportunity efficiency concept. Too little clarity is an important decision-taking risk. Too much clarity, even if it is obtained in a clarity efficient manner, is an unnecessary drain on resources.

It is also worth adding that corporate culture and more general corporate capability issues can be viewed as part of the clarity efficiency and opportunity efficiency concepts, in terms of important objectives with obvious measurability difficulties.

Facilitating creative thinking

The facilitation, demonstration and encouragement of enlightened caution and enlightened gambles discussed earlier are extremely important objectives in their own right. But, they are also extremely important drivers of culture changes associated with a more positive attitude to uncertainty. This positive perspective is extremely important for staff motivation and morale, as well as for the direct payoff in terms of more risk efficient plans and designs, and a more effective approach to achieving efficiency.

An effective PUMP should help to identify difficulties and opportunities to change project base plans or contingency plans that were previously obscure or not recognized. Those responsible for the operation of a PUMP should be motivated to search for such changes, their PUMP should facilitate the search, and they should enlist the support of the project team as a whole to join the search. In this context uncertainty management can be usefully portrayed as a treasure hunt that invites creative thinking – the 'treasure' is increases in risk efficiency and associated opportunity capture through changes in plans. The 'opportunity management area' label in brackets for the competent management area near the risk efficient boundary in Figure 3.3 derives from this perspective, encouraged by the IBM culture change programme mentioned earlier. Dropping the 'risk' management brand in favour of 'uncertainty' management further builds on this perspective.

The authors prefer the 'opportunity management area' label to the 'capable management area' label when working with capable organizations, but it is important to point out that many organizations habitually operate outside that zone, and it is important to be clear that this is incompetent.

We can never be sure that our plans are opportunity efficient. However, we need to search systematically for possible improvements, with a clear understanding of what we are looking for, otherwise we will never find them. This implies that the form of PUMP selected must be geared to a search for opportunities to improve risk and opportunity efficiency. If a project's plans are already very effective and efficient in general terms, usually what is involved is identifying where extra money or other resources expended up-front will reduce later uncertainty, risk and overall expected cost – but more fundamental lateral thinking may be key.

If uncertainty is seen as a 'bad thing' and a source of fear to be avoided, people develop blinkers as a natural defence mechanism. If uncertainty is seen as a 'good thing', a source of opportunity and satisfaction to be seized, then people take off their blinkers. They start to look at all the angles and their expectations and aspirations rise. The following example, adapted from Wheelwright (1978), illustrates the value of lateral thinking involving a different perspective by a different group of people, turning a threat into an opportunity by managing potential delays in a way that improved the project's cash flow. PUMPs should be designed to stimulate and facilitate this kind of creative thinking. This can go well beyond the facilitation of enlightened caution and enlightened gambles, to include entirely new ways of seeing opportunities.

A change of purpose for new production equipment

The established manufacturer of a branded household product suddenly found its market growing rapidly, severely taxing its outdated production process. With outside help, the production manager designed new production equipment that would improve both the consistency of the product and productivity. Although the equipment was new to this application, it was based on known technologies from other fields, and promised twice the output per square foot of plant and per employee, with an investment per unit of capacity comparable with the old equipment. The new process appeared to more than meet cost requirements and the production manager planned to replace the old production equipment with the new as quickly as possible.

At a senior management meeting concern was raised that the production manager had no contingency plan in the event that the new production process experienced unexpected start-up problems. This prompted a discussion of the critical role of additional capacity in exploiting the substantial growth in demand. Further investigation indicated that the cost of creating and maintaining excess capacity was minimal compared to the high margin obtainable on the product. Moreover, if the firm was unable to meet all of the demand for its products, the penalty would not only be a loss in market share, but a waste of advertising dollars equivalent to the capital investment required for 30% idle capacity. The senior management team concluded that, in the short term, the new production equipment should be acquired to provide *additional* production capacity, rather than as a *replacement* for the existing equipment.

Searching for opportunities as 'fun'

When people start searching for opportunities in a broad sense they generally enjoy themselves. Lateral thinking becomes the order of the day, and people start to think of capturing opportunity and containing downside risk as 'fun'. It is fun because it is tackled in advance, in a calm and creative way, while there is time to work around the obvious and important problems. Reactive crisis management is not eliminated, but it is reduced to a tolerable level. *Good* formal analysis processes are not inhibiting, and they are not about 'doom and gloom'; they are about creative thinking, seizing opportunities, and having fun.

While it may not seem so at first sight, this is a *very* serious point. The biggest source of risk and risk inefficient choices is, for most projects and organizations, a failure to attract and keep the best people. If a manager wants to attract and keep the best people, and get the most out of them, morale is a key issue. Good morale cannot be bought, it has to be developed. Good uncertainty management processes can help to build good morale in a number of ways. Encouraging creative and lateral thinking is one way. Other ways include the order-of-magnitude increases in communication between all project staff which tend to flow from the process, breaking down 'them-and-us', enlarging cooperation across group and company boundaries, and so on. These benefits should not simply be allowed to happen. They should be encouraged by designing them into the process.

Constructive insubordination

A common experience for the authors when acting as consultants in an analysis mode is being expected to answer what they soon perceive to be 'the wrong question'. It is important for all analysts, and for all those who ask them questions, to understand that this does not necessarily imply an error of judgement on the questioner's part – it may be the natural consequence of a need for focus prior to the insights provided by analysis. It may be useful for analysts to assume that this is the case, and indulge in 'constructive insubordination', attempting to answer 'the right question', after some time spent attempting to formulate 'the right question'.

Encouraging a dialogue or an interactive process that both facilitates and promotes constructive insubordination, can be an important part of the overall culture change process. It is vital to teams working across different management levels. The following example illustrates what can be involved.

Risk associated with a Canadian offshore gravity platform

An offshore project on the east coast of Canada being planned in the early 1980s involved two possible technologies and a novel source of uncertainty – icebergs from the same source as the one that sank the *Titanic*.

One technology was based on a 'gravity' platform, a larger-scale version of an approach used by the Norwegians for North Sea projects. A large concrete doughnut is cast in a deep-water harbour, sunk, and another section cast on top. This process is repeated until a large concrete 'pipe' about 100 m across and 200 m long is formed. This 'pipe' is then floated and towed to the site. After sinking it at the desired location, it is half filled with iron ore to make it heavy enough to withstand the impact of icebergs. The other half is used to store oil when production begins.

The other technology involved a submarine well-head connection via a flexible hose to 'ship-shapes', effectively tankers, which produce the oil, moving off station if icebergs become a threat.

Political pressures were an important part of the decision process. Gravity platforms would have to be constructed in an east coast Canadian harbour, an area of high unemployment. Ship-shapes could come from anywhere. A number of other factors also favoured the gravity platform approach.

Initially it was assumed that the gravity structure was the preferred approach, and the focus of a risk assessment that Chris Chapman was asked to undertake was on the cost of a gravity platform. However, the initial analysis concentrated on the technology choice question, in terms of uncertainty associated with recoverable oil in the reservoir, the price of oil when it is produced, and the capital costs and operating costs for both technologies. A key issue was the high capital cost and low-operating cost structure of the gravity platform approach versus the low capital cost and high-operating cost structure of the ship-shape approach. This analysis demonstrated that, as things then stood, a gravity platform approach involved unacceptable risk. A low oil volume/low oil price/high platform capital cost scenario involved betting the company – with a risk of losing. A ship-shape approach did not pose this threat, because of its low capital cost.

The company's management was not pleased by this result, addressing a question they had not asked and recommending a course of action they saw as second best for personal as well as corporate reasons. However, they accepted its validity, and managed the risks it identified.

Subsequent to this analysis, further exploratory wells confirmed the anticipated volume of oil, and the risk associated with the gravity approach was managed in other ways, to make this technology (design) choice effective and efficient. The oil price then fell, putting the project on hold for a decade. It proceeded successfully when this source of uncertainty was resolved, but arguably both the additional exploratory well and the period on hold involved important corporate decisions that might not have been.

Generalizing the Canadian offshore project story

The point of the above example is that organizations need people who are prepared to go beyond their basic remit if this seems appropriate, question received wisdom when appropriate, and deliver bad news upwards when appropriate. Everyone needs to see 'the big picture', and say so when their perspective suggests relevant insights. A corporate 'suggestions box' is not enough.

An important motive for PUMPs can be the much more effective working relationships which result from the encouragement of big picture perspectives, the discouragement of tunnel vision, and the encouragement of productive questioning of sacred cows. This does not imply an absence of discipline, or a tolerance of unconstructive insubordination. The goal is a process which is creative and supportive, built on mutual confidence and trust, give and take. It deliberately avoids the assumption that more senior management 'know better' than their juniors, and seeks to liberate the creativity of all levels of management responsibility. Even hard-nosed military commanders in the heat of real battle understand the value of constructive insubordination (the origin of the term) and the obvious illustration of a context in which unconstructive insubordination would not be tolerated.

Conclusion

Best practice in uncertainty management, including both opportunity and risk management – opportunity efficiency – begins with a clear understanding of the scope for application and the objectives that should be pursued. Well-founded trust based on clear thinking and clear communication might be singled out as one key composite objective to be achieved by appropriate analysis and documentation. Another key composite objective is the identification of opportunities to change base plans and develop contingency plans in the context of a search for risk efficiency and a rich view of opportunity and risk management, taking an aggressive approach to the level of risk that is appropriate, with a view to long-term corporate performance maximization. Encouraging and facilitating cultural changes such as a positive attitude to uncertainty, creativity in options generation, and constructive insubordination can also be important. Uncertainty quantification is a vital tool in this process, especially if the full potential value of cultural changes is to be realized, and dysfunctional organizational behaviour associated with confusing targets, expectations and commitments or provisions and contingencies should be avoided. But qualitative analysis and its documentation can also help to capture corporate knowledge in an effective fashion, for use in both current and future projects, and explicit corporate culture management can pay major dividends.

Chapter 4

An overview of generic process frameworks

Some people regard discipline as a chore. For me it is a kind of order that sets me free to fly.
—Julie Andrews

Defining procedures is a common way of ensuring that people are clear about what needs to be done and how to do it. Procedures can also be a way of ensuring that quality and consistency are maintained across different applications over time. If both these objectives are important, effective and efficient procedures need to be simple, transparent and repeatable – but not all processes fit this mould. Some uncertainty management processes need to be sophisticated, subtle and unique in a creative sense. PUMPs of the kind needed for planning offshore projects as discussed in Chapter 3 are at the sophisticated and creative end of the scale. The designs of relatively simple uncertainty management processes, like the BCS and Highways Agency examples discussed in Chapter 2, have to draw on the same general principles as the offshore examples to achieve clarity efficiency. A simplistic basis is not good enough for any context addressed by this book.

For all management processes, the level of detail that is appropriate, and the extent to which a prescriptive approach can be used, depends upon the context and complexity of the overall task. For situations involving limited scope and limited complexity plus low uncertainty, formal, tightly defined processes with specific steps can be used. In the limit, formalization can involve a rigid 'paint by numbers' procedure. Pre-flight safety checks on an aircraft often resemble this, at least until a fault is identified. Where significant scope and significant complexity plus high uncertainty are involved, it is inappropriate to specify procedures in too much detail, and a very serious mistake to make them too prescriptive. Procedures that are too limited or too inflexible to take into account important aspects of application contexts are counterproductive.

A requirement for flexibility and a lack of limitations or bounds imply a need for judgement and knowledge to make appropriate choices about procedures. Attempts to avoid these requirements by 'deskilling' uncertainty management processes involve great risk and need great care. This is a particular concern when managing uncertainty in projects.

Formality is desirable because it provides structure and discipline that facilitates efficient and effective uncertainty management – which achieves opportunity efficiency including clarity efficiency as discussed in Chapter 3. However, this formality is not about the pursuit of a closely defined, inflexible and bureaucratic procedure. Formality in project uncertainty management processes is partly about making sure the right questions get asked and answered, and partly about making sure everyone who needs to know understands the answers. Helping people to develop the right answers in a creative manner is a third aspect. This third aspect lies between the first two in delivery terms. It can be a focus of attention for analysts and process facilitators, but it may be of less concern to others. Giving people the comfort that all the key questions have been asked and appropriately addressed is the basic rationale of a formal process for everyone involved.

Given the variety of contexts in which project uncertainty management might be employed, the range of objectives that might be pursued for such a process, and the complexity of issues involved, it is not appropriate to look for a closely defined, inflexible, 'one size fits all' procedure. Instead, a generic, formal project uncertainty management process is required that provides a guiding framework – highlighting key issues requiring attention, including the need to adapt to different project and organizational contexts as an integral part of the process. A key message of this book is that this kind of formal process must not be a source of restriction, but a facilitator of intelligent, skilful, creative and cost effective analysis and management of uncertainty. In practical terms we need an integrated concept, process and model set that delivers 'clarity efficiency' as part of a broader 'opportunity efficiency'.

Previous chapters have illustrated the desirability of applying performance uncertainty management in each and every stage of the project or asset lifecycle. Each lifecycle stage presents a different context for a PUMP. Consequently, effective and efficient PUMPs should vary in each lifecycle stage to reflect the different objectives for the PUMP, the relevant sources of uncertainty, the tasks involved, and the different people involved.

This chapter outlines the main features of a basic PUMP that provides a framework for PUMPs that suit all lifecycle stages. For convenience and efficiency, we outline a basic PUMP that has been designed, tested and evolved for use in the execution and delivery strategy development (E&D shaping) stage of the Table 1.3 nominal lifecycle. Part II (Chapters 5–11) explains in detail how this E&D shaping PUMP operates. Part III (Chapters 12 and 13) explains how this E&D shaping PUMP needs to be adapted for each of the other 11 stages of the *nominal* life cycle in Table 1.3 – in practice in all stages of any lifecycle portrayal. In brief, the required adaptations involve modest changes for the DOT shaping stage, more significant changes for the concept-shaping stage, quite dramatic changes for the tactics shaping stage and following stages, plus radical changes for the four associated governance stages. For convenience, we shall refer to the set of PUMPs appropriately adapted to suit different life cycle stages as the 'PUMP pack'. Taken together this set of PUMPs provides a complete set of related processes for addressing uncertainty over the whole of the asset lifecycle.

The PUMP pack is a synthesis of earlier specific and generic 'risk management' processes that have been in use since the 1970s, with some new features. The PUMP pack represents an updated description of a coherent set of fully tested operational process concepts, not a new product.

This chapter begins by considering alternative process frameworks, including some of the processes that the PUMP pack builds on. This helps to clarify some of the basic pedigree of the PUMP pack. It also provides a starting point for understanding key differences and associated basic process design choices. One key difference, emphasized at the outset, is attention to the importance of iterations. Limitations of guidelines and standards and a cautionary tale help to clarify this starting point.

An outline description of the PUMP and PUMP pack follow – the core of this chapter, to provide the overview elaborated by Parts II and III.

An historical perspective then shows how the PUMP pack framework has emerged from a synthesis of earlier process frameworks. This historical perspective also sheds some light on the evolution of key ideas which are central to all effective frameworks, and some barriers to effective processes.

Some alternative process frameworks

'Risk management' is a developing discipline, with many different schools of thought, and there have been many attempts by various professional bodies to set out what 'risk management' should involve, with some significant areas of contention. Typical guidance sets out, in varying levels of detail, basic definitions of terms, scoping premises, pertinent organizational arrangements, a description of analytical techniques that can be employed and a summary of key tools. Central to all such guidance is the definition of a process framework that sets out the component steps envisaged in any application of risk management. An illustrative sample of these process frameworks relevant to a project context is summarized in Table 4.1.

For comparison purposes the rows separated by lines in Table 4.1 show the approximate alignment of what we will term 'macro-phases' in each process framework – component steps defined at a fairly macro level. Some guides use alternative terms for the process components we call 'phases' or 'macro-phases', like 'sub-phases', 'processes' or 'activities'.

In Table 4.1 the labels adopted for the macro-phases and component phases in each process framework suggest a superficial convergence between the different process frameworks to the extent that there are macro-phases for: defining the context and planning this particular application; identifying 'risks' (sources of uncertainty); analysis/assessment; response selection; implementation of responses; and subsequent monitoring and review. However, the scope of the macro-phases and associated phases envisaged in each process framework can vary significantly, as can the extent and detail of associated guidance. For example, one of many important differences between the processes portrayed in Table 4.1 is that the PRAM process is the only one that includes structure and ownership issues as separate phases in the process framework.

As another illustration of variations, consider the first macro-phase in Table 4.1. In broad terms, the first macro-phase in all the Table 4.1 process frameworks is about deciding how the risk management process will be carried out in a given project, and how it will fit in with other project management processes. However, the details can be rather different across process frameworks, both in terms of intent and detailed description of what is involved. The OGC Management of Risk (MoR) process first macro-phase, 'identify the context', involves obtaining information about existing risk management policy and process guidance, the nature

Table 4.1 Approximate 'macro-phase' alignments for a sample of process frameworks

Association for Project Management (APM): Project Risk Analysis and Management (PRAM) Guide (APM, 2004)	Institution of Civil Engineers (ICE) and the Actuarial Profession (AP): Risk Analysis and Management for Projects (RAMP) (ICE and AP, 2005)	Project Management Institute(PMI): Project Risk Management (PRM) (PMI, 2008), PMI Practice Standard for PRM (PMI, 2009)	UK Office of Government Commerce (OGC): Management of Risk (MoR) (OGC, 2007)	ISO 31000 (International Standard, 2009)
Initiate: define the project	Organise and define RAMP through the investment lifecycle	Plan risk management	Identify context	Establish the context
Initiate: focus the risk management process	Plan and initiate risk review			
Identify	Identify risks	Identify risks	Identify the risks	Risk identification
Assess: structure ownership estimate evaluate	Evaluate risks	Perform qualitative risk analysis	Assess: estimate	Risk analysis
		Perform quantitative risk analysis	Assess: evaluate	Risk evaluation
Plan risk event responses	Respond to risks	Plan risk responses	Plan (responses)	Risk treatment
Plan project risk responses	Assess residual risks Plan responses to residual risks			
Implement responses	Communicate strategy and plans	Monitor and control risks	Implement (responses and monitor effectiveness)	Monitoring and review
	Implement strategy and plans Control risks			

of the project, and about progress to date. The first macro-phase in the PMI process, 'plan risk management', focuses on defining organizational arrangements, the risk categorization framework, risk tolerances, and reporting formats (PMI, 2008), the project context (objectives, project environment, 'solution approach') and the points at which risk management will be repeated during the project (PMI, 2009). The PRAM guide 'initiate' macro-phase has a somewhat different emphasis. First, it involves definition of the project 'to ensure a common understanding of the project to which the risk management process is to be applied' (APM, 2004, p. 20). Second, it involves focusing the risk management process, tailoring the risk management process to the specific requirements of the project. This includes defining objectives for this particular application of risk management, the 'depth or level at which the risk management process should be applied at each stage of the project lifecycle', and 'due consideration' of 'risk management policy, procedures, methods, organization, roles, infrastructure of staff, skills, and tools' (APM, 2004, p. 21).

Further comparison between these and other process frameworks could be pursued, considering processes described within each phase of different frameworks, but we make only very limited comparisons in this chapter. This is because as soon as we get beyond the spirit of an approach and the level of process detail illustrated by Table 4.1, and attempt to deal with operational details, everything becomes surprisingly difficult to analyse and of limited value to most readers. This difficulty and complexity arises because of differences in basic framing assumptions, like what we mean by risk and uncertainty, how the process relates to the project lifecycle, and whether or not risk efficiency and opportunity efficiency are seen as relevant. Differences in terminology introduce further variation and can further complicate comparisons. Those interested in more details might start with Chapman (2006) and Hopkinson et al (2008).

PRAM, RAMP and the PMI project risk management process are a useful representative subset of this sample of alternative generic process frameworks because their first editions were early in the field and they each take somewhat different perspectives. Any other process frameworks of interest could be characterized in relation to these three plus PUMP within the PUMP pack framework to gain some insights about the relationships, but the basic issues will be similar, and it is the spirit of approaches which matters most. The UK Office of Government Commerce Management of Risk (MoR) guidance (OGC, 2007) is an example of a later guide which builds on these three earlier guides and other sources. ISO 31000 is an example of a recent international standard. Some other examples which may be of interest include a recent version of the Australian/New Zealand standard, AS/NZS 4360 (2004), and three British Standards (2000, 2001, 2008). There are many others, and further forthcoming examples are inevitable.

Limitations of standards and professional guidance

Guidance and associated process frameworks developed and promoted by professional organizations have an important role to play in the development of accepted good practice, if not 'best practice', for a number of reasons. For example, the preparation of guides and standards can bring together experts with different experience, and synthesize that experience in a unique way, and they can tailor completely general common practice approaches to particular types of context, which facilitates constructive detail. However, such process frameworks, and the process of their development, have important limitations that need to be understood. In some cases – for standards in particular – the need for consensus can limit both the scope and detail of what can be said. To achieve agreement, requirements may have to be expressed in outline, often in very brief terms, in order to accommodate a variety of interpretations related to prevailing common practice, with obvious limitations on the extent of the guidance that can be given. In other cases different contributors may write different chapters or sections, and full integration is difficult, leaving ambiguities, if not inconsistencies. In some cases editors attempt to avoid the first two problems by imposing a single view.

Readers unfamiliar with the risk management literature might expect guidance produced by professional bodies to serve as overview summaries of all relevant concepts and recent developments, with special attention paid to contentious or difficult issues, to minimize potential confusion. Arguably this should be the case – but it is not. Guides produced by professional bodies are aimed at a range of different audiences for several different purposes, but they all need interpretation as advice put together by a group of people with three competing objectives to balance:

(1) agreement by all contributors, which if pushed to the limit means what can be said is limited because there is scope for considerable differences of opinion;
(2) consistent style throughout, which if pushed to the limit means one editor is effectively the author whose opinions largely determine what is said;
(3) comprehensive treatment of differences of opinion, which if pushed to the limit means that different styles and messages in the same document are difficult to avoid, which can be confusing.

At present, considerable differences in opinion are a feature of the field, and a wide range of different priorities are adopted towards these three objectives. Limited attention to the last objective in most guidance is a *very* serious problem in our view. This suggests that guides are a part of the literature which those new to the field should address *later* in their exploration of the literature, rather than at the outset, to minimize potential confusion. They should not be a starting point for professional training programmes and qualifications.

Readers new to the literature might expect 'standards' produced by professional bodies to serve as overview summaries of what ought to be the basis of more detailed supplementary guidance produced by professional bodies and standard texts. Arguably this should be the case, but it is not. Standards produced by professional bodies differ from guides in a range of ways, but standards need careful interpretation because they usually reflect ambiguous normative advice focused on the first of the above three objectives with little concern for the third objective.

Stephen Ward served on the committee that produced the BSI 31100 standard on Risk Management (British Standard, 2008) which contributes to ISO 31000, and Chris Chapman has served on working parties for the PRAM and RAMP guides, a direct involvement by the authors in three of the five in Table 4.1. We have both contributed to many other guides and standards, some concerned with operations, strategy and enterprise risk and uncertainty as well as project risk and uncertainty. We both see the role of guides and standards as important in the evolution of the subject, but they need to be interpreted with considerable care by the inexperienced.

A cautionary tale

In 2007 Chris Chapman was approached by a new client who wanted public endorsement of a cost estimate for a maintenance and renewal contract. The client was in dispute with a prime contractor about cost growth in a very large contract. Several years into the contract both parties admitted that initial estimates had proved to be optimistic. But the contractor was claiming that costs would be much higher than the client thought they should be. The difference was hundreds of millions of pounds. Adjudication of the dispute was imminent. Chris was approached at least in part as a contributing author to the RAMP and PRAM guides, which the client claimed to have followed. Chris advised that the client's approach to cost estimating might be interpreted as compliant with PRAM and RAMP, but it was not compliant with his recommended interpretation of either. The client's approach was consistent with common practice, as outlined in the Highways Agency context *prior* to the Nichols report (see the Highways Agency example discussion in Chapter 2). It involved built-in optimistic bias in estimates, because only event uncertainty had been addressed systematically. The client persisted with their claim and won, but the contractor then declared bankruptcy. It soon became clear that actual costs were going to exceed the contractor's estimate as well as the client's estimate, because the contractor's higher estimate was also optimistically biased, probably for the same reason.

The need to avoiding getting into such a position in the first place is the primary message. An important secondary message is claiming compliance with a guide or standard involves an ambiguous message. Those receiving or sending such messages need to understand the implications, as do those producing guides and standards. This book is compliant with ISO 31000, but following ISO 31000 does not mean that results consistent with following this book will be obtained. No guides or standards the authors are aware of actually address freedom from bias, and they certainly do not imply that their processes assure freedom from bias. In some peoples' view, the achievement of unbiased estimates is an unrealistic goal, in part because 'strategic misrepresentation' (wilful conscious bias) is seen as a permanent feature of the landscape. However, there are alternative views that may get tested in the courts before too long, in terms of claims of professional negligence. One goal of this book is defining a 'professional competence' basis for such claims.

This book explicitly avoids detailed critiques of specific guides and standards, primarily because it would not be helpful for most readers. However, it is critical of specific features of common practice, and it is critical of the PMI guides in broad terms because they describe and recommend common practice. Further, it is critical of all other guides and all standards to the extent that they fail to distinguish what they recommend from inappropriate common practice. This book does provide a framework for detailed comparative analysis. Like all views, different processes proposed by different bodies need to be subjected to constructive critique from alternative perspectives. Our collective best interests are served if these processes support each other and move towards addressing common basic concepts and issues. Thus far, explicit criticism in the literature has been muted, and convergence limited. Changing this situation is overdue, and stimulating such change is one objective of this book.

Most guides and standards have useful things to say. In particular, the PUMP pack framework can be seen in part as a synthesis of key features of PRAM and RAMP, building on some of their key contributions.

The key role of planned and unplanned iterations

A basic role of any risk/uncertainty/opportunity management process framework is helping everyone involved to develop sufficient understanding to achieve appropriate clarity about significant sources of uncertainty and what to do about them. What constitutes sufficient understanding and appropriate clarity will depend upon the context, and judgements need to be made about how much detail it is worth going into *for each aspect of the context under consideration as analysis progresses*. This is part of ensuring a 'clarity efficient' process, as explained in Chapter 3. An efficient and effective uncertainty management process involves pursuing clarity efficiency explicitly.

At the beginning of any analysis the relative importance of each aspect of context is part of the uncertainty that needs to be addressed. To address this kind of uncertainty effectively, the uncertainty management process must be iterative, starting with a quick, rough 'first cut' assessment that is progressively refined in subsequent passes as understanding about key issues develops.

This helps to reduce the time spent on relatively unimportant issues and focus effort on the most significant sources of uncertainty.

Iteration involves revisiting or looping back to earlier steps within a phase or to earlier phases in a process or to earlier analysis in any given lifecycle stage or to an earlier lifecycle stage. The purpose of any iteration is to develop, restructure, refine, or reconsider aspects of analysis undertaken to date where this is useful. Efficient analysis will usually warrant several complete passes through the different phases within any given lifecycle stage. It will also usually involve many partial loops, within subsets of the phases or within some phases.

There are costs as well as benefits in iteration, which need to be managed. In particular, planned iterations early in the project lifecycle involving low cost need to be encouraged, but it is very important to discourage the need for late iterations which involve going back to issues that should have been resolved in earlier lifecycle stages, required because of an emergent problem. Costly late iterations need to be minimized by the intelligent use of early iterations. For example, iterations between the phases of a PUMP applied in the concept shaping stage of the asset life cycle, to develop a robust business case for a project, involve a very low cost relative to having to revisit a fragile business case after delivery of the asset.

This flexible approach to a multi-pass iterative process should not be confused with periodic applications of an inherently 'linear' or one-pass uncertainty management process to obtain an updated view of changed circumstances in a project. It is unfortunate that guidelines on risk management processes often refer to 'iterations in the risk management process' when they are merely referring to a recurrent process of risk management carried out at different points in the project lifecycle over time.

Tabular lists of phases or macro-phases in a process framework, like those in Table 4.1, do not capture the planned (highly desirable) or unplanned (less desirable but sometimes essential) iterative nature of processes, and it is typically ignored or given limited discussion in most risk management process guidelines. This is *very* surprising. It may reflect:

- a focus on a 'high level' depiction of processes with an inevitably low resolution portrayal of what is involved;
- concern to keep processes simple, even if this makes them simplistic;
- satisfaction with quick and simplistic methods of identifying key sources of uncertainty;
- lack of concern with second level analysis of the effects of sources of uncertainty and associated response selection;
- reluctance or difficulty in quantifying uncertainty, opportunity and risk;
- a focus on 'risks' in the event uncertainty sense, and a failure to manage *any* other uncertainty effectively, *including uncertainty about what aspects of any given context need priority attention.*

Whatever the explanation, in the authors' view flexible and effective management of iterations is central to clarity efficient uncertainty management with an appropriate level of efficiency. Lack of attention to iteration is a key weakness in most common practice risk management. It is a core reason for clarity inefficiency.

All risk management processes may be iterative *by accident*, because unplanned shortcomings of an earlier pass are discovered later. *Planned iterations* involve revisiting or looping back to earlier phases or steps within a given phase to develop, refine or reconsider aspects of the analysis undertaken to date because the process assumes that a version of the 80:20 rule applies. A 'linear' process designed for one pass will be inefficient because the 20% of issues causing 80% of the problems are unknown at the outset.

If a single-pass, 'right-first-time' approach to all process steps and phases is attempted, it will be highly inefficient, and potentially seriously ineffective. Time will be wasted on issues which turn out to be unimportant, and not enough time will be spent on the important issues not anticipated when the process was started. In a multi-pass process, earlier passes are about making sure we are asking the right questions before spending much time developing suitable answers.

The basic PUMP framework

Table 4.2 provides an overview of the purposes of each of the seven phases of the *basic* (E&D shaping) PUMP. Begin with a look at Table 4.2 as a whole, then consider an overview of the tasks one at a time. A more detailed development is provided in Part II – a complete chapter for each phase.

Table 4.2   An overview of phase purposes for the basic (E&D shaping) PUMP process

Phases	An overview of phase purposes
define the project	Provide an effective common understanding of the project.
focus the process	Provide the basis of a clarity efficient process.
identify *all* the relevant sources of uncertainty, response options and conditions	Identify all the relevant sources of uncertainty using the structured information gathered about the project in the define phase. Represent the uncertainty involved. Treating sources as aggregates when they are not worth decomposing is crucial. To the extent that doing so is worthwhile, identify direct and knock-on consequences for each source of uncertainty, and what might be done about them. When relevant, consider proactive and reactive response options, including secondary sources of uncertainty and associated responses. At an appropriate level of detail, identify all relevant sources of uncertainty to be treated in qualitative terms as assumptions – conditions in quantitative analysis terms.
structure *all* uncertainty	Review and complete the structuring of all uncertainty inherent in the earlier phases, recognizing and making explicit all key interdependencies and links between components. A key aspect of completing the structure is making 'general' and 'specific' response distinctions – identifying general responses which can deal with sets of sources, including unidentified sources and sources to be treated qualitatively. Consider and test simplifying assumptions. Provide simpler, more complex or alternative relationship structures where appropriate.
clarify **ownership**	Allocate *both* financial *and* managerial responsibility for *all* sources of uncertainty. Separate financial and managerial responsibility if this is appropriate. Concentrate on broad concerns like forms of contract initially, details like named individuals towards the end of the iterations.
quantify *some* uncertainty	Clarify relevant conditions and estimate the size of all uncertainty usefully quantified on a first pass. On later passes more and more decomposition of uncertainty is usually useful. Towards the end of the iterative cycling process refining earlier quantitative estimates of uncertainty is usually useful. Both restructuring and refining estimates are about developing a better understanding of uncertainty, opportunity and risk when this is clarity efficient.

(continued)

Table 4.2   Continued

Phases	An overview of phase purposes
evaluate *all* the relevant implications	Synthesize the results of the quantify phase using appropriate dependence assumptions – adding, multiplying and using other required operations to combine sources of uncertainty. Do so two to six sources at a time, building up a nested structure. Understand the uncertainty and how to manage it at the current 'bottom level' before moving up the structure, 'bottom-up'. Remember explaining the analysis will be 'top-down'. A planned hierarchical structure will be needed. To some extent this structure should be designed in the focus phase and evolved in the structure phase, but it will need further consideration in this phase. Interpret the results as sources of uncertainty accumulate, using sensitivity diagrams like Figures 2.4 and 3.2. Use *all* the analysis developed to date to the current level of composition within the nesting structure to evaluate the implications of alternative courses of action. Consider the project outcomes that could result from each identified choice, using decision diagrams like Figures 2.5 and 3.4–3.5. Make provisional decisions about how to revise project plans in response to uncertainty to 'shape' project plans where this is useful – 'project decisions'. Also decide how to restructure and refine analysis on the next pass, if another pass looks useful and time is available. This involves making 'process decisions' about refining and redefining earlier analysis, managing the iterative process.

Define the project

The 'define the project' phase starts by consolidating relevant existing information about the project at a strategic level in a form suitable for analysis in the E&D shaping stage of the project lifecycle. Avoid 'losing sight of the wood for the trees' – it is crucial to keep the perspective strategic and avoid getting involved in any detail that is not directly relevant. Filling in any gaps uncovered in the information consolidation process needs early attention – as does resolving any conflicting views about key issues.

Clarifying all working assumptions is usefully viewed as a basis for identifying any inconsistent assumptions initially – later it will be an important basis for the evaluate phase.

The lifecycle stage and gateway structure is a useful part of the basis for the define phase. The nominal structure of Table 1.3 should be adapted to suit the particular organization and project involved. There is a clear need to build on all earlier lifecycle stage planning, and look ahead at some key later lifecycle issues. The seven' Ws structure is another useful part of the basis of the 'define the project' phase, with a focus dictated by the project lifecycle position. Table 1.4 and Figure 1.3 are useful reminders. The criteria–plan relationship structures are also relevant. The 'define the project' phase can be seen as a form of context capture plus approach development and capture for *the project*. It is important to keep the deliverables of the define phase updated as iterations progress.

Focus the process

The 'focus the process' phase starts by scoping the analysis to be performed at the E&D shaping stage of the project lifecycle. It then provides a strategic plan for the E&D shaping PUMP which reflects both long-term aims and the immediate needs of this lifecycle stage. This is followed by planning the next pass of the E&D shaping PUMP at an operational level.

The 'focus the process' phase can be seen as a form of context capture plus approach development and capture for *the process*. It should clarify relevant *process* working assumptions in conjunction with the define phase *project* working assumptions. These working assumptions will shape all other phases. The goal is seeking clarity efficiency. It is important to keep the deliverables of the focus phase updated as iterations progress.

Identify *all* the relevant sources of uncertainty, response options and conditions

'Identify *all* the relevant sources of uncertainty, response options and conditions' has to limit the complexity introduced to what is relevant in a clarity efficient manner. It involves identifying all sources of uncertainty to be treated separately in quantitative terms. It also involves identifying all sources of uncertainty to be treated separately as working assumptions in qualitative analysis terms, conditions in the quantify phase. On early passes preliminary working assumptions are involved. The PUMP team can change their mind later, but well-judged early views can make later analysis more efficient. Craft skills based on experience are important throughout the process, especially 'problem structuring' skills.

The starting position is at a strategic level within the define phase structure. It is crucial to maintain a strategic perspective and avoid distracting detail. Both opportunities and threats are of interest. Identifying what might be done about each relevant source of uncertainty in terms of reactive and proactive responses can operate at a very specific level or at a more general level. For example, 'what can we do about an activity delay caused by a particular machine failing?' involves a specific response. 'What can we do about delay for some unspecified cause?' involves a general response. Thinking in specific terms often generates general responses, but both may be relevant.

Identifying secondary sources of uncertainty and associated responses can consider contingency plan uncertainty if this is relevant. A 'source' is a convenient short form for 'a source of uncertainty' which *may* matter enough for its identification and separation from higher level composites to be worth while for current assessment purposes. A 'response' is a short form term for things we can do about sources of uncertainty in the conventional proactive or reactive response sense which *may* matter enough for identification and separation from the associated source of uncertainty composites to be worth while for current assessment purposes. Any response option for a particular source of uncertainty may matter enough for its separation from other responses to this source to be worth while for current assessment purposes. General responses are particularly valuable – the 'gold nuggets' in a search for opportunities to improve project performance. Secondary sources of uncertainty arise as a consequence of initiating primary responses. A source of uncertainty and associated responses will matter enough to be worth considering separately if they need to be understood separately in order to:

- estimate expected values, targets or commitments without bias;
- increase sources of risk/opportunity efficiency at any level;
- resolve ambiguity which is a source of concern.

Assumptions that may not hold are sources of uncertainty. As a consequence, they require treatment fully integrated with all other sources of uncertainty, as conditions in quantitative analysis terms. Two categories of working assumptions that will not be treated in quantitative terms need separate identification for integrated qualitative and quantitative treatment.

One category is *project* scope assumptions, which we anticipate will be treated as 'conditions' for any quantitative analysis to follow. Project scope assumptions that apply to the project as a whole should be identified as part of the define phase – for example, the Highways Agency treatment of inflation and EU safety regulation changes as discussed in Chapter 2. More local project scope assumptions need identification during the identify phase – for example, an assumption like 'no work taken off-site' or 'no major fire or accident' applying to a particular activity. Figure 3.2 illustrates examples identified during an 'identify' phase.

A second category is *process* scope assumptions, including modelling assumptions. Examples include assuming no formal response analysis for sources during early lifecycle analysis because the concern is sizing the expected cost and associated uncertainty without shaping the underlying plans, as in the Highways Agency re-estimation exercise. This is an example of a process scope assumption which needs identification in the focus phase. Assuming that the first obvious reactive response which comes to mind on a first pass is to be revisited on latter passes if this source of uncertainty proves important is an example of a process scope assumption that needs further attention in the focus phase.

Both project and process scope assumptions are identifiable working assumptions. It follows that any unidentified working assumptions and all framing assumptions are unidentified sources of uncertainty. The ability to minimize unidentified assumptions is an important skill which PUMP analysts need to develop, decision makers need to look for in their analysts, and governance processes need to exercise due diligence about. Broad uncertainty source composites can be used, like source 3 in Figure 2.4 – other uncertainty sources for which the Highways Agency is held accountable but which have not been considered at portfolio level. This allows us to avoid detail without leaving out any uncertainty. However, the ambiguity involved needs explicit acknowledgement, its role needs to be understood, and avoiding bias means that it needs to be sized appropriately in quantitative terms. Many analysts steeped in common practice project risk management have severe problems coping with any ambiguity concept. Those making decisions including governance decisions need confidence that their PUMP team can treat ambiguity in a competent manner. It will not go away just because it has not been identified.

Regular review and keeping the deliverables from the identify phase up to date is important, as for all other phases.

Structure *all* uncertainty

The 'structure *all* uncertainty' phase starts by reviewing and completing the structuring of all uncertainty inherent in the earlier phases. Recognizing and making explicit all key interdependencies and links between components is crucial. Sometimes this leads to simple dependence assumptions involving well behaved correlation; sometimes it leads to more complex statistical dependence assumptions; and sometimes it leads to a clear need for causal modelling of dependence.

Testing key simplifying assumptions is also crucial. Sometimes simpler assumptions become obvious (a very useful discovery); sometimes more complex structures are needed; and sometimes quite different alternative structures are appropriate.

An important aspect of structuring is distinguishing between responses which are 'specific' in the sense that they are specific to particular sources of uncertainty, and responses which are 'general' in the sense that they deal with sets of sources including unidentified sources. Some general responses may have been recognized in the identify phase, but the structure phase has to ensure that no useful potential general responses are overlooked. General responses may be given other labels, like 'overarching responses' (Hopkinson, 2011), but whatever they are called they are central to a robust and flexible approach. Early pass identification of powerful general responses means that it is clarity efficient to spend less time on responses that are specific to particular sources.

Clarify ownership

'Clarify ownership' involves allocating *both* financial *and* managerial responsibility (separately if appropriate) for specific sources and responses or more generally. Working assumptions for the current pass should reflect the level of clarity needed in the quantitative analysis to follow – any ambiguity about ownership has to be captured in the following quantify phase. The iterative evolution of plans that the PUMP involves means early passes may need to focus on forms of contract issues if these have not been dealt with at a corporate level. Issues like named individuals who are responsible for managing particular sources may not need attention until late iterations or following more detailed planning lifecycle stages.

Quantify *some* uncertainty

The 'quantify *some* uncertainty' phase starts on the first pass by selecting top priority sources for quantitative treatment. Lower priority sources for quantitative treatment can be left for later passes, along with aspects of the project needing less immediate attention. These later passes may be within the quantify phase, or across all phases for just part of the project, or across all phases for the whole of the project. The associated flexibility is important. The flexible iterative process decisions involved are a key aspect of an enlightened approach to iteration management.

Some key assumptions to be treated as conditions for quantitative analysis purposes will need early clarification. However, others can be clarified later, as iterations evolve. The minimum clarity approach discussed in Chapter 2 is the starting point on the first pass unless it is clear that more clarity from the outset is a good investment.

The evaluate phase will help to clarify (a) where restructuring would be a useful next step, on a second or third pass for example, and (b) when refining within a given structure would be useful. Final refining of all estimates if appropriate can be seen as a useful focus for the last complete planned pass of the quantify phase – the planned fourth or fifth complete pass for example. Keeping track of uncertainty treated as conditions at each level in the nested structure is an important aspect of the quantify *some* uncertainty phase.

Evaluate *all* the relevant implications

The 'evaluate *all* the relevant implications' phase involves assessing statistical dependence (dependence not modelled in a causal structure) and using this assessment to synthesize the results of the quantify phase.

Combining sources as specified by the nested structure and interpreting the results in the context of *all* earlier PUMP phases can start with the lowest level of composition. For example, if an activity structure is used for a high clarity analysis, composition can start within each activity using an activity level sensitivity diagram like Figure 3.2. Making decisions about proactive and reactive responses can also start at the lowest level of composition, gradually building up to decisions that address the way uncertainty accumulates across activities. Figure 3.3 illustrates how activity completion uncertainty that has accumulated across activities can be portrayed using sensitivity diagrams. Figures 3.4 and 3.5 illustrate how this duration uncertainty can be transformed into cost to make choices at an activity level using decision diagrams.

Making decisions about refining and redefining earlier analysis is a key issue here. In conjunction with what might be seen as evolving focus phase decisions, analysis can involve complete multi-pass analysis of key sources of uncertainty in key activities before moving on to integrating activities – that is, building up an understanding of what matters most at a decomposed level to provide a firm foundation for decisions at higher levels of composition. This involves iteration loops which are partial in several senses. For example, each activity could be analysed via a detailed iterative qualitative then quantitative process, before moving on to putting key activities together, with diversions into cost if key decisions need to assess cost–time tradeoffs, overall cost being addressed using still later iterations.

Making robust provisional decisions at lower levels before moving up to higher levels of composition reduces the ambiguity otherwise inherent in the higher level decisions. The structure selected to build up the composition/decomposition hierarchy is obviously important. The PUMP team 'feel' for where to start the composition process and what matters most as sensitivity diagrams start to confirm or revise initial views should be exploited, recognizing the value of craft skills based on PUMP experience. A PUMP is a way of thinking, not a checklist procedure, and the ideas developed in Parts II and III need to be understood by aspiring analysts as a foundation for those skills. The quality of their first analysis should not suffer if they take their time, but mentoring will help, and speed should not be expected at the same time as significant learning experiences. Decision makers need to be confident that PUMP team members are collectively providing the level of clarity needed, leaving its efficiency to the PUMP team. Governance should also be primarily concerned about the appropriate level of clarity and the quality of the analysis providing it, but clarity efficiency is an issue. Robustness is an important analysis quality issue – a key aspect of clarity efficiency. And the quality of the PUMP team is an important corporate management issue – another key aspect of clarity efficiency.

Making decisions that help to shape the project and making decisions that help to shape the analysis process are worth distinguishing – some people like to think of them as 'planning' decisions and 'planning the planning' decisions.

Further basic PUMP framework concerns

A simplified process framework description using the three macro-phases defined in Table 4.3 is sometimes useful.

The 'basis for analysis' macro-phase in this PUMP process has two very different key elements: a 'define the project' phase and a 'focus the process' phase. *The rationale for separating these*

Table 4.3 Alignment of a three macro-phase portrayal of the basic PUMP process

Seven phase basic PUMP portrayal	*Basic PUMP portrayal as three macro-phases*
define the project **focus** the process	develop the **basis for analysis**
identify *all* relevant sources, responses, conditions **structure** *all* uncertainty clarify **ownership**	execute the **qualitative analysis**
quantify *some* uncertainty **evaluate** *all* the relevant implications	execute the **quantitative analysis**

phases is clarifying the difference to make them easier to manage – in common with the rationale for all other phase separations. Further, the 'basis for analysis' micro-phase involves qualitative analysis and it is an integral part of the iterative process, which suggests that a simple binary 'qualitative' and 'quantitative' breakdown might be better. Further, some aspects of 'quantitative analysis' are 'qualitative', which suggests that adhering to the seven-phase structure without the complexity of macro-phases might be better for most purposes. The divisions between the seven phases of Table 4.2 are driven by changes in purposes that make separation convenient – they are nominal but useful. We are dealing with a way of thinking – more specifically a process for systematic but creative thinking – not an inflexible procedural basis for a bureaucratic checklist.

Identifying the basic PUMP phases and macro-phases in Tables 4.2 and 4.3 provides only a partial description of the process. A key aspect not fully captured by these tables is the iterative nature of the process. We have tried to convey some feel for the mixture of partial and complete iteration passes which drive effective PUMPs, but we are very aware of the difficulty many people have fully understanding the nature of flexible iterative processes. The basic PUMP process is iterative *by design*, and the design involves significant flexibility *built into the details, as explained in Parts II and III.*

To clearly indicate the pivotal role of the 'evaluate *all* implications' phase in terms of iteration control, the flowchart in Figure 4.1 can be useful. However, it is very important to remember that a variety of forms of partial iteration can also be useful. Some complete iterations are usually useful, as illustrated by Figure 4.1. But less formal partial iterations of various kinds are also an invaluable part of achieving clarity efficiency. Figure 4.2 can be useful to illustrate some of the possibilities. The Figure 4.2 sub-cycle between the 'evaluate' and 'quantify' phases, and the possible loop-back to the 'identify' or 'focus' phase without revisiting the 'define' phase suggested by Figure 4.2, illustrates some of the partial iteration possibilities available. Figure 4.2 can also be useful to illustrate the timing and nominal precedence relationships involved, and to plan a PUMP.

Figure 4.1 portrays the basic loopback iteration structure, from the 'evaluate *all* implications' phase to the 'define the project' phase. Iterations can be selective within this basic loop-back structure in terms of which phases and which aspects of phases are revisited, guided by choices made when evaluating *all* implications. An iterative loopback from the 'evaluate' phase to the 'quantify' phase is sometimes useful after the first pass to refine estimates for sources of uncertainty and responses that evaluation has identified as being important, as illustrated in Figure 4.2. This can be followed by an iterative loopback to reconsider the scope and approach for uncertainty analysis,

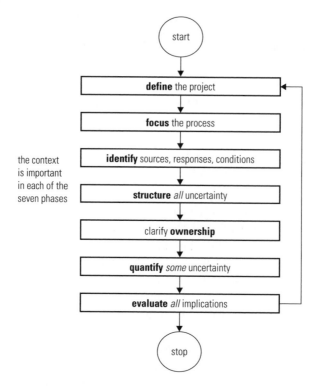

Figure 4.1   The basic PUMP seven-phase flowchart

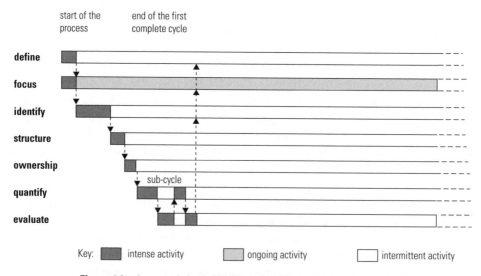

Figure 4.2   An example basic PUMP bar chart (Gantt chart) for the first pass

and refine or revise the identification and structuring of sources of uncertainty, prompted by insights from earlier evaluation. But it may involve first going back to the define phase, to refine understanding of the context, or it might involve accepting the first two phase results and just going back to the identify phase, with all three of these possibilities allowed for by Figure 4.2. Looping decisions are a central function of the evaluate phase, and a flexible approach is a central feature of the basic PUMP approach.

As indicated in Figure 4.2, the define and focus phases can proceed in parallel at the outset for a brief period of intense activity, providing a basis for following phases. Initially they are closely coupled in the sense that they involve different objectives and concerns but they are very interdependent and not easily separated. Focus phase activity is ongoing throughout the basic PUMP process, with intense activity bursts at the start of new iterations, but define phase activity is intermittent.

In all three of the qualitative analysis phases – identify, structure, ownership – it is important to operate at an appropriate level of detail and clarity in each iteration. As indicated in Figure 4.2, a first pass through each of these phases in turn can proceed in series at an initial intense level of activity following a first pass through the define and focus phases.

Following the ownership phase, the quantify and evaluate phases also need serial treatment. On a first pass 'quantify *some* uncertainty' involves sizing uncertainty which is considered to be usefully quantified. On later passes earlier uncertainty quantification may be refined where earlier analysis suggests that this would be both effective and efficient. 'Evaluate *all* implications' is at the core of all the decision taking driven by the iterative nature of the process – decisions about shaping the *project* and decisions about shaping further iterations of the *process*. It builds on all prior analysis to date, qualitative as well as quantitative, in previous lifecycle stages as well as in the current stage.

In practice a linked bar chart like Figure 4.2 can be very useful to plan the first cycle in about 10–20% of the time available for any given application, leaving the remaining 80–90% of the time for further iterations, but without any attempt to plan those iterations. A comparable repeated cycle might be anticipated, but in practice something different may be appropriate. A limited planning horizon involving commitments to action is relevant for reasons explored in Chapter 13.

Figure 4.2 limits itself to the one-word labels for the seven phases in **bold** on earlier figures and tables. These one-word labels are very useful once people are familiar with the terminology, but full descriptions as used in the left-hand column of Table 4.2 and intermediate forms as used in Table 4.3 and Figure 4.1 can sometimes add useful clarity and should not be made redundant. The 'basic PUMP' label is often convenient, but sometimes 'E&D shaping PUMP' is a more helpful label, emphasizing the lifecycle stage for which it was initially designed.

The PUMP pack framework

The nature of the adaptations required for other lifecycle stages will be explored in more detail in Part III, but a preliminary understanding is useful now.

The basic PUMP is the E&D shaping PUMP. The same seven-phase framework can be used for the design, operations and termination (DOT) shaping PUMP. However, the area of focus requires a different basic terminology and different criteria–plan relationship structures are involved. Further, the same basic PUMP with the same basic seven-phase structure can be used for the concept shaping

PUMP, but the area of focus means that even more significant criteria–plan relationship structure changes are involved, along with different terminology, a different discipline base, and more obvious links to corporate strategy. In effect, the basic PUMP is a flexible strategy-shaping PUMP which can take E&D, DOT or concept shaping forms. Indeed, if it is used in a comprehensive manner in the E&D-shaping stage, it needs to review earlier DOT and concept stage decisions. If the nominal lifecycle structure of Table 1.3 is replaced by some other structure, the basic PUMP can still cope with all strategy shaping stages.

The consolidation and governance gateway processes associated with each of these strategy shaping stages is radically different – each is a single phase process designed to link the iterative shaping stage processes, and each has a consolidation role plus an audit role, not a shaping role.

The tactics shaping PUMPs and the tactics gateways are different again, because they involve a transition from strategic plans to action plans requiring commitments at a detailed planning level. More detail is part of the difference, but another important part of the difference is commitment to specific actions while leaving people at the sharp end of a project sufficient room to exercise their expertise. Highly selective detailed planning to test strategy should have been used earlier if this was appropriate, but comprehensive detailed planning for implementation purposes is required for tactics shaping.

Execution and delivery PUMPs are different again. Key reasons include the fact that action is now underway, and replanning selectively coupled to monitoring while trying to implement some tactical plans (which it is too late to change) alters the nature of PUMP objectives.

PRAM involves a variant of the basic (E&D shaping) PUMP in the first three macro-phases of Table 4.1, and the following two macro-phase equivalents are addressed in a more general manner.

RAMP involves an integrated whole lifecycle view of projects, with a business case focus. We believe this perspective is essential. RAMP does not provide detail – referring to PRAM and earlier editions of this book for detailed treatment. However, full integration of the overview provided by RAMP in our nominal 12-stage project lifecycle with the basic PUMP aspects of PRAM is not as simple as it might seem. As the cautionary tale discussed earlier in this chapter suggests, the implications of integrating RAMP and PRAM are not as straightforward as might be assumed.

Key developments since 2000 embedded in the PUMP pack approach include responses to earlier problems driven by a growing recognition of their importance. In brief these developments are:

1. A clear need for *very* low effort approaches that are still clarity efficient and still recognized as professional in a 'fit for purpose' sense. In the limit the transition from formal to informal approaches should be smooth, without a discontinuity or gap, and without dysfunctional distortions of successful informal approaches.
2. The need to explicitly address aspects of uncertainty not currently addressed, the basis of the four uncertainty components (event uncertainty, variability uncertainty, systemic uncertainty and ambiguity uncertainty) outlined in Chapter 1.
3. The need to explicitly address 'bias' in the persistent optimism or pessimism sense, be it unconscious or deliberate.
4. The value of a 'performance lens' and 'knowledge lens' concept to capture the spirit of what is needed to manage both performance related to all relevant objectives and the integration of this aspect of uncertainty management with knowledge management and the rest of project management, as summarized in Figure 1.3.

5. Insight about the way working assumptions are made explicit within a set of framing assumptions which are as unrestrictive as possible allows simple plain English definitions of risk, uncertainty and opportunity to be used to address all relevant aspects of all three in an opportunity efficient manner.

6. Clarity about how 4 and 5 may put formal responsibility for managing some aspects of uncertainty with PUMP pack support staff, but responsibility for risk and opportunity management stays part of basic project, operations, or strategy management, as it should.

7. The conceptual and operational features of a basic PUMP process that can be adapted appropriately to define a PUMP pack for use in all project lifecycle stages.

8. The power of a view of uncertainty management employing plain English terminology which easily adapts to all aspects of uncertainty management in project, operations and strategic contexts – including the very difficult aspects involving social or political goals with regard to environmental concerns and potential fatalities.

9. The importance of *nominal* frameworks and labels explicitly recognized as starting points for adaptation, and the need to *think* in uncertainty management terms while *conversing* in whatever language other people are most comfortable with.

10. The need for clarity about how best to reduce the influence of frameworks promoted by people and organizations who want to impose restrictive definitions, processes and concepts that impede effective approaches to clarity efficiency and more general opportunity efficiency. Ambiguity generated by controversy that is not given adequate public exposure is one root cause of much of the difficulty which needs explicit attention.

Changes in this book relative to its second (2003) edition reflect these ten points in addition to advances in the relevant literature and more clarity in the terminology. Clarifying and then managing *all* the opportunities in projects in the opportunity efficiency sense is the central theme of all these changes.

Ambiguity about responsibility for risk and opportunity

Responsibility for PUMP pack processes does not imply responsibility for managing risk or opportunity. The latter should always rest with those responsible for planning and executing a project or associated operations and strategy.

When uncertainty is understood in the holistic terms a PUMP pack addresses, base plans and contingency plans are shaped over the whole project lifecycle by coordinated project and corporate teams to achieve opportunity efficiency. A PUMP manager and supporting staff may be responsible for the effectiveness of some of the PUMP pack performance uncertainty management process – but this should never be confused with responsibility for managing project risk and opportunity.

Even clarity efficiency is to some extent beyond the direct control of the PUMP team. It is a corporate capability issue, with resourcing, credibility and governance responsibility residing at board level.

Dysfunctional allocation or appropriation of responsibility for uncertainty, opportunity and risk can be one of the important consequences of the common practice 'risk management' label for what is better approached in an 'uncertainty management' conceptual framework. For example, the term 'risk manager' makes sense in a 1950s safety management context, but it does not make sense in a PUMP pack context.

Gateway anticipation

The consolidation aspect of gateways ensures that all changes to base plans and all contingency plans developed by the earlier PUMP are fully embedded, after they have been fully evolved via the iterative shaping process, prior to governance approval of plans. However, earlier approval and embedding of improvements to plans can be an important part of the shaping process and may anticipate likely concerns at the next gateway stage, when this is appropriate. This may involve interim reports and linked formal changes in current plans, but it may just involve informal communication. It does not reduce the importance of formal gateways, but facilitates a flexible 'enlightened gateway' process.

It is always important to make sure that improvements to plans developed by the shaping processes are fully endorsed and used, by the appropriate people at an appropriate time. The common practice notion of 'implement responses' (in PRAM terms) as portrayed by the last row of Table 4.1 becomes part of this enlightened gateway concept. Seamless integration of uncertainty management and project management is the goal, avoiding ambiguity about responsibility for all aspects of plan development and approval.

Ambiguity about the nature and role of governance

Governance should not focus on compliance with a clearly prescribed process, because any clearly specified rigid process cannot deliver clarity efficiency or broader opportunity efficiency. Nor does compliance with ambiguous guides or standards make sense in any project uncertainty management context. Enlightened use of a way of thinking is required by the PUMP team, and by the project team as a whole that they are working with. Enlightened governance is required to ensure that appropriately creative and flexible approaches are delivering what is needed.

What this 'enlightened governance' involves will be clearer by the end of this book. It is unlikely to be obvious now, and there is no easy way to overcome this. Those responsible for governance need to understand in depth what they are dealing with. However, enlightened governance can look for clear symptoms of clarity inefficiency as a starting position, and this chapter does provide some clues about what this involves, just before its conclusion. Consider some relevant history first.

Some relevant history from the late 1950s to the early 1990s

The PUMP pack framework and much of its content is not new. The PUMP label is new, but the PUMP pack framework and content has emerged from the synthesis of earlier project risk and uncertainty management processes and models. These processes and models have themselves evolved over a considerable period of time, as the range of issues addressed was extended.

The nature of these developments may be of interest in their own right, but they are outlined here to illustrate the nature and breadth of the PUMP pack content and provide a rationale for its structure.

The first formal project planning technique to address project uncertainty in an activity-based planning framework was PERT (Program Evaluation and Review Technique) as originally developed in the late 1950s for the Polaris Missile Project (Moder and Philips, 1970). PERT involves a *model* of a project activity network with activity duration probability distributions defined by an approximation of the Beta distribution. Using this model in its original 1950s form, the expected duration of the project is defined by an expected critical path identified using a standard Critical Path Analysis (CPA, sometimes referred to as CPM for Critical Path Method) algorithm with expected durations for each activity. Project duration is assumed to exhibit a Normal probability distribution with an associated variance defined by summing the variances of activities on the expected critical path.

PERT also involves a *process* (or method) involving a series of steps: decompose the project into activities, define precedence relationships, diagram the activities, estimate activity duration probability distributions, and so on. The PERT *process* and associated CPA processes use the *model* in a highly iterative fashion, to develop an initial plan, test for and resolve timetable restrictions, optimize project duration approximately, test for and resolve resource restrictions, and optimize overall project resource use approximately (Chapman et al., 1987, ch. 29). The PERT and CPA processes may have been *designed* in part, drawing on the operations research/operational research, industrial engineering, or systems process traditions of the consultants who designed the models, but in part these processes also *evolved* through use, as captured best practice.

By the 1960s most PERT software used Monte Carlo simulation to avoid assuming that only one path may be critical and that the project duration probability distribution must be Normal. Such software also allowed activity duration probability distributions to be specified that need not be Beta approximations (Moder and Philips, 1970). Modified in this way, PERT is still used by many organizations. However, it is a very primitive approach to project planning in uncertainty management terms, and it can be very misleading unless more sophisticated models are also understood to provide a more general conceptual basis and employed as and when appropriate.

PERT and associated processes, including CPA processes, are implicitly embedded in the basic PUMP, as part of its heritage, and as a special case form of a more general uncertainty management process and model set. The same applies to a series of generalizations considered next.

By the early 1960s, many authors were arguing for the use of decision branches embedded in both deterministic CPA models and probabilistic PERT models. Decision branches in deterministic CPA models reflect alternative ways of approaching particular project activities and activity sets, even if duration variability is not an issue. They are about optimizing technical, resource and duration choices in risk efficient terms. These approaches adopted a 'decision CPM' label (Chapman and El Hoyo, 1972, for example). Decision branches in a probabilistic PERT context usually focused on contingency responses to delays, including loop-back iterations – for example, if a design does not work when a prototype is tested (Moder and Philips, 1970). These approaches adopted a 'generalized PERT' label.

By the late 1960s, some authors were arguing for Markov process probabilistic models involving decision trees embedded in a sequence of time periods. GERT (Graphical Evaluation and Review Technique) is one label used to describe this type of model (Moder and Philips, 1970).

GERT allows activities to be addressed time-period by time-period, greatly enhancing our ability to understand both simple and complex repetitive processes, to accommodate contingency responses that do not wait until an activity has been completed, to deal with time-dependent resource constraints, and to deal with time dependencies like weather windows. Early major users in the USA included the space industry. Working with Acres Consulting Services in 1975, Chris Chapman applied them to a proposed major Canadian oil pipeline project, looking at trade-offs between time, cost and demand for scarce resources. It was this experience that triggered their inclusion in the basic PUMP.

Starting in 1976, working with Acres International Management Services, Chris Chapman and BP International developed probabilistic models for planning and costing offshore North Sea projects which embedded the fault tree and event tree concepts used for safety analysis (NUREG, 1975) in GERT models. SCERT (Synergistic Contingency Evaluation and Review Techniques) is one label used to describe this model in the PERT and GERT tradition (Chapman, 1979). The SCERT approach provided a much more detailed understanding of where uncertainty and associated risk was coming from than earlier Generalized PERT and GERT models. It allowed modelled responses to be specific to a particular source of uncertainty or general in the sense of dealing with the residual effect of combinations of uncertainty sources after specific responses. It also introduced the use of the sensitivity diagram of Figure 3.2 and the decision diagrams of Figures 3.4 and 3.5 to make risk efficient choices involving composite uncertainty – important new tools.

To make effective use of the SCERT models in conjunction with a family of simpler PERT, generalized PERT, decision CPM, GERT, and SCERT derivatives, Chris Chapman and BP International developed an associated SCERT process (Chapman, 1979), a *designed* process that was tested and *evolved* by developing corporate best practice within BP and a range of other organizations in the UK, US and Canada over the following decade (Chapman, 1990). Key insights from the design and testing and evolution of this process included:

1. a recognition of the important role of structured documentation;
2. the need for a formal process which integrated qualitative 'issue structuring' methodologies (Rosenhead, 1989, for example) and quantitative modelling methodologies;
3. the need for a clear understanding of which sources of uncertainty are best modelled quantitatively and which are best treated as assumed conditions;
4. the great value of a formal process in terms of capturing and integrating the knowledge of different people who have different perspectives 'to bring to the party';
5. the great value of a process which indirectly integrates issues which are too complex to model directly, like the 'decision CPM' search for risk efficient activities;
6. the great value of a process which pursues other objectives discussed in Chapter 3, like building trust, eliminating bias, encouraging enlighten caution and gambles, and facilitating an opportunity management culture which attracts and keeps the best people.

During the 1980s and early 1990s, Chris Chapman and Dale Cooper also applied variants of the SCERT models and processes, and some new models and processes, to a range of different contexts and decision types with a range of clients in the UK, Canada and the US, mostly associated with the generic label 'risk engineering' (Chapman and Cooper, 1983a; Cooper and Chapman, 1987; Chapman, 1990). All strategy shaping stages in the project lifecycle were involved. The basis of the approach was designing specific processes or methods tailored to the context, based on generic decision support process ideas developed in both 'hard' and 'soft' OR and related systems areas, as well as experience with earlier specific processes (Chapman, 1992b). The more specific the process design, the more process efficiency could be improved, by exploiting the context characteristics. But the loss of generality carried costs in terms of reduced effectiveness if inappropriate assumptions about the context were made. Managing these tradeoffs was a key process design issue. Designed decision support processes were sometimes used for important single decisions, and sometimes embedded in organizational decision processes. This experience with decision support processes informed subsequent process design work. A relevant generalization was dealing with each of the three 'strategy shaping stages' in the asset lifecycle, one at a time in any given study.

By the early 1960s many organizations were addressing cost uncertainty using a simple cost component structure and a mean-variance model directly comparable to PERT, usually assuming statistical and causal independence between cost components. Building a causal understanding of uncertainty dependence based on the underlying duration and resource usage issues was a key component of SCERT embedded in PUMPs.

Lichtenberg (2000) developed his successive estimation approach in the 1960s as a top-down variant of a mean-variance approach, comparable to early PERT apart from the top-down verses bottom-up distinction. Integration of top-down and bottom-up thinking is a key PUMP feature.

An important example of a top-down approach to dependence issues which can also be embedded in PUMPs is the Systems Dynamics (SD) approach to forensic risk assessment first introduced by Pugh and Associates in the USA (Cooper, 1980), and further developed in Europe by Colin Eden and colleagues (Eden et al., 2000). A qualitative 'influence diagram' version of these SD approaches is a very effective way to understand and explain positive and negative feedback loops.

The use of influence diagrams can be seen as a relatively structured variant of a soft OR or soft systems approach, and all such 'soft' approaches can be viewed as top-down in the sense that they are designed for a holistic approach to 'messes' which resist the initial decomposition inherent in bottom-up approaches. Checkland's Soft Systems approach (Checkland and Scholes, 1990) can be seen as the softest approach on this spectrum.

During the late 1980s and early 1990s, Stephen Ward and Chris Chapman began to widen their project-related interests to address competitive bidding (Ward and Chapman, 1988), contract design (Ward et al., 1991; Curtis et al., 1991; Ward and Chapman, 1994, 1995a), general decision support process issues (Ward, 1989) and process enhancement (Ward and Chapman, 1991, 1995), process establishment within the organization (Ward, 1999), the nature of drivers which shape processes (Chapman and Ward, 1997), linked capital investment decision choice issues (Chapman and Howden, 1997) and linked strategic management issues (Chapman, 1992a). All these developments contributed to the overall shape of the PUMP pack.

The PRAM guide

In the mid-1990s the APM (Association for Project Management) started to develop the first edition of the *Project Risk Analysis and Management (PRAM) Guide* (APM, 1997). PRAM is a core contributor to the heritage of the PUMP process. The first edition PRAM process description was drafted by Chris Chapman, as Chapter 3. It was a distillation of the experience of a large number of UK organizations which had used project risk management processes successfully for a number of years, as understood by a working party of more than 20 people drawn from an APM Project Risk Management Specific Interest Group (SIG) of more than 100 who reviewed working party drafts and provided feedback.

The draft PRAM process was based on a synthesis of designed and evolved processes using a nine-phase structure. The first seven of these phases were similar to the seven phases of Table 4.2, with a focus on the fifth stage of the asset lifecycle – the E&D shaping stage (execution and delivery strategy stage). The eighth and ninth phases, 'planning' and 'management', addressed four following stages of the lifecycle in Table 1.3 – the tactics shaping stage (detailed design and planning stage), the tactics gateways, the execution stage, and the delivery stage.

From an early stage in its development, the PRAM process used more phases than the SCERT process or the various three- to six-phase structures then used by other SIG members. The initial rationale was the need to seek a 'common basis'. Everyone involved wanted to be able to map their process onto the agreed PRAM process. To achieve collective ownership, if possible, a relatively decomposed structure seemed to offer the only way forward. This required more divisions than might otherwise seem sensible, and suggested all the phase divisions as defined by Table 4.2. It was clear that if people could not see how the process they used currently mapped onto what was proposed, they were going to have difficulty accepting it. A new process could add to what they were already doing, and reinterpret what they were already doing, but eliminating what they were comfortable with raised serious problems if they could not see what was 'wrong' with it. The seven phases defined by Table 4.2, plus two more for a total of nine, was the simplest structure that came close to achieving this 'common basis' criterion. *Any* process defined via synthesis involving a group of people and organizations faces a range of similar issues, and how these issues are managed and resolved is important.

The key reason that this seven/nine-phase structure was appropriate in operational terms was the separability (but not the independence) of the phases in terms of different purposes, deliverables and tasks. This suggested that each phase could be thought of as a project in its own right, and the complete set could be regarded as a programme (portfolio of related projects). This in turn suggested that everything we know about good programme and project management could be applied to managing an uncertainty driven risk management process. As for any programme or project, alternative structures are feasible, but this seven/nine-phase structure seemed robust and effective at a generic level, and experience has since confirmed this. Much of the structure was tested operationally prior to the PRAM synthesis, in a SCERT context and in the context of other processes which contributed to its form.

Between agreeing the nine-phase structure (the first seven phases are portrayed by Table 4.2) and the publication of the PRAM guide (APM, 1997), editing to link Chapters 2 and 3 of the PRAM guide resulted in recasting the nine phases as five phases with eight sub-phases, and reinterpretation of the last two phases. A new 'assess' phase was defined, incorporating 'structure', 'ownership', 'estimate' and 'evaluate' as sub-phases. This phase/sub-phase or macro-phase/phase distinction is not an issue of importance, and the alignment between the PUMP process and the first seven phases of the PRAM process is clear. It is mentioned as a useful illustration of minor differences between process descriptions that should matter very little in practice, arising because of understandable pressure within the PRAM working party to 'keep it simple' in terms of well-loved familiar structures. When it is useful to simplify the recommended seven-phase structure of Table 4.2, our preference is for the structure of Table 4.3, for a number of reasons, which should become clear as you progress through this book.

The spirit of the first seven phases of the PRAM process in both its 1997 and 2004 variants is embedded in the PUMP process, and the spirit of the other PRAM phases is embedded in the PUMP pack. To the authors of this book, drafting Chapter 3 of the 1997 PRAM guide and ongoing involvement in the 2004 second edition and further edition discussions provided six very important insights relating to *process* design.

First, 'planning *the project*' in define phase terms and 'planning *the planning of the project*' in focus phase terms are well worth separation, clarified in PUMP by the separation of 'define the project' and 'focus the process' phases. A separate focus phase in PUMP formally acknowledges that there is no one best way to undertake an uncertainty management process for all projects. Deciding how to proceed in a given project context is a particularly difficult process to conceptualize and make operational, therefore recognizing the need for this focus phase is crucial. To some extent the focus phase is familiar territory for skilled consultants, in intuitive if not formal terms, but it is virgin territory for planners or estimators who do not have a sophisticated understanding of decision support processes. If no explicit focus phase is involved in a process description, the process is seriously defective in ways that naive users may not even recognize, using 'naive' in Hillson's (1997) risk maturity sense (discussed later in Part IV). The PRAM working party discussions about the relative value of different approaches in different contexts served as a trigger for the insight that a focus phase is essential.

Second, *both* the define and focus phases have to be part of an ongoing iterative framework, a continually updated 'basis of analysis', not part of a one-shot 'start-up' or 'initiation' phase. The importance of an iterative approach to analysis was recognized early in the development of PERT and CPA, although this insight has been lost along the way by some. It is particularly important with respect to recognizing and reflecting on initial assumptions.

A third insight was that ownership of risk is such an important issue that it deserves attention as a separable phase and as a part of an ongoing iterative process. Isolating it from the iterative loops in a one-shot 'start-up' or 'initiation' phase is not appropriate, and it is usefully conceived as a final part of the 'qualitative analysis' in PUMP terms, because issues not dealt with earlier in the focus phase may need attention prior to quantification.

A fourth insight was that evaluating *all* the implications of earlier analysis, quantitative and qualitative, is a sophisticated phase in terms of managing both the uncertainty management process and the project itself. So far as the authors are aware, PRAM was the first uncertainty or risk management process to have separate explicit define, focus, ownership and evaluate phases built into a designed iterative structure, with an evaluate phase designed with this spirit in mind.

A fifth process design insight was that the Table 4.1 eighth, ninth and tenth PRAM phases ('plan risk event responses', 'plan project risk responses' and 'implement responses'), omitted from Table 4.2, are important parts of the overall uncertainty management process, but they do not require separate treatment in a PUMP pack framework. 'Plan risk event responses' and 'plan project risk responses' are embedded in the basic PUMP and its other shaping plans derivatives – 'shaping plans' is a more general interpretation. 'Implement responses' is embedded in following gateways – enlightened gateways is a more general interpretation. This comment applies equally to other process equivalents, and the macro-phases associated with the last two rows of Table 4.1 indicate the scope of the implications. The monitor and control aspects of some processes noted in the last row of Table 4.1 are deferred until later lifecycle stages in the PUMP pack framework.

A sixth process design insight was the need to restrict the basic process description to a single lifecycle stage, to avoid confusing the last two PRAM macro-phases of Table 4.1 with subsequent use of the same basic process in later lifecycle stages and the monitoring and controlling aspects of other processes.

Where we part company with the PRAM guide is in respect of the ambiguity introduced by attempting to reconcile the features described above with dysfunctional aspects of common practice which some PRAM authors were not prepared to omit. These ambiguity issues are an ongoing concern, with a further edition of PRAM being discussed as this book goes to press.

The RAMP guide

Risk Analysis and Management of Projects (RAMP) was first published in 1998 (ICE & AP, 1998), with a revised 2005 edition edited by Chris Lewin, the chairman of the working party responsible for both editions. This guide is a joint publication of the Faculty and Institute of Actuaries (AP – the Actuarial Profession) and the Institution of Civil Engineers (ICE), with a working party for both editions drawing on members of these institutions.

A key feature of the RAMP approach is a strategic view of projects within a financial model-ling perspective. The RAMP process consists of four activities, which are generally carried out at different times in the lifecycle as indicated below (ICE & AP, 2005, p. 28):

1. Process launch – conducted early in the lifecycle.
2. Risk review – conducted before key decisions or at intervals.
3. Risk management – conducted continually between risk reviews.
4. Process close-down – conducted at the end of the lifecycle or on premature termination.

Each activity is composed of several phases, each of which is made up of a number of process steps. RAMP operates at a more strategic level than PRAM, with a stronger focus on financial issues. It refers to PRAM and to earlier editions of this book for more detailed advice, and uses a less detailed overview process for the whole project lifecycle.

As in the case of the PRAM/PUMP relationship, the RAMP/PUMP relationship involves some differences in definitions and concepts which are not usefully explored here, and concerns about ambiguity are an ongoing issue for the authors.

The PUMP pack involves a synthesis of the PRAM and RAMP approaches at a reasonably detailed level in operational terms to make the best possible use of the spirit of both. In particular, the RAMP notion of starting an uncertainty management process in the first stage of the asset lifecycle and evolving that process as the lifecycle progresses has to be seen as a crucial aspect of corporate best practice. In practice, this is not going to happen unless a process designed for this purpose is available. The PUMP pack is designed for this purpose, at an operational level of detail, which relatively short guides cannot be expected to provide. Managers using PUMP or RAMP or PRAM at different lifecycle stages need to work together in a coordinated manner, and they all need to understand 'the big picture' in the same terms.

The PMI PMBOK guide

The large membership, global reach, and accreditation programme of the Project Management Institute (PMI) makes its *Project Management Book of Knowledge* (PMBOK) chapter on risk management (PMI, 2008, ch. 11) and a linked practice standard (PMI, 2009) an important process description to relate to a PUMP pack approach. From the perspective of this book, the PMI guide is a concise description of common practice. The extent to which it leads or follows common practice is debatable, but it clearly helps to entrench features of common practice which the authors of this book believe ought to be made redundant, like 'qualitative analysis' built on PIGs and an event uncertainty focus in a largely linear process. Neither of this book's authors has contributed to these guides, but we have followed their development from an early release of the first edition (PMI, 1992) and engaged in significant dialogue with their authors over many years. For example, the working party that developed *Prioritizing Project Risks – A Short Guide to Useful Techniques* (Hopkinson et al., 2008) included contributing authors to PMI guidance.

Shortcomings in common practice processes

Based on a number of audits of risk and uncertainty management capability over many years, we list in Table 4.4 a number of shortcomings in common practice processes. In most cases the organizations involved believed they were effectively following a reasonable process framework, although they suspected that their framework was not best practice. In most cases the organizations involved have been surprised at the length of the list of shortcomings in respect of their process, and the serious nature of the issues involved. A wide range of process frameworks were involved.

Table 4.4   Shortcomings of common practice risk management processes

1. A focus phase equivalent which is not used as a flexible basis for adjusting the process to the context of a particular project, or used to modifying the process as the project lifecycle progresses, beginning with concept shaping and ending with project termination.

2. A focus phase equivalent which is unclear about the motives for the process in relation to the various interested parties, or the links between motives for analysis of uncertainty, opportunity and risk and the models selected.

3. A define phase equivalent which is too detailed in terms of activities, and which fails to address *all* seven Ws, the project lifecycle, and linking financial cash flow models in a balanced manner.

4. An identify phase equivalent which is limited to event based uncertainty, which cannot cope effectively with composite uncertainties, and which fails to structure sources of uncertainty and associated risk and responses usefully, often generating excessively long and detailed 'risk registers' that address minor issues in excessive detail.

5. Absence of a structure phase equivalent, with little evidence of robustness testing or effective structuring decisions, including the lack of a significant search for common or general responses and a failure to identify significant linkages and interdependences between important sources of uncertainty.

6. Lack of an explicit ownership phase equivalent, with resulting inadequate attention to the implications of contractual arrangements for motivating parties to manage uncertainty, including inappropriate use of simple contracts.

7. A quantify phase equivalent which is costly but not cost effective, ineffectively linked to earlier qualitative analysis, resulting in biased estimates that are usually highly conditional on scope assumptions and other assumptions which are lost sight of.

(continued)

Table 4.4   *Continued*

8. An evaluate phase equivalent which combines different sources of uncertainty without capturing crucial dependence or without providing the insight to clarify how revisiting earlier analysis can clarify uncertainty where appropriate, develop effective responses where appropriate, facilitate crucial choices to achieve risk efficiency and balance, or demonstrate the robustness of those choices when necessary.

9. Absence of an effective iterative process structure which embeds all seven PUMP phases and a failure to distinguish planned iterations which involve limited costs, successive applications of an iterative process as a project lifecycle progresses, and unplanned iterations to deal with surprises which are costly.

10. Lack of a clear and shared understanding of all relevant objectives, measurable or not, with an orderly process for considering all relevant tradeoffs in opportunity efficiency terms.

This book is about how to address the shortcomings in Table 4.4 in terms of established ideas that have been tested successfully in a range of applications. Table 4.4 can also be interpreted as a list of symptoms of clarity inefficiency plus inappropriate clarity as a starting position for understanding what enlightened governance requires. Parts II and III should significantly enhance the reader's understanding of the nature and implications of these shortcomings. Part IV addresses further related shortcomings in uncertainty management capability at a corporate level.

Conclusion

What this book calls 'uncertainty management' as approached by the PUMP pack is a significant reframing and extension of what is commonly referred to as 'risk management', quite different to some alternative views of project uncertainty management – Cleden (2009) for example. It does not just add to or supplement existing approaches to 'risk management' in a way that leaves existing perspectives unchanged. It widens what is feasible by starting in a different place, introducing more flexibility and power in basic 'framing assumptions'.

Ultimately, all organizations that intend to make extensive use of uncertainty management need to develop a formal process framework that is tailored to the specific kinds of project and context which each organization faces. If an organization is starting from scratch, deployment of a PUMP pack is a good place to start. If an organization has existing risk and uncertainty management processes in place, there will be 'legacy issues' in the form of strong pressures to adapt from the existing basis, rather than start again. For related reasons, readers with some experience of risk and uncertainty management may wish to accommodate preferences and pressures for alternative processes. For example, some readers may want to use an alternative process because they are familiar with it; some readers may see advantages in following a process promoted by a professional organization to which they belong, and some readers may be required to employ a particular process framework mandated by their employer or clients. Nevertheless, whatever their circumstances, *all* readers need a basic understanding of the concepts and issues encompassed by the PUMP pack framework if they are to develop and improve their uncertainty management practice. Comparing the PUMP pack and any alternatives of interest should provide readers with a suitable basis for addressing the process design choice issues.

When doing so, it is important to see opportunity management as the primary goal, risk management as an important secondary goal, and uncertainty management as the vehicle for understanding both. It is also important to see the formal process used as a set of working assumptions to shape creative thinking, and a source of discipline to guide a clarity efficient search for opportunity efficiency. The opening quote for this chapter is a reminder that this discipline should be helpful in a creative sense – its function is ensuring that all the right questions get asked as well as shaping answers in a flexible manner. The discipline provided by a formal process should not be restrictive in a manner that is clarity inefficient.

It is also important to understand that *all* project risk management processes that fail to address *all* components of uncertainty and opportunity efficiency transfer responsibility for what is missed to the rest of project management, with a good chance it will not be effectively dealt with.

Further, *corporate* risk management processes that use a narrower definition of projects – perhaps in an attempt to justify a limited capability to deal with project uncertainty – in effect transfer responsibility for what is missed to the rest of corporate management, with a serious risk it will not be effectively dealt with.

The UK Highways Agency example in Chapter 2 illustrates the adaptation of generic PUMP ideas to a very specific process for a particular organization in transition from common practice to a broader approach. Generic processes have drawn on specific variants with an extensive development history, and they are usefully seen as the basis of all future specific variants. If appropriate specific versions cannot be crafted from existing generic processes, by definition the existing generic process is too restrictive.

Even a very simple specific variant, like that illustrated by the BCS example in Chapter 2, needs to draw on unrestrictive views of what a PUMP can and should do. Part II has to work with fairly high clarity versions of PUMP most of the time – to illustrate the scope of a general approach. But at regular intervals this discussion needs linking to simple examples like that provided by BCS and the Highways Agency.

Part II

The generic process in one key lifecycle stage

Part II elaborates the seven phase generic process framework of the basic PUMP outlined in Chapter 4. It uses one chapter for each phase, Chapters 5 to 11.

As indicated in Part I, a number of drivers should shape any uncertainty management process. It follows that any detailed PUMP description must assume a position in relation to each of these drivers. Each chapter in Part II assumes a focus on the E&D shaping stage – the execution and delivery strategy development stage of the project lifecycle. Part III will relax this lifecycle stage assumption, and consider the additional issues raised by designing and operating an efficient and effective PUMP pack for the whole of the project lifecycle.

In addition, each chapter in Part II makes further common initial assumptions about drivers, such as the need for a high clarity PUMP, but later explores alternative assumptions.

Chapter 5

Define the project

If you are sure you understand everything that is going on, you are hopelessly confused.
—Walter F. Mondale

This chapter explores what the define phase involves. The define phase is the first phase of all strategy shaping PUMPs. The define phase provides a basic foundation for the analysis that builds on it. If the define phase is seriously flawed, everything that follows will be flawed, like the proverbial house or castle built upon sand. However, bedrock foundations may be unnecessary – the key test is 'are deliverables fit for purpose?' This test needs a flexible interpretation based on the analysis to follow before the next updating of the current define phase deliverables, because the define phase is part of the iterative looping process. A strict 'get it right first time' approach is not clarity efficient.

The define phase should be used in the concept shaping stage for all projects, and in each subsequent strategy shaping lifecycle stage, building on earlier lifecycle stage deliverables as the project develops. However, like all chapters in Part II, this chapter's focus is the last of the three nominal strategy shaping stages of the project lifecycle – the E&D shaping stage (execution and delivery strategy development stage) – assuming no earlier PUMP use. The rationale for this focus is threefold.

1. It is important to be able to cope with late initiation of a PUMP approach, because doing so is often essential, a late start in the E&D shaping stage is a useful basis for understanding all late start scenarios, and experience suggests a start in the E&D shaping stage is the most likely late start position.
2. Considerable successful experience to date involves a PUMP initiated for the first time part way through a project life cycle, usually in the E&D shaping stage, and building on this experience base is useful.
3. Low clarity shortcut approaches to the E&D shaping stage, which could be used as part of the concept shaping stage, are best understood in the context of the higher clarity approaches

addressed in Part II. The Part II and Part III ordering of material helps to develop an integrated understanding of all the relevant ideas, because shortcuts are best understood in the context of high clarity approaches when shortcuts are not appropriate.

Although the focus of this and other Part II chapters is the E&D shaping stage, the basic ideas are relevant to all stages; sometimes it is useful to make points relevant to all stages or use examples involving other stages, and sometimes looking at other stages is essential.

During each of the strategy shaping stages the purpose of the define phase is consolidating the project effort to date at a strategic level to define the project in a form suitable for the rest of the PUMP in the present lifecycle stage, resolving any problems this raises. This involves two significantly different but closely coupled tasks:

1. *Consolidate* – Gather and integrate relevant existing information about the project and its management in a suitable form.
2. *Elaborate and resolve* – Fill in any gaps uncovered in the consolidation process and resolve any inconsistencies by stimulating the project team to develop and integrate their plans and management processes in an appropriate form.

The nature of the difference between these tasks means that a different 'mode of operation' is involved, in the sense that if 'consolidation' is stopped to 'elaborate and resolve' when a gap or inconsistency is involved, a different mode of thinking is required.

The deliverables of the define phase in each pass at each stage in the project lifecycle are the basis for a clear, unambiguous, shared understanding of the project and its management processes at a strategic level suitable for the rest of the PUMP to work on.

To understand how the specific 'consolidate' and 'elaborate and resolve' tasks lead to these deliverables, and to employ that understanding in practice, it is helpful to adopt an eight-step structure based on the project lifecycle and seven Ws structures introduced in Chapter 1. Figure 5.1 portrays this eight-step structure, an idealization that helps to capture and illustrate the spirit of the process in simple terms.

Figure 5.1 portrays starting the define phase in 'consolidate' mode. The definition (verbal and graphic descriptions) of the project lifecycle and each of the seven Ws is addressed in turn, and the overall results assessed. If the deliverables are fit for purpose, the define phase is complete and the next phase of the PUMP can start when the parallel focus phase is also complete. If the deliverables are not fit for purpose, loops back to individual steps are initiated as appropriate, in 'elaborate and resolve' mode, to fill in the gaps and resolve inconsistencies. In practice it may sometimes be more effective to aim for separate consolidate-assess-elaborate and resolve loops for each of the eight steps on early passes, as well as using the overarching loop structure of Figure 5.1. The details of eight possible loops shown by Figure 5.1 could be summarized in a single loop back to the beginning as for Figure 1.2, but the detail seems useful here. Our intent is to make Figure 5.1 complex enough to say something interesting and useful, but simple enough to say it clearly and concisely, as a basis for discussion of an effective process which may involve greater complexity, or simplification, depending on the context.

When attempting to implement this phase of the PUMP, the distinction between the steps may seem artificial, with fuzzy overlaps being a routine fact of life. However, the purpose of a detailed specification of the define phase with separate steps is to provide focus, keep the implementation

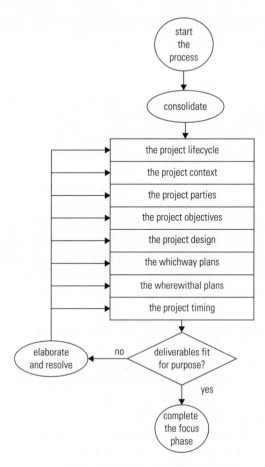

Figure 5.1 Define phase specific tasks

in practice as simple as possible, and avoid serious omissions. Even at this level of detail the method described here is not a 'cookbook' recipe, to be followed blindly. It is more an illustration of culinary techniques, to be used to create specific recipes. Figure 5.1 is not a restrictive definition of the ideal process – it is a caricature, portrayed by convenient working assumptions for discussion purposes.

Both the 'consolidate' and the 'elaborate and resolve' tasks are 'specific tasks' – 'specific' in the sense that they are unique to the define phase. In addition to these two specific tasks, which-which are the basis of Figure 5.1, five 'common tasks' are involved – 'common' in the sense that all PUMP phases require comparable tasks:

1. *Document* – Record in text and tables with diagrams as appropriate.
2. *Verify* – Ensure that all providers of information agree as far as possible, important differences in opinion are highlighted if they cannot be resolved, and all relevant providers are referred to.
3. *Assess* – Evaluate the analysis to date in context, to make sure it is 'fit for purpose' given the current status and purpose of the PUMP.

4. *Report* – Release verified documents, presenting findings if appropriate.

5. *Fit for purpose iteration control task* – Ask 'are the current deliverables fit for purpose?'

Comments on these common tasks are provided in each of the Part II chapters only when particularly relevant, and the first four common tasks are not identified individually in the summary flowchart depictions like Figure 5.1 provided in each Part II chapter and used to structure discussion. However, the final 'are deliverables fit for purpose?' iteration control task has to address all specific and common tasks in each phase, and it does receive separate treatment in each Part II chapter, linked to its portrayal in diagrams like Figure 5.1.

It is convenient to start explaining the details of the define phase by first assuming that a high clarity version of the basic PUMP is required by a project owner, beginning with an example. Generalizing this starting position follows, including lower clarity versions that are often required by both clients and contractors, dealing with some shortcomings in the example version, and exploring further refinements. An extremely refined process may be appropriate in practice if a very high clarity approach is useful because a great deal is at stake, but even if the reader never encounters such circumstances, an understanding of such approaches provides a useful conceptual framework that serves to clarify the implications of short-cuts.

A high clarity example to begin discussion

In the late 1970s a BP version of SCERT involving key ideas embedded in basic PUMPs was used for the first time on the Magnus project, an offshore North Sea project, as part of the process of developing the strategic execution and delivery plans plus the associated capital cost estimate and then seeking board approval. The basis of the process used had been agreed about a year earlier. The details of the process had been developed and approved in the interim using the Ninian project for a retrospective 'passive analysis' – using experienced planning engineers who worked on the Ninian project to ask the question: 'If we were doing this project again, how would we implement the new basic ideas?' A PUMP analyst, who soon became the BP PUMP manager supported by further PUMP analysts, had been selected by BP and briefed by Chris Chapman. This PUMP analyst worked full time on the Magnus PUMP for six months to complete the first Magnus PUMP analysis, assisted two or three days a week by Chris. Over this period about a dozen key players in the Magnus project and supporting company experts provided input and feedback.

Formal use of the seven Ws and project lifecycle structure was not involved, but they were implicit. In seven Ws terms, the initial focus was project duration (the 'when') considering the plans for activities aspect of the 'whichway' and the resource plans for activities aspect of the 'wherewithal' to achieve and demonstrate a minimum expected cost shaping of the project at the E&D shaping stage of the project lifecycle. The define phase equivalent focused on an activity structure suitable for this stage of the project lifecycle for this particular project.

Key activities requiring summary definition were: the stream of activities involved in supplying and laying the pipeline from the platform to the shore, the parallel stream of activities leading to an installed 'jacket' (the platform structure which sits in the water to hold the 'modules' providing production and accommodation facilities), the parallel stream of activities leading to modules ready to install on the jacket, and the activities that integrated these three parallel streams – the hook-up (connecting the pipeline and the platform as discussed earlier), module installation on the jacket, and initiating production. It made sense to understand the pipeline, module and jacket streams first, then their integration, starting with the key activity in the most uncertain stream. A couple of paragraphs of 'description' were provided for each key activity, to clarify simple labels like 'module construction'.

Project lifecycle stage structure

Agreeing a brief, documented outline of the earlier, current and future stages of the asset lifecycle is a useful initial step in the define phase. A summary description of the lifecycle stage structure provides a useful basis for the PUMP identify phase – a framework for thinking about where sources of uncertainty come from over the whole lifecycle. For example, comprehensive early identification of important sources of uncertainty associated with the termination stage has to be based on a clear documented understanding of what this termination stage involves. Designing an offshore oil platform to facilitate its end-of-life removal is an example of this kind of thinking ahead. The scope of the BP process did not include looking at the rest of the asset lifecycle structure in formal terms, but an informal look at 'anything other than activity-based sources of uncertainty' was used. Some relevant sources of uncertainty arising in other lifecycle stages were addressed, like the possibility of growth in the weight of the modules during detailed design leading to more overall module weight than the platform jacket could support. It is now clear that explicit consideration of other lifecycle stages as potential sources of uncertainty in the identify phase is vital for any high clarity PUMP analysis on behalf of a client – whether or not it is explicitly requested. This means that a suitable lifecycle stage structure needs identification in the define phase.

Clarity about the lifecycle can also assist with the PUMP focus phase – that is, clarification of the objectives for current uncertainty management in relation to later uncertainty management. Relevant later uncertainty management can include the identification of uncertainty reduction tasks which are part of the basic project management process, like ensuring timely completion of designs, tests and other project tasks. These tasks will reduce ambiguity uncertainty but they need to be done in an orderly manner for more basic knowledge acquisition management reasons as part of good basic project management.

As noted in Chapter 1, the nominal stage structure of Table 1.3 may be modified for corporate purposes which go beyond uncertainty management in the PUMP sense, and an important part of this modification may involve uncertainty management in terms of knowledge acquisition management. Because Part II of this book is focused on the last of the strategy shaping stages, assuming a more detailed preceding stage structure has little effect on what is involved.

Some clients (project owners) can greatly simplify this very comprehensive perspective, but it is important to understand the implications of doing this. For example, some contractors can afford to think about a project in terms of one lifecycle stage at a time, with an initial focus on 'between now and submitting a bid which gives us a reasonable chance of winning the work'. However, clients need to manage contractor relationships to avoid obvious risks associated with this kind of limited planning horizon.

Project context: the where

A summary description of the seven Ws complements the asset lifecycle structure as a basis for the PUMP identify phase, providing a framework for thinking about where sources of uncertainty come from.

A useful W to begin with is the where. The where is the background framework in Figure 1.2, the basis of the second step in the Figure 5.1 structure, addressing the context of the project.

The context of a project can be very important. For BP it was self-evident that the North Sea was not the same as other offshore locations developed earlier. But experience with a range of organizations since suggests it is important to explicitly think about context issues. For example, if a manufacturing organization which uses a global network of production facilities is considering a new production facility, it clearly has to recognize the geographic, economic, political and cultural implications of the country involved.

If a PUMP approach begins in the E&D shaping stage, experience working on the project owner's behalf with successful high insight PUMP implementations suggests it is very important to provide carefully structured and crafted summary documentation of all the key issues relevant to overall project strategy for all relevant parties over the whole of the lifecycle, context forming part of this picture. The effort this involves will need scaling down to lower levels of clarity when appropriate, and lower levels of clarity may be adequate at the concept shaping stage or for other parties. However, even a minimum clarity approach for a contractor at a bidding stage should not overlook issues like 'is the country in question likely to be stable enough to do business in during the period in question?'

Project context includes the role and strategic implications of the project in all involved organizations. For example, the manufacturing organization discussed above may be considering a new production facility because other facilities in the region are threatened by local politics, and other interdependent global marketing issues may be important. Even a minimum clarity approach for a contractor at a bidding stage should not overlook questions like: 'How does this project fit with other business and overall corporate strategy?'

Project context can have a rich set of implications which are sometimes of obvious importance when overlooked, but quite subtle when identified in advance.

Project parties: the who

The who is about the identity of the key 'parties' to a project, key aspects of the nature of these 'players', and key relationships between these 'stakeholders'. 'Stakeholders', 'players' and 'parties' illustrate a range of different labels usually applied to the who, sometimes with slightly different interpretations. The 'who' is a general project management issue which is inseparable from the management of all aspects of project uncertainty. It is a useful conceptual starting point for the flow of Figure 1.2.

Figure 1.2 had not been developed when early versions of the SCERT process were developed, and the structure of the relationship between the key players seemed clear enough without explicit attention to 'parties' at that time. However, working with a wide range of organizations since has confirmed that the who structure can be both unclear and crucial. Consider a project owner's perspective at the E&D shaping stage of an asset lifecycle when a high level of clarity about the 'who' might be relevant, at least in terms of understanding simplifying assumptions.

In any organizational setting, even very small projects invariably involve two or more parties working together. Parties may be individuals, units of an organization, or organizations as a whole. The relationships between the various parties may be complex, often involving a hierarchy of contractual arrangements. Such relationships bring fundamental complications which have a profound influence on project uncertainty in terms of both opportunity and risk. Later players and other interested parties may require attention as the project evolves, and this will need anticipation for effective strategy development. Indeed, project initiators may cease to dominate. The other interested parties may include regulators and others who are not direct players, but may require careful attention, because they are important sources of uncertainty. It is important to ensure a *broad* view of the who, to include all relevant interested parties, and a *rich* view, to distinguish individual players or groups within single organizations which may have significantly different agendas. For example, in marketing terms distinguishing between the purchaser and ultimate user of a product can be very important. A memorable illustration, for those with very long memories, concerns the launch of a new carbon paper for copy typing which did not make black smudges on secretaries' fingers and clothes. Initial marketing effort was targeted at corporate supply departments. It failed. A revised approach aimed at secretaries was an overwhelming success.

It can be useful to distinguish between 'internal' stakeholders and 'external' stakeholders. Internal stakeholders include project owners who have overall managerial responsibility and power, usually linked to a financial stake, and organizations, teams or individuals who have a contractual relationship with the project owner. The project owner may be a consortium. Other stakeholders are 'external'. External stakeholders may be positive or negative about a project, and they may seek to influence the project through political lobbying, regulation, campaigning or direct action. External stakeholders might include local communities, local government, potential users, regulators, environment groups, and the media.

Analysis involving internal or external stakeholders becomes more complex where:

- the characteristics of the set of main players in a project shift over time through the different stages of the project lifecycle;
- there are multiple objectives, often conflicting, frequently associated with different relative priorities for two or more stakeholders – for example conflicts can include: long-term versus short-term objectives, cost efficiency versus jobs, quality versus quantity, control versus independence (Newcombe, 2003);
- the support of some stakeholders may have a significant influence on the attitudes of other more powerful stakeholders (Newcombe, 2003).

Where stakeholders, particularly external ones, may form coalitions, analysis of possible stakeholder behaviour can become even more complex (Lindquist, 2001; Sabatier and Jenkins-Smith, 1999). With a focus on understanding interrelationships between stakeholders, Chevalier and Buckles (2007) offer a number of techniques in their Social Analysis Systems[2] (SAS[2]) suite of tools, such as 'Stakeholder Identification', 'Social Analysis CLIP', 'Competing Goals' and 'Gaps and Conflicts'. These techniques can be used to identify and compare stakeholder positions, values, power, legitimacy, and ties of collaboration and conflict. Another approach to stakeholder analysis, grounded in soft systems methodology (Checkland and Scholes, 1990), is Engel's RAAKS (rapid appraisal of agricultural knowledge systems) approach. RAAKS is a diagnostic framework and participatory methodology for analysing complex multi-stakeholder situations and for designing effective cooperation and communication strategies. The RAAKS methodology addresses the forms of cooperation between stakeholders, their objectives and their conflicting or shared interests, integration and coordination of activities, relevant knowledge and information networks, and division of tasks (Cummings, 2007).

For define phase purposes it may suffice to draw up a simple list of the project parties, supplemented by a paragraph or two about their nature, and a paragraph or two about each key relationship. This information may be readily available. However, fundamental information is often not available in a concise documented form because it is presumed to be too basic to bother to record.

Two sets of parties often worth distinguishing are 'agents of the client' and 'other parties'. 'Other parties' is a broadly defined residual which includes parent organizations, partners, regulatory bodies, customers and competitors. Competitors are a good example of other parties who are not stakeholders in the usual sense, often overlooked. The 'project owner' or 'client' may have little choice about the involvement of other parties in the project and limited ability to control their objectives and actions, but the ability of these other parties to influence the project and its performance may be substantial. Agents of the client are often assumed to be controllable by the client, but contracts may not control behaviour as anticipated, and this set of parties may include subcontractors who are not directly under the control of the client. The potential for liquidation of both contractors and subcontractors is an obvious concern.

An example of what may not be anticipated, although it later proves very important, is provided by a painful weapon system development project experience. Government managers of this system's development contract believed that no risk was involved because they had a very tight specification with onerous performance penalties. When the prime contractor reported a major shortfall on performance, it was assumed that the contractual provisions could be used. It was discovered, too late, that the prime contractor could pass the liability to a subcontractor, and the subcontractor was owned by the government.

The value of documenting the identity, nature and affiliations of all parties to a project is further illustrated by another example. UK Nirex, a government-established organization with one very big project, 'permanent' disposal of UK intermediate level nuclear waste, was partly owned by its major customers. Defining the project 'who' when considering this overall project was a particularly useful starting point because the uncertainty and risk arising from the built-in potential conflict of interest inherent in the ownership/customer structure was identified formally for the Nirex board of directors by Chris Chapman as part of a board level PUMP. Steps were taken to resolve the potential difficulties, and subsequently the PUMP clearly allocated significant particular sources of uncertainty to specific customers/shareholders in a manner reflecting this resolution.

Generalizing the implications of this example, it is important to understand that 'the home team' is worthy of careful inspection as well as 'the opposition'. For example, two nations which were partners in a new weapon system development project for which Chris provided PUMP advice seemed to want the same thing after high level political agreements. However, one partner was desperate for completion by the agreed date, and the other preferred significant delay. Those involved in the negotiation of the agreements between the two countries understood this very clearly, but those implementing the contract might not, with obvious implications unless this situation was tactfully but clearly identified in documents available to everyone who needed to know. A few pages of background to the agreement making such issues clear to everyone involved were very valuable.

An essential deliverable of the define phase by the end of the strategy shaping stages is a comprehensive list of all the parties who may prove influential in the project. The purpose is to provide sufficient detail for all dependent analysis, in particular sufficient summary information to trigger later recognition of sources of uncertainty which can be generated by all parties to the project.

The effort worth expending by a client with a complex project at the E&D shaping stage will need to be scaled down if a lower level of clarity is appropriate. Lower levels of clarity may be adequate at the concept shaping stage, but arguably this is the best time to sort who issues, which tend to get overlooked later. Contractors can restrict the range of relevant parties, but their clients may not be the only key parties. Even a minimum clarity approach for a contractor at a bidding stage should not overlook issues like 'is this potential client solvent and trustworthy?', to avoid wasting time with definite 'no-way' potential clients, and to avoid learning painful lessons the hard way. In the BCS context discussed in Chapter 2, suppliers needed careful attention as well as customers and subcontractors, and it is hard to imagine a simpler context.

Project objectives: the why

A key aspect of project uncertainty management is appraising the implications of project objectives and related performance criteria or attributes, the project 'why'. 'Risk' for PUMP purposes is defined in terms of unfavourable outcomes relative to expected outcomes (unless an alternative opportunity/risk datum performance parameter is appropriate) for all relevant performance criteria, and 'opportunity efficiency' is defined in terms of tradeoffs involving all objectives. Further, a clear idea of prevailing project objectives is central to basic project management for reasons which go well beyond the PUMP. A clear idea of prevailing project objectives is also important in planning and executing the PUMP, because the structure and form of project objectives ought to drive the structure and form of the PUMP via the criteria–plan relationship structure. It follows that any changes in objectives and performance criteria targets at any stage of the project lifecycle need to be carefully evaluated for uncertainty implications as part of the PUMP. Lack of clarity about project objectives makes this more important, not less important.

In the define phase the assessment of project objectives needs to consider the nature of the objectives, their relative importance from the perspective of all the key players, how they might be measured, and the extent to which tradeoffs can be made between them. For example, project managers must generally consider the relative priorities to be placed on cost, time and quality, recognizing that tradeoffs are possible between these basic performance criteria, and client/contractor perspectives may not be the same. If this is not done, different parts of the project team will make internally inconsistent decisions and the project organization as a whole will show confusion and lack of focus.

It is important to be clear about the full range of relevant performance criteria which may relate to a corporate perspective. For example, corporate concerns about strengthened market position, a more favourable position with regulating authorities, a 'greener' or more ethical public image, may all be important. In the context of an oil major, strengthened market position is a subset of the issues ultimately driving profit, a more favourable position with regulatory authorities is a subset of the considerations driving market position, and a 'greener' or more ethical public image is a subset of the 'corporate responsibility' considerations driving position with regulatory authorities and customers. Each successive member of this quartet (profit–market position–regulatory position–perceived 'corporate responsibility') is more difficult to describe in formal terms. Other performance criteria may not have a simple hierarchical structure like this, and relatively difficult criteria to describe and manage like perceived 'corporate responsibility', may be extremely important. More than one major engineering project has failed as a direct result of a failure to manage these issues, which can be a much more important driver of profit (through revenue, project capital cost and operating costs) than the direct technical choices which tend to receive the attention of technically driven project teams.

It may be appropriate to consider the relative importance of criteria in the context of the project as a whole, although different parts of a project may involve different priorities. In both cases it may be useful to consider these priorities and consequent sources of uncertainty in an analytical structure which records different objectives and related activities explicitly. For example, in projects with a high science content, clarification, detailing and hierarchical structuring of project objectives to correspond with activity structures can be extremely useful. The basis of the rationale is that planned activities are only one way of achieving objectives. Planned activities may currently seem the best way of executing the project. However, serious threats to completion of those activities may be best responded to by doing something quite different, or simply abandoning the associated objective. If the relationship between activities and objectives is made explicit at the outset, in a formally defined criteria–plan relationship structure, the subsequent strategy shaping PUMP effort becomes much more efficient and effective.

If quantification of uncertainty is involved later in the PUMP, the need to be clear about priorities is intensified, because the uncertainty management process must exploit the priority structure and the structure of the uncertainty involved. Further, the evaluate phase has to reflect some aspects of the tradeoffs between objectives in the process structure. Quantification can serve to force organizations to clarify priorities, and an important motive for quantification can be forcing this clarification. Often it is feasible and sufficient to select one primary performance criterion for quantification, and convert other performance criteria into primary criterion equivalents or make qualitative judgements, as discussed in the office manager's photocopier choice example of Chapter 2.

Secondary performance criteria are usefully treated as constraints, and the effect of varying these constraints on performance in terms of the primary criterion investigated to understand tradeoffs, or 'shadow prices' if a mathematical programming perspective is used. This approach is illustrated by an example involving initial priorities which were reconsidered after considerable analysis.

A Canadian client of Acres Consulting Services wanted to build a prototype facility to test the feasibility of using a new production technology in the 1980s. The structure of the initial PUMP assumed that the primary criterion was cost. Delay was treated as a secondary performance criterion, and converted into cost equivalents by assessing (in probability distribution terms) a cost per unit time for delay during construction. Quality (performance in relation to the design specification) was treated as a constraint. Tradeoffs began after the analysis was complete in terms of a representation that all users of the study were satisfied broadly reflected the reality of the situation. In particular, the project as planned at that stage was deemed too expensive, and reengineering was applied to reduce the cost. It was not just a question of reducing quality or increasing duration. The project objectives were revisited and a significant change in approach was adopted, based on insight provided by the initial analysis.

Initial uncertainty analysis often adopts time (duration) as the primary performance criterion. Cost is defined later as a function of time and the variability of other costs which are not time dependent. This was true of all offshore project examples discussed in this book, but not refineries – which were addressed using another PUMP variant. Other ways of relating cost and time, or other possibilities for treating quality, may be preferable in other cases. For example, safety critical software for a weapon system or a nuclear power station may require a very different approach. Functionality may be the primary criterion, followed by cost, with time dependent upon functionality and cost risk choices. These issues are not relevant just because project uncertainty management in the PUMP sense is a concern; they are central to basic project management in very general terms. Further, they drive the basic approach to all uncertainty management – for example, in a North Sea offshore project context it was obvious that project duration uncertainty had to be managed first, then coupled cost rate uncertainty, not the case for refineries.

A further consideration is how project objectives should be measured. If time uncertainty is the key concern, choosing a suitable metric is relatively straightforward, but some important issues need considering. For example, time to milestone payments may be the key concern for a contractor, but time until a system achieves a satisfactory level of performance may be the key concern for a client, and if this leads to different opportunity/risk datum choices, obvious problems can arise. Earlier sensitizing to the 'who' is important if this kind of distinction is going to get recognized. Delay may have very different cost implications for different parties, so which party is considered is crucial. Defining payments in terms of milestones to ensure contractor performance may be the client's ultimate concern, to ensure that a compatible sense of urgency applies to all parties.

For cost uncertainty these issues become more complex. For example, is lifecycle cost the issue or just capital cost? Both can involve a common starting point, but the overall approaches can be very different.

If uncertainty related to 'quality' is the concern, these issues become still more complex. For example, the tradeoffs between complete and partial degradation of a system may raise very complex issues which affect the basic system design. If the PUMP is insensitive to key issues it may prove a costly waste of time, so these issues need up-front treatment.

In some cases it may be useful to define a metric for performance criteria measurement which links time, cost and quality in a more direct manner. For example, computer software projects have a long-standing love/hate relationship with 'the mythical man-month' (Brooks, 1975). 'Standard-months' can be used as a basis for estimating work content, cost and time, with associated performance and efficiency analysis working on a standard-month basis.

The effort worth expending by a client to clarify the why for a complex project will need scaling down if a lower level of clarity is appropriate. Lower levels of clarity may be adequate at the concept shaping stage, but generally who and why should be a central concern at this stage, often overlooked later. Contractors can usually afford a less complex view of the 'who' than clients. But even a minimum clarity approach for a contractor at a bidding stage should not overlook such issues as: 'Do my incentives align with the client's best interests, and if not, what are the implications from my perspective, bearing in mind client reactions if things do not work out as the client expected?' These issues were central even in the relatively simple BCS context described in Chapter 2.

Project design: the what

If a PUMP is implemented at the E&D shaping stage by a project owner who needs a high clarity approach, a review of project design, the project 'what', is an important part of the consolidation, elaboration and resolving inconsistencies process. If ignored, this can involve considerable cost. Further, a carefully crafted strategic level summary of project design issues has been a highly valued feature of many successful project uncertainty management reports concerned with high levels of clarity at the E&D shaping stage of projects not previously assessed in PUMP terms.

Usually the material is selected from design reports prepared by the project team as part of the normal project planning process. In such cases the added value of the PUMP reports is usually simply pulling it together in an integrated form accessible to all project staff. Sometimes this integration process reveals missing detail, occasionally it reveals major flaws. In effect, it is an independent review by a PUMP analyst who is by vocation someone prepared to ask lots of dumb questions, in order to write his or her simplified view of what the design is all about, with a strong drive for internal consistency and clear definitions of relationships. Sometimes the apparently dumb questions have no effective answers, revealing flaws in working assumptions which need serious attention.

The BP version of SCERT did not use a seven-Ws structure as noted earlier. The growth in module weight to a level beyond the capability of the platform jacket is an example source of uncertainty which was picked up, but it might have been missed. A formal focus on the basis of the design helps to avoid overlooking this kind of issue, complementing attention to the DOT (design, operations and termination) shaping stage of the lifecycle. All project owners who want a high clarity approach need to be sure that this kind of issue will not be overlooked.

Four kinds of whichway plans

Four kinds of whichway plans identified in Figure 1.2 may need summary definition, but in the E&D shaping stage the priority is plans for activities.

Plans for activities

The focus of the BP version of SCERT was a high clarity approach to plans for activities as indicated earlier. This may not be the case for other contexts, but short-cut approaches and approaches emphasizing other criteria can build on an understanding of what the BP version was attempting to do and what it achieved. The simplicity of the plans for activities was the key to understanding a high clarity decomposition of uncertainty in terms of sources of uncertainty and response options to shape strategy in an opportunity efficient manner.

The need for a simple project activity structure at a strategic level for uncertainty management purposes during the E&D shaping stage is now widely understood, although not universally practised. If more detailed plans have been developed before strategy is fully shaped, these detailed plans need to be given a summary form. Offshore North Sea projects in the late 1970s could involve total expenditures of the order of £1000 million. Even in the context of projects of this size, aiming for 20 activities in a strategic level activity structure was deemed appropriate, with 50 activities perceived as the upper limit for effective strategic analysis. Example activities were: design the platform jacket, fabricate the jacket, design the modules, fabricate the modules, install the jacket, install the modules, design the pipeline, procure the pipe, coat the pipe, lay the pipe, hook-up, and so on, as noted earlier. Based on this experience, the advice 'target about 20 activities, with an upper limit of about 50', has proven appropriate for a wide range of project types involving major investments, as has the advice to scale this down in a non-linear manner for smaller investments. One activity may be appropriate for very small projects, but five to ten is often more effective.

North Sea project activities like 'lay the pipe' are clearly projects in their own right. Separating components of a project into activities at this strategic level allows for the separation of sources of uncertainty which are largely different and unrelated, the responsibility of different people, or amenable to different types of responses or solutions. Even within a simple strategic structure, there is no point attempting relatively detailed uncertainty management until more strategic issues are resolved. For example, five to ten different types of modules might be involved for one offshore platform project, serving very different functions (power, accommodation, and so on), fabricated by different parties in different locations. It was not appropriate to treat each type of module separately during the E&D shaping stage of the lifecycle, although both preceding and following stages needed this detail. Maintaining this simple structure to shape strategy is never easy. For example, in a 1990s 'next generation' warship study, 20–50 activities were achieved after considerable controversy and proved very rewarding, but in a 2009 discussion of commercial US nuclear power station applications, very high levels of detail remained an unresolved obstacle. Understanding *why* more detail will be needed earlier as well as later, for different purposes, may be the key. The *purpose* of the analysis is certainly central. An important 2010 realization for the authors, explored further in Part III, is the value of a clear distinction between:

- highly selective detailed planning to test strategy when this is important prior to approving a strategy, and
- detailed planning on a comprehensive basis for strategy implementation purposes after the strategy is approved.

It is vital not to assume that sources of uncertainty associated with different activities are independent or unconnected. A useful rule of thumb is 'don't separate activities which involve complex interactions' when defining an initial activity structure for strategic uncertainty management purposes. This can be seen as a corollary of the basic rule of thumb 'keep things as simple as possible'. Only break down an activity into more detailed activities if it seems it will be useful to do so, bearing in mind the drawbacks as well as the advantages of more detail. For strategic uncertainty management purposes, fabrication of all the modules to be installed on an offshore platform might be treated as one activity, and their installation might be treated as another activity, without attempting to deal with the complex interactions within them. Later in the lifecycle, when detailed planning of execution and delivery are addressed for implementation purposes, more detailed definition of the exact nature of interconnections is clearly critical. Further, earlier in the lifecycle when considering design strategy more detail may be critical. But keeping it simple with a view to E&D strategy concerns is the priority in the define phase of the PUMP for the E&D shaping stage. The same lessons apply in an earlier strategy shaping stage analysis, whether or not they are fully integrated. Different corporate groups may have responsibility for the content of associated development and assessment, which adds to the complexity of effective full integration.

The reason it is important to persist with attempts to 'keep it simple' in activity structure terms is simple in principle – if detailed questions are addressed at an inappropriate time we tend to 'lose sight of the wood for the trees'. This does not mean it is always simple in practice. For example, the issues associated with where to decide to draw the lines which divide work content by defining activities are complex. Associated expertise is a craft rather than a science to a significant extent, requiring practice and, inevitably, some mistakes. Some of the iterative looping will be correcting 'mistakes' in earlier working assumptions while they are still easy and cheap to correct, as part of an efficient learning approach.

As an example of simple low clarity variants, the BCS example of Chapter 2 used only three activity/cost items, but Bruce, the BCS proprietor, normally uses 5–15.

Plans for operations

In the E&D shaping stage, plans for future operations are not a central concern, but they still warrant documentation because they complement the design concerns addressed under the 'what' heading above. If a PUMP was not used earlier in the project lifecycle, it is important to address key issues which may have been missed under this heading to complete a high clarity process. For example, one major infrastructure project which Chris Chapman reviewed in the E&D shaping stage was clearly going to suffer from 'quality' problems that would manifest as high operating costs driven by serious maintenance problems. This finding was central to the value of the review. It led to major changes in the project approach, and these changes were arguably the basis of a subsequent successful outcome. In effect, O&S (operation and support) strategy needed attention during the E&D shaping stage because it had not been properly addressed in the earlier DOT shaping stage.

Plans for business case purposes

In the E&D shaping stage, plans for business case purposes may seem off limits, but still warrant documentation because they complement the why concerns addressed above. If a PUMP was not used earlier, it is also important to address key issues which may have been missed under this heading to complete a high clarity process. For example, overly optimistic revenue forecasts may make any subsequent analysis which does not challenge them a complete waste of time, and 'quality' issues may drive revenue issues in ways not considered in the concept shaping stage.

Plans for relationships and contracts

In the E&D shaping stage, plans for relationships and contracts may seem off limits, but still warrant documentation because they complement the 'who' and 'why' concerns addressed above, and they can be central. If a PUMP was not used earlier in the lifecycle, it is also important to define and address key issues which may have been missed under this heading to complete a high insight process. For example, the successful outcome for the major infrastructure project that Chris reviewed (noted just above) was achieved via a change in contracting approach to address the O&S strategy issue, the key review outcome. The ownership phase of the PUMP process for the E&D shaping stage is focused on these plans.

Project resources: the two kinds of wherewithal plans

Two kinds of resources and associated resource-based plans identified in Figure 1.2 need summary documentation. In the E&D-shaping stage, the priority is summary definition of resource plans for activities.

Resource plans for activities

A review of resource requirements implied by the project activity plans must be part of the 'consolidate' and 'elaborate and resolve' tasks because an obvious source of uncertainty is the key resources which may not be available when needed. If a PUMP has not been in place from the outset of the project, the identification of resource requirements is usually part of a process to provide base cost estimates. This process can be somewhat separate from the design and activity planning processes, which may proceed in parallel to some extent.

In large engineering or construction projects, the group of people doing the base cost estimation are not usually the same as the group doing the activity planning; the designers are a third group, and the business case custodians are a fourth group. The various groups often have very different backgrounds, and sometimes these functional and cultural differences are exacerbated by departmental or contractual structures. PUMP analysts often feel as if they have been parachuted into the middle of a 'three-ring circus', with quite separate uncoordinated acts in the three or more rings. They may be viewed by the three acts as a new clown, but they have to operate to some extent as a ringmaster, without offending the ringmaster.

The relationships between professions need to be tackled directly, to avoid associated sources of uncertainty being realized, otherwise they may have to be addressed on a contingency response basis which can prove extremely costly.

Figure 1.2 assumes that the plans for the activities aspect of 'whichway' is addressed *before* the resource plans for activities aspect of 'wherewithal'. For convenience it is usually safe to assume this ordering, but the reverse order may be appropriate if scarce execution and delivery resources driven by design choices dictate how things are done.

Even if constrained resources is not an issue, unit costs for all resources may give rise to important sources of uncertainty, like the cost of coated pipe and the cost of offshore platform jackets and modules. In effect, activity duration is one driver of capital cost uncertainty, but all other resource-based sources of uncertainty need consideration in a systematic manner.

Resource plans for operations

In the E&D-shaping stage, operations resource plans are not a central concern, but they complement design concerns addressed under the 'what' heading considered above, and linked operations plans, with broader links to the 'where' in corporate strategy terms.

For example, in the 1960s, oil refinery operators were among the first serious users of PERT and CPM techniques to identify appropriate planned maintenance cycles, to plan scheduled maintenance execution in cost effective terms considering resource plan issues, and to fully integrate this with inventory and marketing issues.

In any context, strategic resource plans integrated with all other strategic plans to the extent that this is useful are a required deliverable.

Even the very simple BCS context in Chapter 2 involves these issues, with the availability of all the components of a new kitchen or bathroom at the right time being a major source of uncertainty that Bruce has to manage.

Project timing: the when

In the authors' experience it is very important to construct a simple activity-on-node precedence diagram to portray clearly the assumed precedence relationships between the activities selected for the whichway 'plans for activities' portrayal of the project. It is also important to construct a separate (but directly related) Gantt chart to portray the implied timing, the when. Modern linked bar-chart software makes it tempting to combine these two traditional graphs into a single graph, but clarity and generality can be lost if this is done.

At a very detailed planning level, it may seem that precedence relationships are always strict and simple, and defined by the task nature of the activities. The water must be boiled before we make the tea, for example. At a strategic planning level – the level most appropriate for shaping strategy in uncertainty management terms – precedence relationships tend to be fuzzy and complex, and defined by design and resource issues as well as the task nature of activities. This is part of the ambiguity uncertainty inherent in all planning which is not very detailed and tactical. It needs explicit recognition, and formal uncertainty modelling when appropriate. For example, 'deliver materials' and 'construct jacket' might overlap by 3–6 months, depending upon which materials are delayed – an ambiguity which is not resolvable at a strategic level.

In addition, the strategic level views of activity precedence and timing used for project uncertainty management should capture very important alternative approaches to the project which detailed portrayals obscure. Consider two examples.

First, planning the fabrication of modules for North Sea offshore platforms (for accommodation, control functions, and so on) in a conventional critical path network manner, focusing on the plans for activities, naturally assumes that modules are completed before taking them out to install on the platform. In practice it is much more expensive to complete fabrication offshore, but it may be cheaper to do so than missing a weather window. Hence, the planning process had to reflect tradeoffs between the cost of onshore/offshore fabrication and the expected cost of missing a weather window. At a tactical planning level this issue needed addressing directly. At a strategic planning level it needed recognition, but not resolution at a tactical level.

Second, two sequential activities associated with preparing to sink a deep-mining shaft in a UK Nirex 'rock characterization' project were assumed to be on a sub-critical path. When it became apparent that they might be critical, the possibility that they might take place in parallel was raised. It transpired that they had been put in series because it was assumed that the same resources would be used. This was cost effective if this path was sub-critical, but not if it was critical.

Being aware at an early stage of the tradeoffs described in these two examples was essential for good project management, whether or not formal project uncertainty management was an issue. These examples also illustrate interdependency between the project whichway–wherewithal–when trio which needs explicit attention and documentation as part of the PUMP define phase. The questions addressed by 'whichway–wherewithal–when' are not really separable in many situations. However, it is useful to distinguish them for definition consolidation purposes, because they are often treated separately in project planning.

Even though the BCS context in Chapter 2 means that Bruce does not formally plan, these issues are central to the uncertainty he has to manage and his strategic assessment of it for bidding purposes.

Define phase deliverables fit for purpose?

The define phase deliverables for each of the PUMP passes in each of the strategy shaping lifecycle stages is a clear, unambiguous, shared understanding of all relevant key aspects of the project, appropriately documented, verified, assessed as 'fit for purpose' at that stage of the process, and reported on an appropriate basis. The written form of these deliverables may be a single document, or parts of several documents. Whatever its form, a comprehensive and complete define phase in each pass should clarify all the relevant key parts of the project which the PUMP needs to address in a manner accessible to all relevant parties. A single document achieving these ends is often held to be a key benefit of a formal PUMP by senior managers.

The ongoing and integrative nature of the define phase

Part of the purpose of this definition documentation is the provision of a 'reference plan' (starting position plan) for the project, which may be modified and augmented as a result of subsequent PUMP analysis. In practice, ensuring that an appropriate reference plan is available is not just a question of capturing in simplified form an existing common perception of the asset lifecycle and the seven Ws. Usually it involves an assessment of the project planning process itself, which requires responses to errors of omission and commission in the basic project management process. Responses may involve project management changes as distinct from project uncertainty management, involving people and organizations not necessarily part of the PUMP management process.

Even if a PUMP is first implemented when the project is well developed, the define phase as just outlined may reveal gaps in the reference plans which need to be filled and inconsistencies which need to be resolved. In theory, such gaps and inconsistencies should not exist, but in practice they are inevitable, *even if the PUMP process starts in the concept-shaping stage*.

At any stage in the lifecycle, because some aspects of the project may not be clearly defined when the define phase begins, and they may take some time to be defined, important and central aspects of the define phase may be ongoing, and ambiguity uncertainty will be endemic.

Figure 4.2 portrays the way the initial effort associated with the define phase might be timed in a typical basic PUMP process. The initial concern in the first pass should be to make as much progress as possible with the define phase before moving on to the other PUMP phases. In general, the greater the level of unfinished business from the define phase initial pass, the lower the efficiency and effectiveness of the following phases. However, perfection is not feasible, the best shape for the define phase deliverables depends upon their future use, which is inherently uncertain, and fit for purpose assessments are judgements involving risk. PUMP management is a risky business.

To a significant extent the most appropriate shape and content for the define phase deliverables has to be assessed as part of the focus phase, to serve the process objectives determined during the focus phase. This is why the define and focus phases have to proceed in parallel, with the first pass of both completed before starting the first pass of the identify phase. One of the key issues involving the define and focus phase interactions is the nature and role of the criteria–plan and knowledge–plan relationship structures. Their considered is deferred until Chapter 6.

Lower levels of clarity

Low and intermediate levels of clarity may require simplification in a range of different ways, depending on the context. Earlier in this chapter the BCS example from Chapter 2 was used to illustrate low clarity approaches. Some other intermediate level examples were mentioned, but a wide range of intermediate positions will need attention in practice. For example, the Highways Agency example explored in Chapter 2 involved a very simple decomposition of project capital cost into half a dozen components like 'construction', 'land acquisition' and 'traffic management'. These components are high-level activities which locate the expenditure in time, and are important for considering inflation, but duration uncertainty was not considered as a direct driver of cost. 'Construction' cost was further decomposed into three components. Mentioned, but not discussed in detail, are the portfolio of project considerations, the overall budget, and government relationship issues.

Intermediate levels of clarity tend to take a context-specific form somewhere between the BCS/Highways Agency and the BP examples, more usefully explored later.

Conclusion

It is very easy to get confused, even if you think you understand what is going on in a very simple project. The Mondale quotation at the beginning of this chapter is a useful reminder that the basic purpose of the define phase is not complete understanding of the project. The define phase is just a starting point for defining and developing understanding. It can provide useful descriptive material for a range of purposes, including a useful 'executive summary' of what a project involves. However, its basic purpose is not a definitive description in the usual sense of 'definitive'. *The basic purpose of the define phase is getting ready to ask the right questions.* Providing all the relevant answers is part of the role of the final pass of the evaluate phase of the PUMP, after considerable interim effort concerned with posing the right questions.

The define phase has to cover a lot of ground, and it needs intelligence and skill to tackle it in clarity efficient terms. However, it is arguably the most straightforward of the seven basic PUMP phases.

Chapter 6

Focus the process

If the only tool in your toolbox is a hammer, every problem looks like a nail.

—Anon

Generic PUMP pack processes provide a framework for uncertainty management, but the precise scope and detail of analysis in each phase will depend upon the application and corporate context. There is no 'one best approach' for all circumstances. The focus phase of the basic PUMP is about adapting the generic process to the specific project context of immediate interest.

The opportunities for uncertainty management in projects are considerable, pervasive and diverse. Any systematic efforts at project uncertainty management must be carefully designed and managed if 'clarity efficiency' is to be achieved – cost-effective use of uncertainty management resources including process demands on everyone involved, directly or indirectly. Achieving clarity efficiency is the goal of the focus phase.

Part II of this book is focused on using the PUMP process during the last of the strategy shaping stages of the project lifecycle, the E&D shaping stage. As indicated in Chapter 5, using a PUMP in each strategy shaping stage starting with the concept shaping stage is recommended for all projects, but sometimes a later start has to be accommodated. In addition, explaining what is involved in the earlier strategy shaping lifecycle stages at a detailed level is easier if E&D shaping PUMPs are considered first, in part because short-cut versions of later strategy shaping stage applications are needed in the concept shaping stage. For related reasons, it is useful to initially focus on a client (project owner) needing a high clarity approach, later considering short-cuts, lower clarity approaches, and approaches for contractors. This chapter, like all other Part II chapters, follows this approach.

All applications of an E&D shaping PUMP can be viewed as projects in their own right, sometimes usefully identified formally as second-order or higher order projects. This has two implications of immediate relevance. One is a role for a lifecycle structure plus a seven Ws framework in PUMP *process* terms, related to but separate from the *project* versions discussed in Chapter 5. The other is the value of clarity about the difference between strategic and tactical levels of planning in *process* terms. Putting these two implications together, and building on experience crafting both specific and generic process structures, suggests the form of Figure 6.1.

Figure 6.1 portrays starting the focus phase in 'scope the process' mode, a strategic level specific task with six steps. Step 1 involves the process lifecycle, and each of the next three steps involves process Ws. Top-down appreciation of uncertainty in step 5 uses a modification of the Lichtenberg (2000) approach to start with an overview of the overall scale of relevant uncertainty and the nature of the key components. Step 6 involves completing the formation of a process strategy for this pass of the PUMP. If the process strategy is then assessed as fit for purpose, the 'plan the process' mode can begin, a more detailed tactical planning process involving three more

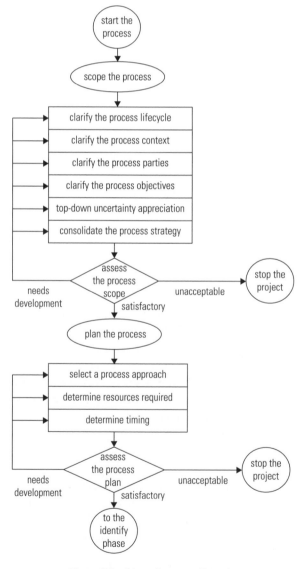

Figure 6.1 Focus phase specific tasks

Ws. If the process strategy is not fit for purpose, normally earlier steps are revisited as appropriate. In 'plan the process' mode, a tactical operational plan is developed for the PUMP application, normally working within the strategy and revisiting earlier 'plan the process' steps if necessary as implied by the second 'deliverables fit for purpose?' iteration control task and feedback structure. Both iteration control tasks can fail to reach an acceptable position, potentially leading to stopping the project unless the PUMP is abandoned. In practice it may be more effective to aim for separate development loops for each of the nine basic steps, with parallel converging strategic and tactical planning processes once the shape of the strategic plan for the PUMP application is in place. Figure 6.1 is not intended to be a restrictive prescription of the focus phase, but an idealization to capture the issues involved at a useful level of complexity and clarity, a portrayal of convenient working assumptions for discussion purposes.

The deliverables provided by the focus phase may be a single document or parts of several documents. Whatever their form, a comprehensive and complete focus phase should clarify all the key aspects of the chosen PUMP approach viewed as a project in its own right, in a manner accessible to all relevant people. The deliverables of the focus phase for each pass at each stage in the project lifecycle form the basis for a clear, unambiguous, shared understanding of a particular PUMP application and its management processes at a level of formal definition suitable for all those who need to understand how the PUMP is going to operate in a given context. Senior managers do not need to understand the details for particular applications, but they should understand what best practice can deliver and be able to distinguish good and poor quality delivery. Trusted, independent advisers are a second best option.

Clarify the process lifecycle

'Clarify the process lifecycle' has to address the PUMP process lifecycle with appropriate anticipation of overall process strategy issues. PUMP objectives associated with current pass concerns in the current primary project lifecycle stage may dominate PUMP process strategy formation, but concerns to be addressed later need joint consideration to design an effective and efficient PUMP pack. For example, if quantification of uncertainty is not an immediate priority, but it will probably be essential soon, the case for very simple immediate quantification is greatly strengthened. There is no need for a detailed formal PUMP plan in lifecycle terms, but an outline of current and future issues agreed by the limited number of relevant players directly involved in the focus phase can pay sizeable dividends. If only one person is responsible for the focus phase, orderly thinking is still essential.

Clarify the process context

'Clarify the process context' can also influence process strategy in a useful manner. For example, if this is the first time a PUMP has been used in an organization, and it is serving as a demonstration and development platform for the organization, time and effort expended is in part an investment that will reap future benefits on other projects, and appropriate clarity level choices should reflect this. As indicated in Chapter 5, the first application of the BP version of SCERT took about six months. Within a year the same process was being completed in about four weeks by the PUMP manager working on his own apart from limited mentoring advice. Part of the reduction in effort was the PUMP manager moving along the process learning curve, part was the organization moving along the process learning curve, and part was corporate learning about offshore North Sea projects via the PUMP process, moving along the project corporate learning curve. *All three aspects reflect an investment in corporate learning with important payoffs.*

Clarify the process parties

'Clarify the process parties' is concerned with clarifying who is undertaking uncertainty analysis for whom, and how the reporting process will be managed. Ambiguity about those who are undertaking a PUMP, and to whom they are reporting, may invalidate all following steps in the focus phase. The key players should be:

- a board level senior manager, to empower the process, to ensure that the PUMP effort reflects the needs and concerns of board level senior managers, and to ensure that it contains the relevant judgements and expertise of all relevant senior managers;
- all other relevant managers, to ensure that it services the whole project management process;
- all relevant technical experts, to ensure that it captures all relevant expertise for communication to all relevant users of that expertise in an appropriate manner;
- a PUMP analyst or analysis team, including a PUMP manager, to provide facilitation and elicitation skills, modelling and method design skills, computation skills, teaching skills that get the relevant messages to all other members of the organization, and the management skills needed to allow PUMP usage to develop and evolve in a way that suits the organization.

Some organizations use the term 'risk manager' to refer to an equivalent to our 'PUMP manager'. Apart from the inappropriate focus on 'risk', this can imply a serious confusion of roles. Uncertainty is a pervasive aspect of a project which can be delegated to uncertainty management process staff in terms of process definition, coordination, facilitation, analysis, and communication for PUMP purposes, but not in terms of the management of associated risk and opportunity, or the size and nature of the underlying uncertainty. Proper integration of uncertainty management and project management generally requires the project manager to take personal overall responsibility for all uncertainty management not explicitly delegated upward to his board or downward to managers of components of the project, plus associated risk and opportunity. As appropriate, all those involved should be supported by a PUMP team and take a share of responsibility for the process, supporting decisions they are responsible for, with no responsibility for risk or opportunity per se remaining with the PUMP manager. In large organizations with large and complex projects, the 'PUMP team' may involve a PUMP manager and analysts, a *process* manager and *process* staff. In a one-person organizations the 'PUMP team' may be a very small percentage of that person's time.

In the context of any given project, the relationship between the PUMP team and other players needs early and clear definition. This can be seen as plans for relationships and contracts in *process* 'whichway' terms. When the PUMP team is part of the project-owning organization, this issue may seem straightforward, but very important issues still need to be addressed in an explicit manner. For example, does the PUMP team report only to the project manager and act solely as a support function for the project manager and the project team, or does the PUMP team also report to the board and act as an auditor of the project team on behalf of the board? In the authors' view the PUMP team should, if possible, be seen by the project team as a support function providing feedback of immediate practical value to the project team. If this is not the case, the cooperation necessary to do the job may not be forthcoming and the PUMP may flounder. However, it is equally important that the PUMP team be seen by the board as unbiased, with a demonstrable record for 'telling it as it is', as providers of an 'honest broker' external review process. If this is not the case, the PUMP may sink without trace.

Another key issue is whether to involve other parties or stakeholders directly in the PUMP or whether to treat them as sources of uncertainty that require appropriate responses to be developed during the PUMP. The timing for involving each relevant stakeholder may be critical. For example, early involvement of external critics of a project may provide enormous benefits if early 'win–win' design changes are feasible. In respect of large infrastructure projects, Flyvbjerg et al. (2003) hold that risk assessment and management should involve citizens and stakeholders such as key institutional actors, various levels of government, industrial interests, scientific and technical expertise, and the media. They argue that 'such involvement should take place in carefully designed deliberative processes from the beginning and throughout large scale projects' (Flyvbjerg et al., 2003, p. 7).

In relation to all key players, the PUMP should be seen as immediately useful and valuable, in the sense that it more than justifies the demands made upon them. If it threatens any of the players, there must be a balance of power in favour of meeting that threat rather than avoiding it.

Often a project planning team provides a high risk environment for uncertainty management. One common reason for this is ineffective project management in relation to uncertainty. Other common reasons include project team members who are not familiar with effective PUMPs, who favour familiar but inappropriate PUMPs, who come from very difficult cultures, or who come from competing organizations or departments.

If the quality of project management or staff is a serious issue, this can be the biggest source of uncertainty for the PUMP viewed as a project, as well as an obvious threat to the primary project itself. If this is the case, it deserves careful management for obvious reasons.

To clarify the importance of the reporting process, consider a simple practical issue. If a PUMP team member reports to the project manager, using information obtained from a set of groups within the project team, it is very important to keep the whole project team on-side. This means that each group must be aware of the implications of their assessments before these assessments go beyond their group, and they must have time to change their minds, perhaps several times, until they are confident about exposing their assessments to the rest of the project team. Some project teams may be fairly uninhibited about this, but others may be extremely sensitive, with consequential major impacts on PUMP plans. A project team made up of contractors who have scope for competition as well as collaboration can be a source of this problem. This issue can be of sufficient importance to warrant a project team design which avoids it.

A common question at seminars is: 'Can I, as a client, ask my prime contractors to do a risk analysis for me?' The answer is 'yes' provided the uncertainty analysis as discussed in this book is implied. But while such an analysis may be a useful starting point for the client, it is only a starting point. The problem here is that to the extent that the client and contractor have different objectives and information, their perceptions of project opportunity and risk will be different. In particular, what the client sees as threats or problems, the contractor may see as opportunities for the contractor. Moreover, the contractor may be unwilling to reveal such opportunities to the client if doing so is likely to lead to a reduction in those opportunities for the contractor.

Addressing the who question associated with the PUMP can also help to clarify who is working for whom in the project team as a whole. To take this a bit further, the 'PUMP who' can be defined in narrow terms as a small team working within a large project team or in a broad sense to include the whole project team, as part of the integration of project management and project uncertainty management. If a PUMP analyst, or the project manager, or some other member of the project team, does not take it upon himself to clarify process party issues in this sense, the issues will be mismanaged or unmanaged. It can be very useful to compare the 'PUMP who' to the 'project who' to check for consistency and clarity.

Clarify the process objectives

'Clarify the process objectives' further clarifies the strategy and scope of the PUMP. For example, an awareness of the purpose and scope of the proposed PUMP can help to determine the desirability of quantification. Consider the following contrasting examples.

An unbiased cost estimate for an engineering construction project

In the 1980s, a Canadian engineering construction project was approaching a board level 'go/no-go' decision at the end of its E&D shaping stage. It was the first project the organization had subjected to a formal PUMP, based on a simplification of BP's SCERT approach, using Acres Consulting Services for process development support. If a 'go' decision was taken, the project would be executed within a few years with no major anticipated changes in management. The project management team wanted board approval for a budget they could live with and control within the organization in an effective manner, but they recognized that if they asked for funds they did not need, they would increase substantially the risk of a 'no-go' decision. This was a very unwelcome possibility. These concerns made a quantitative risk analysis essential, in order to distinguish clearly between targets, expectations, and commitments, and to clarify the bias implications of any scope assumptions, including responsibility for possible changes in scope. However, the PUMP source of uncertainty structure could be kept very simple relative to the BP versions of SCERT on which it was based – there was no need for a complex source of uncertainty structure exploring contingency planning in detail. In retrospect the process used might have been even simpler, building on the Highways Agency approach described in Chapter 2, but reflecting the need to justify reasonably straightforward strategic choices.

A pessimistically biased completion date forecast for a commercial aircraft company

A European commercial aircraft manufacturing company managed airliner production as a programme of projects, with each aircraft treated as a project. Each aircraft was 'costed' on a materials and labour basis, using 'standard hours' for all tasks. Production was planned using standard

CPA (Critical Path Analysis) deterministic planning tools. The basics of most aircraft conformed to a standard production model, but each aircraft involved significant variations according to the instrumentation and finishing requirements of the airline ordering the aircraft. Two sources of uncertainty plagued the manager of each aircraft's production: materials might not arrive when they were required; and staff might not be available when they were required, because another aircraft manager 'stole' them by pleading higher priority, or because of illness and staff turnover.

If materials did not arrive on time they were 'chased', and work was rescheduled to use the materials and staff that were available.

Airlines wanted to know how long it would take to deliver an aircraft when ordering it. Keeping delivery promises was an important aspect of marketing strategy. Forecasting delivery dates to the day over the last 30 days was also a contractual matter, with a cost of about £10 000 per day for late delivery, because of the airline's need to put new aircraft into their service schedules. Consistent failure to deliver on time with substantial variations in performance suggested that a formal uncertainty management system was needed.

The responsible senior manager initially envisioned replacing the CPA approach with an appropriate subset of features from a BP version of SCERT. Discussions with those involved in managing the system suggested that replacing the CPA-based planning system with one capturing the uncertainty involved would hinder rather than help the shop-floor managers. No changes to the existing system were recommended at this level. Work planning in the tactics shaping, execution and delivery stage sense was not the problem, and treating it as if it were the problem would make matters worse. The problem was forecasting before tactical planning took place.

To deal with the forecasting problem, a PUMP approach was suggested that went back to the basic standard hours calculations used for costing, measuring the efficiency associated with converting standard hours into completed work as a function of aircraft percentage completion, and using this model plus forecast staff availability to forecast completion. Measurement of associated uncertainty using simple econometric techniques facilitated balancing penalties associated with under and over provision of time to complete each aircraft. A suitable mild pessimism was built into the forecast for customer information purposes as an appropriately defined contingency – the forecast was a commitment value incorporating an appropriate contingency, not an expected outcome.

The efficiency associated with converting standard hours into work achieved was shown to fall off in a predictable way as aircraft neared completion, because work was increasingly difficult to do out of order due to missing components, and less flexibility was available when rescheduling to cope with shortages of components or key labour.

This form of modelling within a PUMP also provided a 'what-if' capability for addressing higher level programme management questions, such as:

- would it be better to let one aircraft which is in trouble carry on as planned, rather than borrow staff from two others which are currently ahead of schedule, but could be induced to fail if we 'steal from Peter to pay Paul'? or
- would it be a good idea to recruit 10% more staff than we think we need over the next six months? or
- how much is it costing us to have materials arrive late, and what is the most cost effective way to reduce these costs?

Forecasting was the visible problem before the PUMP was developed, and associated strategic planning of the portfolio of projects provided scope for further improvements. There was no need for changes to the tactical work planning for implementation purposes, and it was very important to understand the difference.

Why clarity about process objectives matters

These two contrasting examples illustrate the value of being clear about the purpose of any PUMP before shaping its strategy. In the first example a simple version of a SCERT approach could be used to clarify the budget and associated plans. In the second, applying this kind of simplification applied to tactical planning for implementation would have been counterproductive. Better forecasting of completion times needed a quite different approach. Both examples involved successful outcomes because the very different objectives were recognized. Recognizing the importance of clarity about process objectives can be seen as central to the plans for business case purposes aspect of the process 'whichway'. A basic axiom of those who build successful models for decision support purposes is 'there is no one best model for all purposes'. The same can be said for the processes built around such models. A corollary is that there is no one best way to pursue all uncertainty analyses – much of the need to vary the approach taken hinges on why it is being undertaken. A requirement for effectiveness and efficiency demands that we design or select our models and processes according to our purposes. If more than one purpose is being pursued, we may need more than one model and process, running in a separate but linked manner.

Top-down uncertainty appreciation

'Top-down uncertainty appreciation' provides an overview understanding of uncertainty. Top-down appreciation of uncertainty in holistic terms is an essential ingredient of effective PUMP design for any particular application, and experience suggests that a limited top-down strategic view of all relevant project uncertainty is a useful explicit PUMP step at this point in the process. An approach based on a variant of Lichtenberg's 'successive principle' can be very useful (Lichtenberg, 2000). For example, if project capital cost is the key concern, start with an estimate of an overall plausible minimum cost and an overall plausible maximum cost – a nominal P10 to P90 range. Identify the two or three biggest components, and a residual 'everything else'. Then decompose the biggest component in a similar way – into the two or three biggest components plus 'everything else'. Continue to do this until the relative importance of the main components seems clear to all relevant parties.

Using this approach working directly with the key senior managers has been very helpful on a number of occasions. Sources of uncertainty internal to the project and corporate sources of uncertainty can be related and sized to provide an overview which is immediately useful in its own right, as well as providing a basis for further more detailed analysis. Simple forms of quantitative approaches are usually needed, as illustrated in Part I and further clarified later. Such approaches must recognize that some sources of uncertainty are best left as conditions (assumptions), but semi-quantitative risk ranking approaches like that proposed by Baccarini and Archer (2001) are to be avoided for reasons comparable to the case against 'qualitative' PIG approaches to estimation and evaluation outlined in Chapter 2. Uncertainty at a highly aggregated 'top' level estimated directly without a structured bottom-up analysis basis means that the tendency to optimistic underestimation of uncertainty discussed in Chapter 10 needs to be neutralized as far as possible, by overstating uncertainty when in doubt to manage the downside of inappropriate optimism.

This kind of initial top-down appreciation of uncertainty may reveal levels and forms of uncertainty which some people do not want to address. For example, a board that wants a plus or minus 10% accuracy on capital cost estimates can get very upset if they are told that a P10 to P90 range four or five times bigger is the best they can expect, given current knowledge. However, from a PUMP perspective, it really is a waste of everybody's time to avoid unpleasant truths. If bearing this kind of bad news involves 'constructive insubordination' which is likely to be so unwelcome that it may cut short the messenger's career in this organization, he or she may not wish to divulge this part of the analysis for the time being, and seek appropriate support, but helping to keep bodies buried for any length of time is inappropriate. External consultants have a well-established role delivering bad news, but their use for this purpose should be part of a substantive strategy.

An example illustrates that an important reason for undertaking a top-down view of uncertainty may be to determine where the limits of the project manager's responsibilities for managing project-related uncertainty lie.

Corporate and project boundary interfaces

When Chris Chapman started work on one UK organization's project uncertainty management processes his remit did not include an assessment of corporate strategic threats and opportunities, but an early priority was to persuade the directors that such analysis would be a good idea, because the project manager was convinced that major issues driving his project needed urgent board level decisions. Several preliminary analyses were undertaken to indicate what would be involved. The highly political nature of the project made the issues identified extremely sensitive. A full analysis was not undertaken by Chris, but he was encouraged to provide the directors with a suitable framework and to clarify key sources of corporate uncertainty as he saw them. This process, which helped to shape corporate policy on major strategic issues, was used as the basis for a report to the board, and added substantial value to the overall uncertainty management process.

Apart from its direct value as a strategic analysis for the directors, the strategic overview set the project uncertainty management process in context. It was recognized in a formal corporate sense that a range of major design changes might take place for political reasons, or for reasons related to customer plans. However, those responsible for the design underlying the project were explicitly relieved of responsibility for worrying about such changes, responsibility being formally placed with the board.

For both authors, on many occasions since, it has become clear rather late in the day that this kind of clarity at the outset would have greatly improved overall clarity efficiency.

Consolidating the process strategy and scope

'Consolidating the process strategy' concludes the PUMP strategy formulation involved in all five earlier steps, a concluding step to bring it all together in a form that those immediately involved can understand. 'Process scope' is usefully interpreted as a summary portrayal of 'process strategy' for wider consumption. Process strategy may reside in the heads of the PUMP manager and his team, and include a range of considerations not explicit in the process scope.

Process scope and strategy fit for purpose?

The first 'fit for purpose' test addresses 'process scope' and the underlying process strategy. It provides a convenient place to pause and consider project uncertainty as it is perceived at this point in the PUMP.

Stopping the project may be a possibility needing consideration if the previous steps raise serious questions about the project's viability. However, answering such questions usually becomes central to the objectives of the PUMP, requiring further development of the PUMP strategy and operational plans. At its simplest, the top-down appreciation of uncertainty may identify a single potential 'show-stopper', and the scope and plan the process tasks may then address how best to assess the extent to which this show-stopper can be revised, removed, resolved or dissolved. Deciding whether it is worth undertaking a PUMP to resolve a show-stopper or whether it is better to bring the whole project to a stop without further work can be the key issue.

'The project will probably proceed' is a key working assumption for many reasons. When a project is in serious doubt, a different kind of PUMP is required to one based on the assumption that the project will proceed. It is very important to understand that the whole purpose of project planning *should* change if the viability of a project is seriously called into question, even if everyone else involved in the project fails to see this. If a project that was assumed to be 'a goer' suddenly looks like 'a maybe', project planning and associated uncertainty management need to address the question: 'Is the project worth doing?' Considering how to do the project is appropriate only insofar as doing so is necessary to address the question: 'Is the project worth doing?' Developing details of how to undertake the project will be a complete waste of time should the project be stopped, and resources should be allocated with this potential nugatory expenditure effect clearly in mind.

For obvious basic economy of effort reasons, any issue likely to lead to a 'no-go' decision should be addressed via an appropriate PUMP as early as possible in the project lifecycle. There are linked behavioural issues associated with stopping projects which become more relevant as time goes on. Obtaining unbiased estimates of performance from a project team can become more difficult as their emotional investment in a project grows, particularly if the project team members are threatened by the possibility of the project stopping, and especially if cancellation threatens their livelihood.

Should an acceptable approach to the PUMP prove non-feasible, 'stop the project' is a recommendation that will require justification as discussed in Chapter 12. Fundamental project management failures may be involved, and evidence of such failures may have been uncovered in the parallel define phase tasks as well as in the focus phase tasks, or in earlier passes of the whole PUMP.

Select a process approach

'Select a process approach' is the first 'plan the process' step, as indicated in Figure 6.1. This involves considering how the PUMP is to be carried out in whichway terms at a level of detail suitable for implementation. There are no useful distinctions between plans for operations or activities in whichway terms, and strategic verses tactical shaping distinctions are ignored for simplicity.

It is very important that everyone involved understands that there is no one best approach for all project uncertainty management purposes. We would not expect to use the same approach for the construction of all buildings or the development of all weapon systems or the implementation of all information systems. Even within these industry sectors, we must expect to create plans in a manner tailored to the needs of each specific project. The same applies to planning the PUMP approach.

Planning for a PUMP in terms of this step begins with selecting an appropriate model or set of models. A 'model' in this context is the deliberate simplification of reality we use as a basis for analysis. Most models of interest have a mathematical form, but their associated graphical form can clarify our understanding of the model's implications in important ways, making graphical forms central to clarity efficiency.

Even in an organization with a well-established formal PUMP pack, decisions need to be made, consciously and regularly, about which models to use in individual applications. If these decisions are not made consciously, then decisions are being made by default, which may prove very costly. On some occasions the models used may be too simple, obscuring important issues that should be addressed. On other occasions the models used may be too complex, involving effort that is not cost effective. Using an inappropriate model to analyse uncertainty is an uncertainty management planning error directly comparable to undertaking a construction project with an inappropriate plan. It involves clarity inefficiency that will lead to opportunity inefficiency.

Failing to consider this issue is rather like operating a car hire firm that always offers a Rolls Royce, or a Mini, regardless of the potential customer's wallet or needs. It is difficult to over-emphasize this point because the systematic, generic nature of some frameworks which fail to address it can easily seduce those who ought to know better into the adoption of a single modelling approach for all purposes in all projects, or very ad hoc unsystematic variations. 'If the only tool in your toolbox is a hammer, every problem looks like a nail', is a situation to be avoided.

It is also worth noting that the selection of suitable models for uncertainty management purposes in one project lifecycle stage can influence other lifecycle stage choices, and these issues may need joint consideration. For example, BP's use of semi-Markov process models in the E&D shaping stage facilitated but did not require similar models for tactics shaping, while the commercial airline company approach to forecasting discussed earlier clearly justified a very different approach for tactics shaping.

Choosing an appropriate level of model sophistication in the E&D shaping stage can be left until later in the PUMP if a nested set of compatible models of the SCERT variety is employed. However, specific simplifications in the focus phase which preclude more sophisticated models later can have serious ongoing consequences. Comparable arguments apply to all models used to consider all project Ws.

Determine the resources required

Just as resources for the project require explicit consideration, so too do resources for an effective PUMP, the process 'wherewithal' question. In a given project context, there may be specific constraints on cost and time. Resource questions are likely to revolve around the availability and quality of human resources, including both the availability of key project personnel and the availability of an appropriate PUMP team. The availability of information processing facilities can also be an issue.

Computing power is no longer a significant constraint for most project planning, with or without consideration of uncertainty. Even very small projects can afford access to powerful personal computers. However, software can be a significant constraint, even for very large projects. It is important to select software which is efficient and effective for an appropriate model and method. It is also important to prevent preselected software from unduly shaping the form of the analysis. The authors' longstanding preference to get started is a flexible unstructured software system – any suitable spreadsheet package and '@Risk', for example. This approach is effective in expert hands because it is flexible, but it is not very efficient because it is flexible and requires expert users. When the type of models used and the associated methods or processes have become reasonably well defined, more specific and more efficient software usually deserves attention, perhaps constructed from basic software systems used earlier, or perhaps purchased 'off-the-shelf'.

In the early stages of a PUMP, the PUMP team analysts may be seen as the project planning players doing most of the uncertainty management running. However, as soon as possible it is very useful if all the other parties (as listed earlier) see themselves as part of the team, and push the development of the PUMP as a vehicle serving their needs. This implies commitment and a willingness to spend time providing input to the analysis and exploring the implications of its output.

In any given project, key people's time may become extremely precious. In the terms economists would use, the marginal cost of an extra hour (or the last hour) spent on a PUMP by *all* the staff involved (not just specialist PUMP staff) ought to be assessed in terms of the value of the best alternative use of these hours. At a critical point in the development of a project, the time of the staff involved will be very valuable, perhaps ten times their gross salary cost, and effective use of their time is a key concern. The effects of this are easily observable in terms of the project team which is 'too busy fighting alligators to think about how to drain the swamp they are in'. An effective PUMP should avoid this kind of panic, but crisis management is not going to be eliminated entirely if the project plan is opportunity efficient, and high short-term opportunity costs for the time required for a PUMP is going to remain an issue. In the longer term we need to anticipate the opportunity costs associated with all staff involved in a PUMP, and resource the PUMP accordingly. In a given context, the resources available for uncertainty management are a key consideration in the focus phase, and a core aspect of clarity efficiency.

Determine the process timing

If one of the authors' clients asks 'how long will it take to assess my project's uncertainty?', the quite truthful response 'how long is a piece of string?' will not do. A more useful response is 'how long have we got?' (the process 'when'), in conjunction with 'how much effort can be made available?' (the process 'wherewithal'), 'who wants it?' (the process 'who'), and 'what do you want it for?' (the process 'why'). The answer to this latter question often drives the process 'what' and the 'whichway'. It is important to understand the interdependence of these considerations.

Six months or more may be an appropriate duration for an initial, detailed uncertainty analysis of a major project, but six hours can be put to very effective use if the question of the time available is addressed effectively in relation to the other process Ws. Even a few minutes may prove useful for small projects, or specific decisions, as the following example illustrates.

A formal bidding process initially developed for IBM

A formal bidding process initially developed for IBM UK, now used by a number of organizations experienced in uncertainty management, involves the following steps:

1. At a very high strategic level, decide how to do the project if the bid is successful.
2. Assess the expected cost.
3. Assess the chance of winning, given a bid equal to the expected cost plus a standard mark-up, and given two or three higher or lower bids.
4. Construct a table which shows the expected profit and associated probability of winning for the different levels of bid, with notes about other relevant criteria.
5. Consider the most appropriate bid price in relation to tradeoffs between maximization of expected profit and other criteria.
6. Record the chosen bid and its associated estimate of the probability of winning, and feedback analysis of this information into step 3 the next time a bid is developed.

In the absence of a formal process, most people instinctively spend most of their time on steps 1 and 2, with too much detail and effort on these two steps. Only by articulating *all* the above steps, and spending much more time on steps 3 to 6, is the true relative importance of steps 3 to 6 revealed.

Building on this example

Experience with this process suggests that if only ten minutes are available to prepare a bid, rather than concentrate on steps 1 and 2, a more effective allocation of time would be: two minutes each on steps 1 to 3, one minute on step 4, and most of the remaining three minutes on step 5. Building on this example in more general terms, allocating time and effort to any process has to recognize that most people instinctively spend more time on what they understand, and less time on what they do not understand – a tendency that clarity efficient uncertainty management has to neutralise. *What we do not understand needs more attention, not less, if it matters. Managing uncertainty in the 'incomplete knowledge' sense is central to this, recognizing the difference between lack of information and lack of effective frameworks for thinking about what information is readily available.*

A more sophisticated version of this bidding process is developed in Chapman and Ward (2002, ch. 3), and some of the ideas are developed in Chapter 12 of this book. Fitting a PUMP to available time and other resources is central to the issue of shortcuts, further addressed later.

Whether or not process timing is predetermined by the need to make decisions by particular dates, a linked bar chart like that of Figure 4.2 can be used to plan the first pass of the iterative process, and an allowance made for further passes, as discussed in Chapter 4. The time required for the first and later passes can reflect what has to be done and the resources available to do it. The process 'when' flows from the earlier Ws if the process 'when' is not constrained. If the process 'when' is constrained, the earlier Ws will have to be constrained to make the process feasible.

Process plan fit for purpose?

The second 'fit for purpose' test, the final specific task within the focus phase as portrayed by Figure 6.1, assesses the process plan at a level of detail suitable for implementation by those directly involved. This provides a convenient place to pause and consider the uncertainty associated with the execution of the PUMP. The deliverables of the common tasks – document, verify, assess, and report – which define the process plan with respect to each previous step, need to be consolidated at this point.

A key reason for identifying this specific fit for purpose task is to provide a final go/no-go/maybe decision point in the planning of the PUMP when it is reasonably clear what the PUMP might deliver. One possibility is to move on to the identify phase of the PUMP if the define phase is complete. Another possibility is the need to carry out another pass through the plan the process part of the focus phase, further developing the deliverables of selected steps as appropriate. Stopping the project and the PUMP is a third possibility.

There are inappropriate reasons for stopping the PUMP at this point, such as more uncertainty revealed than the client wishes to see. There are also good reasons for stopping both the project and the PUMP, such as nothing can be done about the key sources of uncertainty for the time being, because they are beyond the control of the organization, and putting the project and the PUMP on hold until the way forward is clearer may save significant nugatory expenditure. 'Stop' need not imply 'abandon' – it may imply 'wind-down further effort until a more favourable outlook emerges'.

It is arguable that both the above example reasons for stopping a project at this point should have been picked up by the strategic level fit for purpose test – this one is really about occasions when 'the devil is in the detail'. However, the high-risk nature of PUMP management and the serious consequences of a 'stop the project' recommendation can mean a provisional decision earlier, confirmed now, is simply prudent process risk management.

Focus phase and define phase joint deliverables

The define phase and the focus phase have to proceed in parallel, with the first pass of both completed before starting the first pass of the identify phase. Several joint issues are worth considering now.

Criteria–plan relationship structure working assumptions

One of the key design and focus phase relationship issues is the nature and role of the criteria-plan relationship structures. As first indicated in Chapter 1, and illustrated since, to understand capital cost uncertainty, we may have to address duration uncertainty first, then uncertainty about quantities of resources needed, then uncertainty about prices for these resources. More generally, we need to clarify working assumptions about this kind of criteria–plan relationship structure before leaving the define and focus phases to start the identify phase, to ensure that those tasked with generating and approving define phase deliverables are comfortable with these working assumptions.

Hard and soft constraint working assumptions

If 'hard' constraints mean that the project must deliver specific operational safety standards or live within specific resource availability, these constraints should be identified and documented as part of the define phase for focus phase purposes. Similarly, 'soft' constraints aimed at balancing cost and duration or various quality measures also need identification and documentation as part of the define phase for focus phase purposes. Both are part of the set of working assumptions associated with the model defined by the focus phase, and those tasked with generating and approving define phase deliverables should be comfortable with these working assumptions.

Project scope assumptions as project wide working assumptions

Project scope assumptions which are project wide need clear documentation as part of the define phase documentation. Examples include 'this project will start execution on a specified date' and 'current EU rules will still be relevant'. In terms of any quantitative analysis that follows, these scope assumptions will need interpretation as 'conditions' in the evaluate phase, along with all other working assumptions treated as conditions.

Process scope assumptions

Process scope assumptions are working assumptions made in the focus phase. They also need appropriate documentation so that they are not forgotten. This includes modelling assumptions like 'we plan to assume a basic PERT structure with no modelling of responses, because shaping plans is not immediately relevant'. A suitable summary included in the define phase documentation can be useful, to ensure that everyone involved understands the implications in broad terms. The PUMP team will need a more detailed understanding of process scope assumptions, including the rational for modelling working assumption choices.

The ongoing nature of the focus phase

A first pass through the focus phase of the PUMP process may be largely concurrent with the define phase, as indicated in Figure 4.2. Updating uncertainty management plans is necessarily ongoing, with further passes initiated by a perceived need to revise the approach to reflect progress. An ongoing intermittent process of minor adjustments may be more important than distinct passes. As a particular PUMP becomes fairly stable in terms of routine updates within a particular lifecycle stage, the 'scope the process' task becomes less relevant, and more detail is required with respect to 'plan the process' issues.

Focus phase short-cuts and specific PUMPs

The spirit of the focus phase structure and the functionality of all its components need to be preserved even if very simple projects with low levels of uncertainty are the concern.

One effective way to reduce the effort involved is to make the focus process more efficient by making the PUMP more specific, pre-specifying its nature in line with prior knowledge about the nature of project issues to be considered. The bidding process example just introduced provides a useful basis for an illustration. If steps 1 and 2 (preparing a very high level strategic plan and costing that plan) are routinely undertaken for common project types, suitable specialized PUMPs can be crafted and tested statistically in relation to project outcomes. If projects that are won fall into similar groups, effective PUMPs used to manage their execution can be used to shape the focus phase for later projects, building on the positives and eliminating the negatives. All relevant experience and data can be seen as an asset to be leveraged to make future PUMPs more efficient and effective. The key caution here is that making PUMPs more specific by definition reduces their flexibility, running the risk they will be used in an inappropriate context.

Another effective way to reduce the effort involved is entrusting the focus phase aspect of PUMP processes to people with more capability for this responsibility. Selection, on-the-job education and training, mentoring and key staff retention are central issues here, further addressed in Part IV. Project opportunity efficiency ultimately depends on the quality of project staff as a team, including the PUMP team. Process clarity efficiency is part of this. Process clarity efficiency is directly dependent upon the quality of focus phase execution and the quality of the PUMP team.

Readers of this book with limited experience of PUMP processes should not anticipate being able to execute a focus phase at this stage in their progress through this book. Apart from reading the rest of this book, they may need suitable experience and mentoring.

A common catastrophic short-cut is ignoring the issues addressed by the focus phase and prescribing a bureaucratic 'one-size-fits-all' process which is both inefficient and ineffective. This undesirable scenario is often aggravated by assuming that relatively untrained staff can use the process because it is simple. Sometimes the justification for simplistic processes is the presumed need for relatively untrained staff to use them without assistance or guidance. *This usually represents a serious corporate failure to understand what is involved, and in governance terms both PUMP manager level and board level implications are important.*

If a PUMP is implemented for the first time in the E&D shaping stage of the lifecycle in the hands of experienced PUMP facilitation staff, a robust strategy developed on the first pass may evolve with minimal effort as the process proceeds through further passes. However, the identification of any serious *process* strategy failures or any serious *project* strategy failures will require a major rethink effort, and unwelcome surprises of this kind should be anticipated. There is no way to avoid such surprises, short of refusing to recognize and deal with unwelcome reality.

Conclusion

Current common practice project 'risk' management process descriptions usually employ a process initiation equivalent to the focus phase which is comparatively limited. A central limitation of common practice is often the use of a 'linear' process – a process that is not iterative by design.

Routine updates are usually recommended, but an effective means of dealing with ambiguity via an efficient multi-pass process is not part of the recommended process.

Current common practice project 'risk' management processes typically restrict the search for 'risks' to uncertain events, sometimes limited to threat or downside risk events. Terminology generally inhibits effective opportunity management, even if opportunity management is officially part of the agenda. Most emphasize a need to identify 'risks' early in each process application, leaving response identification until later, as part of a 'risk reduction' task. Possibly taking more risk to achieve opportunity is not usually on the agenda. Most use a point estimate of 'base' cost, duration and other performance measures, defining associated variability in terms of 'risks'. Most treat independence between 'risks' as a default assumption, with limited guidance about approaches to dependence.

For reasons discussed in Chapter 2, effective risk and opportunity management has to address uncertainty in a broad sense, with early consideration of all relevant sources of uncertainty, decomposing high level uncertainty composites as appropriate. As indicated in Chapter 3, a high clarity approach to the PUMP identify phase involves identifying relevant primary sources of uncertainty associated with base plans, associated relevant primary response options, relevant secondary sources of uncertainty arising from these responses, and so on as appropriate. Even a low clarity approach has to manage estimation bias in a way that reflects ambiguity about these possibilities, with a perceived level of variability reflecting the incomplete knowledge which could be acquired via a higher clarity approach as well as that which cannot be acquired with more data – completing designs, signing contracts and other sources only resolved by advancing the asset lifecycle position.

We can use project duration as an example of a performance attribute needing quantification. If the define phase decomposed the project into a dozen activities, and the focus phase suggested a minimum clarity approach, we could treat each activity as a source of uncertainty, and use a P10 and a P90 estimate to directly size all variability, ambiguity, event and associated systemic uncertainty for each activity. For each activity we could assume a uniform probability distribution, plus a simple scenario description of exclusions/scope assumptions. We could also assume 100% dependence between activities. Higher levels of clarity would involve decomposing these composite sources of uncertainty, including dependence as appropriate, into lower level uncertainty sources. This will include primary sources associated with specific causes for delay, associated response options, and secondary sources and response options. In no circumstances would the PUMP result in PIGs or unstructured risk registers along common practice lines, because this would be a clarity inefficient choice.

For those with significant practical experience of current common practice approaches, the very different nature of the PUMP approach needs to be borne in mind when beginning each of the following Part II chapters. We are starting in a different place, with a very different destination.

Chapter 7

Identify *all* the relevant sources of uncertainty, response options and conditions

Zaphod . . . put on the sunglasses . . . They were a double pair of Joo Janta 200 Super Chromatic Peril Sensitive Sunglasses, which had been specially designed to help people develop a relaxed attitude to danger. At the first hint of trouble they turn totally black and thus prevent you from seeing anything that might harm you.
—D. Adams, *The Restaurant at the End of the Universe*.

Most common practice approaches to project 'risk' management emphasize a need to identify 'risks' early in each linear process application, leaving response identification until later, as part of a 'risk reduction' task. Uncertainty identification beyond events is not addressed. Identification of assumptions to be treated as conditions is not part of the process, because unbiased estimation is not a formal goal. Risk management has limited goals – risk reduction in terms of stopping bad things happening is the primary motive. In our terms this involves using an event uncertainty management process (EUMP) which is not a suitable starting place for understanding PUMPs.

The PUMP approach addresses the identification of relevant sources of uncertainty and response options in a closely coupled manner – in part because unidentified responses are a source of ambiguity uncertainty. Effects or consequences viewed in qualitative terms are part of the glue between sources and responses. For example, some sources involve potential consequences that demand an effective reactive response, but others demand an effective preventative response, and some need both. All relevant assumptions treated as conditions are also treated in a closely coupled manner – in part because they are sources of uncertainty if the associated assumption may not hold exactly, but their nature is somewhat different, and they are approached differently.

A highly iterative process is used. This process initially addresses uncertainty identification in terms of decomposition of overall performance uncertainty to the extent this is useful, within a framework prepared in the define and focus phases. The most useful decomposition structure will depend upon the process objectives. The criteria–plan relationship structure is usually very important, because we are usually interested in more than one objective, and their relationships heavily influence the choices we can make.

Our key overall process objective is usually shaping relevant base plans and contingency plans. This usually means responses are important. Unbiased performance estimates are also usually important. This requires careful attention to ensuring that all relevant uncertainty is considered, including assumptions to be used as conditions later in the process.

In part this very different view of an 'identify' phase flows from a starting position which takes a top-down view of uncertainty related to each performance objective using relevant plans. In part it flows from viewing uncertainty as a composite embracing inherent variability, ambiguity and systemic uncertainty as well as event uncertainty in an integrated manner. In part it flows from integrating top-down and bottom-up perspectives in an iterative framework. In part it also flows from clarifying the terminology of risk, opportunity and uncertainty.

In the identify phase we have to start by addressing the question 'what is the *current* key criteria–plan relationship structure, and where do we need to start within this structure – which performance objectives are most important in the *current* stage of the project lifecycle at the *current* stage of the PUMP, how are associated criteria related to plans we want to manage, and which criterion related to which portion of which plan is an appropriate place to begin?' The identify phase has to use the project objectives and directly linked project plans aspect of the project's seven Ws, plus the process objectives, to structure the sources of uncertainty and responses of immediate interest and to choose a useful place to start. As analysis progresses, other criteria and the rest of the project plans embraced by the seven Ws plus the remaining lifecycle stages will be used to structure all relevant uncertainty. The identification of responses and clarification of assumptions is a closely coupled follow-on within the initial uncertainty about achievement of objectives structure. Understanding complementary use of KUMPs and systemic corporate weaknesses can be important as the identify phase progresses.

As noted in Part I, it is convenient to simplify relevant 'identified sources of uncertainty' to just 'sources' and relevant 'identified response options' to just 'responses' when the meaning is clear, especially in this chapter. 'Conditions' that are relevant are by definition assumptions that we do not plan to treat directly in quantitative terms.

As also noted in Part I, it is important to remember that sources and responses that have not been identified are embedded in higher order composites as part of their ambiguity uncertainty, along with unidentified conditions.

The identify phase involves two specific tasks to address these 'sources', 'responses' and 'conditions', used in a closely coupled manner:

1. *'Search* – Search for all relevant sources, responses and conditions, employing a range of techniques.
2. *Classify* – Classify all relevant sources, responses and conditions to provide a suitable structure, aggregating and disaggregating particular sources, responses and conditions as appropriate.

The key deliverable is a clear, common understanding of *all the relevant sources of uncertainty* facing the project, and *what can be done about them to the extent this is relevant*, explained *at an appropriate level of clarity*.

Opportunities usually need to be identified and managed with the same resolve as threats as part of the same process. Sometimes opportunities and threats are closely coupled, but this need not be the case. Often a PUMP is particularly successful because the process of generating and reviewing responses to threats leads to the identification of important opportunities with implications well beyond the uncertainty that led to their initial identification. The generation of response options ought to involve a systematic facilitation of creativity. The focus phase should be designed to facilitate this kind of creativity, and the identify phase is central to its operation.

The identify phase can be treated as an iterative, six-step process, with each step involving both search and classify tasks, as portrayed by Figure 7.1.

- Step 1 is 'clarify immediate priorities'. On a first pass this involves identifying the current key criteria–plan structure and identifying where to start within this structure. Initially this

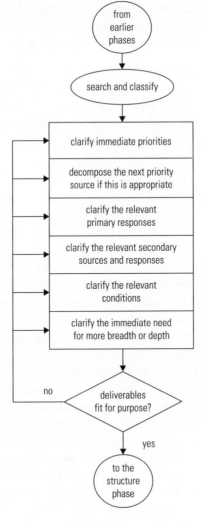

Figure 7.1   Identify phase specific tasks

means working with high level uncertainty composites identified in the define phase. On later passes step 1 involves working at a lower level of decomposition as a more detailed structure evolves. Elements of a top-down approach persist throughout the PUMP, although the structure emerging at the end can be interpreted as a bottom-up analysis.

- Step 2, 'decompose the next priority source if this is appropriate', begins clarification of the nature of the source of uncertainty identified at the top of the list identified in step 1 in terms of underlying 'primary' sources of uncertainty which are worth separate identification – 'primary' implying initiating sources of uncertainty associated with the current base plan.
- Step 3, 'clarify the relevant primary responses', considers any relevant pre-emptive or reactive responses to primary sources of uncertainty.
- Step 4 considers any relevant associated secondary sources and response options.
- Step 5 considers any relevant conditions.
- Step 6 elaborates on the process used in step 1 by exploring priorities that might be addressed in further iterations, including the possible deeper understanding of a particular source and associated responses or conditions, next moving on to other sources, then moving on to other relevant criteria and plans and lifecycle stages, and finally moving on to the structure phase.

A 'deliverables fit for purpose?' iteration control task uses the step 6 analysis to initiate loops back to earlier steps within this phase as necessary, eventually moving on to the next phase.

As with Figures 5.1 and 6.1, the Figure 7.1 portrayal of the identify phase is deliberately simplified, to illustrate the spirit of what is involved, providing a useful target that can help to maintain focus and order.

Clarify immediate priorities

'Clarify immediate priorities' is a particularly crucial first step on the first pass. It shapes the whole analysis to follow. It has strong links to the earlier define and focus phases. It has to use an understanding of the criteria–plan relationship structure to select the initial criterion and plan of interest. It has to begin by considering all relevant objectives for the lifecycle stage of interest, and identify the key criteria. It then has to address the plans most directly linked to this key criterion. Finally, it has to identify what seems to be the biggest source of uncertainty within this basic starting position structure, and consider whether or not its decomposition is desirable.

In the E&D shaping stage of the project lifecycle, an appropriate criteria–plan relationship structure for a high clarity approach usually involves project duration as primary criterion, defined in terms of activity durations, but other starting position frameworks are possible. To explain the highly context specific thinking required, we begin by considering a very specific analysis example – a BP SCERT process manager starting his first analysis of an offshore North Sea project, building on the BP offshore project discussion at the beginning of the Chapter 5. This context provides a convenient basis for an initial explanation of all the steps in the identify phase. A more general view of the first step and its implications will be considered later.

As discussed earlier, when implementing the BP version of SCERT for the first time, the initial focus was project duration (the 'when') considering the 'plans for activities' aspect of the 'which-way', and the 'resource plans for activities' aspect of the 'wherewithal' (in Figure 1.2), to achieve and demonstrate minimum expected cost shaping of the project at the E&D shaping stage of the project lifecycle. Project cost was driven by project duration to a degree that made duration the primary criterion for initial analysis. The initial define phase effort in effect concentrated on the 'activity plans' aspect of the seven Ws as a result – the other Ws were not of immediate interest. About 20 key activities were distinguished, with summary descriptions of each activity as indicated in Chapter 5. In effect the durations of these 20 activities were the 20 basic sources of uncertainty needing initial attention as identified in the define phase.

Early in the discussion of uncertainty levels in each of these key activities, it became obvious that 'pipe laying' was a good activity to start with in the identify phase. The scale and complexity of the uncertainty involved in pipe laying stood out. It was one of the biggest sources of uncertainty. This uncertainty was difficult to understand because of the complex weather window effects, and some weather data that might be useful was available. The joint effect of all these factors suggested that it was probably worth decomposing this source first.

A more intuitive prioritization might be appropriate in some contexts, but a judgement based on current understanding is important.

Decompose the next priority source if this is appropriate

To decompose a source of uncertainty like 'the duration of the Magnus project pipe-laying activity', we need to understand what this activity involves. An illustrative summary description follows. The details given here are a fictional composite of several offshore North Sea projects to illustrate what was involved without revealing any information specific to the BP Magnus project or any other particular project.

The planned pipeline length was 220 km, which might change marginally after a detailed survey of the ocean floor along the proposed route. The pipe was an 18-inch diameter steel pipe with a 6-inch concrete jacket for protection and for slight negative buoyancy when full of air during pipe laying. The pipe-laying barge would carry a stock of pipe sections. After each new section was welded to the pipeline, more of the pipeline would be lowered over the back of the barge in a smooth 's' shape down to the ocean floor, taking up tension on a fan-shaped set of leading anchors. As each anchor line became too short, it would be picked up by a tugboat and reset farther ahead.

The assumed barge would have 1.6 m wave height capability. Given suitable weather and no major problems, this barge could average about 3 km of pipe laying per day. The favourable weather summer season was about 4 months, with a 2–3-month shoulder season either side. Shoulder season operation was feasible, but of increasingly marginal value for cost reasons near the winter season. Viewing 'pipe-laying duration uncertainty' at activity level as a single composite source of uncertainty, a direct estimate was made as a basis for discussing the need to start analysis with this activity. Current knowledge suggested that one season was feasible, with a chance of completing in one season of the order of 90%. The chance of three seasons or more was of the order of 1%, with an implied chance of two seasons of the order of 9%.

A major component of the 'estimated capital cost' generated by this activity was the estimated time to lay the pipe times the cost rate for the barge per unit time. There was one cost rate for 'lay days' (when laying pipe) and another for 'weather days' (when the operator was committed to the BP contract and had planned to lay pipe but was prevented from doing so by bad weather).

Both these rates were uncertain prior to contracting. Another major component of the estimated capital cost generated by this activity was the cost of pipe, defined by an uncertain amount of pipe and an uncertain cost per unit of length. The initial interest was activity duration, but understanding duration at a detailed level would later help with all cost issues.

In this example 'pipe-laying duration uncertainty' is a high level composite of variability uncertainty. Decomposing this high level source began with 'weather'. It was obvious that the weather was a key source of uncertainty for pipe laying, and best treated as a separately modelled source of variability uncertainty. Weather data was available on a sea area and month basis. It indicated the number of days per month the average wave height had exceeded specified levels for the past 20 years. This provided a good objective statistical basis for uncertainty quantification, although a lay barge does not stop as soon as waves rise to its nominal wave height capability and start again as soon as waves go below this level. If bad weather for several days is forecast, the lay barge operator puts a cap on the pipeline end and lowers it to the sea bed before the waves build too much, and picks the pipeline up again after the waves have died down, because picking up and putting down the pipeline is a high risk operation prone to 'buckles', as discussed shortly. This weather data could be used to start quantitative modelling by looking at the effect of weather given no other sources of uncertainty using a month-by-month semi-Markov process model. The basic input specification was a series of 'transition' probability distributions, defining uncertainty associated with how much pipe could be laid each month – March, April, May, and so on, sometimes referred to as 'progress' distributions. Successively adding these 'transition' or 'progress' distributions produced 'state' distributions, defining how much pipe would be laid by the end of March, the end of April, the end of May, and so on, in probability distribution terms, sometimes referred to as 'achievement' distributions. An activity completion date distribution was derived from the probability that the required 220 km would be laid by the end of August, September, October, and so on. This semi-Markov process structure was anticipated in the focus and define phases, but deciding whether or not it is appropriate is an activity-by-activity choice, usefully seen as part of this step.

Uncertainty about how long it would take to lay the required 220 km was quantified in a simple and direct manner during the top-down uncertainty appreciation step of the focus phase, the basis of the 90% chance of one season noted above. Decomposition using a semi-Markov process was identified as potentially useful at that point because it could help to clarify the weather window issue. It was also useful because it allowed consideration of responses on a month by month basis, with some sources of uncertainty requiring immediate reactive responses, and some requiring preplanning of various kinds.

Uncertainty about how much pipe could be laid in March might have been treated as a single composite source of uncertainty with comparable treatment for all other months. However, there was obvious value in identifying 'weather' as a source of uncertainty worth separation. First, effective use could be made of available data to estimate the number of 'lay days' likely each month. Second, barges with levels of capability other than the assumed 1.6 m could be modelled, a more capable 3-m barge for example, clarifying the impact of this kind of pre-emptive response to weather. Third, separation of this and other sources would help to clarify the role of both pre-emptive and reactive response options that were specific to particular sources as well as general responses dealing with sets of sources.

The next source of uncertainty associated with each month's progress which seemed worth separation and quantification was 'buckles' – a kink in the pipeline – which could occur as it is laid, or when the pipeline is put down because the weather is about to get very bad, or as the pipeline is picked up again to carry on when the weather gets better, or while the barge is just hanging on to the pipeline for several possible reasons, like an anticipated very brief period of moderately bad weather.

When 'buckles' were first discussed, it soon became clear there were two very different kinds of buckles which needed clear distinction: 'dry' buckles, and 'wet' buckles.

'Dry' buckles involve no water getting into the pipeline. The lay barge can back-up, pulling the damaged pipe back on board, cut it off, and then proceed. Very little pipe or time is lost. 'Dry buckles' were listed as one example of 'productivity variations', reasons why some days the barge might lay 4 km, other days 2 km, but average 3 km.

'Wet' buckles involve water rushing into the pipeline. The pipeline rapidly becomes too heavy for the barge to hold. It is released quickly, or it tears itself off the barge, sinks to the ocean floor, and fills with water and debris. Wet buckles were a major threat, a source of event uncertainty involving significant potential pipe and time losses.

'Productivity variations' were by definition all the sources of uncertainty not worth detailed identification or discussion – a residual worth quantitative sizing and understanding in top-down terms, but not worth bottom-up decomposition although examples of what this includes are helpful to reduce ambiguity for quantitative sizing and interpretation purposes.

'Productivity variations' is an example of a source of uncertainty treated as a residual composite of only partially identified variability uncertainty *despite* detailed identification and decomposition of other sources. In this case, 'productivity variations' was not worth quantitative decomposition because they could be left to a lay barge operator to deal with without worrying about specific sources or specific responses the operator might use or specific secondary sources.

Further sources deemed worth separate identification at this stage in the process included the lay barge not being available at the contracted date; the lay barge not operating at the expected rate, given no other specific problems; major equipment failures, and so on. In some cases later quantitative analysis was anticipated. In other cases later quantitative treatment was not anticipated, the goal being clarity with respect to scope assumptions and other conditions framing the quantitative analysis.

About 40 sources were identified for this high clarity assessment of a highly uncertainty activity. With hindsight it became clear that the 40 sources identified were at the upper end of a plausible range for effective clarity development. Even a high clarity assessment is usually in the range 10–20 sources plus a 'productivity variations' equivalent, if 20 activities or the equivalent seven Ws components are involved. The range 2–10 separate sources might be effective for a moderate clarity level, with or without modelling a sequence of time periods. The minimum clarity level involves only one source, zero decomposition, sticking to the starting position produced by the define phase.

A PERT special case is clearly too simplistic for offshore pipe laying. In a BCS context a PERT project duration model is too complex – a spreadsheet equivalent with just plausible minimum and maximum activity durations will suffice, *provided* conditions like 'the time estimate to lay a new floor covering assumes that removing the old floor covering does not reveal that the floor is rotten' are agreed in generic terms. Appropriate simplicity – clarity efficiency – is a subtle concept.

A high clarity study of a project might involve some activities needing a medium level of clarity and some activities needing only a minimum level of clarity.

At any level of clarity above the minimum, searching for sources of uncertainty to separate out is usefully addressed in terms of 'wet buckle equivalents' and 'dry buckle equivalents'. That is, before adding a newly identified source to a list of separate sources for an activity, ask the question: 'Is this source like a wet buckle, usefully treated separately, or would treatment like a dry buckle as part of a "productivity variations" equivalent be more appropriate?'

Technical sources of the kind illustrated by the 'weather' and 'buckle' examples are useful for illustrative purposes throughout this book, because they are reasonably unambiguous and easy to understand. Market-related sources and institutional sources may be just as important in practice (Miller and Lessard, 2001). Some technical sources may be much more difficult to deal with (Klein and Cork, 1998), but the same principles apply.

Clarify the relevant primary responses

'Clarify the relevant primary responses' involves searching for and classifying relevant primary responses for each separate source identified in step 2. A qualitative understanding of the effects or consequences of possible outcomes associated with a source is a key component of these judgements. 'Major' or 'minor' qualitative assessments were used for early SCERT analysis focused on threat events, in the spirit of PIG assessments, but more subtle informal assessments recognising systemic and ambiguity uncertainty as well as variability at a composite level are preferable. Documenting what is involved is part of this, as in step 2, building on define phase documentation. Verifying, assessing and reporting at suitable intervals are also part of this.

Often the identification of a possible response to a particular source is a simple task. Once a source has been identified it is frequently obvious how one could respond. However, the most easily identified possible response may not be the most opportunity efficient response to this source, and other response options may be worth identifying and considering because they are potential general responses. Where a source is particularly significant, a systematic examination of a range of possible response options, perhaps with a view to applying several responses in parallel, may be worth while. Further, sometimes relatively minor sources involve general responses of significance. For example, 'pipe coating' was deemed a relatively low uncertainty activity with a one shift operation the standard norm. However, semi-Markov modelling of the inventory of coated pipe available for laying over multiple time periods – bearing in mind the possibility of exceptional pipe-laying progress in very good weather, possibly in conjunction with pipe supply delays – made it clear that a contractual option for second and third shift pipe-coating operation was worth the additional up-front cost.

Eleven generic types of response option can be identified in the literature. They are listed in Table 7.1. The authors' recommended interpretation of methods of handling them are indicated, generalising the common focus on event uncertainty to embrace variability, ambiguity and systemic uncertainty as well as event uncertainty. The rationale for identifying these different response types in Table 7.1 is to provide a checklist of places to start when thinking about response options, 'triggers' for a response generation process.

In the framework used here these 11 generic response types are not mutually exclusive. For example, 'influence probability' associated with outcomes may be the same as 'modify consequences', because uncertainty is not limited to event uncertainty defined as 'risks'. As another

Table 7.1   Generic response types

Type of response	Method of handling uncertainty
Modify objectives	Reduce or raise performance targets expressed as constraints, changing tradeoffs between multiple objectives
Avoid	Plan to avoid specified sources of uncertainty
Influence probability	Change the probability of potential variations
Modify consequences	Modify the possible consequences of variations
Transfer consequences	Transfer consequences to another party via contract provisions or insurance
Develop contingency plans	Set aside resources or make other plans to provide a reactive ability to cope
Keep options open	Delay choices and commitments, choosing versatile options
Monitor	Collect and update data about all sources of uncertainty
Accept	Acknowledge and accept uncertainty, doing nothing about it
Remain unaware	Ignore uncertainty, taking no action to identify or manage it
Optimize all the above	Explicitly recognise the value of selecting an optimal combination

example, when 'develop contingency plans' lead to general responses like a second or third shift in a pipe-coating operation, a contract with the coating facility to allow low cost use of second and third shifts is a form of 'keep options open', which facilitates greater use of 'monitor' and 'accept' responses to a wide range of sources with only specific responses. The checklist function of Table 7.1 response types is useful, but it is important to appreciate that there may be multiple routes from the 'triggers' in column one to the methods of handling uncertainty in column two.

'Modify objectives' is a key response option. For example, as a proactive response, the time allowed to complete a task may be extended before a contract for the work is given because an assessment of the base plan shows that the initial target would be virtually impossible to meet. As a reactive response, selected performance targets may be relaxed by varying amounts during the E&D shaping stages of the project lifecycle, if difficulties in meeting original targets become insuperable or the value of achieving the original targets is reassessed, making appropriate trade-offs between objectives in the process. Setting different levels of cost, time or quality objectives can have varying effects on the achievement of other objectives. These effects depend on a variety of situational factors, not least of which are the nature of the project and the behaviour of the contractors and professionals employed. For example, good quality building work is fostered by allowing contractors time to analyse and properly price what is required, and to conduct the work without excessive haste and paring of costs. In setting goals for attainment on each project objective, tradeoffs must be made between levels of attainment on each objective. Unfortunately, deciding tradeoffs is often complicated by uncertainty about the nature of the interdependencies between the different performance objectives. Thus, a decrease in the time available to complete a project can cause an increase in total project cost, but it may cause a decrease. Similarly, improvements in quality can mean an increase or a decrease in project time associated with an increase or a decrease in project cost.

In the face of these difficulties, a pragmatic approach which is not opportunity efficient is common. Tradeoffs may be expressed simply in terms of one objective having clear priority over another. Alternatively, project objectives are often expressed in terms of satisfying target levels of achievement which are assumed to be mutually compatible. This typically results in a series of ad hoc tradeoffs being made through the life of the project which may be a long way from overall optimality in the opportunity efficiency sense. For example, in a construction project, the client's representative on the building site might accept work of lower performance than specified in the contract where specifications appear excessively tight, in exchange for work of higher performance in other areas, to attempt to secure an overall balance in the terms of exchange. However, the success or failure of this approach may depend upon the compatibility of the personalities of those involved.

'Avoid', the second response type in Table 7.1, is often a feasible and desirable response to uncertainty. However, uncertainty management strategies formulated as avoidance options in practice may operate only as 'influence probability' or 'modify consequences' options. This may still be useful, but the residual uncertainty should be recognized. For example, in a multi-party context transferring uncertainty to another party may be perceived by the transferring party to be an obvious and natural way of avoiding one or more sources of uncertainty. However, uncertainty may not be eliminated for the transferor unless the party receiving the uncertainty adopts appropriate uncertainty management strategies, and the consequences may include secondary sources that fall on the transferor. This is a particularly significant issue in contractual relationships, often with profound implications for project performance. This issue is examined in more detail in Chapter 9.

'Influence probability' is a third generic type of response option. This is a very common starting place when looking for responses. It typically has the intention of reducing the probability of unfavourable (adverse or threat) events occurring. Viewing uncertainty management as opportunity management also involves increasing the probability of favourable (desirable or opportunity) events occurring. In terms of sources of uncertainty more generally, this response involves changing the probability of the various potential outcomes in a favourable manner, often a useful trigger for response generation, even if composites dominated by inherent variability, ambiguity and systemic uncertainty are the concern.

'Modify consequences' can imply a focus on modifying the potential consequences of a realized event on project performance. It certainly includes reducing unfavourable impacts – for example reducing delays likely to be caused should a particular event occur. However, modification may also involve modifying potential consequences by changing their nature, perhaps by transforming an impact on one performance criterion into an impact on another criterion. For example, if an event occurs which will delay the project, it may be possible to counter this by paying for overtime work or other additional resources, like an additional shift in the pipe coating yard. Further, the consequences of inherent variability sources like weather or ambiguity uncertainty like that inherent in a basic PERT model can also start from a search for responses of this type.

'Transfer consequences' is usefully identified as a starting place when transferring financial and managerial responsibility to a contractor or transferring financial implications in part to an insurer is practical. This can leave important residual implications, and generate new sources.

'Develop contingency plans' is a sixth type of response option which can be seen as a starting place. This involves consciously accepting uncertainty but setting aside resources to provide a reactive capability to cope with unfavourable impacts if they eventuate, or looking for other comparable fall-back options. The project manager may set aside a contingency reserve of physical resources, finance or time in case of need. Uncertainty analysis may be useful to determine the appropriate level of contingency provision, like the target and minimum stock of coated pipe in an offshore pipe-laying project, or the appropriate 'management reserve' when giving a project manager a budget that should not include provisions better held at board level or by a customer.

'Keep options open' involves deliberately delaying decisions, limiting early commitments, or actively searching out versatile project strategies that will perform acceptably under a variety of possible future conditions. Supporting this seventh approach via general responses that build in robustness can be crucial.

'Monitor', an eighth type of response, implies a willingness to undertake more active uncertainty management at some point, but the criteria for active management intervention may not be clearly articulated. Delaying uncertainty management is always an option. Uncertainty may decrease (or increase), associated opportunity and risk may change, and the need for real-time problem solving may increase or decrease. Adopting this response ought to involve conscious assessment of the likely costs and benefits of delaying more active responses.

'Accept', with recognition of the risk exposure, but with no further action to manage or monitor associated uncertainty, is a ninth type of response.

'Remain unaware' the uncertainty exists and that something might be done about it is the tenth option – a default option if none of the above options in Table 7.1 is pursued. This makes it a response option in an important practical sense. It is a sensible option in cases where threats and opportunities can be dealt with effectively and efficiently as and when they arise. It has obvious dangers in other cases.

'Optimize all the above' is identified by Hopkinson (2011) as a key component of his top level of maturity, using the risk efficiency concepts in Chapman and Ward (2003). Generalizing this to an opportunity efficient approach is a basic premise of this book. Maturity models including Hopkinson's are discussed later, in Chapter 14.

The scope for complex source-response management is considerable. Robust simple approaches are needed most of the time, but before considering simplification it is useful to explore high clarity approaches developed directly by an effective formal PUMP, illustrating high clarity use of Table 7.1. As an example, consider the potential occurrence of a pipeline 'wet buckle' as described earlier.

One kind of response is purely reactive in an after-the-fact sense using readily available resources: the buckled pipeline can be repaired. This involves sending down divers to cut off the damaged sections and put a cap on the pipeline containing valves. A 'pig', a torpedo-like metal cylinder, is then sent through the pipeline under air pressure from the other end, to 'dewater' the pipeline. The pipeline can then be picked up and pipe laying recommenced.

A second kind of response involves proactive and preventive action up-front which reduces the chance of the source being realized: a more capable lay barge could reduce the probability of a buckle occurring, capability for this purpose being maximum wave height conditions for safe working. This response is also a proactive mitigating response, because a buckle repair can be completed more quickly in the face of bad weather with a more capable barge.

A third kind of response is also after-the-fact, but requires essential prior actions: the buckled pipeline can be abandoned, and a new pipeline started. If the buckle occurs before very much pipe has been laid, and sufficient additional spare pipe has been ordered in advance, this is an opportunity efficient solution because of the time saved. This kind of response is an example of a proactive/reactive combination.

Some responses have important implications for other responses, other sources, or the base plan, all of which need to be identified. For example, a more capable barge reduces the chances of a buckle, and it also allows faster repair of buckles, as noted earlier. A more capable barge also allows faster pipe laying, especially in the face of bad weather, with an impact on base plan performance.

Simply accepting the possibility of a buckle, in the sense of living with it with no direct responses, was not an option. However, oil majors operating in the North Sea in the 1980s often transferred some of the risk associated with buckles to their contractors, via fixed price contracts for a complete pipeline. This did not transfer all the uncertainty, as contractors could not bear the consequential costs or lost revenues associated with delaying the start of oil or gas production. Insurance for such risks was considered, but generally deemed inappropriate.

Designing out the possibility of a buckle, by using flexible pipe and reel barges, was not to our knowledge explicitly identified as a response to 'buckles' in the early days of North Sea pipe laying, but it was considered later. Designing out important sources of risk inefficiency and capturing key sources of opportunity efficiency is an important response.

Now consider another example, where more intuitive PUMPs developed over many years have led to clarity about uncertainty of considerable complexity although the large numbers of people dealing with it use simple 'belt and braces' rules of thumb.

Spending August sailing a small yacht from Southampton to Falmouth in Cornwall and back, along the south coast of England, is Chris Chapman's idea of an enjoyable summer holiday project. Bad weather is the central source of uncertainty. Bad weather can be designed out only by staying at home. Monitoring, keeping options open, and modifying objectives when appropriate, are the basic response strategies.

The trip each way is planned to take a week to ten days, with four or five stops on the way, sailing in daylight. The most desirable stops are anchorages in sheltered bays, which are usable only in certain wind conditions. A buoy in a quiet river is the next preference, a marina a poor third, unless water or fuel is required. Stopovers are for walks, pub meals, and visits to historic houses, gardens and other places of interest. Staying in port is a basic response to a poor weather forecast if a secure 'port' has been chosen. Avoiding planning long passages without alternative ports if the weather is potentially bad is an important variant of this response. If the forecast is bad for a week, going anyway may become almost inevitable as priorities change, but leaving the boat and taking a train home has been used. Once underway, responses include shortening sail (reefing or, in extremes, changing to a storm jib and/or tri-sail), putting on life-lines, and securing the main hatch. The basic objective is enjoyment while on passage, but extensive delays can make getting there more of a priority, and the ultimate priority is the safety of the boat and crew. Sometimes carrying on to the planned destination has to be replaced by heading for the nearest port in a storm, and in extremes that option may have to be abandoned in favour of making sea room.

Many new strategic information system projects for competitive advantage share most of the above characteristics, as do a wide range of other projects, even if having fun is not the basic intent, and ending up dead in the water is not a potential outcome in a literal sense.

Most experienced sailors, and most experienced managers in other contexts where the basis of uncertainty management is monitoring, keeping options open and modifying objectives when appropriate, can recount tales of when it all went wrong, with disastrous or near-disastrous consequences. Yachting magazines carry regular features in this vein, which make educational as well as interesting reading. Corporate disaster stories also receive such attention (for example,

Lam, 1999). Common features are a series of largely unpredicted events whose significance was not recognized, coming together at a time when options were reduced for predictable reasons, and there was a failure to take early enough radical action based on a change of objectives.

In a formal PUMP process centred on monitoring, keeping options open, and modifying objectives when appropriate, a further characteristic of actual or near disasters is a presumed set of primary responses that don't work. For example, on a sailing trip the radio needed for a 'mayday' distress call may not work because the mast carrying the aerial has fallen down, and the emergency aerial, perhaps tested when new, has been stored for many years in a way that has led to its failure. The traditional notion of 'a well found ship' addresses such issues.

In a first pass through the identify phase at least one appropriate response should be identified for each relevant primary source, if only because the consequences of a source cannot be considered without some assumed response. This initial response may be simply 'accept the uncertainty' or 'figure out what to do at the time', but such a response may not be feasible, and a more proactive response may need to be identified. For example, when a wet buckle occurs in an offshore pipe-laying context there is a range of things that can be done, but just accepting the exposure to possible wet buckles is not one of them, and waiting until they happen before deciding what to do would be very unwise. On a first iteration, one response per identified source may be enough, especially for those sources that are clearly unlikely to prove significant. Later iterations can add additional responses for sources of importance. Very important sources may warrant careful consideration of possible options under each type of response in Table 7.1.

Sometimes it is particularly important to stress, and extensively develop, the primary response part of the identify phase as early as possible in the very first pass. One reason is to address low project team morale. Looking for problems can be very depressing when a project which is your sole source of income is already looking decidedly risky. Encouraging the project team to look for responses to each problem before going on to the next can be a vital aspect of success.

Another reason to stress early primary response development arises where a project is based on a design which is so tentative that a major source is best dealt with by redesign.

A third reason arises where a project's objectives are receptive to the response 'if at first it doesn't look like you will succeed, redefine success'. Software projects with a shopping list of deliverables ranging from 'must have' to 'nice to have' are obvious examples, but not so obvious possibilities may be worth consideration in these terms.

In general it is useful to see this early qualitative understanding of consequences and associated response development as part of the process of searching for options with a view to risk and opportunity efficiency which needs to go beyond simple threat management.

Whether or not early primary response development is stressed for the kinds of reasons just cited, it is very important to see responses in terms of all seven Ws and the whole lifecycle as part of a process concerned with maximizing flexibility and enabling appropriate monitoring.

Clarify the relevant secondary sources and responses

'Clarify the relevant secondary sources and responses' involves identifying secondary sources and responses and documenting what is involved where this is worth while in clarity efficiency terms. The extent to which it is worth identifying and documenting secondary sources and responses, including any relevant tertiary and further higher order levels of sources and responses, is very much a matter of judgement, necessarily dependent on a variety of issues. Once again, the key lies in keeping the analysis as simple as possible without overlooking any important issues. Further consideration of wet buckles illustrates this point.

If 'repair' becomes the primary response to a pipe buckle, an important secondary source involves the 'pig' that is sent through the pipe to dewater it, as it may run over a boulder or other debris in the pipe and become stuck. Pig technology is now well developed to clean and inspect pipelines, and modern 'pigs' have closed circuit TV and computers on board, but with or without this kind of technology, a 'stuck pig' is a serious problem. Despite the chuckles it may evoke, it illustrates a secondary source of uncertainty that needs careful attention.

One secondary response is to send down divers, cut off the pipe behind the pig, put a cap on the shortened pipeline, and try again with another pig. This response involves the loss of pipe and time. Another secondary response is to increase the air pressure, hoping to pop the pig through, with the tertiary source that the pipeline may fail to withstand the additional pressure some considerable distance from the stuck pig, resulting in the loss of even more pipe and even more delay.

These two secondary responses to a stuck pig were identified as the only options – both are unattractive, but there was nowhere else to go. It was very important to identify these secondary and tertiary source-response chains, for several reasons.

First, it clearly made sense to assess, well in advance, how far the air pressure should be turned up in the event of a stuck pig. This was not a decision that should be left to a lay barge operator in the midst of a crisis. The decision required the expertise of pipeline designers and pipeline manufacturers, who would understand the safety margins in their design and production, and were best placed to judge the probability of damage and the extent of that damage as the pressure increases. It also required the expertise of those members of the project team who understood the cost implications of delay to the pipe laying, including opportunity costs.

Second, once it was clear that the primary response 'repair' involved considerable scope for loss of pipe, and that additional pipe would have to be ordered if a repair strategy is adopted, 'abandon and start again' began to look a much more attractive option, and fast supply of extra pipe became a key issue.

Third, once it became clear that ordering extra pipe to cope with possible buckles was an issue, what to do with extra pipe if it was not needed became an issue. This triggered consideration of standardising pipeline designs, so that unused spare pipe from one project might be used on other projects. Discussing this thinking with Statoil contributed, at least in part, to their later decision to standardize wherever possible on all aspects of offshore platforms, with substantial overall cost savings.

A key issue illustrated by this example is the insight provided by the identification process. Insight and understanding is what motivates and drives a creative option generation process concerned with opportunity efficiency.

Sometimes it is useful to look at primary source–response–secondary source and response chains within each source, on a chain basis. However, there is also some merit in taking the steps in order for each activity or a larger subset of the project as a whole. We need to be systematic but flexible, adapting to the context, including considerations like availability and convenience for those people involved.

Problems with stuck pigs illustrate secondary sources associated with reactive responses which require proactive thinking and possible proactive responses. Pre-emptive responses can also involve secondary sources needing careful attention. For example, clients often like the response 'transfer the source to a contractor'. But contractors can go broke, and contractors who anticipate expensive transfers can bid as part of a consortium special venture vehicle formed with this exit strategy in mind.

Clarify the relevant conditions

'Clarify the relevant conditions' as an explicit step in the identify phase is new to this edition. Its functions used to be addressed as part of the quantify phase and other phases. We now argue that its role is better understood and executed if a focus is provided at this point in the process. The primary purpose of this step is ensuring that all relevant conditions have been identified and clarified in the sense that all relevant people understand them.

Earlier in this chapter we noted that qualitative treatment as conditions is often anticipated for some identified responses. This step implies 'flagging' (noting in some suitable manner) this intended treatment, confirming or changing this treatment in the quantify phase. If this was all that was involved, a separate step would be a matter of detail of very limited importance. A note about flagging in the sections dealing with identifying sources would suffice. However, there are other concerns to be addressed.

This step can usefully start in the define phase, by documenting *project* scope assumptions applying to the whole project which will be treated as conditions in the anticipated quantification of *some* uncertainty. Any working assumption that may not hold precisely is a source of uncertainty. Project scope assumptions that may not hold, and are treated as conditions, are extremely problematic if everyone involved is not clear about how these assumptions are being treated. In a BP context this was not seen as a central issue, but it was for the Highways Agency example discussed in Chapter 2, and it is now clear that it needs systematic attention in the checking mode as part of the identify phase in any context. For example, in the Highways Agency case 'inflation' was a source of uncertainty passed on to the government unless the Highways Agency signed a contract placing it with a contractor, and unanticipated changes in EU safety regulations was a source passed by each project to the portfolio level management of uncertainty within the Highways agency. All relevant people needed to understand this.

This step can continue in the focus phase, by documenting *process* scope assumptions that could be treated as conditions in the anticipated quantification of some uncertainty which may have wider implications. As an illustrative example, the nominal lifecycle framework used in the PUMP approach assumes that strategy will be approved at the end of the strategy shaping stages before tactical planning for implementation purposes begins. This is a key process assumption. It means that any areas of strategic planning which involve approaches that might prove non-feasible in a way that puts the whole strategy at risk need flagging at this point. The responses may involve detailed planning or design on a selective basis. They may involve proto-types built and tested. They may involve restructuring the whole project – so that all the difficult or problematic aspects have a demonstrated satisfactory approach before the main project goes any further. But direct quantification of associated uncertainty is not a plausible option. In this sense looking for 'risky conditions' which are potential 'show stoppers' missed earlier ought to be a key part of this step. 'Missed earlier' can include ownership phase choices made on earlier passes, or anticipated in later lifecycle stages, particularly important if contractors will be given responsibility for detailed planning or design. If 'the devil is in the detail' we have to anticipate this whenever it might matter enough to make doing so worth while. Now is a reasonable time to make sure that this is done.

We recommend that a clear list of all relevant project and process scope assumptions which apply to the project as a whole is provided as part of the define phase documentation, checked and modified as necessary as part of this step while working in identify mode, and linked to this step's documentation. We also recommend that all more specific project scope assumptions made during the identify phase are listed as part of the identify phase documentation.

For most projects at the E&D shaping stage of the lifecycle, a PUMP undertaken by a client wanting high clarity will involve a significant list of specific sources usefully addressed in qualitative terms as conditions. For example, the pipe-laying activity in the BP North Sea offshore project examples used earlier involved six to ten sources that were usefully quantified: weather, wet buckles, equipment failures, and so on. Of the 40 or so pipe-laying sources typically identified, about 30 were not quantified, but flagged as important 'conditions' – assumptions on which the analysis depended.

As an example, one project involved a source identified as 'management may change its mind where the pipeline is to go' (because the company was drilling for oil on an adjacent site, and a strike would probably lead to re-planning a 'collector network'). It was important to keep the plans – especially potential contractual commitments – as flexible as possible, to respond effectively to a possible change in route. However, the board owned this issue, not the project, and there was clearly no point going to the board with an estimate that said: 'We think there is an $X\%$ chance you will change your mind about what you want, and if you do change your mind, it will cost Y and take Z days longer.'

The identification of conditions of the kind illustrated by the above example can be *much more important* than the identification of sources that are subsequently quantified, and their treatment as conditions is clearly crucial. Such conditions may be the key to effective contract design, claims for 'extras', and risk avoidance or reduction management, which is central to the overall management process.

In the 1980s, statistical analysis of BP project out-turn costs in relation to SCERT based estimates to validate lack of bias clearly demonstrated that lots of relatively minor scope changes were inevitable, and occasional large changes were likely. If a pipeline was 50% longer and bigger because it now served two fields instead of one, nobody was going to quibble (argue) about a change in scope. If a pipeline was 221 km long instead of 220 km because the sea bed conditions, when subject to detailed survey, suggested a minor variation, cost estimators were expected not to quibble about the fine print in their estimate assumptions. Estimators and users of estimates need a joint 'no quibbles' approach.

A more extreme illustration of what is involved here emerged from the Highways Agency (HA) study as discussed in Chapter 2 (Nichols, 2007; Hopkinson et al., 2008). Engineers preparing re-estimates for the cost of major road systems used scope assumptions like 'no inflation' and 'no change in HA quality standards for internal reasons or because of changes in EU regulation' to exclude these components from their quantification of uncertainty, as noted earlier in this section. However, having quantified uncertainty associated with their original estimate plus uncertainty addressed by conventional risk management, they then quantified uncertainty associated with 'anything else a responsible minister could reasonably hold the HA responsible for', a significant 'no quibbles' provision.

The essence of the recommended approach is to use scenario building approaches to clarify in simple terms the key 'no quibbles' scope assumptions, and use an ambiguity uncertainty source with a label like 'project scope changes within the scope of the estimate' to quantify those potential scope changes that would lead to quibbles if they are not included in the estimate. This might be labelled 'the no quibbles provision', but a less frivolous label is important in practice. Also important in practice is linking this 'no quibbles provision' to a residual category, akin to 'everything else we have to take responsibility for not noted above', what some traditional estimators used to call a 'provision for errors and omissions'. It may be useful to couple this with the idea of a 'productivity variations' source, as discussed earlier.

For some projects at some stages in their lifecycle a purely qualitative analysis may be appropriate. For example, in the early 1990s a multi-national weapon platform project was assessed using a simple PUMP variant when it was approaching an early feasibility assessment gateway. It was the first project those responsible had subjected to a formal uncertainty analysis process. Most other uncertainty analyses undertaken elsewhere in the organization involved quantitative 'risk' analysis in the traditional sense. However, while quantitative analysis was an objective, it was not a commitment. When qualitative PUMP analysis clearly defined a small set of 'show-stoppers', uncertainty management focused on managing away the 'show-stoppers'. There was no need at this stage for quantitative analysis, because it would not have served any useful purpose.

By definition, all working assumptions that have not been identified, and all framing assumptions, are unidentified sources of uncertainty – part of the 'unknown unknown'. Framing assumptions are by definition also part of the 'unknowable unknown' – unless a less restrictive framework is adopted.

ABCD assumption based risk assessment (Baxter, 2010) is an interesting example of a focus on assumptions that helps to demonstrate their importance – and is directly relevant to this discussion. However, in the authors' view, its approach to the integration of the subset of assumptions it addresses with other assumptions, and uncertainty management more generally, should be avoided.

Approaches to identification and documentation

Identification of sources, responses and conditions, as discussed in the last four sections for steps 2 to 5 of the identify phase, can be undertaken by one person. It can also involve two or more people in a variety of ways, including a process facilitator interviewing individuals, interviewing groups, or various group processes such as brainstorming and decision conferencing. A key concern is to stimulate imaginative thinking and draw on the experiences of different individuals in a cost effective manner.

Using 'pondering' or more sophisticated approaches

An obvious and simple approach is what might be called 'pondering', involving a single person with 'a clean sheet of paper and a pencil', or the computer-based equivalent, to identify sources, responses or conditions. This is the most basic formal approach possible. It may serve as a default option if other approaches are not feasible or suitable. While simple and potentially limited, pondering should not be dismissed or usurped too readily as a starting point. Most experienced risk analysts start with it intuitively, and provided 'risks' become 'sources, responses and conditions' in the broad sense suggested here, there is nothing basically wrong with this kind of simple starting position.

A straightforward ponder approach to the identify phase in a first pass can be useful, to guide a second pass back through the focus phase, and to provide a basis for further passes through the identify phase. The authors often rely upon it explicitly as part of the ongoing focus phase of the PUMP process, and the subsequent structure phase. Its explicit use before involving other people or undertaking a systematic review of available documentation can be very effective for a number of reasons. For example, it can help to kick off an interview process by providing examples of the level of aggregation of sources of uncertainty of interest, and stimulating other thoughts. The effectiveness of pondering can be enhanced by simple techniques such as prompt lists or identification frameworks. For example, a PUMP team member could consider in turn each of the detailed activities making up each of the project activities consolidated for PUMP purposes, and ask the question 'what are the sources of uncertainty associated with this component activity?'

Alternatively, more resource intensive techniques could be applied from the outset, or applied to selected areas where earlier passes suggest the additional resource commitment would be worth while. Choosing between alternative identification techniques is a question of trading off different levels of analysis costs against effectiveness; a judgement which has to be made in relation to the importance of the uncertainty at all levels. It may require very different approaches in different areas. The most effective approach usually involves successive passes through the whole process on an area by area basis. Early passes are used to distinguish between those areas that warrant the most effective process available and those that do not. Later passes return to apply more effort where this appears to be warranted.

Harnessing creativity and experience

The use of formal procedures to systematically capture personal experience can be very effective in identifying relevant sources and responses. However, it is important that the experiences of a wide range of personnel are sought, particularly early on in the identify phase, to ensure that a comprehensive set of sources, responses and conditions are identified when relevant. Individual project managers may not have sufficient breadth of experience to provide this comprehensive view. Pooling of experience needs to include not only project managers and other project staff, but specialists concerned with all aspects of projects, including, for example, designers, user representatives, engineers, lawyers, financial personnel, and managers responsible for administration, sales, personnel, logistics, and so on. Even with input provided from a variety of sources, the quality of what is obtained depends heavily on the ability of individuals to recall circumstances accurately, without selectivity. Some relevant sources and responses may not be identified because they were effectively managed in the past and are not so readily brought to mind – often a source of consequence if the person who managed them successfully in the past has left the organization.

An obvious limitation of identification based on experience is that such experience may not be entirely applicable to future projects. In particular, it may be of limited value in respect of changing project environments and novel aspects of future projects. A common view is 'the real sources of risk are the one's you can't identify', recognizing that the 'unknown' can have a far greater effect on projects than all of the anticipated sources of uncertainty. For example, Hall (1975) cites examples of firms that were taken by surprise by substantial environmental changes: a mining company's assets seized by a foreign government and the rapid rise in oil price in the early 1970s. Opportunities that need proactive management to be captured can be missed too. For example, an unanticipated decline in business activities may lead to profitable scaling up of a project if the organization involved is ready for the possibility of these circumstances. These are perhaps examples of sources a project manager should be able to regard as 'external' to the project (as discussed in Chapter 6) and indicate a failure to identify and manage 'external' issues rather than a failure to identify and manage 'internal' issues. Although we may wish to place responsibility for 'external' issues higher in the organizational hierarchy than the project manager, the identify phase still needs to identify both 'external' and 'internal' issues, involving all those people necessary to achieve this.

'Thinking the unthinkable' calls for creativity and imagination. One of the best-known techniques for fostering creativity is brainstorming. Brainstorming is often used to improve problem analysis by providing more possible solutions and unusual approaches to a problem. The process typically involves a group of 6 to 12 individuals with a variety of backgrounds in order to facilitate the analysis of a problem from different points of view. In a typical brainstorming session the emphasis is on generating a large number of ideas. In problem-solving situations it is hoped that this will increase the chances of obtaining an excellent idea. In the initial ideas-generation session, wild ideas are encouraged on the basis that ideas are easier to modify than to originate, and participants are encouraged to utilize the ideas of others to develop additional ideas. Throughout this process the judgement of ideas is withheld. Ideas generated are criticized and evaluated in a later stage. Large problems may need to be made more manageable by breaking them into smaller parts, and samples should be available if products are being discussed (Whiting, 1958). There are important pitfalls to overcome (Furnham, 2000), but brainstorming is a valuable and widely used approach.

A less well-known but potentially significant technique is synectics, developed by Gordon (1956, 1968). A synectics team consists of a carefully selected group of individuals best equipped, intellectually and psychologically, to deal with problems unique to their organization. After selection, members are assigned to the synectics team on a full-time basis to solve problems for the entire organization (Crosby, 1968). The synectics process involves two steps. The first step is 'making the strange familiar'. It requires that a problem and its implications be understood. The second step is 'making the familiar strange'. It involves distorting, inverting and transposing the problem in an attempt to view the problem from an unfamiliar perspective.

In the context of source, response and condition identification, creativity techniques such as brainstorming and synectics may be too creative. So many potential sources, responses and conditions may be identified that the project team becomes overwhelmed. Nevertheless, certain features of these approaches are attractive for identification purposes, including: the involvement of individuals with a variety of backgrounds, withholding judgement about identified issues, utilizing the thoughts of others, and attempting to view situations from an unfamiliar perspective.

More recently a number of 'decision-conferencing' techniques have been developed. For example, see Dennison and Morgan (1994), Finlay and Marples (1991), Marples and

Riddle (1992). Decision-conferencing techniques are designed to improve the efficiency and effectiveness of group processes involving the exploration of problems and decision-making situations. Typically decision-conferencing techniques involve a facilitator and real-time computer support operated by one or more analysts. The facilitator manages the group's deliberations, guiding discussion in appropriate directions as necessary. Computer support may be used to help the group to develop an understanding of the different aspects of the problem being addressed and to document the proceedings. For example, Williams et al. (1995a, 1995b) describe the development of a cognitive map during a decision-conferencing process that was used to elicit an enhanced, shared understanding among the project management team of the reasons for project cost overruns.

Knowledge uncertainty management processes (KUMPs)

This book attributes the first use of the KUMP notion to Mike Nichols and the team supporting his Highways Agency report to the Secretary of State for Transport (Nichols, 2007). In effect a KUMP was used by the Nichols team to ask the question: 'What do we need to know by the end of each lifecycle stage to proceed to the next lifecycle stage, as part of the basic project planning process, and as part of the associated PUMP?' It is now clear that KUMPs are usefully seen as an important part of the glue between PUMPs and the rest of project planning. They might be seen as part of the PUMP pack concept, but they can be seen as different in terms of basic purpose.

One aspect of the importance of KUMPs – and their basis in terms of a knowledge lens perspective for looking at uncertainty in terms of incomplete knowledge beyond the PUMP focus – is the way they capture ambiguity uncertainty which is totally 'off the radar' of event based approaches and not immediately obvious from other perspectives. Ambiguity is a particularly important source of uncertainty early in the project lifecycle. If this source is not addressed early estimates of cost, duration and the performance of the project deliverables will be optimistically biased to a serious extent, as illustrated by the Highways Agency example discussed earlier.

A second aspect is the importance of the way this source of knowledge uncertainty is resolved as the project lifecycle proceeds. By the time commitment to a strategy is made, significant ambiguities about designs, contracts and other key working assumptions in the concept-shaping stage will be resolved, and no longer a source of uncertainty or risk – assuming they are resolvable, a key 'risky condition' which sometimes needs attention. By the time a commitment to tactics is made, further uncertainty will be resolved, and no longer a source of risk. The way risk depends upon both commitments and unresolved uncertainty at the time commitments have to be made is of fundamental importance.

A third aspect is the clear demonstration these first two points provide of the need to abandon common practice views of risk management which focus on events and fail to clarify the roles of uncertainty in general terms and commitments, not to mention the difference between commitments, expectations and stretch targets.

A fourth aspect is the scope for new ways to use KUMPs for purposes that might elude PUMPs. For example, while the authors believe that the strategic and tactical planning distinction and ordering underlying the nominal lifecycle structure of Table 1.3 is crucial for efficient and effective shaping of strategy and tactics, it is clear that *sometimes* detailed planning to test strategy is important, as distinct from tactical planning to support following stages. Looking for instances when this might be the case should be seen as part of the identify phase when it may be relevant, but confirming a particular possibility and undertaking selective detailed planning as appropriate might be best seen as part of an allied KUMP. The characteristics of ambiguity uncertainty that should trigger detailed planning to test strategy are 'we have never done this kind of thing before, its feasibility is questionable, the strategy will fail if a feasible tactical plan cannot be developed, and we cannot afford a strategy failure'. The use of detailed planning explicitly for testing strategy as mandated by General Dwight Eisenhower as Supreme Commander of the Allied forces when planning for D-Day (Ambrose, 1994) is an example we will return to later. A linked example is the use of intelligence gathering techniques taking a variety of forms – in the D-Day context key examples included French Resistance movement intelligence efficiently channelled via the British Special Operations Executive (SOE) and secret visits to the beaches to check defences. In a civilian project context, early discussions with potentially hostile regulators and environmental groups are analogous examples, but competitors, future collaborators and customers are also obvious concerns.

Issue lists

Some people who support event-based approaches to risk management use 'issue lists' to capture sources of uncertainty that have a probability of occurring of one, in some cases because they are assumed to be events that have already happened. Managing 'issues' defined in these ways in addition to 'risks' defined as events, but ignoring constraints or any other source of uncertainty, is a seriously inadequate solution to a set of issues that have not been properly understood.

Corporate weakness summary lists

If organizations develop a clear understanding of corporate weaknesses in terms of uncertainty management, as discussed later in Chapter 16, a summary list may provide a useful basis for identifying linked sources/conditions for a particular project. A source of uncertainty and risk with a label like 'the project team do not understand PUMPs' is clearly not a good idea, but diplomatically recognising and managing even more sensitive corporate weaknesses can be crucial. If a board does not understand what they are doing, and nobody reporting to the board can find an effective way to identify and resolve the issue, culpability for the inevitable problems is not limited to the board. For example, significant responsibility may be directly attributable to the person responsible for 'risk management', who may need replacing before the board can develop the necessary capability.

Process ambiguity summary lists

A useful complement to corporate weakness summary lists is a summary of sources of ambiguity that are inherent in the processes and associated models being used – a standardized list of process scope assumptions and their implications for example. As an illustration, if systemic uncertainty is not explicitly identified and modelled, associated bias will need estimation, which should be addressed in a systematic manner across all projects. This kind of list could support the identification of 'risky conditions', like a possible need for selective detailed planning to test strategy prior to the strategy gateway noted above.

Checklists and prompt lists

In the search for relevant sources, responses and conditions it is important to avoid unduly constraining the process if available experience and expertise is to be fully exploited. We explicitly advise against the use of highly structured techniques such as questionnaires which can straitjacket respondents, and strongly caution against over-reliance on checklists to drive the identification of sources, responses and conditions – including corporate weakness and process ambiguity summary lists. Given the popular appeal of checklists, this advice warrants some explanation.

A simple, common practice 'checklist' approach to source identification is often taken on the grounds that a 'quick and dirty' approach can yield substantial benefits despite its conceptual shortcomings. This kind of checklist approach typically takes a view of project uncertainty which is very simple, often limited to event uncertainty. The approach is illustrated in Table 7.2, which shows a typical list of broad headings under which individual, more specific, sources might be identified. Sources are presumed to be independent, and are presented in a standard category framework. This list may be very extensive and cover a variety of categories. It may be extended as experience accumulates over time.

Checklist approaches can be very effective in focusing attention on managing sources of uncertainty, provided they are supported by appropriate administrative procedures, *and they are used appropriately*. For example, a corporate uncertainty manager or PUMP team may operate an internal audit function using checklists as a basis for interrogating project managers at key stages in the lifecycle of projects. More detailed documentation related to individual sources and progress in managing them may accompany these checklists, as considered necessary. However, in our view distributing checklists for others to use is generally not a good idea.

Selection of the sources (including conditions) to be included on a checklist is usually based on experience. An initial list may be drawn up by a small group of experienced project managers, with

Table 7.2   The checklist approach

Source of uncertainty	*Impact*	*Likelihood*	*Exposure*
Definition of project			
Concept and design			
Financing arrangements			
Logistics			
Local conditions			
Resource estimates			
Industrial relations			
Communications			
Project organization			

a view to augmenting the list in the light of new experiences. Even without the help of creativity techniques, checklists developed and added to over several years can become very intimidating, particularly to new members of project teams. Worse still, the length of some checklists may actively discourage further selective analysis of key sources.

A checklist approach is a convenient and relatively simple way of focusing attention on project 'risk' management in the common practice EUMP sense. However, it has a number of potentially serious shortcomings for uncertainty management in the PUMP spirit. Some examples are:

- Important interdependencies between sources are not readily highlighted.
- A list, particularly a long one, provides limited guidance on the relative importance of individual sources.
- Individual entries may encompass a number of important, separate sources implicitly.
- Sources not on the list are likely to be ignored.
- The list of sources may be more appropriate for some projects than others.
- A checklist presents an overly simplistic view of the potential effects of individual sources.
- A checklist does not encourage the development of a more sophisticated attitude to assessing and quantifying uncertainty.
- Individual sources may be described in insufficient detail to avoid ambiguity and varying interpretations, or too much detail, without understanding the composite nature of uncertainty sources.

The main problem is that a checklist does not offer a sufficiently structured examination of sources from which to discover key sources, responses and conditions in a cost-effective manner at a cost effective level of decomposition tailored to each project. In our view, if any kind of 'checklist' is used it should be referred to as a 'prompt list', and used in that spirit as a catalyst and stimulant, not as a definitive statement of possibilities. In a high clarity context it is most effective as a prompt list for 'anything else?' analysis – *after unprompted initial analysis of the project. It should never be used as a starting point and it should never be exposed to everyone involved.*

Further, in our view event uncertainty management process (EUMP) based checklists are rarely suitable for PUMPs, which need to address all forms of uncertainty in flexible composite terms, including associated response and secondary source-response lists, plus assumption lists that may need summary treatment in composite terms. PUMP documentation from earlier comparable projects is much more useful than traditional common practice risk logs or registers.

Documentation

The documentation generated by identification of source–response–secondary source and response chains needs careful management. It also needs linking to the activity structure used to generate it and associated assumptions which may be treated as conditions. Further, some sources may be common to all activities, and some responses may be general in the sense that they can cope with all sources, both these issues needing careful attention. Further still, the approach adopted will need to deal with all seven Ws and lifecycle stages.

For example, generalizing the SCERT approach developed for BP plus later 'risk engineering' versions for other contexts involves a numbering system of the form $u.v.w$ for response w specific to source v arising in the context of define phase component u, where $u = 1, ..., 8$, is defined as follows:

$u = 1$ is concerned with project lifecycle issues

2	context	(where)
3	parties	(who)
4	motives	(why)
5	design	(what)
6	plans	(whichway)
7	resources	(wherewithal)
8	timing	(when)

When relevant, secondary sources and responses involve extending this numbering system to the form $u.v.w.x.y$ for secondary response y to secondary source x. A key increase in process efficiency and effectiveness is provided by the use of simple 'labels' ('handles') for each u, v, w, x and y element, and enough associated text ('descriptions') to clarify what is involved. Being able to access this information flexibly can be very useful – for example, producing a list of sources and responses for which a particular individual or team is responsible.

Illustrating this in the 1970s and 1980s BP version of SCERT context, u was not relevant because the plans for activities structure ($u = 6$) was the focus, but a number like 1.1.1 identified the first response to the first source in the first activity, 'activity 0' was used for sources common to all activities, and 'response 0' or 'response $n + 1$' was used for responses general enough to deal with all specific sources, including 'knock-on delays from earlier activities' when relevant. With hindsight it might have been useful to think separately about resources and timing, instead of linking these dimensions to activities, and to be more formal about other u values, as discussed shortly. For example, a source of uncertainty addressed when looking at 'jacket fabrication' was realizing late in the lifecycle that the actual total weight of all the modules which had to sit on the jacket might exceed the assumed weight when the platform was designed. In general a formal search for this kind of link across lifecycle stages can be very useful.

A simple early pass at identifying relevant primary sources including relevant assumptions and responses for all Ws might involve a simple list of all the relevant sources associated with each W, and brief notes on relevant responses in relation to each source. At any stage in the process the use of a simple label for each source can be very helpful for discussion purposes, while back-up descriptions for each source document what is involved. However, no matter how clear the output looks, if all key sources for all seven Ws have not been properly understood, and that understanding documented and shared by the project team, source identification cannot be complete and effective. For example, failure to consider market and political sources associated with 'why' or 'what' can render detailed planning and uncertainty analysis of plans for activities aspects of 'whichway' and 'when' somewhat superfluous, and market and political sources may be adversely affected by technical choices.

Clarify the immediate need for more depth or more breadth

'Clarify the immediate need for more depth or more breadth', step 6 in Figure 7.1, is concerned with extending the review of immediate priorities in step 1 to prepare for a fit for purpose test which will decide to move on to the structure phase or loop back to step 1. Step 6 also provides a suitable basis for a further pass from step 1 if a loop back is appropriate.

In the context of a high clarity approach to our pipe-laying example with the first pass focused on 'weather' as a key primary source and no consideration of responses, step 6 has to prepare for the following fit-for-purpose test by asking: 'If it looks like we have enough clarity about weather for the time being, is it worth thinking about responses now?' The answer might be 'yes', with a view to a number of passes developing primary responses. Once primary responses seem to be covered in sufficient depth for the time being, secondary sources and responses might be addressed. This might be followed by consideration of relevant constraints – hard constraints imposed by weather or resource availability plus soft constraints associated with tradeoffs between objectives. Once this has been taken as far as seems appropriate, the question might become: 'What other sources might be worth exploring?' The answer might be 'buckles', 'major equipment failures', and so on. Separating 'wet buckle' equivalents from 'productivity variations' equivalents, and deciding whether or not to search for further relevant responses and secondary sources, involves an ongoing process of making judgements about more depth in a particular area of focus versus moving on to the other primary sources within a given activity and other activities. 'Depth of analysis' for the first source addressed might initially relate to primary responses, then secondary sources and responses to 'weather'. Then 'depth' for the first activity might generalize to other primary sources for this activity, which is breadth in terms of separate sources within this activity. Breadth in terms of different activities might follow. In the context of a generalization assuming that a plan for activities was a good place to start, these questions then have to be extended when all relevant activities have been considered to 'which further relevant criteria need attention in terms of which further plans?', and then 'which other lifecycle stages need consideration?'

In the context of a full generalization, other starting places need consideration. This step is more complex than it may at first appear. To address it effectively in general terms a number of aspects need attention, addressed in separate sections to clarify what is involved.

Ordering and considering all relevant performance criteria

One aspect of tailoring the PUMP to each project in the focus phase which needs revisiting and developing as necessary in steps one and six of the identify phase is ordering all relevant performance criteria to facilitate an effective analysis sequence, bearing in mind all the relevant criteria–plan relationship structures and criteria constraint assumptions made in steps one and six. It is not practical to consider many different objectives simultaneously unless a mathematical programming approach is appropriate, and even these approaches usually rely on secondary criteria treated as constraints, so an effective ordering is needed for all relevant performance criteria that should be considered in this pass of the identify phase. Performance criteria are a starting place for analysis using our 'performance lens' for looking at uncertainty about objectives in order to clarify opportunity and risk defined relative to an opportunity/risk datum. In effect the project 'why' has to be decomposed and ordered as a basis for the analysis sequence, starting with the motives of the key party. For example, the key criterion for the BP analysis discussed earlier was duration, but capital cost, substantially driven by project execution and delivery durations at a strategic planning level, had to be addressed later. Tradeoffs between project duration and capital cost could be considered as part of expanding the list of criteria addressed, provided opportunity costs were also part of these tradeoffs at an appropriate level. The underlying concern was capital cost and opportunity costs, but the starting point was uncertainty about activity durations, with linked resource choices. The design, operations and business case strategy decisions which defined 'quality' where taken as 'givens' – project scope assumptions not normally negotiable by those involved in the E&D shaping stage.

Once uncertainty associated with duration was managed for all activities by shaping the execution and delivery plans at a strategic level, making cost-based tradeoffs when doing so, cost uncertainty associated with equipment cost rates and component purchases were considered to obtain overall capital cost estimates. For example, the uncertain duration of a pipe-laying activity was multiplied by the uncertain cost of a lay barge per unit time, to compute lay barge cost. Further, the cost of materials, such as pipe, was assessed in probability distribution terms on a unit basis and scaled up by the number of units required, also defined in probabilistic terms. In addition, components with costs that were not time or quantity dependent in a direct sense had their uncertainty assessed and added.

More generally, project objectives might be viewed in terms of cost, time or quality. Cost might be addressed in terms of capital cost or 'whole life' cost, quality might be divided into technical specification, functionality and appearance, each of which may be uncertain and 'at risk' or a source of opportunities to different degrees. Often performance is perceived primarily in terms of dimensions that can be measured, such as time and cost, or particular aspects of quality. The implication is that variations are possible and measurable, and hence uncertainty exists in respect of these performance criteria. Other criteria that are not readily quantified may be treated as inviolate constraints for project management purposes. This may lead to neglect of uncertainty in these dimensions, even though they represent important performance criteria. It may also lead to inappropriate realized tradeoffs. These problems and opportunities need to be addressed in this step.

In a case like that illustrated by the North Sea examples, it is relatively simple to build cost uncertainty on a time uncertainty and materials quantity uncertainty framework. When a clear plan-criteria relationship structure linking plans and criteria of interest exists, it is worth exploiting. When it does not, more complex approaches may be required, and this complexity requires great care. For example, many common practice approaches to weapon system and information system projects identify sources in terms of time, cost and performance impacts simultaneously, using matrix formats. This may seem sensible for a first-pass approach to the identify phase. However, it poses three somewhat different potential problems. First, it does not facilitate a clear, sequential focus on performance criteria which helps to avoid omissions. Second, it leaves structural and tradeoffs issues to be addressed later, as they must be for quantification, and this is likely to lead to inappropriate quantification too late in the process. Third, it does not clarify the impact of the statistical dependencies involved, never mind the causal relationships which need identification and management, leading to biased estimation, inappropriate choices and missed opportunities. By failing to address the relevant criteria–plan relationship structures it impedes effective quantification, and it impairs the iterative process which is central to a complete PUMP.

Much more detailed analysis of objectives, including their decomposition in a structure directly related to project activities or design components, may be useful in some cases. For example, in a high technology product development project, if a set of components is assessed as very risky, it may be possible to design out the uncertainty by changing the basic nature of the design, perhaps as part of a formal value management process (Green, 1994). This will require a clear understanding of the functional role of the components in the overall design. It involves an interaction between the project 'why', 'what' and 'whichway'. The groundwork for identification of such issues should already have been provided in the define phase.

It is important to address any difficulties associated with these issues explicitly as part of the focus phase or the closely linked structure phase. Detailed guidance on how to manage such difficulties is beyond the scope of this book, but a starting point for those interested is provided by Chapman et al. (1985), Klein (1993) and Chapman and Ward (2002).

Even if only one project party is of concern, it is often very important to define all relevant objectives and their relative priorities in writing. Often different parts of the same organization have different objectives. At the very least, agreed priorities in terms of time, cost, and performance are essential. If differences are very important, treating the different parts of the organization as separate partners may be appropriate. This takes us into different criteria related to different parties, and uncertainty associated with other Ws.

Ordering and considering all other relevant aspects of the seven Ws

Ordering all relevant performance criteria involves a focus on the project 'why' that will order and involve other project Ws needing consideration to some extent, in particular all relevant plans as identified via the criteria–plan relationship structures. For example, the BP initial focus on activity duration in the E&D-shaping stage implied a direct focus on the plans for activities aspect of 'whichway', and an indirect focus on associated 'wherewithal' and 'when' issues. It is usually convenient to start with a focus on the W issues implied by the key criteria for the key party, using a multiple pass approach to develop clarity in these terms, then generalize to consider other criteria from the perspective of the key player, then move on to other Ws in their order of importance, other parties' motives being addressed as part of the 'who'/'why' and the plans for relationships and contracts aspect of 'whichway'. To illustrate this flow, continue considering the BP examples as a starting point, assuming as a consequence that duration is the key criterion, with cost driven by time the underlying concern, and that we now want to use this starting point to ask 'are any other Ws relevant?'

Considering the complete set of Ws in terms of all associated plans can reveal some key sources, associated responses, and in some cases secondary sources, with important interactions that require management. The following subsections consider other Ws in natural groups when relevant, not to generate an exhaustive, generic list of all possible sources, which would be impracticable and inappropriate, but to illustrate the range of areas that could be considered as part of step 6 in Figure 7.1.

Other parties – plans for relationships and contracts and the underlying 'who'/'why'

Chapter 5 indicated the importance of documenting clear descriptions of all the interested parties during the define phase, and how relationships will be managed in terms of explicit and implicit contracts. The concern here is an effective process for identifying sources of uncertainty using this earlier identification of the relevant parties plus the plans for relationships and contracts aspect of 'whichway', linked to systematically exploring all the relevant criteria associated with the 'why' for other parties identified via the 'who'. Examples in Chapter 5 illustrate what is involved to some extent, but consider some other examples.

Joint venture partners are important to address explicitly, in terms of the interests and roles of all the partners. Many offshore oil projects involve a lead partner who takes operational responsibility and other partners who help to fund the project and share the product. A significant change in plans for activities will require approval by all the partners. If they are not all kept informed of the possible need to make such changes, managing the decision to change the plans for activities can be a question of crisis management rather than risk or uncertainty management, adding to the cost of the incidents necessitating the change, or eliminating the possibility of responding to an opportunity. This is an example source that BP addressed as an 'activity 0' source without formally using a seven Ws structure.

Multi-nation military joint ventures, such as the development of new weapon systems or their platforms (aircraft, ships, etc.), make the 'who' dimension very rich indeed, due, for example, to different technical requirements, different needs in terms of timing, and different contracting systems between the partners and their contractors. It clearly complicates the 'why', in the sense that each party's objectives need attention.

Regulators, planning authorities and others providing approvals may also prove to be key parties – requiring careful attention to plans for relationships. For example, combined cycle gas turbine power stations involve warm water discharges into rivers and vapour plumes which are regulated, in addition to the planning permission issues associated with such plant. Nuclear power stations involve obviously increased levels of regulation, including safety standards, which may be changed during construction, necessitating redesigns with delays that yield still more regulation-induced design changes in a vicious circle that can prove extremely expensive – factor of 10 cost increases are not unknown. Channel tunnel rolling stock development and production encountered this kind of difficulty. To manage this kind of source it is important to understand what is driving changes in the regulatory environment, and to endeavour to meet the regulations that will be relevant at the appropriate time in the future, rather than those currently in force. Highways Agency anticipation of EU safety requirements is an example. Early establishment of good working relationships can develop trust based on mutual best interests and appropriate communication.

Competitors for limited resources (wherewithal) can also prove a profitable area of study. For example, oil majors have attempted to avoid bidding up the price for key scarce resources by timing their projects (moving some activities central to the 'when') to avoid excessive competition. If only a half a dozen players are involved, individual study and perhaps direct collaboration may be feasible. More generally, it may be appropriate to look at the markets for specific resources as a whole. Successful commercial property developers are aware of the need to time new building construction, hopefully while the market for resources and cash are depressed, just before the market for office space takes off. Many failed developers are too late in realizing the importance of these considerations.

Much of the uncertainty inherent in project management arises from agents appointed by the client, such as contractors and subcontractors. The client may not be able to rely on an agent performing as the client wishes for reasons related to the nature of the work and the agent's motivation, ability and understanding of the work. In theory, it should be possible for the client to maximize the chances of satisfactory performance by careful selection of a suitable agent, careful monitoring of the agent's activities, and ensuring that the agent is appropriately motivated. Unfortunately, lack of knowledge on the part of the client and the presence of uncertainty can make these things difficult to achieve.

The so-called principal–agent relationship, whether between parties in the same organization, or between a client and contractor, is prone to three fundamental problems: adverse selection; moral hazard; and uncertainty (risk) allocation (Eisenhardt, 1989).

'Adverse selection' refers to misrepresentation of ability by the agent and the principal's difficulty in selecting an agent with appropriate skills. The agent may claim to have certain skills or abilities when hired, but the principal cannot completely verify these skills or abilities either at the time of hiring or while the agent is working. A 'selection' problem can also arise where a contractor misrepresents the work that will be done or the likely final price. 'Strategic misrepresentation' (Flyvberg et al., 2003) is attracting growing interest – an interesting euphemism for deliberate bias or lying. Once a contractor has been hired, it may be difficult for the client to ensure that costs are contained and the work that was promised is what is actually delivered.

'Moral hazard' refers to an agent's failure to put forth the contracted effort. This can be of greatest concern to the principal when it is particularly difficult or expensive for the principal to verify that an agent is behaving appropriately, as when task specifications are inadequate or the principal lacks knowledge of the delegated tasks.

'Uncertainty allocation' in terms of risk and opportunity concerns the manner in which responsibility for project-related sources of uncertainty (sources and responses) is allocated between principal and agent. Uncertainty allocation is very important because it can strongly influence the motivation of principal and agent, and the extent to which uncertainty is assessed and managed. Insofar as principal and agent perceive risk and opportunity differently, and have different abilities and motivations to manage uncertainty, then their approach to uncertainty management will be different. In particular, either party is likely to try to manage uncertainty primarily for their own benefit, perhaps to the disadvantage of the other party.

The uncertainties arising from problems of adverse selection, moral hazard and uncertainty allocation are more likely to arise where principal and agent are separate organizations, as in most client–contractor relationships. Where principal and agent belong to the same organization it might be expected that such problems would be less likely to arise, to the extent that the parties can share information, responsibilities and objectives more readily. Unfortunately, this is not always the case and there can be significant issues in allocating uncertainty in a hierarchical structure within organizations. Chapman and Ward (2002, ch. 6) explores 'internal contracts' to address such issues.

Sources associated with the plans for business case purposes aspects: the 'whichway'

Later passes of the basic PUMP might usefully address sources of uncertainty associated with assumed revenues and other business case plans not identified elsewhere. For example, many serious project failures are a result of a failure to rigorously assess uncertainty and control estimation bias associated with revenue estimates. This might be picked up by identifying 'customers' as part of the who, and customer relationship plans as part of the 'whichway'. If not it needs attention as part of the plans for business case purposes aspects of the 'whichway'.

Sources of uncertainty associated with project timing: the 'when'

Project timing, the when, can be an important primary source of uncertainty over and above the timing implications of delay to plans for activities considered earlier. Viewed as an integration of all plan-based timetables, the when is a recipient of impacts from a large number of plans, which can generate important second-order effects. Formal documentation of the Ws is concerned with making sure these issues do not fall down cracks and get lost from sight until they generate a crisis. For example, in Chapter 5 a UK Nirex deep mining shaft project was used to illustrate a timing/resource link, in terms of overstated time uncertainty if common resource usage is overlooked. Other examples of this kind of link include regulatory changes and prototype failures which lead to redesign of the product of the project at a late stage, perhaps half way through construction.

Even if no first- or second-order implications are involved, project duration is an economic choice that needs explicit attention. For example, a 1974 Acres Consulting Services study of a proposed large diameter gas pipeline to bring Arctic gas to US markets was initiated to explicitly address the question 'what is the optimal target project duration?' in response to political pressure for a shorter duration. Even if no one outside the project team asks questions about project duration, the issue of tradeoffs between time (indirect cost) and direct cost is important. At this stage in the process the question of direct and indirect cost tradeoffs needs to be raised in broad terms. For example, if the proposed project duration is five years, the question is why not four, or six? If the answer is not clear, further attention to the issue will be required, and the need to give it attention should be flagged. From the outset it is important to be clear what level of overhead costs per unit time will be incurred in relation to any project extensions.

Sources associated with project design and plans for operations

Many of the important sources associated with a project relate to the specific physical nature of the project and its design, to the what of the project and the way it will be operated and supported in the operations stage of the asset lifecycle. The relationship may be direct and obvious or indirect and easily overlooked. For example, many risk management methods for high technology products (such as advanced weapon systems) suggest an explicit focus on technical issues arising from design because using a design based on the latest technology may involve sources associated with technical failures or reliability problems. Using a design based on established technology may avoid certain technical sources but involve other sources associated with more aggressive competitors who are willing and able to manage the uncertainty involved in new technology.

That is, avoiding a technical source may involve generating a competitor-based source, but where the choice of technology is implicit, competitor based sources may not be seen as a related issue.

Design changes are often a major threat. However, freezing the design is often not a viable option. Hospitals, military equipment, computer software, and comparatively simple consumer products may require design updates during development and production to remain viable. Anticipating these changes in needs may be the key to successful design, as well as the key to a successful project more generally. Attention to procedures for 'change control' (design changes) should be recognized as central to any project involving a design that is neither simple nor stable.

Effective anticipation of design changes is part of the PUMP pack concept. Links to other Ws may be quite simple but very important, requiring an understanding of the 'what', with the 'whichway' and 'why' assumed to have been covered earlier, and the 'wherewithal' and 'when' yet to be considered. For example, property developers will be sensitive to issues like how many car-parking places a planning department may require for a new building now, and whether or not this is likely to increase by next year. A design that fails to reflect this sort of change can seriously threaten a project. At the very least it requires a clear understanding of the technologies involved, and the interface between technological choices and related issues. For example, the development of computer-controlled fly-by-wire technology revolutionized aircraft design because inherently unstable designs, which previously would not have been able to fly, became feasible, but a whole new set of sources were generated that were not all anticipated at the outset.

It is important to appreciate that what is the recipient of influences or effects from other Ws as well as a primary source, and these effects can generate substantial second-order effects. For example, if some combination of problems from a variety of sources threatens the viability of the target project completion time or date, or its cost, the response may be a change in design. This may have the desired effect, or it may make the situation worse. This impact is well understood in theory in terms of the standard time–cost–quality triangle (Barnes, 1988), but it is often overlooked in practice. Part of the role of documenting the seven Ws in the define phase, and review of this documentation in the identify phase, is explicit identification of these issues.

The importance of effective consideration of how the product of a project is going to be used when the project lifecycle reaches the O&S stage is becoming increasingly obvious. Even if the PUMP of immediate interest is concerned solely with the E&D shaping stage, overlooking key concerns not effectively addressed in the earlier DOT shaping stage can be very serious. At the very least, 'constructive insubordination' requires a quick test of all earlier lifecycle stage decisions if an effective PUMP was not used earlier, including concept shaping stage decisions, as illustrated by the 'constructive insubordination' example in Chapter 3.

Sources of uncertainty associated with project resources: the 'wherewithal'

The importance of uncertainty management involving resources, the 'wherewithal' of the project, is obvious. Lack of the right resources in the right place at the right time is a source of serious opportunity inefficiency. Making sure this does not happen is central to project management. In Chapter 5 a relatively low-key illustration of resource-related sources was provided. Now consider an example when the availability of one resource was a major issue.

The 1974 Acres study of an optimal duration for a major Arctic gas pipeline with political pressures for a shorter duration [mentioned a few pages ago] was significantly driven by the impact of a scarce resource – welders. The availability of welders was central to the project because political pressures were forcing a short project duration (a 'when' issue) which required a significant proportion (of the order of 10%) of the suitably skilled welders available in Canada. Other factors influencing the availability of welders also needed to be understood, such as immigration rules that would make importing labour difficult or impossible, and a recognition that Arctic construction of this kind often leads to a pattern of employment that involves long hours (and weeks) for an extended period when cash is accumulated by the workforce, followed by a spell on a sunny island until the cash runs out, the duration of both periods depending upon the welders' circumstances and whims. This study used a conventional semi-Markov process GERT framework, in part because weather windows and contingency planning were important, and in part because a dynamic approach linking these issues to resource constraints was vital. It was part of the basis for the BP SCERT model developed soon after.

Potential shortage of various resources is not the only resource-related source of uncertainty. For example, in the context of computer software projects, there is a widely held view that adding more staff to a software project that is running very late is rather like attempting to drown a fire by pouring on petrol. This kind of feedback loop dependency has much wider implications and applications.

A further set of issues is linked to the idea that usually economic usage of resources suggests self-imposed constraints even if there are no externally imposed constraints. For example, employing 300 people one week, 100 the next, and 200 the next, is generally very uneconomic compared with 200 throughout. If all the resources required are readily available in the required quantities at the required times with no difficulties associated with quality or performance, and no costs associated with highly variable resource usage patterns, the 'wherewithal' issue is not worth pursuing, but this is very rarely the case. At the very least it is worth confirming a working assumption that this is the case, in writing if appropriate.

It may be convenient to identify and describe resource plans for activities within the activity 'whichway' structure, and resource plans for operations within the operations plans 'whichway' structure, but resources shared with other projects or operations mitigate against this, making separate 'wherewithal' documentation useful. If a project is subject to political pressure to employ local labour or other resources in construction or operations terms it makes obvious sense to identify this type of consideration in relation to those resources that are relevant, as this has implications for how the resource units are defined. As in the case of activities and sources, the basic rule of thumb is disaggregate resource types only when it looks useful to do so.

Sources associated with the context: the 'where'

Context is often an issue, and thinking about sources of uncertainty generated by the context is potentially important. For example, 1980s BP North Sea offshore oil and gas projects shared some important features with earlier and concurrent projects in other parts of the world, but there are also obvious differences that are very relevant when basing any assessments on experience in another context. Even North Sea experience several years earlier needed interpretation with care because of the learning curves climbed in the meantime. BP did not need a seven Ws structure to understand this, but some organizations can find a seven Ws 'where' the basis of helpful discipline in a creative sense.

Sources in other stages of the project lifecycle

If, as in the BP SCERT examples, the PUMP is designed for high clarity at the E&D shaping stage in the project lifecycle, with design, operations and business case strategy beyond the scope of the PUMP, it might seem unwise, as well as inappropriate, to address other lifecycle stages. However, experience with a wide range of clients provides clear evidence that often this is not the case. Steps 1 and 6 of the identify phase addressed in the previous sections of this chapter were concerned with ensuring that relevant performance criteria and other relevant Ws did not get ignored. A further important check in later passes of a high clarity approach is making sure that relevant sources of uncertainty that may not materialize until later stages in the project lifecycle, plus all relevant sources that may have been overlooked in earlier stages, are addressed now.

As noted in Chapter 1, many important sources are associated with the fundamental management processes that make up the asset lifecycle. A fair number of sources are implicitly acknowledged in lists of project management 'key success factors'. Potential sources typically identified in this way are listed in Table 7.3. The structure of Table 7.3 follows the lifecycle stage structure of Table 1.3 apart from omitting the gateway stages.

The identification of these sources of uncertainty in the project management literature is based on substantial project management experience, but it is somewhat haphazard. Different writers identify different success factors or problem areas, describe them in more or less detail, or identify as single problem areas what may in practice be a whole series of separate issues. Another difficulty is that sources of uncertainty are identified as adverse effects rather than in terms of underlying causes or uncertainties. For example, potential problems in the execute stage of a project can often be related to weaknesses in particular earlier stages of the project: 'failure of prototype to pass performance trials' may be a consequence of faulty workmanship, unreasonable performance requirements or a choice of new technology or novel design features. The uncertainty management issues associated with the E&D shaping stage should have been picked up as part of the processes already described. The others are a useful a basis for considering earlier and later lifecycle stages at this point in the process – addressed stage by stage in following subsections.

Concept-shaping

A common source of overall project opportunity inefficiency is a failure to carry out the equivalent of steps one through six of the identify phase in the concept shaping stage at an effective level of clarity. Stakeholder expectations associated with a concept shaping stage that is not subjected to formal uncertainty management until the end of the strategy stages can be a major issue, as can assumptions about the relative priorities of performance objectives. These are just two examples of common major problems which can become increasingly large 'elephants in the room' that everyone seems to see except those who are responsible for dealing with them. This is never an acceptable reason for avoiding these issues, but it can make managing a PUMP with a focus on what really matters at a strategic level a very high-risk operation. Even if a very effective PUMP process has been applied at the concept shaping stage, it can be important to revisit concept shaping issues as part of the E&D shaping stage PUMP in terms of an integrating update incorporating information and views that may have been overlooked earlier.

Table 7.3   Typical uncertainty management issues in each stage of the project lifecycle

Lifecycle stages	Uncertainty management issues
Concept shaping	Level of definition Definition of appropriate performance objectives Managing stakeholder expectations
Design, operation and termination (DOT) shaping	Novelty of design and technology Determining 'fixed' points in the design Control of changes
Execution and delivery (E&D) shaping	Identifying and allowing for regulatory constraints Concurrency of activities required Capturing dependency relationships Errors and omissions
Tactics shaping	Adequate accuracy of resource estimates Estimating resources required Defining responsibilities (number and scope of contracts) Defining contractual terms and conditions Selecting capable participants (tendering procedures and bid selection)
Execution	Exercising adequate coordination and control Determining the level and scope of control systems Ensuring effective communication between participants Provision of appropriate organizational arrangements Ensuring effective leadership Ensuring continuity in personnel and responsibilities Responding effectively to sources which are realized
Delivery	Adequate testing Adequate training Managing stakeholder expectations Obtaining licences to operate
Operations and support (O&S)	Provision of appropriate organization arrangements Identifying extent of liabilities Managing stakeholder expectations Requirements for efficient and effective maintenance Changing regulatory environment Changes in use and demand for the project deliverable
Termination	Appropriate design and organizational arrangements Identifying extent of liabilities Managing stakeholder expectations

Identifying concept shaping stage risky conditions in project and process terms can be a useful focus, relating them to what has been learned since the concept gateway. Chapter 12 will clarify some of these issues.

Design, operation and termination (DOT) shaping

Another common source of overall project opportunity inefficiency is a failure to carry out the equivalent of steps one through six of the identify phase in the DOT shaping stage at an effective level of clarity. The result is a project proceeding through to execution with insufficient clarity about uncertainty associated with design or operations or termination and insufficient management of that uncertainty. During delivery or operation or termination this gives rise to difficulties necessitating additional design development and operations planning plus ongoing adverse effects on the performance criteria of cost, time and quality. Related opportunity inefficiency associated with 'premature definition' is also difficult to avoid entirely, except on very routine, repeated projects, and the problem is most acute in novel, one-off projects involving new technology. The basis of both problems is that it is extremely difficult to specify in advance how every part of the execution, delivery, operations and termination stages of the lifecycle will unfold; neither is it cost effective to seek to do so. In any case, some uncertainty about operating conditions and related factors outside the control of project management will always remain. Inevitably, judgements have to be made about the degree of detail and accuracy practicable in the DOT shaping stage, and some will be well worth revisiting by the end of the E&D shaping stage as part of an overall assessment of strategy. Identifying DOT shaping stage risky conditions in project and process terms can be a useful focus, relating them to what has been learned since the DOT gateway. Chapter 12 will also clarify some of these issues.

Tactics shaping

The tactics shaping stage is a significant task involving decisions about project organization, identification of appropriate agents, and allocation of tasks between them. Much of the detailed planning in large projects may be done by different parties as part of a contracting and follow-on subcontracting process. As noted in the previous section, the introduction of an agent is prone to the three problems of adverse selection, moral hazard and uncertainty allocation. In particular, this stage of a project can introduce several sources of uncertainty with significant risk inefficiency implications:

- participants have different priorities and risk/opportunity/uncertainty perceptions;
- unclear specification of responsibilities, including those relating to uncertainty;
- communications between different departments or organizations;
- coordination and control tasks.

Even if client and agents all work for the same organization, the problems presented by these uncertainties can be substantial. When agents are different organizations, these problems can be particularly challenging.

In a client–contractor situation, the client exerts influence over the contractor primarily via conditions laid down in a contract between the two parties. The contract sets out what is to be produced, what the client will pay, how the client can assess and monitor what the contractor has done, and how things should proceed in the case of various contingent events. In theory, the contract seeks to reduce uncertainty about each party's responsibilities. In practice substantial uncertainties can remain associated with items such as:

- inadequate or ambiguous definition of terms (specifications; responsibilities of parties to cooperate, advise, coordinate, supervise);
- inappropriate definition of terms (performance specifications; variations; extensions);
- variations (powers to order; express and implied terms; pricing and payment mechanisms);

- payment and claims arrangements (timing and conditions for payment);
- defects liability (who has to be satisfied; who could be responsible; extent of liability).

Effective uncertainty management towards the end of the E&D shaping stage should look forward and anticipate these issues, putting effective responses in place. It should also raise the question 'could the devil be in the detail in tactics shaping terms?' That is, should selective detailed planning be undertaken before strategy is agreed and comprehensive detailed planning and design begins?

Execution and delivery

During the 'execution and delivery' stage the essential process issue is the adequacy of coordination and control procedures. Thus coordination and control ought to include uncertainty management practices as 'good project management practices' which amount to:

- milestone management;
- adequate monitoring of activities likely to go wrong;
- ensuring realistic, honest reporting of progress;
- reporting problems and revised assessments of future issues.

A common source of opportunity inefficiency in the execution and delivery stage is the introduction of design changes. These late design changes can lead to major schedule disruptions, with knock-on implications driven by resource plans, affecting cost, time and quality measures of performance directly. A potentially serious concern is that changes are introduced without a full appreciation of the knock-on consequences. Apart from direct consequences, indirect consequences can occur. For example, changes may induce an extension of schedules, allowing contractors to escape the adverse consequences of delays in works unaffected by the change. Changes may have wider technical implications than first thought, leading to subsequent disputes between client and contractor about liability for costs and consequential delays (Williams et al., 1995a, 1995b; Cooper, 1980). Standard project management practice should establish product change control procedures which set up criteria for allowable changes and provide for adequate coordination, communication and documentation of changes. However, adjustments to production plans, costs, and payments to affected contractors ought to be based on an assessment of how project uncertainty is affected by the changes and the extent to which revised uncertainty management plans are needed.

In an operational context involving repetitive actions, human failings can be a significant source of risk inefficiency. Studies of accidents and disasters often identify 'human error' and 'management error' as major contributory causes (Engineering Council, 1993, app. 3; Kletz, 1985). Such risk inefficiency may be evident in a project setting. Although the novelty of a project can discourage complacency and carelessness to some degree, the project context is often characterized by sufficient novelty, complexity, work pressure, and uncertainty as to increase greatly the likely significance of human failure or error.

In any organizational context, a number of factors influence the performance of an individual participant, as shown in the left-hand column of Table 7.4. Failure in individual performance, whether amounting to inadequate or incorrect performance, may be related to one or more of these factors in a wide variety of ways, as shown in the right-hand column of Table 7.4.

Table 7.4   Possible causes of inadequate or incorrect performance by individuals

Factors	Sources of opportunity/risk inefficiency
Task perception	Following instructions which are incorrect Failure to realize responsibility Personal interpretation of a task required Mistaken priorities, such as taking short cuts through safety rules to save time
Capability and experience	Lack of appropriate training or skills to perform a task Failure to follow instructions Lack of appreciation of consequences of actions Inappropriate choice of procedure to achieve desired outcome Jumping to conclusions about the nature of a situation
Work environment	Information overload makes it difficult to identify important pieces of information and easier to ignore or delay scrutiny Task overload impairs ability to monitor developments and formulate reactive or proactive responses Difficult working environment Inadequate work environment, equipment, or procedures increase the chance of mistakes
Mistake	Random slips Failure to detect very unusual situations or rare events Incorrect assessment of a situation
Motivation	Lack of incentive for high level of performance Lack of concentration on a task Personal objectives
Actions of others	Failure to communicate information Frustration of actions Incorrect or faulty components supplied Insufficient quality of contribution

In a project context, sources of opportunity/risk inefficiency of the kind listed in Table 7.4 could feature in any stage of the project lifecycle. However, seeking to identify such sources associated with individuals at every stage may represent an excessive level of analysis. More usefully the factors in Table 7.4 might be applied to particular groups of individuals or to individual participating organizations. In the latter case it is easy to see how the sources of risk inefficiency of Table 7.4 might be associated with individual departments or whole organizations acting, for example, in the capacity of contractors or subcontractors.

At the very least, looking forward to the execution and delivery stage at this point should raise the question: 'Could the devil be in the detail in execution and delivery stage terms?' That is, should selective trials of execution and delivery techniques and associated training be undertaken before strategy is agreed – what the building industry see as 'buildability' issues.

Operations and support (O&S)

Looking forward to the O&S stage and developing appropriate responses for key sources while still in the E&D shaping stage can reduce or eliminate potential later problems at relatively low cost.

This can be seen as what should have happened in the DOT shaping stage if an effective PUMP was used, updated when that stage was addressed as discussed a few subsections earlier. If not, it needs attention now. At the very least looking forward to the O&S stage at this point should raise the question: 'Could the devil be in the detail in O&S stage terms?' That is, should selective trials of O&S techniques and associated training be undertaken before strategy is agreed – what might be called 'operability and supportability' issues. The key here is identifying which sources of uncertainty need this attention before the end of the three strategy shaping stages of the life-cycle, and which do not.

Termination

Looking forward to the termination stage while still in the E&D shaping stage can also prove very productive. 'Terminability' probably does not work as a useful term, but the concept should be clear. The key is identifying any important termination stage sources needing identification before strategy shaping is concluded.

Links and dependencies anticipated in the identify phase

It is convenient to leave a search for links and dependences between sources of uncertainty and responses until the next phase, as discussed in the next chapter. However, in practice PUMP management embodied in the ongoing focus phase has to anticipate what the structure phase might provide when deciding to move on to that phase instead of probing more deeply in the identify phase.

One way to reduce the need to consider statistical dependencies later in the process is the identification of associated underlying causal relationships now, via greater depth. For example, if overheating of markets for key resources is a common problem for many activities, separate identification of this source of uncertainty will allow more detailed causal explanations and models of its effects and appropriate responses.

Looking for more breadth within the seven Ws and project lifecycle structure is a matter of completeness which evolves over successive passes. Looking for more depth is usually a matter for late passes once it is clear what is important, but whether enough depth has been achieved may be an issue on any pass.

Generalizing 'more depth'

What more depth might involve beyond the kind of source–response–secondary source chains described in terms of pipe laying wet buckles is worth brief clarification here, after first reviewing the integration of top-down and bottom-up analysis central to PUMP.

As noted in Chapter 6, an important aspect of the PUMP focus phase is a top-down appreciation of uncertainty, to determine where the limits of the project manager's responsibilities for managing project-related uncertainty lie, and to size the big uncertainty areas, as a basis for PUMP design. This involves identifying which sources are 'internal' to the project and therefore the responsibility of the project manager, and which are 'external' and therefore the responsibility of higher level management. It also involves a first pass, top-down view of internal project uncertainty, quantifying this in terms of cost, revenue, duration and other performance measures as appropriate.

It is important to appreciate the three separate roles this kind of top-down perspective can provide. It provides a background initial view of uncertainty from a senior management perspective. It provides a basis for designing a bottom-up detailed PUMP process. And it provides a consistency check against a bottom-up analysis. Top-down and bottom-up analysis should confirm each other, and adjustment to one or both pursued until they do.

In order to allocate analysis effort efficiently and effectively, the bottom-up PUMP as a whole as described in Part II needs to start at a reasonably simple level on the first pass, and facilitate deeper (lower level) subsequent analysis on later passes, wherever this is clarity efficient. That is, the level of 'the bottom' needs to be moved down selectively as successive iterations unfold. Further, is important to appreciate that the PERT/Generalized PERT/GERT/SCERT model set which underlies the structure of this analysis in a 'whichway' dimension, and comparable structures for other Ws, may be complemented or replaced in some areas by alternative frameworks which better capture the structure of issues. As we go deeper, dependencies become more and more important, and a switch to other Ws can require major model structure changes, depending upon the process objectives. For example the use of a systems dynamics model structure to capture positive and negative feedback loops may prove useful as an alternative to a SCERT structure in some circumstances (Williams et al., 1995a, 1995b; Williams 2005; Ackermann et al., 2007).

Even if the structure remains the same, further decomposition of categories of uncertainty can be undertaken in subsequent iterations through the steps in Figure 7.1. One key consideration is ensuring that deeper levels of uncertainty are identified whenever appropriate, as distinct from more detail at the same level. Another key issue is understanding the sources identified well enough to identify responses in an effective manner. Consider an example, described in more detail elsewhere (Chapman, 1988), which illustrates one way of considering uncertainty at different levels.

Beaufort Sea oil project

A proposed Beaufort Sea oil project was being considered by Gulf Canada. It involved oil production on artificial islands. The oil would be sent through pipes to the shore in a sea area known for very deep ice-scours in the ocean bed. These deep scours would threaten a pipeline even if it were buried 3 or 4 metres beneath the sea bed, many times deeper than conventional pipe burying. The key source of uncertainty associated with a key performance criterion that Chris was asked (by the project manager) to address was 'ice-scour damage' to the pipeline. This composite source of uncertainty question was addressed via decomposition. The question 'what was the chance of ice-scour damage?' involved two components:

1. What was the chance ice would strike the pipeline?
2. What was the chance that an ice strike would seriously damage the pipeline?

Chris was also asked to take the first of these questions to still deeper levels of analysis by the company ice-scour experts, addressing the questions:

1. What was the uncertainty in their data, with a view to assessing what type of additional data would be most useful (more seasons or a wider area within a season, for example)?
2. What was the uncertainty in the statistical model used to estimate the likelihood of scours at different depths?

Deeper levels of analysis could be associated with the alternative mechanisms associated with generating scour (ice heave during freezing versus grounded ice during thaws), and so on. Further, deeper levels of analysis for pipe failure mechanisms given an ice strike would involve very different questions and models. Any project's 'wet buckle equivalents' might be approached in a similar manner to provide greater clarity via greater depth of analysis. The issue always is 'would it pay?'

Different contexts leading to different starting positions

It was convenient to outline what the identify phase involves in all six steps using a single BP example as a starting point for most early discussion. However, reconsider 'clarify immediate priorities', step 1 of the identify phase, if a very different context is involved.

The project lifecycle and seven Ws structure, as developed in the define phase, remain central, as do the criteria–plan relationship structures. In the E&D shaping stage, overall project duration and associated timing is usually important, but the starting place may be somewhat different. For example, the first oil refinery project cost uncertainty analysis addressed by BP with support by Chris, shortly after the Magnus exercise, began the identify phase equivalent of an E&D shaping stage analysis by ignoring construction activity duration uncertainty and taking a direct interest in market factors influencing the cost of major components and materials over the period prior to letting the key procurement contracts. The view of the project staff involved, supported by the subsequent analysis and outcomes, was timing all contracting and the start of associated work in relation to markets becoming hotter or seriously overheated was the key source of uncertainty that could be directly managed, and how long the project took once contracts were in place was a directly dependent second order concern. Anticipating this for subsequent refinery cost assessments affected the define and focus phase, but this kind of change should also drive both via the iterative process within any given project, even if it is the first project of this kind.

If other lifecycle positions are involved, the differences can be more fundamental. For example, when a Canadian oil major was considering concept stage assessment of the offshore project involving icebergs discussed in Chapter 3, how much it would cost to build a gravity platform had to be assessed in terms of a very preliminary design, with design ambiguity a key component, largely driven by contributing ambiguity about operating conditions affecting the platform. Project and associated activity duration was not an immediate issue. Indeed, the two biggest relevant sources of uncertainty had little to do with the gravity platform of immediate interest. They were how much oil was in the reservoir, and what price would it fetch per barrel in the market place over the lifetime of the field? The key component of the seven Ws needed to start an appropriate analysis was the cash flow model driving the plans for business case purposes, and revenue was more important than cost.

If a very different starting position is adopted, the details of the analysis that follows will look very different. But to ensure relevant base plans and contingency plans are shaped in opportunity efficient terms, the basic structure of the Figure 7.1 process still applies, the lifecycle and seven-Ws structure remain central, and the role of the criteria–plan relationship structure remains critical.

Keeping it simple when lower clarity is appropriate

Keeping it simple when a lower level of clarity is appropriate is *always* a *very* important issue. However, to avoid being simplistic – using inappropriate simplicity – it is useful to start by understanding what clarity efficient approaches delivering high clarity involve. That is why this section has been delayed until now, with a comparable pattern in other Part II chapters.

Lower clarity approaches should be viewed as effective shortcuts based on a clear understanding of what a high clarity approach ought to deliver and what it ought to cost, bearing in mind associated uncertainty, and the full range of low and intermediate clarity options available. The ability to select an appropriate lower level clarity approach has to depend upon relevant knowledge and experience.

Lower clarity may be appropriate for a variety of reasons. For example, politicians may want an estimate of the cost of a new road or a new aircraft carrier which *might* be built in ten years time, *if* in five years time it is deemed an affordable priority. It *may* not be worth detailed assessment of how either possibility would be built or what would be built if it may not be built, except insofar as this information might be needed to obtain as unbiased view of the expected cost and related overall uncertainty. This is particularly important on a first pass, when an unbiased order of magnitude figure may indicate that the idea should be dropped as non-feasible, any more effort being a clear waste of time and money.

The simplest version of the identify phase, on the first pass of an exploratory process, simply assumes a single composite source for each of the relevant seven Ws components identified in the first pass of the define phase. If activities are involved and the process goes on to direct quantification, a basic PERT model is implied, perhaps simplified to P10 to P90 range estimates assuming uniform distributions, a minimum clarity quantitative model as discussed earlier. Comparable approaches would be involved for all other W structures.

If it is not obvious that a high clarity approach is needed, overall clarity optimization in clarity efficiency terms suggests this kind of minimum clarity approach on the first pass, then adding a little more clarity where doing so would clearly pay in later passes, unless the cosmetic effects of more apparent precision is worthwhile on the first pass. For example, using three-point estimates and asymmetric smooth curves may make some users more comfortable than P10 to P90 ranges to define linear cumulative probability distributions, and this may justify cosmetic detail.

A wide range estimate on the first pass might suggest a second pass which looks for one or two 'wet buckle' equivalents, and a 'productivity variations' equivalent. If responses are not immediately relevant, the first reasonably robust response identified might be assumed. If semi-Markov processes to explore effects over a sequence of time periods have no obvious immediate value, they should not be used.

In a case like the Highways Agency example discussed in Chapter 2, three sources of uncertainty were used to capture *all* the relevant uncertainty associated with the construction cost aspect of a road's capital cost in a simple composite level manner, using decomposition to assist unbiased estimation, not to generate responses. Decomposition is always about more clarity, but what provides the biggest increase in clarity for the least additional effort will depend on the purpose of the exercise.

The level of clarity sought in the identify phase clearly needs to be coordinated with the level of clarity sought in the earlier define phase and the later estimate phase. Coordination of these decisions is part of the ongoing focus phase.

The key to understanding what is needed is an understanding of the composite nature of any simple quantitative estimate of uncertainty or its qualitative equivalent, and the benefits of decomposition, given what that decomposition would provide and cost. If an offshore North Sea project's overall cost estimate has a P10 to P90 range like £1.2 to 1.9 billion, it is clearly worth decomposing this uncertainty as discussed earlier in this chapter before a responsible board releases the funds to build it. However, this level of uncertainty may be entirely acceptable at the concept shaping stage given a much more modest decomposition to explain its nature. If a possible new road cost estimate has a P10 to P90 range like £1.2 to 1.9 million, a very different level and kind of decomposition may be relevant when it still has no political commitment or priority.

Identification phase deliverables fit for purpose?

Figure 7.1 shows the current pass of the identify phase terminating once the identification of relevant sources, responses and conditions is 'fit for purpose' on this pass. It can be difficult to decide when this point has been reached.

On the first pass and on following early passes it is very important to anticipate a return to the identify phase from later phases in the PUMP as insights and issues from the analysis as a whole emerge. On a first pass aim for much less detail than is likely to be necessary – to avoid a detailed analysis that would later prove wasted.

This principle should be followed less aggressively on subsequent passes. There is always a risk that further iterations will not happen. Further, inefficiencies associated with too much iteration to get to a given level of analysis in a given area may add to the cost of analysis significantly, depending upon how iterations are managed. This reinforces the case for making the identify phase as complete as possible in terms of breath and depth before proceeding to the next phase. Part of the basic overall case for completeness reasonably early in the iterations is the value of specific responses which serve as general responses, building in robustness with less pressure for specific response detail. Another part of the basic case for early completeness is that whenever sources, responses, and associated secondary issues (response chains) are not properly understood, any subsequent uncertainty management can be a complete waste of resources. Risky conditions that are not understood have similar implications.

Bearing all this in mind, time management pressures and the availability of key people may require getting on with some of the next phase while the identify phase is still in progress. Further, sometimes it can be useful to treat PUMPs for different parts of a project as concurrent parallel projects.

Delays associated with an incomplete define phase can aggravate the complications this leads to. Regarding a PUMP as a project or portfolio of projects in its own right, this is 'fast tracking' in a fairly extreme form, rather like starting to put up a building before the foundations are fully in place. Any attempt to 'fast track' a PUMP needs to be managed with great care.

Conclusion

The identify phase involves the identification of at least one source of uncertainty for each activity or other plan component associated with the seven Ws identified in the define phase. If a detailed decomposition of this basic source structure is relevant, identified and decomposed, responses may also prove relevant. A generic 'do nothing' or 'cross your bridges when you come to them' response is one option, but this will not be appropriate in some cases. A generic 'do nothing or something unspecified' is inevitable if sources of uncertainty are high level composites like PERT activity duration variability with no intention to deal with explicit responses.

If a high clarity approach is needed, and an activity structure is the priority place to start, a first pass through the six steps of the identify phase should provide a preliminary list of obvious 'wet buckle' equivalents plus a 'productivity variations' equivalent for all key high uncertainty activities. This first pass should also provide a 'repair' equivalent reactive response option plus a reasonably rich set of other options whenever this may be relevant. As in earlier Part II chapters, it is useful to start by assuming a high clarity approach for a client without the experience to take short-cuts, and it is always important to take short-cuts understanding what is gained and lost. Even when high clarity overall is clearly needed, detailed lists of response options may be deferred until later passes for those sources that prove significant, but early identification of response options can form the basis of a concerted opportunity identification process that goes beyond simple threat management. Risk and opportunity efficiency is about generating options which may lead to better plans, responses to sources providing the starting point from a PUMP perspective.

Some guides have descriptions of identify phase equivalents which concentrate initially on assessing the effects of 'risks' (sources) without reference to associated responses, leaving consideration of responses until later, and then only consider alternatives in relation to major issues. Most ignore the composite nature of uncertainty assessments considering *all* sources of uncertainty, including assumptions. The authors recommend an early proactive approach to responses in an iterative framework as indicated above when high clarity is needed, simplified for lower levels of clarity without losing sight of what simplification costs as well as its benefits. The essence of the matter on early passes is:

- do not waste time considering the details of a decomposed structure of primary sources if a higher level composite perspective is adequate;
- when considering responses to primary sources do not waste time considering alternative responses if the first is both effective and efficient;
- do not overlook key responses;
- do not overlook key reasons why key responses may not work;
- do not overlook any apparently minor problem that has no effective fix once it occurs;
- identify opportunities that may have implications beyond the issues that triggered their consideration;

- always emphasize the opportunity management aspect of the process if it looks like it might pay to do so;
- do not overlook sources treated as conditions.

On later passes explore deeper levels of uncertainty where this is particularly important and when it becomes clear that it is important.

The quotation at the beginning of this chapter can be linked to the notion of uncertainty as a composite which may be clarified at different levels to reveal opportunity and risk. A high clarity approach like BP's version of SCERT supplemented by more recent ideas such as those developed for the Highways Agency will put a wide and rich range of sources in clear view, complete with responses and secondary sources. A lower clarity PUMP approach like that used by the Highways Agency for their simple re-estimation exercise will not provide this clarity, but it may provide a huge improvement on common practice in terms of eliminating estimation bias while reducing the effort involved – greater clarity efficiency. Clarity efficient PUMPs are like good quality prescription sunglasses – they filter out the glare of unwanted light, but they do not blind the wearer. Common practice approaches which are limited to event uncertainty are roughly comparable to Zaphod's sunglasses with scratches. The scratches provide glimpses of some potentially dangerous events, but completely eliminate all other serious approaching dangers from vision, and most important opportunities.

This chapter is long relative to all other chapters in this book because the identify phase has to cover a lot of ground if high clarity is needed, all of which needs understanding to take effective shortcuts. However, the identify phase is not particularly complex to implement once its role in relation to the PUMP as a whole is understood. It is arguably one of the simplest of the seven phases to execute most of the time given a clear understanding of what is involved.

Chapter 8

Structure *all* uncertainty

… for want of a nail the shoe was lost; for want of a shoe the horse was lost; and for want of a horse the rider was lost.

—Benjamin Franklin, 1758

The define phase provides a basic seven Ws and project lifecycle structure. The identify phase extends this structure to *all* identified sources of uncertainty, some treated as conditions, plus relevant response options. The structure phase is concerned with completing the associated qualitative analysis apart from the ownership issues addressed in the next phase. The objective is to improve understanding of the relative importance of different sources given a qualitative view of consequences and identified response options, to explore relevant interactions, and to test the assumptions implicit or explicit in all earlier steps. This can lead to refinement of existing response options and prompt the development of new responses which are more effective. It can also lead to more effective forms of analysis.

In general, we want the structure used to be as simple as possible, but not misleadingly so. The structure phase involves testing simplifying assumptions and developing alternative assumptions when appropriate. More complex structure or simpler structure may improve clarity efficiency.

Failure to deal with complexity can render analysis dangerously misleading. For example, assuming a large number of sources of uncertainty are independent will allow their individual effects to tend to cancel out when considering the overall effect, on a 'swings-and-roundabouts' basis. But, if, in practice, they are positively correlated (things tend to go well or badly at the same time), this assumed cancelling effect will be significantly reduced. Such circumstances need to be appreciated, counter-balanced if appropriate, and overall residual bias in assessments taken into account. Conversely, failure to simplify when appropriate can mean unproductive effort which reduces overall effectiveness. For example, sometimes simple, slightly pessimistic assumptions about dependence will suffice until we see if associated variability matters.

Failure to structure effectively can also lead to lost opportunities. For example, some responses to particular sources operate in practice as general responses in that they can deal with whole sets of sources, possibly all sources up to that point in a project, including sources which have not been identified. It is *very* important to recognize the opportunities provided by such general responses.

The structure phase involves four specific tasks:

1. *Develop orderings* – Develop an ordering of sources and associated responses for several purposes, including priorities for project and process planning and convenience for expository purposes (reports, presentations and discussion).
2. *Explore interactions* – Review and explore possible interdependencies or links between the key plan components (project activities, for example), other plan and seven W components, sources and responses, seek to understand the reasons for these interdependencies, and further adjust orderings to reflect them.
3. *Refine classifications* – Review and develop where appropriate existing source of uncertainty classifications, in the sense that a 'new' response may be defined because the understanding associated with an 'old' response may be refined, and in the sense that a new classification structure may be introduced, distinguishing between specific and general responses, for example.
4. *Other selective restructuring* – Insights derived from the above may lead to revisions to precedence relationships for activities assumed in the define phase, and comparable relationship adjustments in terms of the other Ws.

Sometimes these four tasks are usefully seen as different modes of analysis best treated separately in the sequence shown, but in general a prescribed sequence is not helpful, and parallel progression on all four may be appropriate.

Most generic risk management process frameworks do not promote an explicit, separate, stand-alone structure phase, although PRAM does use one, and is the first generic process to do so. Some traditional modelling approaches, such as basic PERT, may seem to have no need for a separate structure phase, because the approach used inherently assumes a particular simple standardized structure. However, even in this case, testing the way the standard structure is implemented is very useful and is normally built into standard iterative process descriptions. A conventional management science approach to the use of any model-based approach requires such a step, usually referred to in terms like 'test the model'.

A variety of techniques have been developed by a number of individuals and organizations that are directly relevant to structuring in a PUMP context. This chapter attempts to integrate these considerations in a five-step process, as shown in Figure 8.1. Each of these steps may involve all four of the above specific tasks, as well as the four common tasks – document, verify, assess and report. Figure 8.1 portrays the process in a simplified form, consistent with Figures 5.1, 6.1 and 7.1.

This five-step process is more detailed than any other implicit or explicit project uncertainty management structuring process the authors are aware of, and we hope it offers some useful new insights. The approach to the first four steps is comparable to the 'ponder' approach associated with a first pass through the identify phase, prior to considering alternative approaches. It is the sort of approach a single analyst could take – and should use as a check on any specific diagramming techniques adopted in the fifth step.

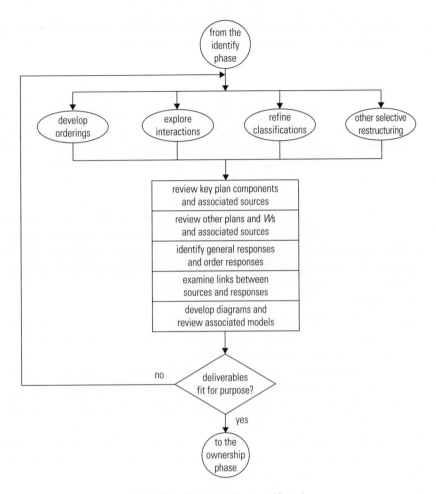

Figure 8.1   Structure phase specific tasks

As in other Part II chapters, the concern is the E&D shaping stage of the lifecycle, and a client seeking high clarity is assumed initially.

Review key plan components and associated sources

In the E&D shaping stage the key plan components are usually activities. It simplifies exposition if we assume that this is the case for present purposes.

Chapter 5 indicated the need for a summary level project activity structure represented by an activity-on-node (precedence) diagram and a Gantt chart. Part of the purpose of the 'review key plan components and associated sources' step when activities are the focus is to ensure that no important sources of precedence flexibility have been overlooked and that the constraints on precedence flexibility are clearly defined where they are important. A simple and direct approach to this task is to question each and every precedence assumption, to make sure that no potentially significant assumptions of convenience are treated as inflexible imperatives. The potential value of considering this explicitly was illustrated by the Nirex deep mine construction example of Chapter 5 – a precedence sequence was assumed so that the same resources could be used, but the rationale for the precedence relationship was not documented.

Part of the rationale for the top-down uncertainty appreciation of Chapter 6 is to clarify the difference between internal sources owned by the project and external sources owned by the corporate management team or some other party. This, together with subsequent source-response analysis, has to be used to clarify which aspects of the project are relevant for uncertainty management purposes. Important judgements about discarding or acquiring aspects of project responsibility are essential somewhere in the overall process. This step is concerned with ensuring that they are not overlooked. Important links may drive these decisions, as illustrated by the following example.

In the mid-1970s, Acres Consulting Services developed uncertainty management processes for the engineering and construction of a major pipeline planned to take Arctic oil to markets in the USA, mentioned earlier in the context of a resource constraint associated with welders. The project manager assumed that associated regulation issues were 'external' (corporate) issues. However, preliminary analysis of the permissions process, using lawyers experienced in such processes, indicated that regulatory uncertainty was a major source of project uncertainty, and management of this uncertainty could not be effective if it was treated separately from the management of technical and construction issues. Consequently, the project was redefined to recognize the need for this integrated treatment, and the regulatory risk lawyers became key players in the project uncertainty management team.

When clarifying project boundaries, it is often useful to recognize pervasive activities, sometimes associated with pervasive sources of uncertainty. For an environmentally sensitive project, 'maintain public confidence' may be such an activity, linked to one or more specific permission process activities, but also linked to other specific corporate activities within and beyond the project. It may be very important to recognize such pervasive activities formally, in order to ensure that basic things get done to avoid the obvious associated threats. They can be worth seeing as other relevant Ws without the detail mapped onto the activity framework.

A further aspect of this step is making sure that all activity definitions correspond to a common date for the 'snap-shot' that the PUMP will provide. This is a change control aspect of the PUMP (as distinct from the project). However, addressing change control for the PUMP may serve as a reminder to ensure all necessary project change control processes are in place, as part of an assessment of the project management process. This illustrates the cross-checking which a PUMP can stimulate. Having captured one new important idea or link, the instinctive question that should be asked is: 'Does this idea or link apply anywhere else?'

A goal of this step is a documented structure for the activities that reflect interactions with all other aspects of the analysis and portray the 'plans for activities' aspect of the project whichway in terms that are both effective and efficient. Some of the interactions will be clarified later in the structure phase, as part of the iterative nature of this phase, but drawing together all the interactions and their effects that have been identified earlier in the PUMP is a sensible part of this first step.

In the define phase, a key skill is the ability to choose an activity structure that is *both* effective *and* simple. This skill is tested in the structure phase. A similar issue arises when identifying source and response categories. For example, if two important sources both warrant the same response, it may be sensible to aggregate them, while if different responses are involved, separation is important. One way to address this is to formally identify some sources as 'collectable', to indicate that they need to be collected together into a pool of the 'productivity variations' variety, leaving a relatively small residual of sources treated separately. Anticipation of appropriate choices in the identify phase is a key skill, illustrated by the 'wet buckle' and 'dry buckle' distinctions discussed in Chapter 7.

The basic rules of thumb for collective/separate treatment at this stage in the process on a first pass are:

1. Put all sources involving significant opportunity or risk into the 'separate' category if their responses are unique, into the 'collective' category if they share common effective responses.
2. Put all sources involving limited opportunity or risk into the 'collectable' category if an effective response is available.
3. Consider all intermediate cases on their individual merits, in terms of the value of the clarity expected from separate treatment versus the cost/effort/time required.

Statistical dependence is one of the issues that can make judgements related to the third category complex. Any difficult decisions are best deferred until a later pass, after initial quantification to size the relative importance of sources has taken place.

There is a natural tendency to omit recording some sources altogether in the identify phase because they are immediately considered to be of a minor nature. The merit in not doing so, using a 'collective' treatment designation audited now, is to ensure that:

- there is a complete audit trail, to protect organizations and careers should such sources prove important and questions are asked about their identification;
- apparently minor issues which do not have an effective response are less likely to be overlooked;
- prior to any estimation effort, sources are given an effective and efficient estimation structure, with separate treatment of sources which are worth separate treatment, and collective treatment of those which are not;
- the nature of the sources treated collectively is clarified, with a rich range of examples to make underestimation of the effect of such sources less likely.

Review other plans and Ws and associated sources

Analogous sources may need to be dealt with for other plans and Ws, and some basic structural linkages between the Ws usually require attention. Consider some illustrations.

A Gantt chart, defined by the precedence relationships between activities and base estimates for activity durations, provides a base estimate of the overall project 'when'. It may be useful to ensure that formal links between Gantt charts and activity-on-node network diagrams are in place in terms of a joint computer-based model at this stage. This allows rapid assessment of the effect of a change in the plans for activities on the 'when' and vice versa.

Project resource usage can be linked to Gantt charts via standard activity-based resource planning models. If resource usage is a potential area of restriction, it may be worth using these models to explore just how much flexibility is available. In the limit, some projects are resource driven and should be managed in a manner which reflects this.

Project direct and indirect costs can be linked to Gantt charts via resource usage and cost, or directly via time–cost functions. These can be used to explore the flexibility associated with the project 'when', in overall project terms, and in relation to specific activities. The possible use of such models was alluded to in Chapter 7. At this stage, ensuring that such a model is not required if it is not already in place becomes an issue.

It may be useful to recognize formal links between project 'whichway–when–wherewithal' issues and the project 'what'. By way of an illustration, in the framework of a generalized PERT model decision trees can be used to embed design change decisions into a base plan network, using what are called decision nodes as well as precedence nodes. For example, if a test on a high risk component is successful, the project proceeds using it, but if the test fails, an alternative approach is adopted.

In some circumstances plans for activities may be less important than other plans, particularly if other lifecycle stages are involved, and using a more general label for the first step is useful. Part III will explore some relevant examples.

Identify general responses and order responses

Responses require development in the structure phase for some of the same reasons as the sources and associated activities or other plans and W components, leading to useful selective restructuring if more or less complexity increases clarity efficiency. Two new aspects of this selective restructuring development are worth highlighting:

- distinguishing between specific and general responses;
- ordering specific and general responses.

Distinguishing between specific and general responses

Some responses are specific to particular sources. For example, if a pipeline 'wet buckle' occurs as discussed in Chapter 7, 'repair' or 'abandon and start again' are feasible specific responses. Other responses may be identified in the context of a particular source, but serve as general responses in the sense that they offer a solution to a wide range of sources, including important unknown sources. This calls for a careful and systematic search for all general responses. As a simple, practical matter, all project managers should try to make sure that they have at least one general response available to deal with combinations of sources, including sources they may not have been able to identify. Consider a further extension of the Chapter 7 discussion of wet buckle responses.

It was recognized that more than one wet buckle could occur, leading to very serious delay. A possible response to this specific source was identified – using a second lay barge working from the other end, with a submarine connection to join the two parts of the pipeline. It soon became clear that this response was unlikely to work unless a contractual option on a second barge was in place. It then became clear that the cost of such an option was too high if it's only role was dealing with two or more buckles. However, it was then recognized that this response was a general response. It would recover time lost due to any combination of buckles, bad weather, equipment failures, a delayed start to pipe laying and a wide range of other difficulties, including some that may not have been identified in the first place.

Planning to lay pipe from both ends using two barges was not a cost effective base plan. Nor was it a cost effective response to two or more wet buckles in isolation. However, being able to use a second barge in this way as a contingency plan provided a very powerful way to buy back lost time resulting from earlier delays triggered by a wide range of identified sources, and a source of comfort in relation to unidentified sources. This made the purchase of an option on the use of a second barge in case of need a particularly important issue. If this powerful general response was not available when needed because the importance of the option was not recognized earlier, a major failure of the proactive high clarity PUMP would have occurred.

The Chapter 7 second or third shift pipe coating option is a closely linked example from the same project. The Chapter 2 example concerned with the implications of a National Power demonstration project involving a take-or-pay gas contract for a gas turbine electricity generating project provides a further illustration of the important role of this step in the process. Using standard British Gas supplies for testing purposes was a viable response to possible delay caused by a wide range of factors, including those not identified. This option was identified as a direct result of implementing this step in the SCERT equivalent of the structure phase.

The key is being aware of any particularly useful general responses and ensuring that they can be implemented if necessary whenever this is opportunity efficient.

General responses can be viewed as a source of flexibility and resilience, building in flexibility and resilience being a key generic response to uncertainty which deserves attention from several perspectives. Hopkinson (2011) emphasizes the same point, using the expression 'overarching responses', and observing that commercial solutions that foster constructive behaviour between the parties are often effective general responses.

Ordering specific and general responses

It is useful to identify a preliminary ordering of responses in a preferred sequence in terms of which response is the most effective first choice, and if that fails, what is the next best choice, and so on. Ordering of responses may be useful for each set of specific responses associated with particular sources and for each set of general responses associated with particular activities. While comparable to the ordering of activities in precedence terms to some extent, ordering of responses is a rather different process, with no prior formal analysis to provide its basis. In early iterations the judgements may be purely intuitive. At a later stage, analysis can be used to test these intuitions when appropriate.

Other selective restructuring

One example of possible further selective restructuring is identifying a general response that is so powerful that it makes further consideration of complex separate source and specific response combinations redundant. Another example is reordering sources of uncertainty so that their order corresponds to the sequence in which they might be experienced to improve ease of review and discussion. Reordering of sources to clarify discussion was recognized as important in the very early BP studies. A particularly important example, recognised relatively recently, is simplifying a summary description of all project scope conditions and all process scope conditions when this is useful. This kind of 'other selective restructuring' is part of all five steps, usefully mentioned specifically in this step. Looking for effective ways to simplify is always important and often worth while.

Examine links between sources and responses

Examination of links between sources and responses involves a systematic search for dependencies between sources and responses associated with all seven Ws of the project. One aspect of examining these links involves reassessing all specific and pervasive sources in the light of preferred responses and secondary issues. The basic approach is to ask, for each source, the question: 'Could this source initiate problems in any directly or indirectly related source, response, base activity or other project W?' Another aspect of examining these links is to ask, for all identified responses which are reasonably likely to be implemented, the question 'If this response is implemented will it affect other activities, responses, or sources?' One product of this search will be the identification of responses that are mutually exclusive or incompatible, or affect other activities in an adverse manner. Alternatively, economies of scale or synergies between possible responses may be identified which offer opportunities for further improvements in project performance.

Ensuring any pervasive sources have been identified as pervasive is an essential starting point, comparable to, and linked to, the search for pervasive activities and general responses. Pervasive sources may be sources that operate as underlying causal factors for several different sources, or sources that impact on a number of different activities or responses. Consider an example – weather as a pervasive source in North Sea projects.

'Weather' was a major source of uncertainty when considering pipe laying in the North Sea in the 1970s. As discussed earlier, a 1.6 m lay barge was a barge deemed capable of working in wave conditions up to a nominal 1.6 metres maximum height, so 'weather' in terms of wave height was a direct source of uncertainty in relation to pipe-laying performance.

In addition to this direct effect, bad weather greatly increased the chance of a buckle, and the probability of a buckle increased significantly as the amount of work in the 'shoulder seasons' (early spring or late autumn) increased because of the weather implications. It was important to recognize and model this dependency effect to understand the implications.

Often dependence between different sources can be identified in causal terms. Sometimes the relationship is not clearly definable in these terms, and may be best described in terms of statistical dependence. For example, preliminary 'macro' level assessments of the relationship between capital cost items associated with BP refinery projects suggested about 60 to 90% dependence – equivalent to a coefficient of correlation of 0.6 to 0.9 approximately. (Dependence measures and approaches to dependence are discussed in Chapter 11.) This level of dependence was driven by the prevailing level of construction activity and other specific market pressures, as well as more general economic conditions. Attempts to describe this dependence between cost items or associated activities in causal terms were not fruitful, in the sense that too many different factors were clearly driving a similar joint movement to make individual identification and modelling of the factors worth while. However, it became clear that it was essential to model this statistical dependence to avoid bias which otherwise made cost uncertainty estimates misleading to an excessive degree. Further, it became clear that exploring market cycles and their impact on the project as a whole could be very useful.

Statistical or causal dependencies can also be generated by responses. For example, if, in a construction project based on the use of two cranes, one crane should fail and the response is to press on using only one crane, a significant increase in use may be required from the surviving crane, possibly increasing its failure probability. In the limit, such dependencies can cause a cascade or domino effect. Reliability engineers are familiar with the need to understand and model such effects, but many project managers are not.

It may be important to address dependence very carefully. Failure to do so, as in using a basic PERT model and assuming an independence between activity durations that does not exist, can be dangerously misleading, as well as a complete waste of time. For example, in the context of a basic PERT network, with activity A followed by activity B, the durations of activities A and B may be positively dependent. If A takes longer than expected, B may also take longer than expected. This can arise because the sources for A and B are common or related. Causal relationships underlying this dependence might include:

- the same contractor is employed for both activities, who, if incompetent (or particularly good) on activity A, will be the same for activity B;
- the same equipment is used for both;
- the same labour force is used for both;
- the same optimistic (or pessimistic) estimator provided estimates for both activity duration distributions using the same methodology.

An important form of dependency is the 'knock-on' or 'ripple' effect. In the simple example above, when things go wrong in activity A, the cost of activity A goes up and the delays impact on activity B. The cost of activity B then increases as a consequence of contingency responses to stay on target and knock-on effects – resources set aside may no longer be available for example, and attempts to catch up lost time may lead to double or treble shift operation or changes to more expensive technology. As a consequence of contingency responses, which induce negative time dependence, the positive statistical dependence between the durations of A and B tends to partially disappear from view. However, the negative dependence introduced into the activity duration relationships by contingency planning induces strong positive dependence between associated costs. If A costs more than expected, B tends to cost very much more than expected, because of the need to keep the project on target, quite apart from other market-driven sources of dependence and knock-on effects. Put another way, cost and duration modelling of uncertainty which does not explicitly consider contingency planning tends to estimate time uncertainty erroneously (usually optimistically), and it tends *grossly* to underestimate direct cost uncertainty. Projects that cost two or three or even ten times their estimated cost generally reflect this kind of 'knock-on' effect. Considering the impact of contingency planning will clarify apparent time uncertainty, and increase apparent direct cost uncertainty.

Common causes of 'knock-on' effects are design changes and delays, which not only have a direct impact but also cause 'ripple' effects, commonly referred to as 'delay and disruption'. Often direct consequences can be assessed fairly readily in terms such as the number of person-hours required to make a change in design drawings and the person-hours needed to implement the immediate change in the project works. However, 'ripple' effects are more difficult to assess, and may involve 'snowballing' effects such as altered work sequences, conflicting facility and manpower requirements, skill dilution, undetected work errors, and so on. Consider two examples.

Example 1 – Cooper (1980) has described how a computer simulation based on influence diagrams was used to resolve a $500 million shipbuilder claim against the US Navy. By using the simulation to diagnose the causes of cost and schedule overruns on two multi-billion dollar shipbuilding programmes, Ingalls Shipbuilding (a division of Litton Industries Inc.) quantified the costs of disruption stemming from delays and design changes due to the US Navy. In the settlement reached in June 1978, Ingalls received a net increase in income from the US Navy of $447 million. It was the first time the US Navy had given such a substantial consideration to a delay and disruption claim.

Example 2 – In 1991 apparently small changes in the design of fire doors on Channel Tunnel rolling stock was expected to lead to a delay of up to six months in providing a full service for car and coach passengers, substantially reducing expected revenue for Eurotunnel, operators of the tunnel. The problem was caused by the insistence of British and French authorities that the width of the fire doors separating the double-deck car shuttles should be widened from 28 inches to 32 inches (Taylor, 1991). In the event this and other knock-on impacts were successfully demonstrated (Williams et al., 1995a and 1995b) using a variant of Cooper's (1980) methodology. A useful more recent review of such effects is Williams (2005).

The situations described in Cooper (1980), Williams et al. (1995a, 1995b) and Williams (2005), involved what some people call 'forensic risk management'. In such cases, it is obviously unfortunate that the very considerable benefits of constructing cognitive maps to explore source-response dependencies were sought *after* these projects got into serious difficulties, rather than *before*. However, the learning points provided make this kind of analysis very useful beyond their forensic role, in several ways.

The need to appreciate fully the implications of 'knock-on' effects in a project is clear, especially for activities late in an overall project sequence, which may be considerably delayed, with possible contractual implications of great importance. As the Eurotunnel and Ingalls examples both demonstrate, this process of appreciation can be greatly facilitated by appropriate diagramming of activity–source–response structures and their interdependencies.

Develop diagrams and review associated model structures

The use of a range of diagrams is advantageous throughout the structure phase to document and help to develop insights in the structuring process. Precedence networks and Gantt charts are key documents because they capture key aspects of the project base plan. However, other diagrams are important in terms of capturing a range of wider considerations. For example, if a formal model is used to link Gantt charts to resource usage and associated resource constraints, these issues will require appropriate diagrams. If direct/indirect cost models are used, other standard diagrams will be required. Of particular concern here are diagrams that summarize our understanding of source–response structures, and links between activities, sources and responses.

Ensuring that the earlier steps in the structure phase result in a set of diagrams that summarize the classification, ordering and linking involved is extremely important. Complexity is inherent in most projects, but it must be made manageable to deal with it effectively. A summary diagram structure, which all those who need to be involved can discuss as a basis for shared understanding, is very important. Organizations that have used such diagrams often stop doing so because they are difficult to construct, but start using them again because they realize that these diagrams are difficult to produce precisely because they force a proper disciplined understanding that is otherwise not achieved. One such diagram is the source–response diagram initially developed for offshore oil projects and subsequently adopted by a range of organizations, illustrated in part by Figure 8.2.

Figure 8.2 is based on the same example as the source of uncertainty sensitivity diagram of Figure 3.2. It provides an illustration of the core features of source–response diagrams in the context of the fabrication of an offshore platform jacket, the first section of a BP diagram which went on in the same vein for several pages. A more complete version may be found in Chapman et al (1987).

Primary sources are represented by circles along the diagram's horizontal centre line and linked parallel lines. The 'yard not available' source is the first source in a time of realization sense. It implies that the yard is not available because another jacket is still under construction in the contracted yard (a dry dock construction area like a big shipyard), and our jacket has to await its completion. A close second in this 'time of realization' sense, shown slightly to the right, is 'start-up problems' – we can get access to the yard, but it has not been used for some time, so it will take time to get up to speed.

These two sources are mutually exclusive – we can have one or the other, but not both. This is why they appear in parallel. All the other sources shown are in series, indicating that they can all occur, without implying additive or multiplicative effects at this stage. Their sequence

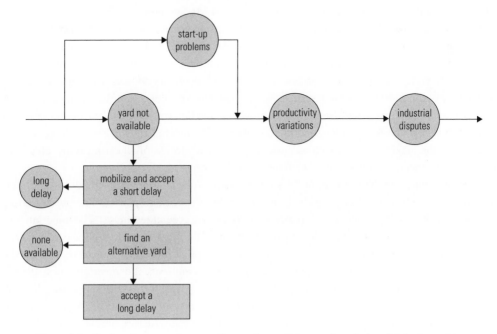

Figure 8.2   Portion of a source-response diagram for an offshore project platform fabrication activity

is nominal. Dependence relationships could be indicated on the diagram and lead to ordering sources, but independence is assumed with respect to those sources shown.

Responses are represented by boxes, ordered to reflect the preferred implementation sequence. Secondary sources are represented by circles by the side of primary response boxes. For example, if the yard is not available, the preferred response is to 'mobilize' (get ready to start work, making temporary use of another site) and 'accept a short delay'. The secondary source here is a 'long delay', which would lead to the secondary response 'find an alternative yard', hopefully limiting the delay to something shorter than 'long'. The secondary source here is 'none available', at which point 'mobilize' and 'accept a long delay' are the only remaining options.

The BP version of these diagrams illustrated in Chapman et al (1987) shows more primary sources, response boxes and secondary sources for all the sources, a way of linking successive pages, links from earlier activities discussed in notes along the top of the diagram, and notes about key assumptions under some of the response box sets. Links could appear as arrows between sources and responses, with links out to other diagrams if appropriate. For example, if 'productivity variations' led to the response 'move work offsite', the probability and the impact of 'industrial disputes' might be increased, and industrial disputes for 'jacket construction' might lead to industrial disputes for other activities. Identification of all these links, dependence and ordering issues is part of the structure phase steps identified earlier. Whether or not they will need formal modelling is a decision to be made later, in the quantify and evaluate phases of the PUMP, coupled to decisions about assumed responses and triggers for reactive responses, using and building on diagrams produced in this phase if appropriate. For example, it might be decided later to tolerate productivity variations to a significant extent in order to avoid industrial disputes before initiating any potentially provocative responses. A specified trigger point for moving on to such responses might be indicated, like 'more than 15% degradation of rate of progress per week sustained for three weeks'. This kind of high clarity modelling might imply a semi-Markov process with statistical dependence between progress distributions in successive months. However, a lower clarity first pass might just assume that all productivity variation delays will be tolerated and all sources will be modelled without modelling month-by-month effects, to keep it simple if this activity does not look critical.

These dependencies involving sources, responses and secondary sources illustrate further the complexity of the generic types of response we may have to consider to capture the most effective response to uncertainty. They also make it clear why a diagram to capture the structure provided earlier is a very good test of understanding that may lead to redefinitions in earlier steps. Indeed, completing the diagram can be seen as a useful part of the process of all earlier steps, plus later model building steps, not just a final step test of earlier steps.

The final source on the last page of the source–response diagram for each activity is a collector/ dummy source which represents residual uncertainty after specific responses. The ordered boxes which appear below this residual uncertainty collector are the general responses. The importance of the structuring process as a whole is highlighted by the need for this feature. It also indicates that the residual uncertainty of real interest is the combined effect of all individual sources (net of specific responses) less the effect of general responses. This serves to emphasize the importance of structure. Further, it clarifies the nature of the ambiguity uncertainty involved if this structure is not clarified.

Implicit in a high clarity approach to the identify phase is a very complex decision tree which will remain an implicit, ill-understood 'bushy mess' unless the structure phase is pursued until source–response diagrams like that of Figure 8.2 can be drawn. Completion of such diagrams by the PUMP team, and subsequent verification by all relevant players on the project team, is a watershed in a high clarity implementation of the overall PUMP.

In principle, a numbering system of the kind described in Chapter 7 (*u.v.w.x.y.z* designations), could be used to drive an 'automatic' computer-generated version of Figure 8.2 in terms of basic layout. National Power asked one of the authors (Chris) to assess the feasibility of such software. However, adding all appropriate links indicating dependencies as discussed in the last section would have to be 'manual'. Key links can influence the most effective diagram layout, and approaches using computer graphics in a 'manual' mode when appropriate have been employed to date by all users the authors are aware of.

The 'short delay', 'medium delay' and 'long delay' possible impacts portrayed by the three response boxes under the 'yard not available' source circle in Figure 8.2 suggest and allow comparison of this portrayal and the PIG of Figure 2.3. Both figures portray a source of uncertainty that involves an event that may or may not happen, with three possible levels of impact. However, a tick in a box in Figure 2.3 is a totally different basis for analysis, with no attempt to tease out alternative response options, dependencies that may be crucial, the accumulating effect of successive specific responses that are only partially successful, and the backstop of general responses that may provide significant opportunities, like the National Power 'start the project early and capture the opportunities' response discussed in Part I.

Decision trees

Decision trees, as explained in standard decision analysis texts, underlie source–response diagrams. Low or medium clarity implementation of a PUMP can sometimes make good use of the basic or standard form. Part of the process of developing diagrams is reviewing the associated model structure – asking the questions:

1. Would a simpler form of this model capture what matters?
2. Would a more complex form of this model be worth the effort?
3. Would an alternative form of model be more clarity efficient?

Simple decision trees can sometimes usefully simplify the model underlying Figure 8.2, and sometimes complex decision trees in a textbook format are more useful than the Figure 8.2 integration of decision trees and fault or event trees.

Fault trees and event trees

Two common approaches used in a system-failure analysis context, which underlie the Figure 8.2 approach, are fault-tree analysis and event-tree analysis. It can be useful to adopt these approaches in their basic or standard forms as a preliminary or an alternative to the use of the Figure 8.2 source–response diagram format. A classic reference is NUREG (1975).

Event-tree analysis involves identifying a sequence of events that could follow from the occurrence of particular source–response configurations, and then representing the possible scenarios in a tree diagram where each branch represents an alternative possibility.

In fault-tree analysis the process is reversed, working backwards from a particular event known as the top event, in an attempt to identify all possible sequences of events giving rise to the top event. Ishikawa or fishbone diagrams (Ishikawa, 1986) adopt a similar approach, showing necessary inputs to a particular final position.

Influence diagrams

Event-tree and fault-tree analysis approaches do not guarantee completeness in the set of possible failure modes included, and they are not very effective tools for thinking about complex feedback forms of dependence. A versatile representation of causes and effects in feedback terms can be achieved with 'influence diagrams', as used in 'systems dynamics' (Forrester, 1958, 1961; Rodrigues and Williams, 1998; Senge, 1990) and 'cognitive mapping' (Eden, 1988). The process of construction and interpretation of influence diagrams goes beyond identification of direct source–response and cause–effect relationships between key factors. It also assists in identifying potentially important links, such as particular sources that influence many other sources either directly or indirectly (Eden et al., 2000; Howick, 2003).

One advantage of influence diagrams over tree diagrams is that much more complex interactions can be shown, including feedback and feed-forward loop effects, as might be expected given their control theory origins. As noted earlier, Williams et al. (1995a, 1995b) describe a study of a large design and manufacturing engineering project which was undertaken as part of a 'delay and disruption' litigation. Design changes and delays in design approval would have caused delay to the project. In order to fulfil tight time constraints, management had to increase parallel development in the network logic, reducing delay, but setting up feedback loops that markedly increased the total project spend. Cognitive mapping, using specialist computer software called 'Graphics Cope', was used to elicit the relationships. The resulting cognitive map contained some 760 concepts and 900 links. Over 90 positive feedback loops were identified, illustrating the complex dynamics of the real situation. Figure 8.3 summarizes some of the key feedback loops.

One of the key learning points diagrams like Figure 8.3 provide is a clear illustration of the importance of positive feedback loops in terms of project 'runaway' – vicious circles leading to loss of control. Another is that some management actions can dampen positive feedback, but some can exacerbate it – two boxes in Figure 8.3 illustrate the latter – more parallel activities and enforced work on unfrozen items. Williams (2004 and 2005) explores these learning effects further. All readers need to understand the broad nature and implications of these learning points, to avoid making comparable mistakes in their projects.

In addition to their background learning role to prevent comparable mistakes, an understanding of the scale of potential dependence effects is important in terms of understanding why 100% dependence and comparable correlation coefficient of unity assumptions are closer to reality than independence in many circumstances – simple minimum clarity models using 100% dependence *may* be slightly pessimistic, but they may be optimistic, and they are prudent in a realistic manner. If sense testing results suggest that less dependence than 100% is credible, more detailed assessment of dependence *may* be appropriate. However, simply assuming less than about 60% dependence without more detailed assessment is usually very unwise.

When more detailed understanding of dependence looks useful, influence diagrams like Figure 8.3 can be a very useful exploratory tool, used as a complementary tool for Figure 8.2, or as an alternative.

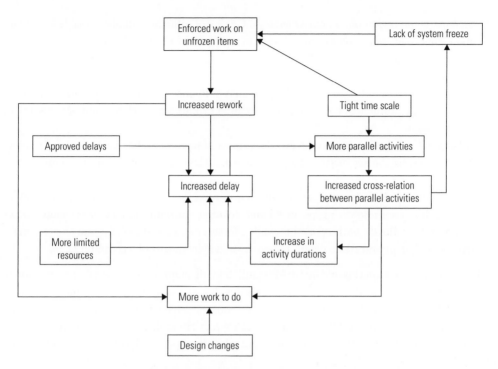

Figure 8.3   Example of cognitive mapping portrayal of key feedback loops
Reproduced by permission of the Operational Research Society

Influence diagrams such as Figure 8.3 are essentially a qualitative tool, but they can provide a starting point for systems dynamics models which are quantitative, and there are well-developed methodologies for a systems dynamics route to quantification (Rodrigues and Williams, 1998; Eden et al., 2000; Howick , 2003; Howick et al., 2008). Influence diagrams do not indicate the magnitudes or the timing of influence relationships that would be quantified in systems dynamics model simulations. Thus a link between two factors X and Y does not indicate the strength of the link, whether it is continuous or intermittent, and whether the impact on the influenced factors is immediate or delayed. Nevertheless, an influence diagram can be a useful aid to understanding a complex situation, particularly if effectively interpreted. It explores positive and negative feedback loops in a way that Figure 8.2 does not facilitate directly, providing a very useful complementary or alternative technique. Diffenbach (1982) suggests a number of guidelines for interpreting influence diagrams:

1. *Isolated factors* – A factor not linked to any other factor suggests that the isolated factor is not relevant to the depicted situation, or that not all important links and factors have been identified.
2. *Influencing only factors* – A factor that influences other factors but is not itself subject to influence from other factors prompts questions about overlooked links and factors that might influence this factor.
3. *Influenced only factors* – A factor that does not influence any other factors prompts questions about overlooked links and factors by which this factor might be influenced.

4. *Secondary and higher order consequences* – Chains of influence suggest possible secondary and higher order consequences of a change in a given factor in the chain.
5. *Indirect influences of A on B* – Chains can reveal potentially significant indirect influences of one factor on another.
6. *Multiple influences of A on B* – One factor may influence another in more than one way; these multiple influences could be direct (by link) or indirect (by chain) and of the same or opposite sign.
7. *Self-regulated loops* – A chain with an odd number of negative links that cycles back to meet itself is a self-regulating, negative loop; successive cycles of influences result in counteracting pressures.
8. *Vicious circles* – A chain with zero or an even number of negative links that cycles back to meet itself is a self-reinforcing, positive loop. However, since it is unlikely that vicious circles will operate endlessly, with no countervailing forces, one should look for one or more negative loops that are interrelated with the positive loop by means of a common factor.

The process of constructing and interpreting influence diagrams can go beyond identification of direct source–response and cause–effect relationships. It can also assist in identifying potentially important links, such as the nature of source–response chains associated with vicious circles, or particular sources which influence many other sources either directly or indirectly. Increased understanding of cause–effect relationships can also prompt the formulation of additional responses.

In a study of roles, responsibilities and risks in management contracting, Curtis et al. (1991) used relatively simple influence diagrams to indicate the main factors affecting performance of the management contractor and their interrelationships with other project parties in construction projects. This task was simplified by breaking the construction procurement process down into three relatively independent subsystems, centred on the management contractor as the key participant: the pre-contract stage; the pre-construction stage; and the construction stage. At each stage, an influence diagram portrayed the main influences on the project and management contractor behaviour. This was useful in highlighting underlying principles of behaviour and in formulating recommendations for applying management contracting.

An influence diagram approach can be seen as a precursor to structuring source–response diagrams with a view to ensuring that positive feedback loops do not occur and negative feedback loops are exploited. This has been their role in the authors' consulting to date. However, some advocates of influence diagrams and systems dynamics approaches see them as an alternative approach. For example, see Ackermann et al. (2007) for discussion of a study in a systemic risk management context which complements the current discussion but does not address uncertainty in all the aspects of interest here. Three key points flow from this:

1. If an alternative PUMP to one which ultimately uses a source–response diagram conceptual basis as described here is going to be used, in principle this should be recognized in the focus phase, and the rest of the PUMP adapted accordingly.
2. In practice, the need for an alternative approach might be picked up in this step of the structure phase, as part of the testing of the structuring assumptions made in the focus phase, and a structure phase test of robustness for the structuring aspect of the PUMP methodology is important.

3. While the authors have yet to find alternative approaches useful as a host methodology, they have found many other frameworks useful as supporting methodologies.

The situation can be different in earlier lifecycle stages, and some PUMP users might find quite different processes advantageous in some circumstances. Whatever host framework is used, the habit of always testing *all* working assumptions is very important, and the structure phase is the place to make sure that this has been done on a comprehensive basis.

More general soft systems models

The use of influence diagrams can be viewed as a reasonably 'hard' special case version of a range of 'soft' management science approaches usually referred to as soft systems, soft Operational Research (OR), or other labels which span the two, like problem (situation) structuring methods (Rosenhead, 1989; Rosenhead and Mingers, 2001; Checkland and Scholes, 1990). All these ideas are directly relevant to the structure phase.

Managing 'constructive tensions' and 'multi-methodology' concerns

Some pioneers and advocates of 'soft' approaches have viewed them as a reaction to 'hard' approaches, avoiding 'reductionism' inherent in hard science methodology, and inherently incompatible with such approaches. Others have taken the view that either can be embedded in the other (Chapman, 1992b). There is a tension between hard and soft approaches. The issue here is managing it as a 'constructive tension', along with other constructive tensions.

'Multi-methodology' is the current Operational Research (OR) term – for example, see Williams (2008) – for making sure that different methodologies used together are compatible. However, the basic idea that models and associated processes need internal consistency is not new or unique to an OR perspective, and it is central to the 'clarity efficiency' concept that underlies this book. At a more philosophical level, *Zen and the Art of Motorcycle Maintenance* (Persig, 1999) addresses this issue and the linked notion of 'quality'.

There is a sense in which a PUMP approach takes a top-down reductionism view of uncertainty about performance objectives, treating the seven Ws and the project lifecycle as the framework for a 'closed system' analysis. However, an effective PUMP demands creativity, lateral thinking and an 'open systems' mentality some of the time, especially in the identify phase. The robustness analysis aspects of the structure phase can be seen as testing the reductionism of earlier phases – 'sense testing' in qualitative terms. The search for dependencies and other links can be seen as using 'open system' exploratory approaches to support this. In particular, it is useful to see part of the role of the structure phase as looking for issues of importance that have not been effectively dealt with earlier. Systemic uncertainty is central to this search, which means that all useful approaches to 'systemic risk' need consideration. So is seeking a coherent overview, via an effective marriage of whatever approaches best provide this overview, all top-down approaches being of special relevance. 'Sense testing' in the craftsman's 'does it look and feel right?' sense can be seen as the ultimate test. An important implication is the need for craft skills.

Structure phase deliverables fit for purpose?

As with other phases of the PUMP process, the structure phase is itself an iterative process. In particular, we cannot assess the importance of some sources until we have identified responses and considered possible interactions between sources and responses. However, some prior assessment of the importance of identified sources is necessary to guide the initial structuring, to avoid too many or too few source and response categories.

The structure phase clearly connects to all previous phases, because it is a form of robustness analysis associated with all earlier phases, as well as ordering sources and responses and associated Ws for subsequent phases. Figure 4.1 limits the nominal feedback structure to one loop-back from the evaluate phase to the define phase, but selectively revising earlier structuring is important, and a loop-back from the structure phase is an obvious possibility that can be exploited to maintain internal consistency for all deliverables to this point in the process.

Before moving on to the ownership phase, the structure phase should always be as complete as possible given the progress made in the identify phase and the overall level of clarity being sought on this pass of the PUMP.

In terms of the opening quote for this chapter, a sound structure phase is about making sure your horse's shoes have a full set of nails before setting off on the full gallop implied by quantification of uncertainty. A missing nail which leads to a lost shoe which leads to a lost horse which leads to a lost rider is a classic illustration of systemic risk. Comparably minor details missed in the structure phase can lead to realizing catastrophically damaging process threats, and missed opportunities can be almost as important.

Low and intermediate levels of clarity

If a low level of clarity was appropriate in the earlier phases, proportionate simplicity is needed in the structure phase. For example, the BCS example discussed earlier involved 5–15 activity durations with a single source involving measured uncertainty for each – uncertainty for which the BCS proprietor Bruce would take responsibility if an 'estimated cost' contract was selected by the client. The associated structure phase is limited to making sure that no important tasks have been omitted or double counted. For example, clean-up time each day is easy to overlook. The 'structure phase equivalent' in the BCS bidding process has to remind Bruce to ask the question 'have I allowed for clean-up time?' *plus* 'are there any other omitted items that need a separate or collective provision?'

When intermediate levels of clarity are appropriate, thinking about where more or less detail would be productive in clarity efficiency terms can be an important aspect of the focus phase, usefully reconsidered in conjunction with specific deliverables of the structure phase.

To illustrate the potential tradeoffs involved, less activity detail with more source detail might involve the same level of effort but more clarity – more clarity efficiency. This is usually the case if 500 activities are used with a simple PERT model. Less extreme cases will involve less obvious judgements that may be helped by specific examples.

Another example of the tradeoffs which are worth consideration is more use of semi-Markov process models to model uncertain progress in successive time periods, and less detailed assessment of sources within each associated transition distribution. A further example is more time spent using influence diagrams to consider feedback dependency structures, and less detail of other kinds.

Designating 500 activities, making no attempt to understand dependence, and creating a risk register listing 500 independent 'risks', is a parody of common practice that is grossly inefficient in terms of relevant clarity tradeoffs. It should be obvious that this is territory that all organizations should avoid. But as clarity efficiency is approached, the tradeoffs become less obvious, and the need for judgements based on experience-driven craft becomes more important.

Conclusion

The structure phase as described here is a very important part of the PUMP approach, especially if clarity efficiency matters in a high clarity context. It is about transforming the information generated earlier into a qualitative model of project uncertainty, ideally summarized in diagrams, and testing the robustness of the qualitative model. The richer the information generated in the define and identify phases, and the greater the uncertainty associated with focus phase choices, the greater the need for care in the structure phase, to provide a sound basis for inferences to follow.

In the authors' experience some key points to bear in mind in the structure phase are as follows:

1. Independence, or lack of it, is one of the most significant assumptions made in any modelling of uncertainty.
2. In a cost dimension, high levels of positive dependence are endemic, and in a duration dimension important instances of both positive and negative dependence are endemic, with important interdependencies between durations and costs.
3. Making inappropriate assumptions about dependence or avoiding quantification because of dependence are potentially dangerous cop-outs which may negate the whole process. It is the difficult bits that can be particularly important.
4. There is a general tendency to deal with the bits we understand and omit consideration of the bits we do not understand. Vigorous action is needed to neutralize this tendency.
5. The most effective way to understand uncertainty dependence is to model it in causal terms.
6. 'Statistical' dependence is best thought of as a causal dependence of several kinds that cannot be sorted out, or it is not cost effective to sort them out at this stage.
7. Ensuring a simple but effective structure for sources and responses as well as activities is greatly facilitated by a diagram like Figure 8.2.
8. Being prepared to experiment with different forms of diagram, like Figure 8.3, can greatly enhance the PUMP as a whole.
9. It is important to understand that serious positive feedback effects take dependence effects way beyond simple correlation concepts, with implications that do not seem plausible unless the vicious circle effects are understood.
10. The flip side is management actions that induce negative dependence or create virtuous circles are major sources of opportunity efficiency.

Making sure that *all* relevant aspects of uncertainty have been structured is more important than the details of the specific structure employed. Any missing aspects of uncertainty are analogous to the missing nail in the shoe of the horse that Benjamin Franklin had in mind. They can bring down the horse, the rider and the mission the rider was pursuing. Risky conditions, including those which are part of the unknowable unknown because they involve framing assumptions, are particularly noteworthy. Any process without the equivalent of a focus phase and a structure phase is particularly exposed to this kind of process risk.

Chapter 9

Clarify ownership

It is an equal failing to trust everybody and to trust nobody.

—18th-century English proverb.

Making sure that every relevant source of uncertainty and response option has an appropriate owner is recognized as basic good practice – in principle. In practice this worthy ambition is rarely achieved. One obvious reason is a failure to identify particular sources of uncertainty and response options early enough in the project lifecycle. A second reason is a failure to implement an effective allocation of ownership to the parties involved in a project which works for both identified and unidentified sources of uncertainty and response options. A third reason is a failure to achieve an alignment of objectives of the relevant parties. A fourth is a failure to identify key relationships between sources of uncertainty, response options and the alignment of objectives which later prove to be important. The latter may be due to perverse incentives to ignore sources of uncertainty and response options associated with some objectives as a result of excessively strong incentives on other objectives. All four reasons involve uncertainty management process failures, and all four are the concern of the PUMP ownership phase. They can be seen as a hierarchy to some extent, and they are worth consideration separately and jointly.

Failures of uncertainty management associated with the allocation of ownership tend to arise because an 'ownership phase' is not recognized explicitly, or not given sufficient attention. Source of uncertainty and response option allocation always occurs in any situation where more than one party is responsible for the execution of a project. Just as roles and responsibilities are allocated to parties concerned, so too are uncertainty management issues associated with the enterprise. However, allocation of uncertainty, opportunity and risk can take place by default – it need not be explicit, intentional or clearly articulated. The consequences of an allocation, particularly a default allocation, may not be fully appreciated, and the manner in which allocated responsibilities are to be managed may be unclear, if they are managed at all. All forms of relationship can be interpreted as informal contracts for some purposes, and all contracts can be interpreted as incentive contracts. This perspective can be useful for examining implicit and unclear implications, including perverse incentives.

This chapter aims to provide a framework for efficient and effective ownership allocation processes, in terms of an explicit clarity efficient ownership phase in the PUMP process. Locating the ownership phase after the structure phase is appropriate because in some respects the ownership phase involves a particular kind of structuring, usefully treated separately because it deserves special emphasis, and usefully treated after the structure phase because it builds on it. Locating the ownership phase before the quantify phase is appropriate because some ownership issues need attention before starting the quantify phase. However, some ownership phase tasks can be completed quite late in terms of PUMP iterations within any lifecycle stage, and just before the gateway exit in the E&D-shaping stage.

The ownership phase has five purposes linked to the four reasons for failure noted at the beginning of this chapter:

1. to select or develop a suitable basic plan for relationship and contracting strategy which aligns objectives as far as possible for all relevant parties;
2. to distinguish the sources of uncertainty and associated response options which the project client (owner or employer) is prepared to own and manage from those the client wants other parties (such as contractors) to own or manage, in terms of all relevant objectives, including sources of uncertainty, responses and objectives which have not been identified in explicit and unambiguous terms;
3. to allocate responsibility for managing uncertainty owned by the client to named individuals as appropriate at this stage in the project lifecycle;
4. to approve, if appropriate, ownership/management allocations controlled by other parties;
5. to test the robustness of the overall approach plus the operational details as appropriate at this stage in the project lifecycle.

The first two of these five purposes should be achieved before moving on to a first attempt at the quantify and evaluate phases of the PUMP process. Some organizations will consider the first purpose as part of a concept-shaping project strategy development process or underlying corporate strategy, which the PUMP define phase should identify. Deferring achievement of the third and fourth purposes until later PUMP iterations is usually appropriate. Early attention to the fifth purpose, sustained throughout the PUMP, can be very important unless very robust approaches are guaranteed by earlier experience.

Ownership issues are often so important that it is particularly useful to treat this phase as a project in its own right, with attention to the associated seven Ws, in a manner comparable to the earlier focus phase. Ownership issues can sometimes be given a fairly simple treatment like that illustrated by the BCS approach in Chapter 2, but they are often so complex that they are considered in more detail in Part IV as part of a corporate perspective on relationship and contract plans.

Ownership issues may involve formal or explicit contracts, like a legally binding contract between a client and a contractor. Additionally, ownership issues may involve informal or implicit contracts, like the relationships between a project manager, project staff, and heads of departments in the same organization providing project inputs like the design of what the project will produce. For the purposes of this chapter, 'contracts' includes both explicit and implicit contracts. The term 'relationship and contract plans', interpreted in the very broad Figure 1.2 seven

Ws sense, will be simplified to 'contract plans' for some current discussion. Formal contracts are usually the key concern, and in most contexts the initial focus can be limited to formal contracts, but informal contracts can prove crucial. The longer but more general 'relationship and contract plans' terminology will be used sometimes as a reminder.

The deliverables provided by the ownership phase are clear allocations of ownership and management responsibility, efficiently and effectively defined, and legally enforceable as far as practicable when appropriate. The tasks required to provide this deliverable may be very simple or extremely complex, depending upon contract strategy. For expository purposes we assume no fixed corporate contracting policy. In these circumstances the ownership phase involves two specific tasks which are the focus of two modes of analysis:

1. scope the contracting strategy, and
2. plan/replan the contracts.

'Scope the contracting strategy' (including informal contracts defining all important relationship plans) must reflect the context (where). It has to concentrate on issues like:

- 'what are the objectives of the contracting strategy?' (the contract 'why'),
- 'which parties are being considered?' (the contract 'who'), and
- 'what aspects of uncertainty and associated opportunity/risk require allocation?' (the 'what' of the ownership phase viewed as a project).

This mode culminates in a strategy for ownership allocation (relationship and contract plans at a strategic level). 'Plan/replan the contracts' builds on the earlier definition of the contract plans at a strategic level. It considers:

- the implementation details of the approach (the contract 'whichway'),
- the instruments (the contract 'wherewithal'), and
- the timing (the contract 'when').

This mode transforms ownership strategy into operational form (relationship and contract plans at a level of detail suitable for implementation). Figure 9.1 elaborates the structure of the ownership phase.

Figure 9.1 portrays starting the ownership phase in 'scope the contracting strategy' mode. Three Ws are addressed in turn in the first three steps, followed by a switch to plan/replan the contracts mode for three more Ws. All six of these Ws are addressed in a 'where' context established in the define phase. The first 'deliverables fit for purpose?' iteration control task initiates possible loops back to the first three steps, until the strategy is 'fit for purpose'. This iteration control task is not shown immediately after the first three steps because of the difficulty in separating uncertainty appreciation and contract design issues at the levels of contracting strategy and a detailed contracting plan. It is an example of appreciating that 'the devil may be in the detail' and we cannot afford to settle on a strategy until a broad understanding of what the detail implies is clear. A second 'deliverables fit for purpose' iteration control task initiates loops back to the last three steps to refine the detail until the contract plan is 'fit for purpose' – what some people call 'dotting the i's and crossing the t's'. A final deliverables fit for purpose iteration control task considers the fully refined overall ownership approach, possibly in gateway terms explored in

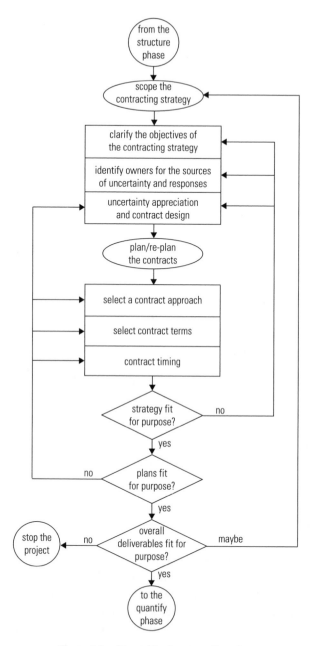

Figure 9.1   Ownership phase specific tasks.

Chapter 12, with stopping the project as an option to reflect the common need for critical review by people who may not have been involved earlier, judging the issues from wider perspectives.

Figure 9.1 is an idealization to capture and illustrate the spirit of the ownership phase process, recognizing that in practice more complex processes may be effective, in common with Figures 5.1, 6.1, 7.1 and 8.1. The lack of separability implied by the three deliverables fit for purpose iteration control tasks is a somewhat different complexity, with implications addressed towards the end of this chapter. As in previous phases, the recurring common tasks of document, verify, assess and report are not shown, to keep the diagram simple, but they play an important role.

Clarify the objectives of the contracting strategy

From a client's point of view, the fundamental reason for being concerned about who owns what sources of uncertainty and associated responses is that this will influence how uncertainty is managed and whether it is managed in the client's best interest. This suggests a need to consider explicitly who the uncertainty owners could be and make conscious decisions about how uncertainty and associated response option management should be allocated to various parties.

A fundamental point is that different parties involved in a project frequently have different perceptions of project uncertainty, associated opportunity and risk. They also have different abilities and motivations to manage these issues. As a consequence, they may wish to adopt different strategies for managing project uncertainty. One reason for this is that different parties typically have different knowledge and perceptions of the nature of sources of uncertainty. Another reason is that different parties are likely to have different objectives, or at least different priorities and perceptions of performance objectives.

Consider one common situation in which these considerations are important from three different perspectives:

1. uncertainty analysis by the client prior to putting a contract out to competitive tender;
2. uncertainty analysis by a bidding contractor prior to submitting a tender;
3. post-tender uncertainty analysis by the winning contractor.

In each case the scope of the uncertainty analysis undertaken will be influenced by the predominant concerns of the party undertaking it and the information about uncertainty available.

Analysis of uncertainty by the client prior to putting a contract out to competitive tender will be developed to manage uncertainty in the client's best interests. Tender documentation and the contract may be drafted to allocate uncertainty to the contractor. However, even with the help of advisers, the client may not be in a position to assess many of the sources of uncertainty associated with the project, particularly in terms of the most efficient and effective response options. Such sources may be better assessed by potential contractors. Some of the key sources will be associated with contractor selection and contract terms.

Analysis of uncertainty by a bidding contractor prior to submitting a tender could be based on the client's uncertainty analysis if it is provided in the tender documentation. The greater the detail provided by the client in relation to the uncertainty which is to be borne in whole or in part by the contractor, the less the contractor has to price for risk related to the contractor's uncertainty about what the project involves. Opportunity and risk analysis here needs to evaluate uncertainty about the tasks required to perform the work specified in the tender documents. This analysis also needs to assess bids that give an appropriate balance between the risk of not getting the contract and the opportunity/risk associated with profits and losses if the contract is obtained. Some of the key sources of uncertainty will be associated with client selection (addressing questions like 'is the client's business secure?') and contract terms.

Post-tender analysis of uncertainty by the winning contractor should be undertaken to reduce uncertainty and risk associated with the contractor's profits, to pursue opportunity efficiency and check the risk/expected profit balance. If the client has already undertaken such an analysis, and provided it to all bidding contractors, the winning contractor can use it as a starting point. If the contractor has to start from scratch, two drawbacks are involved:

1. The scope for modifications to the project specification and base plan will be less than would be the case during the client's uncertainty analysis. This implies a less efficient project specification and base plan.
2. The level of detail adopted by the contractor will be determined by the benefit to the contractor of more or less detail. Sources of uncertainty which involve costs which can be recovered from the client, and contingency plans associated with the contractor's possible bankruptcy, will not be relevant. This implies less efficient project specification, base and contingency plans.

It may be that these two effects discourage contractors from undertaking effective uncertainty analysis. They certainly strengthen the case for a client's uncertainty analysis prior to the development of tender documentation. If the client chooses the wrong contractor, or the contractor chooses the wrong client, or either agrees to inappropriate contract terms, both may have serious problems on their hands which require crisis management more than uncertainty management in the PUMP sense. Part IV returns to these problems and their management.

As a first step in the ownership phase of the PUMP process, 'clarify the objectives of the contracting strategy' is not usually about project specific issues. The key principles are usually generic ones, applicable to all comparable projects undertaken by the organization. Nevertheless, it is useful to distinguish this step to ensure that these principles are duly acknowledged by the appropriate personnel.

If a PUMP is being applied for the first time in the E&D shaping stage, identifying a failure to address the substance of this first step earlier in the project can raise fundamental concerns, of 'show stopper' magnitude. If this is the case, they need urgent resolution.

Most of this chapter maintains the Part II perspective and the common working assumptions for each Part II chapter – a focus on the E&D shaping stage PUMP assuming no prior PUMP processes, with an initial concern for a client seeking high clarity. However, this section is an obvious exception, and ownership issues do deserve serious attention as early as possible for both clients and contractors, even for contractors who need minimal clarity.

As an example of the need to consider plans for relationships which go beyond formal contracts, some enlightened oil companies which want to develop oil wells in sensitive areas plan their relationships with local communities very carefully, providing community services and community assets as part of a 'social contract' formally recognized in these terms. Others have to face criminal and rebel military threats which require very different planning.

Identify owners for uncertainty and response options

The second step in 'scope the contracting strategy' mode involves identifying parties who could be expected to own all relevant sources of uncertainty and associated response options. Ownership of sources of uncertainty implies responsibility for bearing financial and other consequences.

Ownership of associated response options implies management responsibility. Different parties may be involved for each.

An obvious starting point is the list of key players identified in the define phase. As noted in Chapter 5, this list includes agents of the client such as contractors and subcontractors, 'other stakeholders' such as parent organizations, regulatory bodies, competitors and customers. Clearly not all of these parties are relevant for source of uncertainty or response option ownership purposes, although potential owners need not be confined to the client and agents of the client. Other potential owners might have been implicitly identified in the consideration of responses in a first cut of the identify phase. These might include particular groups and individuals within the client, contractors, subcontractors' organizations, and third parties, such as insurers.

Within the client's organization, it is clearly important to distinguish between 'the project' and 'the board'. Further subdivisions within the project are often important, in terms of project financing and the associated ownership of sources of uncertainty and response options. For example, if the project is an information systems (IS) project undertaken by an external third party and managed by an internal IS group for an internal client, issues associated with the external third party, the internal client, the IS group and the board may need to be identified and managed separately.

In a given project, different divisions of labour and organizational arrangements may be possible, and the choice between these may be usefully driven by uncertainty management considerations as well as the physical nature of the project works. For example, the UK Nirex deep mine project mentioned earlier involved PUMP variants which included examining all the major components of the project in relation to their key sources of uncertainty and response options with a view to minimizing the number of these issues which would require managing across contractor boundaries. The number of contractors and the division of work between them were designed to minimize problems with uncertainty management during construction. The need to do this arose because using local contractors was part of the corporate strategy, and none of these local contractors was big enough to act as a prime contractor. Using a PUMP to design work packages is a good example of one possible deliverable of an overall PUMP process driven by ownership phase concerns. This can be achieved in a reasonably simple manner mid-way through the iteration process in the E&D shaping stage of the project lifecycle. The scope for complexity when considering various forms of contracting systems for construction projects is substantial. To get a flavour of this complexity, consider just one kind of contracting approach, 'management contracts'.

Management contracts are widely advocated and used whenever the client does not have in-house expertise to manage contractors on a time and materials basis and the client may not be clear at the outset what is needed in terms clear enough for a fixed price tendering process. For example, a hospital trust may want a new hospital built.

Management contracting systems involve the employment by the client of an external management organization to coordinate the design and construction phases of the project and to control the construction work. The concept underlying management contracting systems is that the management contractor (MC) joins the client's team of professional advisers and devotes efforts unequivocally to pursuing the client's objectives. The MC is able to do this by being employed on a fee basis so that there is no conflict of interest on the MC's part between looking after the client and protecting the MC's own earnings. The MC normally accepts no liability for the site works other than any detriment to the client which is attributable to the MC's negligence.

The MC is normally brought in at an early stage in the preconstruction period in order to contribute management and construction expertise to the design, and prepare a construction schedule linking works packages with design decisions. Competitive tenders are sought by the MC from construction contractors for specific packages of construction work. As the construction work is let in a succession of packages, each one can reflect the particular conditions and sources of uncertainty applicable to that part of the work. In this way the issues can be looked at separately and decisions made upon the extent to which issues need to be incorporated in a work package contract.

Four types of management contracting system can be distinguished in the construction industry:

1. basic management contracting;
2. construction management;
3. design and manage;
4. design, manage and construct.

'Basic management contracting' involves the MC directly employing works contractors to undertake all construction packages. The MC does none of the construction work, but exercises coordination, time, cost, and quality control over the work package contractors and provides facilities for their common use. The permanent works are constructed under a series of construction contracts placed by the MC after approval by the client.

A variation of this system which is more frequently used in North America is termed 'construction management'. It involves the MC performing the same coordination and control functions, but contracts for construction are formed between the client and the work package contractors. This arrangement gives the client more direct contractual involvement with the construction work, but can reduce the managerial impact of the management contractor.

Recognition of the importance of managing design has led to the emergence of a third variation, the 'design and manage' system. This system gives the management organization a specific responsibility to oversee the design work on behalf of the client. This responsibility is normally exercised in a purely professional manner, and gives the management organization a seniority among the designers that ostensibly enables it to impose a stronger discipline.

The fourth kind of management contracting system, 'design, manage and construct', places a degree of responsibility upon the MC for the performance of the construction operations. It moves the MC away from a purely professional role which restricts the MC's liability to negligence in performing contractual duties. The additional liability can occur in two ways. First, the MC is allowed to take on some elements of the construction work using the MC's own workforce. Second, the MC is expected to accept some responsibility for achieving cost and time targets, and for meeting quality specifications.

Each system gives rise to somewhat different sources of uncertainty and allocations of responsibilities, and each system varies in its ability to manage project opportunity efficiency and risk. Choice between the different systems is not clear cut. It depends on a variety of factors, including the nature of the project and performance criteria, the skills of the management contractor, and the role the client is willing to take during project execution. A detailed discussion of these issues is given in Curtis et al. (1991).

Design and build (D&B) and design, build, operate and transfer (DBOT) are examples of further variants without a MC element but with other common elements – see Chapman and Ward (2008) for example.

Uncertainty appreciation and contract design

As noted in Chapter 6, an important part of scoping the PUMP for a project is deciding what issues are 'internal' to the project and therefore the project manager's responsibility to manage, and which are 'external' to the project and therefore issues which the project manager is not expected to manage.

Usually ownership of a source of uncertainty implies responsibility for the management of response options for that source as well as responsibility for bearing its consequences. However, it is often important to distinguish between responsibility for managing responses and responsibility for bearing the consequences of the source of uncertainty and associated response options. In particular it may be desirable to allocate these responsibilities to different parties, recognizing that the party best able to manage responses may not be the party best able to bear the consequences. For example, a contractor may be best placed to manage a source, but it may not be appropriate or desirable for the contractor to bear all the associated financial consequences, and other consequences may have to remain with the client, like loss of reputation. The following example illustrates the nature of this question.

Why some sources have consequences that project managers should not own

In the early 1980s the BP version of SCERT was used to analyse a North Sea oil pipeline which had to cross three other existing pipelines. Given the way lay barges were positioned, with lots of anchors in front under considerable tension, the chance of damaging one (or more) of the existing pipelines was seen as significant. The consequences if an existing pipeline was fractured were very significant. The environmental impact and clean up costs, the compensation required by the other pipeline owners, and all associated reputation costs, would be colossal. In addition, the pipe-laying equipment would have to be diverted from the task in hand to sort out the damaged pipeline, which would involve the loss of a weather window and cost a season.

This source of uncertainty provides a good example of a low-to-medium probability source of event uncertainty with a large impact that does not average out with other sources. Such events either happen or they do not, with a major impact either way relative to the expected outcome. For example, assume a £200 million impact in this case, a 0.10 probability, an expected cost of £200 million $\times$ 0.10 = £20 million. If this source had been quantified and rolled into the analysis used by the corporate board to set the budget for the project, the implicit effect would have been to give the project manager financial ownership of this potential event with a budget of £20 million. If the potential event subsequently occurred, this budget would not have sufficed and the project manager would have had to go back to the board for more money. If the potential risk was not subsequently realized, the project would have had £20 million to spend on other things which the board might not have appreciated. Further, some of the £200 million might be associated with lost sales as a consequence of loss of reputation, not an issue the project can bear in any meaningful sense. Whatever the outcome, it would not be appropriate for the project to bear the full financial consequences of this kind of event. Responsibility for this source of uncertainty in financial and reputation terms had to be retained by the board, along with a portfolio of other similar sources of uncertainty associated with other projects, and the detailed management of reputation risk needed delegation to specialists in this area.

It was clearly important for the project team to accept responsibility for physically managing the immediate implications and direct response options associated with this source, including developing procedures and plans to avoid the potential adverse event being realized, and developing contingency plans should it happen. It might have been worth indicating to those responsible for avoiding this source of uncertainty what sort of unpleasant futures might be forthcoming if the event was realized. But there was no point in making the project financially responsible for it with an extra £20 million in the budget. Nor was there any point in making the project directly responsible for corporate reputation management response options. All aspects of this understanding were part of the implicit 'contract' between the board and the project, part of their 'relationship plans'.

With hindsight a widely available corporate policy document capturing this understanding might have been useful. It has obvious links to the 2010 Deepwater Horizon context.

Generalizing this kind of clarity about ownership of sources

In addition to distinctions between project management and board level financial and reputation responsibilities, some organizations are moving towards distinguishing between sources of uncertainty including associated response options owned financially by the project manager, those owned by those at the sharp end of specific aspects of the project, and those owned by a number of intermediate management levels, in the context of control budgets which recognize the target, expected value and commitment distinctions discussed in Part I. Control budgets and associated issue allocations in a hierarchical structure represent an interlocking set of organizational agreements, all of which can be viewed as 'contracts' for present purposes. External contracts and subcontracts with other organizations extend this structure. It is important to define, and in some instances to design, this structure. Chapman and Ward (2002, ch. 6) consider these concerns in terms of internal and external contracts designed to manage good luck as well as bad luck, generalizing aspects of Goldratt's 'critical chain' perspective (Goldratt, 1997). This kind of analysis suggests that uncertainty appreciation and contract design should be a step which is an integral part of both contracting strategy and more detailed contract planning.

Hopkinson has pointed out that aligning ownership of financial consequences and influence over outcomes often involves tradeoffs between insights about what needs to be done and authority to implement the necessary responses. If relatively junior management levels have more insight but lack authority, this can imply that ownership has moved too far up the hierarchy. However this tension is managed, communication clarity is clearly important.

Select a contract approach

The specific task 'plan/replan the contracts' involves considering how the contracting strategy is to be implemented, in terms of formal and informal contracts, first addressing the 'select a contract' approach or 'whichway' question, to expand on the closely related 'what' or contract design question.

The contract approach adopted is highly dependent on the parties involved in working on the project and the way in which project tasks have been divided and distributed between these parties. For example, the novelty and technical nature of a construction project may warrant the employment by the client of an architect, engineer, quantity surveyor, prime contractor and a variety of subcontractors. The presence of these parties may imply clear allocation of particular issues to particular parties. A very different and perhaps simpler allocation strategy is implied for a client who opts for a 'turnkey' contract to procure a building, where the client has only to deal with a single prime contractor.

In a client–contractor situation the client exerts influence over the contractor primarily via conditions laid down in a contract between the two parties. The contract sets out what is to be produced, what the client will pay, how the client can assess and monitor what the contractor has done, and how things should proceed in the case of various contingent events. The contract may identify and allocate sources and responses explicitly, but very often particular issues are not identified explicitly and allocation of issues is implicit in the nature and size of contract payment terms. In these cases, the consequences of such allocation may not be fully appreciated. In particular, the manner in which issues are to be managed may be unclear.

From an uncertainty management perspective, with a view to both opportunity and risk, it is usually very important to identify sources of uncertainty which are:

* controllable by the contractor;
* controllable by the client;
* not controllable by either party.

Different payment arrangements should usually be adopted for each of these categories, implying different levels of sharing information for each category, so that appropriate allocation and positive management of uncertainty in each category is encouraged where possible.

The acquisition of information about sources of uncertainty plays a key role in the ability of contractual parties to allocate and manage associated uncertainty. Given the potential conflict of contractual party objectives, a central question is the extent to which contractual parties can obtain mutual benefit by sharing relevant information. A related question is how this information can be used to allocate sources and responses on a rational basis and in a mutually beneficial way.

Select contract terms

The 'whichway' and 'wherewithal' in an ownership phase context can be associated with contract details, including budgets, fees and penalties, the operational details which make internal or external contracts work.

This is one reason for the development of a wide range of 'standard' forms of contract which serve as familiar 'models' for the contracting process. For example, the Institution of Civil Engineers' (ICE, 1995) *New Engineering Contract* (NEC) Engineering and Construction Contract (ECC) was designed so that its implementation should contribute to rather than detract from the effectiveness of management of the project works. This is based on the proposition that fore-sighted, cooperative management of the interactions between the parties can shrink the risk (and risk inefficiency) inherent in construction work. The ECC main options offer six different basic allocations of sources and responses between the 'employer' (client) and contractor, and whatever variations in strategy between different contracts within a project are adopted, the majority of the procedures will be common to all contracts.

Internal contracting, and associated incentive and target-setting mechanisms, have not received the same attention, but the problems can be equally complex and equally important. Intelligent choices which reflect the circumstances can be crucial to effective and efficient allocation and subsequent management of issues. Chapman and Ward (2002, ch. 6) consider this question in some detail.

Determine the timing of responsibility transfers

'When should transfers of responsibility take place?' is an important basic question with a number of associated questions which need early consideration. Where project issues are ongoing, answering this question can substantially alter the allocation of sources and responses between parties. Obvious examples include the length of warranties, or the determination of 'vesting' or handover dates. Such issues cannot be addressed in detail until earlier steps in the ownership phase have been addressed comprehensively. However, failure to consider them early enough in the PUMP can lead to project delays and contract arrangements which are not opportunity efficient.

A further important (but often neglected) aspect of ownership assessment timing is the time allowed for tenders and contract negotiations. In particular, bidding contractors ought to be given sufficient time to price for the uncertainty they will be expected to carry.

Three separate fit for purpose tests?

It is almost always useful to seek effective shaping of strategy before engaging with the details of shaping effective tactics. The project lifecycle structure of Table 1.3 reflects this separability, with a strategy/tactics planning watershed after three strategy-shaping stages plus associated gateways. The focus phase structure illustrated by Figure 6.1 also reflects this separability, in terms of 'scope the process' and 'plan the process' separability. This kind of separability is never strictly 'true', in the sense that 'the devil may be in the detail', but it is usually robust enough to prove a useful working assumption.

In an ownership phase context it seems worth dropping this separability, sketching out at least a first pass at the detail before deciding whether or not the strategy looks viable, and further shaping the plan detail before the overall fit for purpose test. That is the implication of the 'strategy fit for purpose?' test following the 'contract timing' step instead of the 'uncertainty appreciation and contract design' step, and a final overall 'deliverables fit for purpose' test. It is less efficient, but arguably the increase in effectiveness is clarity efficient.

The basis of the rationale for strategy/tactics planning separability in the project lifecycle is that most people involved in overall project strategy shaping have sufficient experience of subsequent detailed planning and execution phases to anticipate the key implications of strategic choices. This kind of separability does not seem to be the case in terms of ownership phase strategy. If people cannot anticipate the key implications of the detailed planning and execution when considering strategy, separability is not a viable working assumption.

The final overall 'fit for purpose' test provides a convenient place to pause and consider the issues associated with the overall contracting strategy as a whole, as well as individual planned contracts developed to this point. Allowing for possible gateway status can be useful. It emphasizes the need to see formal contracts and less formal relationship plans as crucial choices which everyone involved needs to understand, plus the possible need for independent audit. The possibility of multiple contracts with many parties makes this overall integrative assessment crucial. For example, if the constraints imposed by other parties collectively put the project at risk in unacceptable ways, it may be worth explicitly addressing the possibility of stopping at this stage, or going back to re-scope the basic project strategy as well as the contracting strategy.

The ongoing nature of the ownership phase

Assuming the PUMP is being applied for the first time in the E&D shaping stage of the project lifecycle, on behalf of a client with limited PUMP experience, a first pass through the ownership phase should focus on contracting strategy. This is because initial concern in the next phase of the PUMP, the quantify phase, may be restricted to issues the client proposes to own or issues contractors are prepared to own, as identified in the ownership phase. Subsequent passes through the ownership phase can then focus on contract planning at a more detailed level, considering issues like work package design as illustrated by the UK Nirex example. This can be followed by quantifying and evaluating contractor costs and verifying contractor cost estimates. This will require evaluation of the implications of all relevant sources and associated responses, possibly using a somewhat different approach and different people than those involved in evaluating client owned issues. Verifying the feasibility of assumed response options and their effects is part of the rationale for being clear about who owns sources of uncertainty and response options before quantification and evaluation. For example, client-initiated redesign is a response that may invalidate all allocations of risk to a contractor, with knock-on cost implications which are orders of magnitude greater than the cost of the redesign itself. Approved, named individuals responsible for all key response options in all contracting organizations are an example of the final detail prior to execution which should be anticipated from the outset, but which may be left open until the last minute where appropriate.

A simple example

The scope for complexity in the treatment of ownership issues should be clear from the earlier management contracting examples. However, it is always vital to make these issues simple in an appropriate way for each particular context. Clarity efficiency demands it, practicality being a key aspect of clarity efficiency.

To emphasize the scope for this kind of tailored simplicity, reconsider the ownership strategy and detailed plan associated with the BCS example introduced in Chapter 2. Recall that BCS is a one-person organization.

Bruce, the proprietor of BCS, refurbishes kitchens and bathrooms for domestic clients. Bruce uses no formal planning once a contract is in place, and the context requires a very low effort approach to bidding and contracting.

A spreadsheet package designed by Bruce's brother Andy allows Bruce to put an estimate together with the client on a lap top computer, as part of a trust-building integration of estimating, tendering and contracting. For a carefully selected example of one of the 5–15 activities Bruce commonly uses, like 'remove existing floor covering and prepare for new floor', Bruce starts by entering a 'target minimum' number of hours, 4 for example. He explains that this is how long he believes it will take in a 'no problems' scenario. He then enters a 'target maximum' number of hours, 10 for example. He explains that this is how long he believes it might take him in terms of a 'bad news for the client' scenario, when the glue has gone hard, the surface left is rough and requires skimming, and so on. He explains that this does not include any *very* bad news for the client' scenarios, e.g. the floor is rotten and needs extensive replacement, which might run to 50 hours. He indicates that any very bad news for the client scenarios must be owned by the client. He explains that he will estimate target minimum and maximum durations for each item, with the client. He explains that his software will apply his cost per hour to both to provide an indicative target cost range, and take the mid-point of this range to estimate the expected cost of his labour given no very bad news for the client scenarios. He indicates that the software will then add a 10% contingency to the mid-point to provide the labour cost basis of an 'estimated cost contract'. If the client wants a 'fixed price' contract, *conditional on no very bad news scenarios for any item*, Bruce will agree to this estimated cost with a 10% contingency – an 'estimated price contract option'. The 10% is to pay for the marginal 'bad news/very bad news scenarios' Bruce might have to accept, the unpleasant nature of discussions about marginal cases of this kind, and the risk Bruce is taking surrounding arguments about liability for very bad news scenarios. Bruce indicates the client can expect to save the 10% contingency if they trust him and opt for a time and materials contract. He explains a true 'fixed price contract' is simply not feasible – Bruce would have to estimate the probability of all possible very bad news scenarios and make provisions for them, or lie about his willingness to take all such risks, neither of which he is prepared to do. Most of his clients like the approach and accept a time and materials contract.

The most important sources of risk Bruce has to manage are clients he cannot trust and clients who do not understand the limitations of any cost estimate, the two together constituting a 'very bad news for Bruce' scenario. 'Very bad news for Bruce' scenarios can be partially controlled by advance payment requirements, but they are best avoided by developing experience based rules of thumb for avoiding potentially difficult clients.

The BCS context is so simple it is hard to imagine a contractor who can afford a less sophisticated approach, or a client who should not be suspicious of a contractor offering a less sophisticated approach.

Other low clarity examples involving clarity efficiency

From the perspective of BCS clients the approach outlined in the last section is particularly clarity efficient if they trust Bruce and opt for a time and materials contract and Bruce does not damage this trust. Trust is central to clarity efficiency at any level of clarity for all parties. In the memorable words of a contributor to the Curtis et al. (1991) research project into management contracts discussed earlier, 'the moment contracts come out of the drawer everyone is in trouble'. There are those who believe in 'win–lose' solutions where they always win, and many have a track record which suggests there really is 'a sucker born every minute'. But a working assumption here is that 'WIN–win' simulations should be sought, with 'WIN' for the home team being the focus, and 'win' for all other relevant parties to the extent that this is feasible being part of an enlightened view of what 'WIN' means. 'WIN' is a big win in all respects, 'win' a more modest but acceptable win overall, including issues like pride, confidence, mutual respect and self respect. This working assumption approaches the status of a basic, framing assumption, but there are times when doing business with parties who cannot be trusted is preferable to not doing business at all, or is the only viable choice.

A simple sealed bid competition with the lowest price being accepted is the obvious choice for a client *provided*:

- the client knows exactly what they want,
- the client can specify what they want without ambiguity of any kind, and
- there is a healthy market place involving a good supply of competent and honest contractors who are willing and able to bear the risk associated with fixed price contracts.

The reality is that these target working assumptions never hold exactly. When a low level of effort is appropriate, clarity efficiency is about robust but simple remedies to the key failures in these target working assumptions. Consider a few illustrative examples.

Driving tunnels is a notoriously risky aspect of any project. A fixed price contract for a tunnel would involve a huge gamble for the contractor, in effect a bet on what ground conditions might be discovered. A well-tested solution is an agreed 'fixed' contract price which is conditional upon a particular 'base scenario' set of ground conditions with a pre-specified adjustment for a plausible set of alternative ground condition scenarios, and an agreed arbitration process for interpolating, once the tunnel is complete and the actual ground conditions have been documented. In effect, the bet on the ground conditions is taken by the client, the most appropriate party in most circumstances. All other uncertainty, in risk and opportunity terms, is left with the contractor, assuming the client can specify clearly what they want and the contractor can be motivated to perform effectively and efficiently with objectives aligned to the client's by this approach. Generalizing this example, any limited set of clearly defined sources of uncertainty best borne by the client can be separated out in this way, with residual uncertainty borne by a contractor.

'Partnership contracts' of various forms have proven popular for several decades, and some notable successes stand out from the failures. The approach to building retail stores adopted by Marks and Spencer is often cited as a success. The basic formula as recounted by many is: Pick the most capable and cooperative contractor you can find, pay them well on a time and materials basis, tell them exactly what you want with a focus on quality, and make it clear they will continue to build all your shops unless they let you down. In short, make it clear to a 'winner' that they want to stay on your team, a simple but effective alignment of objectives which can be applied in many other circumstances.

Conclusion

A WIN–win approach to contracts can be interpreted as avoiding both trusting everybody and trusting nobody in an opportunity efficient manner, a useful response to the opening quote for this chapter. A WIN–win approach is a useful default goal for the ownership phase. However, achieving this goal is not easy, and there are no simple foolproof approaches to all contexts.

This is a short chapter, because the concerns addressed are not usually treated as a part of the mainstream process of project risk management, and we do not want to unduly interrupt the flow of the other chapters. However, the issues involved are of fundamental importance, and they should be addressed in a clarity efficient manner in any PUMP. Part IV revisits some of the more complex issues from a corporate perspective.

Chapter 10

Quantify *some* uncertainty

But to us, probability is the very guide of life.
— Bishop Joseph Butler, 1756.

This chapter, and the next, may seem too technical to be of interest to senior managers. In our view this is not the case – no senior manager should be unaware of the key points made in this chapter and the next, and those responsible for opportunity/uncertainty/risk management have a responsibility to ensure that there is a corporate understanding of all the key issues at a suitable level of clarity by all relevant players. Probability as it is addressed here is not high science – it is practical common sense captured in a manner which provides structure to guide decision making. The 'how to do it' details are not relevant to senior managers, but the 'what needs to be done' principles discussed in this chapter and the next need to be understood by everyone involved in uncertainty management, along with their rationale and implications.

The key deliverable provided by the quantify phase of the PUMP is probability estimates of *some* uncertainty associated with sources of uncertainty and response options identified earlier in the PUMP. These numeric estimates of uncertainty associated with cost, duration, or other measurable project performance criteria provide a basis for making choices which shape the project to achieve opportunity efficiency. They also provide a basis for understanding which sources of uncertainty and associated responses are important, perhaps worth more attention, and which are relatively unimportant.

The notion 'you cannot manage what you cannot measure' is not true, but it is much easier to make risk efficient decisions and demonstrate this has been done if credible quantification is feasible for some aspects of uncertainty. Credible quantified analysis carefully linked to interpretation of qualitative treatment of all features not addressed in numeric terms is the key to overall opportunity efficiency.

The quantify phase involves two central modes of analysis which are different but related:

1. size sources of uncertainty in probabilistic terms (on a first pass);
2. refine earlier quantification of uncertainty (on subsequent passes).

An effective quantify phase involves a clarity efficient approach to both these modes of analysis. A single-pass approach to the quantify phase is rarely either effective or efficient. In the E&D-shaping PUMP, as in all PUMPs, we want to minimize the time spent on relatively minor sources of uncertainty with simple response options, so as to spend more time on major sources of uncertainty involving complex response options. The quantify phase plays a key role in achieving this with clarity efficiency in an iterative PUMP. A first pass through the quantify phase involves a focus on sizing sources of uncertainty which were deemed worth separate quantification on a first pass through the identify phase. Subsequent looping back for further passes from the PUMP evaluate phase to the define phase, or an intermediate phase, can refine our understanding of those sources and responses which are identified as important. To begin with, this refinement will usually seek greater clarity in terms of structure – more detailed identification of primary sources and response options, for example. As it becomes clearer which of the sources of uncertainty matter most, and what the most appropriate source–response structure looks like, sources of uncertainty can be quantified with greater refinement if this is worth while. When the key sources that are usefully quantified separately and associated response options are understood, further sources can be quantified at an appropriate level of detail.

At the beginning of this iterative process all uncertainty that will not be quantified must be described in clarity efficient qualitative terms. The basis of quantifying sources is clarity about closely coupled conditions – treatment of linked uncertainty in qualitative terms – so this basis needs confirming at the outset and revising as needed as the process continues.

Some common practice approaches to project risk management suggest a non-numeric approach initially, using likelihood and criteria ranges associated with scenario labels such as 'high', 'medium' and 'low', commonly referred to as a 'qualitative assessment', with numeric measures later if appropriate. At the beginning of this chapter it is worth emphasizing that qualitative statements of beliefs about uncertainty in a PIG sense are often of limited use because they are open to different interpretations by different people. This chapter has to address simple but effective approaches to clarity which overcome this 'weak communication problem'. Merkhofer (1987) provides an illustrative example.

As part of a seminar on decision analysis conducted for a private company, the seminar leader included a demonstration called the 'Verbal Uncertainty Exercise'. This exercise was designed to show that different individuals assign very different probabilities to the same qualitative expressions. In the exercise the seminar participants were individually asked to assign probabilities to common expressions such as 'very likely to occur', 'almost certain to occur', etc. The seminar leader had just completed the demonstration and was about to move on to another topic when the president of the company said, 'Don't remove that slide yet.' He turned to one of his vice presidents and, in essence, said the following: 'You mean to tell me that last week when you said the Baker account was almost certain, you only meant a 60 to 80% chance? I thought you meant 99%! If I'd known it was so low, I would have done things a lot differently'.

This 'weak communication problem' can be linked to a widespread underlying 'irrational objectivity' condition (Chapman and Ward, 2002) which involves a failure to grasp the inherently subjective nature of all practical applications of objective probability based tools. In part this is what Bishop Joseph Butler was talking about in his 1756 quote – clearly not a new problem. However, general acceptance in the literature of a full role for subjective probabilities had to wait until 'modern decision analysis' and the 1960s, and many people with a limited formal exposure to probability theory and practice are still not convinced.

Using data to develop 'objective' estimates

Sometimes good data is available to provide 'objective' estimates, in terms of probability distributions for a parameter of interest, or the probability of a particular event occurring. One of the benefits of breaking out various sources of uncertainty is the ability to use such data. Consider an example, building on earlier discussion of a BP version of SCERT. Equipment laying pipe in the North Sea is designated in terms of maximum wave height capability in metres: 1.6 m, 3 m, and so on. Even in the early days of North Sea offshore projects, weather data by sea area spanning 15 or so years was available which indicated the number of days in each month that waves were above various nominal heights (see, for example, Mould, 1993). This historical data provided a very good basis for estimating how many days per month a lay barge might be able to operate or not due to weather conditions.

The recommended *basic* approach to using this kind of data involves starting by constructing a frequency based, common interval, rectangular histogram form of probability distribution for the possible number of lay days per month. Figure 10.1 illustrates a typical common interval rectangular histogram of this kind. It uses three intervals to span the range 7.5–22.5 lay days per month, based on past observations of the number of lay days in the month of April. If we had ten observations in the range 8–22 days inclusive, each to the nearest day, with three observations in the range 8–12, five in the range 13–17, and two in the range 18–22, using this data to generate the Figure 10.1 portrayal would be convenient and effective. Four or five intervals would be

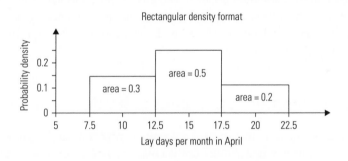

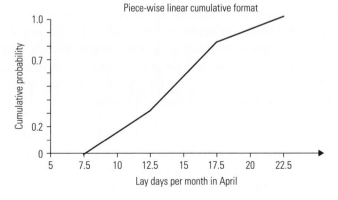

Figure 10.1   Example of a three interval representation of variability

feasible, as would one or two, but three intervals with central (class mark) values of 10, 15 and 20 days is a clarity efficient starting point based on the data available.

For reasons noted earlier, there is a gap between this data based probability distribution estimate and the reality of a 'lay days achieved' probability distribution. In practice, a lay barge operator does not wait until waves go above the equipment's nominal wave height before stopping operations, and start again as soon as the waves drop below the nominal wave height. For important practical reasons, judgements are made about carrying on for short spells of bad weather, stopping early for anticipated prolonged bad spells, and starting later after prolonged bad spells, because starting and stopping pipe laying may involve picking up or putting down a pipeline – operations prone to 'buckles'. However, it was reasonable in this case, as a first order approximation, to ignore this gap – a convenient working assumption known to fail a reality test, but reasonably robust in the context of the inferences eventually drawn.

This example illustrates the inevitable introduction of a subjective element into the probability assessment process, even if no subjective adjustments are made. There is always a gap between the circumstances assumed for data analysis purposes and the actual circumstances. At the very least the future is never exactly the same as the past. Decisions about whether or not to ignore such gaps are always required. The basis of any associated adjustments is inherently subjective, and the validity of any unadjusted estimates is an equally subjective judgement. In this sense *there is no such thing as a truly objective probability estimate for practical situations*. Even the card or dice player has to make important assumptions about bias and cheating. All practical estimates are conditional upon assumptions which are subjectively assumed to hold, and we need to recognize that such assumptions are working assumptions which never hold exactly. The issue is the extent to which these assumptions fail to hold. In this sense, all practical 'objective' estimates are conditional, and any 'objective' conditional estimate is necessarily 'subjective' in the form required for practical analysis.

Subjective estimates when data is limited or absent

Some people argue that quantitative analysis is a waste of time if it has to be based on subjective estimates of event occurrence probabilities or the range of possible outcomes. There are obvious concerns about the validity of subjective estimates, reinforced by the recognition that no event occurrence probability assessment (except 1 or 0) can be proven to be wrong. However, given that individuals are guided by their perceptions of uncertainty whether or not quantification is attempted, it often makes sense to articulate these perceptions so that uncertainty can be dealt with as effectively as possible. In addition to the general benefits of quantifying uncertainty set out earlier in Chapters 2 and 3, quantifying subjective beliefs encourages more precise definition of issues, motivates clearer communication about uncertainty, and clarifies what is important and what is not.

Very often there are aspects of a project where uncertainty is very important but appropriate data is not available. Even where past experience is relevant, the required data may not have been collected, may not exist in sufficient quantity or detail, or may not have been recorded accurately or consistently. In such situations, quantification may have to rely heavily on subjective estimates of probability distributions.

For example, when estimating the probability of a wet buckle per kilometre of pipe laid, BP planning engineers in the 1970s obtained data on the number of wet buckles to date for North Sea projects and divided it by the number of kilometres laid At the time they then argued that a better estimate involved dividing this number by 2, because equipment was getting better and operators were becoming more experienced. Following the statistical traditions of the day, a point estimate of the probability obtained in this way was used, and it was robust enough for the inferences drawn. It was clearly much better than ignoring the subjective judgements involved. However, with hindsight a more robust approach providing additional clarity would have been to use a distribution like that of Figure 10.1 to portray uncertainty associated with the most appropriate adjustment factor. That is, instead of just assuming an adjustment factor of 0.5, a variant of Figure 10.1 could have been used with intervals centred on 0.25, 0.50 and 0.75, associated with the most appropriate adjustment factors subjectively estimated with reference to everything known about the data base and progress over the time periods in question. The shape of the resulting distribution would probably be different to Figure 10.1 and more or fewer intervals with a different range could be used. However, such a distribution clearly exists, and the special case with an adjustment factor of 0.5 given a probability of 1.0 is not as plausible as a subjectively determined assessment of the variability and ambiguity uncertainty involved. In this framework failing to make any adjustment is equivalent to a subjective version of Figure 10.1 indicating a probability of 1.0 for an adjustment factor of 1.0 – clearly inappropriate.

It is worth recognizing that probability distributions for probability values are often more important than probability distributions for associated outcomes. For example, the time taken to repair a wet buckle was modelled in terms of a 'lay days' probability distribution comparable to Figure 10.1 with 10–20 intervals, subjectively estimated without formal data analysis because appropriate data was not readily available. The variability involved was significant, as was the asymmetry of the distribution shape, but this was probably less important than the variability associated with probability of a wet buckle occurring. With hindsight, less precision for this repair time distribution, and explicit treatment of wet buckle occurrence probability uncertainty, would have been more clarity efficient.

BP typically used more than three intervals whenever uncertainty was modelled, in part for high clarity definition of distribution shapes, in part because their evaluate phase computer software employed a discrete variable probability tree probability calculus approach instead of Monte Carlo simulation, for reasons not worth exploration here (Clark and Chapman, 1987; Cooper and Chapman, 1987).

If in doubt about the value of three intervals versus more intervals, a simple first-pass shortcut is to use just one interval – the minimum clarity approach discussed in Chapter 2 – with a view to using more intervals on subsequent passes if the associated uncertainty matters.

Assessment of some sources of uncertainty may be best handled by identifying them as conditions, with associated assumptions clearly defined in a suitable form, deliberately avoiding estimation in the usual quantitative (probability based) sense. Earlier chapters have emphasized the importance of this part of the process, and its implications need exploring in this chapter and the next.

On occasion, any estimation in the usual quantitative terms may be a waste of time and best eliminated: for example, if on a first pass the concern is identifying and then managing any 'show-stoppers', the 'quantify *some* uncertainty' phase may involve a very special case when *some = none*, and the quantify phase as a whole reduces to looking for show-stoppers.

An outline of the quantify phase

The key deliverable of the quantify phase is the provision of a basis for understanding the importance of sources of uncertainty and associated response options using quantification in probability terms when appropriate. This must be linked to clarification of uncertainty treated as conditions when quantification is not appropriate, building on earlier phase qualitative analysis.

Based around the two modes of analysis set out earlier, eight specific tasks are required to provide this key deliverable. Figure 10.2 indicates their relationships.

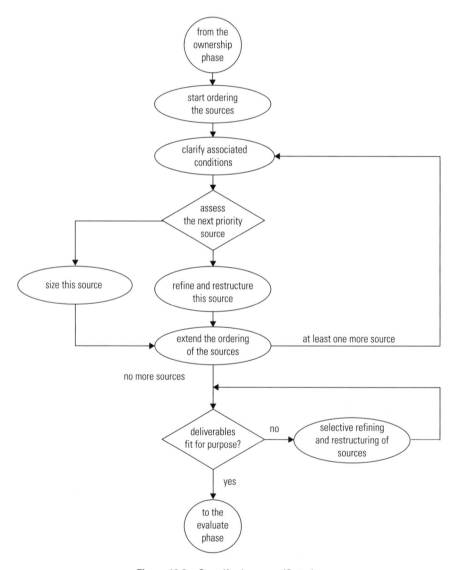

Figure 10.2   Quantify phase specific tasks

A summary of what each task involves follows:

1. *Start ordering the sources* – As the basis of the process, list the obviously important sources needing treatment on this pass of the overall PUMP in priority order.
2. *Clarify associated conditions* – Clarify all relevant project scope conditions, including any specific to this source and more general conditions.
3. *Assess the next priority source* – Decide whether the next priority source needs initial quantification or refinement of earlier quantitative estimates.
4. *Size this source* – When initial quantification is appropriate, provide a simple probability estimate, based on data only if it is readily available, drawing on the current perceptions of the individual or group with the most appropriate knowledge, to 'size' the uncertainty associated with the source in probability terms.
5. *Refine and restructure this source* – When the implications of uncertainty sized earlier warrants, refine the initial sizing estimate, perhaps in conjunction with refining the response-related decision analysis or the earlier definition of the source and its context – what might be referred to as modest 'local' (within this phase) restructuring.
6. *Extend the ordering of sources* – Extend the list begun in task 1 and loop back to task 2 until no more sources need assessment on this pass of the overall E&D-shaping PUMP.
7. *Deliverables fit for purpose?* – A test with a positive outcome expectation, moving on to the evaluate phase if achieved.
8. *Selective refining and restructuring of sources* – If there is obvious room for improvement without making use of the evaluate phase, take a shortcut by making local refining and restructuring changes immediately.

Two streams reflecting two different modes of analysis are separated by the task 3 assessment, as illustrated by Figure 10.2. Task 8 is a variant of task 5. Now consider each of these eight tasks in more detail.

Start ordering the sources

Getting started on the quantify phase during the first pass of the PUMP is the immediate concern. Getting started on later passes is a follow-on concern.

Starting the quantify phase by selecting the sources of uncertainty which earlier phases on this pass of the PUMP suggest are the most important is a simple and effective rule of thumb. Successive selections can be based upon a perceived overall ordering of the relative importance of sources, usually within activities or other subdivisions of the project, which in turn may be selected because of the relative importance of these aspects of the project as currently perceived. No matter how crude the basis of this ordering judgement, it is preferable to using an arbitrary ordering.

Any probability estimation process and any linked approach to understanding conditions associated with estimates requires 'getting up to speed'. Even if everyone involved is experienced in this kind of analysis, if they have not done it for a while they may need to refresh their memory of what is involved. If inexperienced people are involved, 'going down a learning curve' is an important part of the process, in the sense that new skills need to be taught and absorbed.

It makes sense to spend extra time on the most important sources and to couple this to 'learning curve' and 'getting up to speed' issues. It also makes sense to grip people's interest and involvement by starting with particularly important *and interesting* sources, which are *fun* to look at in the non-trivial sense explored in Chapter 3. When in doubt, err on the side of sources that have aspects which intrigue or touch on common experience, to motivate exploratory learning, provided this is a cost effective use of the time involved.

Clarify associated conditions

All probability distributions used for making practical decisions are conditional. At the very least we usually assume that the world is not going to end in the next few minutes. The question addressed in this section is 'how do we clarify important assumptions best treated as conditions?'

The short answer is 'this is best done earlier, as part of the qualitative analysis phases', with a focus in the identify phase as discussed in Chapter 7. However, everyone involved in the estimation process needs reminding at this point.

For example, in a BCS context, the BCS proprietor needs to explain to customers that all his 'target maximum' estimates are conditional on no 'very bad luck for the customer' scenarios, e.g. he discovers a floor to be retiled needs replacing. As another example, in a Highways Agency quick re-estimate context there are three categories of uncertainty addressed as separate sources, and a set of assumptions defining uncertainty which the estimator can treat as conditions because they are beyond his 'project'. Uncertainty that is owned by the Highways Agency at portfolio level or the government is one example. Even in a high clarity context like the BP North Sea examples, it is important to be clear that specific conditions like 'no change in pipeline route' mean no significant changes, and all minor scope changes are accommodated in a 'no quibbles provision' with a suitable label.

Assess the next priority source

Assessing the next priority source for sizing treatment or refining and restructuring involves a default 'size the source' decision if this has not already been done. The top priorities for quantification in the BP versions of PUMP were sources like 'weather' and 'wet buckles'. Assume that this is the context of interest for the moment, on the first pass through the E&D-shaping PUMP.

Size a source using a histogram approach when data is available

If good data is available for an important source, as in the 'weather' example associated with Figure 10.1, it makes obvious sense to use this data from the outset. We recommend employing rectangular histogram forms of probability distribution like Figure 10.1, optimizing the number of distribution intervals in a data efficient manner which also reflects the advantages of simplicity for subsequent analysis. For example, in the Figure 10.1 example central (class mark) values of 10, 15 and 20 are very convenient, but a central value of 30 raises complications if common intervals between interval boundaries are wanted. Such complications may be best avoided, depending upon the best tradeoffs between technical assumptions that are not worth exploring here. Note that an assumed wave height capability is embedded in the quantification of this source of uncertainty – part of the response option choice for this source. Note also that a variability uncertainty source is involved, plus some ambiguity uncertainty associated with working assumptions. Further, note that a separate estimate is required for each relevant month – to use a semi-Markov process model, the 'weather' source was in effect decomposed into a set of sources for each relevant month earlier in the PUMP.

If data is available but subjective adjustment is needed, as in the case of 'wet buckle' probability of occurrence, it makes sense to use the data but assess the uncertainty associated with both the data and the adjustment. As discussed earlier, a point estimate of the probability of a buckle occurring was not clarity efficient. A variant of the Figure 10.1 histogram approach for both the probability of a wet buckle occurring, and its impact if it occurs, would be clarity efficient.

If no data is available, as in the case of estimating the impact of a wet buckle in terms of delay, the standard 1970s BP 10–20 interval variant of the rectangular histogram illustrated by Figure 10.1 probably involves more detail than needed for a first-pass estimate. Three or four intervals would probably be clarity efficient for a first pass, and a suitable judgement needs to be made.

Note that in this wet buckle case a basic response is assumed – repair the buckle. On a first pass the possibility of stuck pig during the repair operation might be assumed, but the implications might not be explored beyond supposing a longish tail for the impact distribution. Note also that an event uncertainty source is involved, plus ambiguity uncertainty associated with working assumptions. By definition, working assumptions involve ambiguity uncertainty which needs sizing to understand robustness in qualitative terms, if not in quantitative terms. Two estimates of uncertainty are involved, one for the probability of occurrence of the event, and a second for the impact if the event occurs, in effect decomposing the 'wet buckle' source into two component sources. The event uncertainty source could be further broken down – into uncertainty associated with what the data says about observed past wet buckles, and use of this data to forecast future wet buckles. More than these two or three sources would be involved if wet buckles were not assumed to be dependent upon the expected number of lay days but otherwise independent of weather or month. This assumption is an important aspect of the inherent dependence issues.

All estimates associated with any event uncertainty source could take a rectangular histogram form for sizing purposes, with a minimum of one class defined by P10 and P90 values, the minimum clarity approach discussed in Chapters 2 and 3. This special case reduces to a point estimate only if the P10 and P90 are the same for the level of precision being used. If this *basic* approach is taken, in all cases the number of intervals used should be clarity efficient for sizing purposes unless it is obvious that more clarity will be needed later, and it is a sound investment to obtain it now. Alternatives to this basic approach will be discussed later. There is a general need to choose a level of clarity consistent with earlier phases in the current pass of the PUMP, anticipating a consistent level of clarity in the following evaluate phase, to achieve overall clarity efficiency.

Judgement about the number of intervals to use should err on the high side if the parties involved are used to and expect high clarity smooth curves. This was part of the reason for 10–20 intervals in the 1970s BP context. Experience suggests that relatively few intervals capture unbiased expected values, spreads and skew in a clarity efficient manner for expert users. However, lumpy distributions can be a concern for those not used to them. A lack of trust in crude quantification is the flip side of unwarranted trust in elegantly smooth curve results based on unfounded probability distribution function assumptions that are a complete nonsense.

Size a source without data using a simple scenario approach

In the absence of readily available data, a 'simple scenario' approach to sizing uncertainty is recommended. The 'minimum clarity' (minimum effort) approach introduced in Chapter 2 is a special case of a 'simple scenario' approach in estimation terms.

The simple scenario approach can be illustrated in terms of a purely subjective approach to the estimation of Figure 10.1, assuming there is no available data to estimate the variability uncertainty source 'weather'. Seven basic steps are involved.

Step 1 – a pessimistic outcome scenario

The first step in the sizing uncertainty task using a simple scenario approach is to locate the pessimistic end of the range of possible outcomes. Commencing with a pessimistic outcome scenario is a useful way to minimize optimistic bias, but some people may be uncomfortable with this, and reversing steps 1 and 2 is an option. This estimate should be a 'nominal' pessimistic outcome in the sense that it has:

- a rounded value, to make it easy to work with, and to indicate clearly its approximate nature;
- an initially perceived chance of being exceeded of the order of 10% for criteria like cost or duration, 90% for criteria like revenue or lay days.

Using Figure 10.1 as an example, ten days is an illustrative pessimistic scenario estimate, working to the nearest five days.

Step 2 – an optimistic outcome scenario

The second step is to estimate a complementary optimistic outcome scenario. This estimate should be nominal in a similar sense, in that it has:

- a rounded value on the same scale as the pessimistic outcome scenario, to make it easy to work with and indicate clearly its approximate nature;
- an initially perceived chance of being exceeded of the order of 90% for a criteria like cost or duration, 10% for criteria like revenue or lay days.

Using Figure 10.1 as an example, 20 days is an illustrative optimistic estimate, working on the same five-day interval scale.

Step 3 – intermediate outcome scenarios

The third step is to decide whether one interval is sufficient or three or more are needed. If only one interval is needed, the minimum clarity special case applies. Simple geometry can be used to produce the Figure 2.1 simplification of Figure 10.1. Two intervals is a rather special case considered later. If the preferred choice is three or more intervals, usually it is convenient to choose values for intermediate scenarios such that the distances between each pair of adjacent scenario values are equal, with a default choice of three intervals in total, with one intermediate interval. Using the Figure 10.1 example, one intermediate interval with a central value of 15 is the obvious choice.

Step 4 – outcome interval widths

The fourth step is to define interval widths centred on each of the outcome scenario values. Usually it is convenient to make these interval widths equal to the distance between the scenario values, the five-day interval used here. More sophisticated processes embedded in suitable computer software could dispense with the use of a common interval size, while keeping the basic simplicity of a simple scenario approach.

The rationale for steps 1 to 4

The rationale for this procedure in terms of beginning with the extremes, initially the pessimistic extreme, is to mitigate against 'anchoring' bias effects which are discussed later, and ensure that residual bias is conservative (safe), while 'keeping it simple'. With a bit of practice, optimistic and pessimistic outcome scenarios on a common scale with one or two intermediate points on the same common scale can be selected quickly and easily. The simplicity of the scenario set is more important than whether the probabilities associated with values exceeding or being less than the extreme scenarios are closely in line with the guidelines. The priority is 'keep it simple'.

If one interval is chosen, the simple scenario approach simplifies to the minimum clarity approach, ending in step 3. Three or more intervals mean the next part of the simple scenario process is concerned with assessing the probabilities associated with each of the designated intervals, working to one significant figure as a basic default option unless greater precision looks useful. For 'size the uncertainty' purposes it is convenient to assume that all values in a particular interval are equally likely, as shown directly by the rectangular histogram density format in Figure 10.1, indirectly by the corresponding piece-wise linear cumulative distribution format.

Step 5 – optimistic outcome probability

Step 5 involves assessing the probability of an outcome in the interval centred on the optimistic outcome scenario value. Working to one significant figure is usually convenient to start with, and is assumed here. In the context of criteria like cost or duration, given the nominal P10 interpretation of the optimistic outcome scenario, a probability of 0.2 is a reasonable estimate for this interval. In the context of criteria like revenue or lay days, a nominal P90 percentile interpretation also suggests a probability of 0.2 for this interval. An estimate of 0.3 may be preferred, and 0.1 is a possibility. However, usually these are the only viable choices, a simplicity driven by the optimistic outcome scenario definition. Even modest experience makes selecting the most appropriate value in the context of this first-pass process fairly quick and efficient. Using Figure 10.1 as an example, the default probability of 0.2 has been chosen.

Step 6 – pessimistic outcome probability

Step 6 involves assessing the probability of an outcome in the interval centred on the pessimistic outcome scenario value. Given an estimated 0.2 probability for the interval centred on the optimistic outcome scenario value, and the complementary nominal 90 or 10 percentile interpretation of the pessimistic outcome scenario, 0.3 is a reasonable expectation, rounding up to reflect the usual asymmetry of both cost/duration and revenue/lay day type criteria distributions, as illustrated by Figure 10.1. Relative to expectations, there is usually more scope for things to go badly than there is for things to go well. An estimate of 0.2 may be preferred, and 0.4 is a possibility, but 0.1 would be a cause for query. As in the context of the optimistic outcome probability, the process is efficient and quick for participants of even modest experience, with a simplicity driven by the scenario interpretations.

Step 7 – intermediate outcome probabilities

Step 7 involves assessing the probability of outcomes in the central intervals. If a single intermediate outcome scenario is involved, the associated probability is simply a residual – in the Figure 10.1 context, $(1 - 0.2 - 0.3) = 0.5$. Two intermediate scenarios require a split, rounding to the nearest 0.1. Again simplicity is the key. A little practice should make the process easy, fast and efficient.

The rationale for the sequence of steps 5 and 6

The rationale for the sequence of steps 5 and 6 is to encourage an assessment which spreads the distribution. Reversing the order will tend to yield a narrower distribution: 0.2 followed by 0.1, instead of 0.2 followed by 0.3. The literature on bias and most peoples' practical experience tells us very clearly that optimism bias is more common than pessimism bias, so when we have a choice, making a choice which tends to neutralize this bias makes obvious sense.

The overall basic rationale for the simple scenario approach

The overall basic rationale for this simple scenario estimating process is that we know people tend to underestimate uncertainty, and we have a choice about the sequence we use to elucidate information, so it makes sense to order the steps of our elucidation process to minimize the anticipated bias. We want enough clarity to understand the size of the uncertainty, and the associated expected value, but skew and distribution shape more generally may not be of importance for sizing purposes.

Event uncertainty sources

The basic approach discussed above addresses a variability source, like the number of lay days available in a month. When sizing an event uncertainty source, like 'wet buckles', it is desirable to consider the range of possible impacts separately from the probability that an event will occur. The simple scenario approach can be used to first assess the likely range of impacts given that the event happens, and then to assess the probability of the event happening. The rationale for this order is clarifying the overall nature of the outcome probability distribution given that the event occurs before estimating the probability that the event will occur.

Broader interpretation of all first-pass estimates and revisions

Whatever the approach used to define first-pass estimates, they need the broader interpretation associated with a minimum insight approach in Chapter 2. That is, clarifying the distinctions between stretch targets, commitments and expectations discussed in Chapter 2 needs attention as part of the first pass, and these broader interpretations also need updating with revisions. Indeed, these distinctions need clarification throughout the evaluate phase as well, but we will avoid saying so repetitively.

Refine and restructure a source

A first pass through the quantify phase will be primarily concerned with sizing sources of uncertainty in order to identify which sources warrant further attention, to help to allocate estimating time effectively and efficiently, unless it is obvious that more clarity is a sound investment. This section assumes that sizing uncertainty has been done. It assumes that each source of uncertainty worthy of further attention in terms of refinement has been identified, and that refinement of estimates might lead to local and limited restructuring. This involves important tradeoffs between refining and restructuring in local and more general terms.

The purpose of refining earlier estimates is to add more clarity in an efficient manner. Concerns associated with refining estimates include:

1. deciding what level of detail to aspire to – 'how many intervals?' in the context of our basic rectangular histogram approach;
2. exploring alternatives to histogram approaches to obtaining more detailed estimates;
3. assessing the reliability of estimates;
4. determining how best to manage the elicitation of probabilities;
5. clarifying the relationship between objective data and subjective probabilities.

The following five sections address each of these concerns in turn. Their interdependence and the general nature of some of the issues involved mean they have structuring implications in other phases of the PUMP.

How many intervals for a rectangular histogram approach?

Suppose the source in question is the uncertain effect of weather in a given month as characterized by Figure 10.1 and Table 10.1.

Table 10.1 provides a probability distribution for the number of days in discrete terms using the class mark values associated with the central values in intervals, a tabular format probability tree equivalent to Figure 10.1. The simple common interval rectangular histogram density

Table 10.1   Tabular format discrete value probability tree for interpreting Figure 10.1

Days	Probability	Contribution to expected value (days times probability)
10	0.3	$10 \times 0.3 = 3.0$
15	0.5	$15 \times 0.5 = 7.5$
20	0.2	$20 \times 0.2 = 4.0$
Expected number of days (via third column sum)		14.5

format of Figure 10.1 and the associated piece-wise linear cumulative format mean that the expected value for the continuous variable form is the same as the expected value for the discrete variable form of Table 10.1. One of the advantages of the format of Figure 10.1 is its easy conversion to a discrete variable equivalent, facilitating the use of probability trees to understand conditional dependence and decision trees to understand option choices.

Even if a source is of only moderate importance, presenting results to the project team may raise unnecessary questions if the portrayal is too crude, particularly if members of the project team are inexperienced in the use of low clarity approaches. All sources modelled separately may require more probability distribution detail if only as a cosmetic issue, but further precision and accuracy may be required because a source is recognized as important. Still more precision and accuracy may be required because demonstrating the validity of decisions dependent on the issue is important. The task here is to assess how much precision and accuracy may be appropriate with respect to this particular pass through the quantify phase for a source defined using Figure 10.1 and Table 10.1.

Provide more probability distribution detail using a 'second-cut' approach

A reasonable concern about estimates like those of Table 10.1 and Figure 10.1 is their clearly crude or nominal nature. People may be uncomfortable making significant decisions based on estimates which are so overtly crude. Assume for the moment that Figure 10.1 and Table 10.1 were not based on hard data – they were estimated on a purely subjective basis by an engineer with appropriate experience.

More detail can be associated with Table 10.1 outcomes using a 'second-cut' refinement of a 'first-cut' simple scenario estimate without significantly altering the intended message, as illustrated in Table 10.2.

The 'second-cut' probabilities of Table 10.2 illustrate the impact of working to the nearest 0.05 instead of to the nearest single significant figure, increasing precision by a factor of 2 by using a 20-division probability scale instead of a 10-division scale, and pushing an estimator to provide more detail in the distribution tails, when the estimate is purely subjective. We will argue later that most probability elicitation techniques are biased in terms of yielding too small a spread. The design of the second-cut process described here is explicitly concerned with pushing out the spread of distributions, to deliberately work against known bias, maximizing this effect by associating a 0.10 probability with the class mark value 5, instead of 0.05, which would preserve an expected outcome of 14.5. But note that the second-cut approach reduces the expected value by

Table 10.2   Second-cut example

Days	First-cut (Table 10.1)	Second-cut
5		0.10
10	0.3	0.20
15	0.5	0.50
20	0.2	0.15
25		0.05
Expected value	14.5	14.25

less than 2%, and it tells much the same story in terms of spread. Further, note that if subjective estimation was simplified to a P10 to P90 range minimum clarity approach, with P10 = 10 and P90 = 20, the expected value is (10 + 20) / 2 = 15, an increase in expected value of less than 4%, which would be neutralized by a more plausible P10 = 9 and P90 = 20 with an expected value of (9 + 20)/2 = 14.5.

Provide more probability distribution precision in a rectangular histogram framework

The main conclusion to be drawn from these simple numerical illustrations is that *more detailed estimates add very little in the way of precision with respect to expected outcomes*. Bias is an issue needing careful control, and precision is relevant to the control of bias, but precision on its own is a largely cosmetic issue if expected values are the concern.

A second conclusion to be drawn is that a difference in expected values between successive cuts is a function of the skew or asymmetry of the distribution, which is modest in this case. Extreme skew would make more intervals more desirable. However, to some extent the minimum clarity approach deals with this, as effectively, or even more effectively, than three or more intervals. For example, a P10 = 9 and a P90 = 20 is arguably a very likely and plausible estimate outcome if Figure 10.1 was entirely consistent with the available data.

A third conclusion to be drawn is that the variance (spread) increases as more detail is provided. This is a deliberate aspect of a process for adding more detail which is focused on the tails. However, it is worth noting that the second-cut level of precision used in Table 10.2 (five intervals) provides all the precision needed for most purposes in terms of variance. Further, it is worth noting that a minimum clarity approach also performs well in terms of unbiased variance estimation.

A fourth conclusion is that this subjectively based second-cut process could also be used to adjust a purely data based first pass. For example, if Table 10.1 and a linked Figure 10.1 were based on 3, 5 and 3 observations in three class intervals, second-cut adjustments shown in Table 10.2 might reflect bad weather effects being understated if short periods of good weather are not long enough to use effectively, with long periods of good weather being particularly useful.

Finally, it is worth noting that any probability distribution shape can be captured to whatever level of precision is required by using more intervals – the common interval rectangular histogram approach involves no restrictive assumptions at all, and it facilitates tradeoffs between precision and estimation effort which are clear and transparent.

If very wide ranges and heavy skew are involved, a useful modification of the basic approach is moving to logarithmic scales with order of magnitude estimates. This improves precision with no fundamental change to the basic rectangular histogram approach.

Alternatives to rectangular histogram approaches

A range of well-known alternative approaches to providing more detailed estimates which may improve precision are available, which may or may not help in a given situation. One of the most common approaches is to use a particular probability distribution function.

Probability distribution function approaches

Specific probability distribution functions *may* provide more reliable estimates than the minimum clarity approach or its generalized common interval rectangular histogram parent described above, *if* the assumptions they are based on clearly hold and a limited data set can be used to estimate distribution parameters effectively. However, while specific probability distribution functions usually provide more precision, this additional precision is often spurious, and specific probability distributions often provide less accurate estimates, because the assumptions underpinning the specific probability distribution are not appropriate and they distort the issues modelled. In general it is counterproductive and dangerous to employ specific probability distributions if the nature of the assumptions underpinning a specific probability distribution are not clearly understood and are not clearly applicable. For example, Normal (Gaussian) distributions should not be used if the 'Central Limit Theorem' is not clearly understood and applicable. Table 10.3 indicates distributions often assumed, and associated assumptions.

Instead of estimating parameters for a particular theoretical distribution, an alternative approach is to fit a theoretical distribution to a limited number of elicited probability estimates. This can serve to reduce the number of probabilities that have to be elicited to produce a complete probability distribution.

This approach is facilitated by the use of computer software packages such as 'MAINOPT' or '@Risk'. 'MAINOPT' is a tool which models 'bath-tub' curves for reliability analysis. The generic 'bath-tub'-shaped curve shows the probability of failure of a component at a particular time given survival to that point in time. The analyst specifies parameters which indicate the timing of the 'burn-in', 'steady-state' and 'wear-out' periods, together with failure rates for each period. The software then produces appropriate 'bath-tub' and failure density curves. Woodhouse (1993) gives a large number of examples in the context of maintenance and reliability of industrial equipment.

A popular choice for many situations is the triangular distribution. This distribution is simple to specify, covers a finite range with values in the middle of the range more likely than values at the extremes, and can also show a degree of skewness if appropriate. As shown in Figure 10.3, this distribution can be specified completely by just three values: the most likely value, an upper bound or maximum value, and the lower bound or minimum value.

Table 10.3   Applicability of theoretical probability distributions

Distribution	Applicability
Poisson $P(n) = \lambda^n e^{-\lambda} / n!$ mean $= \lambda$ variance $= \lambda$	Distribution of the number of independent rare events, n, that occur infrequently in space, time, volume or other dimensions. Specify λ, the average number of rare events in one unit of the dimension (e.g. the average number of accidents in a given unit of time).
Exponential $f(x) = \begin{cases} e^{-x/k} / k, \ k > 0; \\ \quad 0 \leq x \leq \infty \\ 0 \ \text{elsewhere} \end{cases}$ mean $= k$, variance $= k^2$	Useful for modelling time to failure of a component where the length of time a component has already operated does not affect its chance of operating for an additional period. Specify k, the average time to failure, or $1/k$ the probability of failure per unit time.
Uniform $f(x) = \begin{cases} 1/(U-L) \\ \quad L \leq x \leq U \\ 0 \ \text{elsewhere} \end{cases}$ mean $= (U+L)/2$ variance $= (U+L)^2/12$	Where any value in the specified range $[U, L]$ is equally likely. Specify U and L.
Standard Normal $f(x) = \exp(-x^2/2) / \sqrt{2\pi}$ mean $= 0$, variance $= 1$	Appropriate for the distribution of the mean value of the sum of a large number of independent random variables (or a small number of Normally distributed variables). Let $Y_1, Y_2 \ldots Y_n$ be independent and identically distributed random variables with mean μ and variance $\sigma^2 < \infty$. Define $x_n = \sqrt{n}(\bar{Y} - \mu)\sigma$ where $\bar{Y} = \sum_{i=1}^{n} Y_i$. Then the distribution function of x_n converges to the standard Normal distribution function as $n \to \infty$. Requires μ and σ^2 to be estimated.
Standard Normal $f(x) = \exp(-x^2/2) / \sqrt{2\pi}$ mean $= 0$, variance $= 1$	If y represents the number of 'successes' in n independent trials of an event for which p is the probability of 'success' in a single trial, then the variable $x = (y - np) / \sqrt{np(1-p)}$ has a distribution that approaches the standard Normal distribution as the number of trials becomes increasingly large. The approximation is fairly good as long as $np > 5$ when $p \leq 0.5$ and $n(1-p) > 5$ when $p > 0.5$. Requires specification of p and n.

Alternatively, assessors can provide 'optimistic' and 'pessimistic' estimates in place of maximum and minimum possible values, where there is an X% chance of exceeding the optimistic value, and a $(100 - X)$% chance of exceeding the pessimistic value. A suitable value for X to reflect the given situation is usually 10%, 5%, or 1%.

In certain contexts, estimation of a triangular distribution may be further simplified by assuming a particular degree of skewness. For example, in the case of activity durations in a project planning network Williams (1992) and Golenko-Ginzburg (1988) have suggested that durations tend to have a 1:2 skew, with the most likely value being a third along the range (that is, $2(M - L) = (U - M)$ in Figure 10.3).

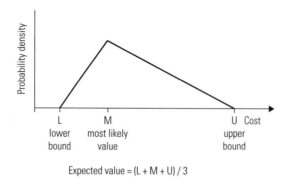

Expected value = (L + M + U) / 3

Figure 10.3 The triangular distribution

The triangular distribution is often thought to be a convenient choice of distribution for cost and duration of many activities where the underlying processes are obscure or complex. Alternative 'theoretical' distributions such as the Beta, Gamma, and Berny (Berny, 1989) distributions can be used to model more rounded, skewed distributions, but analytical forms lack the simplicity and transparency of the triangular distribution (Williams, 1992). In the absence of any theoretical reasons for preferring them, and given limited precision in estimates of distribution parameters, it is doubtful whether use of Beta, Gamma or Berny distributions has much to offer over the use of the simple triangle distribution.

In our view, for reasons indicated earlier, it is doubtful that triangular distributions offer any advantages over the use of a minimum clarity approach generalized as appropriate using common interval rectangular histograms as illustrated by Figure 10.1, and they may cause significant underestimation of extreme values. The use of an absolute maximum value also raises difficulties discussed in the next subsection, whether or not the absolute value is solicited directly from the estimator.

Fractile methods

A common approach to eliciting subjective probabilities of continuous variables is the 'fractile' method. This involves an expert's judgement being elicited to provide a cumulative probability distribution via selected 'fractile' values.

The basic procedure as described by Raiffa (1968) using the percentile (P) notation adopted earlier is:

1. Identify the highest (P100) and lowest (P0) possible values the variable can take. There is no chance of values less than P0. There is a 100% chance that the variable will be less than P100.
2. Identify the median value (P50). It is equally likely that the actual value will be above or below this figure (i.e. 50% chance of being below P50 and a 50% chance of being above P50).
3. Subdivide the range P50 to P100 into two equally likely parts. Call the dividing point P75 to denote that there is a 75% chance that the true value will be below P75and a 25% chance that it will be in the range P75 to P100.

4. Repeat the procedure in step 3 for values below P50 to identify P25.
5. Subdivide each of the four intervals obtained from step 3 and step 4, depending on the need to shape the cumulative probability distribution.
6. Plot the graph of cumulative percentage probability (0, 25, 50, 75, 100) against associated values (P0, P25, P50, P75, P100). Draw a smooth curve or series of straight lines through the plot points to obtain the cumulative probability curve.

A variation of Raiffa's procedure is to trisect the range into three equally likely ranges, rather than bisect it as in step 2 above. The idea of this variation is to overcome any tendency for the assessing expert to bias estimates towards the middle of the identified range.

In our view this approach is fundamentally flawed in the context of most practical applications by the dependence upon identification of P100 in the first step. Most durations and associated risks are unbounded on the high side (there is a finite probability that the activity may never finish), because the project may be cancelled, for example. This means any finite maximum is a conditional estimate, and it is not clear what the conditions are. Further, it is very difficult in practice to visualize absolute maximums. For these reasons most serious users of PERT models redefined the original PERT minimum and maximum estimates as P10 and P90 values forty years ago, as discussed, for example, by Moder and Philips (1970). The recommended minimum clarity approach and its common interval rectangular histogram generalization avoid these difficulties. However, variants of Raiffa's approach which avoid the P0 and P100 issue may be useful, including direct interactive plotting of cumulative probability curves.

Relative likelihood methods

A common approach to eliciting subjective probabilities of discrete possible values like those of Table 10.2 is the method of relative likelihoods (Moore and Thomas, 1976). The procedure to be followed by the assessing expert as Moore and Thomas describe it is as follows, using the M = most likely value notation of Figure 10.3:

1. Identify the most likely value of the variable (M) and assign it a probability rating of 60 units.
2. Identify a value below M which is half as likely to occur as M. Assign this a probability rating of 30 units.
3. Identify a value above M which is half as likely to occur as M. Assign this a probability rating of 30 units.
4. Identify values above and below M which are a quarter as likely as M. Assign each of these values a probability rating of 15 units.
5. Identify minimum and maximum possible values for the variable.
6. On a graph, plot the probability ratings against associated variable values and draw a smooth curve through the various points.
7. Read off the probability ratings for each intermediate discrete value. Sum all the probability ratings for each value and call this R. Divide each individual probability rating by R to obtain the assessed probability of each discrete value.

The above procedure may be modified by identifying variable values which are, for example, one-third or one-fifth as likely to occur as the most likely value M.

Other alternatives and hybrids

Some other less common and hybrid approaches are possible. An example hybrid approach is adding Normal or log-Normal distribution tales to Beta distributions at their P5 and P95 values, popular with some BP engineers in the 1980s, because it allowed them to continue with the familiar PERT basis but reinterpret minimum and maximum values as plausible scenarios, avoiding the bias inherent in absolute maximum or minimum values.

Our recommendation

In our view a second-cut approach to refining a rectangular histogram approach which generalizes the simple example illustrated by Table 10.2 is simpler and more effective, using as many classes as needed to obtain the desired precision, and logarithmic transformations if this is useful. However, some of the ideas associated with the Moore and Thomas procedure or other alternatives can be incorporated in a generalized rectangular histogram-based approach if desired. Further, occasional use of specific probability distributions when their assumptions are sound is useful, and what matters most is a robust approach to bias which all those involved are comfortable with.

The reliability of subjective estimates of uncertainty

The reliability of subjective estimates of uncertainty is of obvious interest in the context of a 'refine the source' task, but it is a more general issue too, also directly relevant to the 'size the source' task.

Techniques used to encode subjective probabilities ought to ensure that estimates express the estimator's true beliefs, conform to the axioms of probability theory, and are valid. Testing the validity of estimates is extremely difficult, since it involves empirical observation over a large number of similar cases. However, it is possible to avoid a range of common problems, if these problems are understood.

An important consideration is ensuring honesty in estimates, and that explicit or implicit rewards do not motivate estimators to be dishonest or biased in their estimates. For example, a concern to avoid looking inept might cause estimates to be unrealistically optimistic. There is a growing recognition that deliberate lies are a major issue, sometimes using euphemisms like 'strategic misrepresentation' (Flyvberg et al., 2003).

Even if honest estimating is a reasonable assumption, estimates may still be unreliable. In particular, overwhelming evidence from research using fractiles to assess uncertain quantities is that people's probability distributions tend to be too tight (Lichtenstein et al., 1982, p. 330). For example, in a variety of experiments Alpert and Raiffa (1982) found that when individuals were asked to specify 98% confidence bounds on given uncertain variables, rather than 2% of true values falling outside the 98% confidence bounds, 20–50% did so. In other words, people tend to underestimate the range of possible values an uncertain variable can take. The second-cut approach illustrated by Table 10.2, deliberately pushing out the tails, helps to overcome this tendency. However, arguably it falls well short of what is needed.

Slovic et al. (1982) suggest that 'although the psychological basis for unwarranted certainty is complex, a key element seems to be people's lack of awareness that their knowledge is based on assumptions that are often quite tenuous'. Significantly, even experts may be as prone to overconfidence as lay people when forced to rely on judgement.

The ability of both the lay person and experts to estimate uncertainty has been examined extensively in the psychology literature (e.g. Kahneman et al., 1982). It is argued that, as a result of limited information processing abilities, people adopt simplifying rules or heuristics when estimating uncertainty. These heuristics can lead to large and systematic errors in estimates.

Adjustment and anchoring

Failure to specify adequately the extent of uncertainty about a quantity may be due to a process of estimating uncertainty that makes adjustments to an initial point estimate. The initial value may be suggested by the formulation of a problem or by a partial computation. Unfortunately, subsequent estimates may be unduly influenced by the initial value, so that subsequent estimates are typically insufficiently different from the initial value. Moreover, for a single problem, different starting points may lead to different final estimates that are biased towards the starting values. This effect is known as 'anchoring' (Tversky and Kahneman, 1974).

Consider an estimator who is asked to estimate the probability distribution for a particular cost element. To select a highest possible cost U (using Figure 10.3 notation, or P100) it is natural for some estimators to begin by thinking of a best (central) estimate of the cost and to adjust this value upward, and to select the lowest possible cost L (using Figure 10.3 notation, or P0) by adjusting the best estimate of cost downwards. If these adjustments are insufficient, then the range of possible costs will be too narrow, and the assessed probability distribution too tight. Other estimators may naturally start with a 'no problems' estimate of U, compounding range bias with central value bias.

Anchoring bias can also lead to biases in the evaluation of compound events. The probability of conjunctive 'and' events tends to be overestimated while the probability of disjunctive 'or' events tends to be underestimated. Conjunctive events typically occur in a project where success depends on a chain of activities being successfully completed. The probability of individual activities being completed on time may be quite high but the overall probability of completion on time may be low, especially if the number of events is large. Estimates of the probability of completing the whole project on time are likely to be overoptimistic if based on adjustments to the probability of completing individual activities on time. In this setting, unbiased estimation of completion time for identified activities can be achieved with appropriate project planning software, but the anchoring may be an implicit cause of overestimation when a number of conjunctive events or activities are not explicitly treated separately.

To overcome these problems in a minimum clarity estimate context, asking for a P90 first, then a P10, is the obvious choice. If an estimator cannot think about these questions in that order, anchoring bias should be anticipated and engineered out in other ways.

The availability heuristic

The availability heuristic involves judging an event as likely or frequent if instances of it are easy to imagine or recall. This is often appropriate insofar as frequently occurring events are generally easier to imagine or recall than unusual events. However, events may be easily imagined or recalled simply because they have been recently brought to the attention of an individual. Thus a recent incident, recent discussion of a low probability hazard, or recent media coverage, may all increase memorability and imaginability of similar events, and hence perceptions of their perceived likelihood. Conversely, events which an individual has rarely experienced or heard about, or has difficulty imagining, will be perceived as having a low probability of occurrence irrespective of their actual likelihood of occurring. Obviously experience is a key determinant of perceived risk. If experience is biased, then perceptions are likely to be inaccurate.

In some situations, failure to appreciate the limits of presented data may lead to biased probability estimates. For example, Fischoff et al. (1978) studied whether people are sensitive to the completeness of fault trees. They used a fault tree indicating the ways in which a car might fail to start. Groups of subjects were asked to estimate the proportion of failures which might be due to each of seven categories of factors including an 'all other problems' category. When three sections of the diagram were omitted, effectively incorporating removed categories into the 'all other problems' category, subjects overestimated the probability of the remaining categories and substantially underestimated the 'all other problems' category. In effect, what was out of sight was out of mind. Professional mechanics did not do appreciably better on the test than laypeople.

Such findings suggest that fault trees and other representations of sources of uncertainty can strongly influence judgements about probabilities of particular sources occurring. Tables 10.1 and 10.2 generalized to incorporate event uncertainty can be interpreted as a way of exploring the importance of these kinds of issues.

Presentational effects

The foregoing discussion highlights that the way in which issues are expressed or presented can have a significant impact on perceptions of uncertainty. This suggests that those responsible for presenting information about uncertainty have considerable opportunity to manipulate perceptions. Moreover, to the extent that these effects are not appreciated, people may be inadvertently manipulating their own perceptions by casual decisions about how to organize information (Slovic et al., 1982). An extreme but common situation is where presentation of 'best estimates' may inspire undue confidence about the level of uncertainty. The approach recommended here is designed to manipulate perceptions in a way which helps to neutralize known bias.

Managing the subjective probability elicitation process

It should be evident from the last section that any process for eliciting probability assessments from individuals needs to be carefully managed if it is to be seen as effective and as reliable as circumstances permit.

Spetzler and Stael von Holstein (1975) offer the following general principles to avoid later problems in the elicitation process:

1. Be prepared to justify to the expert (assessor) why a parameter or variable is important to the project.
2. Variables should be structured to show clearly any conditionalities. If the expert thinks of a variable as being conditional upon other variables, it is important to incorporate these

conditions into the analysis to minimize mental acrobatics. For example, sales of a new product might be expected to vary according to whether a main competitor launches a similar product or not. Eliciting estimates of future possible sales might be facilitated by making two separate assessments, one where the competitor launches a product and one where they do not. A separate assessment of the likelihood of the competitor launching a rival product would then need to be made.

3. Variables to be assessed should be clearly defined to minimize ambiguity. A good test of this is to ask whether a clairvoyant could reveal the value of the variable by specifying a single number without requesting clarification.

4. The variable should be described on a scale that is meaningful to the expert providing the assessment. The expert should be used to thinking in terms of the scale used, so in general the expert assessor should be allowed to choose the scale. After encoding, the scale can be converted as necessary to fit the analysis required.

Developing the second point in a slightly different manner, if a number of potential conditions are identified, but separate conditional assessments are too complex because of the number of variables or the partial dependency structure, the minimum clarity approach can be developed along the lines of the more sophisticated approaches to scenario building used in 'futures analysis' or 'technological forecasting' (Chapman et al., 1987, ch. 33; van der Heijden, 2005). That is, estimation of the P10 and P90 scenarios can be associated with consistent scenarios linked to sets of high or low values of all the conditional variables identified. This approach will further help to overcome the tendency to make estimated distributions too narrow. For example, instead of asking someone how long it takes them to make a journey which involves a taxi in an unconditional manner, starting with the pessimistic P90 value, suggest that it could be rush hour (so taxis are hard to find and slow), raining (so taxis are even harder to find), and the trip is very urgent and important (so Sod's law applies).

An instructive case study which illustrates many of the issues involved in probability elicitation is described by Keeney and van Winterfeldt (1991). The purpose of this study, funded by the US Nuclear Regulatory Commission, was to estimate the uncertainties and consequences of severe core damage accidents in five selected nuclear power plants. A draft report published in 1987 for comment was criticized because it:

- relied too heavily on scientists of the national laboratories;
- did not systematically select or adequately document the selection of issues for assessing expert judgements;
- did not train the experts in the assessment of probabilities;
- did not allow the experts adequate time for assimilating necessary information prior to assessment;
- did not use state-of-the-art assessment methods;
- inadequately documented the process and results of the expert assessments.

Following criticisms, project management took major steps to improve substantially the process of eliciting and using expert judgements. Subsequently, probabilistic judgements were elicited for about 50 events and quantities from some 40 experts. Approximately 1000 probability distributions were elicited and, counting decomposed judgements, several thousand probability judgements were elicited. Given the significance of this study, it was particularly important to eliminate discrepancies in assessments due to incomplete information, use of inappropriate assumptions, or different meanings attached to words. Nevertheless, uncertainties were very large, often covering several orders of magnitude in the case of frequencies and 50% to 80% of the physically feasible range in the case of some uncertain quantities.

Various protocols for elicitation of probabilities from experts have been described in the literature (Morgan and Herion, 1990, Chapter 7). The most influential has probably been that developed in the Department of Engineering–Economic Systems at Stanford University and at the Stanford Research Institute (SRI) during the 1960s and 1970s. A useful summary of the SRI protocol is provided by Spetzer and Stael von Holstein (1975), and Merkhofer (1987). A similar but more recent protocol is suggested by Keeney and van Winterfeldt (1991) drawing on their experience of the study of nuclear power plants outlined above and other projects. Their procedure involves six stages, as follows:

1. identification and selection of issues;
2. identification and selection of assessing experts;
3. discussion and refinement of issues;
4. assessors trained for elicitation;
5. elicitation interviews;
6. analysis, aggregation and resolution of disagreements between assessors.

For completeness each stage is described briefly below, but it should be noted that stages 1 to 3 relate to the PUMP define, focus, identify and structure phases examined in previous chapters. In particular, stages 1 and 2 are comparable to a first pass of the define, focus, identify and structure phases and stage 3 is comparable to a first pass of the structure phase plus restructuring via looping back for another pass in a PUMP context.

Stage 1 – identification and selection of issues

This stage involves identifying questions about models, assumptions, criteria, events and quantities that could benefit from formal elicitation of expert judgements and selecting those for which a formal process is worth while.

Keeney and van Winterfeldt (1991) argue for the development of a comprehensive list of issues in this stage, with selection of those considered most important only after there is reasonable assurance that the list of issues is complete. Selection should be driven by potential impact on performance criteria, but is likely to be influenced by resource constraints which limit the amount of detailed estimation that is practicable. This stage encapsulates the spirit of the define, focus, identify and structure phases discussed in earlier chapters.

Stage 2 – identification and selection of experts

A quality elicitation process should include specialists who are recognized experts with the knowledge and flexibility of thought to be able to translate their knowledge and models into judgements relevant to the issue.

Analysts are needed to facilitate the elicitation. Their task is to assist the specialist to formulate the issues, decompose them, to articulate the specialist judgements, check consistency of judgements and help to document the specialist's reasoning. Generalists with a broad knowledge of many or all project issues may be needed in complex projects where specialists' knowledge is limited to parts of the project. This stage also encapsulates the spirit of the define, focus, identify and structure phases discussed in earlier chapters.

Stage 3 – discussion and refinement of issues

Following issue and expert selection, a first meeting of experts and analysts should be organized to clearly define and structure the variables to be encoded. At the start of this first meeting, the analyst is likely to have only a rough idea of what needs to be encoded. The purpose of the meeting is to enlist the expert's help in refining the definition and structure of variables to be encoded. The aim is to produce unambiguous definitions of the events and all other uncertain quantities that are to be elicited. For all uncertain quantities the meaning, dimension and unit of measurement need to be clearly defined. All conditioning events also need to be clearly defined.

At this stage it is usually necessary and desirable to explore the usefulness of disaggregating variables into more elemental variables. Previous chapters have discussed the importance of breaking down or disaggregating sources and associated responses into appropriate levels of detail. A central concern is to ensure that sources are identified in sufficient detail to understand the nature of significant project uncertainty and to facilitate the formulation of effective management strategies. From a probability elicitation perspective, disaggregation is driven by a need to assess the uncertainty of an event or quantity derived from a combination of underlying, contributory factors.

Often more informed assessments of an uncertain variable can be obtained by disaggregating the variable into component variables, making judgements about the probabilities of the component variables, and then combining the results mathematically. In discussions between analyst and assessor a key concern is to decide on an appropriate disaggregation of variables. This will be influenced by the knowledge base and assumptions adopted by the assessor.

Disaggregation can be used to combat motivational bias by producing a level of detail that disguises the connection between the assessor's judgements and personal interests. Disaggregation can also help to reduce cognitive bias (Armstrong et al., 1975). For example, if each event in a sequence of statistically independent events has to occur for successful completion of the sequence, assessors are prone to overestimate the probability of successful completion if required to assess it directly. In such circumstances it can be more appropriate to disaggregate the sequence into its component variables, assess the probability of completing each individual event, and then compute the probability of successful completion of the whole sequence.

Cooper and Chapman (1987, ch. 11) give examples of disaggregation in which more detailed representation of a problem can be much easier to use for estimating purposes than an aggregated representation. These examples include the use of simple Markov processes to model progress over time when weather effects involve seasonal cycles as in the pipe-laying context referred to in earlier chapters. Disaggregation also facilitates explicit modelling of complex decision rules or conditional probabilities and can lead to a much better understanding of the likely behaviour of a system. Disaggregation includes deciding that a simple PERT model that treats each activity duration as a single source of uncertainty is too crude, prompting the need for decomposition in terms of more than one source for each component of the basic framework, whether or not Markov processes and associated decision rules are modelled. All such disaggregation is the basis of and rationale for looping back to refine the structure of the analysis framework in later passes of the PUMP, having used earlier passes to identify the aspects where more detail would pay the biggest dividends.

The basis of the top-down approach to uncertainty decomposition embodied in the PUMP can be seen as a generalization of these ideas.

Stage 4 – training for elicitation

In this stage of the elicitation process the analyst leads the training of specialist and generalist assessors to familiarize them with concepts and techniques used in elicitation – to give them practice with assessments, to inform them about potential biases in judgement, and to motivate them for the elicitation process.

Motivating assessors for the elicitation process involves establishing a rapport between assessor and analyst, and a diplomatic search for possible incentives in which the assessor may have to prove an assessment which does not reflect the assessor's true beliefs.

Training involves explaining the nature of heuristics and cognitive biases in the assessment of uncertainty and giving assessors an opportunity to discuss the subject in greater depth if they wish. Training may also involve some warm-up trial exercises based around commonplace variables such as the journey time to work. This familiarization process can help assessors to become more involved in the encoding process and help them to understand why the encoding process is structured as it is. It can also encourage assessors to take the encoding process more seriously if the analysts are seen to be approaching the process in a careful and professional manner (Morgan and Herion, 1990).

In the Keeney and van Winterfeldt study (1991) outlined earlier the elicitation process worked largely due to the commitment of project staff to the expert elicitation process and the fact that the experts were persuaded that elicitation of their judgements was potentially useful and worthy of serious effort. Training of experts in probability elicitation was crucial because it reassured the experts that the elicitation process was rigorous, and showed them how biases could unknowingly enter into judgements.

Stage 5 – elicitation

In this stage structured interviews take place between the analyst and the specialist/generalist assessors. This involves the analyst reviewing definitions of events or uncertain quantities to be elicited, discussing the specialist's approach to the elicitation, including approaches to decomposition into component sources of uncertainties, eliciting probabilities, and checking judgements for consistency.

Conscious bias may be present for a variety of reasons, such as the following:

• An assessor may want to influence a decision by playing down the possibility of cost escalation, or by presenting an optimistic view of possible future revenues.
• A person who thinks they are likely to be assessed on a given performance measure is unlikely to provide an unbiased assessment of uncertainty about the performance measure. Estimates of the time or the budget needed to complete a task are likely to be overestimated to provide a degree of slack.

- A person may understate uncertainty about a variable lest they appear incompetent.
- For political reasons a person may be unwilling to specify uncertainty that undermines the views or position of other parties.

Where such biases are suspected, it may be possible to influence the incentive structure faced by the assessor, and additionally to modify the variable structure to obscure or weaken the incentive for bias. It can also be important to stress that the encoding exercise is not a method for testing performance or measuring expertise.

Spetzler and Stael von Holstein (1975) distinguish three aspects of the elicitation process: conditioning, encoding and verification. Conditioning involves trying to head off biases during the encoding process by conditioning assessors to think fundamentally about their judgements. The analyst should ask the assessor to explain the bases for any judgements and what information is being taken into account. This can help to identify possible anchoring or availability biases. Spetzler and Stael von Holstein (1975) suggest that the analyst can use availability to correct any central bias in estimates by asking the assessor to compose scenarios that would produce extreme outcomes. Careful questioning may be desirable to draw out significant assumptions upon which an assessment is based. This may lead to changes in the structure and decomposition of variables to be assessed.

Encoding involves the use of techniques such as those described earlier, beginning with easy questions followed by harder judgements. Spetzler and Stael von Holstein (1975) provide some useful advice for the encoding analyst:

- Begin by asking the assessor to identify extreme values for an uncertain variable. Then ask the assessor to identify scenarios that might lead to outcomes outside of these extremes and to estimate the probability of outcomes outside the designated extremes. This uses the availability heuristic to encourage assignment of higher probability extreme outcomes to counteract central bias that may otherwise occur.
- When asking for probabilities associated with particular values in the identified range, avoid choosing the first value in a way that may seem significant to the assessor, lest subsequent assessments are anchored on their value. In particular, do not begin by asking the assessor to identify the most likely value and the associated probability.
- Plot each response as a point on a cumulative probability distribution and number them sequentially. During the plotting process the assessor should not be shown the developing distribution in case the assessor tries to make subsequent responses consistent with previously plotted points.

The final part of the elicitation stage involves checking the consistency of the assessor's judgements and checking that the assessor is comfortable with the final distribution. Keeney and van Winterfeldt (1991) suggest that one of the most important consistency checks is to derive the density function from the cumulative probability distribution. This is most conveniently carried out with on-line computer support. With irregular distributions, the cumulative distribution can hide multi-modal phenomena or skewness of the density function. Another important consistency check is to show the assessor the effect of assessments from decomposed variables on aggregation. If the assessor is surprised by the result, the reasons for this should be investigated, rechecking decomposed assessments as necessary.

Stage 6 – analysis, aggregation and resolution of disagreements

Following an elicitation session, the analyst needs to provide feedback to the assessor about the combined judgements if this was not possible during the elicitation session. This may lead to the assessor making changes to judgements made in the elicitation session.

Where elicitation of a variable involves more than one assessor, it is necessary to aggregate these judgements. This may involve group meetings to explore the basis for consensus judgements or resolve disagreements. Keeney and van Winterfeldt (1991) found that whether or not substantial disagreements existed among expert assessors, there was almost always agreement among them that averaging of probability distributions (which preserved the range of uncertainties) was an appropriate procedure to provide information for a base case analysis.

An overview of all six stages

It should be clear from all the discussion in this section that probability encoding is a non-trivial process. Eliciting probability values needs to be taken seriously for credible results. To be effective, the encoding process needs to be carefully planned and structured, and adequate time needs to be devoted to it. The complete process should be documented as well as the elicitation results and associated reasoning. For subsequent use, documentation should be presented in a hierarchical level of detail to facilitate reports and justification of results in appropriate levels of detail for different potential users. In all of these respects the encoding process is no different from other aspects of the uncertainty management process.

Dealing with contradictory data or a complete absence of data

As argued earlier, purely subjective estimates for the first pass of a PUMP are useful even if relevant data exists, to clarify whether or not it is worth spending time accessing and analysing the data. If no data exists, subjective estimates to capture what situation experts know in softer terms are essential, to identify which aspects of a situation are worth further study. To reject the use of such understanding, whether or not data is available, is irrational. For those who like labels, it is a form of 'irrational objectivity' (Chapman and Ward, 2002, ch. 12).

Where no data exists, or the data is contradictory, or relevant domain experts have very different opinions, it can be useful to employ sensitivity analysis directly. For example, a reliability study for PetroCanada undertaken by Acres Consulting Services (Chapman et al., 1984) involving liquefied natural gas (LNG) plant failures, used order of magnitude increases and decreases in failure probabilities to test probability assumptions for sensitivity. Where it didn't matter, no further work was undertaken with respect to probabilities. Where it did, extensive literature searches and personal interviews were used. It transpired that LNG plant failure probabilities were too sensitive a matter to persuade operators to provide data or estimates directly, but operators were prepared to look at the Chapman et al. estimates and either nod or shake their heads.

In retrospect, drawing on a minimum clarity approach, it is now clear that most use of sensitivity analysis in a context like this is based on a common framing assumption which no longer makes sense – the assumption that we can quantify variability and uncertainty about the

attack every two thousand years justified the expenditure, a clear decision to spend it might have been the result.

A middle ground result is not a waste of time. It indicates there is no clear case one way or another, based on the assumptions used. If loss of life is an issue, a neutral analysis result allows such considerations to be taken into account without ignoring more easily quantified costs.

The key issue this example highlights is that *the purpose of analysis is insight, not numbers*. At the end of the day we usually do not need defendable probabilities. We need defendable decisions, whatever the outcome. The difference can be very important.

Extend the ordering of the sources

In Figure 10.2, 'start ordering the sources' kicks off the quantify phase, and 'extend the ordering of the sources' simply carries on this process with one significant new feature – identifying when there are no more sources to be considered *on this pass of the PUMP* and it is time to move on to a 'fit for purpose' test.

If the PUMP is initially focused on activities, as for the BP examples, it may be sensible to complete several full PUMP cycles for a given activity such as 'pipe laying', before moving on to other activities. It may even be sensible to complete several complete PUMP cycles for 'weather' before moving on to wet buckles and other pipe-laying sources of uncertainty. To some extent these judgements will be influenced by where all the people involved are on their learning curves. It will also be influenced by issues like 'how much time is available?' and 'how many complete PUMP iterations look appropriate?' and 'who is available to obtain information from?' It is a judgement clearly requiring coordination with earlier process management judgements, like 'how deeply should we explore each source of uncertainty?', 'to what extent is proactive response option choice optimization an issue?', and 'what kind of source structure looks sensible to start?'

If the PUMP is planned as a one-pass process to estimate cost, as for the BCS example, the proprietor Bruce has a standardized 'prototype' list of items to use as a prompt list, and when that list is exhausted he needs to ask the client 'is there anything else you can think of which should be part of the estimate?' If the answer is 'no', omitted items are at least in part the responsibility of the client.

A key difference between clients and contractors is that clients have responsibility for anything that is omitted from explicit consideration by default, given common working assumptions – contractors cannot depend on these working assumptions, but clients cannot depend on avoiding them.

The fit for purpose test

In Figure 10.2, the expectation in the 'fit for purpose' test is moving on to the evaluate phase. Iterations within the quantify phase are primarily about making sure that all sources of uncertainty have been considered on a first pass and refined as suggested by the evaluate phase on earlier passes of the PUMP. However, revisiting a source to refine its treatment may be part of the within phase looping structure, and sometimes it may be obvious that either refining or limited restructuring of a source or response structure would be useful – there is no need to move on to the evaluate phase to see that minor adjustments to the structure would be beneficial. This 'fit for purpose' test is a flexible shortcut, facilitating small local adjustments.

Selective refining and restructuring of sources

If a very low clarity initial sizing estimate is used on a first pass, it may be immediately obvious that a source of uncertainty is much more important than originally thought. Noting this and picking up on it via this specific task before moving on to the evaluate phase might involve refining the estimate as discussed earlier.

However, small local adjustments to the source and response structure may use *restructuring* rather than *refining* to achieve more insight in a clarity efficient manner, and we did not discuss this kind of restructuring earlier. These adjustments could take a wide variety of forms. For example, the initial modelling basis might assume a response that impact estimation suggests is clearly inadequate. Then it makes sense to immediately reconsider the assumed response, perhaps drawing on identify phase consideration of alternative responses, perhaps extending what was considered at an earlier point in the process. This section has two key points to make.

The first is that 'restructuring' includes changing assumed responses to test alternative response assumptions. In this context revised base plan assumptions may be involved, or revised contingency responses, or both. This is the basis of shaping E&D strategy, a primary goal of the PUMP being opportunity efficient shaping of strategic plans.

The second key point is the very important difference between refining and restructuring at a local level. An example may help to illustrate the refine/restructure difference, and refine/restructure tradeoffs, which have wider implications basic to the PUMP as a whole. A separate section has been used because of these wider implications.

An example illustrating refine/restructure tradeoffs

A 1990s review of an organization's project risk management practice by Chris Chapman involved interviewing senior users of risk management results to assess their concerns. Putting issues raised by a senior major programme manager and the budget holder for the total portfolio of programmes and projects together provides an example that has been useful to highlight potential tradeoffs in estimating between two approaches:

1. *refining* the quantification of sources in a given source structure, a central concern of the quantify phase, and
2. *restructuring* sources in the extended decomposition of sources sense, which is the basic concern of the define, focus, identify and structure phases, with minor local adjustments sometimes useful as part of the quantify phase.

The example begins with a problem posed by the programme manager – 'how should his staff estimate how long it will take to get a design change approval with financial implications?' There is a 'corporate standard' duration of 3 weeks, with a debatable interpretation, ranging from a stretch target to a commitment target. Past data the programme manager is aware of involves five observations: 3, 7, 6, 4 and 15 weeks. The organization suffers from a 'conspiracy of optimism', as observed by the major budget holder. This is a catchy label for a 'can-do' approach that covers for a variety of behaviours – like unwillingness to show lack of understanding or to let the team down once commitments are made. The organization also suffers from 'irrational objectivity', a label for belief in objective numbers when subjective alternatives are clearly better. See Chapman and Ward (2002, ch. 12) for more detailed discussion of such behaviours.

One conventional starting place is using the available data to estimate an expected duration for design change approvals: the sum of the five values divided by 5,

$$(3 + 7 + 6 + 4 + 15)/5 = 7.$$

Assuming that this is done, the conventional next question is what probability distribution function should be assumed to characterize the shape and spread of associated uncertainty. An attractive possibility for some is a Normal (Gaussian) distribution – but the 15 does not look as if it comes from a Normal distribution. A tempting way around this for some is to reject the 15 as an outlier, especially if it arose because the project was in trouble and head office was giving the project manager a bad time as a consequence, or the estimator is convinced this project is not going to get into trouble, or the estimator is not going to admit it if it is likely to do so! Rejecting the 15 lowers the expected value to

$$(3 + 7 + 6 + 4)/4 = 5.$$

Another conventional starting place begins with a probability distribution function – a Beta distribution approximation as used for basic PERT models for example. In this case the range is 3 to 15, defined by data-based optimistic and pessimistic values, and the expected value is their sum plus four times the most likely value all divided by six. Assuming a plausible but unobserved most likely duration of 5, this yields an expected of duration 6.3. More refined versions of this kind of approach could be used, like treating the duration of 3 as a P10 value and the duration of 15 as a P90 value, a Beta distribution over the P10 to P90 range, and Normal distribution tails. A minimum clarity approach can reasonably treat 3 as a P10 value and 15 as a P90 value, and divide the sum by two for an expected value estimate of 9. This interpretation involves using the Figure 10.4 version of Figure 2.2.

If more clarity is required, a sensible next step is to treat the 3, 7, 6 and 4 observations as typical of a 'normal' scenario, and the 15 as illustrative of an 'abnormal' scenario. The data can be interpreted as suggesting a one in five or 0.2 probability of 'abnormal' scenarios, a four in five or 0.8 probability of a 'normal' scenario. A data driven minimum clarity approach to the 'normal' scenario can assume a P10 = 3, a P90 = 7, with a mean of 5. A minimum clarity approach to the 'abnormal' scenario can start with a mean of 15 associated with the one observed instance, perhaps linked to the 'project in trouble being punished' context. In traditional objective statistical analysis terms there are no degrees of freedom left to estimate uncertainty associated with the 0.2 probability or the 15 weeks impact. However, speculation on other potential reasons for an unusual outcome might suggest key staff on holiday (summer time or other school holidays for

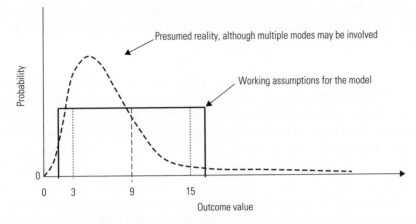

Figure 10.4 Simple estimate portrayal for design change approval.

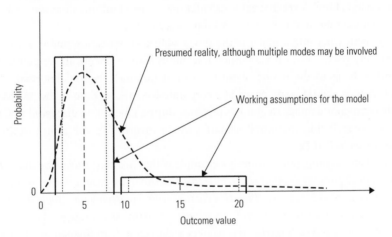

Figure 10.5 Two-scenario portrayal for design change approval.

example) or end of financial cycle constraints. This might lead to an 'abnormal' scenario probability P10 = 0.1 and P90 = 0.3, an abnormal scenario impact P10 = 10 and P90 = 20. Figure 10.5 portrays the implications.

The two-scenario portrayal of Figure 10.5 is crude, but it captures the long tail of the presumed reality in more informative terms than an assumed distribution function to approximate its shape, because it gets people thinking about why the abnormal might happen, and what might be done to avoid such problems, like making sure that any design change requests avoid holiday periods and end of financial cycle periods.

In short, using these two 'normal' and 'abnormal' scenarios is an alternative to a 'two-interval' version of the simple scenario description earlier. It is not a refinement of the one-interval minimum insight approach. It is a restructuring, heading in the direction of the high insight BP version of SCERT. The 'normal' scenario is a variant of the BP pipe-laying 'productivity variations' source. The 'abnormal' scenario involves separation of all 'wet buckle equivalents', without trying to model them separately. A two interval refinement would be much less effective. Indeed, a three or four interval refinement would not provide the same level of clarity.

More recent 2010 discussions with the same client organization suggested it might be worth extending this 'two scenario restructuring approach' to a 'four scenario restructuring approach'.

The third scenario would be a 'highly abnormal' scenario, perhaps a 'one in a hundred' interpretation in probability expected value terms, with a correspondingly high impact of 100 weeks in impact expected value terms. This would add about $100 \times 0.01 = 1$ week to the expected value, ignoring the $5 \times 0.01 = 0.05$ weeks reduction if the 0.01 probability for the 'highly abnormal' scenario is taken from the normal scenario. It clearly emphasizes the need to consider extreme values which are unlikely to be observed in small samples. We have to ignore such possibilities (with obvious bias and error implications) or resort to subjective estimates based on speculating about a general class of 'unknown unknowns' involving low probability high impact scenarios.

The fourth scenario would be the 'project cancelled' scenario, with no chance of completion. It would be excluded from expected value calculations to avoid infinite durations, which emphasizes the obvious conditional nature of any finite expected value.

Thinking about what might underlie these two additional scenarios, and how to avoid them, might prove very useful, even if very crude minimum clarity models are employed for all scenarios. Further, it opens discussion about the extent to which 'highly abnormal' and 'project cancelled' scenarios should be managed at a corporate level rather than at the project level. The BP example of 'anchor damage to another pipeline' during pipe laying discussed in Chapter 9 is illustrative of what 'highly abnormal' scenarios might involve. We will return to this aspect of managing sources in Part IV.

The immediate learning point from this example is that *restructuring using more decomposition of uncertainty sources is often more effective than refining estimation of sources, and it is usually a good idea to seek a clarity efficient structure before worrying too much about refinement of effectively sized sources of uncertainty*. In a sense, structure is a strategic choice, refinement a tactical choice, and it is worth getting the strategy right before worrying too much about tactics.

A 'cube factor' view of bias control

On occasion there is a need to make very important subjective adjustments to data-based estimates to reflect issues known to be important, even if these issues are not immediately quantifiable in objective terms. For example, there is sometimes a need to acknowledge the potential effect of 'unknowns' or inherent optimism bias in estimating processes when they are significant. When Chris Chapman had a university student summer job with IBM in Toronto in the 1960s, advice provided by a 'wise old timer' on the estimation of software costs was 'work out the best estimate you can, then multiply it by 3'. The wise old timer, Ted White, was still in his twenties at the time, but he was president of IBM Canada within a decade – he knew what he was talking about. A more recently suggested version of this approach is 'multiply by pi', on the grounds that pi ($\pi = 3.14$) has a more scientific ring about it, it is bigger, and it is closer to reality on average'. Such advice may seem silly, but there is a serious point here. A significant provision for what has not been considered in any formal process is dispensed with only by the very brave, who can be made to look very foolish. What we need is a formal explanation for such uplifts, and a way of sizing them.

All relevant project scope assumptions treated as conditions plus all relevant process scope assumptions, which are also conditions whether or not they are seen as such, can be labelled 'known unknowns', and appropriate adjustment for them treated as the first of three adjustment steps. For example, the notion of a 'project scope changes within the scope of the estimate' source of uncertainty (a 'no quibbles factor') can be identified and defined in terms of 'known unknowns'. If this 'no quibbles factor' is then quantified and added to the basis of the estimate, it becomes part of a 'no quibbles' estimate. This approach, used to reduce bias in estimates associated with project scope assumptions frequently treated as outside the estimate, is a very important first step in a broader approach to bias control. The conditions it addresses can be extended to include working assumptions like assuming independence (known to be untrue) or a particular form of contract (which may not happen). Process scope assumptions are more difficult to assess than project scope assumptions, but they can be even more important. For example, if PIGs have been used in a context like the Highways Agency estimates prior to the re-estimation exercise, a significant provision is suggested to accommodate process scope assumption uncertainty.

If this is done, a second step is adjusting for 'unknown unknowns', the relevant project and process scope assumptions involving conditions that have not been identified. This involves a quality judgement on the scope for important sources that have been overlooked – even very careful high clarity approaches will miss some unknown unknowns, but low clarity approaches usually offer more scope.

A third step is adjusting for 'bias' in the sense of 'all other sources of bias', like assuming statistical independence when systemic uncertainty is important and it was not picked up as part of the 'known unknowns'. In principle the first two categories might make the third redundant, but in practice we need a residual to sweep up anything missing from the first two, including conscious bias or outright lies, for example.

Bias may be conscious or unconscious, pessimistic or optimistic, and clues about the existence of bias may be available or not. For example, in respect of large infrastructure projects, Flyvbjerg et al. (2003, p. 20) conclude: *the cost estimates used in public debates, media coverage and decision making for transport infrastructure development are highly, systematically and significantly deceptive. So are the cost–benefit analyses into which cost estimates are routinely fed to calculate the viability and ranking of projects.* Consequently, Flyvbjerg et al. (2003, p. 65) argue that estimates by construction and user groups of economic growth resulting from a proposed infrastructure project should be treated with caution where infrastructure projects are likely to generate benefits for these groups while the major part of costs is often borne by taxpayers. Similarly, environmental impact assessments for infrastructure projects may be deficient due to lack of accuracy in estimates of impact predictions, limited scope, and the time horizons considered (Flyvbjerg et al., 2003, p. 49). Aside from bias derived from the self-interest of providers of estimates, uncertainty of estimates is further compounded if related activities are not well defined, relatively novel, or complex, or there has been limited opportunity for estimators to develop a high quality estimate. The latter can be a common problem for contractors preparing competitive tenders with limited time to develop detailed cost estimates.

This three-step 'kuuub' factor adjustment (known unknowns, unknown unknowns and bias) can be spelt 'cube', given a three dimensional 'cube' interpretation, and used in various ways

(Chapman and Ward, 2002). The key point here is the need to use such an adjustment framework to appreciate the overall quality of an estimate, adjust estimates when this is vital, and engineer bias out of estimates when this is desirable. It can be interpreted in relation to expected value estimates as a basic starting position, but then reflect contingency adjustments to provide a suitable estimate of an appropriate commitment value. To illustrate the basic nature of this cube factor adjustment role, consider the design change approval example of the last section.

If our project manager is presented with an estimate of 3 weeks for the design change approval, because the estimator wants a simple objective basis for estimates, and the 3 week 'corporate standard' is suitably objective in the estimator's view, multiplying by 3 or π or 4 might be sensible. Uncertainty has been ignored by the estimator, so a simple rule of thumb is needed, and a cube factor of 3 or 4 or somewhere in this range is much better than a cube factor of 1. Better still is an explicitly uncertain cube factor – with say a P10 value of 2 and a P90 value of 6 with a P50 expected value of 4 to be on the safe side with estimators who are grossly insensitive to uncertainty.

If our project manager is presented with an estimate of 9 weeks for design change approval based on a minimum clarity approach, the crude nature of the estimate is obvious, but its robust nature is less obvious, and very useful. The uniform density function shape helps to offset the impact of the long right hand tail in the way Figure 10.4 illustrates. More generally, we can engineer simple approaches to manage bias, overestimating dependence effects providing a very useful way to offset suspected optimism from any sources. This is discussed further in the next chapter.

If the project manager of the last section's example is presented with an estimate of 7 weeks based on a 'normal' and 'abnormal' scenario approach, complete with suggestions about how to control and reduce the uncertainty associated with the 'abnormal' scenario, the reduced expected value may seem plausible because of the obvious improvement in clarity and capability. But an expected value of 8 weeks based on including a 'highly abnormal' scenario would seem to be better still.

The Highways Agency re-estimation approach discussed earlier (Hopkinson et al., 2008) replaced a data based 'optimism adjustment factor' approach advocated by HM Treasury (2003a, 2003b). Average cost overruns for past projects were calculated when risk management had not been used for a range of different types of projects to estimate adjustment factors based on average outcome/estimate ratios. These factors were used to uplift estimates unless a formal risk management process had been used, but dropped completely if the pre Nichols report risk management process had been applied. This approach lacked the necessary judgement about the quality of the basic estimate or the uncertainty management process, and it ignored any induced bias associated with an anticipated adjustment process that was indifferent to quality. Quality should matter. Systems that assume that quality does not matter are not addressing what matters. The kind of data analysis used for optimism adjustment factors could be useful for background pi factor assessments, but only as an indication of what happens on average, and its treatment as a basis for 'errors and omissions provisions' is usually preferable.

In general, simple approaches need to be engineered to deliver quality in clarity efficient terms, replacing the need for a background pi factor via consideration of all uncertainty, appropriate provisions including 'no quibble provisions', clarity about exclusions, and balanced treatment of all other bias sources in a cube factor framework. The PUMP as a whole needs to have these ideas built in. The technical details can normally stay in the background, but the fact that these ideas are built in, and the implications of this, needs to be clear to everyone involved.

Quantify phase treatment of dependence

Some implications of dependence are conveniently addressed in the next chapter, but some aspects need to be addressed in earlier PUMP phases, and some may need attention in the quantify phase.

The identify phase and the structure phase are directly concerned with identifying systemic uncertainty and structuring the models used to manage it in causal terms. For example, decomposing uncertainty associated with weather and buckles in an offshore pipe-laying activity is concerned with understanding and managing causes and effects, addressing systemic uncertainty in terms of causal modelling.

Any significant systemic uncertainty which is not dealt with in causal dependence terms must be dealt with in statistical dependence terms. By definition, statistical dependence is unidentified causal dependence, a form of ambiguity uncertainty.

The simplest way to deal with statistical dependence at an overall level in the quantify phase involves estimating all pessimistic scenarios assuming all other sources involve pessimistic scenarios – Sod's Law (or Murphy's Law or cynical pessimism or whatever else you care to call it) applies on a global basis. This can be scaled down to separate sets of sources, portions of the whole.

A very simple intermediate level of clarity is provided by percentage dependence or coefficient of correlation assumptions discussed in the next chapter.

A more sophisticated intermediate level of clarity is provided by conditional specifications. For example, if the Figure 10.1 and Table 10.1 specification of weather uncertainty is used for each month, and wet buckle probabilities are conditional on how many lay-days are available in a month, this could be modelled via a conditional specification – a different wet buckle probability distribution for each relevant lay days interval.

In practice dependence may need considerable attention in the quantify phase, but for easier exposition, further, more detailed discussion of this topic is left until the next chapter.

Conclusion

Quantification of uncertainty is an important way of increasing understanding of what matters and how it matters given assumptions about future conditions. However, it is not possible or even desirable to attempt quantification of all sources of uncertainty. Carefully linking quantitative treatment of some uncertainty to a qualitative treatment of the residual is crucial.

Practical considerations require an approach to quantification of some uncertainty and structuring the qualitative residual that is both useful and cost effective. This implies a process of quantifying uncertainty and dealing with the residual that is iterative, initially starting with rough quantitative estimates of key sources of uncertainty and refining or restructuring these estimates when and where this increases understanding of uncertainty and informs decision making. This chapter suggests a particular quantification process for *some* uncertainty, a basic common interval approach to rectangular histograms, with a range of variants and alternatives. It involves a scenario interpretation of P10 and P90 estimates, rather than a strict percentile value interpretation. It also suggests linked approaches to qualitative treatment based on scenario analysis. Further, it suggests linking approaches like a 'no quibbles' adjustment and a 'cube factor'.

Recognizing that much uncertainty may be best treated as conditions, and that qualitative and quantitative analysis need clear integration, requires explicit management. The identify phase is a useful focal point for developing clarity about all relevant conditions, but their implications are very important in the quantify phase.

A common situation is not knowing what format to collect data in until quantitative analysis based on subjective estimates demonstrates the value of such data. How much effort it is worth expending on data capture and analysis is often worth formal assessment by starting an iterative process using subjective judgements based on minimal data capture and analysis effort. Simple analysis of any readily available and relevant data is usually a good starting point, but extensive data analysis and further data collection is usually best reserved for special cases once it is clear the effort will be worthwhile.

Even when good data is available, the assumptions used to formulate probability distributions which describe the future are necessarily subjective. Thus it is appropriate to think of all probability distributions as subjective, some based on realistic data and assumptions, others more dependent upon judgements made in a direct manner. To capture the difference between the observed past and the anticipated future, subjective adjustment of estimates based on data is usually essential. Unfortunately, this subjectivity can be a potential major weakness in any estimating process, and concerns about the basis for subjective estimates of probability and their validity are reasonable concerns. Consequently, any method used to elicit probability estimates from individuals needs to address these concerns, drawing on a full understanding of modern subjective probability approaches, as well as traditional objective probability approaches based on data driven perspectives. However, elicitation methods have to be simple and practical in clarity efficient terms.

The role of probabilities associated with quantified estimates is to help us to make decisions which are consistent with the beliefs of those with relevant expertise and knowledge, integrating the collective wisdom of all those who can usefully contribute. The integration of views of different people is a key issue which qualitative approaches cannot address. The validity of probabilistic estimates themselves is not really relevant unless misconceptions lead to ill-advised decisions. Ultimately the quantification process is about understanding why some decision choices may be better than others.

Chapter 11

Evaluate *all* the relevant implications

'Five to one against and falling ... four to one against and falling ... three to one ... two to one ... probability factor of one to one ... we have normality ... Anything you still can't cope with is therefore your own problem.'

—D. Adams, *The Hitchhiker's Guide to the Galaxy*.

Evaluation of *all* the relevant implications of uncertainty is central to clarity efficient development of insight about the nature of project uncertainty, which is in its turn central to the understanding of effective responses to manage that uncertainty in an opportunity efficient manner. In this sense the evaluate phase is at the core of understanding uncertainty in order to clarify its implications and plan responses to it when this is appropriate.

The evaluate phase does not need to be understood at a deep technical level in order to manage simple forms of uncertainty. However, some very important concepts, like statistical and causal dependence, need to be understood properly at an intuitive level in order to manage *any* uncertainty effectively. An understanding of what is involved when probability distributions are combined is part of this. This chapter endeavours to build on earlier chapters to provide for everyone interested in uncertainty a basic intuitive understanding with a minimum of technical detail that goes beyond a basic foundation. Those who want to play an active role in managing subtle or complex uncertainty should see this chapter and the last as a basis for deeper exploration. Some starting point discussion and references are provided, but there is a huge relevant literature.

The purpose of the evaluate phase is combining the results of the quantify phase in the context of all earlier PUMP phases and evaluating all relevant decisions and judgements. The evaluate phase includes the synthesis of individual source of uncertainty quantification, the presentation of results, plus the interpretation of results, bearing in mind all relevant sources that were not quantified and treated as conditions or assumptions. It includes process decisions like: 'Do we need to refine earlier quantitative or qualitative analysis, and if so where?' It also includes project decisions like: 'Is plan A better than plan B, and do we also need a plan C plus an exit strategy plan D?'

The deliverables will depend upon the depth achieved in preceding phases. Looping back to earlier phases before proceeding further is likely to be a key and frequent decision. An important early deliverable might be a prioritized list of sources of uncertainty and associated option choices, while a later deliverable might be a diagnosed potential problem or opportunity associated with a specific aspect of the base plan or contingency plans, plus suggested revisions to these plans to resolve the problem or capture the opportunity. The key deliverable is diagnosis of any and all important opportunities or threats, and comparative evaluation of responses to these opportunities or threats.

As indicated in Chapter 10, the quantify phase should be used to drive and develop the distinction between two different tasks involved in the early passes of the PUMP – refining analysis and restructuring analysis. A first pass can be used to portray overall uncertainty and the relative size of all contributing factors. A second pass can be used to explore and confirm the importance of the key issues, obtaining additional data and undertaking further analysis of issues where appropriate. Further passes can further refine and restructure our understanding.

In some risk and uncertainty management process descriptions, some of these decisions and judgements are viewed as part of other phases. This may not involve any material differences. However, it is important to treat the diagnosis of the need for such decisions, and the development of the basis for appropriate judgements, as part of the iterative structure which precedes tactical planning for implementation.

It is convenient to consider the specific tasks of the evaluate phase under five 'modes of operation' headings:

1. *Select an appropriate subset of sources* – As the basis of a process of combining successive subsets of sources of uncertainty and associated option choices, choose an appropriate place to start, and each successive source on later passes, using a structure which reflects the causal structure of dependence, the structure of the overall model being used, and the most effective story line to support cases for changes;
2. *Specify dependence* – Specify the dependence between the selected sources in an appropriate structure;
3. *Combine the subset of sources* – Combine the sources, using addition, multiplication, division, greatest operations or other operations as appropriate, computing summary parameters as appropriate;
4. *Portray the effect* – Design a presentation for overall and intermediate results to provide insights for the analysts in the first instance, to tell useful stories for analysis users as the plot of these stories emerges;
5. *Diagnose the implications* – Use the presentation of results to acquire the insight to write the appropriate stories and support associated decision taking.

Figure 11.1 portrays the way these five modes of operation relate to the fit for purpose assessment task which is the pivotal PUMP iteration control task.

Figure 11.1 portrays starting the evaluate phase in 'select an appropriate subset of sources' mode. Initially the objectives are making sure that the selected subset of sources is the most appropriate place to start, for reasons comparable to those discussed in Chapter 10. The rationale becomes more complex later, when dependence becomes a key issue, and developing and telling stories becomes the concern. Then grouping issues within the underlying model structure may become important. For example, if time (duration and delay) uncertainty is the focus of early

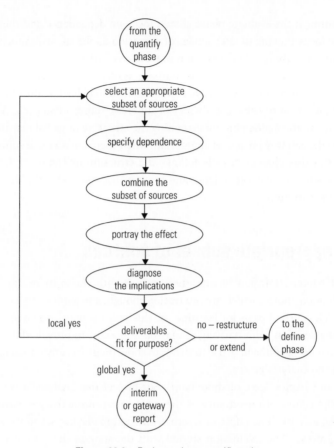

Figure 11.1   Evaluate phase specific tasks

passes, the project activity structure is the natural and obvious framework, and the way activities accumulate delay over the project duration may define the story line sequence. Later passes may extend analysis to other plans and Ws, and at some point overall integration may be crucial – for example, a net present value (NPV) or multiple criteria framework using a balanced scorecard approach (Kaplan and Norton, 1996) may be essential. Early anticipation of this evolution can be very useful, but responding to surprises is also very important.

'Specify dependence' could be regarded as part of the structure phase or the quantify phase, and in some cases earlier attention in both these phases is essential, but it is most conveniently discussed at this point in the evaluate phase, and simple approaches make this an operationally convenient point to address it.

'Combine the subset of sources' involves a complex range of considerations, but the objective can be simply stated – effective and efficient synthesis of all the earlier analysis, with a view to understanding what matters and what does not. 'Portray the effect' is comparatively straightforward and obvious.

'Diagnose the implications' is the most complex mode of operation, and it is arguably the most crucial task in the evaluate phase and the PUMP as a whole, the basis of the pivotal iteration control task that follows.

Early passes through the evaluate phase should focus on dependence and the combination of sources, with the focus moving to later modes of operation as the iterative process matures, but important exceptions to this gradual evolution in focus may arise.

At the bottom end of Figure 11.1 a fit for purpose assessment task controls iterations – the key PUMP iteration control task. A positive result means a loop back within the evaluate phase with a view to moving on to selecting a wider or different subset of sources. A negative result leads to a loop back to the define phase if extending the structure or global restructuring is called for. Proceeding to the gateway process is appropriate when there are no more sources to integrate.

The structure of this chapter broadly follows the structure of Figure 11.1, with two tasks merged for convenience (specify dependence and combine the sources) and additional exploratory sections when this is useful.

Select an appropriate subset of sources

As indicated in Chapter 10, it may be important to start with one or more subsets of sources of uncertainty and option choices which are interesting enough, and sufficiently familiar to all those involved, to provide a useful basis for learning. At this point it may also be important to throw light on a pressing decision. Alternatively, it may be important to provide those contributing to the PUMP with results of immediate use to them, to show them an early return for the effort they have invested in the analysis process.

As explained in Chapter 7, for offshore North Sea project risk analyses it was often useful to start with the core source of uncertainty in the most uncertain activity – weather uncertainty in the pipe-laying activity. The effect of weather on the pipe-laying schedule was modelled as a semi-Markov process. The calculation started with the state of the system when pipe laying begins (no pipe laid). A progress probability distribution for the first time period was applied to this initial state to define the possible states of the system at the start of the second time period. A progress probability distribution was then applied to this state distribution to define the possible states of the system at the start of the third time period, and so on (Cooper and Chapman, 1987, provide a numerical example).

Only after this central source of uncertainty had been modelled and understood, and tentative decisions made about the best time of year to start pipe laying for a particular project, did the analysis move on to further sources. Further sources were added one at a time, to test their importance and understand their effect separately. Each successive source was added in a pair-wise structure to the accumulated total effect of earlier issues. Because some of these sources (like pipe buckles) were themselves weather dependent, it was essential to build up the analysis gradually, in order to understand the complex dependencies involved.

If semi-Markov processes are not involved, and dependence is treated in simple terms, it may be appropriate to treat the subset of time or schedule issues associated with each activity as a base-level source, then move on to other Ws and overall evaluation as indicated earlier.

As a low clarity illustration, the BCS example in Chapter 7 involved 5 to 15 sources treated as a single set. Each source was defined by duration uncertainty for a component of the project like 'take up the existing floor' and 'lay a new floor', transformed by a cost per unit time rate into a cost item, and summed over all items. No iterations were involved in the PUMP.

Specify dependence and combine the selected subset of sources

A central task of the evaluate phase is combining two or more sources of uncertainty so that their net effect can be portrayed. To demonstrate the nature of dependence, both of a statistical and causal nature, to illustrate its potential significance, and to indicate the range of approaches to combining probability distributions available, this section begins with a subsection which considers independent addition of two quantified sources employing the simple 'common interval' (CI) form of probability specification introduced in Chapter 10 plus basic discrete probability arithmetic as used for probability and decision trees.

Independent addition using basic discrete probability arithmetic

To keep explanation as simple as possible, start by assuming that we are combining the costs of item A and item B, each with the same probability distribution of costs represented by three values as shown in Table 11.1, defining C_a and C_b.

Table 11.2 shows the basic discrete probability arithmetic calculation of the distribution of $C_i = C_a + C_b$ assuming the costs of A and B are independent.

The calculation associated with the joint cost of 16 involves the product of the probabilities of individual costs of 8, the 0.04 probability reflecting the low chance of both items having a minimum cost. Similarly, the joint cost of 24 reflects the low chance of both items having a maximum cost. In contrast, a joint cost of 20 has a relatively high probability of 0.37 because it is associated with three possible ways of obtaining a cost of 20: 8 + 12, 10 + 10, or 12 + 8. The probabilities associated with joint costs of 18 (via combinations 8 + 10 and 10 + 8), or 22 (via combinations 10 + 12 and 12 + 10), are closer to the 20 central case than they are to the extremes because of the relatively high probability (0.5) associated with $C_a = 10$ and $C_b = 10$.

Table 11.1 Cost distributions for items A and B

Cost (£k), C_a or C_b	Probability
8	0.2
10	0.5
12	0.3

Table 11.2 Distribution for $C_i = C_a + C_b$ assuming independence

Cost (£k), C	Probability computation	Probability
16	0.2 × 0.2	0.04
18	0.2 × 0.5 + 0.5 × 0.2	0.20
20	0.2 × 0.3 + 0.5 × 0.5 + 0.3 × 0.2	0.37
22	0.5 × 0.3 + 0.3 × 0.5	0.30
24	0.3 × 0.3	0.09

Successive additions of further cost items using the same common interval (2£k) will make the probability of extreme values smaller and smaller. For example, ten items with this same distribution will have a minimum value of 80, with a probability of 0.2^{10}, zero for all practical purposes, in a simple cost context.

Summary statistics and a mean-variance approach

The most useful summary statistic of a variable or combination of variables is the 'mean' or 'expected value'. It is computed as the sum of all the possible outcome values for the variable weighted by the associated probabilities of each value.

The expected value is a point estimate of what will happen on average – one very important reason expected values are useful. Expected values have the very useful property that they are additive under some conditions. That is, the expected cost of a sum of costs is equal to the sum of the expected values for each individual cost – *provided independence or simple dependence can be assumed.*

It is important to distinguish between the expected value and other 'measures of central tendency' associated with a distribution, such as the 'median' (that value which has a 50% chance of being exceeded), and 'the most likely value' (the most probable value, often referred to as the 'best estimate'), which do not have this additive property unless assumptions are made which are generally inappropriate. For example, consider the two cost items A and B associated with Table 11.1. Each item has an expected value of

$$[(8 \times 0.2) + (10 \times 0.5) + (12 \times 0.3)] = 10.2 \text{ (£k)}.$$

This means that the expected cost of the two items is

$$2 \times 10.2 = 20.4 \text{ (£k)},$$

also obtainable from Table 11.2 using the sum of the products of the possible values and their probabilities,

$$[(16 \times 0.04) + (18 \times 0.20) + (20 \times 0.37) = (22 \times 0.30) + (24 \times 0.09)] = 20.4 \text{ (£k)}.$$

This means that the expected cost of a thousand such items is

$$1000 \times 10.2 = 10\ 200 \text{ (£k)},$$

and of more general use, expected values for n items with any distributions can be added to define the expected value of the sum, for any value of n, provided the independence or simple dependence assumption holds.

The most likely cost of 10 for each item cannot be added or multiplied in this way to obtain a most likely value for more than one item. The median cost will lie between the expected cost and the most likely value of total cost. The 2% difference between the expected value of 10.2 and the most likely value of 10.0 is negligible, but it is small only because of the nearly symmetric shape of these distributions. For completely symmetric distributions, this difference would be zero. If 8 were the most likely value, with a probability of 0.5, while 10 and 12 had probabilities of 0.3 and 0.2 respectively, the expected value would be

$$[(8 \times 0.5) + (10 \times 0.3) + (12 \times 0.2)] = 9.4.$$

With this skewed distribution the difference between the most likely value and the expected value is substantial, some 18% of the most likely value. Such a difference in magnitudes is common, arising from much less extreme asymmetry but much longer distribution 'tails'. In general, the more low probability/high impact event uncertainty sources a probability distribution embodies, the longer the right-hand tail of the distribution, and the greater the gap between the expected value and the most likely or median values. Chapman and Ward (1996) provide a plausible nuclear power cost per kWh example where the expected cost is more than double the most likely cost, explored in more detail in Chapman and Ward (2002, ch. 11).

While the expected value of a variable is a useful measure of what will happen on average, management of uncertainty and risk needs to consider the range of possible values that a variable could take. The simplest common practice alternative to the discrete probability approach of Table 11.2 is a 'mean-variance' approach, a special case of a class of approaches known as 'moment-based approaches'.

The 'variance' of a probability distribution is a useful measure of the average amount of dispersion or spread in a distribution, and variances for *independent* random variables are additive. That is, the variance of a sum of statistically independent costs is equal to the sum of the variances for each individual cost. Independence induces a square root rule reduction in variability as n increases. For example, each of the cost items A or B of Table 11.1 has a variance (in $£^2k^2$) of

$$[(8 - 10.2)^2 \times 0.2] + [(10 - 10.2)^2 \times 0.5] + [(12 - 10.2)^2 \times 0.3] = 1.96.$$

Compared with a single item $(n = 1)$, the sum of four cost items like A or B $(n = 4)$, decreases total variability by a factor of 2, $n = 16$ decreases total variability by a factor of 4, $n = 64$ increases total variability by a factor of 8, and so on. This means that the variance of a thousand such items is

$$1.96 \times 1000 = 1960$$

and the standard deviation (square root of 1960) is about 44 (£k). The standard deviation of the cost of one of our cost items, 1.4 (square root of 1.960), is about 14% of 10.2, but 44 is about 0.43% of 10 200, a reduction by a factor of about 32 (equal to the square root of 1000).

By the Central Limit Theorem the expected or mean value of a sum of n independently sampled values from a probability distribution with mean μ and standard deviation σ is approximately Normally distributed with mean μ and standard deviation $\sigma/\sqrt{n}$ as n becomes large. In practice, quite small n will produce a Normal result for most practical purposes. A simple practical illustration is provided by the distribution of outcomes when rolling dice (n die: $n = 1$ (uniform), 2 (triangular), 3 (already looking roughly Normal), and so on – see for example, Anderson et al. (2010). Using standard Normal tables, this implies that the expected value of the sum of our 1000 cost items (all with the same cost distribution), should fall in the range 10 200 ± 44, that is within one standard deviation of the mean, about 68% of the time, and almost certainly falls within the range 10 200 ± 132, defined by three standard deviations either side of the mean (a 99% confidence band).

This result suggests an extraordinary degree of certainty about the sum of our 1000 cost items! It generalizes for any reasonably large n with any component distributions. In most project contexts such a result should be recognized as absurd, a major reason for this being that cost items are rarely if ever completely independent, and the more cost elements we seek to distinguish the greater the likelihood that many will be dependent to a greater or lesser extent. The absurdity of this result highlights the need to avoid simplistic independence assumptions, and the importance of understanding and capturing dependence when combining probability distributions for a number of variables together.

Dependence in a mean-variance framework

The mean-variance approach can be generalized to consider well-behaved dependence in terms of correlation or covariances, the basis of Markowitz's approach to risk management for portfolios of securities or other investments. However, simplicity is lost – n securities involve $n^2/2 - n$ covariances. Simple common patterns of dependence are the usual practical way to balance the need to consider dependence but keep that consideration reasonably simple.

Monte Carlo simulation

The original PERT approach used a mean-variance approach assuming only one critical path, defined by expected values, *plus* independence. To avoid the first of these assumptions, since the 1970s the task of combining activities in a PERT network is typically carried out with the aid of computer software based on Monte Carlo simulation. Monte Carlo simulation is easy to write general purpose software for, and it is a particularly useful approach when complex relationships are involved – like multiple paths in a network. Because general purpose software is widely available, Monte Carlo simulation has become the basic common practice approach for most applications involving the combination of probability distributions, including sums of cost items and cost and revenue and discounting calculations (Hertz, 1964; Grey, 1995). Monte Carlo simulation is based on 'sampling'. For example, to add the probability distributions for cost of items A and B of Table 11.1 assuming independence to define $C_a + C_b = C_i$, we start by taking a 'sample' from the cost distribution for A. The mechanics of this 'sample' reduce to using a 'pseudo random number generator' to obtain a random number in the range 0–1, using this sampled value to reference the probability scale of a cumulative distribution, and reading off the corresponding cost. For example, a generated random number value of 0.1 would yield a sample cost of 8. Assuming the random numbers are uniformly distributed over the range 0–1, this can be shown to result in costs sampled from the assumed distribution for C_a. A similar sample of possible cost for item B can be added to define a sample for $C_a + C_b = C_i$. Repeating this procedure, say, a hundred times, results in a frequency distribution for C_i that approximates the true integration with sufficient accuracy for most purposes.

This simulation (sampling) approach makes it relatively straightforward to add large numbers of probability distributions together in a single operation to assess the overall impact of a set of sources *provided independence or some simple common form of dependence is assumed.* Unfortunately, this convenience can seduce analysts into a naive approach to integration that assumes independence between sources and overlooks the importance of dependency. It also encourages analysts to set up the combination calculations to present the end result and ignore intermediate stages. Both these effects are aggravated if the mechanics of how individual distributions are combined is not transparent to the user. Together these factors can lead to serious clarity inefficiency due to a failure to appreciate insights from considering intermediate stages of the combination process and dependencies between individual sources of uncertainty.

Monte Carlo simulation can deal with simple forms of dependence and a wide range of situation specific complex forms, including causal dependence modelling. *Appropriate* Monte Carlo software is a very powerful and general tool. But simplistic use of Monte Carlo simulation, sometimes encouraged by inappropriate software, can be a serious source of clarity inefficiency. As Hopkinson has put it, tools which are designed to make Monte Carlo easy and 'disengage the brain from the modelling process' are dangerous. Yet vendors are often driven in this direction by customers who insist on ease of use whilst also arguing that a tool that sells well must support good practice. Common practice seems to be riddled with paradoxes of this kind, and why this should be the case is an intriguing question.

The practical implications of the effect of inappropriate independence assumptions

The first two subsections used simple numerical examples and basic theory to indicate how independence assumptions lead to variability cancelling out. Now consider some practical implications of inappropriate independence assumptions starting with a fairly extreme actual practice example.

A PERT model of a complex military hardware project involving several hundred activities was used to estimate overall project duration. Individual activity probability distributions were estimated for each activity which those involved felt were reasonable. Assuming independence between the duration of individual activities, the PERT model suggested overall project duration would be 12 years about ± 5 weeks. However, the project team believed 12 years ± 5 years was a better reflection of reality. It was recognized that modelling a large number of activities, and assuming independence between them, effectively assumed away virtually all the real variability, making the model detail a dangerous waste of time. The project team's response was to use fewer activities in the model, but this did not directly address the question of dependence. It obscured rather than resolved the basic problem. There is a good case for suggesting this made matters worse. It made *very* silly results plausible, so people believed them when outright rejection of the independence assumption would have been much more helpful. For example, perfect positive correlation might have been assumed, or some suitable intermediate position.

In practice, assuming independence is always a dangerous assumption if that assumption is unfounded. It becomes obviously foolish if a very large number of items or activities are involved. However, it is an apparently plausible understatement of project uncertainty that is the real evaluation risk – when a modest number of items are combined assuming independence to produce a result which may seem plausible but actually underestimates variability by several hundred percent. This is compounded if those involved would *prefer* limited variability results.

For example, some boards look for ±10% precision for capital cost estimates when −50% to +200% would be more credible P10 and P90 values. This has directly related bias implications for expected values, compounded if dependence is complex, and further compounded if there is corporate confusion about measures of central dependency.

Positive dependence in addition

Positive dependence is the most common kind of statistical dependence, especially in the context of cost items. If item A costs more than expected because of market pressures, and B is associated with the same market, the cost of B will be positively correlated with that of A. Similarly, if the same estimator was involved, and he or she was optimistic (or pessimistic) about A, the chances are they were also optimistic (or pessimistic) about B.

Table 11.3 portrays the distribution of $C_p = C_a + C_b$ assuming perfect positive correlation.

The possible outcomes shown are twice those of Table 11.1 and the probabilities shown are the same as for values of C_a and C_b as in Table 11.1 because the addition process assumes the low, intermediate and high values for C_a and C_b occur together. That is, the only combinations of C_a and C_b possible are 8 + 8, 10 + 10, and 12 + 12.

Table 11.3 shows clearly how the overall variability is preserved compared with C_i, the addition of $C_a + C_b$ assuming independence. In this special case where A and B have identical cost distributions, C_p has the same distribution with the cost scaled up by a factor of 2.

Successive additions assuming perfect positive correlation will have no effect on the probability of extreme values. For example, ten items with the same distribution will have a minimum scenario value of 80 with a probability of 0.2. Compare this with the independence case cited earlier, where the probability of the minimum scenario value is 0.2^{10}.

Figure 11.2 portrays the addition of possible costs for A and B assuming perfect positive correlation. Figure 11.2 can be plotted directly from Table 11.3, interpreting 16 as the central value for the interval 14 to 18, 20 as the central value for the interval 18 to 22, and 24 as the central value for the interval 22 to 26.

A more general form of 100% dependence addition implying a form of perfect positive correlation is avaable using the continuous variable cumulative forms introduced in Chapter 10 and procedures discussed at length elsewhere (Cooper and Chapman, 1987). In brief, the two component distributions in their cumulative forms are added horizontally. That is, in terms of the simple A plus B example of Figure 11.2, the addition assumes that costs of 7 for A and 7 for B

Table 11.3   Distribution for $C_p = C_a + C_b$ assuming perfect positive correlation

Cost (£k), C	Probability
16	0.2
20	0.5
24	0.3

occur together, costs of 8 and 8 occur together, and so on. More generally, all percentile values occur together, whatever the component distribution shapes and class structure.

Figure 11.3 re-plots the C_p curve of Figure 11.2 in conjunction with a cumulative curve for C_i derived directly from Table 11.2.

For C_i the minimum cost of 15 in contrast to the minimum cost of 14 for C_p reflects a small error in the discrete probability calculation of Table 11.2 if it is assumed that the underlying variable is continuous. For example, if A and B are both uniformly distributed about the central value 8 in the interval 7 to 9, precise integration to obtain their sum yields a triangular distribution over the interval 14 to 18, not a rectangular distribution over the interval 15 to 17. The geometry

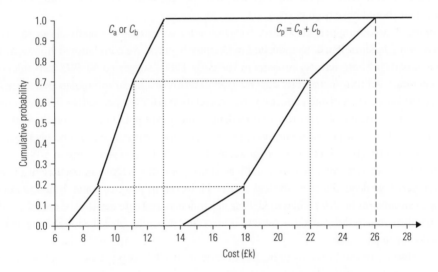

Figure 11.2 $C_p = C_a + C_b$ assuming perfect positive correlation

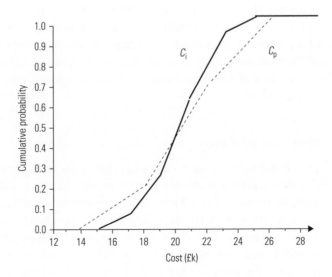

Figure 11.3 Comparison of C_p and C_i cumulative probability curves

involved means that a probability of 0.04 / 8 = 0.005 should have been allocated to the range 14 to 15, not the zero assumed by the Figure 11.3 plot of Table 1.2. All other classes involve comparable errors, which can be calculated and used to adjust the results – see Cooper and Chapman (1987, ch. 3) for a detailed discussion. This error is of no consequence in the present discussion, apart from a slightly distracting discrepancy in the end points for the two Figure 11.3 curves. This is easily overcome at a reasonable level of precision by simply joining the end points.

Figure 11.3 demonstrates the difference between an independence assumption and a perfect positive correlation assumption with just two components added. If more components are involved, the gap between the curves widens rapidly, illustrated earlier in terms of extreme value probabilities, and in terms of the military hardware project with an estimated duration range in weeks which should have been years.

In practice, assuming perfect positive correlation for cost items is usually closer to the truth than assuming independence. As indicated in Chapter 8, extensive correlation calibration studies associated with onshore refinery projects in the early 1980s suggested 60–90% dependence was the usual range, defining 'percentage dependence' in terms of a linear interpolation between independence (0% dependence) and perfect positive correlation (100% dependence). The two curves of Figure 11.3 demonstrate 0% and 100% dependence, linear interpolation between them any intermediate level. For most practical purposes, percentage dependence is approximately the same as 'coefficient of correlation' (defined over the range 0–1, with 0.5 corresponding to 50%).

Monte Carlo-driven software can usually accommodate dependence in coefficient of correlation or percentage dependence equivalent forms. However, in practice some 'industry standard' packages can cause difficulties when modelling dependence, and care needs to be exercised. PUMP team members undertaking analysis need to understand dependence well enough to realize when results do not make sense.

In the absence of good reasons to believe otherwise, if 100% dependence is not an acceptable assumption because it is deemed excessively pessimistic, the authors assume about 80% dependence for cost items, a coefficient of correlation of 0.8, representing a slightly conservative stance relative to the average observed for BP onshore refinery projects. For related reasons, 50% is a reasonable working assumption for related project activity duration distributions, unless there is reason to believe otherwise. This avoids the extreme optimism of complete independence when assuming 100% dependence is unduly pessimistic. If this approach to dependence is too crude, a higher clarity treatment of dependence is required. More optimistic assumptions without justification are asking for trouble.

Negative dependence in addition

Negative dependence is less common than positive dependence, but it can have very important impacts, especially in the context of successive project activity durations, and 'insurance' or 'hedging' arrangements. For example, if A and B are successive activities, and B can be speeded up (at a cost) to compensate for delays to A, the duration of B will be negatively correlated with that of A (although their costs will be positively correlated, as discussed in Chapter 8).

In terms of the simple discrete probability example of Table 11.1, perfect negative correlation (−100% dependence) implies that when C_a takes a value of 8, C_b is 12, and vice versa (overlooking for the moment the different probabilities associated with these outcomes). Call the distribution of $C_a + C_b$ under these conditions C_n. In terms of the continuous variable portrayals of Figure 11.2, C_n is a vertical line at a cost of 20 (overlooking the asymmetric distributions for A and B). Negative correlation substantially reduces variability, and perfect negative correlation can eliminate variability completely.

From an uncertainty management point of view when risk is important, positive correlation should be avoided where possible, negative correlation should be embraced where possible. Negative correlation is the basis of insurance, of 'hedging' bets, of effectively spreading risk in a portfolio of investments. Its value in this context is of central importance to risk management. The point here is that while independence may be a central case between perfect positive and perfect negative correlation, it is important to recognize the significant role that both positive and negative dependence have in specific cases and the fact that positive and negative dependence cannot be assumed to cancel out on average.

Other combining operations

Evaluation of uncertainty in a cost estimate may involve multiplication ('product') and division ('quotient') operations. Evaluation of profit may involve subtraction ('difference') operations. Evaluation of precedence networks can involve 'greatest' operations at a merge event. The mathematics can become more complex. In particular, simple common interval calculations become much more complex than the calculation of Table 11.2. However, the principles remain the same, and the effects of positive and negative correlation can become even more important. For example, if costs are perfectly positively correlated with revenues, profit is assured, while perfect negative correlation implies a high gearing up of the risk.

Conditional specifications of dependence

One of the obvious difficulties associated with non-expert use of percentage dependence or coefficient of correlation assessments of dependence is the need for mental calibration of what these measures mean. If this is an issue or if dependence is too complex to be captured adequately by simple measures like percentage dependence, conditional specification of dependence is an effective solution. Table 11.4 provides a simple example, based on the cost of item A with the same C_a distribution as in Table 11.1, but with the distribution of the cost of item B, C_b, dependent or conditional on the level of C_a. It involves a form of positive dependence which makes extreme values for the second distribution very likely when extreme values of the first occur – but not inevitable.

Table 11.5 shows the calculation of the distribution of the cost $C_c = C_a + C_b$ assuming the conditional specification of Table 11.4.

The computational effort is not increased by the conditional specification. In this particular example it is actually reduced. However, specification effort is increased, and it would increase exponentially if we wanted to consider three or more jointly dependent items in this way. It is this specification effort which constrains our use of conditional specifications to occasions when it adds value relative to simple percentage dependence or coefficient of correlation specifications.

Table 11.4   Conditional cost distribution for C_b given C_a

C_a (£k)	Probability	C_b (£k)	Probability
8	0.2	8	0.7
		10	0.3
10	0.5	8	0.2
		10	0.5
		12	0.3
12	0.3	10	0.3
		12	0.7

Table 11.5   Distribution for $C_c = C_a + C_b$ assuming the specification of Table 11.4

C_c (£k)	Probability computation	Probability
16	0.2 × 0.7	0.14
18	0.2 × 0.3 + 0.5 × 0.2	0.16
20	0.5 × 0.5	0.25
22	0.5 × 0.3 + 0.3 × 0.3	0.24
24	0.3 × 0.7	0.21

Comparison of C_c with 'bounds' provided by C_i to C_p is provided in Figure 11.4.

The C_c curve of Figure 11.4 involves the same kind of approximation error as the C_i curve. It is larger in the region of the extremes because extreme values are more likely, but even if this error is allowed for, Figure 11.4 should make it clear that a simple dependence structure like that of Table 11.4 does not yield a simple interpolation between C_i and C_p. For most practical purposes 60–90% dependence is a reasonable interpretation of the level of dependence portrayed by Table 11.4, but conditional specifications can imply relationships which are not the same as well behaved correlation. By 'complex dependence' we mean any dependence relationship other than 'well behaved' 'simple dependence' relationships which do not affect expected outcomes. Other special types of dependence relationship and other levels of dependence could be mentally calibrated and explored in a similar manner. More values and suitable software to yield smoother curves would obviously help.

This example should help to make it clear that very high levels of dependence are both plausible and common. Indeed, a conditional approach could be used to portray non-linear knock-on effects which are more complex than those illustrated by Table 11.4 but very common. For example, to illustrate what might be involved: if the duration of A is 8 then B is likely to be 8, and if A is 10 then B is expected to be 10 with more variability, but if A is 12 then B is expected to be 16 with huge variability on the high side – because making a complete mess of A implies both a lack of competence and knock-on effects. Cooper and Chapman (1987) explore such cases in detail.

If 'knock-on dependence' over and above 'well behaved dependence' is identified as a separate source of uncertainty, it can be estimated directly using a variant of this kind of conditional impact of events but not uncertainty about the probability of events. Modern decision analysis (see Raiffa, 1968, for example) makes it clear that point estimates of probabilities may be convenient, but they are a first order model easily replaced by a second order model recognizing uncertainty about probability values. Given this insight, instead of increasing and decreasing the LNG plant failure probabilities by an order of magnitude one at a time in a traditional sensitivity analysis framework, the same insight could be obtained much more simply by defining P10 and P90 estimates in terms of order of magnitude increases and decreases, then using evaluation phase tools discussed in the next chapter. We will return to this example in Chapter 11.

In some situations, where experience and data is extremely limited, individual assessors may feel unable or unwilling to provide probabilistic estimates. In such situations providing the assessor with anonymity, persuasion, or simple persistence, may be sufficient to obtain the desired cooperation (Morgan and Herion, 1990, ch. 7). However, even where assessors cannot be persuaded to provide probability distributions, they may still provide useful information about the behaviour of the variables in question. This information could be used in the P10 and P90 range sense suggested above, as an alternative to sensitivity analysis.

Nevertheless, there can be occasions where the level of understanding is sufficiently low that efforts to generate subjective probability distributions are not justified by the level of insight that the results are likely to provide. In deciding whether a probability encoding exercise is warranted, the analyst needs to make a judgement about how much additional insight is likely to be provided by the exercise. Sometimes a parametric analysis or simple order-of-magnitude analysis may provide as much or more insight as a more complex analysis based on probability distributions elicited from experts, and with considerably less effort. In the following example, probability estimates were unavailable, but it was still possible to reach an informed decision with suitable analysis.

Deciding whether or not to protect a pipeline from sabotage

During a study of the reliability of a water supply pipeline undertaken by Sir William Halcrow and Partners for a UK regional water authority, Chris Chapman was asked by the client's board to provide advice on the risk of sabotage. The pipeline had suffered one unsuccessful sabotage attack, so the risk was a real one, but with experience limited to just one unsuccessful attack there was clearly no objective basis for assessing the subsequent chance of a successful attack. Any decision by the client to spend money to protect the pipeline or not to bother needed justification, particularly if no money was spent and there was later a successful attack. In this latter scenario, the senior executives of the client organization could find themselves in court, defending themselves against a charge of 'professional negligence'.

The approach taken was to turn the issue around, avoiding the question 'What is the chance of a successful sabotage attack?', and asking instead 'What does the chance of a successful sabotage attack have to be in order to make it worth while spending money on protection?' To address this latter question, the most likely point of attack was identified, the most effective response to this attack was identified, and the response and consequences of a successful attack were costed. The resulting analysis suggested that one successful attack every two years would be necessary to justify the expenditure. Although knowledge was limited, it was considered that successful attacks could not be this frequent. Therefore, the case for not spending the money was clear, and could be defended, if necessary in court after a successful attack. Had a successful

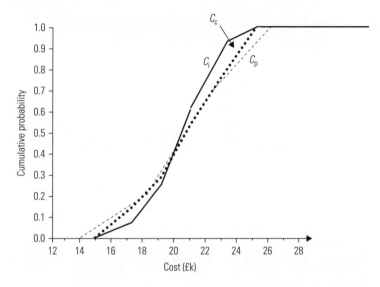

Figure 11.4   Comparison of C_c with C_p to C_i bounds.

specification, in relation to any group of sources at any level which gives rise to it. Stephen Cresswell, one of the informal reviewers for this book, first recognized this possibility, and provides software support to implement its use.

Causal model structure for dependence

In addition to the use of conditional specifications like Table 11.4 to calibrate simpler dependence measures or model 'knock-on dependence' as a separate source of uncertainty, this form of specification is very useful for more complex forms of dependence (Cooper and Chapman, 1987) as just noted. In this context the use of conditional specifications can become a form of causal structuring of dependence, asking questions about why B ought to vary with A in a particular pattern. Once these questions are raised, it is often more practical to explicitly address the possible need for a causal modelling structure. Indeed, complex models of the SCERT variety discussed earlier can be seen as a way of addressing dependence in this spirit.

If, for example, the reason the costs of items A and B are correlated is that they will be the responsibility of either contractor X or contractor Y, contractor X being very efficient and Y being very inefficient, but political pressures determining the outcome, it may be useful to model this choice directly, as indicated in Table 11.6.

Table 11.7 computes the associated cost distribution, defined as C_m, the 'm' subscript denoting causally *modelled.*

Those who do not follow the probability tree calculations imbedded in Table 11.7 do not need to worry about the computational detail. What matters is the simplicity and clarity of a format like Table 11.6, its relationship with a format like Table 11.4, and the quite different results they yield. The result provided in Table 11.7 involves much stronger dependence than even C_p, with very little chance of a value of 20, and values of 16 or 24 much more likely. That is, the example

Table 11.6   Causal model of dependence example specification

Probability X will be responsible for both A and B = 0.6

Probability Y will be responsible for both A and B = 0.4

Cost (£k) for A or B if X responsible	Probability
8	0.8
10	0.2

Cost (£k) for A or B if Y responsible	Probability
10	0.1
12	0.9

Table 11.7   Distribution for $C_m = C_a + C_b$ assuming the causal model of Table 11.6

Cost (£k)	Computation	Probability
16	0.6 × 0.8 × 0.8	0.384
18	0.6 × 0.8 × 0.2 + 0.6 × 0.2 × 0.8	0.192
20	0.6 × 0.2 × 0.2 + 0.4 × 0.1 × 0.1	0.028
22	0.4 × 0.1 × 0.9 + 0.4 × 0.9 × 0.1	0.072
24	0.4 × 0.9 × 0.9	0.324

provided by Tables 11.6 and 11.7 has been chosen to illustrate a 'bimodal' result which can be so extreme as to virtually eliminate any chance of a central value, one or other of the extremes becoming the likely outcome. This is an even more extreme form of positive dependence than the perfect positive correlation illustrated by C_p, which some people see as a very pessimistic extreme or bound on the impact of positive correlation. Put slightly differently, *perfect positive correlation is not a pessimistic assumption in practice, it is actually quite optimistic.* Perfect positive correlation is optimistic because it assumes no complex dependence knock-on relationships which systemic risk research clearly indicates are the real problem in many cases.

Perfect positive correlation and perfect negative correlation are the most extreme forms of *simple dependence which is well behaved,* but more complex forms of dependence can produce extremes which go significantly beyond the bounds of simple perfect correlation, and they frequently do so. Cooper and Chapman (1987) develop these ideas in more detail.

If a causal structure that can be articulated underlies any complex form of dependence, it is usually clarity efficient to explore that structure using some form of probability or decision tree. An important part of the overall process is defining the structure in a manner which simplifies our understanding of complex issues. Cooper and Chapman (1987) also develop these ideas in more detail. Chapman and Ward (2002) build on this in a less technical and broader context. Other authors taking a compatible line include Spetzler and Stael von Holstein (1975) and Lichtenberg (2000).

Three points that all readers need to clearly understand are:

1. The PUMP process as described in this book addresses exploring causal relationships that underlie complex dependences in a clarity efficient fashion.
2. Users of PUMP results do not need the technical understanding of issues like dependence obviously required by PUMP analysts.
3. Users of PUMP results do need well-founded confidence in the capability of PUMP analysts.

Operational sequence

If simple dependence approaches like percentage dependence or correlation are used, often a convenient basis for first pass analysis, it makes sense to specify dependence after choosing an appropriate subset of issues, prior to integrating them, as part of the evaluate phase. If a conditional structure for statistical dependencies used, then it may be useful to see dependence specification as part of the quantify phase. If a conditional structure is used to portray a causal structure, then it is useful to see dependence specification as part of the define or structure phases, with estimation implications in the quantify phase. Some of the looping back from the fit for purpose assessment task in Figure 11.1 will reflect these choices.

Explicit bias engineering

Some people argue that assuming independence is a very simple approach and that sometimes a very simple approach is best. The authors would not argue with the 'sometimes a very simple approach is best' part. But assuming independence because the nature of any dependence involved is unclear, is simplistic to an extreme extent – simple in a seriously inappropriate manner. Independence is rarely a clarity efficient *working* assumption unless there is reasonable empirical evidence for it, and failing to consider the validity and robustness of independence assumptions is negligent. Analyses that use independence as a *framing* assumption (which implies a failure to understand or test the assumption) are seriously flawed in very fundamental terms.

Assuming 100% (perfect positive) correlation is a working assumption that is often both simpler and more appropriate than independence. It is simpler because we can just add P10 and P90 or any other percentile values when addition is the operation involved, and easily generalize this approach to other operations. In a simple context like the BCS example of Chapter 2, this means that simple spread sheet calculations – there is no need for probability trees or simulation in Monte Carlo terms – 'soft quantification' is involved. Indeed, adding P10 and P90 values doesn't even need a spread sheet – the traditional back of an envelope will do!

The 60–90% correlation for cost items noted earlier suggests 100% correlation is closer to the truth than 0% if a simple sum of cost items model is involved, with a useful bias on the conservative side to offset the usual optimism when uncertainty is estimated subjectively. That is, assuming 100% correlation is more robust, in addition to being simpler. 'Simple' and 'robust' are both important characteristics, but 'robust' is most important.

The argument for a conservative (deliberately pessimistic) approach to dependence to ensure robustness becomes particularly important if there are any reasons to believe that the net effect of all other sources of bias is optimistic. Some PUMP users become very worried about even a hint of deliberate pessimistic bias, perhaps because they instinctively prefer less uncertainty to more uncertainty and they do not fully understand the scope for dysfunctional bias. The key to effective reassurance is to recognize that early passes are about sizing uncertainty to see if it matters – if it doesn't matter then a little bit of pessimism doesn't matter – if it does matter, deeper understanding may be important. Crucially, 'robustness' demands a slightly conservative approach to avoid assuming something doesn't matter which later proves crucial. The 'cube factor' discussed in Chapter 10 can be a useful basis for discussing 'bias engineering' – we do not want a numeric cube factor comparable to a 'pi factor' if we can avoid it, but balancing sources of optimistic and pessimistic bias is a simple and sound pragmatic approach.

If users are uncomfortable with what they see as excessive pessimism, the next step up, in terms of more clarity for more effort, is to incorporate an appropriate percentage dependence assumption using Monte Carlo simulation software.

The more sophisticated portrayals outlined earlier in this section can be used by expert users for still more clarity. Such portrayals are outlined in this chapter in part to set out the basis of an expert PUMP team tool kit. But their prime purpose for all readers is clarifying 'the nature of the beast' – everyone involved in uncertainty management needs to understand the general nature of dependence and the extent to which dependence matters.

If the PUMP team believe that quantify phase estimation of probability distributions is on the optimistic side, despite their endeavours to neutralize this bias, accepting further optimistic bias on dependence estimates is clearly undesirable, and pessimistic bias on dependence estimates can provide less overall bias.

Portray the effect of a set of sources

Graphs like Figures 11.3 and 11.4 are clearly useful when assessing the nature and importance of dependence, and for assessing the possible need to reconsider the way dependence might be modelled. Such figures help to develop the story that a completed analysis will tell. Even if dependence is not involved, this story needs to be developed a bit at a time, as each successive distribution is combined with the subset of parameters considered to date, or at intervals as subsets are compiled.

Figure 11.5, a copy of Figure 3.2, illustrates a high clarity version of the sensitivity diagram that is a key tool for understanding and explaining uncertainty. Even a low clarity analysis can benefit from use of this diagram format as a framework for interpretation. It is not always feasible, *but its absence when it is feasible and potentially useful is a clear symptom of clarity inefficiency*. To begin to explore the rationale for this important assertion, consider a high clarity situation, building on the Part I discussion of the Figure 3.2 version of Figure 11.5 and the Chapter 8 discussion of the Figure 8.2 source–response diagram associated with the same example.

Figure 11.5 portrays the build-up of six sources of uncertainty within a given project activity. As discussed in Chapter 3, the activity is the fabrication of a steel jacket for an offshore North Sea project, and delay has been modelled assuming a focus on this activity. The curve labelled '6' incorporates all six sources. The curve labelled '1' involves just the first source, the curve labelled '2' is the combined effect of the first two, and so on. The gaps between the curves indicate the relative

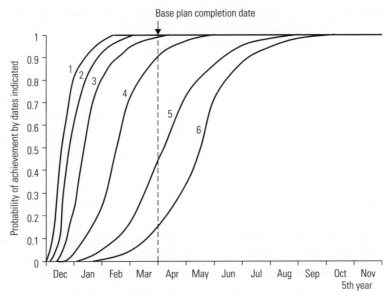

Probability curves show the cumulative effect of the following issues:

1. yard not available, or mobilisation delays
2. construction problems / adverse weather
3. subcontracted nodes delivery delays

4. material delivery delays
5. industrial disputes
6. delayed award of fabrication contract

Notes:
1. the curves assume a minimum fabrication period of 20 months
2. no work is transferred offsite to improve progress
3. no major fire, explosion or other damage

Figure 11.5   Sensitivity diagram: activity level output for an offshore project

importance of each contribution, source 5 ('industrial disputes') being the most important in this example.

If the sources involved are assumed to be independent in causal and statistical terms, the working assumption for this example, the build up of the curves can be chosen in a manner that reflects the planned focus of discussion, as indicated in Chapter 3. However, if source 2 is dependent upon 1, not vice versa, the 1–2 ordering is important, and if source 3 is dependent on the outcome of sources 1 and 2, the 1–2–3 ordering is important.

Users of PUMP deliverables and most PUMP analysts do not need to understand the more complex dependence alternatives, but all need to understand that dependence relationships of all the statistical and causal kinds discussed in the last section can be captured in these pair-wise relationships, if appropriate. For example, if a senior manager reviewing Figure 11.5 expressed the view that source 5 (industrial disputes) had about a 50% dependence relationship with source 2 (construction problems/adverse weather), with no other dependencies, and asked to see the implications, reordering these sources 1–2–5–3–4–6 (or any other 3–4–6 sequence) would capture this dependence exactly and revising the computation would be straightforward. If the same manager then expressed the view that source 2 had about a 40% dependence relationship with source 1 (yard not available or mobilization delays) and source 5 had about a 60% dependence relationship with source 1, an average 50% dependence working assumption is simple to achieve for the 1–2–5 sequence, but if this is deemed too crude, looking at the underlying causal structure would probably be the most useful way forward.

Each activity in a network can be portrayed using the format of Figure 11.5. Less important sources can be combined, to keep the story simple, with or without underlying analysis, six separate sources or source subsets being close to the upper limit of effective portrayal in this format. For example, source 1 (yard not available or mobilisation delays) involves two mutually exclusive event uncertainty sources as discussed in relation to Figure 8.2, and a decomposition of source 1 could portray these two component sources separately. If they were important enough, each of these two components could be further decomposed. A nested hierarchy can decompose this activity level view of uncertainty to whatever level of detail is useful.

Relationships between a sequence of activities and relationships involving merging streams of activities can then be portrayed using the same sensitivity diagram format, but with the slightly different appearance of Figure 11.6.

Curve 7 in Figure 11.6 shows offshore installation of the jacket complete, the gap between curves 7 and 6 the additional uncertainty associated with jacket float-out and installation. Curve 6 in Figure 11.6 incorporates uncertainty about the fabrication of the jacket captured by curve 6 in Figure 11.5. However, Figure 11.6 portrays that uncertainty in the context of a structured decomposition of uncertainty about preceding contracting and delivery activities and milestones beginning with award of a design contract for the jacket.

This sensitivity diagram format could be used again to show a top level portrayal of the 'start of production' milestone, with components for 'jacket installation', 'modules installation', 'pipeline hook-up', and so on.

In parallel with activity durations, capital cost components driven by durations and equipment costs per unit time can be calculated. Overall capital cost can be built up in the same way, using duration uncertainty, materials volume and cost uncertainty, and equipment cost rate uncertainty. Built bottom-up, such curves are normally used top-down to explain what is involved at all levels relevant to assessing option choices.

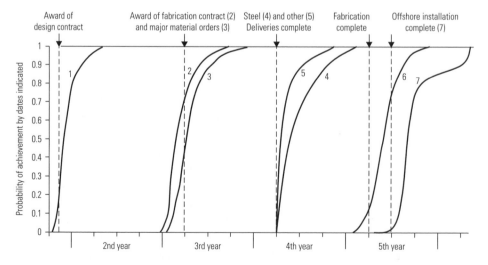

Figure 11.6   Sensitivity diagram: intermediate level of output for an offshore project

A low clarity 'soft quantification' approach like that adopted by BCS in Chapter 2 using the 'sensitivity table' spreadsheet format of Table 2.2 instead of a 'sensitivity diagram' can be portrayed using the sensitivity diagram format of Figure 11.7.

Figure 11.7 shows an overall cost defined by A + B + C. This example is restricted to just three components for simplicity. The simplest interpretation in relation to dependence is perfect positive correlation, or 100% dependence, but more sophisticated interpretations are feasible and can be very useful. If component A is defined by P10 and P90 values, these values can be plotted on the 10 and 90 percentile lines to produce the linear cumulative probability distribution implied by a minimum clarity interpretation, the A curve of Figure 11.7. If B is also defined by P10 and P90 values, these values can be added to the comparable A values with the sums plotted on the 10 and 90 percentile lines, the A + B curve of Figure 11.7. Addition of uncertainty about the cost component C follows in the same way. The simplicity of the linear form means more than six curves might be feasible in one diagram, but nested composition/decomposition with no more than five or six curves per diagram is recommended to make sensitivity analysis interpretation as easy as possible when sensitivity analysis is relevant – it was not for BCS. The Figure 2.4 Highways Agency sensitivity diagram approach involves a minimum clarity 'hard quantification' variant of Figure 11.7 and the BCS spreadsheet approach.

An initial top-down uncertainty characterisation study for the UK Nirex 'rock characterisation facility' (a deep mine for testing the suitability of an intermediate level nuclear waste repository), used to design more detailed bottom-up approaches shaping project plans, illustrates a variant of the BP refinery approach outlined earlier.

The starting point was a 'base cost' estimate already in place, and a list of sources of uncertainty defined in terms of conditions or assumptions, mostly explicit, which had been made when producing this 'base cost' estimate. Senior members of the project team provided a subjective estimate of the variability associated with the base estimate given all the conditions held, defining a distribution called 'B' for 'basic uncertainty'.

Conditions were then grouped into four sets of 'specific sources', the first three of which were assumed to share a high level of common dependence within each group:

'G (geology) sources' – all related to geological uncertainty with direct cost implications;

'GD (geology/design) sources' – all related to design changes driven by geology uncertainty;

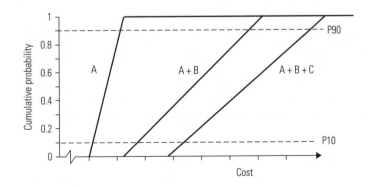

Figure 11.7 Sensitivity diagram: addition of items A, B and C

'GP (geology/planning) sources' – all related to planning approval sources driven by geology uncertainty;

'I (independent) sources' – which could be assumed to be largely independent of each other and other specific sources.

Various experts contributed to subjective estimates of 'direct cost' (ignoring the knock-on effects of delay) probability distributions within each of these four sets, designated: G1, G2, etc.; GD1, GD2, etc.; GP1, GP2, etc.; I1, I2, etc.

Based on discussions with the experts during the elicitation of these distributions, Chris Chapman provided initial estimates of a percentage dependence level within and between each set. These were used with the estimates to provide five figures in the Figure 11.5 sensitivity diagram format. Four were defined by:

G = G1 + G2, etc.
GD = GD1 + GD2, etc.
GP = GP1 + GP2, etc.
I = I1 + I2, etc.

The fifth was the sum of these four subsets of sources, defined by:

S = G + GD + GP + IR

In the light of earlier discussions about specific sources, senior members of the project team then provided estimates of the probability of delay to the project (D), and the probability distribution for the indirect cost of delay per unit time (CT). Further sensitivity diagrams in the format of Figure 11.5 showed:

CD = CT × D
C = B + S + CD

As indicated, the final curve for C was built bottom-up, but the complete set of underlying sources of uncertainty were explained using sensitivity diagrams presented top-down in three levels:

1. C = B + S + CD
2. CD = CT × D
   S = G + GD + GP + I
3. G = G1 + G2, etc.
   GD = GD1 + GD2, etc.
   GP = GP1 + GP2, etc.
   I = I1 + I2, etc.

The project team as a whole then discussed these results in relation to the underlying assumptions in order to assess:

- whether the results portray an overall story which was consistent with their beliefs;
- where the uncertainty was a cause for concern which needed attention in terms of a clear need for more data and analysis of those data;

- where the uncertainty was a clear cause for concern which needed attention in terms of exploration of alternative ways of addressing the seven Ws.

The kind of analysis illustrated by this example can be undertaken in days or weeks, hours if really pressed, as part of a top-down uncertainty appreciation (as discussed in Chapter 6), and used to drive the start of a more detailed bottom-up analysis.

Diagnose the implications

Diagnosis of the implications of all earlier analysis is central to the uncertainty evaluation process, and to providing support for associated decisions. It is discussed here using the sensitivity diagram portrayal of sources of uncertainty first, starting with the most obvious and straightforward concerns needing early treatment in early passes of the PUMP. Discussion then moves on to the more subtle concerns. To some extent the sequencing of aspects in this section reflects the way focus might evolve over a sequence of passes, but the last aspect addressed may need attention on the first pass. A more accurate interpretation of the sequence used to discuss aspects of diagnosis in this section is ordering for clarity of exposition, moving from special cases to more general concepts, moving from local project concerns to global corporate concerns, and moving from the key objective with a measurable attribute and quantified uncertainty to other objectives which matter.

Sensitivity analysis

All effective quantitative modelling requires sensitivity analysis, so that the analysts and the users of analysis can understand the relative importance of the components and working assumptions which the analysis uses. Sensitivity analysis is a key analysis tool – to test and demonstrate robustness, and to provide guidance about where to seek better definition if a 'problem' is emerging from the 'messes' of systemic and ambiguity uncertainty being considered. Sensitivity diagrams like Figures 11.5–11.7 provide a direct built-in sensitivity analysis in a clarity efficient manner as already discussed. The case for sensitivity diagrams begins with their clarity efficiency as a basic form of sensitivity analysis – there is no better lower effort approach available when the pair-wise separability implicit in their use is not a problem. If partial results are not accumulated and displayed in the way portrayed by Figures 11.5–11.7, the sensitivity analysis information they provide is lost.

There are ways of partially recovering such information if it has to be lost because assuming a pair-wise separability structure is not appropriate. For example, a common approach when n parameters are involved is to hold parameters 2 to n at their expected values, let parameter 1 vary over its plausible range, and then repeat this procedure for all other $n - 1$ parameters. The results can be portrayed graphically. One common variant of such graphs is known as a 'tornado' diagram. Another is commonly known as a 'cat's whiskers' diagram. Both are alternative forms of a 'sensitivity diagram'. In effect, our 'sensitivity diagram' is a particular form of sensitivity diagram based on successive accumulation of uncertainty portrayed using cumulative probability distributions. However, if feasible, a nested structure using the sensitivity diagram approach illustrated by Figures 11.5–11.7 is almost as simple to compute and *very much simpler to use*. It requires planning the sequence of the distribution combination operations in advance, and viable associated separability working assumptions, but in practice this a very small price to pay for the convenience and insight which follows such integration operations when they are appropriate.

There are two important barriers to the use of sensitivity diagrams like Figures 11.5–11.7 which need explicit mention. One is a lack of readily available software. BP developed their own software, based on discrete probability arithmetic, used by agreement for other Acres clients in the 1970s and 1980s. Since then the authors have usually relied upon skilled users of fairly general Monte Carlo simulation-based packages like '@Risk' and related graphics packages to manage all computations and presentation material. The software market supply of 'tornado' diagrams and their equivalents has discouraged some risk management users from adopting sensitivity diagram alternatives in the Figure 11.5–11.7 sense. This may change, but as of 2011 it is still an issue.

The other barrier is the higher level of uncertainty analysis skill needed to cope with nested composition structure development. This needs attention as part of a broader issue – the need for corporate investment in uncertainty management capability. Clarity efficiency at high levels requires a significant investment in uncertainty management corporate capability by board level senior managers who understand in broad terms what that clarity efficiency will buy. It also requires governance processes which ensure corrective action if the level of clarity efficiency delivered is not good enough.

In some circumstances alternative forms of sensitivity analysis may be preferred, but some form is essential. The issue now is what should be done with this information on the first and successive passes, beginning with what PUMP team members need to do.

Data, decision and knowledge needs

One important aspect of the iterative approach to the PUMP is its use to allocate data acquisition and analysis time efficiently. It is rarely clarity efficient to spend a significant amount of time looking for and analysing data before undertaking a first-cut analysis. It is usually more effective and efficient to spend the time thinking about the structure of the issues, do a first cut based on subjective assessments of possibilities, then look for data where it matters. This assumes that reasonably expert judgements are being used in terms of the structure of the issues, but if this is not the case, data requirements are usually the least of the problems needing attention.

Figure 11.5 reflects the story told by a first-cut analysis based on subjective probability estimates provided by the group responsible for this activity, as discussed in Chapter 3. Figure 11.5 suggests a probability of achieving the 'base plan' completion date of about 0.15. This was an unsatisfactory outcome. When the relative importance of 'industrial disputes' was observed, industrial dispute data for all the yards likely to be used for the fabrication of the jacket was gathered and analysed. The analysis confirmed the relative importance of industrial disputes, and the sizing of this source in Figure 11.5. It was worth spending extra time on data acquisition and analysis for this issue, but not on comparatively unimportant issues.

Once it was confirmed that the picture portrayed by Figure 11.5 was valid, improving the prognosis was in order, by changing the base plan or contingency plans, with particular reference to key sources. As indicated in Chapter 3, in the process of 'industrial dispute' data acquisition and analysis, the hypothesis that a carefully drafted contract with the yard would be an effective response was explored, usefully anticipating what might have been a separate second step. That is, after getting data as appropriate to confirm a first-cut quantification of uncertainty, a reasonable next step is considering alternative decision options. Analysis of the data suggested that such contracts actually had little effect on these industrial disputes. Such industrial disputes mainly occurred during the last 10% of a contract if no more work was anticipated in that yard on completion. Recognition of this cause led to addressing the only effective response identified – smoothing the flow of work to yards to the extent possible by all the oil companies involved. It was recognized that this approach would resolve the particular problem diagnosed by Figure 11.5, and the more general 'industrial disputes' problem. It was also recognized that a smoother work flow for yards would reduced jacket fabrication costs by avoiding bidding up the price when demand peaked. Both these changes would contribute to improved opportunity efficiency, at the project level and at the corporate level. Identifying decisions that need to be made, and assessing how they should be made to achieve risk efficiency at all levels for all objectives, is part of the process of seeking opportunity efficiency. This is a deeper and more fundamental issue than simply assessing data needs, although both are illustrated by the 'industrial disputes' source of Figure 11.5.

Data needs are a subset of a wider set of 'knowledge' needs. Decision needs can be seen as a formal part of this wider set of knowledge needs, as just illustrated by the second part of the industrial disputes example above. Other aspects of imperfect knowledge can also be involved. For example, Figure 11.5 suggested that 'material delivery delays' (curve 4) and 'delayed award of fabrication contract' (curve 6) both needed deeper understanding, including delays linked to the award of the design contract and subsequent design progress.

Generalizing, a first-cut analysis often indicates what additional knowledge would be useful when that knowledge is not a matter of information in the 'data needs' sense, or a particular set of choices in the form of contract and collaborative timing in the 'decision needs' sense. Sometimes useful additional knowledge concerns understanding of what systemic uncertainty relationships underlie the uncertainty of immediate interest, as illustrated by the underlying role of design information in Figure 11.6.

The KUMP and PUMP relationship here

If this aspect of the evaluate phase generates a need for more data which changes project plans in a direct way, it can be seen in terms of a feedback relationship with the KUMP considered in the identify phase discussion of Chapter 7. Separating the PUMP and KUMP roles was useful in the identify phase, because different processes concerned with different objectives intersect, and avoiding confusion may be helped by understanding the distinction. The KUMP and PUMP distinction in the evaluate phase is of no immediately obvious benefit, but it might be useful. Indeed, if we think of a PUMP pack including KUMPs being applied to the process as a higher order process, a KUMP focus may become dominant.

Identifying risk efficient options

When a decision needs to be made between identified options, provided at least one objective involves a measurable attribute and associated uncertainty is usefully measured, decision diagrams to facilitate option choices like Figures 11.8–11.10 are extremely useful in terms of formulating and explaining recommendations.

Superficially these decision diagrams resemble the sensitivity diagram format of Figures 11.5–11.7, but their nature and role is quite different. The curves in decision diagrams of Figures 11.8–11.10 represent mutually exclusive choices, alternative courses of action. The curves in the sensitivity diagrams of Figures 11.5–11.7 represent component sources of uncertainty for one selected course of action, nested if many sources are involved to keep each diagram simple.

Figure 11.8 is a copy of Figure 3.4. Underlying the Figure 11.8 diagram was a nested hierarchy of sensitivity diagrams in Figure 11.5–11.6 format. As discussed in Chapter 3, the cost curve for the 3-m barge option is risk efficient relative to the 1.6-m barge option because its expected cost is lower, and if risk is interpreted as the possibility of a cost greater than the expected cost (of the lowest expected cost choice – the opportunity/risk datum – to be more precise), the overall relative position of the two curves indicates a lower level of risk. This is a simple generalization of a Markowitz mean-variance approach introduced in Chapter 3. Defining risk relative to expected outcome (the mean value) of the best choice in expected value terms is a plausible working assumption. Measuring risk as 'variance' is not a plausible working assumption even if the same expected values are involved, because of the typical asymmetric shape of probability distributions. However, the format of Figure 11.8 does not require us to measure 'risk' at all – all relevant higher moment implications are illustrated directly by the gap between the two cumulative probability distribution curves. 'Risk' can be defined and portrayed precisely via quantified uncertainty in terms of cumulative probability distributions, but 'risk' is not a measurable criterion, and in terms of an uncertainty management approach, there is no useful purpose served by working assumptions which attempt to reduce 'risk' to a directly measurable form like variance.

Figure 11.9 is a copy of Figure 3.5. As discussed in Chapter 3, the 3-m barge option curve has been shifted to the right so its expected cost is now higher than the 1.6-m barge option. This means that both choices are risk efficient. The key issue is that tradeoffs between risk and expected outcome need consideration to make a choice. The same generalization of a Markowitz mean-variance approach is involved, but it is now important to recognize that risk-return tradeoffs are not a preference issue at a project level. In this case corporate level risk efficiency needs consideration to decide whether or not taking the additional risk at a project level is worthwhile.

Figure 11.10 is a copy of Figure 2.5, discussed in Chapter 2 in terms of an office manager's photocopier choice example. Figure 11.10 illustrates a low clarity version of the same decision diagram format as Figures 11.8 and 11.9, in the sense that linear cumulative curves are an obvious and convenient shortcut.

Figure 11.10 portrays a comparison between approach C and approach B in terms of cost cumulative probability distributions, a simplified context and format for the same message as Figure 11.9. As noted earlier, it shows that in terms of cost as measured, both are risk efficient. Tradeoffs are involved. Approach B has a lower expected cost, but the tail of the distribution crosses that of approach C, implying more risk. In this case most organizations would find this risk worth taking, but the more profound the overlap and the closer the expected outcomes, the more difficult the choice.

Figure 11.10 also portrays a comparison between approach A and either C or B which delivers a message directly comparable to Figure 11.8, but the absence of an overlap plus the linearity makes the message even clearer.

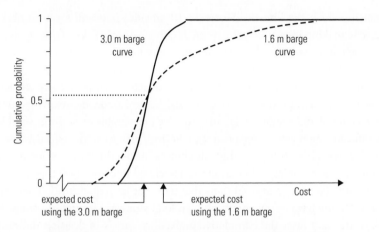

Figure 11.8 Decision diagram: one risk efficient choice example.

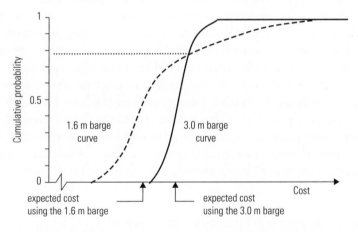

Figure 11.9 Decision diagram: two risk efficient choices example.

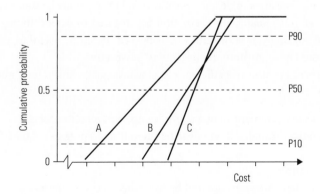

Figure 11.10 Decision diagram: comparison of approaches A, B and C.

The simplicity which the linearity Figure 11.10 provides is useful for a number of reasons. One advantage is making it easy to estimate such curves. Another is making it easy to interpret the messages the curves portray which facilitates discussion of other objectives. For example, in terms of cost it is clear that A dominates B and C. If A is not available, it is clear that B has a lower expected cost and the additional risk should be taken to achieve corporate risk efficiency. Further, it is relatively straightforward to start to explore risk-reward tradeoffs involving other objectives (like photocopier speed and colour) which may involve measurable or non-measurable attributes.

A clarity efficient approach to opportunity efficiency has to make effective use of decision diagrams like Figures 11.8–10 for any difficult choices, measuring at least one important objective if measurement is feasible, and quantifying associated uncertainty if this is useful, but also addressing relevant objectives and conditions that have not been quantified. These option choice decisions can be at any level in the analysis – high level strategic alternatives or low level tactical alternatives. At the very least the cumulative probability curves of decision diagrams provide a conceptual framework for thinking about risk–reward tradeoffs in purely qualitative terms – but they also provide a basis for other relevant considerations. For example, recall the BCS context described in Chapter 2. Bruce, the BCS proprietor, has to manage cost quantified variability over the P10 to P90 range via his estimating process and contract option choices – but he also has to visualize the importance of a client understanding – or not – the conditions associated with ownership of 'very bad news' scenarios in simple qualitative 'very bad news for Bruce' terms. At a higher clarity level, IBM UK and many other organizations have found versions of Figure 11.10 directly useful. At a still higher level of clarity, BP and many other organizations have found versions of Figures 11.8–11.9 directly useful. Multiple objective versions of Figures 11.8–11.9 involve a level of sophistication explored with a very limited number of clients by the authors so far, but the scope for very wide application is now much clearer. So is the need for organizations to start with simple versions, seeking more clarity only when doing so looks potentially advantageous, but understanding always what the route to more clarity involves, in terms of costs and benefits.

'Treasure hunts' involving project risk efficiency

Often possible improvements in risk efficiency are not flagged in the way discussed above, and sometimes there is no need for a diagram to demonstrate why improvements should be pursued. This may be because they are simple and very obvious, but they may be subtle and very complex. In *all* such cases we must search for them, and be prepared to defend them, with diagrams if need be, but not using analysis effort unless it is needed. It can be useful to see this search as a 'treasure hunt', from an 'opportunity management' perspective.

Typical examples at a project risk efficiency level which can be linked to implicit or background use of Figure 11.8 include:

- using more capable equipment than the minimum requirements suggest;
- using more resources initially, then releasing them if rapid progress is made;
- starting earlier;
- purchasing insurance;
- designing out the key threats recognized by this stage in the analysis;
- writing contracts to allow more flexible responses to possible threats and opportunities.

This aspect of the diagnose task is about using the insights gained from earlier discoveries to search for such changes in an effective manner. 'Earlier discoveries' clearly applies to earlier in the PUMP for the current project. It should also include earlier discoveries from earlier projects, both those internal to the organization and those external projects discussed in the literature or private information forums like The Major Projects Association. It can also include insights provided by the examples in this book, as a basis to get started.

Overall opportunity efficiency needs to be sought at all levels by an integrated approach to all the aspects discussed so far, beginning at the lowest level addressed, gradually moving upwards and outwards towards overall opportunity efficiency at a corporate level.

'Treasure hunts' involving corporate risk efficiency

Figure 11.9 illustrated tradeoffs between risk and expected cost which may require attention because they can lead to a gain in *corporate* level risk efficiency although they may seem to expose the *project* to a high level of risk. Often such opportunities do not make themselves obvious – they must be searched for. Further, often they reflect opportunities people are not prepared to take and would prefer not to see if they are not protected from the 'bad luck/bad management confusion'. These are key opportunities to address, particularly in the early stages of introducing formal uncertainty, opportunity and risk management processes into an organization.

Typical examples are the flip side of the examples cited in the last subsection context of risk efficiency improvements if the numbers (probabilities) are different. They include:

- using less capable equipment than maximum requirements suggest;
- using fewer resources initially, with fall-back plans in place when appropriate;
- starting later;
- not purchasing insurance (self-insuring);
- designing in the possible ability to capture possible opportunities recognized at this stage of the analysis.

'Treasure hunts' involving tradeoffs between objectives

Using decision diagrams like Figure 11.10 (in asymmetric S curve form when appropriate and with underlying sensitivity diagrams when appropriate) to portray the comparative implications of alternative options is one way to evaluate changes in 'base plans' and 'contingency plans' that involve tradeoffs between additional objectives that may or may not be measurable over and above a key directly measurable attribute and associated quantified uncertainty. They provide a way of portraying what the tradeoffs involve so that those responsible can make informed choices considering opportunity efficiency at a corporate level, as well as a project level, in terms of all relevant objectives and associated risk.

Decision diagrams used in conjunction with underlying sensitivity diagrams can also be used as a basis for thinking about a systematic search for opportunity efficiency which may reveal further 'hidden treasure' opportunities. For example: if an activity was given a less generous time provision, would the direct cost increase be less than the revenue increase; if the quality specification for a component was decreased, would the related decrease in time or cost be worthwhile; and so on. The more mature the iterative process, the more the focus of analysis should shift towards this step, but it may prove important on the first pass. For example, if the first pass suggests that corporate targets for early completion are not feasible, seeking feasibility may be the initial focus of attention.

Formal imposition of hard and soft constraints

Some constraints may be 'hard' (in the sense they cannot be relaxed) for everyone involved. For example, if building a jacket for an offshore North Sea oil production platform requires one of six feasible yards and they are all busy, a wait may be inevitable. Formal imposition of hard constraints can be a key aspect of the diagnose aspect of the evaluate phase. Such constraints may be identified earlier, in the context of the seven Ws in the define phase, or in the identify phase. However, a formal test for *any* violations of relevant hard constraints is important. Where relevant violations are identified, a loop back to reshape the strategy will be needed.

Some constraints may seem 'hard' to those who need to comply, but at a corporate level they are 'soft' – in the sense they can be relaxed at a cost – possibly an opportunity cost. For example, if the board of an oil company decides it wants first oil by a fixed date to meet world wide sales targets in a cost effective manner, that constraint may seem hard to project staff, but it could and should be relaxed by the board if meeting it in the face of major difficulties is more expensive than deferring sales or acquiring oil elsewhere.

Balancing all relevant objectives, in the sense of seeking an optimal set of tradeoffs between all objectives, is usefully viewed in operational terms as moving soft constraints. As a simple example, if shorter duration is desired for an activity or a whole project, more expensive resources can be used, or the quality of the deliverable can be reduced, tradeoffs within the seven Ws structure elaboration of the classic 'cost-time-quality' triad. Working assumptions about soft constraint representations of objectives may have been identified earlier, as for hard constraints. However, a formal test for *any* violations of relevant soft constraints is important. This should include relevant tradeoffs between risk and reward for all relevant objectives, as well as tradeoffs between objectives, including objectives which do not have measurable attributes. Where relevant violations are identified, a loop back to reshape the strategy will be needed.

Formally meeting all soft constraints in terms of an appropriate risk of exceeding them is an integral aspect of the 'treasure hunt' concept, as is moving relevant soft constraints appropriately. However, the presence of hard constraints involves an additional aspect.

The ordering of the three earlier 'treasure hunt' aspects, plus this hard and soft constraints aspect, reflects the need to start the first pass of the PUMP with a clear understanding of the criteria-plan relationship structure, and with a focus on key measurable objectives at the level of key activities and sources of uncertainty, gradually broadening and widening the concerns addressed. This does not imply that opportunities involving tradeoffs between objectives should not be embraced as soon as they are discovered, or that relevant hard constraints do not need immediate attention. As noted earlier, the ordering of all these aspects is convenient for conceptualization and it loosely relates to a shifting focus, but it is not an operational ordering.

Formal recognition of conditions and robustness

Whenever quantification is used to understand some aspects of a situation, it is easy to overlook what has not been quantified. This is perhaps the second biggest mistake an analyst or the users of analysis can make. It is vital to minimize the risk of this mistake. The conditions noted in

Figure 11.5 illustrate attention to this aspect of interpreting quantification of uncertainty, and other examples have been used earlier, like the 'very bad news for Bruce' BCS scenario.

A deeper part of the same basic aspect is clarity about the implications of all other working assumptions and any framing assumptions. For example:

- if independence has been assumed inappropriately, estimates of variability will be biased on the low side, perhaps by a factor of 10 or more;
- if 'uncertainty' as quantified is limited to event uncertainty, expected outcomes may be so biased as to be meaningless;
- if a minimum clarity approach assuming 100% dependence has been used, marginal pessimistic bias *might* be involved, depending upon other assumptions.

Probably the biggest mistake an analyst can make is failing to understand or communicate effectively the relevance of working or framing assumptions which ought to condition the interpretation of an analysis. Probably the biggest mistake any user of analysis can make is believing an analyst who makes this mistake.

The robustness of any interpretation needs formal attention in the structure phase of the PUMP, as an aspect of 'diagnose the implications'. It will need further attention later.

Building clarity in successive evaluation passes

The ordering used for successive aspects in this section of the process description is in a rough way inversely related to their importance and their impact on project performance improvements. As the iterative nature of the process matures, it will become clearer why the investment in the earlier iterations of the PUMP provides insights that can be used to improve project performance in the later iterations. The focus of attention moves from the tactical or strategic at an activity level to the strategic at the level of interfaces between the project as a whole and the corporate strategy it is embedded in, perhaps via an intermediate programme level. We see the forest as a whole in terms of a limited set of trees in clearly defined relationships. The issues are defined in terms of sources that matter and effective response choices within a seven Ws and project lifecycle framework that is holistic and integrated. The depth of understanding that emerges will have to be explained to others top-down, but the insights are built bottom-up within each pass of the PUMP using the structure developed in earlier phases. If the sequencing of the aspects addressed in successive layers of analysis is optimized, major surprises leading to major revisions to the shaping strategy should be limited, but some surprises are inevitable. Skilled management of the evaluate phase is craft, not science, and being delighted by interesting surprises is a very useful motivating objective for PUMP team members.

All the above aspects of diagnosis require attention as and when appropriate as the set of sources of uncertainty analysed and option choices grows. Effective and efficient choices which are relevant at any point need provisional choices – most choices cannot be left until all the sources have been jointly evaluated. Careful attention to partial results as the evaluation process proceeds will suggest changes to those looking for such changes. In particular, conditions or scope assumptions associated with partial aggregation of quantified sources may need careful attention. Such conditions or assumptions can become crucial at the stage when all quantified sources have been aggregated – as when defining a budget or a delivery date, for example. When all quantified sources have been combined, interpretation needs to address the importance of all assumptions as an integrated set, including scope conditions which have not been associated with quantified uncertainty and all other relevant assumptions.

Analysis fit for purpose?

Following a given pass through the diagnose step, results of analysis may suggest no further effort is needed on this pass of the PUMP for this particular subset of sources – a 'local yes' result for the following 'fit for purpose' test. This implies a loop back to the top in Figure 11.1, to evaluate the next subset of sources.

If a particular subset of sources does need revisiting, a 'restructuring' loop back to earlier PUMP phases, nominally the define phase, may be needed, as illustrated by the discussion of the Figure 11.5 example. However, this larger loop back, between phases, might await complete assessment of all other subsets of sources currently quantified, suggesting a loop back within the evaluate phase first, perhaps completing full consideration of all sources quantified so far within the evaluate phase before a larger scale 'restructuring' loop back to the define phase. For reasons discussed earlier, in practice flexibility about how iterations are managed is important. Whether 'restructuring' loops back involve separate sets of activities initially treated separately, or a sequential sequence starting with the most important, all the initially decomposed and then quantified subsets of sources will need assessment.

All 'restructuring' loops can include 'refining' of selected quantification, and refining/restructuring tradeoffs addressed as part of this task.

When the initially decomposed and quantified sources have been analysed in a satisfactory manner, broader and wider concerns will need to be addressed via 'extending' loops, nominally back to the define phase, although in practice the identify phase or later phases may be the focus of the extensions. For example, minimal 'extending' loops might involve quantifying more sources, more substantial extending loops might involve identifying more sources, and still more substantial extending loops might involve widening the Ws and objectives addressed. The distinction between 'restructuring' and 'extending' loops is important, but again flexibility is important.

When the analysis has been extended as far as it needs to go, and all analysis thus far is fit for purpose, but a gateway process is not imminent or appropriate, a 'pausing' loop back to the define phase may be appropriate, with an interim report if appropriate. That is, the PUMP may be put on hold, to be restarted when appropriate. A further possibility here is analysis fit for purpose suggesting major changes in earlier strategic decisions, requiring an exit from the iterative PUMP phases to an interim reporting process discussed in Chapter 12 via the 'global yes'.

When the analysis has been extended as far as it needs to go, all analysis thus far is fit for purpose, and a gateway process is now imminent and appropriate, a 'global yes' ends all iterations for the present lifecycle stage, taking the process on to a gateway, the overall strategy gateway for present purposes.

There is no provision for going to a gateway process without a recommendation to proceed or to reconsider an earlier strategic decision, because this implies a PUMP failure. Managing this risk implies starting the PUMP early enough in the life cycle or admitting PUMP failure.

This final fit for purpose task is the pivotal point for the PUMP as a whole within the stage of the lifecycle being addressed.

An overview of alternative integration procedures

Those not interested in computational issues, computer software selection or hands-on analysis may be inclined to skip this section. It is arguably the least relevant section in this book for senior managers. However, at least a skim read is advisable for all readers.

As noted earlier, Monte Carlo simulation is the usual method employed to combine probability distribution in standard risk analysis software packages like '@Risk' (Grey, 1995, for example). However, an outcome interval with a probability of the order 0.01 will require a thousand samples or more to estimate with reasonable precision, a similar number being required for a resulting curve which is smooth, without visible sampling error. Using ten thousand samples gives the same level of precision as a controlled interval and memory (CIM) procedure with about 30 classes, the latter being about a thousand times faster (Yong, 1985). A CIM approach is a generalization of the simple discrete probability examples used for Tables 11.1–11.7, developed in Cooper and Chapman (1987).

Non-random sampling procedures ('Latin Hypercubes', for example) can be used to speed up the production of smooth curves in a Monte Carlo simulation context. In principle, such procedures are a partial move towards the completely systematic sampling procedure which CIM procedures use, partially reducing sampling error while possibly inducing some systematic error. In practice, the systematic error is unlikely to be important, though it can be.

Simple discrete probability methods suitable for manual computations in a decision tree or probability tree context, and controlled interval and memory (CIM) developments of these methods (Cooper and Chapman, 1987), provide alternatives to Monte Carlo simulation. The key points about the CIM process in the present context are:

- it requires combining successive pairs of sources of uncertainty, for computational reasons;
- this requirement encourages thinking about a structure for these successive pairs which reflects dependence and the story to be told;
- a by-product of this computational structure is built-in sensitivity analysis, as discussed in relation to Figure 11.5;
- for reasons discussed in relation to Figure 11.5, the use of CIM procedures or exposure to the results of their use should persuade any expert analyst or user of analysis without access to CIM software to use Monte Carlo-driven packages as if they were CIM driven to some extent, if not to the point of always using a pairing structure.

The approach described in this chapter assumes Monte Carlo simulation-driven software will be used, but the lessons from CIM-driven analysis learned by the authors are worth incorporating in the process. In the long term, software which uses expert system technology to select CIM or Monte Carlo processes as appropriate might be practical as a means of making computation more efficient, achieving the same level of precision with less effort, but the authors do not anticipate it in the short term. In any case any sampling software which allows for dependence used with reasonable care should prove just as effective.

Earlier 'industry standard' methods based on statistical moments, typically 'mean-variance', as used in the original PERT calculations (Moder and Philips, 1970), and by Lichtenberg (2000) in his 'successive estimation principle', need not assume independence, and an expert system-driven probability evaluation package could usefully embrace moment-based approaches as well as CIM and Monte Carlo. Moment-based approaches offer speed and precision when appropriate assumptions hold, but catastrophic systematic errors (bias) when appropriate assumptions do not hold.

The 'soft quantification' approach using simple spread sheet addition of plausible minimum and maximum values illustrated by the BCS example can be seen as a special case of a minimum clarity approach using a 100% dependence assumption and an underlying Figure 11.7 interpretation, but more than one view of what this kind of approach should involve is possible. For example, if all items are estimated independently, dependence levels less than 100% simply imply that ranges for sums may have a P5 to P95 or a P1 to P99 range interpretation rather than P10 to P90, depending upon how many items are involved and what level of dependence is involved. Alternatively, if successive items are estimated in a manner conditional on plausible maximum or minimum values of earlier items, along the lines illustrated by the Highways Agency example in Chapter 2, P10 to P90 range interpretation can be preserved for any level of dependence – including cases involving complex systemic uncertainty relationships. This broader interpretation means 'soft quantification' is usefully thought of as a fourth approach to integrating uncertainty, with a range of simple and sophisticated variants.

To summarize this section, four types of procedure for combining probability distributions can be considered, each with their advantages and disadvantages. Current 'industry standard' software based on Monte Carlo simulation is effective if used by experts with adequate understanding of dependence in a manner reflecting the usage of CIM approaches, but it is not a simple, efficient solution to all evaluate phase issues. It needs to be used with care, and better software is feasible, even for the simple treatment of dependence discussed in this chapter. The basic common interval discrete probability approach used in this book is useful at a conceptual level, even if it is replaced by a Monte Carlo simulation approach for operational purposes. Mean-variance approaches are also conceptually useful, but need great care when used in practice, especially if they tempt people to assume independence which does not exist. 'Soft quantification' using simple range estimates show considerable promise as a flexible minimum effort approach which can be generalized to more sophisticated approaches capable of dealing with complex systemic uncertainty in relatively simple terms.

Conclusion

The evaluate phase is the pivotal PUMP phase which directs where and how successive iterations develop the analysis. Figures 4.1 and 11.1 indicate that all iterations loop back to the beginning of the evaluate phase or the define phase, but in practice selective loops back to other phases (like the structure phase) can provide effective shortcuts.

Effectiveness and efficiency for uncertainty management as a whole depends upon how well this iterative process works. This depends on the ability of PUMP team analysts to detect what is important and what is not, before spending too much time on the unimportant, without overlooking important threats or opportunities that do not stand out initially, plus the team's ability to communicate all implications to all relevant users of their results. Extensive probabilistic analysis based on carefully researched data can be very useful, but often such analysis is not appropriate. What is usually essential is an initial rough sizing of uncertainty associated with *all* the key sources that require management, followed by refinement in some areas where that refinement is worthwhile. In general, the goal of a first pass through the PUMP should be a focus on sizing uncertainty in order to evaluate the best way to use later passes. A sizing first pass provides the initial understanding of which areas need the most attention, and which can receive less attention. This assessment is itself prone to risk which must be managed – but treating all aspects of project uncertainty as equally important in a single pass process is rarely sensible. The risk invariably realized is that too much time is spent on some issues which do not matter and too little time is spent on issues which do matter.

First pass estimates used to initiate the evaluate phase should be seen as simple statements of belief by those reasonably able to judge, brought together to provide a basis for discussing what matters and what does not. The numbers should be simple order-of-magnitude assessments, with a clear overall health warning to the effect that no one will be held accountable for their accuracy. Only when and if it becomes clear where data analysis and more objective probabilistic estimates might be useful, should the accuracy of such estimates become a concern.

The evaluation approach recommended here is based upon a need for efficient and effective decision taking – opportunity efficiency in overall optimality terms including clarity efficiency. As pointed out in Chapter 10, the probabilistic estimates used are a means to an end, not an end in themselves. Conditions or assumptions which quantitative analysis is based on also need to be understood – they can be crucial.

The results we get when we combine probability distributions of component sources of uncertainty are critically dependent upon the dependence assumptions used. Assuming independence between component sources when this is not an appropriate assumption renders probabilistic analysis misleading and potentially dangerous, not just useless. Those who are not prepared to understand and reflect on important dependencies should avoid probabilistic risk or uncertainty analysis. *Those using common practice risk analysis results provided by others should pay particular attention to the understanding of dependence displayed by their analysts, and totally reject any probabilistic analysis which suggests a failure to deal with dependence between any variables quantified in probabilistic terms in an appropriate manner.*

If the range of values associated with an important variable is clearly misjudged by a factor of 10, the associated analysis is clearly suspect. If independence is assumed between half a dozen key variables when 50% dependence (or a coefficient of correlation of 0.5 or some equivalent level of dependence) is appropriate, the associated analysis of risk can be much more misleading. A factor of 10 error on the size of a single variable may be a trivial error in comparison.

Understanding dependence and understanding structure are related issues. The most effective way to deal with dependence in a statistical sense is to give it a causal structure which explains it. Statistical dependence is causal dependence we have failed to identify and structure.

Sometimes a causal structure for dependence is not feasible, and sometimes developing a causal structure may be feasible but not cost effective. In such cases experienced analysts can effectively employ measures like percentage dependence or coefficients of correlation. However, to develop that experience, working with causal structures and conditional specifications is an important part of the learning process.

Combining uncertainty estimates quantified in the previous phase is just the starting point for a really effective 'evaluate *all* relevant implications of all uncertainty phase'. When interpreting quantitative analysis, an effective and efficient way of summarizing and interpreting *all* qualitative analysis assumptions and associated conditions is very important. We have provided clues about how to do this, such as notes on a sensitivity diagram like Figure 11.5. But it deserves careful attention which we have not fully illustrated because it is so context specific. Some of the ideas developed in scenario planning may prove useful here – for example, see Schoemaker (1995) and van der Heijden (2005).

Other key issues needing careful attention which are addressed in this chapter, but require further context specific development, include the following:

- An effective and efficient way of minimizing bias associated with quantitative analysis, building on 'cube' (kuuub) factor notions.
- An effective and efficient approach to sensitivity analysis, building on Figures 11.5–11.7.
- An effective and efficient framework for making decisions at all levels, building on Figures 11.8–11.10.
- Effective and efficient management of the iterative process.
- Use of risk efficiency.
- Considering risk efficiency at project and corporate levels, for all objectives, measurable or not.
- Considering tradeoffs between all objectives, for opportunity efficiency in overall optimization terms, using 'soft constraint' notions.
- Considering clarity efficiency as part of the opportunity efficiency concept.
- Maintaining clarity about robustness – never making working assumptions with potentially dangerous implications that are not understood, and avoiding framing assumptions which have restrictive implications that are not understood.

A key feature of the approach described in this chapter is the use of nested sensitivity diagrams portraying the way uncertainty accumulates using successive cumulative probability distributions like those of Figures 11.5–11.7 to build up a picture of combined sources of uncertainty. A second key feature is the use of decision diagrams where alternative mutually exclusive course of action choices are portrayed by cumulative probability curves like those in Figures 11.8–11.10. Joint use of these two forms of diagram provides the basis of a formal process of seeking understanding of what matters, spending more time on what matters, and moving towards overall opportunity efficiency. The authors believe these two tools used together in this way are central to the achievement of clarity efficiency for a very wide range of contexts. They are practical tools developed and used at various levels of clarity over a period of more than three decades.

One feature of their use is clarity about tradeoffs between risk and expected performance in terms of all relevant objectives. Optimal choices in terms of this issue are influenced by the level of decomposition involved. As the E&D shaping PUMP progresses, lower level of decomposition means that risk becomes more of an issue, and Part III considerations will intensify this issue.

Part III

The generic process in all lifecycle stages

Part II assumed one key lifecycle stage to describe in detail the seven-phase generic PUMP framework outlined in Chapter 4 of Part I. Part III relaxes this assumption to address the whole lifecycle. However, what might be regarded as other 'unfinished business' also has to be addressed, concerned with designing and operating efficient and effective PUMP pack processes which integrate with project management as a whole for a holistic lifecycle process.

Chapter 12 explores the implications of fully integrating the strategy development stages – all the stages prior to a watershed when strategy development ends (in principle) and strategy implementation begins. In practice, strategy implementation will have to revisit strategy formation as detailed plans evolve and execution and delivery progress.

Chapter 13 explores the implications of fully integrating the strategy implementation stages.

Chapter 12

Fully integrating the strategy shaping stages

> *Plans are nothing, planning is everything.*
>
> —Napoleon Bonaparte

Part II discussed PUMPs in the execution and delivery strategy shaping stage of the project lifecycle – E&D shaping PUMPs. It was assumed that a PUMP had not been applied in earlier life-cycle stages. This chapter generalizes the Part II discussion by considering the use of PUMPs in all the strategy shaping stages and associated gateway stages of the project lifecycle. Table 12.1 shows the relevant portion of the Table 1.3 stage structure with Table 3.1 roles for PUMPs elaborated for exploration in this chapter.

As a starting point, recall that the seven Ws structure of Figure 1.2 is a basic framework applicable to all stages of the project lifecycle, but the focus shifts as the lifecycle evolves. In the concept shaping stage, the chain of concern of the PUMP and other project planning is the 'where–who–why–what' and plans for business case purposes, plus plans for relationships and contracts, plus integration of all plan-based timetables, including preliminary versions of plans for operations, activities and resources. In the DOT shaping stage, the chain of concern of the PUMP and other project planning is the 'where–who–why–what' component-based design plans, plus plans for asset operation, plus resource plans for operations, usually with a focus on the component-based design framework, although all other Ws involved are relevant. In the E&D shaping stage the chain of concern of the PUMP and other project-planning activity is the 'where–who–why–what', plus plans for execution activities, plus resource plans for activities, although all other Ws involved are relevant.

We need somewhat different PUMPs for each of the three strategy shaping stages – more if a more sophisticated lifecycle structure is needed for reasons mentioned in Chapter 1. The seven-phase framework of the basic PUMP remains clarity efficient for all strategy shaping stages, but the differences need clarifying.

Table 12.1   Roles for PUMPs in the strategy shaping stages of the project lifecycle

Lifecycle stage	Stage purposes	Roles for the associated PUMP
Concept shaping	Concept, project objectives and business case development in corporate strategy terms	Confirm the initial concept from a corporate perspective Identify stakeholders and their expectations Identify appropriate performance objectives Provide unbiased initial estimates of business case outcomes Evaluate the concept and business case in corporate strategy terms
Concept gateway	Consolidation Governance	Consolidate the base and contingency plans Confirm expectations about the deliverables
DOT shaping	Design, operations and termination (DOT) strategy development from a design and operations management perspective	Confirm the design basis from a design and operations perspective Develop lifecycle operations performance criteria Assess the feasibility of the design strategy Assess the likely costs and benefits of design changes Evaluate the operations and termination strategy Test the reliability of designs and their operations effectiveness
DOT gateway	Consolidation Governance	Consolidate the base and contingency plans Confirm expectations about the deliverables
E&D shaping	Execution and delivery (E&D) strategy development from a project management perspective	Confirm the execution basis from an execution perspective Estimate the resources required at a strategic level Identify and allow for regulatory constraints Assess contracting strategy at an overview level Assess the feasibility of plans Assess the likely duration of execution Assess the likely cost of execution and delivery Determine the appropriate milestones Determine the appropriate levels of contingency funds Assess the effect of changes to plans
Strategy gateway	Consolidation Governance	Consolidate the base and contingency plans Confirm expectations about the deliverables

The ordering of material in Part II and this chapter is designed to keep the discussion as simple as possible, first considering the strategy gateway PUMP, then working backwards from the E&D shaping stage. The connectivity of the issues addressed is very high, so keeping the discussion as simple as possible is important.

The first section of this chapter considers strategy gateway PUMPs. Strategy gateway PUMPs are crucial in their own right, but they are also useful as a model for all other gateway processes. Gateway PUMPs are key components of the PUMP pack – very different to shaping PUMPs, but closely coupled to preceding shaping stage PUMPs. The following sections begin with PUMPs for the design, operations and termination strategy shaping stage – DOT shaping PUMPs. DOT gateway PUMPs are considered next. Consideration of concept shaping PUMPs, then concept gateway PUMPs, conclude the sequence.

A further section considers a contractor perspective, to generalize from the client focus of Part II. The final sections emphasize the importance of considering all relevant perspectives.

The case for implementing a PUMP process at the outset of the concept shaping stage and applying compatible PUMPs throughout the whole of the strategy shaping stages of the project lifecycle should be clear by the end of this chapter.

Strategy gateway PUMPs and associated interim reports

This section addresses strategy gateway PUMPs. It maintains the Part II assumptions that a PUMP was not applied until the start of the E&D shaping stage of the project lifecycle and that our focus is a client perspective. 'Strategy gateways' are particularly important gateways, sometimes worth referring to as 'overall strategy gateways' to emphasize the way they conclude the strategy shaping part of the lifecycle as a whole.

The deliverables that a strategy gateway process should provide are in two basic forms. One is commitment to strategic plans consisting of base plans, contingency plans, and commitment plans, approved by the overall gateway process. The other is PUMP background documentation associated with the development and justification of these plans, including the reference plans which served as their starting point.

As a reminder of ideas central to this chapter which were established earlier, we use the term 'base plans' as a generic label for 'no-problem, stretch target plans' – what should happen if we capture all relevant opportunities and manage all relevant threats using a clarity efficient PUMP *and we are lucky*. Effective capture of good luck requires the implementation of base plans of this kind. These base plans *may* resemble reference plans *after* removal of provisions and contingencies plus adjustments involving proactive responses to uncertainty and other changes suggested by earlier PUMP shaping phases. Base plans incorporate proactive responses – but not reactive responses.

'Contingency plans' are the operational form of recommended reactive responses, which include trigger points (decision rules) initiating the reactive responses. They reflect anticipated potential departures from base plans which deserve planning attention now, whether or not resource commitments are involved.

'Commitment plans' are plans to which it is sensible to commit, bearing in mind the cost of failing to meet commitments, the cost of adding too much contingency allowance when defining commitment values, *the scope for being unlucky*, and *the overall implications of being unlucky*. For example, base plans might have a plausibly optimistic P10 scenario interpretation, and commitment plans a plausibly pessimistic P90 scenario interpretation.

It is useful to identify the specific tasks of the strategy gateway under two 'mode of operation' task headings:

1. consolidate and explain,
2. support and convince.

The 'consolidate and explain' task has to consolidate PUMP documentation as a basis for formal approval, and provide a 'snapshot' of the current state of play of the background documentation deliverables. It also has to extract a clear strategic plan, defined in terms of base plans plus contingency plans including trigger points for contingency decisions and commitment plans. Explaining the strategic plans in terms that all those involved can understand is the goal of the 'consolidate and explain' task.

The 'support and convince' task has to explain why the deliverables associated with the 'consolidate and explain' task achieve opportunity efficiency, including clarity efficiency for this stage in the lifecycle. Providing a case for all relevant players that has as much clarity as the analysis to date will allow is the goal. Setting that goal appropriately at the outset and adjusting it as the process evolves is clearly important.

Figure 12.1 portrays the way the two specific 'mode of operation' tasks might be used if the first step associated with 'consolidate and explain the strategy' provides a PUMP report in written form, and the next three steps extract summary base, contingency and commitment plans. The 'support and convince' task uses these deliverables in presentations. In practice 'consolidate, explain, support and convince' have to overlap, with informal communication and feedback playing important roles.

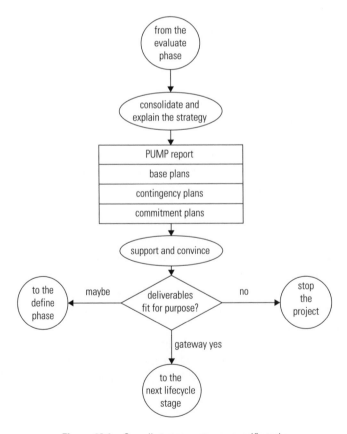

Figure 12.1   Overall strategy gateway specific tasks

The process depicted in Figure 12.1 does not involve basic PUMP phase equivalents. It is usefully conceived as a very different process, involving only one phase. It follows on from the linked earlier E&D PUMP, in a closely coupled relationship. However, at the gateway stages all the tasks have a different set of purposes, and control of the 'deliverables fit for purpose' test involves different players.

A particularly important difference is that there are no *planned* iterations in Figure 12.1. The process *as planned* is a non-iterative (linear process) bridge between:

1. the finish of the evaluate phase of the PUMP in the E&D-shaping stage of the lifecycle, and
2. the start of the tactics-shaping stage of the lifecycle.

PUMP pack gateway processes assume that a 'gateway yes' will normally be the result from the 'deliverables fit for purpose' test. However, a 'maybe' result can lead to unplanned iterations back to the PUMP define phase within the E&D-shaping stage. Such iterations are problems to be managed, not opportunities to be seized, but the 'fit for purpose' test has to be unbiased and rigorous. Unplanned iterations back to earlier lifecycle stages may be required, but a loop back to earlier stages this late in the project lifecycle suggests earlier process failures that are serious, or significant changes in circumstances. A gateway 'no' may lead to stopping the project. Stopping a project this late in the lifecycle suggests earlier process failures which were very serious, or very significant changes in circumstances for reasons beyond our control.

The defining difference between the end of the strategy-shaping stages and the start of the tactics-shaping stage is usually a dramatic increase in the rate of expenditure on the project which drives a corresponding increase in the immediate cost and knock-on complications of iterations back to earlier phases. As painful as any outcome other than a 'gateway yes' may be, an unwarranted 'gateway yes' is very risky.

In some cases a 'gateway yes' may be linked to 'going public' with the insights generated by the strategy-shaping process. This is a further reason for ensuring an appropriate decision on grounds that will stand up to general 'public scrutiny' as well as later governance processes.

Governance processes built into this 'fit for purpose' test need careful attention for a wide range of reasons. The bottom line is: mistakes at this point can be very expensive.

Let us now consider what is involved in the Figure 12.1 process in more detail, starting with the reference plans that underlie the first step of 'consolidate and explain the strategy'.

Reference plans

Consolidation and explanation of strategy should begin with a discussion of reference plans to the extent that this is relevant. Reference plans reflect the project description at a strategic level captured in the E&D-shaping PUMP define phase. As indicated in Chapter 5, senior executives and directors often comment on the immense value to them of a carefully crafted simple explanation of the nature of the project that reference plans should provide. Ensuring that an appropriate reference plan is available in an appropriately polished form is the essence of this step of the strategy gateway process, drawing to an effective conclusion a process that started at the outset of earlier PUMPs.

Reference plans can usefully capture some earlier misconceptions, to provide convenient 'straw men' to be knocked down by uncertainty analysis in order to demonstrate the value of the PUMP. For example, the BP Magnus project manager was happy to expose to the board the reference plan for a 1.6-m lay barge to undertake the hook-up discussed in Chapter 3 and later chapters, to demonstrate a key change from a reference plan to a base plan. He argued that this change made a case for using the process his team had pioneered for all future large or sensitive BP projects world wide, and this argument was accepted by the board. Sensible disclosures of reference plans which needed revision in this very open way will be selective. However, there is a case for a confidential record of all original reference plans pre-PUMP as a basis for unbiased assessment of the value of a PUMP and as a basis for a more general 'lessons learned' approach to knowledge management.

Reference plans need not be credible given the latest appreciation of project uncertainty. If reference plans are prototype base plans developed prior to applying a PUMP, they may not embed proactive responses, they will not assume that contingency and provision have been stripped out, they will not be linked to clearly defined contingency plans, and they should not assume good luck. If reference plans are prototype commitment plans developed prior to applying a PUMP, they may not be feasible because they include unacceptable unintended consequences for a number of reasons, such as a failure to understand the scope for bad luck and potential adverse changes in the environment of a project.

It is important to recognize that some reference plans may not be worth revealing, and it can be tactful to bury others. If reference plans seriously embarrass any major players, revealing them can put the whole PUMP pack analysis at risk. Helping all major players to bury their embarrassing earlier misconceptions by revising reference plans may be a key part of a successful PUMP *when this is appropriate*. Selective memory is often expedient. A key purpose of pre-strategy gateway PUMPs is to uncover aspects of project reference plans or associated project planning processes which need changes. However, provided that all necessary changes are made, sometimes some changes are best kept confidential to the analyst and those responsible, to avoid any unnecessary embarrassment. Assuring everyone involved that this will be the case can be an important starting point at the beginning of earlier PUMP applications. This is comparable to the confidentiality agreement that any consultant signs before he or she starts work, except that it is informal, and it is a separate understanding with each individual player. The operative words here are *avoiding unnecessary embarrassment, provided that necessary changes are made*. The practical reason why it is important to adopt this position, and make it very public at the outset of any PUMP, should be obvious. If this is not done, people will be inhibited and defensive in a way that is both natural and entirely reasonable given their perspective, to the detriment of the project as a whole from the project owner's perspective. Our ultimate purpose is to help the project's owners succeed. 'Impartial science' operating like a loose cannon will be recognized as a danger by all concerned and properly treated as such. That said, once an organization has an effective PUMP pack capability in place and fully integrated with project planning, the interpretation of reference plans as starting point base plans or starting point commitment plans weakens the case for burying anything, because standards of professional competence change and people who are confident about their competence are less sensitive about their fallibility.

The PUMP report

As a minimum the PUMP report should include a comprehensive list of strategic level threats and opportunities, assessed in terms of 'eight key deliverables':

1. sources of uncertainty which decompose *all* relevant uncertainty about *all* relevant objectives in a clarity efficient manner, quantified in a clarity efficient manner when quantification is appropriate;
2. related conditions and other qualitative considerations structured in a clarity efficient manner;
3. clarity about the implications given recommended proactive and reactive responses;
4. an assessment of relevant alternative potential proactive and reactive responses;
5. an assessment of alternative potential tradeoffs between all relevant objectives and expected reward–risk tradeoffs in terms of all relevant objectives;
6. cumulative probability distribution portrayal of 1–5 where measurement of attributes and probabilistic portrayal of risk is appropriate;
7. suitable scenario portrayal of 1–5 where measurement is not appropriate;
8. a summary extraction of the base, contingency and commitment plans.

PUMP-based analysis needs to be documented to explain all associated recommendations. Controversial recommendations need special care and explanation in 'support and convince' mode when presenting. An explanation of the need for key proactive and reactive responses is part of this. A bottom-up analysis process involves a bottom-up documentation process, but it needs to be presented top-down, to explain the overall position first, then elaborate on what is driving the uncertainty that matters, using nested sets of sensitivity diagrams like Figures 11.5–11.7, supported by decision diagrams like Figures 11.8–11.10.

The process of interpreting uncertainty via PUMP documentation in top-down terms can be regarded as the essence of this step in the overall strategy gateway process. This top-down perspective can produce new insights, and it is important to give it the time and space it deserves. Like writing the executive summary for a report, attempting to explain what we understand can be an important process in clarifying and developing that understanding.

Communicating insight to allow decision takers to make choices reflecting *all* relevant issues is the goal. Formal analysis has serious limitations, and a failure to address these limitations when attempting to offer advice is a *very* serious mistake.

The base, contingency and commitment plans

Consolidating and explaining project base plans at a strategic level using the PUMP deliverables is an important task. The base plans may not need a document which is separate from a PUMP deliverables document, but a clear summary of the base plans is useful, and for some purposes a separate document may be useful. For example, it may be prudent to limit some people's' attention to what they should be trying to do, as long as there is transparency about the implications of failure for reasons beyond their control. In conceptual and operational terms it can be useful to see base plans as an entity which can be separated from the process used to derive them.

For similar reasons it is usually helpful to formally summarize and explain reactive responses associated with any well-developed contingency plans, including trigger points and decision rules, for all significant threats and opportunities which are not fully dealt with via proactive responses. Such contingency plans may be the only effective way to deal with important uncertain events which have a low probability and a high impact. They will inevitably be the only opportunity efficient way to deal with the implications of an accumulation of a wide range of sources of uncertainty involving inherent variability, ambiguity and systemic relationships as well as events. A separate document for contingency plans may not be required, and a simple summary list of recommended reactive responses may be all that is needed, within or separate from the main PUMP deliverables documentation. However, it can be useful to see contingency plans as separate entities in conceptual and operational terms.

When seeking approval for a project strategy defined in terms of base plans and contingency plans, it is *very* important to set out in very clear terms the commitments involving all relevant objectives and all relevant parties. Expected outcomes may not matter a great deal, provision/contingency distinctions may not matter at all, and the details of contingency plans may not matter to many of those involved, but who owns provisions plus contingencies, and who owns sources of uncertainty not incorporated in either, usually matters a great deal to everybody.

A common seminar observation and follow-up question is 'my boss/organization will never understand the difference between

1. stretch target values and associated base plans,
2. commitment values with clear exceptions and associated commitment plans,
3. expected outcome values involving provisions but not contingencies,

so what should I do?' The short answer is

1. reveal only the commitment plans and commitment values,
2. emphasize the exceptions/conditions in simple summary terms,
3. work on your boss's/organization's enlightenment,
4. consider contingency plans which include a new job.

Part IV explores some longer answers.

Support and convince at a strategic level

Convincing those responsible for a project go/no-go/maybe decision to agree to a 'go' can be associated with a change in the mode of operation at this point in the strategy gateway PUMP, from carefully crafted writing of the report to effective presentations plus all other relevant aspects of selling the recommendations of the report. It can be useful to make this change explicit, just to acknowledge the need for going beyond writing a good report. However, once this is done, it becomes obvious that the selling process, more generally defined as taking all key players with us, needs to start much earlier. There is a relevant Operational Research tradition which holds that selling a solution to a problem (or a means of resolving a messy set of problems) has to begin at the beginning of the problem definition process.

The 'support and convince task' is concerned with providing an interface between analysis as reported in formal documents and a clear understanding of the issues in holistic terms. It is also concerned with changing people's' perceptions in advance of formal reporting when culture change issues are involved, and it may involve important aspects of bargaining to achieve this – for example, see Harwood et al. (2009).

Assess the strategy to gain approval or to seek formal approval for rejection

Assessing the project strategy to gain approval in the sense of the Figure 12.1 'fit for purpose' test should reflect a governance process designed to ensure corporate objectives are served by further investment in the project, testing the conclusions drawn in the Figure 11.1 'fit for purpose' test in the E&D stage. Earlier steps in the strategy gateway PUMP can be managed by the PUMP team, but this step needs independent corporate leadership reflecting its audit role.

The strategy gateway PUMP should continue to focus on uncertainty at a strategic level, not the details. Indeed, this assessment should begin with a top-level overview of all objectives, and then focus on key objectives relevant to choices being considered. It has to work top-down to address specific sources of uncertainty and relevant response options, starting with the difficult issues, not the easy issues. One key reason for an *overall* strategy gateway assessment prior to tactical planning is to ensure that strategic focus does not get lost in premature detailed planning issues.

It is usually easier to maintain a strategic focus if detailed tactical plans have yet to be developed, but they may have been needed for other purposes, in which case a formal summary may be important. For example, sometimes highly selective detailed planning to test strategy is important, to ensure that 'the devil is not in the detail'. If it is clearly understood that this kind of selective detailed planning may be needed, earlier attention to this possibility may be warranted via strategy shaping PUMPs or linked associated KUMPs.

In practice more than one 'overall' strategic gateway may be important, and this kind of elaboration of the 'nominal' structure for the strategy shaping stages of the lifecycle is easily accommodated. However, a failure to clearly distinguish the final overall strategic gateway 'watershed' from tactical planning and gateways is a common source of serious clarity inefficiency.

A fit for purpose 'gateway yes' decision, a 'go' decision for the project, should be the default and usual working assumption at this stage in the PUMP. If this is the case, no significant project management errors of omission or commission at a strategy-shaping level should remain. Sometimes it is not feasible to produce such a plan, because of crucial unresolved issues. This is usually a clear sign of impending problems which require immediate management, making a 'maybe' decision for the project the prudent choice. In terms of Figure 11.1 and Figure 12.1 used in an integrated manner, 'maybe' decisions should be part of the Figure 11.1 evaluate phase. An unanticipated 'maybe' decision as part of a formal strategy gateway indicates a PUMP failure in the last of the strategy shaping stages.

At this point an unanticipated 'not fit for purpose' decision, a 'no-go' decision for the project, should be seen by all concerned as a failure of the project-planning process as a whole, unless there has been a very significant change in the circumstances that were anticipated, and this anticipation failure was reasonable. Failure of the planning process as a whole may include a failure of uncertainty management as a whole. However, if the PUMP pack has done its job effectively, a project 'no-go' recommended by the PUMP-based overall strategy gateway may be the only sensible way forward, and it may be essential to take that decision to a formal gateway-equivalent process, a consolidation of the 'no-go' in Figure 11.1. The reputation of the PUMP team and the project team should be able to survive a 'no-go' recommendation when this is appropriate, wherever it occurs.

Early detection of a clear case for a 'no-go' or 'maybe' decision may mean that a very limited report is needed, and a very informal process. However, there may be associated 'lessons learned' which need documentation to avoid future nugatory effort.

Assuming a 'go' decision is achieved, this triggers transition from the last of the strategy shaping stages to the tactics shaping stage of the lifecycle.

If a project proceeds beyond the strategy gateway, further clarity efficient development of proactive and reactive responses in the tactics shaping stage should narrow the P10 to P90 ranges and comparable ranges for non-measurable objectives, reducing uncertainty prior to making tactical commitments as well as getting ready to manage that uncertainty.

As indicated in Chapter 4, 'enlightened gateways' can involve incorporating improvements to plans prior to the formal gateway consolidation process when this is appropriate. This is akin to an informal gateway process overlapping the shaping process. It can involve interim reports or less formal communication. It can be seen as part of the integration of PUMP team effort and the rest of project management. It should not diminish the importance of a formal gateway stage.

The strategy gateway process is a key component of the PUMP pack, but it is usefully distinguished from the associated E&D shaping PUMP. It has different purposes, and responsibility for its overall effectiveness involves corporate governance issues which need care in terms of corporate ownership and competence.

DOT shaping PUMPs

An appropriate PUMP process within the DOT shaping stage of the lifecycle will always pay dividends, considering design, operations and termination strategy decisions jointly, even if the project does not proceed to an E&D shaping stage. If DOT and E&D shaping stages use a comparable PUMP methodology, integration of DOT PUMP analysis with E&D PUMP analysis is easier and more effective. This section explains how the E&D shaping PUMP can be adapted to provide a basic framework for the preceding DOT shaping PUMPs.

A key concern here is linking design issues and components to performance objectives or benefits of the project in a structured way. The criteria–plan relationship structures may not be as familiar or as straightforward as those that need attention in the E&D shaping stage, but even science-based projects, like research or research and development projects, can benefit from formalization of these links. Formally integrating consideration of the 'where–who–why–what' component-based design plans with operations plans and operations resource plans is an obvious step to take, provided organizational arrangements that may prevent it can be set aside.

Indeed, it is difficult to see an argument against moving in the direction of one common but adaptable strategy shaping PUMP used in both the DOT and E&D shaping stages, apart from difficulties associated with traditional management silos, and there is growing support for moving quickly and decisively in this direction (Allport and Ward, 2010).

Two applications outlined in the following two subsections provide usefully contrasting illustrations of what is involved in a DOT shaping PUMP. A discussion and comparison of these two examples follows, using the basic PUMP seven-phase structure recommended for all strategy shaping PUMPs.

A liquid natural gas storage pilot project example

In the early 1980s, Acres Consultancy Services realized that variants of the BP version of SCERT methodology applied in the E&D shaping stage, and its supporting software, could be transposed to a range of other contexts, including analysis in the DOT shaping stage of project lifecycles. The first application of this SCERT variant methodology in a DOT shaping context involved a design decision for the storage of liquid natural gas (LNG) for PetroCanada (Chapman et al., 1984). A small Acres team, driven by three people based in Niagara Falls, Ontario, executed the study. The design decision concerned the volume of storage required for a LNG facility on Melville Island in the Canadian High Arctic. This storage facility was to act as a buffer between the production of LNG and the arrival of ice-breaking LNG carrying ships that would transport the LNG to east coast US ports. The 'activity' structure of offshore oil projects used in an E&D shaping context could be transformed in a DOT shaping context into a design 'component' structure for an LNG production facility with about ten components (subsystems), such as the compression chain, the cooling system, the storage facilities, and so on. A semi-Markov process framework addressed 'how much LNG can we produce in a day?' rather than the E&D question 'how much pipe can we lay in a month?' The sources of uncertainty were no longer 'risks' in the sense of threat of delay or opportunity for early completion, but 'reasons for potential outages' in the reliability and maintainability sense. Risk (uncertain event) probabilities became 'mean times between failures'. The objective was to minimize operating costs in order to maximize operating profit. Quantified sources of uncertainty included all 'outages' relevant to sizing the LNG storage, but those not relevant to storage – major fires for example – could have been quantified if a wider scope had been of interest. Possible responses were after-the-fact repair strategies and pre-emptive design changes. A key deliverable was a clear case for avoiding the single compression chain design that had been assumed in order to save money because the project was a marginal 'pilot' project intended to assess the potential feasibility of high arctic LNG production. The PUMP process identified better ways to save money and improve performance, thereby enhancing opportunity efficiency.

Yukon river crossing example

The second application of the BP version of SCERT in a DOT shaping context was also a design decision. It addressed how best to take a large-diameter gas pipeline (48 inches) across the Yukon River (Chapman et al., 1985). The client was the Fluor Corporation. Acres American executed the study using a team of about 30 people located near Washington. This study illustrates an effective approach to a strategic design decision involving many different parties with many different objectives. The obvious design choices were to put the gas pipeline in a spare pipe-rack on a bridge built to carry a large-diameter oil pipeline which followed the same route, or build a separate pipe-rack. A separate aerial crossing was an obvious third option, added for completeness with limited thought about how it would be done. A separate submarine crossing was a similarly unrefined option, triggered halfway through the study by recognition that relatively independent sources of uncertainty threatened the bridge and a submarine crossing.

The bridge had been built by the owners of the oil line, but its ownership was then passed to the State of Alaska, and it was a significant state asset in road traffic terms. The loss of the bridge would affect road traffic, oil flow, gas flow, and national energy security. It would also involve environmental issues related to oil spill and gas release, with obvious local and international implications. The 'activity' structure for the project was very simple – just one component, the river crossing structure. The time structure used to consider the future operating stage of the project in reliability process terms was also very simple – reliability in successive annual periods. The complexity of the study was driven by the structure and measurement of performance objectives, the wide range of potential threats beyond 'natural' threats like seismic events and 100-year return period storms, and the very differing interests of key stakeholders. For example:

- what was the cost to the oil pipeline owners of a lost day of production?
- to what extent might the US government and US population see the same lost day of oil production cost as a future benefit – of great value when other oilfields have been used up? and
- what was the chance of wilful sabotage by enemy agents or vandals?

A key resulting deliverable from the analysis was a clear case that all parties could support for a separate submarine crossing which was better from the perspective of all parties. As noted above, this separate submarine crossing was not on the initial list of options – it was generated by the creative nature of the DOT shaping PUMP employed.

The define phase

Reviewing the basic PUMP define phase approach discussed in Chapter 5, what needs changing and what is the same for a DOT shaping PUMP?

Begin with some basics which stay the same. It is helpful to be clear that the same asset lifecycle stage structure as portrayed in Table 1.3 (or some alternative developed from this nominal basis) is relevant, to focus current lifecycle stage concerns and put them in context. Further, the same seven Ws as portrayed in Table 1.4 and Figure 1.2 apply, although the focus now shifts to the way the 'where–who–why–what' quartet drives and is driven by plans for operations and resource plans for operations instead of plans for execution activities and resource plans for these activities. In addition, the same considerations apply in terms of keeping the basic Ws structure simple – a target of about 20 components for a high clarity approach, scaled down in a nonlinear manner for lower clarity. However, while the use of 10–15 components for the LNG study was clearly consistent with this advice, only one component for the river crossing might look inconsistent. The reason this exception does not disprove the rule is two-fold. First, in physical terms the river crossing was very simple: the pipeline could be put into an existing spare pipe-rack constructed by the oil pipeline owners when the bridge was built in case it was needed for oil pipeline purposes, or a separate pipe-rack could be built, the two favoured options. The terms of reference for the LNG study were very focused on design and operation issues, but the broader nature of the Yukon River crossing study meant that some time and effort went into deciding that the operations stage of the project dominated the execution and delivery stage – both were relevant, and an execution and delivery strategy stage assessment might have followed.

The focus phase

Reviewing the PUMP focus phase approach of Chapter 6 this time, what needs changing and what stays the same for the DOT shaping stage?

The same general set of models and related process ideas can be used. In the LNG case, the PetroCanada models and processes were directly comparable to an uncanny extent with the BP SCERT approach used in other E&D shaping contexts, given the appropriate changes in terminology. 'Activities' became *'components'*; 'risks', using the terminology of the day for 'sources of uncertainty', became reasons for *'outages'*; and so on. Further, the semi-Markov process features of the BP SCERT software and the word-processing structure for documenting the activity–risk–response structure developed by BP were used without modification or extension.

In the Yukon River crossing case, the same software and word-processing structure applied, but extensions to deal with the novel complexities noted earlier were seriously taxing. Chris Chapman designed the methodology strategy as part of a comprehensive bidding effort. Chris and Dale Cooper then had to deliver a detailed plan for implementation while immersed in its execution as part of a team of about 30 people working on this 'study project'. Chris reported to a pragmatic ex US Army Corps of Engineers study manager (Chuck Debelius) who was kind and patient, but low on tolerance of dithering or lack of clarity. At the outset of the study Chuck insisted that the study would not be complete until he had a one-page executive summary that justified the key recommendations that *anyone* could understand without looking at the main report. The main report was clearly going to run to many hundreds of pages, and address some very complex issues. Chuck drove home his demand with an apocryphal story. His commander had once asked for a half page report. When Chuck delivered a whole page report, his commander folded it over neatly, pressed the crease, tore it in two, read the first half, and said 'this report is not complete!' An important lesson learned by Chris was the immense value of this level of clarity as a top-down deliverable. Seeking this kind of clarity is a useful motivating goal from the outset.

The identify phase

One common feature in the two DOT shaping examples is that the identified 'sources of uncertainty' may be primarily 'event uncertainty' as suggested by 'fault tree' and 'event tree' approaches that underlie most reliability, availability and safety modelling. However, sources of uncertainty may also involve variability uncertainty composites that include inherent variability, event uncertainty, ambiguity uncertainty and systemic uncertainty. For example, basic performance assumptions may involve ambiguity because design has not been finalized, and systemic failures 'when all the holes in a Swiss cheese align' are well-known phenomena (Reason, 1997, p. 9). Another common feature is response options which may be preventative or reactive, plus some relevant secondary sources and responses.

In the LNG case, the three people driving the study had no LNG experience, they had only limited access to individuals with related LNG plant experience, and there was a very limited availability of published literature about LNG facility outage experience. This raised obvious difficulties not previously encountered. Operators of existing LNG facilities contacted were very helpful, but were constrained by understandable confidentiality concerns. In the Yukon River crossing case the large team assembled provided comprehensive coverage of most aspects at a reasonable level of experience, but unambiguous identification of what was involved for sources of uncertainty like sabotage and vandalism, and the value of a barrel of oil in 30 years' time, clearly pushed the credibility of any 'expert' assessment into territory not encountered earlier.

The structure phase

One feature of both the DOT shaping examples is the need for a carefully structured sequence for building up composites of all the relevant sources of uncertainty to the top level, so sensitivity diagrams showing uncertainty components built bottom-up can be explained top-down. The more subjective and debatable the assessment of individual components becomes, the more important this kind of clarity becomes. Sensitivity diagrams in the format of Figures 11.5–11.6 were central to the management of the assessment process in the equivalent of the evaluate phase, and they were central to the formal reports, in both the LNG and the Yukon River crossing cases.

In the LNG case no new structuring issues were encountered, but the value of a general response (like a second compression chain) and a willingness to go beyond the study remit when marginal constructive insubordination looked useful, had its value confirmed.

In the Yukon River crossing case the value of a general response was closely linked to the importance of systemic uncertainty. Failure of a separate aerial or submarine crossing would not impact the bridge, an important independence in terms of effects. However, in addition, most of the sources of uncertainty that might lead to failure of the bridge or a separate aerial crossing would not involve the same level of threat for a separate submarine crossing. This provides a further form of independence in terms of sources of uncertainty, and this was a key attraction of the submarine crossing option.

The ownership phase

Ownership was not an issue for the LNG study, but it was central to the Yukon River crossing case. Identifying an option which was optimal for all interested parties in terms of all relevant objectives was a crucial outcome. It was achieved because of the independence aspects of the submarine crossing. This was a classic case of aligning interests as far as possible. It was central to a simple explanation for an unanticipated recommendation. This helped to satisfy the one-page executive summary objective as well.

The quantify phase

One common feature of both the LNG and Yukon River crossing cases was the use of subjective probability estimates for all uncertain event impacts and variability uncertainty that it was useful to quantify. A histogram representation of these probability distributions was a second common feature. The use of point estimates for event probabilities, in keeping with the common approach at the time, was a third. In both cases sensitivity analysis for these point estimates of probabilities took an obvious common practice form – debatable estimates were increased and decreased one at a time by an order of magnitude to see if it mattered. If it mattered, more attention was given to this source, to understand it better, manage it better, and estimate its importance with more precision. In both cases subsequent reflection now suggests that a simple interval estimate approach to all event probability uncertainty would have provided a significant improvement in clarity efficiency, that is, much better understanding with a lot less effort, incorporating event probability uncertainty into the sensitivity diagram output format of Figures like 11.5–11.7. Much more effective treatment of dependence could have been part of this. For example, the cost of the loss of oil flow for a few months in a time of peace and plenty might be quite low from the perspectives of the US federal government and the US population, but might be very high in a time of conflict or war, which is clearly linked to the probability of a sabotage attack on the bridge. This added analysis power, plus greater clarity about the limited need for detailed data gathering and analysis if the preferred option choices clearly dominate alternatives, might have saved further analysis effort in the Yukon River crossing case, and might have provided more confidence for the LNG results. It is not always sensible to capture uncertainty within a model in this way. One or two key sources which are *very* contentious may be best left outside the model, so decision takers can make their own uncertainty sizing assumptions given sensitivity analysis as a basis, including parameter 'flip' point evaluations as discussed later in this chapter. However, if we are not sure which uncertainty matters most, putting it inside the model in this way can greatly improve clarity efficiency, even if we later decide to take it outside the model again for one or two key sources.

The evaluate phase

The use of Figures 11.8–11.9 format decision diagrams as well as Figures 11.5–11.6 format sensitivity diagrams in a hierarchical structure was a feature in both the LNG and Yukon River crossing cases. The value of such diagrams could have been reinforced and extended as discussed in the last subsection, and further enhanced by other lessons learned since, lessons that are reflected in Chapter 11.

Alternative DOT shaping PUMP methodologies

There is scope for a wide range of alternative methodologies to uncertainty management in the DOT shaping stage. Safety, reliability, maintainability, supply chain and operations management – to mention just a few – may be interpreted as directly relevant disciplines replete with methodologies. Further, some techniques, like discrete event simulation, cross all these boundaries – for example, see Pidd (1996, ch. 9). To some extent a general management science perspective can attempt to span all these disciplines and techniques – for example, see Pidd (1996) and Williams (2008). However, in the authors' view it makes sense to adapt all useful alternatives to the seven-phase basic PUMP structure – adjusting that structure if necessary – to achieve compatible methodologies in different lifecycle stages. As we need compatible processes, we have to start somewhere to achieve this compatibility, and attention to generality built into the basic PUMP and all underlying uncertainty management concepts makes a basic PUMP framework a useful place to start.

Safety objectives in the DOT shaping stage – some key issues

To illustrate the scope for the uncertainty management perspective of this book in what might be regarded as a separable discipline, consider the question of safety objectives in the DOT shaping stage as safety is often a very important consideration in DOT shaping stage analysis. A common definition of 'risk' for safety purposes is

$$\text{'risk} = \text{probability} \times \text{impact'}$$

a measure of *expected* outcome in the 'what happens on average' sense.

As an illustration of the difficulties this approach can lead to, there is a good case for arguing that the corporate failure of Railtrack in the wake of the October 2000 Hatfield train crash, and the more serious Ladbrooke Grove train crash a year earlier, was a consequence of assessing rail safety using this approach. Chapman and Ward (2002, ch. 7) explores why. The basis of the explanation is that the *expected* cost of accidents in terms of fatalities, injuries and other consequences clearly needs minimization, but large *deviation*s from what happens on average is what drives public perceptions of railway risk and railway management competence. It could be argued that Railtrack panicked after two serious accidents about a year apart; at least in part because large deviations from what the public expected – and what Railtrack had achieved – were not an integral aspect of their formal risk management process. It is reasonable to measure risk in a safety context relative to a zero datum point – any deaths or injuries or other costs are risk in a zero target sense, and a zero target and opportunity/risk datum point makes sense. However, the public need to be conditioned to the inevitability of occasional serious accidents which may exceed average outcomes by a factor of 10 or more, and the chance that two or more may follow in a short time period, as part of a formal process of managing risk in this 'departures from targets and averages' sense, as well as a separate DOT commitment concept understood by regulators and other relevant parties. People may understand why buses usually arrive in twos and threes, but applying that thinking to rail crashes may be very a different matter. Confusing targets, expectations and commitments because the difference is not discernible in the basic framework is extremely dysfunctional. Figures 11.5–11.7 format sensitivity diagrams dealing with *all* relevant uncertainty associated with interval estimates for event probabilities, as discussed above, could be used to consider the composition of the 'equivalent fatalities' metrics commonly employed. That is, an 'equivalent fatalities' measure aggregates actual fatalities with different levels of injuries, and the weighting factors are clearly debatable within plausible ranges. Further, to consider design and operating option decisions, equivalent fatalities measures are sometimes transformed into monetary units by a nominal 'value of a fatality avoided', but these are also uncertain and debatable within plausible ranges.

These ideas can be used to clarify the safety aspects of any project's DOT shaping stage. This is not current mainstream safety management, but these ideas expand the conventional safety perspective without losing sight of current safety concerns, by providing a more general framework that can consider current practice as a special case. In effect, current 'risk' measures become first-order expected outcome measures, with a clear case for higher order possible deviations from expectations measures. Sensitivity diagrams in the Figures 11.5–11.7 format also provide a clear basis for making effective treatment of safety part of the E&D shaping stage PUMP when this is appropriate.

The basis of Chapman and Ward (2002, ch. 7) is an unsuccessful consulting assignment in the late 1990s. Chris was commissioned by Railtrack to undertake a strategic review of their approach to safety about two years before their corporate failure. He recommended an uncertainty-based approach consistent with this book's PUMP-based approach. Railtrack expressed interest in the report, and it led to some interest in the wider safety community, including an invited ICE (Institution of Civil Engineers) lecture, but no policy changes the authors are aware of. However, we believe in learning from failures as well as successes – unsuccessful consulting assignments are sometimes the basis of successful research and follow-on applications.

A recent successful application of a PUMP approach to the safety aspects of open pit coal mining can be viewed as operations safety management in a PUMP framework. Two senior executives of Cerrejon Coal in Columbia, one of the largest open pit coal mines in the world, spent a brief period in the UK developing an approach in outline with Chris in 2007, now implemented to replace a more traditional approach.

The authors do not expect a rapid conversion to uncertainty management thinking in the safety management community. However, readers of this book with responsibility for safety cannot afford to wait until the safety management community becomes more enlightened. Readers may have to work with a range of people with limited views of shared problems. How one deals with this will obviously depend on the context. But the starting position should be a clear understanding of what they are saying in a framework which clarifies the limitations of their thinking.

DOT gateway PUMPs and interim reports

The strategy gateway process of Figure 12.1 is easily adapted to define DOT gateway PUMPs addressing design, operations and termination strategy. Clarity about the difference between reference, base, contingency and commitment plans is just as important (perhaps obvious in relation to many operations and termination plans), but with crucial implications in the safety context addressed in the preceding subsection. Clarity about governance issues may be marginally less important, but it can be very important to distinguish between decisions to iterate through the DOT shaping stage by a PUMP team, and decisions to revisit issues by a corporate group who can judge the value of continuing or stopping a project in terms of corporate objectives.

The reports produced by the LNG and Yukon River crossing cases were not gateway reports in the overall strategy gateway, or DOT gateway, sense – they were interim reports. Both faced other design gateways and business case gateways, and the LNG case report by Acres was part of a larger design and operation feasibility study involving several other consulting companies. However, both cases reinforce the authors' view that interim and gateway reports during the DOT strategy stage ought to be comparable to and compatible with interim and gateway reports during the E&D shaping stage, even if subsequent lifecycle stages building on earlier stages is not a concern. When a whole lifecycle perspective is a concern, this kind of compatibility is clearly a potential asset worth exploiting. Indeed, as Part II should make clear, if everything that a clarity efficient DOT shaping PUMP should do has not been done, a clarity efficient E&D shaping PUMP should address the omissions, even if a client does not ask for this to be done. A similar argument applies to the concept shaping PUMP and following stage PUMPs.

Concept shaping PUMPs

Given the limited information typically available in the concept shaping stage of the asset lifecycle, plus the obvious direct links to corporate strategy, it might be argued that a clarity efficient concept shaping PUMP ought to be a very different process to PUMPs designed for later lifecycle stages. This section explores the extent to which a clarity efficient concept shaping PUMP has to be different in a substantive sense.

As noted in Table 1.3, the primary focus of the concept shaping stage is the development of an outline business case for a proposed asset. Consequently, the discipline of economics, and financial economics in particular, is the usual basis of concept shaping stage methodology because base plans for business case purposes require a discounted cash flow model. The models used in later lifecycle stages can be used to build a discounted cash flow model, but such models are different in important respects which shape how they are traditionally approached.

If we start looking at a concept shaping PUMP in financial economics terms, it is evident that we have to estimate a range of cost and revenue parameters that draw on a summary of plans not yet developed. In their current conceptual form these plans involve significant incomplete knowledge, involving ambiguity uncertainty that will be resolved in later stages of the lifecycle, assuming that early stage gateways are successfully negotiated. In the cash flow framework of an initial business case model, capital cost will be one parameter. It will require estimation via a simple version of the E&D shaping PUMP needed later, assuming that the project proceeds to the E&D stage. Operations stage costs will be additional parameters, requiring estimation via a simple version of the DOT shaping PUMP needed later in the DOT shaping stage. Operating revenues or benefits will also need comparable consideration, as will the sources and costs of capital, corporate resource constraints in terms of finance, and other constrained resources.

Concept shaping stage decisions necessarily rest on summary/short-cut versions of more detailed strategy shaping processes, so there is value in treating them in a fully integrated manner from the outset. In the define phase of a PUMP designed for the concept shaping stage, it clearly makes sense to anticipate treating the three (or more) strategy shaping stages (concept, DOT and E&D shaping) in an integrated manner. Further, resolving ambiguity as the lifecycle progresses also needs effective integration by effective knowledge acquisition management as part of the basic project management process.

If this first lifecycle stage starting position is adopted, and we want to adopt the idea of a fully integrated clarity efficient PUMP pack approach to all strategy shaping stages, the first step of the PUMP identify phase in each of the strategy shaping stages can start with the most important criterion for that stage of the lifecycle, using the same seven Ws and lifecycle structure, but starting in a different place.

There are some important new issues if a PUMP is employed in the concept stage. These issues are associated with the need to integrate project strategy and broader corporate strategy at this stage, with ongoing update implications in later lifecycle stages. For example, capital rationing for new capital investments has to be considered in terms of all available opportunities, and some projects may be platforms for facilitating other corporate opportunities. Sometimes the risk of pursuing a project is specific to that project's technology, but sometimes the risk of not pursuing a project that is a platform for other projects has much broader implications.

The ongoing nature of these integrative aspects will be clarified shortly, using three examples. Start with the most complex example context.

Permanent disposal of nuclear waste

In the mid-1990s Chris Chapman was engaged by UK Nirex to provide advice on an E&D shaping PUMP for the construction of a 'rock characterization facility' – a deep mine to be instrumented for testing the suitability of an enlarged mine complex to store UK intermediate level nuclear waste, as discussed earlier in Chapter 11. This rock characterization project was a component of the one large project UK Nirex was set up to execute – long-term 'permanent' storage of nuclear waste on behalf of all UK waste producers, with ongoing operations implications over a virtually infinite operations and support stage. A year or so into the development of an E&D shaping PUMP for the rock characterization facility, the Department of Energy (DoE) undertook a review of the overall permanent storage project, with a view to deferring this project for 50 years. The E&D shaping PUMP for the rock characterization facility was given a simple form to consider the duration and capital cost of the initial construction phase of the project as a whole, building on earlier cost estimates. This framework was then used to consider a version deferred for 50 years. Operations issues after 50 years were assumed to be the same, but operations issues during the deferral period were studied to assess the cost of ongoing 'temporary' storage of nuclear waste on the surface in simple DOT shaping PUMP terms. These results fed into a DoE discounted cash flow model, as did a HM Treasury mandated 6% real discount rate (HMSO, 1991). The result suggested a £100 million advantage for deferral, and consequently the DoE recommended deferral (DoE, 1994).

At the time Chris and Nirex argued that the 6% real discount rate assumption was not appropriate and that the basis for such a figure was highly uncertain (Chapman and Howden, 1997; Chapman and Ward, 2002, ch. 8). A lower rate of about 3% seemed more defensible. The Treasury has since revised its discounting recommendations to a rate which starts at 3.5% and reduces over time to 1% in a multiple test framework (HM Treasury, 2003a). A somewhat different multiple test approach is recommended by Chapman et al. (2006), using a real discount rate of the order of 3% based on different basic economics. Whichever framework is used, a 3% real discount rate suggests that a £multi-billion decision error was made by the DoE, other things being equal. There is, of course, considerable room for argument that 'other things' are not equal, and the authors would like to make it clear that we are neither pro- nor anti- nuclear – we are pro-clarity of thought and anti-ambiguous cases. In the event, the rock characterization facility failed to get local planning approval, but a decade later this issue was back on the UK central government agenda, with proposed changes in planning procedures.

The need for a multiple test gateway framework arises because deciding to proceed with a project or not is a corporate level strategic decision that usually involves a number of considerations and objectives which can only be collapsed into a single discount rate test if unrealistic working or framing assumptions are made. In the nuclear waste disposal case, the cost of capital, government energy policy, intergenerational transfer of welfare issues, and risk associated with either choice, makes a decision rule based on a single discount hurdle rate basis defective in obvious ways. Once the basic problem is understood, PUMPs which accommodate it in simpler contexts can be designed. Simpler examples will help to clarify what is involved.

Alaska power authority hydroelectric power project

Before we explore what was learned from the nuclear waste case, consider another somewhat simpler case that underlay Chapman and Howden (1997).

In the late 1970s the Alaska Power Authority had to choose between a major hydroelectric power project and incremental development of coal-fired power units. Acres Consulting Services were providing support on a range of issues, and possible adaptation of the BP SCERT methodology ideas was explored. An impediment to choosing the hydro option was the very long payback period and the 'risk' that seemed to be implied by a long payback period. A very simple PUMP was developed to assist with this decision (Chapman and Cooper, 1983b). At the time it seemed to set aside what had been learned about strategy-shaping PUMPs from the BP SCERT applications, and start in a very different place. It avoided direct probabilistic modelling of any of the parameters of the standard net present value (NPV) decision framework, because the key parameter uncertainties involved issues such as the rate of inflation of fuel prices relative to general inflation and the terminal value (at a nominal planning horizon) of a hydroelectric power unit, which are by nature highly correlated and only amenable to highly subjective probability distribution estimates. The approach developed was 'parametric' in that it systematically identified how far parameters had to move from their expected values to change ('flip') the decision, comparing that movement to plausible ranges of values to identify the relative importance of uncertainty associated with all key parameters. It facilitated identifying the key parameter followed by exploration of a simple qualitative understanding of associated uncertainty in a framework most suited to the key parameter. The parametric analysis suggested that the key parameter was the value of the hydro facility at the end of a planning horizon of 40 years, when a coal-fired power station alternative conventionally has a terminal value of zero. There was a plausible case for arguing that the value of this particular hydroelectric facility 40 years on in today's money before discounting was greater than the cost of construction. It was clearly likely to be much more than zero. About 90% of the capital cost was roads, dams and other civil works that might be much more valuable in 40 years if properly maintained, given inflation in construction costs and further relative escalation in fuel costs. The 10% of total capital cost associated with turbines and generators might be worth zero after a conventional 50 years planning horizon, but even this was debatable. It was useful to determine what minimum value for the hydroelectric facility in 40 years' time would indicate that hydro was the preferred choice under various expected value assumptions for other parameters. It was also useful to recognize both the likely modest losses in NPV terms if hydro was selected and energy prices fell, and the likely massive losses if hydro was not selected and energy prices rose, with implications linked to the rest of the Alaska economy and the cold climate. The decision addressed in this example is complex, but it involves a moderate level of complexity relative to the nuclear waste disposal example, and the qualitative 'parametric' approach provided a useful complementary methodology which underlay the nuclear waste approach.

Insulating the walls of a house in the UK in the 1980s

Before confronting the complexities of the UK Nirex or the Alaska Power Authority examples, a third, simpler, example is useful. A house owner-occupier in the UK in the 1980s is considering insulating the walls of his home. This involves a decision very similar to that faced by the Alaska Power Authority, with useful simplifications and differences. The similarities include the need for a framework considering a potentially appreciating asset, very uncertain energy price considerations, and discounting considerations over a time horizon which might be very long.

Now consider a concept-shaping PUMP in terms of the basic PUMP seven-phase approach, starting with common basics, using the home insulation example when notation needs defining, and then generalizing to consider the hydro and nuclear waste examples when appropriate.

The define phase

The PUMP define phase discussion in Chapter 5 assumed application in the E&D shaping stage of the project lifecycle. What needs changing, and what is the same, if we want to outline a clarity efficient concept shaping PUMP define phase?

Begin with some basics which stay the same. The same seven Ws as portrayed in Figure 1.2 apply, but now the initial focus is the way the 'where–who–why–what' quartet drives, and is driven by, the business case. This is extended to the way the business case is driven by and drives the plans for relationships and contracts, plans for operations, plus all other plans, and the integration of all plan-based time tables.

Significant differences in a concept shaping PUMP, compared with later strategy shaping stage PUMPs, flow from the NPV cash flow framework required by a business case, the way the business case has to drive and be driven by all other aspects of the seven Ws, and the necessary links between project strategy and corporate strategy.

To illustrate this, consider the simplest of the three examples introduced above – whether or not to insulate the walls of a UK home by an owner-occupier.

A key parameter is the discounted payback period, the number of years the householder lives in the house before selling it to recoup the insulation cost in discounted NPV terms. Like hydro-electric power, insulation is likely to prove an appreciating asset, as fuel costs escalate at a rate higher than general inflation. However, in this case the biggest source of uncertainty is how long the owner will keep the house. Moving soon after insulating would involve a small loss. Staying a long time without insulating would involve a very large loss.

The most basic parameter structure starting point involves a planning horizon of n years, a time period index $t = 0, 1, 2, \ldots, n$, with $t = 0$ serving for the capital investment starting point, and a 'current value' or 'money of the day' differential cash flow (for the 'nominally preferred' 'option A – insulate' less the fall-back 'option B – do not insulate') measuring net cash flow in at the end of time period t, X_t.

The most effective initial calculation involves three parameters:

1. C: differential capital cost at $t = 0$ (the full installed cost of the insulation),
2. F: differential operating cost for $t = 1 \ldots n$ (the fuel cost saving per annum), and
3. S: differential 'scrap' value (the value of the installed insulation = the value of the house with insulation less the value of the house without insulation) tomorrow if insulation is installed today ($t = 0$).

This initial simplification can then be linked to three 'rate of change' parameters and a discount rate:

1. I: a general inflation rate factor,
2. E: a real escalation rate factor for F (inflation above the general rate),

3. A: a real appreciation rate factor for S (the installed insulation appreciation rate),
4. D: a real discount rate factor defined as:

$$D = (1 + r/100)$$

where a real discount $r = 5\%$ means $D = 1.05$ for example, with comparable interpretations for I, E and A.

In these terms a basic NPV formulation means the differential NPV of insulating over not insulating is given by:

$$V = -C + \sum_{t=1}^{n}\left(FI^t E^t/I^t D^t\right) + SI^n A^n/I^n D^n.$$

The general inflation terms cancel out, so we can work in 'real' terms to assess 'economic desirability' in terms of values for V greater than zero.

In the hydro/coal example, C becomes the capital cost of the hydro approach less the capital cost of a coal fired equivalent, F becomes an operating cost differential driven by coal prices, and S is the value of the hydroelectric facility less the value of the coal-fired station assuming a zero value for the coal station at the standard 40-year planning horizon for coal-fired power stations. In this case S is in effect the 'value' of the hydro facility 'tomorrow' if it is built 'today' (ignoring construction duration issues as a working assumption), perhaps equated to C, with A defining the way that value changes over time. In this context there was no point in separate S and A parameters, the two being combined in a parameter defining the value of the hydro facility in money of today after 40 years. A potentially useful alternative interpretation involves the way the value of the Alaska Power Authority as a whole changes over time given selection of the coal or hydro routes.

In the nuclear waste defer/proceed-now example, C becomes C_0, the capital cost of the disposal facility if proceeding now, and F becomes the operating cost differential driven by surface storage costs if deferral is selected. S is no longer a relevant concept, but there is a new parameter C_{50}, the capital cost of the disposal facility if building it is deferred for 50 years. In this case S and A are replaced by C_{50} for estimation purposes, the capital cost of the disposal facility in 50 years' time.

In practice notation changes may be convenient for any particular context, in some cases 'appreciation' may become 'depreciation', and in some cases short-term inflation or escalation cycles thought to be predictable and multi-year construction periods might need calculated adjustments to simple model results. However, in general it pays to simplify the basic model even further, by further composition of the simple basic parameter set. Using the insulation example terminology, we can define

$$R = \sum_{t=1}^{n} E^t/D^t \qquad \text{(a composite discount parameter)},$$

$T = S A^n / D^n$ (the terminal value of the insulation in present value terms),

$N = C - T$ (depreciation of the insulation asset over the horizon in present value terms),

so that

$V = FR - N.$

This gives us a constructively simple top down perspective for the decision rule: 'if V is greater than zero, then select the nominally preferred option A, otherwise use the fallback option B'. This simplicity has a number of benefits. First, $V = 0$ defines a 'flip point' as parameters change, which we can rewrite as the condition

$N = FR.$

We can then use a range of tests equivalent to 'V greater than zero?' which include:

1. is D greater than the 'correct' D? (an internal rate of return (IRR) approach),
2. is n greater than the 'correct' planning horizon? (a discounted payback period approach),
3. is N greater than FR? (a planning horizon cost and benefit view),
4. is F less than N/R? (an annualized benefit and cost view),
5. a terminal value version of S equivalent as used for the hydro/coal decision.

This means we can select whichever approach best suits our particular context – a discounted payback period for the insulation decision for example – once we understand which parameter uncertainty is most important.

Second, it becomes obvious that unless we want to model presumed 'knowledge' about the immediate future, it is long-term averages that we need, and short-term fluctuations generally cancel out, in addition to general inflation.

Third, less obvious but also important, escalation rate (E) and real discount rate factor (D) positively correlated variations cancel out, as do F and R negatively correlated variations, with an amplified effect if the opposite correlations apply.

In brief, we can use a simple top-down focus to identify sources of uncertainty which really matter at a composite level, decomposing only where it clearly matters, to avoid getting lost in the detail of an impenetrably complex NPV calculation.

Given this very simple but general starting point structure, the define phase of the concept-shaping PUMP can use simple versions of the later phase PUMPs to develop an early view of all the relevant parameters. Most important, it can start to consider other relevant objectives for all the relevant parties. For example, the householder considering insulation may be interested in a warmer house or the kudos of 'green credentials' in addition to cash savings. The electric power authority may be thinking about Alaska's future in a very cold climate when the coal and other fossil fuel run out. And a government contemplating nuclear disposal needs to think about the environmental consequences of a nuclear waste disposal strategy, 'low carbon' concerns, energy policy implications, linked economic policies and security implications.

This multiplicity of relevant objectives and the implications of constraints is the basis of multiple tests, implemented during the evaluate phase addressed below.

In effect, the criteria–plan relationship structure in the concept-shaping PUMP requires reference to the integrated lifecycle and seven Ws structure. Simplification is feasible, but it requires great care, and how it is approached matters a great deal.

The focus phase

Reviewing the PUMP focus phase discussion of Chapter 6, it is important to emphasize that the focus phase addresses different concerns with different outcomes depending upon the context, and which stage of the project lifecycle is involved is a very important aspect of the context. In the concept-shaping stage there is a particularly obvious need for a simple top-down view of all relevant uncertainty in relation to all objectives for all relevant parties, with a clear view of what is sensibly quantified, and what has to be addressed in qualitative terms.

Corporate learning processes need to recognize that it can be very helpful to understand that useful general lessons learned in very different contexts can be applied in other contexts provided the frameworks being used are compatible. This is important because it makes experience portable, richer and more relevant. For example, the Alaska Power Authority hydro/coal decision outlined earlier prompted a rejection by Chris Chapman of quantification of uncertainty in probabilistic terms, but the later UK Nirex studies and the development of minimum clarity ideas has led to a more balanced approach embracing quantitative analysis where this is useful, as discussed below. Any organization working across all strategy-shaping stages ought to make similar connections.

The identification phase

Uncertainty identification in the concept-shaping stage requires a top down perspective that is dominated by variability uncertainty composites which include inherent variability, event uncertainty, ambiguity uncertainty and systemic uncertainty. However, specific event based sources of uncertainty may need identification and appropriate responses.

For example, in the house insulation case two basic options were considered:

1. a lower cost option involving injecting expanded polystyrene into brick cavity walls,
2. a higher cost option using rock wool.

The lower cost option was rejected because of the risk of rising damp if building subsidence subsequently takes place. Analysis focused on the decrease in the differential scrap value S and an increase in associated risk which more than offset the increase in C, all other parameters remaining unchanged. In effect, an event uncertainty source was usefully identified and part of the model that was used to make a choice.

In the hydro case the dam silting up or failing due to earthquakes was addressed. In the nuclear waste case, the preferred site becoming non-feasible for political reasons, if a 50-year deferral took place, was addressed. However, most other uncertainty was not linked to specific identified events. The value of a very simple top-down perspective as a starting point is particularly obvious at the concept-shaping stage – involving just one composite source for each parameter discussed above, like C, F and S. As in other lifecycle stages, identification in the concept-shaping stage also needs to recognize response options which may be preventative or reactive, plus some relevant secondary sources and responses.

An important aspect of response recognition in the concept stage is the formulation of a project management strategy that offers a suitably robust and generic response to uncertainty associated with the project. As noted in Chapter 1, projects involving speculative product development or the application of novel technology, or high levels of complexity, warrant careful, early attention to project management strategy, starting with design of an appropriate lifecycle structure. Rather than simple sequential progression through the lifecycle stages in Table 1.3, more complex parallel trials and iterative cycles of activity maybe appropriate. In particular highly uncertain elements of a project raise questions about knowledge gaps, assumptions, or what is feasible. The project management process then needs to contain activities designed to answer those questions, recognizing that answers may well force significant modifications to designs, plans and performance objectives (Lenfle and Loch, 2010). This is an illustration of the knowledge lens perspective outlined in Chapter 1.

Considering uncertainty in general terms suggests general responses in the form of 'resilience' and 'agility' built into the project management process. In broad terms, this might involve balancing control and flexibility, a focus on learning processes, parallel working, intensive communications, adaptability, trial and error, frequent testing, fast feedback, decoupled dependencies (Laufer et al., 1996; Augustine, 2005; Loch et al., 2006; Fernandez and Fernandez, 2008; Cleden, 2009). In principle, consideration of all such project management strategies are within the scope of a PUMP pack, highlighting the desirability of integrating PUMPs into project management processes, particularly in the concept stage.

The structure phase

As with PUMPs in other lifecycle stages, there is the need for a carefully structured sequence for building up composites of all the relevant sources of uncertainty to the top level. However, a striking difference based on experience to date is the lack of use of sensitivity diagrams like Figures 11.5–11.6 showing the relative importance of uncertainty components for the basic parameters discussed above. The reasons for this will be explored shortly.

The ownership phase

Ownership was not an issue for the home insulation case, apart from its role in terms of a planning horizon defined by selling the house, but ownership was an issue in both the Nirex and Alaska Power Authority examples. In the nuclear waste case, one important issue was benefits enjoyed by one generation of UK citizens (low cost energy and defence) that are paid for by later generations (left to cope with the waste). This intergenerational transfer issue was equally important in the Alaska Power Authority case, but for somewhat different reasons. Conventional funding approaches coupled to US regulation of electricity utilities meant that new financing approaches were necessary to avoid overcharging current generation electricity consumers and undercharging future consumers. 'Financial feasibility' had to be distinguished from 'economic desirability' (Chapman and Cooper, 1985).

The quantify phase

As noted already, the insulation and hydro/coal cases limited themselves to parametric analysis using expected value starting points for all parameters and related plausible ranges without an explicit minimum clarity basis. The nuclear waste example caused a rethink of this position, moving to a more general position that makes use of quantification when it is useful. With hindsight we now recommend fully adopting the minimum clarity basis outlined in Chapters 2 and 10, plus a modest increase in minimum clarity when significant asymmetry is involved, even if probability distributions are not needed in an explicit form. For example, the insulation case might start by estimating the expected value of n – the planning period duration – by estimating a P10 value for n of 2 years and a P90 value of 20 years, then assuming the expected period before moving house is about 5 years, clearly implying significant asymmetric uncertainty without bothering to quantify the probability distribution formally. This approach to all the parameters, as a mandated minimum acceptable clarity, would provide a clear and simple basis for sizing uncertainty associated with all expected values, and help to control bias in estimates from the outset.

The nuclear waste case involved a number of parameters where full quantification was useful. For example, C_0 uncertainty had already been quantified, and it was useful to use this as a basis for quantifying C_{50} uncertainty, observing that strong positive correlation was probable. Further, a semi-Markov process model of costs over consecutive time periods gave those estimating an expected value for the cost of temporary surface storage of nuclear waste a lot more confidence in the average cost per annum of surface storage. They could only approach this task in a way they were comfortable with by defining the condition of the waste at a starting point, thinking about what measures would have to be taken given that state, and then thinking about what this would imply for the following year. A semi-Markov process was part of their planning and costing perspective, with good reason, and it made sense to accommodate this perspective directly. Further, the DoE accepted an 80% probability (expected value) that another site would have to be found if deferral took place, effectively doubling the current money expected value of C_{50} relative to C_0.

The evaluate phase from a project perspective

As noted earlier, the use of Figures 11.5–11.6 sensitivity diagrams in a hierarchical structure was not part of the nuclear waste case at the top level, and this way of portraying uncertainty was not considered for the hydro/coal or insulation cases. Also the use of Figures 11.8–11.9 decision diagrams was not part of the top-level DoE approach either. This is worth exploring briefly here.

In the house insulation example, expected value NPV analysis using example parameter estimates indicated a positive V for insulation of £152 assuming 5 years before moving house. Parametric analysis of all the parameters discussed earlier indicated that the only associated risk of significance was a possible move before the 5-year expected duration. Table 12.2 shows V values for $n = 1$ to 10.

Table 12.2 $V(£)$ as a function of n for the insulation example

n	0	1	2	3	4	5	6	7	8	9	10
V	-150	-100	-45	15	80	152	230	315	408	510	621

This table shows modest losses if moving within a year of installing insulation proved to be the outcome ($n = 1$ and $V = -100$). The example assumes $C = £400$ and $S = £250$, an overnight depreciation of £150 when insulation is installed ($n = 0$ and $V = -150$). However, this table also clearly shows losses turn into gains between $n = 2$ and 3, with a nonlinear increase in NPV resulting in a substantial payoff by year 10. Put into simple story terms, in a 1980s UK home context, if you insulate there is a low probability of low losses if you move unexpectedly early, but the opportunity for savings if you stay a long time is much more important. Put the other way around; if you do not insulate you run a massive risk of losing this opportunity. Plus you can be more comfortable and greener if you insulate, with no risk of unintended consequences like rising damp. Simple stories which do not need complicated graphs to communicate the key insights should be kept simple.

That said, if what was at stake was much more important, and the relative advantage differential was much smaller so that more clarity becomes desirable, might it help if we drew further on Part II ideas and Figures 11.5–11.10 in particular? The answer is a tentative 'yes', with reasons worth understanding, although we will not attempt a full illustration.

Keeping with the insulation case: if uncertainty about n was assumed to be the only source of uncertainty about the NPV of insulation, and we formally quantified this uncertainty using a P10 = 1, a P90 = 9 and a P50 = 5 assumed to be the expected value with an associated uniform probability density function assumption, we could use the results in Table 12.2 to plot a cumulative probability curve for V representing the NPV of option A over option B.

We need to recognize that Table 12.2 (or its graph equivalent) allows users to implicitly use their own probability curve for n to interpret the same information, which can be useful. If different people may have different views of the appropriate probability distributions, or less effort is involved using a parametric presentation, it can be better to give users the basic parametric relationships without the probabilities, to avoid possible discussions about difficulties in assessing probabilities or differences in views that may not matter.

However, *if* uncertainty about other basic parameters is treated in the same way by people with special expertise in each area, and *if* they collectively think about, and agree, suitable dependence assumptions, and *if* the results are combined using Figures 11.5–11.6 format sensitivity diagrams with a summary Figures 11.8–11.9 format decision diagram, then there is a good case for arguing that more clarity has been provided in an efficient manner. At the very least, it is worth understanding that the use of Table 12.2 format parametric analysis is a short-cut version of a higher clarity quantitative approach using Figures 11.5–11.10. Put a bit differently, Figure 11.5–11.10 curves can be key tools in PUMP evaluation in all lifecycle stages, but in the concept-shaping stage parametric approaches may be more clarity efficient.

In the nuclear waste example as addressed by Chapman and Howden (1997), the Table 12.2 equivalent was Table 12.3.

Table 12.3 shows a £100 million advantage for deferral if a real discount rate of 6% per annum is assumed, as was required by HM Treasury at that time, dropping to zero just below 6%, becoming

Table 12.3 V (£ millions) as a function of r = the real discount rate (% per annum) for the nuclear waste example

r	0	2	4	6	8
V	−9250	−3600	−1100	100	740

a disadvantage of £1100 million with a real discount rate of 4%, £3600 million with a discount rate of 2%, and £9250 million at 0%. The significance of the real discount rate assumption and the 2003 HM Treasury move to annual discount rates ranging from 3.5% to 1% prompted Chapman et al. (2006) to propose a 'traffic light' decision process for public sector projects.

The evaluate phase from an overall strategy perspective

Full development of the details of the Chapman et al. (2006) 'traffic light' process are not appropriate here, but the approach as a whole has a number of features worth understanding by all readers of this book. Consider in outline how the 'traffic light process' operates. Start by considering the concerns of those who are directly interested in public sector (government funded) projects. As will become clear, those who are interested in private sector projects, or intermediate public/private sector partnerships, and even personal domestic projects, can apply the same ideas to achieve a clarity efficiency that is not available from common practice discounting approaches. It starts with a corporate portfolio review process, and it takes a corporate strategy perspective throughout, while facilitating quick independent decisions for all clearly desirable projects.

1. The process for each project starts with a 'bond test' focus in the evaluate phase, which asks the question: 'Does a proposed project have a positive NPV using an estimated actual cost of money discount rate linked to any bond funding which would be necessary?' This involves the only use of discounting, employing an assumed actual cost of the money needed.
2. If this bond test is passed, the evaluate phase focus shifts to a 'return test'. A government must constrain how much it invests in all sectors, with priorities for different sectors which change with circumstances and political priorities – defence, education, health, and so on. The return test facilitates this balancing of priorities, without using the discounting process. Capital rationing and tradeoffs between different sectors are treated in constraint terms, with revealed shadow prices which are not embedded in the discounting process. Embedding any opportunity costs in discount rates induces bias – in favour of 'quick buck' projects, against long payback projects. Different opportunity costs for different investment areas will simply vary the bias.
3. If this return test is passed, the evaluate phase focus might shift to a 'risk test' next – the ordering of tests can be altered to suit the context. There is always a risk that we will make the wrong decision in NPV terms because we got the NPV parameters wrong or we were unlucky in terms of anticipated NPV uncertainty. For example, we insulated the walls of a house and then moved immediately because of an unexpected job offer without getting our money back, or the UK decided not to dispose of nuclear waste in the 1990s because HM Treasury insisted on a real discount rate of 6% but post-2003 HM Treasury believe that about

3% is appropriate. All associated uncertainty has to be addressed in risk efficiency terms via Figures 11.8–11.9 or Tables 12.2–12.3 equivalents. However, often the real risk has nothing to do with the NPV parameters in a direct sense. It involves additional objectives not considered in NPV terms. For example, permanent disposal of nuclear waste may lead to radiation leakage with serious environmental and health implications. Not disposing of nuclear waste may lead to collapse of domestic nuclear power capability, energy security and cost problems, knock-on general economic problems, further knock-on social and political problems. All these risk issues need serious attention in a holistic framework at individual project levels and at higher strategic levels. If they are not addressed directly in an integrated way, what often happens is that a 'risk premium' is added to the discount rate. This compounds the bias against safe long payback projects like hydro, favouring quick payback solutions, which ironically may be very high risk 'quick buck' projects. It also ignores the real issues – serious systemic risks involving a number of crucial strategic objectives are taken without recognizing the implications. When dropping the 6% real discount rate and moving to a multiple test approach, HM Treasury (2003a) indicated that taking a risk premium out of the discount rate was in part the motivation for their changed approach.

4. If a risk test is passed, the evaluate phase focus might shift to a 'legacy test'. A government must constrain how much it redistributes costs and benefits across generations – generally society does not want to live well now at an extortionate cost to our grandchildren, or vice versa. At a strategic level, overall balance in these terms needs to be sought. For example, if most current government expenditure favours current generations at the expense of future generations, projects which work the other way should be viewed favourably, but projects which make matters worse should be discouraged, with a simple and transparent means of managing this effect. When dropping the 6% real discount rate and moving to a multiple test approach, HM Treasury used an economic framework that treats this issue in discount rate terms. However, this issue needs to be addressed at a portfolio level, without confusing it with the treatment of the estimated actual cost of money, the latter being a project level issue whenever finance is contingent upon the project being addressed.

5. Further tests are possible in any context, and other contexts raise further issues. For example, this 'traffic light' process could be adapted for a highly geared private sector utility company like a UK water and sewage utility. In the early 2000s most UK water and sewage utilities became about 80% bond funded because of regulatory pressure on equity returns. To match available water to growing demand, two options from a larger set of possibilities are replacing old cast-iron leaking water mains with new plastic pipes and advertising water conservation measures. There is a good case for treating new water mains as bond funded, advertising as working capital funded, with real discount rate differences. Both sources of funding may be constrained, but rationing in both cases needs an 'appropriate return' test. An opportunity cost increase in the discount rate will seriously bias the case against long-term returns associated with investments like new water mains. An opportunity cost increase in the discount rate will also bias against investments like advertising to encourage reduced consumption, with short- and long-term implications. Further, constraints on the rate at which new water mains can be installed economically may arise because of a limited supply of appropriate contractors. This warrants an additional 'test', with comparable resource constraints in other contexts, like limited project management resources.

This 'traffic light' process could also be adapted to a private individual considering insulation. If the cost of insulation is easily added to an existing mortgage, usually a low cost source of finance, this defines the actual cost of capital and the relevant discount rate. If mortgage funding is limited by 'hard' or 'soft' constraints, a return test equivalent is important to assess the different insulation possibilities in conjunction with other potential calls on the house mortgage funding. Risks that need consideration include unintended consequences like rising damp, but also any threats to the householders' ability to pay a larger mortgage, like sudden unemployment in an economic downturn.

In summary, a single hurdle rate test as advocated in most basic finance texts depends upon assumptions which clearly do not hold in the nuclear waste context. Once it is clear why, and how a simple multiple test approach could work in a government context, private sector equivalents become obvious, and the shortcoming of common practice single hurdle rate approaches incorporating opportunity costs and risk in the discount rate become obvious in any context. Even simple personal decisions should be clearer – such as how far to take energy conservation measures like insulation in any reader's home. Further, the need to link project selection decisions to corporate strategy becomes clearer, at all levels – from private households, to large corporations, to national governments.

The multiple test approach at a project level exploits the multiple objective and hard/soft constraint management features of the evaluate phase as discussed in Chapter 11 in a different manner, but no fundamental new features are involved. The multiple test approach at a portfolio level does involve a new feature relative to Part II. It needs to be understood and applied for the first time for each project in the concept shaping stage. But this consideration of the link between projects and the corporate strategy they are embedded in needs to be revisited throughout the life of the project as circumstances and knowledge changes. In the authors' view it is useful to acknowledge the different emphasis and PUMP features needed for concept shaping PUMPs, but to see concept shaping PUMPs as variants of the same basic PUMP process used for all strategy shaping stages. Indeed, once the complete PUMP pack is understood and in practical day-to-day use, there is a good case for re-designating the 'basic PUMP' as a concept shaping PUMP, to ensure that both DOT-shaping PUMPs and E&D shaping PUMPs update the overall strategy tests as the lifecycle progresses.

The authors do not anticipate an immediate radical change in approaches to discounting along the lines proposed in this section, by HM Treasury or any other collection of economists. However, those who want a clarity efficient approach to their projects or their corporate strategy with opportunity efficient outcomes cannot afford to wait.

Concept gateway PUMPs and interim reports

The strategy gateway PUMP of Figure 12.1 is easily adapted to define a concept gateway PUMP which can form the basis of interim reports. Clarity about the difference between reference, base, contingency and commitment plans is even more important at the concept gateway, because uncertainty is greater. Arguably the need is even greater to see the concept gateway PUMP as a separate component of the PUMP pack – clearly distinguished from the concept shaping PUMP.

All strategy gateway PUMPs include a fit for purpose test which in effect audits the linked strategy-shaping PUMPs. It follows that the competence required to judge PUMP-based plans must include an understanding of all relevant PUMP pack concepts. The controversial nature of common practice 'risk management' and the nature and extent of common practice failings makes this an issue for all strategy gateway PUMPs – but it is probably most important for concept gateway PUMPs.

The concept gateway reports produced by the nuclear waste and hydro/coal cases were comparable to the BP E&D gateway case reports in some ways, but the parametric flavour was different, and they were not gateway reports in the same sense. Both faced other business case gateways involving several other parties. However, these examples reinforce the authors' view that interim and gateway reports during the concept shaping stage ought to be comparable to and compatible with interim and gateway reports during later stages of the project lifecycle, even if subsequent project lifecycle stages building on earlier stages is not an immediate concern. When a whole lifecycle perspective is a concern, this kind of compatibility is a potential asset worth exploiting.

Generalizing the use of the Figure 12.1 gateway process in this way means that all strategy-shaping stages can use variants of the same basic strategy gateway process, and the PUMP pack needed during these strategy shaping stages and their gateway processes involves just two basic process types: strategy shaping PUMPs and strategy gateway PUMPs.

NatWest Bank information systems example

As an example of what might be achieved using a PUMP pack from the concept phase onward, consider one organization which did this with a successful very large-scale information systems project.

In the 1990s NatWest Bank undertook a very large organizational change programme based on computerization of branch banking. Consultants based at Cranfield Business School helped the NatWest team develop a 'balanced scorecard' approach to the business case for the change – see Kaplan and Norton (1992) for examples of this approach. Chris Chapman helped the NatWest team to develop a 'benefit risk management' approach to the delivery of forecast business case benefits within the cost and time envelope defined by the business case. The benefit structure used to justify the project in the concept-shaping stage was formally mapped onto the system design and the tasks required to achieve the product of the project, and the sources of uncertainty associated with the tasks and design were linked back to the benefits. This integration of PUMP ideas and balanced scorecard ideas was very successful for NatWest, and it demonstrates the scope for beginning with a business case expressed in terms of the full range of relevant commercial concerns – some not easily measured – and managing all relevant uncertainty through to completion of a complex programme. Other lessons learned from observing NatWest's success include the importance of clear thinking about intended and unintended operations implications before embarking on any major project, the immense value of pilot projects to reduce the cost of learning by doing and leveraging the payoffs from learning generated by pilot project operations staff, and the general importance of corporate learning processes.

A contractor's perspective on the strategy shaping stages

It was convenient in exposition terms to focus on a client's perspective throughout Part II and the early part of this chapter. This section considers a contractor's perspective, addressing issues that both contractors and clients need clarity about. There are two key differences in a contractor's perspective as it is addressed here:

1. A client is ultimately responsible for all uncertainty not explicitly taken and effectively managed by contractors, while a contractor has significant control over accepting responsibility for uncertainty.
2. A client can decide to use a willing contractor or not, but a contractor has to persuade a client to accept their proposition or bid in the face of competition from other potential contractors.

A case study initially developed with a senior IBM executive for a 1990s IBM UK culture change project provides a useful illustration of the issues involved in recognizing these differences. It was discussed briefly in Chapter 6. It is developed in more detail here. Chapter 3 of Chapman and Ward (2002) elaborates this analysis. It is an example of the whole of the strategy-shaping stages collapsed into one stage from a contractor's perspective.

The Transcon case study

The Transcon case study uses a basic single-stage bidding context. The client, Transcon, a European road haulage organization created by the merger of two different firms with different international markets, has used consultants to scope a 'systems integration' project. This project involves the supply of new hardware, new software, revisions to existing software, revamped physical facilities, and retrained staff. Transcon has invited sealed tenders by a stated time for this project, and indicated they will select one with no further negotiation. The authors used this case study about 40 times with IBM staff as part of the 1990s culture change programme noted earlier. With IBM's permission and with adjustments for various reasons, we have used it ever since with a very wide range of seminar participants, changing the bidding organization's name to 'Astro'. A summary of part of the story told by the case when it is reviewed by the seminar leader after its use in syndicate groups is the focus of what follows here.

Suppose Astro wants to develop a bid for Transcon's systems integration project using the following uncertainty management process.

1. At a very high strategic level, decide how to do the project if the bid is successful.
2. Assess the expected cost.
3. Assess the chance of winning, given a bid equal to the expected cost plus a standard mark-up, and given two or three higher or lower bids.
4. Construct a table which shows the expected profit and associated probability of winning for the different levels of bid, with notes about other relevant criteria.
5. Consider the most appropriate bid price in relation to tradeoffs between maximization of expected profit and other criteria.
6. Record the chosen bid and its associated estimate of the probability of winning, and feedback analysis of this information into step 3 the next time a bid is developed.

Suppose Astro addresses step 1 using a simplified version of the PUMPs discussed earlier to translate the scope requirements of Transcon's consultant's report into an execution and delivery strategy, making strategic choices about technical options and alternative subcontractors in order to shape a strategic approach. Suppose Astro uses the results of step 1 to address step 2, and derives an estimated expected direct cost for the project of £13 million, to the nearest million.

Suppose corporate policy on contribution to overhead (fixed costs) plus profit suggests a mark-up of 15%, implying a 'nominal price' (nominal cost to the client given standard mark-up) of £15 million to the nearest million.

Now suppose Astro addresses steps 2 to 6, beginning by assessing a 'probability of winning' curve like that of Figure 12.2, the solid part of the curve defining the plausible bidding range.

Then suppose Figure 12.2 is used together with the expected cost of £13 million to produce Table 12.4. It is convenient to round expected direct cost, mark-up and bid values to the nearest

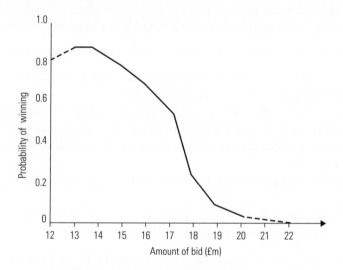

Figure 12.2   Probability of winning against amount bid

Table 12.4   Contribution to profit (margin) for the plausible range of bids

Bid (£m)	Probability Astro wins	Margin if Astro wins (£m)	Expected margin (£m)
13	0.90	.0	0
14	0.88	.1	0.88
15	0.80	.2	1.60
16	0.70	.3	2.10
17	0.55	.4	2.20
18	0.25	.5	1.25
19	0.10	.6	0.60
20	0.05	.7	0.35

million, but two decimal places on probability values in the tabular form is useful to give the piece-wise probability curve a plausible shape and interpretation.

Some of the implications of Figure 12.2 and its tabular portrayal in the first two columns of Table 12.4 usefully drawn from the case study material or linked working assumptions noted here are:

- a bid of £20 million is a plausible maximum, with a chance of winning of around 5%, because the client indicated this was as high as they were prepared to go to Astro staff (and probably to all Astro competitors);
- as Astro drops its bid from £20 million, the probability of winning increases at a modest rate over the range from £20 million to £19 million, it then increases rapidly in the range £19 to £17 million, where most competitors are most likely to bid, reducing to a more modest rate again in the range £17 to £14 million;
- from £14 million to £13 million involves a negligible increase in probability, and attempting to 'buy the work' with a bid below £13 million is counterproductive,
- winning the bid with certainty is not possible, because the client will assume that Astro does not understand what is needed if a bid below a plausible minimum of £13 million is submitted.

Some further implications of Table 12.4 usefully drawn from its development and discussion are:

- each £1 million added to the bid increases the 'margin if Astro wins' (a conditional expected margin given Astro wins to be more precise) by £1 million;
- each £1 million added to the bid increases the 'expected margin' (an unconditional expected margin defined by the product of columns two and three) by an amount which peaks at a £17 million bid, thereafter declining because the decline in the probability of winning dominates the increase in the bid;
- bidding at the nominal price of £15 million involves a lower expected margin than bidding £17 million;
- bidding at £17 million is the 'text book optimal solution', the opportunity efficient choice in terms of the numbers used and the objectives addressed explicitly.

However, in practice it is vitally important to avoid providing the decision takers with a simple recommendation 'bid £17 million'. What they need is Table 12.4 and the underlying Figure 12.2 as a basis for discussion. This discussion has to consider opportunity efficiency in terms of *all* objectives that matter. It also has to consider the robustness of the analysis. Consider some of the issues which need to be addressed.

If the expected direct cost is of the order of £13 million, and if Figure 12.2 is roughly consistent with the beliefs of the Astro staff with appropriate knowledge, then bidding at £17 million will maximize short-term expected margin. However, if Astro is short of work and bidding opportunities at present, or winning this bid has important long-term profit implications, a £16 million bid deserves serious consideration. The decline in expected margin is only £0.1 million, and the increase in the probability of winning is from 0.55 to 0.70. At the very least, a refined analysis of bids in the range £16–17 million may be worth consideration, including descriptive scenario assessments of the softer issues with summary labels added to Table 12.4.

A bid of £15 million increases the chance of winning from 0.70 to 0.80, with an expected margin reduction of £0.5 million – a smaller increase in the chance of winning for a larger decrease in expected margin. However, if Astro is very short of work and bidding opportunities at the moment, or this is a very important contract to win for long-term marketing advantage reasons, a refined analysis in the range £15–17 million may warrant serious consideration, formally addressing the qualitative issues.

A bid of £15 million for reasons just discussed may be sensible, but a bid of £15 million because this yields the 15% mark-up required on average as corporate policy is not a good idea. Using a standard mark-up and ignoring Figure 12.2 plus Table 12.4 implications involves over-pricing in tough markets, under-pricing in favourable markets, which is an opportunity inefficient pricing policy. Opportunity efficiency requires consideration of the Table 12.1 tradeoffs plus all associated tradeoffs including non-quantified objectives.

These tradeoffs will not be significantly affected by minor changes to the expected direct cost or Figure 12.2, and any decision takers' 'what ifs' are amenable to modelling. These 'what ifs' modelled for greater clarity could include explicit treatment of 'semi-variable overhead costs' – costs which are not strictly 'direct' (variable) or fixed.

'What ifs' of particular interest may include sources of uncertainty and risk which can be transferred to the client, perhaps without making this too obvious, and features of the bid competitors may not have which increase the chance of Astro winning.

If this kind of analysis is used regularly, then recording the probability of winning as forecast by curves like Figure 12.2 will allow feedback to correct significant bias in the estimation of such curves. For example, if ten bids each have an estimated probability of winning of 0.5, but only one is won, optimistic bias is obvious. Simpler linear curves in a narrower plausible range can be used to get started or just to keep it simple. A complete lack of relevant data is not a good reason for avoiding formal quantitative analysis. A probability of winning curve like Figure 12.2 is implicit in any bidding process, as are the tradeoffs which lead to departures from the short-run margin maximizing bid, and they are clearly relevant. Keeping them invisible does not mean they go away. Capturing them with explicit working assumptions allows appropriate exposure and discussion, resulting in more informed judgements.

The use of a table like Table 12.4 allows quantification and data accumulation to test subjective estimates where this is feasible and useful, facilitating the use of this information in conjunction with management judgements about softer issues such as long-term market advantages associated with winning a bid, and the advantages of work to keep otherwise idle or redundant staff busy.

One major source of uncertainty that contractors have to deal with, but clients do not, is the chance that the contractor's bid will not be accepted. For a contractor to address this source requires the special PUMP features illustrated by Figure 12.2 and Table 12.4, generalized if need be, to more complex bidding processes. However, contractors do not have to accept responsibility for a source of uncertainty if they can place it with the client, and they need not make this clear to the client, if it does not pay them to do so.

Clients who believe they should adopt a tough stance with their contractors, in a 'zero-sum game' sense, often overlook the tendency of such a stance to evoke features of 'the winner's curse'. The winner's curse means the winning contractor is the contractor most likely to have:

1. least understood the task, or
2. is the most hungry for work because they are the least capable, or
3. is prepared to tell the biggest lies, or
4. some combination of all the above.

Using this case study to ensure that seminar participants who are very client oriented understand their contractor's perspective, and the issues associated with the winner's curse, has usually been very much appreciated. The message they take away is the importance of understanding how their actions will be responded to by their contractors.

Contractors attending the same seminar usually enjoy syndicate group working with the staff of clients they do business with, or potential clients, for obvious but also subtle reasons related to general understanding of what matters and how issues should be approached. Even if the client-oriented participants with whom they share a seminar are from very different industries, they usually take away a better understanding of client behaviours. This kind of learning generalizes.

Having a clear view of relevant stakeholder perspectives

Going back to the original use of the Transcon case for IBM, involving 40 or so different culture change process group applications, it was successful at least in part because each seminar syndicate group of about six participants mixed sales, systems, and a full range of other staff.

What may be self-evident – but is nevertheless worth emphasis – is the importance of common understanding by all project parties of how relationships can and should work. This includes regulators, lawyers who deal with contractual issues, bankers who provide funding, and so on. A whole lifecycle view of the PUMP pack encourages and facilitates the interactions necessary to achieve this common understanding. Any organization contemplating a full lifecycle implementation of PUMP pack concepts might use their own variant of IBM's Transcon case study approach to get all relevant parties working together in a context all can relate to.

Portfolio/programme/project boundary issues

If all projects are addressed from their concept stage initiation through to their strategy gateway via a common PUMP pack approach, it should be clear that some projects may be usefully seen as 'programmes' in specific 'portfolio of project' terms (with common aims and shared resources for example), while corporate strategy might be usefully defined in other 'portfolio of projects' terms. This book does not address alternative views of what constitutes a 'programme' or a 'portfolio' as distinct from a 'project', because it uses 'project' in inclusive terms. Indeed, we argue that clarity about project uncertainty management in the sense addressed by this book needs to be part of any meaningful distinctions. Although providing appropriate boundary definitions is not an arena we wish to enter at present, it might be useful to note that those who want to emphasize distinctions like 'programmes are about delivering benefits, while projects have more directly defined deliverables', are talking about 'projects' in our terms in both cases. The need to consider portfolios in the Highways Agency sense as discussed in Chapter 2 raises obvious additional issues, like which sources of uncertainty are best treated at portfolio and project levels, but misses no insurmountable difficulties.

To emphasize the inclusive nature of 'projects' addressed in this book, reconsider the UK Nirex example discussed earlier. The 'rock characterization project' addressed initially was in effect one phase or stage of the one big project the organization was set up to address – long-term storage of UK intermediate level nuclear waste. The whole enterprise became the focus when the DoE became involved in deferring the overall project. And a key issue from the outset was ownership by some of the main customers – ambiguity about client/contractor/customer relationships – which needed early attention at board level if the scientific and engineering programmes were to achieve the coherence they needed. It is just not sensible to argue that conceptually different and incompatible approaches are needed because we are addressing different slants on an organization like UK Nirex. One coherent framework needs to be general enough to cope with all aspects, and adaptable enough to provide clarity efficiency in any given application.

However we define big and complex projects and programmes, we need a coherent way of breaking them down and putting them together again that reflects important considerations such as shared goals, shared resources, and the scope for both competition and collaboration.

Further, however portfolio management is approached, it needs to reflect all the concept stage considerations addressed in this chapter.

A platform for managing these tensions needs to be part of any portfolio/programmes/project boundary structure that avoids potentially limiting framing assumptions. That is the aim of a PUMP pack approach.

Conclusion

For many years in many organizations, an early review of the project 'what' has been an important component of PUMPs primarily concerned with execution and delivery. Formally embracing the seven-Ws structure of Figure 1.2, and integrating its treatment over all the project lifecycle stages portrayed by Table 1.3, are obvious steps to take if the organizational traditions that may prevent it can be set aside. In particular, full integration of a PUMP with an appropriate level of clarity during the concept-shaping stage of the lifecycle will always pay dividends. A basic business case cash flow framework raises issues associated with discount rates, multiple objectives and multiple constraints. More 'soft' issues may become apparent and in urgent need of structured thinking. Further, addressing concept-shaping intensifies the problems associated with different disciplines using very different framing assumption perspectives. The need to link projects to overall corporate strategy is also a new dimension – but relevant for all following stages.

One of the key messages from fully integrating the concept-shaping stage with the rest of the strategy stages in PUMP terms is that the necessary tests of robustness and flexibility applied to all assumptions have to include assumptions of convenience adopted by some widely used financial economics approaches. Economists have understood the bias associated with using an inappropriate discount rate for at least 50 years. If the discount rate is too high, long payback projects which should be accepted are rejected, and 'quick buck' projects which should be rejected are accepted. An estimate of the actual cost of capital is usually appropriate. Increasing the discount rate by adding opportunity cost to the discount rate is convenient because it avoids a second hurdle test, and it avoids thinking about the funding constraints associated with sources of finance, but it is a source of systemic bias as important as 'strategic misrepresentation'. This is a source of bias which needs to be avoided at government, corporate and domestic decision levels. The associated assumptions are not fit for purpose in any context. Further increasing the discount rate by adding a risk premium to the discount rate makes matters worse, drives decisions towards 'quick buck' projects which are risky. Moreover, such an approach will obscure risk associated with objectives not measured by the cash flow estimates that may be part of the wider strategic context. Project strategy cannot be addressed in isolation from corporate strategy without a range of problems, some obvious, some not so obvious.

Simplicity is central to understanding, in the sense that we have to make simplifying assumptions to deal with the complexities of a messy reality. However, untested framing or working assumptions which distort our perception guarantee failure, and repeated use of any assumptions which demonstrably distort our view of reality is negligent.

Using a detailed year by year cash flow model and elaborate financial modelling to assess a decision like deferring nuclear waste disposal, while failing to address uncertainty and risk that really matters, involves a tragic lack of balance about what to simplify and where to add complexity that pays, even if all UK citizens are lucky and 'the right' decision has been made. The authors are not in a position to judge the right and wrong decision, because we do not understand the full strategic context. But it is now clear that even relatively simple household energy conservation decisions are probably biased in the same way, and there is a general need to be very careful about all assumptions we routinely accept without fully understanding their implications.

A key area for method development is finding more formal and structured ways to link the corporate objectives or benefits of a project to concept shaping issues, project and corporate portfolio relationship issues, buyer and seller (client and contractor) issues, design issues and operations issues. As noted earlier, even science-based projects, like research or research and development projects, can lend themselves to formalization of these links, as clearly demonstrated by scientists involved in the UK Nirex rock characterization project. As noted in the NatWest example, the development of benefit management processes for information technology projects can play a similar role in more commercial projects.

One of the key messages from fully integrating the DOT shaping stage with the rest of the strategy stage PUMPs is that the same concepts and models apply, but the language changes significantly.

Consolidating and explaining the strategy is the first mode of analysis for the strategy gateway PUMP. The material this is based on must be produced in the required form from the outset. In a very real sense, 'writing the final report' should begin on day one of a concept shaping PUMP. However, finishing this strategy report effectively involves a lot of craft, a very clear understanding of why analysis was undertaken, and an ability to explain what is important about what was discovered in preceding PUMPs. The systematic structure provided by contributing PUMPs does not replace craft skills. It makes craft skills more useful, and the absence of craft skills more visible. This enhanced visibility may be perceived as a threat by the incompetent, but it is an opportunity for both the competent and their managers.

The authors hope that the case for full integration of the strategy shaping stages in a PUMP framework is convincing. We also hope the case made here for a PUMP pack that includes separable gateway processes, with due care given to all governance issues, is convincing. Certainly it is difficult to see an argument against moving in the direction of one common but adaptable PUMP pack for concept, DOT and E&D shaping stages – all strategy shaping stages whatever lifecycle structure is used. The only real problem we are aware of is the cultural silos and legacy implications of planning processes that maintain separation of these strategy-shaping stages. However, it would be a serious mistake to underestimate the importance of these factors as barriers to change, and we return to them in Part IV.

Chapter 13

Fully integrating the strategy implementation stages

I have never known a battle plan to survive a first contact with the enemy.
—A military quotation, sometimes attributed to Bismarck,
frequently cited in non-military contexts.

This chapter builds on Chapter 12 and all the Part II chapters by considering the application of PUMPs in the lifecycle stages that follow the strategy gateway. Table 13.1 shows the relevant portion of the Table 1.3 stage structure with Table 3.1 roles for PUMPs elaborated for exploration in this chapter.

Commencement of the tactics shaping stage following successful transition through the strategy gateway stage is a watershed for several reasons. One reason, noted earlier, is that from this point sunk costs tend to increase at an accelerating rate. Another reason is that subsequent to progressing through the strategy gateway, there is an increasing resistance to strategic changes by those responsible for strategic choices. Such resistance is often compounded by a significant number of new people becoming involved, who may see it as inappropriate to seriously question earlier thinking and assumptions, perhaps because they have a job description which requires them to refine the details and get on with implementing the strategy.

The transition from strategy gateway to tactics shaping requires an important change in perspective – implementing a strategy assumed to be robust involves a mindset change everyone needs to understand in a common manner. Sometimes this change is highlighted by a contractor taking responsibility for the development of plans previously developed by the client, or different client staff groups taking responsibility, but this need not be the case.

The transition from strategy gateway to tactics shaping is also a natural dividing line for the discussion of how the PUMP needs to vary in each of the lifecycle stages of Table 1.3.

Plans agreed at the strategy gateway using a PUMP pack should be opportunity efficient, anticipating an uncertain future as effectively and efficiently as possible. However, these strategic

Table 13.1   Roles for PUMPs in the tactics shaping and later stages of the project/asset lifecycle

Lifecycle stage	Stage purposes	Roles for the associated PUMP
Tactics shaping	Detailed design and planning for execution, delivery, operation and termination purposes	Help to shift the perspective to implementation Consolidate the strategic plans for implementation purposes Develop detailed designs and plans Develop resource allocation and contracting criteria Estimate the resources required at a more detailed level Assess the contracting strategy at a more detailed level Evaluate alternative procurement strategies Define contractual terms and conditions Determine appropriate risk sharing arrangements Assess the implications of contract conditions Assess and compare competitive tenders Determine the appropriate target costs and bid prices for contracts Evaluate detailed designs and plans
Tactics gateways	Consolidation Governance	Consolidate the base and contingency plans Confirm the deliverables
Execution	Execution	Support the execution of the plans Coordinate, control and monitor progress Modify all targets, commitments and resource allocations as needed Revise estimates of cost on completion or completion time Provide ongoing execution evaluation Assess the implications of changes to designs or plans Support responding to crises and disasters
Delivery	Delivery	Support the delivery of the asset created by the project Identify issues impacting delivery Assess the feasibility of delivery schedules Assess the feasibility of meeting performance criteria Assess the availability of commissioning facilities Assess the reliability of testing equipment Assess the resources needed to modify the delivered asset
O&S	Operation and support (O&S)	Support the operation of the asset created by the project Assess the effectiveness of uncertainty management strategies Provide ongoing uncertainty management of all relevant concerns Update assessments of asset performance Support the design and planning of maintenance Assess appropriate levels of resources required Support responding to crises and disasters
Termination	Termination	Assess options for replacement, decommissioning, or transfer Identify the extent of future liabilities Support the termination of the asset

plans need tactical shaping then implementation. For this strategy implementation process we need PUMPs with some significantly different components to those considered in Part II and Chapter 12. However, all PUMPs should be compatible, and their use needs to be integrated across lifecycle stages as well as across project, operations and strategy boundaries.

Following discussion works through the post-strategy gateway lifecycle stages in the natural order of Tables 1.3 and 12.1, beginning by assuming that the project strategy will be implemented as approved.

Tactics shaping PUMPs and tactics gateway PUMPs

Initiating a PUMP in the tactics shaping stage of a project when no earlier lifecycle stages have used a PUMP is not recommended. Managers who claim that detailed designs and plans are needed before uncertainty or risk can be addressed might be right in certain very special circumstances, but in the authors' experience such managers usually do not understand uncertainty in a PUMP sense, and they are usually thinking in terms of common practice risk management with very little scope or ambition. To rescue a project that has reached a detailed planning stage without prior PUMP attention is usually very difficult, and often exceedingly unpleasant. If it needs to be done, those doing it need extensive experience, credibility and clout. 'Speak softly, but carry a big stick', can be a credo worth remembering.

The purpose of PUMPs in the tactics shaping and tactics gateway stages of the project lifecycle is to use all the analysis of preceding strategy shaping stages as a platform for developing opportunity efficient detailed plans that will pass appropriate assessments and result in a project ready for execution and delivery. Figure 13.1 provides a simple overview of what a PUMP-based approach to tactics shaping and tactics gateway approval involves, addressing two stages in one diagram: formulating tactical plans, followed by 'supporting and convincing' at the tactics gateway. Following subsections focus on new PUMP pack features underlying Figure 13.1.

'Tactical plans' are base plans, contingency plans and commitment plans – directly comparable to the 'strategic plans' concept discussed at the beginning of Chapter 12, but more detailed, as observed earlier. Tactical plans include action plan designation of base and contingency plans where appropriate. 'Action plans' are the front-end tactical plans which involve a commitment to implementation in terms of taking specific actions. Organizations that do not distinguish between stretch targets and firm delivery commitments at both strategic and tactical levels have a common but serious basic problem, even if they distinguish contingency plans. However, organizations that fail to distinguish between action plans and contingency plans compound these problems.

All tactics shaping PUMP deliverables involve choosing an appropriate level of detail for tactical planning, and rolling that planning forward within the boundaries provided by the strategic plans to reach a plausible tactical horizon. Achieving what is required by the strategic plan is the basic goal. If the whole of the tactical plan looks feasible, committing to the action plan component can follow.

A key difference between the strategy shaping PUMPs discussed in previous chapters and the tactics shaping PUMPs of interest now is the nature of the PUMP define phase. In a tactics shaping PUMP following earlier use of strategy shaping PUMP approaches, the define phase should involve initiating tactical planning within an agreed strategy in terms of the basic plans plus contingency plans developed earlier. Tactical plans developed before an opportunity efficient strategy is approved are often a waste of time – and they may be a very dangerous waste of time, because they tend to inhibit free thinking about shaping strategy. In some circumstances there may be valid reasons for selectively developing detailed tactical plans prior to agreeing strategic plans in order to test a strategy – but to assume that detailed plans developed before a strategy is approved will be suitable for implementation is usually asking for trouble.

Strategic planning should involve input from those who will have to implement the strategy where appropriate. Oversight of tactics by those responsible for strategy may also be important,

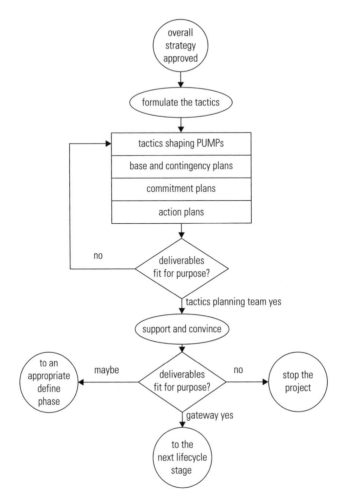

Figure 13.1   An overview of tactics shaping and tactics gateways

but a significant degree of devolution is usually implied by the transition from strategic to tactical planning. This devolution is motivated by the need for effective and efficient use of more people operating at a more detailed level. It usually involves a range of important implications.

One important implication is the use of different tactics shaping PUMPs by different tactical planning groups to pursue their own objectives within the overall project strategy. Using a North Sea offshore production platform project example, the strategy team member who provided input about the 'modules' which sit on the 'platform jacket' may now have to manage a team planning the details of half a dozen very different modules designed and constructed in different places by different organizations. He or she may need a very different PUMP to the leader of the group responsible for the jacket or the pipeline, and each of these PUMPs may be different to the portion of the strategy shaping PUMPs used earlier for these components of the project. For example, at a strategy level Magnus project 'module installation' was a short duration activity modelled in very simple PERT terms to capture considerable ambiguity without the associated detail, but tactical planning involved extensive simulation studies to explore complex decision sequences, using discrete event simulation techniques (Pidd, 1996, ch. 9).

Decomposition of plans and uncertainty

The level of detail and the tactical/strategic emphasis are drivers that should significantly shape the PUMPs used at different levels of planning, along with related issues like the objectives of the analysis. This may have significant modelling implications. For example, at a strategic level, ambiguity associated with activity precedence relationships may require probabilistic modelling (Cooper and Chapman, 1987), and may make some standard network planning software inappropriate. However, at a tactical level, reasonably strict precedence relationships may be a viable assumption.

Significant decomposition of plans and associated uncertainty has important implications for the nature of clarity efficient approaches to planning. In general, the greater the decomposition, the simpler PUMPs should be expected to be, because less is at stake, and more plans need attention. However, there may be important exceptions, like the Magnus module installation example above. More than one level of decomposition may be involved.

For example, an offshore North Sea project treated in terms of 40 activities in the strategy shaping stages might involve 10–100 times more activities for tactics shaping purposes. As indicated above, a strategy level activity like 'fabricate the modules' which did not distinguish different types of platform modules earlier can now be decomposed into half a dozen sets of activities to consider each module individually, recognizing different lead times for different items of equipment and some very different sources of uncertainty. A lower level PUMP necessarily involves much more detail in terms of the activity structure and the other six Ws, and usually it will involve much less payoff for effective uncertainty management, so the use of simpler models should be anticipated on average. However, some situations may warrant significant sophistication. For example, one very useful study involved in the Magnus project looked at onshore versus offshore completion of several particular platform modules, trading off the factor of 10 increases in cost for offshore completion with the benefits of getting all modules installed earlier.

Continuing with this illustrative example, for large projects involving a lot of uncertainty it may be worth seeing the lower level PUMP at this point as a 400 activity mid-clarity variant of a 40 activity high clarity PUMP used earlier, and embedding a minimum clarity 4000 activity PUMP variant in it to reach the level of detail needed for implementation. The minimum clarity variant might use P10 and P90 value estimates interpreted as stretch targets and commitments, but use a basic deterministic critical path analysis algorithm to compute target and commitment planning dates. That is, a single level of detail approach to uncertainty management for complex projects is very ineffective, because it does not distinguish strategy and tactics effectively. At least two levels are recommended to increase effectiveness efficiently. Three or more levels might be appropriate in some cases, implying intermediate planning levels which may need a distinguishing label. This is consistent with the notion of hierarchical network structures often used for planning large projects.

Whether or not even a very large project requires more than two levels of detail, with a very decomposed activity level structure at the bottom, will depend on issues like the extent to which work is done in-house or contracted out, the extent to which in-house work is managed centrally or locally, and so on.

Small projects involving modest levels of uncertainty might use only five to ten activities at the strategic planning level, and a purely deterministic approach to planning in stretch target terms at the tactical level. This two-level approach might be suitable for quite a wide range of projects if the number of activities at the strategic level is treated as variable, but a deterministic approach to stretch target tactical planning is preserved. When and how project size and uncertainty makes simple and more complex uncertainty management approaches appropriate at different levels is not clearly definable in general terms. However, a minimum of two levels is useful for most projects, and it is important to link the levels in terms of a nested structure.

A deterministic approach to tactical planning in stretch or commitment value terms does not mean that important features of the generic PUMP should not be preserved. For example, deterministic tactical plans in activity terms should still embed proactive responses, identified sources of uncertainty should still be linked to contingency plans, ownership of uncertainty in financial and managerial terms still needs clear definition, and a judgement that this collective uncertainty is effectively captured by the strategic level portrayal of it is essential. The only thing that may be missing is a bottom-up probabilistic analysis to confirm the strategic level's top-down view of what has now been decomposed in order to clarify the detail for implementation purposes.

These different levels in terms of activity decomposition should be reflected in related treatment of the other six Ws – the level of detail in terms of timing, resource definition and allocation, design detail, and the management of different party motivation issues.

Base plans and contingency plans deliverables

Developing distinct contingency plans at a tactical planning level suitable for strategy implementation may be very important. That is, reactive responses may need to be identified, and associated trigger points and other decision rules may need to be developed, prior to committing to associated tactical base plans. It is important to extract base plans plus contingency plans at the end of the tactical plan formulation process, as a summary for those who have to execute the plans without needing to read the PUMP documentation that explains their development. However, it can be very beneficial to provide PUMP reports and briefings to everyone who might do their job better as a result. This implies tailoring PUMP reports to their readers, and to more than one set of readers in many cases.

Commitment plans deliverables

There is an obvious need for commitment plans in the P80 or P90 scenario sense at a tactical level where tactical plans intersect with overall strategy or the tactical planning of other groups. However, these commitments will be limited in number relative to the detail of the base and contingency plans, and they may operate at a higher 'summary' level. This issue can be linked to General George Patton's belief (Ambrose, 1994), paraphrased here as 'You should tell people what needs to be done, but not tell them how to do it – you will be amazed at the ingenuity people have if you give them the opportunity'. Patton's views about letting those responsible for executing plans lead detailed planning articulates a widely held view in military circles which makes sense anywhere. It clearly had a central role in one of the most successful actions on D-Day, undertaken by a small British unit, explored in detail in *Pegasus Bridge, June 6, 1944* (Ambrose, 1988). For all projects it is an important issue over the whole of the strategy-shaping stages as well as during the tactics-shaping stages as is a two-way dialogue and gateway processes which reflect these issues.

Action plans deliverables

What we will call 'action plans' are plans requiring commitment to action if an overall plan is approved. For example, contracts put in place to undertake activities, supply resources or components will be expensive to change. It is important to distinguish such plans, and associated action planning horizons, and clearly identified tactical plans which are also action plans should be deliverables from the tactics-shaping PUMPs.

Clarified action and tactical planning horizons as a basis for all deliverables

Uncertainty management for projects usually requires early consideration of appropriate planning horizons with respect to project plans at a strategic level. Often these are captured in the definition of distinct project phases managed as separate sequential projects. For example, a project planned to take 15 years may involve a 'phase one' component project, which is effectively the first three or four years, followed by several subsequent phase component projects, in the form of Figure 1.1a. Usually these component projects are defined in terms of deliverables, such as feasibility, development, permission to proceed from a regulator, an operational prototype, production of the 'first of class', and so on. This kind of phase structure may serve several purposes, but an important motive is usually controlling commitments – if the first phase does not achieve its objectives, later phases will be reconsidered, and there may be little benefit in going below a strategic level of planning for later stages until their approval looks imminent.

Whether or not a phased approach is used for strategic planning, planning horizons are also important for lower level tactical planning. Even within a single layer of tactical planning, there is a clear need to adopt different levels of detail for different purposes. Also there is no need for detailed planning too far into the future. Further, there is a clear need to distinguish plans that involve a commitment to action with linked planning horizon concerns.

Prior to implementation, tactical plans require explicit consideration of an appropriate planning horizon, a 'tactical plans horizon'. A key driver of an appropriate tactical plans horizon is the range of associated 'action plan horizons', the initial period of the tactical plans horizon that requires detailed action plans *plus* firm commitments in terms of taking specific actions because of lead time considerations.

It would be very convenient for planners if all the appropriate action horizons were a single time period, say three months, associated with a regular review and revision of plans as necessary. However, different action horizons will be appropriate where there are different lead times for different resources. For example, ordering critical materials or contracting for critical equipment may involve relatively long lead times. Hence, it is usually useful to choose a shortest common denominator review period for tactical plans, like a week or a month, but recognize longer action horizons for specific types of resource.

It would also be convenient if detailed planning could be confined to the action horizon. However, tactical horizons longer than action horizons are usually required, and a longer common tactical horizon allows optimization of action plans with effective consideration of what follows the different action horizons.

Experience with and without PUMPs suggests that too much detailed planning beyond a plausible tactical horizon is wasted effort. It usually involves largely deterministic planning effort which would be better spent on uncertainty management at this or a higher level of planning, with detailed planning for implementation purposes restricted to a much shorter planning horizon. Detailed planning of actions beyond a plausible tactical horizon is typically undertaken on the implicit assumption that this plan is what will happen – the one thing we can be fairly sure will not happen. Sometimes it is undertaken to reduce uncertainty, a purpose usually better served by a PUMP, allowing for exceptions when detailed planning is used to test strategy, as noted earlier.

Effective use of tactical horizons to produce a significant saving in detailed planning effort usually involves a culture change. In the absence of PUMPs, detailed planning can give people more confidence in higher level plans (or strong nerves), but such confidence is often misplaced. Once people become used to detail being limited to a plausible tactical horizon, they become grateful for the avoidance of what is then seen as unnecessary effort, in addition to seeing the saved time being better spent on a PUMP.

More effective use of action horizons, and more effective change control more generally, are related culture change issues. Once people get used to making the distinction between action plans and other plans, they become more focused on exploiting opportunities associated with flexibility and on resisting costly changes in commitments.

The 'deliverables fit for purpose?' iteration control test and planned iterations

Iterations within PUMPs used to develop opportunity efficient tactical plans from strategic plans should be planned for, in the same way as iterations in the strategy shaping stages of the project lifecycle should be planned for. Formulating tactics in the tactics shaping stage of the project lifecycle is a lower level version of shaping strategy. There are important differences, but both need an iterative approach for comparable reasons.

The first 'deliverables fit for purpose?' test of Figure 13.1 should be associated with each different area of planning. This separation by 'area' may involve activity/component distinctions – like modules, platforms and pipelines in offshore North Sea projects. It may also involve seven Ws distinctions – detailed design, detailed relationships and contract planning, and so on. However, all areas need joint consideration before moving on to an overall tactics gateway unless separate gateways are used for concurrent detailed planning and execution approaches. This kind of concurrency is an obvious source of uncertainty – and risk as well as opportunity.

Support and convince with respect to tactics

When a tactics planning team are convinced that no more iteration is necessary, because they have a suitably developed action plan, they need to produce a suitable case for gateway approval. Supporting and convincing with respect to project tactics should be straightforward relative to supporting and convincing with respect to project strategy. For a start, it may be the project manager and his senior support team who need convincing – not the board. However, there is still a need to ensure effective communication of all the relevant issues considered by those who prepared the plans to those responsible for approving choices, whose judgement may have to reflect further concerns and issues.

Support and convince tasks interface the abstraction of analysis with the messy details of reality, accommodating the need for different people with different perspectives and concerns to use analysis to reach joint decisions. Finding the most effective manner to interact with people during the process of analysis is a craft, not a science, and it is an important aspect of the craft skills required to achieve a successful PUMP implementation.

The 'enlightened gateway' ideas touched on in Chapters 4 and 12 can become more important as planning moves from strategy to tactics to implementation – in particular the need to overlap shaping plans and consolidate plan improvements, integrating PUMP team effort and the rest of project management.

The 'deliverables fit for purpose?' gateway test and gaining gateway approval

This final 'fit for purpose' test, or set of tests, before the project execution stage or stages begin, ought to be straightforward relative to the earlier strategy gateway assessment. However, sometimes the tactics planning team for a particular area will miss issues picked up by different perspectives brought to bear by an effective gateway process. Sometimes this just means looping back to the define phase of the tactics shaping PUMP for the tactics development team directly involved – a fairly straightforward 'maybe' outcome. However, sometimes several tactical planning teams may be involved. Further, sometimes adjustments to strategy which take the PUMP process back to the define phase at a strategy level is the implication of the 'maybe' outcome. Anticipating and looking for all these possibilities is part of what tactics governance should be about.

Adjustments to strategy which are 'refinements' should be received graciously and accommodated with a minimum of fuss, but they should be avoided if possible. Adjustments to strategy which require a complete rethink will effectively reveal serious earlier errors of judgement or major changes in circumstances. 'Better now than later' is a usefully positive frame of mind to adopt, but 'better still if threats or opportunities had been responded to earlier' is the clear message. Stopping the project at this stage will raise questions about the competence of the project team, and threaten careers. It may also raise questions about the effectiveness of the PUMP pack and associated project management processes. This means that the associated governance process has to have sharp eyes and very sharp teeth if strategic misrepresentation or other biases are possible.

Budgets used for financial control purposes are usually part of what is approved at this stage, and associated estimates and controls should reflect base plan, contingency plan and commitment plan distinctions. The use of estimates for control purposes also requires an understanding of which issues are the responsibilities of which parties, and how parties are motivated to behave. Chapman and Ward (2002) explore these concerns in some detail, especially in chapters 4, 5 and 6. Within the PUMP pack processes these concerns are addressed in the ownership phases. Final details may receive further attention in a still lower level PUMP within the execution and delivery stages, but strategic issues should have been resolved during the earlier project-shaping stages.

As at earlier gateways, approval should be conditional on mutually understood assumptions, including assumptions about major sources of uncertainty that were deemed best treated qualitatively. This implies a need to revisit approval if such assumptions no longer hold. Some 'wiggle room' may be important for those charged with implementing tactics, but 'clarity efficient ambiguity' at an appropriate level from a corporate perspective is a useful framework for viewing it.

Separating gateway approval at a strategic level and gateway approval at a tactical level, with separate associated support and convince tasks, is important both in conceptual terms and at a practical level. In particular, it helps to ensure that a sound strategic plan is in place before detailed planning begins. This makes time that might otherwise be wasted on redundant detailed planning available for uncertainty management at both strategic and tactical levels. This is often an important opportunity to discover and exploit uncertainty for organizations that currently base their confidence in project plans on detailed deterministic planning. For organizations that currently see no need for this distinction, it may be useful to question the level that their risk and uncertainty processes operate at. If it is *de facto* at a tactical level, because of the level of detail used from the outset, the opportunity to address strategic planning issues using PUMP packs appropriate for strategic issues is of considerable importance, and it should be pursued at board level.

Execution and delivery PUMPs

Initiating a PUMP pack in the execution and delivery stages of a project when no earlier stages used a PUMP is not recommended, and there is no plausible case for deferring PUMP initiation until these stages.

If project 'management' is decomposed into 'planning' and 'control', a classic binary division, beginning the execution and delivery stage of the project lifecycle means we are now leaving the realm of pure 'planning'. We are moving into 'control', but maintaining an ongoing interest in 'planning'. Even the very best of plans need adjusting in the heat of battle, and use of a PUMP at this point in the lifecycle is also about the combination of ongoing planning and creative initiative plus training. This combination is essential to bridge the gap between understanding what needs to be done and making plans work during the execution and delivery stages. Execution and delivery involves quite different processes and skills from earlier planning focused stages.

The basic message of this section is that once execution and delivery starts, PUMP use has to be embedded in four quite different 'macro' tasks involving very different modes of operation to the specific or general tasks within PUMPs addressing earlier lifecycle stages:

1. manage planned execution and delivery actions,
2. roll execution and delivery action plans forward,
3. monitor and control,
4. manage crises and be prepared to respond to disasters.

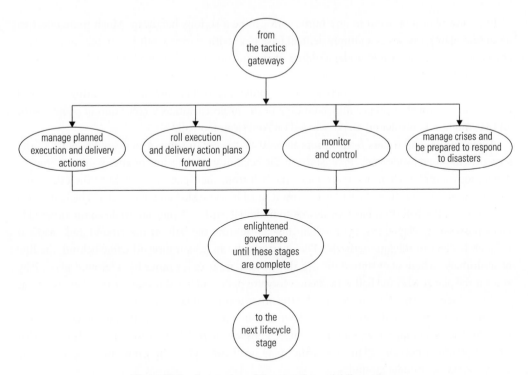

Figure 13.2   An overview of the execution and delivery stages

The 'doing' rather than 'planning' focus of all four macro-task modes is fundamental, and the 'enlightened' and continuous aspects of gateway consolidation and governance are important. Consequently, these four macro-tasks have to be managed in parallel, as indicated in Figure 13.2. The format of this section follows Figure 13.2.

Effort on all four parallel tasks may not be continuous, but effort must be concurrent on all four fronts. This has important practical implications. For example, for a large project, if one person is formally responsible for all four parallel specific tasks, problems are almost inevitable if they fail to delegate each task to a suitable champion, and they do not regularly remind themselves of the need to manage all four simultaneously.

A unique characteristic of the execution and delivery stages relative to earlier lifecycle stages is the 'enlightened governance' mode of operation task following the four parallel macro-tasks *throughout* the execution and delivery stages. This enlightened governance task is conveniently considered after the four parallel tasks, but it has implications for each of these parallel tasks.

Manage planned execution and delivery actions

Operational plans for the immediate 'action horizon' require implementation now, but translating plans into actions is seldom entirely straightforward. Some see the key as planning detail. We see the key as insight about what we want to happen and what might happen, as distinct from what we hope will happen, with particular reference to the motivation of the parties involved, and a clear vision of what really matters.

Excessive planning detail in any framework can be a serious handicap. Much more effective for action plan purposes is a simply defined base plan with clarity about its stretch target status embedded in even a simple understanding of the uncertainties involved, plus relevant contingency plans. It can also be much more 'fun' for those involved, 'empowering' them to make decisions which encourage 'seizing opportunities', providing 'ownership', and generating improved performance through a proper understanding of the project team as a collection of people, with all that implies. Consider an analogy based on American football.

American football differs from European football (soccer to some Americans) because of the structure imposed by 'downs'. 'Play' starts at the beginning of the game or after scoring (a 'touchdown', for example) when one team kicks the ball from their end of the field to the other end. The 'receiver' who catches the ball runs with it until he is tackled and play stops. The team with possession of the ball then has four downs to make 10 yards – if they fail to do so the other side takes possession. Play starts again when the 'centre' lifts the ball off the ground and passes it through his legs to the 'quarterback'. The quarterback can pass it forward while behind 'the line of scrimmage' where play started on this down, or hand it to a runner for a 'ground play'. Play stops if the player with the ball is tackled. A forward pass which is dropped means play restarts at the line of scrimmage. An interception by the other team changes possession.

In this very structured context, each down involves an action plan within a one-down action horizon. Each set of four downs after a change of possession or 10 yards are achieved is a minimal tactical planning horizon. Planning further play until the end of the game might be viewed as a tactics/strategy middle ground.

Each down is separated by a period of re-organization for the next 'play'. This allows detailed planning for the next play in the 'huddle' – all the players on the team with possession form a ring, shoulder to shoulder, to hear the quarterback's instructions. When the quarterback says '93' (play number 93), each player knows what he is supposed to do. The plan for a play specifies base plan actions for all players. On most plays, a score is the planned result if everyone does what they are supposed to, and the opposition behave as expected. The self-evident failure to score with every play does not detract from the value of the planning. Nor does the planning inhibit a skilled running back (ball carrier) or a skilled blocker.

Most project plans are not pre-specified plays, and most projects follow their base plans more closely than American football players. However, the analogy has value in terms of clarifying the distinction between successive action plans and what has to be done to actually move the ball forward. Formal planning in terms of what the plan specifies for each play requires additional informal planning by each player. More generally, the higher the skill levels of the players, the less players need to be instructed in detail, and the more they are able to interpret plans flexibly and effectively in response to what is happening on the ground in 'real time'. Effective use of contingency plans can be seen as part of the training, not part of the plan *per se*.

Routine project planning meetings concerned with implementing planned actions should have some of the characteristics of an American football 'huddle', including each member of the team being reminded what everyone else is planning to do, clarifying how and why they may fail, and reaffirming team 'bonding'. Project activity between meetings should have some of the characteristics of a successful offensive American football play, including each member of the team doing his best at his own prescribed task, capitalizing on opportunities, and minimizing the impact of team-mate failures.

European football (soccer) involves less formal play planning, without the 'downs' structure. This book's failure to develop the analogy to include European football should not be seen as a matter of bias. Some time was spent speculating on European football and other sporting analogies, but their development is left to the reader.

Roll execution and delivery action plans forward

The notion of action horizons embedded in a tactical planning horizon developed earlier in this chapter is very important, to avoid wasteful and inhibiting detailed planning. So is their creative interpretation, as discussed in the last subsection. They are vital parts of knowing what is important and what is not. If the importance of these distinctions is grasped, rolling action plans forward becomes a vital ongoing aspect of the execution and delivery stage use of a PUMP pack.

Rolling action plans and the associated tactical planning horizon forward implies an ongoing tactical planning gateway cycle. Approving new PUMP-based tactical plans on a regular cycle – weekly, monthly, or every six months for example – is a built in feature of a PUMP-based approach. Project review cycles are common practice, with coupled re-planning, so approving new tactical plans on a similar cycle is not a radical departure from most common project management practice.

In terms of the American football analogy, we need to call the next play. The formality of calling the next play may be an appropriate analogy for present purposes, but a chess analogy also has value. In a chess player's terms, we need to plan moves as far ahead as our capabilities and the context allow. The next move is the key priority, but thinking further ahead at a tactical level is also important. Even chess 'masters' do not plan games to 'checkmate' from the outset, but thinking several moves ahead and anticipating what other people are likely to do is what distinguishes good chess players. A tactical planning horizon and its action plan front end needs to be approached in a similar spirit. Until we see what happens, some aspects of detailed planning are an inhibiting waste of time. But anticipation needs to go beyond the next move or play. A key difference between chess masters and other chess players is the effectiveness of the way they anticipate what will happen without detailed analysis of all possible moves. Devices which can be useful in this context include:

- updated detailed base (stretch target) plans for all activities to be undertaken during the action horizon, with ownership of, and responsibility for, sources of uncertainty and contingency plan responses clearly indicated, as well as anticipated progress and commitments which may imply knock-on implications if not met;
- less emphasized but clearly defined tactical plans for the rest of a common tactical horizon;
- a short prioritized list of sources of uncertainty and responses requiring ongoing management attention, with changes in priority emphasized and trends assessed, and both ownership in financial terms and managerial responsibility clearly defined.

Monitor and control

In the context of the monitor and control task, the American football analogy demonstrates a clear distinction between formal and informal monitoring and control at different levels of authority.

For example, a running back with the ball under his arm has to monitor play and respond instinctively in fractions of a second. At the end of each play, the quarterback has to monitor progress to choose the next play. The coach will also monitor at this level, and may intervene, directly specifying the next play. The manager may get involved at this level, and will do so in terms of half-time and end-of-game reviews. End-of-game and end-of-season reviews may involve still higher levels of monitoring and control.

Projects involve very important informal monitoring as well as formal monitoring and change control processes at various levels. As in most other aspects of project management, simple devices are usually the best unless there is clear reason for more complex devices. A device which has proven useful for a century is the Gantt chart, indicating planned progress in relation to progress achieved to date in a simple, visual manner.

A useful update on the classical statistical control chart (plotting actual outcomes within pre-plotted confidence bands) are charts plotting actual outcomes (in cost, duration or other performance measure terms) in relation to pre-plotted target, expected, and commitment values.

Each time the project plan is reviewed, eliminating the sources of uncertainty which have now been resolved, confidence band assessments should contract, unless new sources of uncertainty have been identified, or the sizing of identified sources revised. Plotting how this process is progressing can be useful, especially if some serious setbacks have been experienced but the chance of achieving commitments is stable or improving. However, this is an example of a relatively complex portrayal of the monitoring process, best used infrequently at high levels. The lower the level, and the more frequent the monitoring activity, the simpler the monitoring devices have to be.

It is worth remembering that people directly involved in a project are usually all too well aware when things are going wrong. Usually the concern is not a need for devices to detect when things are going wrong; it is having ways of explaining what is going wrong in order to persuade appropriate people to take appropriate action. More generally, the concern is to ensure that processes are in place that encourage this level of communication to take place in an effective manner.

The distinction between target, expected value, and commitment estimates is of substantial importance in relation to the monitor and control task. The location of the agreed opportunity/risk datum can also be important. Managing the process of reconciling what actually happens to these three types of estimates is essential if the monitoring process is to facilitate an understanding of the implications of departures from base plans.

Given a monitor and control task that is defined to reflect these links and generate responses using the PUMP pack deliverables outlined earlier, monitoring is not a mechanical reactive task. It is a flexible and creative proactive task, concerned with understanding what is happening in 'real time' in relation to what was planned, anticipating future departures from plans, and initiating all necessary revisions to earlier plans.

In some literatures 'weak messages' are a concern – along with the ability of people monitoring to pick up on soft or ambiguous information. A good example is the external auditor of a company's accounts who sees an unusual number of big BMWs in the company car park – not evidence of fraud, but a hint that more than usual diligence might be sensible.

Re-planning selectively using a PUMP pack at both tactical and strategic levels is what control means if a PUMP has been used earlier. The provision for both on a regular basis has to be built into the progress review process. This regularity should not inhibit special reviews when conditions of importance associated with earlier approvals no longer hold. For example, if the off-shore pipe-laying operation, crossing three other pipelines discussed in Chapter 9 severely damaged another pipeline, and immediate re-planning at both strategic and tactical levels is obviously imperative. Less obvious cases near the boundary need clear rules.

Manage crises and be prepared to respond to disasters

Managing planned actions can embrace the variations from base plans that do not warrant contingency plans, as well as the management of variations via contingency plans. A major concern of formal uncertainty management is to avoid nasty surprises that give rise to crises, which then require crisis management. However, it is very unwise to be totally unprepared for crisis.

A 'crisis' might be defined as 'a significant surprise', 'a time of acute danger or difficulty' or 'a major turning point'. The best responses in general terms are based on insight, effective and efficient information systems, being prepared, being able to respond rapidly, and being decisive. Viewing crisis management as contingency management for significant unspecified and unanticipated events, a more effective crisis management strategy will make it effective and efficient to devote less time to contingency planning for specified and anticipated events. This view connects with the concern to develop 'general responses', as discussed in Chapter 8 for example.

A 'crisis' in the 'major turning point' sense noted above may be the result of extreme bad luck or extreme good luck in terms of identified sources of uncertainty as well as 'unknown unknowns'. For example, if a P90 estimate of sales in the first month of a new product are exceeded by a factor of 10 and production capability cannot cope, we have a crisis which becomes a golden opportunity if dealt with, a public relations nightmare if bungled.

If we accept 'crisis' in the sense defined above as something we must be prepared to manage, it follows that a 'disaster' in the sense of 'a crisis we fail to manage effectively' is something we need to be prepared to respond to. At the very least there may be legal liability issues.

Very different kinds of PUMPs are needed for routine planning, crises, and disasters. Some of the key ideas in this book are relevant to crises and disasters, but synthesis with very different literatures is essential, and this synthesis is not attempted here. The focus of this book is 'routine' planning, but those who want to explore relevant crisis and disaster management literatures might start with Smith and Elliott (2006); and Drennan and McConnell (2007).

Enlightened governance

Regular reviews associated with rolling detailed plans forward, re-planning and revisiting both tactical and strategic gateway approvals because associated conditions did not hold, are only part of an integrated approach to governance. The extra is holistic judgement of the project to date on a continuous basis that considers in enlightened terms optimal tradeoffs between all project objectives (both strategic and tactical objectives) plus optimal tradeoffs between project and broader corporate objectives. In terms of all these objective sets, both quantifiable and non-quantifiable objectives are important. This topic will be developed more in Part IV, but three points are worth making now.

First, the absence of enlightened governance is clearly observable in projects that do not achieve their original objectives or a reasonable reassessment of those objectives, because they are held to budgets or timescales that were approved subject to conditions that no longer hold. This may arise because project staff failed, but this does not excuse the governance failure involved. It can be useful (although not necessarily fair) to see any strategic failure as a prima facia governance failure, in the sense that those responsible for governance are presumed guilty unless they can demonstrate innocence. 'Strategic misrepresentation' is central to this issue, as are the responsibilities and presumed capabilities of boards and board of director equivalents.

Second, enlightened governance should start when PUMP pack development starts, at the beginning of the concept-shaping stage. Enlightened governance should be seen as implicit in all Part II discussions in this book, and all the earlier life cycle stages and PUMPs.

Third, if 'planning the planning' in a PUMP focus phase sense is generalized to treat all planning in each lifecycle stage as a project in its own right, then a variant of Figure 13.2 becomes explicit for each lifecycle stage, as an overview of execution and delivery of the *planning process* in that stage. That is, PUMP pack management in each lifecycle stage is a high uncertainty project that can benefit from a PUMP perspective, including enlightened governance.

Moving on to the next lifecycle stage

Completing the execution and delivery stages does not involve a gateway process. However, delivery acceptance tests and compliance tests may have some similar characteristics. In practice, there may be important further overlaps between project lifecycle stages at this point. For example, pilot delivery and operation may involve important 'trial and error' learning processes before 'rollout' of the main programme, and 'leveraging the earlier learning'. These were key features of the success in the NatWest Bank example introduced in Chapter 12.

Operations and support (O&S) PUMPs

Many people involved in projects will very reasonably regard completion of delivery as the end of a project. Some of those concerned with a whole lifecycle perspective may regard delivery as the beginning. For present purposes Figure 13.3 is a convenient summary of the implementation of the operation and support (O&S) strategy approved at the strategy gateway.

Figure 13.3 is very similar to Figure 13.2. One difference is the initial link – from the strategy approval gateway instead of from the details gateway. The other is the inclusion of the tactics-shaping for operations and support before the O&S stage begins. An O&S details gateway may be needed, but it is not shown. These changes are obviously coupled, and both are important; otherwise Figures 13.2 and 13.3 are effectively identical, and this is also important. Conceptually, the rolling process of managing planned actions is the same for both stages, as is (a) the process of rolling action plans forward, (b) the monitor and control process, (c) managing crises and being prepared to respond to disasters, and (d) enlightened governance, until this stage is complete. Even the process of moving on to the next stage may be comparable, with overlaps between the O&S and termination lifecycle stages – for example, if electricity utility plant is reduced to

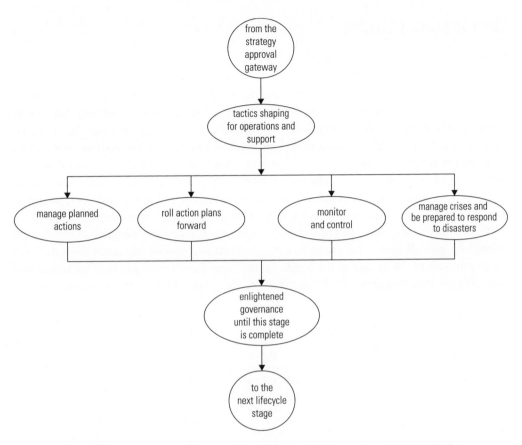

Figure 13.3   An overview of the operations and support (O&S) stage plus prior tactics shaping

emergency use or mothballed. That is, operations management and project management involve directly compatible processes at this level.

Some of the points made in the last section about the execution and delivery stages are worth brief reiteration, to emphasize their importance in both contexts, and the slight differences.

For example, tactical planning for a stable operation may involve seasonal and weekly and even daily cycles with associated demand uncertainty that has to be integrated with supply uncertainty. Running a company making, bottling and distributing beer and running an electricity utility company both have these short-term planning concerns. Tactical planning for an evolving operating environment may add additional uncertainty. Further, integration of maintenance and redundancy and new build decisions may be essential, as in the case of an electricity utility. Further still, strategic operations planning and linked corporate strategic planning have to interface at this stage. Operations management as a whole 'owns' this stage, and strategic operations management thinking needs to be fully integrated with corporate strategy. Changes not anticipated earlier in the lifecycle need corresponding ownership, and governance needs to address responsibility for unanticipated changes that carry high costs which could have been avoided.

Termination PUMPs

For present purposes termination management is usefully summarized by Figure 13.4.

Figure 13.4 is identical to Figure 13.3 apart from the tactics-shaping addressing termination instead of operations and support. The extent of this similarity is also very important. For example, tactics shaping for termination does not have to start immediately when strategy is approved, but it must be completed before termination actions start, a tactics gateway may be necessary, the devil may be in the detail, and tactical plans may not survive their first contact with reality.

Termination from the perspective of the project owner may be carefully pre-planned years in advance, as in the termination of offshore oil production or the decommissioning of a nuclear power station. However, it may be linked to selling an asset once it has proved itself, or market conditions allow, or some other conditions are met, which imply changes in ownership perspective.

These changes in perspective can require a whole project lifecycle perspective to clarify what is involved from all angles. For example, a design, build and operate contractor for a road will see termination of the project as the handover date after a contracted period of operation, perhaps 20 years after completion of the construction stage. After 20 years the government agency

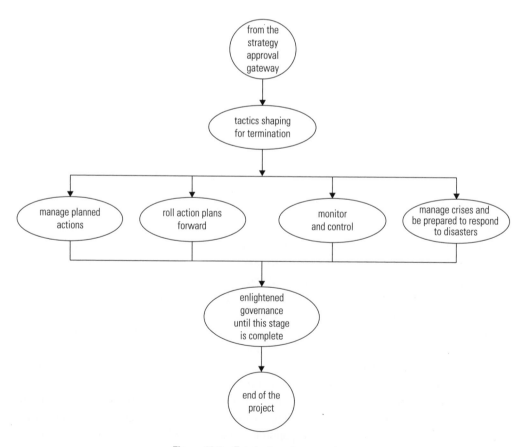

Figure 13.4   Termination stage overview

responsible for the road acquires maintenance obligations which were contracted out earlier, as part of a contract also transferring design and build responsibilities, so their version of the project is ongoing. The basic rationale of this kind of contract is usually shaping contractor incentives – to encourage the contractor to design and build maintenance considerations into the original road. Such incentives can work very well. However, if the contractor's *actual* cost of capital is very different from the government's *actual* cost of capital, both project evaluation and the actual economics of the road may be changed by the choice of contracting approach in ways that are not understood by the agency, the government or the public. This effect could be managed – by the government providing a form of mortgage for the road to the contractor, at a government bond-funding interest rate. However, if those responsible do not see the uncertainty involved in advance, they cannot manage it, and others may never see it. The wide variety of public sector and private sector partnership approaches to contracts currently used in the UK and elsewhere involves similar issues – PPP (Public Private Partnership), PFI (Private Finance Inititive) and Tif (Tax increment funding) for example.

Project, operations and strategy linkages

Thus far the focus of Part III has been the extension of PUMPs and PUMP pack use to all asset lifecycle stages with minimal attention to the strategy – operations – project links that shape projects. When considering the concept-shaping stage, links to corporate strategy were developed in terms of multiple test alternatives to single hurdle rate discounting approaches. The need to align project and corporate objectives at that point, and update this alignment thereafter, was noted. However, we deferred considering formulating and updating the strategy – operations – projects relationships that drive projects by assuming that a project would be implemented as approved. Several aspects of seeking full integration between projects, operations and strategy now need to be explored. The example of strategic planning in Ontario Hydro introduced in Chapter 1 provides an initial basis for discussion.

Ontario Hydro strategic planning example

At the beginning of the 1990s, Ontario Hydro sought Ontario government permission to adopt a strategy which involved ten new nuclear power stations over a planning horizon of 25 years, as out-lined in Chapter 1. The Independent Power Producers Society of Ontario (IPPSO) were concerned that their commercial interests would suffer if 'too much' nuclear power was provided relative to demand given all the relevant uncertainty, because of the way 'avoided costs' determined the tariffs for privately produced electric power. Consequently, as official interveners, IPPSO initiated a critical study, funded by Ontario Hydro, of Ontario Hydro's approach to strategic planning (Chapman, 1992a).

A fundamental criticism in the resulting report was the lack of appreciation of uncertainty in Ontario Hydro's approach, as noted in Chapter 1. This lack was closely coupled to a need for a *medium*-term planning horizon, in addition to the short and long-term horizons employed, recognising that all three horizons involve very different aspects of uncertainty which need to be approached in different ways.

The long-term planning horizon of 25 years involves the question 'what mix of hydro, nuclear, thermal and other renewable power or conservation should Ontario Hydro aim for in 25 years time?' This is a classic portfolio analysis problem, with high level strategic risk associated with estimating long-term costs incorrectly and getting locked into an inappropriate portfolio of power sources. This problem needs answering in terms of 'what should Ontario Hydro aim for now, bearing in mind plans can be changed as time unfolds?' Current priorities for 'new build' are defined by the gap between where Ontario Hydro is now, and the optimal mix in 25 years' time as assessed now. The stage Ontario has reached now is defined by current operating plant, planned refurbishments, and planned retirements.

The medium-term horizon of about 1–5 years involves the question 'At what point should Ontario Hydro commit to which new power stations, bearing in mind new build priorities, planned refurbishments and retirements, plus anticipated demand?' This is a classic decision analysis problem, with medium level strategic risk associated with new capacity coming on stream too soon or too late, additional costs for an interim period because power needs to be imported at higher prices, or old and inefficient plant needs to be run, or plant needs premature shutdown, or power needs to be exported at lower prices. The same risk and opportunity efficiency concepts are involved as for the long-term horizon, but the nature of the uncertainty, opportunity and risk are very different.

The short-term horizon of about one year involves the question: 'Which plant needs to be run on load and on standby for the next hour, the rest of today, the rest of the week, and so on?' This is a classic short-term operations analysis problem which most utilities are very good at, needing no further comment here or in Chapman's (1992a) report. It was the medium and long-term distinctions that Ontario Hydro's strategy proposals did not make, and that some other organizations need to make more clearly.

There are important connections that need to be made between the different uncertainty management processes within these different horizons. For example, if all electric power generation units selected at the highest level are very large units, this means reserve capacity has to be larger than would be the case if smaller units were selected, because any plant failures will be bigger. This should be reflected in the cost estimates used at the top level as well as in medium and low level plans. However, there is enough separability to be useful.

In these terms the focus of projects–operations–strategy joint decisions are medium-term planning decisions, within a long-term framework which has to roll forward on a regular review basis – the 25-year horizon will never be reached, and commitments to build can be made in stages. The equivalent of a concept gateway approval might put a project in a queue for possible building in 10 years' time. The equivalent of a tactics gateway might mean the start of construction as soon as possible. Intermediate gateways have intermediate implications.

From a PUMP pack for projects perspective, a key feature of the recommended Ontario Hydro approach to three horizons and associated gateways was early ordering of new facilities in concept-shaping stage terms, followed by investment in further lifecycle stage planning in an orderly manner, with detailed planning just before the start of execution and delivery. An important aspect of this planning is flexibility to respond to shifts in the perceived 25-year horizon targets, with minimal impact on projects about to be executed. This flexibility is directly linked to a concern to avoid opportunity inefficient choices in terms of building facilities that involve higher costs than alternatives because of uncertainty about future electric power generation costs.

This implies projects need to change with corporate strategy changes at each stage in their lifecycle *where this is cost effective*, but preferably not during detailed planning, and hopefully not during execution and delivery.

More details of the associated strategic planning framework are provided in Chapman and Ward (2002, ch. 11). The concern here is the interface between projects and both operations and strategy planning in the medium and long term, and the extent to which comparable frameworks for other kinds of projects and organizations have similar implications.

Generalizing the planning horizon and gateway implications

All organizations have to develop their own approach to integrating operations–strategy–project issues, and such approaches may take a very different form to that suggested for Ontario Hydro in the example above. However, all organizations need to address the same basic questions. What planning horizons are needed? How are these horizons linked to project gateways?

Most organizations do not have to deal with such large-scale physical asset choices involving such long lives and unpredictable operating costs as faced by utility companies such as Ontario Hydro. By way of a very different example, when NatWest Bank undertook the branch banking computerization programme outlined in Chapter 12, the 'asset' was a new way of doing business, a mixture of hardware, software, business process, organizational structure and marketing projects usefully viewed as a corporate change programme. The equivalent of the 25-year target portfolio of power stations was a business model target at a much shorter horizon. The equivalent of the medium term involved pilot projects to introduce early versions of new hardware and software and staff training, to learn from carefully selected branch staff before attempting rollout of the main programme, which would itself be updated and revised as the organization as a whole learned from the change experience. The same basic questions included: 'What planning horizons are needed for the pilots and the main rollout?' 'How are they linked to programme gateways?' and 'How should gateway and horizon interfaces be managed to avoid making technical and financial commitments earlier than necessary?'

Change management programmes can look very different from traditional asset creation projects, and the language can reflect a very different perspective. However, some of the fundamentals do not change, including the need to address horizons and gateways which interface the strategy–operations–project trio in the way outlined in this section.

Lifecycle and contract structure interfaces

For organizations building and operating power stations, roads, oil fields, nuclear waste disposal facilities, weapon systems, commercial computer systems, or any of the other 'client side' examples used earlier, a common problem is: 'What kind of contracts should be used?' This simple question does not have a simple answer. Ward and Chapman (2008) and Chapman and Ward (2008) provide recent hints at general answers by the authors. However, a specific issue which is worth attention here is the need to address asset lifecycle and contract structure interfaces.

In the 1970s, BP's version of SCERT reflected an approach to contracting based on BP understanding and managing uncertainty over the whole project lifecycle, addressing risk and opportunity in risk and opportunity efficient terms, using contractors largely employed on a time and materials basis. In the 2010s, most client side organizations do not have the in-house capability to take this approach. They need contractor input to design strategy and all detailed planning as well as execution and delivery, either for political or economic reasons. This raises problems about contractual structures that cross lifecycle stages, because this implies gateways embedded in the middle of contracts, and difficulties associated with competitive bidding and continuity. For example, if the Highways Agency uses one contractor to undertake the design, operations and termination strategy-shaping stage for a major road programme, how can they use the same contractor to undertake the execution and delivery strategy-shaping stage, the tactics-shaping stage, and then the execution and delivery stages – with obvious continuity benefits – without loss of benefits associated with competitive bidding for each stage? The short answer is a design and build contract, which might be extended to a design, build and operate contract. Choices about contractual structures are not just about continuity benefits. They are about benefits associated with motivating contractors to do the best they can for clients and those their clients serve, by aligning motivation with 'enlightened incentives'.

These choices are *very* important; they need to be made fairly early in the project lifecycle – if not at a corporate level for all projects – as they substantially impact on PUMP pack deliberations and associated governance processes for the whole of the remaining project lifecycle.

Conclusion

The first part of this chapter considered particular features of a PUMP applied after the strategy gateway watershed, in the detailed planning part of the lifecycle designated in Table 1.3 as the tactics-shaping and tactics gateways stages. Building on earlier PUMPs to help shape and test plans at a tactical level is the core of what is involved. The tactics-shaping PUMP provides a bridge between the output of the strategy shaping stages as approved at the overall strategy gateway and the action plans needed to start the execution stage of the project lifecycle. Craft skills, and a clear grasp of purposes and possibilities, are important.

In subsequent execution, delivery, and utilization stages, PUMP use has to be embedded in four quite different 'macro' tasks:

- manage planned execution and delivery actions;
- roll execution and delivery action plans forward;
- monitor and control; and
- manage crises and be prepared to respond to disasters.

The 'doing' rather than 'planning' focus of all four of these macro-tasks involves very different modes of operation to the specific or general tasks within PUMPs addressing earlier lifecycle stages. Additionally, these four macro-tasks have to be managed in parallel, and on a continuous basis throughout each post-planning stage, accompanied by enlightened governance over all these four tasks.

It could be argued that the relatively simple treatment of the above tasks in this chapter seriously understates the importance of the 'doing' as opposed to 'the thinking about the doing'. However, this chapter concentrates on building on the platform provided by earlier use of PUMP pack concepts to assist the overall project management process at a level of detail consistent with getting readers started down the road to enlightened planning. There is no intention to play down the importance of post-planning, implementation issues.

Success in all projects needs a great deal more than the PUMP pack ideas developed thus far, and it is important to be clear about the key additional organizational and human behavioural factors such as effective governance, supporting infrastructure, appropriate organizational culture, employee capabilities, incentives, and motivation that can influence both planning and implementation of projects. Such issues have been recurring underlying themes throughout this book and are central to the discussion in Part IV.

One obvious example of what is important beyond PUMP concepts is the organizational structure of a project owning organization, and the place of key project parties within it. Another example is variations in risk taking and leadership styles linked to the personality of key managers. Ambrose (1994, 1988), Dixon (1987) and Furnham (2003) provide interesting and pertinent analyses of such human characteristics. For example, according to Ambrose: during World War II General Eisenhower thought General Montgomery was too risk averse; Eisenhower was prepared to take big risks if he had to, but only after careful calculation; Eisenhower did not have the flair to cope with highly adverse contexts where the opposing General Rommel often excelled; both Rommel and Eisenhower were highly suited to the roles they had to play. Both Ambrose and Dixon offer a number of insights based on the planning and decision-making behaviour of commanders in military contexts where uncertainty and risk were very significant. However, aside from any hindsight bias when seeking lessons about risk taking and decision making after the event, we need to be careful about too much emphasis on project management analogies based on warfare and competitive games with adversaries. Especially in the context of implementing strategy, the role of collaboration and a 'community' view of players instead of a client/contractor/ customer relationships perspective can be *very* important. Project teams can involve complex tensions between cooperation and competition. How these tensions are managed once the action starts is particularly critical. It is part of the process of avoiding 'vicious circles' and building in 'virtuous circles', building teams that operate effectively, dealing with all the complexities of personal relationships and chemistry, and providing 'enlightened governance' that is integrative and holistic. The managerial behaviour aspect of project management seems a rich area for research, provided interpretation uses an appropriate uncertainty management framework.

Part IV

Key corporate implications

Chapter 14 takes a corporate perspective on project opportunity and risk management processes and considers what is involved in establishing and sustaining an organization's PUMP pack capability. This is in part a matter of using what we have learned in Parts I to III to address all relevant corporate implications, in part a practical guide to starting to plan a corporate change that may be needed.

Chapter 15 considers contracts and governance as frameworks for enlightened relationship management. This is in part a question of generalizing the meaning of 'contracts' and 'governance' to accommodate uncertainty associated with the way people behave, in part a practical guide to what this means.

Chapter 16 looks at further important corporate implications of adopting a PUMP approach. This highlights the significant limitations of common practice enterprise risk management. Chapter 16 also considers the corporate capabilities that organizations should develop to support and deliver effective management of uncertainty, opportunity and risk. These capabilities include organizational learning, an appropriate organization culture, appropriate human resources capability, and decision support for addressing uncertainty.

Chapter 14

Developing PUMP capability as a project

All men are equal – all men, that is to say, who possess umbrellas.

—E.M. Forster

Thus far this book has been largely about how to achieve effective and efficient uncertainty management in the context of a single project. From Part I onwards we have argued for the use of a PUMP pack for all individual projects. Part II discussed what is involved in each phase of the basic PUMP in the E&D shaping stage of the nominal lifecycle framework. Part III considered modifications to the content of each PUMP pack member when applied in other project lifecycle stages. However, important corporate implications of this kind of approach to uncertainty management that have not been addressed need attention now.

In this chapter we consider what is involved in establishing and sustaining appropriate project uncertainty management capability for an organization. The issues involved can be explored more systematically if we consider the establishment and operation of this capability as a project in its own right, and examine this project in terms of the seven Ws framework plus the project (asset/change) lifecycle framework of Chapter 1. This approach shapes the structure of this chapter.

As noted in Chapter 6, the application of a PUMP to a given project can be a high risk project in its own right, warranting particular attention to the *process* 'who' question in the focus phase of the PUMP. The process of instituting formal project uncertainty management procedures as a standard corporate policy is also not without risk. The essential threat is that the policy fails to bring sufficient benefits. This may arise because procedures are inappropriate, not properly implemented, or only partially adopted. Different parties or all parties involved may be at fault. Once difficulties are encountered, the credibility of the initiative may suffer, making it very difficult to revive a project uncertainty management capability initiative at a later date. Such threats and their underlying causes need to be recognized and managed in much the same way as they would in any significant organizational change.

Walsham (1992) has suggested a management framework that views organizational change as a jointly analytical, educational and political process where important interacting dimensions are the context, content, and process of the change. Significant aspects of context include: stakeholders' perspectives and relationships between those affected by a particular project, the history of existing procedures and systems, informal networks and procedures, and infrastructure needs (for example, skills and resources required). The process of change involves the dynamics of interaction between participants in a project and others who are affected by it or who can affect it. Significant aspects of process include power-politics and organizational culture. Implementing a significant change like the introduction of a PUMP capability needs to take these dimensions into account.

Other writers on the management of change have related the implementation process to Lewin's (1947) model of planned change which involves three phases: unfreezing–changing–refreezing. Each phase is concerned with changes in the balance of (psychological) forces in the organization and the degree to which they restrain or drive change. Unfreezing involves disturbing the equilibrium of the status quo by increasing the balance of driving forces over restraining forces, decreasing restraining forces, or a combination of these. Effective unfreezing generally involves increasing driving forces while managing a reduction in restraining forces to reduce resistance to change. Refreezing involves the systematic replacement of the temporary change-inducing forces with more permanent forces which can maintain the new status quo.

Forces for change in terms of building project uncertainty management capability are likely to be derived from senior management recognition of the potential benefits as noted earlier. Resistance to change coming from other parties may be due to some or all of the following:

1. parochial self-interest in maintaining the status quo;
2. inability to perceive a need for change;
3. pressure of other work;
4. concern about the costs of introducing new procedures;
5. individuals concerned that they will be unable to carry out the new procedures;
6. uncertainty and suspicion about the nature of the change.

Most people are very reluctant to understand or accept the idea that *their* conceptual framework is flawed. However, they readily understand what is wrong with common practice concepts and tools imposed by their organization if they can see how more general tools can make better use of what they understand, and they usually embrace change which will involve less effort for greater reward. Initial change management is often most effective if it aims for what some people call 'the low-hanging fruit' – the changes that offer clear benefits which are easy to make.

That said, change management is always difficult, and for some people 'sticks' as well as 'carrots' are essential – punishments are needed as well as rewards to stimulate action. A common problem for the authors, when working as consultants, is dealing with risk management professionals and other staff who have a vested interest in preserving inappropriate practice for a range of reasons. In our experience this can be a serious impediment to change that is *very* easy to underestimate. Relatively junior level managers charged with significant project uncertainty management capability development can face related difficulties with other staff at the same, higher or lower levels. Such difficulties need sensitive but firm management, including early and candid discussion with appropriate senior staff. In terms of 'managing downwards', this might include a declared willingness to apply the well-known change management maxim: *'If you can't change the people, change the people.'* This captures the idea that if some staff are not willing to make the necessary changes to their thinking and approach, they should be replaced by people who will. It can be very important to do this sooner rather than later, so that their potential for acting as a brake on change is minimized. In terms of 'managing upwards', there are comparable strategies.

Suggested strategies for reducing resistance to change often include education, communication, participation and involvement, facilitation and support, and offering incentives. Discussing the introduction of strategic planning processes as a significant organizational change, Ansoff (1984) has argued that maximum resistance is produced by a change process which seeks to impose administrative systems before addressing sources of behavioural resistance to change. In contrast, Ansoff argues that minimum resistance is created when a change process builds acceptance of change before introducing administrative systems. In the context of introducing formal PUMPs, the minimum resistance route implies a process which first clarifies the need for and relevance of formal uncertainty management, seeks to improve stakeholders' understanding of what is involved, and provides motivation for individuals to use the new formal processes. Additionally, there is a need to ensure that uncertainty management skills are developed, and that individuals have sufficient time and resources to operate the PUMP on individual projects. Subsequently, administrative systems for coordinating and monitoring the application and effectiveness of PUMP applications can be introduced.

A seven Ws perspective

Effective development of an organization's project uncertainty management capability requires recognition and critical evaluation of where and how project uncertainty management already occurs in the organization, decisions about where attempts to develop the use of PUMPs should be made, and further decisions about who should be involved and what skills and capabilities they need. When considering these issues it is useful to employ a project definition process based on the seven Ws, as depicted in Figure 1.2. This framework can be simplified and scaled back if pre-existing capability is extensive. However, when simplifying in this way, it is important not to confuse project uncertainty management capability as defined in this book with common practice project risk management capability (based primarily on simple risk registers and probability impact grids, for example).

Where: what is the context?

As noted in Chapter 1, the 'context where' is an obvious influencing factor on the development and subsequent operation of corporate capability in project uncertainty management. In particular, important aspects of the organizational context include:

- the position of project uncertainty management capability in relation to other capability development projects or change initiatives;
- the broader economic, political, environmental or technological context and associated expectations held by stakeholders about appropriate uncertainty and risk management capability;
- the organizational infrastructure within which uncertainty management capability must take place and draw on for support.

Clarification of the 'where' context issues for a project uncertainty management capability project need to include a candid critique of all current processes and capabilities relevant to the changes required. Some see this as a task usefully addressed via 'maturity models' that provide a means of benchmarking current capability against external or previous internal capability with a view to moving up a maturity level, towards a top level defined by a maturity model.

Benchmarking project uncertainty management capability deserves attention because any organization that starts a process of development for its project uncertainty management capability will want to monitor progress, and organizations that want comfort or need a spur to action may seek external comparisons.

One approach to developing generic benchmarks involves the concept of a 'risk maturity model' (Hillson, 1997). Risk maturity models attempt to simplify the bench-marking process by defining a specific number of 'maturity levels' ranging from organizations with no formal risk management processes to a state of fully integrated risk management. Three 'risk maturity model' approaches to project uncertainty management capability benchmarking are directly relevant (De Loach, 2000; Hillson, 1997; Hopkinson, 2011).

Table 14.1 summarizes two examples. The first, from De Loach (2000), is an adaptation of a capability maturity model for software engineering organizations developed by the Software Engineering Institute (SEI) of Carnegie-Mellon University (Paulk et al., 1993, 1995). It identifies five levels of maturity: initial, repeatable, defined, managed and optimizing. The second example, from Hillson (1997), is also influenced by the SEI maturity model (Hillson's model). It identifies just four levels of maturity: naive, novice, normalized and natural. Hillson recognizes that some organizations may not fit neatly into the specified categories of maturity, but argues that his four levels 'are sufficiently different to accommodate most organizations unambiguously. ... more than four levels would increase ambiguity without giving sufficient additional refinement to aid use of the model' (Hillson, 1997, p. 37).

In both maturity models, each level is described in terms of a set of characteristics, the main ones being summarized in Table 14.1. DeLoach (2000) provides a short, unstructured list of features for each maturity level. Hillson (1997) provides substantially more detailed characterisation of each maturity level, identifying features under four attributes: 'culture', 'process', 'experience' and 'application'. Hillson then goes on to list the problems facing an organization that wishes to progress from one maturity level to the next, and he suggests lists of actions appropriate for increasing risk maturity.

More recently, Hopkinson (2002, 2011) describes a project risk maturity model (RMM) assessment tool developed by HVR-CSL, now part of QinetiQ, a leading UK listed engineering technology and services company. Using Hillson's four-level capability structure, the RMM assesses project risk management capability in terms of six perspectives:

1. project stakeholders;
2. risk identification;
3. risk analysis;
4. risk responses;
5. project management;
6. risk management culture.

The RMM comprises a collection of 50 questions, each with possible responses corresponding to each of the possible levels of maturity. For a given project, responses contribute to a weighted

Table 14.1 Two examples of risk management maturity models (Ward, 2005)

Example 1 (DeLoach, 2000)

			Maturity Level		
Description	**1 Initial**	**2 Repeatable**	**3 Defined**	**4 Managed**	**5 Optimizing**
Capability	(Ad hoc/chaotic) No institutionalized processes Reliance on competence of individual	(Intuitive) Processes established and repeating Reliance on individuals reduced	(Qualitative/quantitative) Policies, processes and standards defined and uniformly applied across the organization	(Quantitative) Risks measured and managed quantitatively, and aggregated enterprise wide Risk/reward tradeoffs considered	(Continuous feedback) Emphasis on taking and exploiting risk Knowledge accumulated and shared

Example 2 (Hillson, 1997)

			Maturity level	
Description	**1 Naive**	**2 Novice**	**3 Normalized**	**4 Natural**
Definition	No structured approaches for dealing with uncertainty Reactive crisis management Reliance on competence of individuals	Experimentation via nominated individuals and specific projects No effectively implemented organization wide process	Generic risk policies and procedures formalized and widespread	Proactive approach required to risk management in all aspects of the organization Common organization wide understanding of activities, roles and responsibilities for risk management Standard processes and tools tailored to specific applications Formal assignment of responsibility for risk management Organization wide training

rating assessment of risk management capability in respect of each of the six perspectives. The overall assessment of project risk management capability is assessed as the lowest rating across the six perspectives. The rationale for this approach is that process capability in each of the six perspectives is critical to overall risk management capability, so overall capability is only as strong as its weakest capability perspective.

Maturity models provide a pragmatic method for roughly assessing the level of risk management capability in an organization. The main purpose of this is to facilitate the recognition of areas where improvements in risk management processes can be made. In the absence of any other frameworks, such advice is potentially very helpful. However, maturity models do not facilitate appreciation or consideration of the full range of possible choices for opportunity and risk management development.

Some concerns can be raised from a common practice risk management perspective. For example, anchoring advice on a few specified scenarios (the maturity levels), which may not correspond particularly closely to prevailing risk management practices in a particular organization, and the limited way in which maturity levels are described.

More serious concerns include the need for critical analysis from a more general project uncertainty management perspective when introducing a PUMP pack approach. What is missing needs assessment in significantly different terms using a PUMP and KUMP approach to all relevant uncertainty. This implies more ambitious end points and intermediate levels than a Table 14.1 portrayal. Further, ambiguity about longer term strategic plans and goals needs to be balanced by clarity about short-term action plans using a series of activities or component projects. For example, the concept-shaping stage of the overall change project might itself be defined in 'Mark 1' terms using an initial uncertainty management education, buy-in and strategy formation project, followed by an initial demonstration project, followed by a consolidation and strategy review project, and so on, addressing all the issues mentioned earlier. This might be followed by a design and operations-shaping stage for the Mark 1 demonstration project context plus a parallel new concept-shaping stage built around another demonstration project. Embracing enterprise wide uncertainty management via a programme of linked projects might involve an emergent corporate strategy building on the 'Mark 1' concept-shaping stage as it evolves to embrace all aspects of all projects, operations and strategy formation.

Who: who are the parties ultimately involved?

The parties involved in establishing, developing, implementing and maintaining an organization's project uncertainty management capability include those who might champion the initiative, the individuals or project teams responsible for making it happen, those who use the associated uncertainty management systems and procedures, those who subsequently support and maintain the capability needed, and those involved in the associated governance processes. Outside parties may also be influential, such as suppliers, banks or major customers. The experience, seniority and role of the corporate capability project manager are obviously of critical importance. That such a manager is appointed with these responsibilities is a basic tenet of effective project management.

An obvious issue is the location and size of any corporate uncertainty management support unit, and how it relates to uncertainty management across the whole organization. In a project-based contractor organization, three alternative modes of support indicating one dimension of the possibilities included:

1. no specific uncertainty management support for project managers, but limited training in uncertainty management techniques;
2. the provision of a central analysis support unit which project managers can call on as necessary; or
3. project managers provided with uncertainty management support in the form of a full-time, dedicated analyst or team built into the project team.

All three of these modes need PUMP facilitators, a PUMP team which could be outsourced if occasional training courses comprise 'mode 1' support, or dependence upon consultants is not an issue, perhaps because they come from a parent organization. A PUMP team involving more than one analyst will need a PUMP manager to manage the PUMP team. However, whatever the size, shape and corporate location of the PUMP team, from the outset, it is important to be clear that the role of PUMP facilitators is to *help other project staff to manage uncertainty*. The PUMP team *do not manage risk or opportunity, they are not opportunity or risk managers, and while they help to enlighten governance, they are not directly responsible for good governance*.

Why: what do the parties want to achieve?

As Figure 1.2 shows, the objectives of a project are driven by the project parties (the project 'who'). The objectives is project uncertainty management capability development in this case. The danger – a serious risk – is that objectives are inappropriately restricted by particular parties. What is needed is a project champion who is aware of the potential benefits that can accrue from an effective project uncertainty management capability from a corporate perspective, and who has the will and the influence to maintain an ambitious view of what can and should be achieved.

Setting priorities among possible objectives and applications for uncertainty management requires an appreciation of the full range of potential benefits obtainable plus a well-informed appreciation of key areas of uncertainty. For example, building on our earlier discussion of bidding by a contracting organization, contracting organizations might choose to focus initial effort on improved competitive bidding processes aimed at:

- improving transparency about the quality of cost estimates;
- ensuring that simple cost estimates with 'requisite' clarity for bidding purposes are unbiased;
- devising procedures to address uncertainty about the probability of winning with different bids;
- establishing efficient computer-based uncertainty analysis processes which can produce analyses in the short timescales required;
- being able to evaluate the implications of proposed contractual conditions;
- rapidly evaluating alternative ways of carrying out components of the proposed contract.

In dictionary terms 'requisite' means 'required by circumstances, necessary for success'. In bidding contexts 'requisite clarity' can be a useful term for very limited departures from a minimum clarity approach, emphasizing the minimum effort aspect.

For contractors facing an increasingly competitive environment and ever more demanding customers, the prospect of obtaining a new core competence should be a major incentive to adopt more systematic uncertainty management. Chapman and Ward (2002, ch. 3) developed some of these bidding process ideas further. But bear in mind the obvious fact that those who benefit from winning bids that later lose money, may not be enthusiastic about processes that interfere with their ability to get away with inappropriate low bids or inappropriately sloppy thinking. Any context change may involve losers as well as winners, and the behaviour of both needs effective management from a corporate perspective.

The benefits of formal PUMPs, as described in Chapter 3 and developed in Parts II and III, have tended to focus on the manner in which improvements in performance of individual projects can be obtained. A more long-term corporate view is to consider the benefits of effective PUMPs in terms of improved corporate performance over a stream of projects. Part of the role of formal uncertainty management is clarifying the value of a wider set of motives, as well as helping to pursue them.

To illustrate the scope of corporate benefits that may be long term and very important, Figure 14.1 offers a view of corporate benefits that the application of PUMPs for all projects might bring in a contracting organization.

Figure 14.1 incorporates the benefits of documentation and corporate learning described in Chapter 3 in a direct manner, with other benefits working through 'ability to manage uncertainty'. Assuming that a contracting organization undertakes uncertainty management prior to and after tendering, then a number of interrelated benefits can accrue, all driving up profitability, through lower level benefits such as the following:

- keener pricing, better design and stronger uncertainty management abilities provide competitive advantage and improve chances of winning contracts;
- better appreciation of uncertainty means more realistic pricing and the avoidance of potential loss-making 'disaster' contracts where uncertainty is too great;
- ability to manage sources of uncertainty means lower project costs with direct profit implications;
- reduced tendering costs mean higher profits.

Figure 14.1 can be generalized to portray comparable benefits for a client organization. For example, better integration of project shaping and selection with strategic and operations management of uncertainty is a broad concern all organizations ought to address, especially client organizations with complex relationships between these areas that need explicit attention.

What: what is it the parties are interested in?

In physical terms the 'what' of project uncertainty management capability might be considered to be the formalized procedures, documentation and information systems that support and facilitate an effective PUMP for individual projects. In these terms the 'what' question relates to the nature of the formal PUMP framework to be adopted and the resulting documented deliverables as discussed in Parts II and III.

Information systems design could revolve around what is needed to carry out particular steps in a generic PUMP pack framework. At a basic level this involves the collation of information

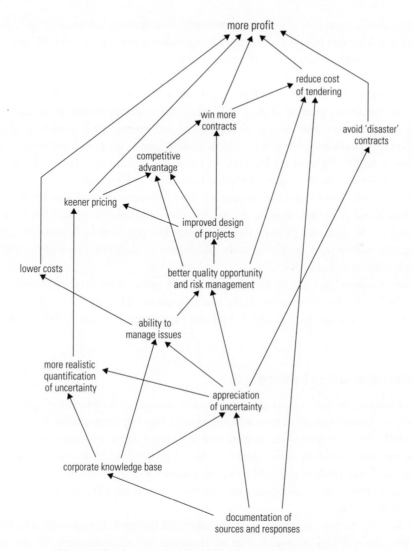

Figure 14.1 Corporate benefits of effective uncertainty management

about identified sources of uncertainty, consideration of how this information will be used and by whom, what information to include related to individual sources of uncertainty, and how frequently this information will be updated. Additional issues include the extent to which information from particular PUMP applications will be made available for other future applications, and how this pooling of information will be organized and coordinated. An intranet data facility centrally controlled is an obvious approach, but the cost effectiveness and reliability of such a system requires careful assessment. Proprietary software databases can be useful, but care needs to be taken in considering the facilities such packages offer. The problem is that facilities provided, such as simplistic risk ranking, may drive an organization's uncertainty management processes and perceptions of what they are about. This can pre-empt future deployment of more efficient and effective PUMP approaches.

A further consideration in deploying uncertainty management information systems is the desirability of linking this information with other information systems. If a PUMP approach is to become 'integrated' with operational, strategic and project planning and decision making, wholly separate PUMP information systems may be inappropriate. Indeed, the feasibility and value of augmenting existing information systems and associated decision-making procedures should be a primary consideration. An obvious priority is linkage with information systems to support strategic planning.

The deployment of decision support software is less problematic. Such software might include spreadsheets plus simulation software to help to quantify and evaluate risk and sources of uncertainty. This is readily deployed for local use in particular applications. However, effective and efficient uncertainty analysis requires specialist knowledge and sometimes expert assistance to construct appropriate models for a given context. This can warrant significant corporate investment in centralized analytical support. *Ad hoc* reliance on bought-in consultants to undertake specific analyses is always an option. However, given the potential in most organizations for expanding uncertainty management activity, developing an in-house capability is likely to be much more efficient and effective.

At a more strategic level, the target 'what' may be an 'effective uncertainty management culture' with the benefits like those noted in the previous section. The role of formal PUMPs is then to facilitate and encourage the attitudes, beliefs and ways of working that comprise this culture.

Whichway: how is it to be done?

In terms of building project uncertainty management capability, the 'whichway' question relates to *all* plans for initial implementation and subsequent ongoing development of applications of formal PUMPs both on individual projects and associated corporate issues that are not part of specific projects. As indicated in Figure 1.2, the 'what' drives the 'whichway' to a significant extent. Four different kinds of plans are involved: plans for relationships and contracts; plans for business case purposes; plans for operations; and plans for activities directly involved in developing the capability 'what'.

'Plans for relationships and contracts' are about all informal contracts or understandings between all parties as well as more formal relationships. For example, early BP analysts had a clear understanding with all parties that they normally worked for, and reported to the project manager, but they could be trusted by the board to 'tell it like it is', an 'honest broker' reputation being very important.

'Plans for business case purposes' include preserving the case made for the project uncertainty management capability project in the first instance at each stage in the capability evolution process.

'Plans for operations' include ongoing operation of the project uncertainty management capability in corporate terms once it is established.

'Plans for activities' are the obvious 'what has to be done to create the project uncertainty management capability of interest'.

A common practice approach to building risk management capability is to begin with a simplified risk management process and tool kit, perhaps limited to PIGs and simple risk registers, introduced fairly rapidly with a minimum of piloting. Following rapid introduction, the intention is to continue operating the simplified process in a well-defined administrative framework, without major changes in format. We argue against this approach, because to achieve effective uncertainty management it is essential to understand the nature of a comprehensive PUMP. Ideally, this understanding needs to be developed in a methodical fashion on a widespread basis, not confined to one or two individuals charged with the rapid introduction of an approach with limited, short-term ambitions.

When the introduction of formal PUMPs into an organization is part of a long-term change in project management and organizational culture – usually a desirable position to adopt – it is very important to see early applications as part of a corporate learning process. The approach advocated in this book is the pilot or demonstration study approach, applying a comprehensive PUMP to a carefully selected *initial* 'demonstration project' to learn on, later extending the scope of the PUMP pack with *further* 'demonstration projects'. A suitable demonstration project usually has three characteristics:

1. It has been very well managed to date.
2. Despite its successful management to date, important sources of uncertainty raise concerns which need to be addressed to the satisfaction of those granting sanction.
3. There is sufficient time to undertake a comprehensive uncertainty management process.

This builds on successful experience with BP and National Power, as discussed in earlier examples; and has been a successful approach for clients ever since. A pilot study approach of this kind should ultimately lead to relatively effective uncertainty management procedures, but it may be relatively slow as a learning process. In contracting organizations, retrospective analysis of recently completed projects may provide more time for the necessary analysis and learning, divorced from tight time schedules associated with tender formulation.

Early applications might target areas of project planning where the benefits from project uncertainty management will be greatest, and use this experience as a learning process before attempting more widespread use of PUMPs. For example, in a project-based organization, an obvious starting place is at project manager level for E&D shaping stage support, working down into supporting project components and teams. Further development of uncertainty management capability might then be targeted at later and earlier project lifecycle stages, following the pattern of this book's Part II and Part III structure.

Over time, an understanding of both the costs and the benefits of PUMP variations can be developed that will inform choices about short cuts in subsequent applications. This implies that the first project an organization subjects to a PUMP should be carefully selected to facilitate these longer term benefits.

As a simple analogy, consider planning to sail a yacht across the English Channel from Southampton to Cherbourg for the first time. Reading a few sailing magazines will soon make it clear that it is a good idea to make the first crossing in daylight, in spring (when days are longest), starting at dawn, with stable weather conditions forecast for several days ahead. Given this starting position, project planning and an associated PUMP based on a simple approach to navigation would suffice: assuming you take the Isle of Wight on your left, head due south from the Needles until you hit the French coast, then turn right. Such easy crossings allow time for refining navigation skills, making course corrections which are designed to enhance knowledge rather than minimize crossing time, making frequent checks with positioning instruments, and using visual checks where feasible. Developing effective and efficient navigating skills for other conditions requires practice using formalized methods with ample time to compare and contrast alternative ways of determining the position (location) of the yacht. This learning process should be fun. Most people who go into project management as a career need a measure of fun to keep them on the job, as well as the stimulation of challenges to meet. A bit more fun and a bit less challenge than the norm can be a useful bias for early learning experiences. The saying 'there are old pilots and bold pilots, but no bold old pilots' does not apply directly to project staff, but some of the bolder young project staff need to be explicitly taken on a few 'Channel crossings' with a pleasurable learning experience before letting them attempt more challenging 'crossings' like the Atlantic Ocean, never mind the Southern Oceans. Navigating through a high-risk project can be much more difficult than crossing the Channel in a yacht and in general warrants more attention to formality, not less.

The above ideas apply to choosing an appropriate level of sophistication in the first attempt at a PUMP of the kind discussed in this book, as well as choosing an appropriate project. As most people who have acquired some of their wisdom via the 'school of hard knocks' know, making mistakes is the only way to learn some of life's more important lessons, but it is important not to make mistakes which kill or cripple future opportunities. If mistakes are inevitable, we need to make mistakes we can live with.

Continuing the Southampton to Cherbourg sailing analogy, it is advisable to aim to hit the French coast several miles up-tide and/or up-wind of the destination, because it is comparatively easy to alter course at the last minute in a down-wind and down-tide direction, but comparatively difficult to do so up-wind against the tide. We know we will get it wrong to some extent, and the error is not symmetric in its effect, so we aim for low cost errors. The magnitude of error assumed should reflect our proven navigation skill. Choosing a low level of sophistication for a first PUMP and observing the results is like hitting the French coast in the dark with no position-finding instruments and no knowledge of the coast. However, if you can safely assume you are up-tide and up-wind of Cherbourg, then you can drift down-wind and tide until what looks like a major harbour comes into view. This is comparable to choosing a high level of sophistication for a first PUMP with a view to adjusting towards simpler PUMPs as experience is gained. If you don't know which side of Cherbourg you are on, you have a potential major problem on your hands. If you start with sophisticated PUMPs, then simplify as experience is gained, you will be clear 'which side of Cherbourg you are on' in PUMP terms.

An excessively sophisticated PUMP will be a handicap, as will an excessively difficult project. But learning requires a challenge, and only by using a bit more sophistication than we need can we recognize when and where it is safe to take shortcuts. As experience is gained, the emphasis can move from PUMPs as a general corporate level uncertainty management learning experience in the context of effective use from the outset for all projects considered, to PUMPs as an effective *and efficient* way to deal with immediate concerns in particular projects. Shortcuts can be taken in the light of an understanding of how much effort will be saved by the shortcuts and what the likely impact will be on the effectiveness of the project management process as a whole.

Evolution in project uncertainty management support

In 1976 BP International began the development of its London-based project uncertainty management capability for offshore oil and gas projects in the North Sea. A senior BP project manager was convinced by an Acres Consulting Services colleague to arrange an internal seminar for a group of senior BP project managers given by Chris Chapman. They agreed to fund 'passive project' development of a suitable BP approach, later labelled SCERT for publication purposes, using Chris and a senior BP engineer who had recently been involved in the Ninian project. Their brief was to develop Chris's ideas, based on earlier Acres studies of US and Canadian energy projects, into a BP uncertainty management process assuming another chance to redo the E&D shaping stage for the Ninian project – answering the question: 'If we were planning Ninian again at the E&D shaping stage, how would we proceed?'

A BP senior management group later approved the resulting BP SCERT process. They selected the Magnus project (already late in the E&D shaping stage of project strategy development and approaching a gateway to approve release of funds for detailed planning) as the first 'live project' test of the BP SCERT process. They arranged for the appointment of a carefully selected BP engineer as their first 'uncertainty analyst' – to undertake 'project uncertainty management' in this book's terms, although different terms were used at the time. For the first three months this first uncertainty analyst had extensive and almost continuous external consulting support from Chris. Over time, consulting support became less intense, and largely concerned with generic methodology for new considerations – a contract for a few days a month as needed was in place after about two years, the relationship continuing in various forms for about a decade.

The first Magnus study took about six months. It was successful, for reasons discussed in Chapter 3, and similar studies of other projects began. Within about a year the same depth of analysis and level of clarity was achieved inside six weeks. Shortly after this the first 'uncertainty analyst' became the 'uncertainty process manager' and a group of analysts were working in the same way, to cover all projects, often earlier in the project lifecycle, sometimes later. This group of analysts reported directly to the project managers for the most part, as a service function for project managers, independent of the design, planning and costing functions. Sometimes they served an audit function, reporting to the board. The 'uncertainty process manager' was recognized as a high-flyer, but the standard corporate practice of moving all employees on to a more senior post after a limited time span was suspended to allow corporate capability to develop with appropriate continuity.

After a few years, a more senior BP engineer was made head of the uncertainty analysis function and the planning function, effectively integrating planning and uncertainty management formally when the original uncertainty process manager was promoted. Then a still more senior person was made responsible for uncertainty management, planning and costing, extending the integration.

As time went on analysis was undertaken earlier and earlier in the E&D shaping stage of project lifecycles. Plans were not tested by uncertainty analysis after building them using other modes of analysis – they were built using uncertainty analysis. To the authors' knowledge PUMPs did not get integrated into the DOT shaping stage, which had separate risk/uncertainty analysis support, with a somewhat different (safety, reliability and availability) focus. Nor, so far as we know, did BP uncertainty management processes linked to SCERT get integrated into the concept shaping stage. BP SCERT-based processes were simplified and used for detailed planning and later strategy implementation stages.

Wherewithal: what resources are required?

The 'wherewithal' question concerns the extent of resources formally invested in developing and maintaining a project uncertainty management capability. Such resources include personnel in terms of both numbers and expertise, the time allocated to uncertainty management, and the provision of supporting infrastructure such as information systems and appropriate software. The greater the investment in such resources, the easier it will be to move towards more effective uncertainty management in terms of the other Ws, and choices made in respect of the other W questions may be influenced by the resources available. As Figure 2.1 indicates, ongoing operations plans need attention as well as immediate activity plans.

In terms of personnel, resourcing choices include decisions about the number, expertise and location of dedicated uncertainty management personnel deployed, the resources available to them, and the extent of training to develop the expertise of other employees.

Formal allocation and resourcing of time dedicated to uncertainty management is another important aspect of 'wherewithal' choices. For example, a senior management directive that formal project review meetings should also consider uncertainty management issues may not result in much additional uncertainty management if it has to be squeezed into already busy one-day meetings. A directive accompanied by an expectation that uncertainty management deliberations should involve an additional full day's consideration is a rather more substantial resource commitment. Similar observations apply to the establishment and maintenance of information systems to support uncertainty management.

When: when does it have to be done?

In a project uncertainty management capability context, the 'when' question concerns the timing of initiatives to establish the project uncertainty management capability. As indicated in Figure 1.2, the 'what', 'why' and 'who' drives the 'when' to a significant extent in terms of the timing of implementation via six different kinds of plans. A pilot approach fostering learning can be very effective, but assumes that time is available for this. A situation to be avoided is an external 'who', such as a bank or a major customer, driving the project uncertainty management capability 'why' and 'what' in their interest, and forcing a rushed programme to establish and operate an uncertainty management process that is inappropriate for the real needs of the organization.

A project lifecycle perspective

The seven Ws framework points to a number of important aspects for consideration in establishing project uncertainty management capability. Taking a project lifecycle perspective of the project 'establish a project uncertainty management capability' provides a complementary, chronological perspective, and additional insights into those issues that need to be addressed.

The concept shaping and concept gateway stages

As noted when discussing Table 1.3, the concept shaping stage involves an outline specification of the deliverable to be produced and clarifies the purpose of the project. When establishing project uncertainty management capability in a selected initial demonstration project area, this stage should be reasonably straightforward in that the purpose and deliverable are readily identifiable. The purpose is to obtain the benefits described in the 'why' section above, in Chapter 3, and in Part III, in a specific context. The long-term overall strategic project deliverable is the application of formal uncertainty management processes in all projects, fully integrated with all other corporate uncertainty and risk management, with the PUMP as a recommended process framework. However, the immediate Mark 1 project can focus on a specific context and an initial view of what appropriate capability involves.

As with any corporate initiative, senior management support is crucial to empower the project, and to ensure that it reflects the needs and concerns of senior management. All relevant managers, but especially project managers as future users of formal PUMPs, need to become involved at this early stage, to ensure that their concerns are addressed at this stage.

Ideally, a manager for the project uncertainty management capability project should be appointed in this stage so that he or she can actively participate in elaborating the project uncertainty management capability concept and clarify its purpose before the more detailed DOT shaping and E&D shaping stages. It may be very important to ensure that this project manager operates at board level, and that he or she is not also the PUMP manager. In the National Power example, the uncertainty management process project manager was the Director of Engineering, a senior board member. The PUMP manager was a relatively junior engineer, with a department of one to start. This National Power approach worked very well for the several years Chris was involved.

To facilitate the design and introduction of associated procedures and infrastructure, it can be useful to involve a wider group of parties, including individuals in functional departments in the organization, key customers, key contractors or subcontractors, potential partners, and external consultants.

The need for an independent governance gateway will depend upon the context, but it can be important, especially if some of those involved have personal agendas that could get in the way of appropriate objectivity from a corporate perspective.

The design, operation and termination (DOT) shaping and gateway stages

As noted in Chapter 1, the focus of the design aspect of the DOT shaping stage is giving substance to the 'what' of the project uncertainty management capability as discussed earlier, although some consideration of the other Ws will be involved. It is assumed that the PUMP framework can form the basis of the formal processes ultimately needed. The aim is to build effective project uncertainty management capability which can pursue flexible tactics within the scope of a comprehensive process framework. If administrative processes for a simplified uncertainty management process that is limited in scope are introduced, this may delay and even discourage development of uncertainty management expertise.

Another design consideration is the range of projects that will be subject to a formal PUMP. A simple answer, adopted by many of our clients, is 'all projects'. We support this approach. However, it implies that different levels of PUMP will be cost effective for different sizes and types of projects. This transforms the question into: 'What kind of PUMP should be used over the range of projects of interest?' In general, comprehensive uncertainty management will tend to be most useful when projects involve one or more of the following:

- substantial resources;
- significant novelty (technological, geographical, environmental or organizational);

- long planning horizons;
- large size;
- complexity;
- several organizations;
- significant political issues.

In time, organizations institutionalizing project uncertainty management may use different guidelines for applying PUMPs to different kinds of projects, dependent on the degree of presence of the factors listed above. However, such sophistication needs to wait on the development of experience with a comprehensive PUMP on selected projects.

A further design consideration is at what stage of a project's lifecycle PUMPs will be applied. Part III discussed this issue in detail, making the observation that, in general, PUMPs are best applied as early as possible in a project's lifecycle – in the concept-shaping stage – with coordinated and integrated further application of the same basic process and concepts for all further stages until termination is complete. This is a significant issue for organizations with major projects involving the creation of long-lived assets, but it is also significant for contracting organizations involved in only part of a client's project lifecycle. As indicated in Chapter 9, contractors may usefully undertake uncertainty analyses in respect of a given contract, first as part of tender development to help to determine whether to bid or not and at what price, and second, as ongoing uncertainty management of a contract that is actually won. Contracting organizations ought to institute PUMPs that incorporate uncertainty management at each of these stages. As indicated in Figure 14.1, this may lead to strategic decisions about the amount of effort to be applied to submission of tenders, the level of profits expected on individual contracts, and an appropriate target success rate for submitted tenders.

The relationship between design and operations is important here, as is the anticipated evolution of design and operations. However, while, 'termination' of the project uncertainty management capability project might be usefully viewed as a threat to be avoided, 'termination' is not a relevant project lifecycle stage for planning purposes – uncertainty is not going to go away, and learning more about how to deal with uncertainty in clarity efficient terms has no obvious end-point.

A separate gateway involving objective governance can be important. If clients and their contractors are working together in a coordinated manner, governance issues can be particularly important and subtle.

The execution and delivery (E&D)-shaping and strategy gateway stages

The E&D shaping stage of establishing project uncertainty management capability involves determining how the design will be executed and delivered, what steps to take in what order, what resources are required in broad terms, and how long it will take. This involves determining specific targets for establishing an operational PUMP development, particularly in terms of the scope of the projects to be covered and the time scale in which this is to be achieved. To a large degree these targets will depend on the impetus behind the initiative, related to the parties involved and perceived need.

Plan development needs to include arrangements for capturing existing risk management expertise, generalizing it to effective uncertainty management expertise, and disseminating it as part of developing uncertainty management thinking and expertise in individual personnel. This may include in-house training courses and special interest group seminars – as a form of 'quality circle' for example.

A separate objectives governance gateway stage is usually important to assess overall strategy, especially if earlier gateways were not used.

Details shaping and details gateways

As noted in Chapter 1, the details shaping stage involves decisions about project organization, identification of appropriate participants, and allocation of tasks between them. From a corporate perspective, responsibility needs to be clearly allocated for:

* development of PUMP documentation and guidelines;
* implementation of PUMPs;
* monitoring compliance with guidelines, and the effectiveness of PUMPs.

A key aspect is the choice of roles allocated to corporate and business unit 'uncertainty officers', project managers, support function managers, analysts, internal audit, and other specific functional areas.

Most organizations introduce project *risk* management processes using a 'risk manager' or 'risk analyst' who may be an external consultant, an internal consultant, or a member of the project team who has undertaken some form of training or self-study programme on risk management. A sizeable team of analysts may be involved, or the part-time efforts of a single individual. Most organizations with mature project *risk* management capability maintain a risk analysis team led by a 'risk manager'. We prefer a term like 'project uncertainty process manager', or 'project uncertainty capability manager', or 'PUMP manager'. In large organizations this team may be dedicated to project uncertainty management, but it may work alongside operations and strategy uncertainty management teams, part of what some refer to as an 'enterprise uncertainty (or risk) management' function, usually designated ERM although EUM is more appropriate. In small organizations this EUM/ERM 'team' may be a single individual with other responsibilities. Even a very small organization needs somebody to act as the repository of uncertainty management skills and to facilitate formal uncertainty management.

This team or individual may undertake uncertainty analysis for individual project managers. However, they should not be regarded as risk or uncertainty *managers*, since proper integration of project uncertainty, risk and opportunity management and project management more generally requires that the project manager take personal responsibility for all uncertainty that is not explicitly delegated upwards to more senior managers or downwards to managers of components of the project.

The provision of analytical support, while useful, is only part of institutionalizing PUMPs and associated project uncertainty management capability. There is an additional need to ensure widespread, effective application of uncertainty management guidelines, to monitor the quality of PUMP applications, and to ensure that uncertainty management experience is captured and used to improve the management of uncertainty in subsequent projects.

Some organizations have details gateways for each project which focus governance on compliance with a very specific, mandated risk management process – usually a very limited and restricted process. Gateways for individual projects should focus on 'sense testing' the project's detailed planning, using an unrestricted project uncertainty management capability perspective with a focus on the robustness of key recommended decisions. There is scope for more than one judgement about the suitability of process choices and probabilities. Project decisions and associated possible outcomes should be the focus of governance concerned with process substance and spirit, rather than process form and superficial compliance with process guidelines.

Execution

The steps in the execute stage of the project lifecycle shown in Table 1.3 are:

1. coordinate, control and monitor progress;
2. modification of all targets, commitments and resource allocations as needed;
3. ongoing execution evaluation.

These steps, carried out in a continuous iterative process, are part of the ongoing management of PUMP applications. From this perspective, the project uncertainty management capability project never terminates, and the delivery, operation and support stages become part of the execute stage. However, a first pass through the execute stage might usefully involve a pilot exercise applying the proposed formal PUMP framework to a suitable project, as indicated earlier. Lessons from this experience may influence the design of the PUMP in a subsequent pass back through the earlier stages before application of the PUMP on another project. This experience might also provide data in respect of sources of uncertainty and the efficacy of responses of direct relevance to other concurrent and subsequent projects. Such feedback clearly need not wait for termination of the subject project. As a general principle, the institutionalizing of a formal PUMP framework should include arrangements to disseminate the latest experience in managing uncertainty as rapidly as possible. In this context, it may be useful to see the project uncertainty management capability project as a programme of projects, in the sense of all aspects of Figure 1.1.

Delivery

As indicated in Chapter 1 the delivery stage of a project involves commissioning and handover, with the steps shown in Table 1.3:

1. basic deliverable verification;
2. deliverable modification;
3. modification of performance criteria and stakeholder expectations about delivery and operational performance;
4. delivery evaluation.

These steps are worth addressing periodically to check and appraise the effectiveness of PUMP procedures. Over time this can lead to significant changes in the way PUMPs are coordinated and controlled.

Operations and support (O&S)

As indicated in Table 1.3, the O&S stage of a project involves the following steps:

1. basic operations and support verification;
2. ongoing development of operations and support criteria;
3. ongoing development of operations and support;
4. ongoing operations and support evaluation.

There is a need to provide continuing support for uncertainty management in future projects in both a facilitating and supervisory sense. Aside from analytical expertise which may be called upon by project management teams, there may be a need for corporate management involvement in scrutinizing individual PUMPs to ensure an appropriately rigorous approach, to facilitate improvements in uncertainty management practice, and to monitor the effectiveness of PUMPs. The level of such support will need to be reassessed periodically to ensure it remains cost effective. As noted in the BP example early in this chapter, the level of analytical support may need to be increased over time, and it may need to change qualitatively, depending on the expertise and resources available within the project teams. Policy decisions may need to be made about the composition of project teams if the need for uncertainty management increases. Apart from analytical support, senior management scrutiny of uncertainty analyses and uncertainty management plans may be well worth maintaining indefinitely as part of standard project appraisal procedures. This will help to maintain and improve standards of uncertainty management, particularly through changes in personnel at all levels.

Termination

As pointed out above, there should be no termination stage, unless the project uncertainty management capability project fails, and oversimplification or loss of capability is a threat which needs explicit attention. Those who manage uncertainty in a security or safety context have a particularly obvious version of this problem. If nothing happens, because the organization's uncertainty is effectively managed and they are lucky, justification of ongoing expenditure on capability is vital. If a major incident occurs, because the organization is unlucky and there are any weaknesses in the organization's uncertainty management, the courts may assess uncertainty management competence, and the survival of organizations and individual careers may be at stake. This is just part of the more complex issue of sustaining corporate opportunity efficiency.

Ongoing PUMP review as a corporate process

Following each application of the chosen PUMP framework to a project, a systematic appraisal of the PUMP application is appropriate to evaluate the likely relevance and usefulness of both project specific results and process experience, to inform both future projects and future uncertainty management practice. Periodically, a broadly based review of PUMP procedures and supporting infrastructure is appropriate to draw out lessons from the operation of PUMP procedures across the organization. This might be visualized as a 'lessons learned' stage at the end of each project lifecycle – part of the Table 1.3 structure. However, it is more usefully seen as a separate *corporate* process, or as part of the ongoing development of corporate capability in uncertainty management. We return to this topic in Chapter 16.

Conclusions

Establishing a corporate capability to carry out PUMPs in appropriate projects can be regarded as a project in its own right. This perspective suggests considering what such a project involves by using the seven Ws and lifecycle stage frameworks as described in Chapters 1 and 5. Clearly it would be possible also to apply the processes discussed in Chapters 6–13 to such a capability development project. This has not been pursued here, but in the context of a particular case the reader may find it useful to do so.

A central message of previous chapters is that the benefits from a well-developed PUMP capability are considerable. This means that PUMP capability is worthy of significant and sustained investment. This in turn implies development that involves implementation of a comprehensive PUMP, selectively to begin with, targeting areas of project planning where the need is greatest, then using this experience as a learning process before attempting more widespread deployment of PUMPs.

The reasoning behind this approach is that to achieve effective uncertainty management, it is essential to understand the nature of a comprehensive PUMP. Rapid, corporate-wide introduction of simplistic risk management processes in a narrowly defined administrative framework may seem attractive, even expedient given some organizational imperative, but this runs the risk of freezing out more sophisticated approaches, and ultimately, much more valuable uncertainty management development.

Most organizations first use a formal common practice 'risk management' approach because of an organizational imperative, sometimes imposed by 'nature', sometimes imposed by regulators, bankers or other interested parties. Organizations progressing to the application of a PUMP of the kind discussed in this book often do so for similar reasons. However, once formal PUMPs are in place, most organizations using them have expanded their uncertainty management capability as the benefits have been more deeply understood and appreciated.

Some organizations have later been seduced by short-term convenience and cost savings associated with oversimplification and loss of in-house uncertainty management capability. This is a risk that needs vigilance at board level – as part of ongoing governance processes that use external expertise whenever and wherever appropriate.

In terms of guiding ongoing development of project uncertainty, opportunity and risk management capability, benchmarking risk maturity models offer a potentially useful way forward if they can make the transition from a common practice risk management perspective to an uncertainty management perspective. However, the number and scope of the attributes considered is typically limited, as are the descriptions of levels of maturity. Together, the seven Ws and the project lifecycle stage frameworks point to additional attributes or 'dimensions' of uncertainty management application and capability that should also be considered in any benchmarking exercise.

Chapter 15

Contracts and governance as frameworks for enlightened relationship management

We must indeed all hang together, or most assuredly we shall all hang separately.
—Benjamin Franklin

Some people view contracts through a 'legal lens', as legal instruments designed to preserve the interests of different parties in a legal sense, in a court of law if need be. However, *once the contracts come out of the drawers, everybody is in trouble*, as noted in Chapter 9. The opening quote for this chapter, attributed to Benjamin Franklin – as a remark to John Hancock during the signing of the Declaration of Independence on 4 July 1776 – has resonance in any important undertaking when the key players do not 'hang together' in the 'work together for a common goal' sense of this phrase. Benjamin Franklin's remark is a generalization of the contract specific comment repeated above – it applies to some extent to all relationships of interest in this chapter. Contracts between clients and contractors are a central concern, but governance and other relationships are also relevant aspects within the seven Ws framework.

The PUMP ownership phase, as discussed in Chapter 9, is concerned with allocating responsibility for managing project uncertainty to appropriate project parties in each individual project. As noted previously, the issues involved are of fundamental importance, because allocations can strongly influence the motivation of parties and the extent to which project uncertainty is assessed and managed by each party.

Insofar as individual parties perceive sources of uncertainty and associated opportunities and risks differently, and have different abilities and motivations to manage uncertainty, then their approach to uncertainty management will be different. In particular, each party is likely to try to manage uncertainty primarily for their own benefit, perhaps to the disadvantage of other parties. If one party, typically the client (project owner), is in a position to allocate uncertainty, then this party may regard allocating all uncertainty to other parties as perfectly acceptable, even if doing so antagonizes the other parties and leads to an inappropriate loss of opportunities for *all* parties. The fundamental weakness in this simple but extreme strategy is that it involves unenlightened relationship management that may not be in the best interests of the client. For example, the use of exculpatory contract clauses by a client to unfairly transfer risk to the contractor can cause contractors to increase their prices and destroy the contractor's trust (DeMaere et al., 2001). This can increase defensive behaviour and conflict, reduce the potential for establishing long-term or partnering relationships, and jeopardize project success. In most situations, a more considered uncertainty allocation strategy can produce a situation where uncertainty is managed more effectively, to the benefit of all parties concerned.

All these issues need corporate attention as well as special treatment within each project, and ensuring a common corporate understanding of the best approach to all contracts and other relationships is the focus of this chapter.

The authors believe it is important to see contracts and governance as formal frameworks for enlightened relationship management, using an 'enlightened relationship' lens to view *all* aspects of *all* relationship and contract planning. We use the word 'enlightened' here in the common 'enlightened self-interest' sense, driven by the client's best interests, but reflecting the need to encourage a collaborative relationship whenever this serves the client's best interests in opportunity efficiency terms, even if 'war is best seen as a continuation of diplomacy by other means'. The generality of this enlightened relationship perspective complements the generality of the uncertainty, opportunity and risk concepts underlying the PUMP approach to managing ambiguity and systemic uncertainty.

An enlightened relationship management approach to contracts

An enlightened relationship management approach to contracts requires that there is:

1. appropriate clarity about the specification of the required activities and *all* associated sources of uncertainty;
2. appropriate clarity about the sources of uncertainty allocated to each party in managerial, financial and other terms;
3. sufficient capability to manage *all* the sources of uncertainty;
4. appropriate motivation to manage *all* the sources of uncertainty to achieve opportunity efficiency for the client.

The rationale for allocating sources of uncertainty between the client and other parties ought to be based on meeting these conditions as far as possible.

If condition 1 is not met, then effective uncertainty management is impossible because not all sources of uncertainty that need to be managed will have been appropriately identified and clarified. However, the composite nature of uncertainty means very detailed specification may not be necessary – a simple overview level may serve in some contexts, as illustrated by the Highways Agency example discussed in Chapter 2.

If condition 2 is not met, parties may not be aware of their responsibilities, or what the client and other parties are expecting from them in terms of uncertainty management. Again the composite nature of uncertainty is important. As illustrated by the BCS example discussion in

Chapters 2 and 9, a common joint understanding of the spirit of the dividing line between client and contractor responsibility is crucial, but it may not be sensible to attempt detailed itemization of relevant sources of uncertainty.

In respect of condition 3, as any manager knows, assigning a task to an individual, team, or organization unit is only appropriate if the assignee has the skills and capacity to carry out the task. An appropriate combination of skills and capacity is necessary for effective (and efficient) performance. Condition 3 captures the spirit of the frequently touted maxim that 'risk should be allocated to the party best able to control and manage the risk', with our preferred term 'source (of uncertainty)' replacing 'risk' to ensure all aspects of uncertainty are addressed, including opportunity and the ubiquitous ambiguity which causes so much grief in contractual relationships. But it goes much further, recognizing competence as a significant source of uncertainty, systemically linked to other sources, and needing explicit attention

Condition 4 is about ensuring appropriate motivation of *all* project parties to manage sources in the *client's* best interests – opportunity efficiency defining those best interests. Basic motivation theory and common sense tells us that parties will be motivated to do this to the extent that this serves their *own* interests, and to the extent that the expected rewards are commensurate with the effort expended. This calls for a significant degree of alignment of the objectives of all parties with those of the client, and difficulties arise when project parties have different objectives which are not congruent. Unless a shared perception of project success criteria is possible, these different, conflicting criteria may imply very different perceptions of project-related opportunity and risk, and different priorities in project uncertainty management.

Differences in perception of project success arise most obviously in client–contractor relationships. The question of 'success from whose point of view?' matters to even the most egocentric party. For example, in a simple single client and single contractor context, if the client or the contractor push their luck, mutual trust and cooperation may be early casualties, as noted above, and in the limit the other party may walk away or go broke and cease to exist.

When making uncertainty allocations, it is important to distinguish between responsibility for managing a source of uncertainty and responsibility for bearing the consequences of that source in financial or other terms. In particular, as noted in Chapter 9, it may desirable to allocate these responsibilities to different parties, recognizing that the party best able to physically manage an issue may not be the party best able to bear the financial or other consequences of that issue.

Different people within the same client or contractor organization can give rise to essentially the same problems, as can multiple clients or multiple contractors, and relationships between different parties involved in governance relationships. Equally, agreements about source of uncertainty allocation in a hierarchical structure or between different units in the same organization can be viewed as 'contracts' for present purposes (Chapman and Ward, 2002, ch. 6).

To address these concerns this chapter begins in the context of a simple two-party situation involving a client and contractor to illustrate the basic issues.

Consequences of two simple contract payment terms

Two basic forms of risk allocation via contract payment terms are the 'fixed price' contract and the 'cost plus fixed fee' (CPFF) or 'reimbursement' contract. In the fixed price contract the contractor theoretically 'carries all the risk' in conventional terms, 'owns all the uncertainty' in our terms – with risk and opportunity implications. In the CPFF contract the client theoretically carries all the risk or owns all the uncertainty. From an uncertainty management perspective neither is entirely satisfactory under all circumstances. Fixed price contracts are by far the most common and frequently used inappropriately, but consider the CPFF alternative first.

Cost plus fixed fee contracts

With a cost plus fixed fee (CPFF) contract the client pays the contractor a fixed fee and additionally reimburses the contractor for all costs associated with the project: labour, plant and materials actually consumed are charged at rates that are checked and approved by open-book accounting. The cost of overcoming errors, omissions, and other charges is borne by the client.

Advantages for the client include the following: costs are limited to what is actually needed; the contractor cannot earn excessive profits; and the possibility that a potential loss for a contractor will lead to adverse effects is avoided.

However, CPFF contracts have a serious disadvantage as far as most clients are concerned, in that there is an uncertain cost commitment coupled with an absence of any incentive on contractors to control costs. Under a CPFF contract, the contractor's motivation to carry out work efficiently and cost effectively is considerably weakened. Moreover, contractors may be tempted to pad costs in ways which bring benefits to other work they are undertaking. Examples include expanded purchases of equipment, excessive testing and experimentation, generous arrangements with suppliers, and over-manning to avoid non-reimbursable layoff costs, a problem which is more pronounced when the fee is based on a percentage of actual project costs.

A further difficulty is that of agreeing and documenting in the contract those items that are allowable costs on a given project. However, it is important that all project-related costs are correctly identified and included at appropriate charging rates in the contract. Particular areas of difficulty are overhead costs and managerial time. To the extent that costs are not specifically reimbursed, they will be paid for out of the fixed fee, and contractors will be motivated to minimize such costs.

The use of a CPFF contract also presents problems in selecting a contractor who can perform the work for the lowest cost. Selecting a contractor on the basis of the lowest fixed fee tendered in a competitive bidding situation does not guarantee a least-cost outcome. It could be argued that it encourages a maximum-cost outcome.

Fixed price contracts

Common practice is for clients to aim to transfer all risk to contractors via fixed price contracts. Typically, a contract is awarded to the lowest fixed price bid in a competitive tender, on the assumption that *all* other things are equal, including the expertise of the tendering organizations and the extent to which they are motivated to look after the client's best interests. Competitive tendering is perceived as an efficient way of obtaining value for money, whether or not the client is relatively ignorant of the underlying project costs compared with potential contractors.

With a fixed price contract, the client pays a fixed price to the contractor regardless of what the contract actually costs the contractor to perform, in theory. The contractor carries all the risk of loss associated with higher than expected costs, in theory, but benefits if costs turn out to be less than expected, in theory and in practice.

Under a fixed price contract, the contractor is motivated to manage project costs downwards. For example, by increasing efficiency or using the most cost effective approaches the contractor can increase profit. Hopefully this is without prejudice to the quality of the completed work, but the client is directly exposed to quality degradation risk to the extent that quality is not both completely specified and verifiable. The difficulty of completely specifying requirements or performance in a contract is well known. This difficulty is perhaps greatest in the procurement of services as compared with construction or product procurement. For example, it is very difficult to define unambiguously terms like 'cooperate', 'advise', 'coordinate', 'supervise', 'best endeavours' or 'ensure economic and expeditious execution', and it is unrealistic to assume that contractors have priced work under the most costly conditions in a competitive bidding situation.

In the case of high uncertainty projects, where uncertainty demands explicit attention and policy or behaviour modification, a fixed price contract may appear initially attractive to the client. However, contractors may prefer a cost reimbursement contract and require what the client regards as an excessive price to take on cost uncertainty within a fixed price contract. More seriously, even a carefully specified fixed price contract may not remove all uncertainty about the final price the client has to pay. For some sources of uncertainty, such as variation in quantity, or unforeseen ground conditions, the contractor will be entitled to additional payments via a claims procedure. If the fixed price is too low, additional sources of uncertainty are introduced: for example, the contractor may be unable to fulfil contractual conditions and go into liquidation, or use every means to generate claims. The nature of uncertainty and claims, coupled with the confidentiality of the contractor's costs, introduce an element of chance into the adequacy of the payment, from whichever side of the contract it is viewed (Perry, 1986). This undermines the basic concept of a 'fixed price' contract and at the same time may cause the client to pay a higher than necessary 'risk premium' because sources of uncertainty effectively being carried by the client are not explicitly so indicated. In effect, a cost reimbursement contract is agreed by default for sources of uncertainty that are not controllable by the contractor or the client. This allocation of uncontrollable risk may not be efficient. Client insistence on placing 'fixed price' contracts with the lowest bidder may only serve to aggravate this problem. Further, a fixed price contract means that a contractor able to generate an 'opportunity discount' to supplement their 'risk premium' will keep it to themselves and pursue opportunity efficiency from their perspective – not the client's.

Oil majors like BP with North Sea projects in the 1970s typically took a very 'hands-on' approach to uncertainty management. They paid their contractors on a piece or day rate basis for pipe laying, for example. Some sources of uncertainty, like bad weather, they left to their contractors to manage, while monitoring performance, but they accepted the cost consequences of unexpected bad weather and all other external risks of this kind, like buckles. They also took the opportunity efficiency benefits of all the uncertainty within their control. The rationale was based on the size and unpredictability of sources of event uncertainty such as buckles, the complexity of uncertainty, the ability of the oil companies to bear related risk relative to the ability of the contractors to bear it, the charges contractors would have insisted upon if they had to bear it, and the risk they would go bankrupt if both parties were unlucky. However, by the late 1980s, many similar projects involved fixed price contracts for laying a pipeline. The rationale was based on contractor experience of the problems, and lower charges because of this experience and market pressures. There may be other reasons driving similar changes in approach within any organization over time. For example, the UK Ministry of Defence (MoD) moved from 'hands-on' to 'hands-off eyes-on' (as the use of fixed price contracts is referred to in the MoD) for a range of motives – which included political considerations. Both these examples illustrate the way the rationale for a particular uncertainty allocation can change within a given organization.

The above observations suggest that fixed price contracts should be avoided in the early stages of a project, when specifications may be incomplete and realistic performance objectives difficult to set (Sadeh et al., 2000). A more appropriate strategy might be to break the project into a number of stages, and to move from cost-based contracts for early stages (negotiated with contractors that the client trusts), through to fixed price competitively tendered contracts in later stages as project objectives and specifications become better defined.

Normally, the client will have to pay a premium to the contractor for bearing the cost uncertainty as part of the contract price. This premium can be seen as a 'risk premium' less an 'opportunity discount', but as the opportunity efficiency pursued by the contractor will be defined from the contractor's perspective, the 'discount' aspect of the net premium may be ambiguous. From the client's perspective, this net premium may be excessive unless moderated by competitive forces. However, the client will not know how much of a given bid is for estimated project costs and how much is for the bidder's 'risk premium' less his 'opportunity discount' – unless these elements are clearly distinguished. In the face of competition, tendering contractors (in any industry) will be under continuous temptation to pare prices and profits in an attempt to win work. Faced with the difficulty of earning an adequate return, such contractors may seek to recover costs and increase earnings by cutting back on the quality of materials and services supplied in ways that are not visible to the client, or by a determined and systematic pursuit of claims – a practice common in the construction industry. This situation is most likely to occur where the supply of goods or services exceeds demand, or clients are price conscious, or clients find suppliers difficult to differentiate. Even with prior or post bidding screening out of any contractors not deemed capable, reliable and sound, the lowest bidder will have to be that member of the viable set of contractors who scores highest overall in the following categories:

1. Most optimistic in relation to cost uncertainties. This may reflect expertise, but it may reflect a willingness to depart from implicit and explicit specification of the project, or ignorance of what is required.
2. Most optimistic in relation to claims for additional revenue.
3. Least concerned with considerations such as the impact on reputation or the chance of bankruptcy.
4. Most desperate for work.

Selecting the lowest fixed price bid is an approach which should be used with caution, particularly when:

- uncertainty is significant;
- performance specifications are not comprehensive, clear and legally enforceable;
- the expertise, reputation and financial security of the contractor are not beyond question.

The situation has been understood in conventional risk management terms for many years, as summed up by Barnes (1984):

> *The problem is that when conditions of contract placing large total risk upon the contractor are used, and work is awarded by competitive tender, the contractor who accidentally or deliberately underestimated the risks is most likely to get the work. When the risks materialize with full force he must then either struggle to extract compensation from the client or suffer the loss. This stimulates the growth of the claims problem.*
>
> *The remedy seems to be to take factors other than lowest price into account when appointing contractors. In particular, a reputation gained for finishing fast and on time without aggressive pursuit of extra payment for the unexpected should be given very great weight and should be seen to do so.*

Barnes' use of 'total risk' equates to 'risk' in our 'possible unfavourable outcome' sense plus 'opportunity' in our 'possible favourable outcome' sense, without clarity about expectations from different perspectives and associated risk/opportunity datum issues, and his use of 'risks' equates to 'sources of uncertainty' in our terms. Because opportunity is treated indirectly as upside risk, it does not get emphasized, and risk efficiency and its opportunity efficiency generalization may not be in evidence. Developing the implications of clarity about these issues is useful.

An underlying issue is the extent to which clients and contractors wish to cooperate with an attitude of mutual gain from trade, seeing each other as partners. Unfortunately, the all too common approach is inherently confrontational, based on trying to gain most at the other party's expense, or at least seeking to demonstrate that one has not been 'beaten' by the other party. This confrontational attitude can breed an atmosphere of wariness and mistrust. A 'win–win' notion is not part of the agenda. It appears to matter greatly whether the client is entering a one-off non-repeating contractual relationship, or a relationship that may be repeated in the future. To the extent that the client is not a regular customer, the client can be concerned only with the present project and may have limited expertise in distinguishing the quality of potential contractors and bids. Competition is then used to 'get the best deal'. This is often manifested as seeking the lowest fixed price on the naive and rash assumption that all other things are equal. As indicated above, this practice brings its own risk, often in large quantities.

Well-founded willingness to own uncertainty

Many of the problems with claims and arbitration arise because of contractual parties' preoccupation with transferring uncertainty to other parties, generally under fixed price contracts. To the extent that either clients or contractors believe that uncertainty can be transferred or off-loaded onto the other, or some third party such as a subcontractor, then any assessment or management of project uncertainty on their part is likely to be half-hearted. Consequently, many contracting parties do not assess sources of uncertainty or share information about uncertainty in any systematic way. Some address 'risks' in the 'event uncertainty' sense, but fail to address inherent variability, ambiguity and systemic uncertainty in a comprehensive manner; and many fail to understand that transferring uncertainty involves opportunity as well as risk. As we have seen in the previous section, this behaviour may not be in the best interests of either party.

Abrahamson (1973) has commented on the problem in the following way, using 'risk' in both the 'source of uncertainty' sense and the 'unfavourable/favourable outcome relative to an opportunity/risk datum defined by expectations' sense:

> *The strangest thing is that the pricing of risk ... is resisted by both sides. Some contractors prefer a contentious right to their extra costs to a chance to price a risk, and indeed rely on the increase in their final account from claims to make up for low tenders. On the other hand, some clients and engineers prefer to refer to risks generally or as obliquely as possible, presumably in the hope of finding a contractor who will not allow for them fully in his price.*
>
> *These two attitudes are equally reprehensible and short sighted. What a sorry start to a project when they encounter each other!*

Arguably the focus of Abrahamson's comments is 'risk' in the downside sense, with insufficient emphasis of the upside in opportunity efficiency terms. Such behaviour is often encouraged by legal advisers concerned to put their client's legal interests first. In legal circles debate about risk allocation in the downside implications of uncertainty sense is usually about clarifying and ensuring the effectiveness of allocation arrangements in the contract. Lawyers are not concerned with the principles that should guide appropriate allocation of uncertainty between contracting parties in a truly general opportunity efficiency sense from their client's perspective. It could be argued that they are pursuing their own future interests by maximizing conflict, implicitly if not explicitly.

Limiting the focus on uncertainty to event uncertainty, 'risks' in the common practice sense, adds inappropriate limitations and confusion, making a bad situation worse.

At first sight, appropriate allocation of all relevant uncertainty might be based on the willingness of parties to take on uncertainty (Ward et al., 1991). However, willingness to accept ownership of uncertainty will only result in conscientious management of project uncertainty to the extent that it is based on:

1. an adequate perception of project uncertainty;
2. a real ability to bear the consequences of risk eventuating;
3. a real ability to manage the associated uncertainty and thereby both mitigate risk and capture opportunities and associated rewards;
4. a reasoned assessment of risk–reward tradeoffs.

Willingness to own uncertainty should not be a criterion for uncertainty allocation to the extent that it is based on:

1. an inadequate perception of project uncertainty;
2. a false perception of ability to bear the consequences of a risk eventuating;
3. a need to obtain work;
4. a view that transferring uncertainty to another party is costless.

As noted earlier, these latter conditions can be an underlying reason for low tender prices on fixed price contracts.

To ensure that willingness to own uncertainty is well-founded, explicit consideration of uncertainty allocated between the contracting parties is desirable, preferably at an early stage in negotiations or the tendering process, addressing all aspects of uncertainty at a suitable level of clarity. In particular, contractors ought to be given an adequate opportunity to price for all the uncertainty they will be expected to carry. Unfortunately, the following scenario for a construction project is often typical.

A construction project that had taken several years to justify and prepare was parcelled up and handed to tendering contractors who were given just a few weeks to evaluate it from scratch and commit themselves to a price for building it. Each contractor tendering had been through an extensive and costly pre-qualification exercise that was designed to determine their capacity to undertake the work. Having the gratification of being considered acceptable, they wanted to be allowed the time to study the tender documents in detail and to consider carefully their approach to the work. Instead they were faced with a tender submission deadline that only permitted a scanty appraisal of the complex construction problems and uncertainty involved. Consequently, each tenderer proceeds along the following lines.

A site assessment team, which might include a project manager, estimator, planner, geologist and representatives of specialist subcontractors, is assembled and despatched to the site, with instructions to gather all the method- and cost-related information needed for preparing the bid. This information, together with quotations from materials suppliers, subcontractors and plant companies – and advice on the legal, insurance, financial and taxation implications – is assessed by the estimating team working under great pressure to meet the deadline. Various construction techniques have to be investigated and compared, and temporary works proposals considered and designed. Lack of information on ground conditions, plant availability, materials supply, subcontractor capacity and many other important factors have to be overcome by further investigation and inspired guesswork. The contractual terms have to be explored to elicit the imposed 'risk strategy' of the client. An assessment has to be made of the client's reaction to any qualifications in the bid. Possible claims opportunities are evaluated.

In the absence of adequate time and information, any evaluation and pricing of potential risk exposure is on an *ad hoc* basis. Evaluation of uncertainty begins by questioning experienced managers in the contractor's organization and arriving at a consensus of the 'gut feelings' expressed. The overall level of uncertainty is assessed by looking at the overall programme, checking if it is very 'tight', considering the effects of delays by suppliers, and checking the basic conditions for any extension of time. Few, if any, calculations or references to specific results on previous contracts are made, the rationale being that any such references are unlikely to be applicable to the circumstances of the contract in question, even if any relevant data existed. The chairman ends up by pulling a figure out of the air based upon his feelings about the advice obtained.

Even if the contractor is prepared to undertake appropriate analysis of project uncertainty, a lack of information about project sources of uncertainty coupled with a lack of time to prepare a tender may preclude proper evaluation.

Joint identification of sources of uncertainty by the client and the tendering contractors is desirable, on efficiency grounds in terms of cost effective identification of a comprehensive list, and to ensure that both parties are fully aware of the uncertainties involved. If tendering contractors were simply given more time to tender without client involvement, they might undertake an adequate analysis of the project uncertainty. However, while many sources of project uncertainty may be best assessed by knowledgeable contractors, it may be more efficient for the client to undertake an analysis of certain sources to expedite the tendering process and to ensure that all tenderers have similar information. For example, contractors should not be expected to bear uncertainty that cannot be cost effectively quantified with sufficient certainty, such as variable ground on a tunnelling project. In such cases the price ought to relate to what is actually encountered (Barber, 1989). If clients are unduly concerned about bearing such uncertainty, then it will be appropriate for them to undertake the necessary in-depth analysis themselves, and require tendering contracts to price for the uncertainty on the basis of the client's analysis. Sharing such risk is always an option, as discussed later. Obviously, the greater the detail provided by the client in relation to sources which are to be borne in whole or in part by the contractor, the less the contractor has to price for uncertainty about what the project involves.

In determining a final bid figure, contractors need to consider several other factors besides estimates of the prime cost of performing the contract (Ward and Chapman, 1988, 2008). The intensity of the competition from other contractors, the costs of financing, insurance and bonding, the financial status of the client, terms of payment and project cash flow, the level of provisions to cover all sources of uncertainty and the level of the contingency allowance to cover risk, all affect the mark-up that is added to the prime cost of construction. This also applies to the contractor's view of opportunities and opportunity efficiency issues. The tendering contractors' uncertainty, opportunity and risk analysis will have additional dimensions to the client's analysis. In addition, each contractor requires a bid that gives an appropriate balance between the risk of not getting the contract and the uncertainty associated with possible profits or losses if the contract is obtained, as illustrated in the IBM UK bidding example discussion of Chapter 12.

Transparent pricing

Apart from allowing contractors sufficient time to properly consider the pricing of uncertainty, clients need to be able to assess the extent to which contractors' tender prices are based on a well-founded willingness to take on project uncertainty. A useful 'transparent pricing' strategy is for the client to require fixed price bids to be broken down into prices for expected project costs (including appropriate provisions) and risk premia (which reflect asymmetric penalties associated with contingency allowances plus fees for bearing risk) for various sources of uncertainty. Different contractors' views of opportunities should be built into their expected costs, and different estimates associated with such differences plus bias. The nature and control of all bias should be understood. Supporting documentation should show the contractors' perceptions of uncertainty upon which these assessments were based, to allow meaningful audit of bias for example. As in insurance contracts, pricing based on broad categories of uncertainty, rather than related to small details, is a realistic approach. An important consideration in performing uncertainty analysis is the identification of key factors which can have a major impact on project performance. However, detailed uncertainty analysis may not be necessary to determine the relative significance of some project sources of uncertainty. Pricing need not consider all project uncertainty in detail, but it does need to be explicitly related to major sources and it does need to be comprehensive – without large 'unknown unknown' gaps.

An important benefit of a 'transparent pricing' strategy to both client and contractor is clarification of categories of uncertainty remaining with the client despite a 'fixed price' contract. For example, there may be project sources of uncertainty associated with exogenous factors, such as changes in regulatory requirements during the project, which are not identified or allocated by the contract. Such factors are unlikely to be allowed for in bids, because tenderers will consider such factors to be outside their control and the responsibility of the client.

A further benefit of 'transparent pricing' is that it helps to address an important potential 'adverse selection' problem. Contractors who can provide honestly stated, good-quality uncertainty pricing may price themselves out of the market in relation to those who provide dishonestly stated, poor-quality uncertainty pricing at low prices, if there are sufficient clients who are unable to distinguish between good and poor quality, honesty and dishonesty. As Akerlof (1970) argues in a paper entitled 'The market for "lemons": quality uncertainty and the market mechanism', poor quality and dishonesty can drive good quality and honesty out of the market. Clients can address this problem by requiring transparent pricing of uncertainty in tenders and by requiring tender submissions to include plans for managing uncertainty. In this way, comparisons between tenderers in terms of the extent of well-founded willingness to bear uncertainty can be made on a more informed basis.

In practice, tenderers experienced in uncertainty management may be able to demonstrate well-founded willingness to own uncertainty *and* submit lower tender prices than competitors, by exploiting opportunity efficiency defined from the client's perspective. In such cases 'transparent pricing' should help to consolidate their advantage over less experienced contractors, but they may have to 'educate' their clients to develop 'enlightened relationships'. 'Enlightened relationships', driven by clients who educate their contractors as necessary, are a more robust way forward.

Efficient allocation of uncertainty

It is often suggested that cost uncertainty should be allocated to the party best able to anticipate and control that uncertainty, usually replacing the term 'uncertainty' by 'risk' – frequently in the event uncertainty sense – although variability, ambiguity and systemic uncertainty may also be involved. On this basis, a tentative conclusion is that fixed price contracts are appropriate when sources of uncertainty are controllable by the contractor, CPFF contracts are appropriate when sources of uncertainty are controllable by the client. However, this conclusion ignores the relative willingness and ability of each party to own uncertainty in terms of associated risk in the possible unfavourable outcomes sense – to bear risk in our terms. In particular, it ignores the pricing of uncertainty in terms of bearing risk, the client's attitude to tradeoffs between expected cost and carrying risk, and the contractor's attitude to tradeoffs between expected profit and carrying risk. Further, it fails to address questions about how any uncertainty that is not controllable by either party should be allocated.

In principle, decisions about the allocation of uncertainty ought to be motivated by a search for opportunity efficiency, including favourable tradeoffs between risk and expected performance as described in Chapter 3. Given the opportunity, a client should favour opportunity efficient allocation of uncertainty between parties to a project which simultaneously reduces risk and improves project performance for the client, be it in terms of lower expected cost or higher expected profits, or some other measure of performance. An obvious example is decisions about purchasing insurance cover. Insurance is best regarded as one way of developing contingency plans (one of the types of generic response listed in Table 7.1), where payment of an insurance premium ensures the ability to make some level of restitution in the event that an insured risk eventuates. The basic maxim for risk efficient insurance purchase is: Only insure risks that you cannot afford to take, because (a) an uncovered event would cause serious financial distress that would distort other basic operations, or (b) dealing with an uncovered event would cause other forms of distress it is worth paying to avoid. For example, employment injury liability insurance may be worth while on both counts. A project may not be able to meet large claims without financial distress, but it may be just as important to avoid a position of conflict with employees over claims. The insured party may take steps to reduce the possibility of loss or mitigate the impact of any insured risk, and reasonable efforts to do this may be required by the insurer. Insurers are third parties who take on specific risks with a view to making a profit; therefore, if the premium they can charge is not greater than the expected cost of underwriting the risk (giving them a positive expected profit), they will not take on the risk. In this sense they are subcontractors, competing for sources of uncertainty which might be better left with other contractors or the client.

Elsewhere (Chapman and Ward, 1994), we show in detail how the allocation of uncertainty might be guided by consideration of the risk efficiency of alternative forms of contract payment terms. In choosing between a fixed price or a CPFF contract, the criterion of risk efficiency implies choosing the contract with the preferred combination of expected cost and risk. As explained in Chapter 3, if one option offers both lower expected cost and lower risk, then this is a risk efficient choice.

The approach in Chapman and Ward (1994) distinguishes three basic types of project cost uncertainty: contractor controllable uncertainty, client controllable uncertainty, and uncontrolled uncertainty. The analysis suggests that different contractual arrangements may be appropriate for each type of uncertainty, in each case dependent on the relative willingness of the client and contractor to accept project-related risk in the possible unfavourable outcome relative to expectations sense used in this book. If a project involves all three types of uncertainty, the contract should involve different payment terms for each. To the extent that individual sources of cost uncertainty independently contribute to each of the three categories, it may be appropriate to subdivide categories and negotiate different payment terms for each major independent source. One simple, practical example of this approach is where a client undertakes to pay a lower fixed price by agreeing to carry a designated source of uncertainty via cost reimbursement in respect of that source.

The analysis highlights the need for clients to consider project cost uncertainty explicitly in the form of a 'PC curve' (PC = Probability distribution of Costs), and to identify T (the clienT's 'equivalent' certain cost), corresponding to the maximum fixed price the client is prepared to pay. In the envisaged procedure, the client first identifies appropriate constituent groupings of project risks, constructing associated PC curves and identifying T values for each. The PC curve for the project as a whole is then obtained by combining the component PC curves. The total project PC curve together with the associated T value is used later for checking consistency and completeness of submitted bids rather than to determine a single payment method for the whole project. Tenderers are asked to submit for each group of project sources of uncertainty designated by the client:

1. fixed price bids R (the contractoR's 'equivalent' certain cost);
2. the contribution to profit, or fee, K (a constant), required if a CPFF contract is agreed.

In addition, tenderers might be required or choose to submit their perceptions of constituent source of uncertainty PC curves (which need not match the client's perceptions), to demonstrate the depth of their understanding of the project sources of uncertainty and to justify the level of bids, should these be regarded by the client as unusually low or high. Equally, a client might provide tenderers with the client's perceptions of constituent source of uncertainty PC curves to encourage and facilitate appropriate attention to project cost uncertainties. If a spirit of cooperation and willingness to negotiate mutually beneficial uncertainty sharing arrangements prevailed, the client and individual tenderers could exchange perceptions about constituent risk PC curves with a view to developing a consensus view of project uncertainty. Such views expressed as PC curves would facilitate the negotiation of mutually beneficial uncertainty sharing agreements without the necessity for the PC curves themselves to have any legal status in the contract.

In assessing bids, the client would be concerned about the relative sizes of R and T values for each constituent source of uncertainty PC curve. The contractor bidding with the lowest total sum of R values would not necessarily be the contractor with the most preferred pattern of R values.

Our analysis (Chapman and Ward, 1994) concludes the following about the risk efficiency of fixed price and CPFF contracts:

1. a fixed price contract is usually risk efficient in allocating contractor controllable uncertainty;
2. a CPFF contract is usually risk efficient in allocating client controllable uncertainty;
3. in respect of uncontrollable uncertainty, a fixed price contract is risk efficient if the contractor is more willing to accept risk ($R < T$), but a CPFF contract is risk efficient if the client is more willing to accept risk ($T < R$).

An important conclusion is that even where client and contractor share similar perceptions of project cost uncertainty, a fixed price contract may be inefficient for the client, if the contractor is more risk averse than the client. In this situation the contractor will require a higher premium to bear the risk than the client would be prepared to pay for avoiding the risk. This situation can arise where the client is a relatively large organization for whom the project is one of many, but the contractor is a relatively small organization for whom the project is a major proportion of the contractor's business, a fairly common scenario.

We believe the results this analysis suggests are robust. These are not abstract arguments which will not withstand the impact of practical considerations. However, some clients have appeared to be willing to enter into CPFF contracts only as a last resort. For example, Thorn (1986) notes an experience in the UK Ministry of Defence in which the desire to avoid taking risk has frequently led to non-competitive contracts being placed on a fixed price basis, even when the specification has been insufficiently defined for a firm estimate to be agreed:

> In such cases, the contractor is unwilling to commit to a fixed price without a substantial contingency to cover any unknown risks, and the Authority is unable to accept the high level of contingency required by the contractor. The result is that prices have been agreed at such a late stage in the contract that the amount of risk eventually accepted by the contractor is substantially reduced and, in some cases, removed altogether. The Review Board has frequently expressed concern at delays in price fixing, and has advocated the use of incentive contracts. These are intended to be used when the risks are too great to enable fixed prices to be negotiated, but not so great as to justify the use of cost plus contracts.

Part of the problem here is the need to distinguish between the common use of 'risk(s)' in the source of uncertainty sense, with an expected outcome value, and risk in the 'possible unfavourable outcomes relative to expectations' sense used in this book, the basis of risk efficiency and opportunity efficiency.

Incentive contracts

Incentive contracts, often referred to as 'target cost' or 'cost-plus-incentive-fee' contracts, offer the possibility of sharing uncertainty between the client and the contractor and an intermediary position between fixed price and CPFF contracts. Sharing uncertainty implies sharing both opportunity and risk in a related manner. This is potentially a more opportunity efficient alternative for both the client and the contractor.

In the simplest form of incentive contract, where

C = the actual project cost (which is uncertain at the start of the project),
E = target cost,
b = the sharing rate, $0 < b < 1$,
F = the target profit level,

and E, b and F are fixed at the commencement of the contract, payment by the client to the contractor is

$$C_T = F + bE + C(1 - b),\qquad(15.1)$$

and the profit to the contractor is

$$P = F + b(E - C).\qquad(15.2)$$

When $b = 1$, the contract corresponds to a fixed price contract. When $b = 0$, the contract corresponds to a CPFF contract.

Note that, in Equation (15.2), if the cost C exceeds E by more than F/b, then the profit to the contractor becomes negative (the contractor makes a loss).

In the situation described by Equation (15.2), which is sometimes referred to as a budget-based scheme, tendering firms select a budget (target cost), and incentive profit is proportional to budget variance (Reichelstein, 1992). Three parameters are required to specify the contract: the sharing rate b, the target cost level E, and the target profit level F. In theory, the target cost level should correspond to the expected value of project costs. In practice, it is very important that this is understood, lest misunderstandings about the status of this figure arise. Instead of specifying F, a target profit rate r may be specified, where $F = rE$. With this specification the client must decide which (if any) values to preset for E, b and F or r prior to inviting tenders.

An alternative form of Equation (15.2) is

$$P = d - bC\qquad(15.3)$$

where d is a fixed profit fee, with

$$d = F + bE.\qquad(15.4)$$

In Equation (15.3) only two parameters are required to specify the contract: the sharing rate b, and the fixed profit fee d. Tenders may be invited in the form of d if b is pre-specified by the client, or for both b and d. Typically, if a 'uniform' value for b is pre-specified by the client, the contract is awarded to the contractor submitting the lowest fixed profit fee d.

The economic literature focuses on linear incentive contracts in the form of Equation (15.1), but in practice incentive contracts often involve more than one sharing rate over the range of possible project costs, and they may incorporate minimum and maximum levels of allowable profit. Two main types of incentive contract are usually distinguished: the fixed price incentive (FPI) contract and the cost plus incentive fee (CPIF) contract. These differ mainly in the treatment of cost overruns beyond some ceiling. In both forms of contract the contractor's profit from cost underruns is subject to a ceiling value, but uncertainty sharing takes place for costs in some range around the target or expected cost. With an FPI contract the contractor assumes a higher share of risk for cost overruns outside this range, and may carry all risk above some set cost level. With a CPIF contract the client takes all cost risk above some cost level and the contractor receives a minimum level of profit.

Selection of an appropriate sharing rate

Uncertainty sharing arrangements may be opportunity efficient from the client's point of view when contractors are risk averse, have superior pre-contractual information, or limited liability under the proposed contract. The desirability of uncertainty sharing will also depend on whether the cost uncertainty is controllable by the contractor, controllable by the client, or controllable by neither. In the latter case, the party owning the uncertainty acts as a quasi-insurer (Ward et al., 1991), and the desirability of uncertainty sharing is related to the relative levels of risk aversion of the contractor and client. In the case of cost uncertainty that is controllable to some extent by either party, uncertainty sharing influences incentives to manage those sources of uncertainty.

An inherent problem with uncertainty sharing is the reduction in a contractor's sensitivity to adverse outcomes as the proportion of cost uncertainty borne by the client increases. In the case of contractor controllable sources of uncertainty, the contractor's motivation to limit cost overruns and seek cost savings will be reduced as the client takes on more uncertainty. It follows that different levels of uncertainty sharing may be appropriate for categories of uncertainty which are (a) controllable by the contractor, (b) controllable by the client, and (c) not controllable by either.

Samuelson (1986) shows that, under 'general conditions', *some* level of uncertainty sharing, with $0 < b < 1$, should be preferred by the client to either CPFF or fixed price contracts. The general nature of Samuelson's analysis does not lead to any specific optimal values for b, but the optimum value of b increases as the client becomes more risk averse, and as more costs are controllable by the contractor. A further complication is that contractor risk aversion affects the actual level of contractor effort on controlling costs once the sharing rate b has been negotiated. The greater the perceived risk of loss in a contracting situation, the more vigorously contractors strive to reduce costs for the sake of avoiding loss as well as for the sake of gaining increments of profit (Scherer, 1964). A similar difficulty exists in considering the efficiency of sharing client controllable uncertainty. However, in specific situations, the client may be able to identify and cost various options available and evaluate these under different sharing arrangements.

In the case of uncertainty which is not controllable by either the client or the contractor, a plausible variation to the uncertainty sharing arrangement in (15.1) and (15.2) is to set $F = K + b^2(V - E)$, where K is the fee required by the contractor if a cost reimbursement CPFF contract were to be agreed, and V is set to the value R or T referred to in the previous section. Assuming that variance (Var) is an appropriate measure of risk, this sharing arrangement reduces the contractor's risk from $\text{Var}(E - C)$ to $\text{Var}\ b(E - C) = b^2\ \text{Var}(E - C)$. Therefore the contractor's risk premium should be reduced from $(V - E)$ to $b^2(V - E)$ under this sharing arrangement. With agreement between client and contractor on the value of the expected cost E, this arrangement is risk efficient for both client and contractor for a wide range of circumstances (Chapman and Ward, 1994).

Of course, difficulties in specifying an optimum, risk efficient level for the sharing rate need not preclude the use of incentive contracts and pragmatic definition of sharing rates by the client. In practice incentive contracts, or target cost contracts, often specify different sharing rates for costs above, below and close to the target cost, as in the case of FPI and CPIF contracts noted earlier. This provides substantial flexibility to design incentive contracts which can reflect the particular project context, and the relative willingness and ability of the client and the contractor to bear financial risk. Broome and Perry (2002) describe several examples of incentive contracts and the different rationales underlying each one, usefully illustrating many of the considerations involved in effective and efficient allocation of risk. The underlying principle, as Broome and Perry put it, is:

> the alignment of the motivations of the parties so as to maximize the likelihood of project objectives being achieved, taking into account the constraints and risks that act on the project and the strengths and weaknesses of the parties to it.

Determining an appropriate target cost

A further problem in ensuring an opportunity efficient incentive contract is determining an appropriate value for the target cost E. Ideally, the client would like the target cost to correspond to the contractor's true estimate of expected cost. Obviously, the benefit to the client of an incentive element in the contractor's remuneration will be undermined if the target cost is higher than the contractor's true estimate of expected cost.

Suppose firms are invited to tender values for b and E. A disadvantage of this invitation is that it can encourage a generally high level of tender values for E. But the client would like to encourage truthful, unbiased estimates of the expected costs from tenderers. In principle, the client could achieve this by offering higher values of b for lower estimates of E. Then submitting an overestimate of expected cost will be less appealing to the contractor because the associated lower sharing rate limits the contractor's ability to earn large profits when costs turn out to be low. Conversely, if a contractor truly believes that costs will be high, the threat of low profits if costs turn out to be high will dissuade the contractor from submitting an underestimate of expected costs.

Thus, the client could offer a menu of contracts, in terms of values of F and b for different values of E. By submitting a cost estimate, a tendering firm chooses one particular incentive contract given by the corresponding F and b values. Provided F and b are suitably defined, such a menu of contracts can induce firms to provide unbiased estimates of project cost.

A practical application of this menu approach for rewarding sales personnel in IBM Brazil is described by Gonik (1978). Gonik describes an incentive system which gears rewards to how close staff forecasts of territory sales and actual results are to the company's objectives. A sales forecast S is made by each sales person for a given period and sales region, and this is used to determine each person's level of bonus P. If the company quota is Q, actual sales achieved are A, and a base level of bonus payment preset by the company is B, then each person's level of bonus payment P is given by

$$P = BS / Q, \text{ where } S = A \tag{15.5}$$
$$P = B(A + S) / 2Q, \text{ where } S < A \tag{15.6}$$
$$P = B(3A - S)/ 2Q, \text{ where } S > A \tag{15.7}$$

In general, for a given sales forecast S, bonuses increase as A increases, but for a given A, payments are maximized if $A = S$. Thus, sales personnel receive more for higher sales but are also better off if they succeed in forecasting actual sales as closely as possible. In principle, a similar system could be adopted in contracting to encourage contractors to provide unbiased estimates of project costs and control these costs to the best of their ability (see, for example, Reichelstein, 1992).

Selection of efficient contractors

If the client presets b and F (or r where $F = rE$), the selection of the contractor who bids the lowest value for E (or d) is not guaranteed to minimize procurement costs for the client. There may still be difficulties in selecting the most efficient contractor. For example, McCall (1970) has argued that incentive contracts awarded on the basis of the lowest bid leads to 'inefficient' firms being selected. McCall's analysis implies that relatively inefficient firms, whose actual costs are high, tend to submit estimated costs (bids E) that are lower than actual costs, because they can share some of their losses with the client. Conversely, relatively efficient firms, whose actual costs of production are low, tend to submit estimated costs (bids) that are higher than actual costs. With the client sharing in any cost underrun, the less an efficient firm's expected cost, the more it must bid to secure a profit equal to that obtainable elsewhere. Hence, if a client chooses among firms on the basis of the lowest bid, then it is possible that it will select relatively inefficient firms (high actual costs) instead of relatively efficient ones (low actual costs). The probability of selecting a high-cost instead of a low-cost firm increases as the declared sharing rate decreases.

In addition, where F and b are fixed by the client, Baron (1972) shows that if two firms are bidding for a contract, other things being equal, the more risk-averse firm will submit the lower bid (in effect the lower estimate of E from Equation (15.4)), and the probability of a cost overrun will be greater if that firm is selected. Thus a low bid for d may reflect a contractor's wish to reduce the risk of not winning the contract rather than ability to perform the contract at low cost. This possibility is generally recognized in both fixed price and CPFF contract situations.

However, the above arguments by Baron and McCall are of limited relevance where clients do not preset the sharing rate b. More usually, it might be expected that the fixed profit fee d and sharing rates would be determined together, so that clients would bargain simultaneously for both low cost targets *and* high contractor share rates. Thus, in general, the tighter the negotiated cost target, the higher the sharing proportion desired by the client. In these circumstances, Canes

(1975) showed that there is a systematic tendency towards cost overruns, because contractors tend to submit bids below their actual estimate of expected costs. According to Canes only a subset of efficient firms will be willing to compete by simultaneously increasing the share rate they will accept and reducing their target cost bid. Inefficient firms and the remainder of efficient firms will prefer to charge for higher share rates by raising target cost bids, and in Canes' analysis these firms correspond to the set of firms which submit bids below their expected costs. To the extent that tendering contractors are observed to charge for higher share rates in this way, cost overruns can be expected from such contractors. As a contract letting strategy, Canes suggests setting the target profit rate r (and hence the target profit level F) at zero while allowing firms to choose share rates subject to some minimum rate greater than zero. Canes argues that this policy should minimize clients' costs of procurement while inducing firms to reveal their true opportunity costs of production.

However, an important assumption in the analysis of Canes (1975) and McCall (1970) is that the contracting firms are assumed to be risk neutral (maximizers of expected profit). In situations where contractors are significantly risk averse, their conclusions need to be treated with caution.

Multidimension incentive contracts

Consideration of incentive contracts, based on sharing the consequences of cost out-turns different from an expected cost figure, provides a useful starting point for considering the alignment of the motivation of contractor with client objectives. As noted earlier, pragmatic variation of risk-sharing rates for cost out-turns above, below, or close to target costs, can provide additional flexibility to reflect a particular project context and the relative capabilities of client and contractor to control costs, or bear the financial consequences of cost overruns. However, such contracts are limited in their ability to align contractor motivation with client objectives because they only address the cost dimension of performance. Thus an incentive contract based on costs will not adequately address the management of uncertainty about performance in other dimensions, such as project duration and quality of deliverables. A cost-based incentive contract leaves the contractor free to exploit contractual ambiguities in respect of time and quality performance by making tradeoffs between cost, time and quality that optimize payments to the contractor based on cost outcomes. Such interdependent management of cost – time – quality aspects of project performance may not be in the best interests of the client.

A more general approach is to adopt multidimension incentive contracts that incentivize the contractor to manage uncertainty about various attributes of performance in a manner that is aligned with the interests of the client. For example, in a design and build contract, the client may be interested in performance in respect of capital cost, time to build, subsequent operating and maintenance costs, physical appearance, and various aspects of functionality. A central issue here is that managing uncertainty with respect to the different performance criteria will involve making tradeoffs in performance with respect to these criteria, and these tradeoffs should be opportunity efficient tradeoffs with respect to the client's objectives.

Any contract with a supplier ought to reflect these concerns of the buyer, and specifically provide incentives for the supplier to manage uncertainty and the inevitable tradeoffs between performance criteria in a way that aligns with the buyer's interests. This requires a *'balanced incentive and risk sharing'* (BIARS) contract. Given the adoption of buyer and supplier as a useful general characterization of the parties to a contract, use of the acronym BIARS (pronounced 'buyers'), seems apt.

Not surprisingly, a key requirement to operate any form of BIARS contract is that the buyers must first be clear about their own objectives and performance criteria for the product or service they seek. Specifically, the buyers need to:

1. identify pertinent performance criteria;
2. develop a measure of the level of performance for each criterion;
3. identify the most preferred (optimum) feasible combination of performance levels on each criterion;
4. identify acceptable alternative combinations of performance levels on each criterion;
5. identify the tradeoffs between performance criteria implied by these preferences.

The five steps above are not just applicable to buyers contemplating a BIARS contract. These steps should be undertaken by any project owner, particularly in the early conception and design stages of a project. Undertaking these steps should be part of the process of understanding the relationships between the seven Ws of the project, and managing uncertainty about project performance. The process of identifying and considering possible tradeoffs between performance criteria is an opportunity to improve performance. It should enable a degree of optimization with respect to each performance measure, and it is an opportunity that needs to be seized.

Adopting an iterative process may be the most effective way to complete these steps. The information gathered from these steps can then be used to formulate a BIARS contract by selecting some or all of the performance criteria for inclusion in the contract, developing payment scales which reflect the acceptable tradeoffs, and negotiating acceptable 'risk sharing' ratios for each contract performance criterion with the supplier. Effective BIARS contracts involve three basic principles:

1. congruent motivation,
2. expected values as a basis for triggers, and
3. consistent risk-sharing ratios.

The best way to obtain congruence between the motivation of supplier and buyer is to ensure that the actions of the supplier result in pain and gain in the same proportions as the buyer will experience between all performance criteria of significant interest to the buyer that are not predetermined free of uncertainty and ambiguity. This significantly reduces the moral hazard problem for the buyer.

Expected values should be the basis for pain/gain triggers. In a single dimension, an incentive contract based on cost pain and gain sharing rates may vary with performance relative to a target cost E, most appropriately an unbiased estimate of expected cost, as noted earlier. In the mult-dimensional case, the E_k for the k different performance criteria are best referred to as 'trigger' points above and below which pain and gain sharing rates may vary. The term 'target' is no longer appropriate since risk efficient tradeoffs may involve deliberately aiming for performance above or below any one particular E_k value. Departures from this expected value basis need care – building in a reasonably high chance of meeting targets to avoid perceptions of 'failure' is tempting, but the expected bonus implied needs to be offset, and this can raise difficulties.

Consistent risk sharing ratios are also crucial. Pain and gain adjustments to the expected cost or price should be driven by risk sharing rates set with respect to each of the k performance criteria that reflect the relative variability and importance to the buyer of each performance criterion.

Capital cost is an obvious place to start, as a basic performance criterion. Starting with the premise that the supplier should take 50% of the risk associated with potential variations about a 'trigger' cost seems a plausible place to start unless there are obvious reasons for more or less. The obvious next step is balancing this capital cost incentive with a duration incentive which reflects the actual and opportunity costs to the buyer of delay and early delivery. Consideration of such opportunity costs is a basic aspect of planning that can be pursued through an appropriate iterative process, with or without uncertainty. That is, having developed in outline a plan with what seems a suitable expected cost and duration, replan it to answer the questions:

- 'How much would it cost to take a week (or month) off the schedule?' and 'would it be worth it?'
- 'If a week (month) is worth it – what about two?'
- 'If a shorter duration isn't worth it – what about a longer duration?'

If these questions have not been addressed then appropriate duration–capital cost tradeoffs have not been addressed, and there is no reason to assume that what is proposed is appropriate. This indicates a very basic project planning failure, whether or not uncertainty is an issue.

Balancing capital cost and duration against operating cost seems a very obvious next step. This involves an iterative approach to seek an answer to the question: 'If we redesign and replan the project to reduce capital cost by allowing operating costs (broadly defined) to increase, will there be a net saving over the holding period for the asset?' Operating costs involve a 'cash flow', in the case of a building associated with costs like electricity for light (which may vary with design, for example), fuel for heating (which will vary with insulation specification, for example), painting and other routine maintenance, refurbishment, alterations associated with use changes, off-setting rental income and so on. This cash flow needs to be considered over the lifecycle of the asset of interest, or perhaps a planned holding period. A lifecycle of many years means that net present values must be used for comparison with capital cost at the same point in time. There has been a lot of attention given to 'whole life costing', but there is little evidence that trigger contracts of the kind suggested here have been used to deliver a balance between operating cost, capital cost and duration. Addressing these three criteria is a 'minimalist' defensible position for most projects.

A first pass estimate of the size of annual operating cost variations as a function of design might suggest that lighting efficiency, heating efficiency, the cost of adapting the layout to revised use, or some other component of 'operating cost', is particularly important. In these cases it would be no more than common sense to pay particular attention to this component when seeking preferred or optimum tradeoffs between capital cost and operating cost. For an office park built primarily to rent out, rentable values (income) may be usefully treated separately in considering possible tradeoffs.

More generally other performance criteria may be relevant in considering tradeoffs. For example, in a railway system, air traffic control system or road system, all the above performance measures may be relevant, plus new ones such as safety, reliability and availability. Each of these new criteria poses measurement difficulties, in terms of measures which can be compared directly to capital cost. Chapman and Ward (2002, ch. 7) indicates how this could be done in relation to safety, and why there is no alternative if we want to consider safety properly in relation to competing demands on finite resources. Opportunity management in the sense of joint optimization with respect to all relevant criteria may require us to look at criteria that can only be evaluated indirectly, like safety, as well as criteria that can be measured directly, like capital cost, and intermediates like project duration.

It is important to appreciate that this search for optimum tradeoffs applies to *each* performance measure and relevant components of concern to the buyer. That is, capital cost expenditure allocations need to be optimized at least approximately within any given total cost. This is largely a 'design issue' linked to the operating cost aspects of design. Activity duration allocations also need to be optimized at least approximately within any given total project duration. This is a planning issue linked to design, and hence to capital and operating costs. These component optimization problems may be treated as separable to some extent, but they are certainly not independent.

The presence of uncertainty in costs and durations demands attention to risk efficient tradeoffs in relation to all performance measures. The only effective practical approach is to make the best guesses we can in all relevant dimensions, and then iteratively test the working assumptions involved in these best guesses.

Intra-organizational relationships and governance

As noted earlier, enlightened relationship management within a particular organization needs to address similar issues to those associated with uncertainty management involving inter-organizational contracts. The intra-organizational parties involved may be individuals, teams, different organizational units, or different levels of management in the organizational hierarchy. While formal contracts between such parties within an organization are not usually present, written or unwritten agreements serve a similar purpose, and issues related to aligned incentives and appropriate allocation of risk and responsibility for managing sources of uncertainty are similar to the inter-organizational contexts.

A project client's board can exercise governance on all projects via budgets and associated understandings with the project manager, a form of contract between the board, representing the organization as a whole and a corporate view of the project, and the project manager, representing those aspects of the project which the project manager is responsible for. One question this raises is: 'Are objectives suitably aligned?' If they are not, perverse incentives may operate. For example, it may not be in the project manager's best interests to reveal significant cost escalation which might lead the board to cancel the project and end the project manager's contract.

Another question this raises is: 'Does the division of ownership of uncertainty via project budget setting make sense?' Generally the project manager has responsibility for managing project-related uncertainty, but financial governance considerations drive how far the project manager has financial control in terms of the allocated project budget. Setting project budgets below the expected cost of a project may seem an effective way of increasing performance by squeezing the project team, but on the average the project manager will need to seek approval for additional funds, with direct approval process costs. More serious are the indirect costs of project staff frustration and unenlightened gambles encouraged by funding levels which are inherently inefficient because they are too low. Such inefficient finance allocation can be avoided by setting project budgets at a thoughtfully selected level above the expected cost of a project by including a contingency allowance that should not be required on average if the expected cost has been properly determined. The sizing of this contingency should be based on all relevant issues. A common governance problem is that contingency allowances are often fully used. This suggests poor estimating, inadequate management of uncertainty, a failure to consider behavioural issues, a lack of incentives for project managers to control costs, or some combination of these issues.

In corporate governance terms, when setting project budgets there is a tradeoff to be made between excessive control costs if budgets are set too low and potential loss of control if budgets are set too high. Even if budgets set at expected cost plus a contingency are well managed, the allocation of contingencies to a portfolio of projects represents an inefficient deployment of the contingency allowance elements from a corporate financing perspective. This needs to be balanced against inefficiencies associated with excessively tight controls. A common pragmatic compromise aims to assign to the project manager a budget of expected cost plus contingency that lets him or her manage about 80% of anticipated variability, so that about 20% of the time project budgets will be exceeded, leading to an immediate audit of performance.

Part of the reason for exceeding the project budget may be the occurrence of 'explicit extreme events' involving a large potential impact value relative to the expected value of their impact. Such risks are best owned at a business unit or corporate level in terms of the potential financial liability (Chapman and Ward, 2002, ch. 6). In operational terms, the business unit or board acts in a corporate self-insurance role involving a self-insurance premium in the form of a provision for a loss. Should the project need to call on funds beyond the agreed project budget, any request from the project manager would be subject to a loss-adjusting process comparable to an insurance company paying a claim.

If the board cannot accommodate self-insurance in this way, it may be appropriate for the board to externally insure an appropriate part of the risk. The board is in business to take appropriate risk up to limits of its ability to do so. It should pass on risk (and expected profit) only when not to do so would increase the threat of corporate difficulties to an unacceptable level if a serious extreme event were to occur. When transferring risk via external insurance, the board should be very selective. A common basis for such selectivity is only insuring losses above some acceptable threshold. That is, if £100 million were deemed the maximum event risk the company should run, a re-insurance approach to extreme event costs above £100 million should be used in conjunction with self-insurance of the first £100 million of any such event.

Governance concerns might also address, at a subproject level, incentives for organizational units working on the project to manage uncertainty in the interests of achieving project objectives. In principle, the issues associated with budget setting for a project and higher level risk financing of extreme events might arise at a subproject level in terms of scaled-down equivalents in the management hierarchy below the project manager. However, extreme events are not the dominant issue at subproject level. The dominant issues are who owns uncertainty, and understanding who should own uncertainty, driven by the need to be able to distinguish between good luck and good management, bad luck and bad management, and bias in estimating future performance.

The essence of the project manager's problem is that the teams or departments responsible for undertaking the sequence of activities in a project may not be motivated to manage uncertainty in the best interests of the project, and the project manager may have limited direct control over their activities. For example a pipeline delivery project might involve in-house activities involving engineering design staff to design the pipeline, and procurement staff to place orders for the pipeline with external suppliers. The design task might have uncertain duration primarily because of uncertain demand in design staff time from other projects and other parts of the same project. An additional factor affecting both time and quality, and therefore cost, might be the quality of the design staff allocated to the task. Similar reasons for task duration variability might apply to the procurement staff, plus potential difficulties associated with suppliers and the ability of procurement staff. In such a context if each activity is assigned a base plan duration set at the 80% confidence level, it is easy for each department to regard the 80% duration figure as a target and lack any incentive to finish their task earlier than this 80% duration. Taking several sequential activities together, a very plausible scenario is that each activity takes the 80% confidence level duration and 20% of the time takes even longer. Chapman and Ward (2002, ch. 6) provide a detailed example and discussion of these dysfunctional effects on project performance. They then go on to show in detail how an appropriately designed internal BIARS contract could incentivize each contributing party to make appropriate tradeoffs between quality, cost and duration, and to finish earlier than the 80% duration.

Governance of the board by a public company's shareholders in terms of project performance can be addressed in related terms. If a company's projects always come in over budget, the incentives in the implicit contract between the board and the shareholders are clearly not working – they are not enlightened and they need to be changed. More appropriate uncertainty sharing may be needed, but other dysfunctional incentives may be involved.

Governance of a government department by a government minister or watchdog can also be addressed in related terms. The Nichols report to the Secretary of State for Transport discussed in Chapter 2 (Nichols, 2007) was the result of a House of Lords Select Committee review of Highways Agency performance. Its success was in part attributable to the enlightened relationship management approach adopted by Mike Nichols. It was not just a critical review of existing practice within the Highways Agency; it addressed uncertainty that needed ownership at Department for Transport and Government levels, emphasized Highway Agency strengths as well as weaknesses, and provided incentives and tools to improve current practice, and motivate the changes needed.

Conclusion

Addressing uncertainty ownership issues in this chapter has been focused on the client–contractor relationship because this is one of the most common and clear-cut contexts in which ownership issues arise. It is also a useful context to illustrate basic ownership issues which apply in most multi-party situations, including intra-organizational contexts where legal contracts are replaced by various forms of agreement ranging from formal terms of reference, written undertakings, informal 'understandings', to traditional working practices. Even with limited client–contractor focus, uncertainty ownership issues are not simple, and only an overview has been provided. Those seriously touched by these issues need to follow up the references provided.

Despite the risks inherent in the fixed price contract this is still a very common form of contract. CCFF contracts have weaknesses for the client/project owner which severely limit its use by risk-averse client organizations. Incentive contracts offer a variety of middle ground positions, but do not appear to be as widely used as they might be. This may be because of a lack of awareness of the shortcomings of typical fixed price contracts, because of a lack of appreciation of the value of incentive contracts in motivating contractors, or because of an inability to design effective incentive contracts. The additional complexity of incentive contracts makes them difficult and time consuming to negotiate, and both parties have to understand complex contract design issues. In particular, there are problems in selecting the lowest cost contractor, and appropriate values for the sharing rate b and the target cost E, not to mention ensuring that the contractor always acts in the best interests of the client with respect to all the client's objectives – measurable or not. Unless firms can be motivated to provide unbiased estimates of costs (perhaps by arrangements such as those described above), client organizations may be wary of incentive contracts when they are unable to formulate realistic project cost targets for themselves, never mind formulating their preferred tradeoffs between all objectives so this can be built into the contract. Incentive contracts may be confined to procurement projects where the client has a sound basis to estimate contract costs, there are uncertainties that make a fixed price contract impractical, but the uncertainties are not so great as to justify the use of cost plus contracts (Thorn, 1986). However, a general problem with incentive contracts is that the evaluation of the consequences of a particular incentive contract is not straightforward when project objective tradeoffs are uncertain. This can make it very difficult to carry out negotiations on a fully informed basis, but such difficulties are not insurmountable (Ward and Chapman, 1995a; Chapman and Ward, 2002, chs 5 and 6). In particular, the 'Balanced Incentive And Risk Sharing' (BIARS) contract approach developed in Chapman and Ward (2002) provides an operational approach to resolving all the issues the authors are aware of, provided the client is prepared to assess preferred tradeoffs between attributes of interest, like cost, duration and various measures of 'quality'. For this reason, it might be better to think of BIARS contracts as 'Balanced Incentive, Opportunity and Risk Sharing' (BIORS) contracts to better reflect this book's terminology – Chapman and Ward (2008) further develop linked ideas. Perhaps the most significant obstacle to greater use of incentive contracts and uncertainty sharing is the still widespread unwillingness of parties entering into procurement contracts to explore the effects of project uncertainty and the possibilities for effective uncertainty management, as distinct from conventional views of risk.

Negotiating a fixed price contract with a trusted contractor may be a preferred alternative for knowledgeable clients, especially if trust is based on previous experience, and perhaps also worth pursuing by less knowledgeable clients. Also, a move away from 'adversarial' contracting towards 'obligational' contracting (Morris and Imrie, 1993) may be mutually beneficial for both clients and contractors using these contracts, and give rise to an atmosphere of increased trust and sharing of information. In these circumstances there will be opportunities for increased mutual understanding and management of contract uncertainty.

The flexibility of incentive contract forms of payment is very attractive. More widespread use of such contracts will depend on the development of more 'obligational' contracting, rather than 'adversarial' contracting, in addition to concern about uncertainty, opportunity and risk in the sense developed in this book. However, the use of a BIARS/BIORS framework is essential for the achievement of effective uncertainty management in opportunity efficiency terms. When operating cost tradeoffs with capital costs are fully considered, a whole-life asset lifecycle view of projects and associated contractual relationships becomes crucial. Similar issues arise calling for similar remedies, in respect of intra-organizational uncertainty ownership and management.

Chapter 16

A corporate capability perspective

'Not everything that can be counted counts, and not everything that counts can be counted'.
—Albert Einstein

The focus of this book is the development and application of efficient and effective processes for managing project-related uncertainty, opportunity and risk. In this final chapter we complete the relaxation of a project focus to consider the corporate implications of the issues and processes discussed in previous chapters in wider terms.

Relaxing the project focus raises an immediate question about the wider applicability and transferability of a PUMP approach to all aspects of organizational activity. We argue that the basic PUMP approach together with attendant concepts apply to corporate and operations management as well as all levels of project over the complete asset lifecycle in an organization. There are some new issues, but most of the new issues are joint, needing coordinated treatment. This has significant implications for existing common practice risk management, including corporate processes that operate under the label enterprise or enterprise-wide risk management.

Whether or not organizations take on board uncertainty management via PUMPs, there are a range of generic concepts and uncertainty management issues that all organizations need to recognize and address, whatever the decision-making context. In particular, there are a number of corporate capabilities that organizations should develop to support and deliver effective management of uncertainty, opportunity and risk. These capabilities include organizational learning, an appropriate organization culture, appropriate human resources capability, and decision support for addressing uncertainty.

Wide application potential for a PUMP approach

The effectiveness and efficiency of a PUMP approach to uncertainty was evident in Part I, in terms of the comprehensive nature of the uncertainty concept introduced in Chapter 1, the approach to making choices provided by the opportunity efficiency, risk efficiency and clarity efficiency concepts developed in Chapters 2 and 3, and the rich range of objectives developed in Chapter 3.

The wide scope for potential applicability of a PUMP approach to managing uncertainty in organizations was also evident in Chapter 1, in terms of the way projects were contextualized, the 12-stage project (asset/change) lifecycle of Table 1.3, and the seven Ws. The overall task of managing organizations was considered in terms of three basic aspects: operations, projects, plus a corporate perspective addressing corporate strategy, resourcing, capability issues and governance. Project creation is driven by strategic decisions which are influenced by current and desired future operational capability, and future operations are facilitated by projects that maintain or enhance operational capability. Projects often involve physical asset creation or maintenance, but sometimes they are centred on intangible asset creation and maintenance, and they usually involve both tangible and intangible assets – corporate reputation is a concern common to most projects. Projects are embedded in a hierarchy or portfolio of projects reflecting long, medium, and short-term planning objectives. Major, long-term projects involve strategy implementation. Small, short-term projects may be part of a complex programme of component projects contributing to a strategic initiative, or they may be small parts of operations instigated to maintain or enhance operational performance. In the limit, 'small' projects are part of 'business as usual' operations management, and 'large' projects are part of the strategic management agenda. We have seen that the PUMP can be applied to any 'size' of project whether or not it has strong strategic or operational characteristics.

Characterizing projects via a nominal asset lifecycle explicitly links the application of a PUMP to all stages of the lifecycle, from conceptualization as part of corporate strategy through to utilization of the underlying asset/change as part of corporate operations. In Part III, Chapters 12 and 13 outlined how the PUMP concepts can be applied to the different stages of the lifecycle. In principle the PUMP concepts could be applied solely to single stages in the lifecycle, to inform significant investment decisions whether the focus is a corporate perspective, projects, or enhancement and maintenance of operations. For example, a PUMP could be applied at intervals during the operation and support stage of a long-lived infrastructure asset to support decisions about maintenance, improvements, possible replacement and decommissioning. However, the approach advocated in this book is for the successive use of a PUMP in each stage of the asset lifecycle.

If PUMPs are used to manage operations uncertainty in the design, operations and termination strategy-shaping stage (DOT shaping stage) of all project lifecycles, as discussed in Part III, this can become a natural basis for operations management-led aspects of detailed planning, delivery, operations and termination for both individual projects and their integration. Operations management PUMPs developed via a DOT shaping stage intersection with project management in this way will need full collaboration across operations and project management boundaries.

Further, if PUMPs are used to manage strategic uncertainty in the concept shaping stage of all project lifecycles as discussed in Part III, this can form the basis of integration with all other aspects of corporate strategy shaping and delivery. As with operations management PUMP development and integration, a wider opportunity is involved, with correspondingly wider challenges.

The Ontario Hydro example outlined in this book starting in Chapter 1, and elaborated in Chapman and Ward (2002, chapter 11), indicates one example of how this might be done.

Organizations might start with PUMP-based approaches to project management, and use this to begin linked corporate change processes in specific aspects of operations management and strategic management as discussed in Chapter 12, using this as a starting point for a complete corporate transformation. However, current enterprise risk management (ERM) processes and concepts will be challenged by this approach, and a more direct or top-down route involving a direct challenge to current ERM needs to be understood, even if it is not the chosen route.

Enterprise risk management

In recent years ERM has become a focus for corporate risk management development – with good reason. A representative definition of ERM is 'a truly holistic, integrated, forward looking and process orientated approach is taken to manage all key business risks and opportunities – not just financial ones – with the intent of maximizing shareholders' value for the enterprise as a whole' (DeLoach, 2000, p. 5).

The term 'holistic risk management' is sometimes used in the simple sense of the management of *all* sources of risk (Hopkin, 2002). Miller and Waller (2003, p. 99) clearly regard this as a necessary part of their view of integrated risk management as they state: 'The essence of integrated risk management is consideration of the full range of uncertain contingencies affecting business performance.' However, in its proper sense, 'holistic' implies a systemic perspective, which recognizes system properties that are distinct from the properties of system components. In this sense, holistic risk management would imply recognition and management of interactive effects between an organization's activities and associated risks. Waring and Glendon (1998, p. 56) argue that 'holism does not imply consideration of every possible aspect of the particular whole, but a consideration of the essence of all the significant aspects. Holism is in contrast with reductionism whereby significant features may be lost deliberately (and often in ignorance of the adverse effects on understanding and outcomes) in the search for simplicity, elegance and convenience.' From this perspective many corporate risk identification exercises are more reductionist than holistic, in that little effort is directed at considering the interactions between identified areas of risk and associated 'risk events'. In our terms the focus is event uncertainty, with inadequate attention to variability uncertainty, systemic uncertainty and ambiguity uncertainty.

The term 'integrated risk management' is frequently used by corporate risk managers to refer to the joint management of all risk management functions in the organization. However, the term is also well established in the financial risk management literature, where integration relates to the combined treatment of the various sources of financial risk, recognizing interdependencies between both sources of risk and management responses. Integrated risk management in the financial sense is concerned with employing insurance, debt, equity, and financial derivatives in a coordinated manner to manage the organization's overall financial position (for example, see Doherty, 2000). A somewhat different definition of integrated risk management uses the word 'integrated' to mean the embedding of risk management processes into all aspects of decision making. For example, AIRMIC's integrated risk management special interest group define the achievement of integrated risk management as 'when risk management is integrated (or embedded) into all of the functions and processes within the organization' (AIRMIC, 1999, p. 4).

Common practice ERM in essence involves compiling and collating risk registers which are then used to produce risk profiles for various levels or parts of the organization. Typically risk registers capture brief descriptions of potential adverse events, estimates of their probability of occurrence, size of impact, an outline description of a possible response, and a designated risk owner, responsible for managing the risk. Such processes often involve substantial administrative effort via hierarchical risk committees supported by proprietary software. Such processes may provide a degree of comfort that risks are being identified and managed, and that external expectations for corporate governance are being met. However, the extent to which such processes are either truly integrated into planning and decision making, or 'holistic' in the sense of capturing interdependencies and systemic issues, is questionable. Such processes also lack important features that are necessary for effective and efficient management of significant uncertainty related to future performance. When viewed from a PUMP perspective, the following are significant shortcomings that taken together have a cumulative deleterious effect.

1. A focus on risk reporting and control of possible reductions in future performance. There is little attention to other objectives that might be pursued to enhance future performance (see Chapter 3), or the idea that an uncertainty management process might have different objectives in different application contexts (see Chapter 6).

2. A focus on 'risks' as adverse events or threat events, rather than the full range of sources of uncertainty that can influence future performance (see Chapters 1 and 7). A focus on a limited subset of a 'risk' or 'risk and opportunity' list defined in event terms, with no way of addressing everything this leaves out, is in effect a seriously dysfunctional and ill-considered decomposition of all uncertainty. Accompanying use of probability impact grids, using a simplistic 'quantitative' perspective which is actually just weak quantitative analysis, just makes matters worse.

3. A process that encourages an initial starting point of 'what might go wrong', typically using a generic 'source of risk framework' to generate a 'comprehensive' list of sources of risk, often described in varying levels of detail that do not reflect their relative importance. The process often fails to relate the identification of sources to key performance criteria at different levels or in different parts of the organization (see Chapter 7).

4. A single-pass process that discourages a progressively more detailed interactive analysis of significant sources of uncertainty. Moreover, this concept of an iterative process is further obscured by the use of the term 'iterative' to refer to identification processes that are merely repeated at intervals to update the 'risk picture' (see Chapters 4 and 6).

5. The absence of a structure phase, whereby significant linkages and interdependencies between sources of risk (uncertainty), and associated performance criteria, are systematically explored (see Chapter 8). Instead, entries in the risk register are treated as separate, independent adverse events to be separately managed. Structuring is limited to simplistic ranking of 'size' or importance of each identified risk according to simplistic mapping of identified risk events based on single value or qualitative estimates of impact and of the probability of impact, for each event. A 'conditions' or 'scenarios' interpretation of 'events' does not deal with the basis of this problem, although some people act as if it does.

6. Typically ERM is operated as a largely qualitative process that provides no framework for quantitative analysis of uncertainty and associated risk. Estimating, understanding the

combined effects of sources, and evaluation of alternative courses of action or risk responses are all unaddressed in a typical ERM process framework. In particular there is no part of the ERM framework that addresses:

(a) quantitative estimation of uncertainty and risk beyond simplistic probability-impact grids;

(b) understanding the combined effects of sources of uncertainty;

(c) evaluation of alternative courses of action or risk responses;

(d) potential tradeoffs between different performance criteria and the implications for choosing between alternative courses of action (see Chapter 3);

(e) the appropriateness of performance objectives, and the potential distinction between targets, expected outcomes and contingency allowances;

(f) issues associated with biased estimates and communication failures.

Taken together, the above list illustrates the severe limitations of common practice ERM as a process for managing uncertainty, opportunity and risk. Despite the somewhat overblown name, ERM is far from representing a comprehensive, best practice process for informing key planning and decision making processes. This is not to deny the usefulness of some ERM type processes. As a minimum they can provide a widely acceptable, low technology mechanism for focusing management attention on some key performance issues. However, the promulgation of common practice ERM processes, involving apparently very simple processes and tools, may be encouraging managers to take an inadequate and simplistic approach to the management of uncertainty and risk. Worse, it creates a very poor and misleading impression to third parties of what best practice in uncertainty management should involve. Some would go so far as to argue that enlightened common sense might be preferable.

Further implications of a PUMP approach – a corporate perspective

As should be clear from the previous section, improvements in common practice ERM could be made by adopting PUMP-related processes and concepts. That said, application of PUMP phases with a corporate rather than project perspective raises some generic issues and considerations worth outlining here. For convenience the discussion is structured around each of the seven basic PUMP phases in turn.

Define the context

Chapter 5 considered the define phase as providing an unambiguous, shared understanding of the project context and its management processes at a strategic level, to serve as a basic foundation for subsequent analysis. More generally, this phase is warranted in any uncertainty management context.

Such a phase is conspicuous by its absence in most ERM characterizations, perhaps because the implicit corporate context is assumed to be understood by all concerned and needs no explication.

In practice this can be a rather naive and optimistic assumption. From a corporate perspective, an explicit effort to provide an 'executive summary' of key features of the corporate context to guide further analysis is likely to be a very useful exercise in its own right. As noted in Chapter 5, an important aspect of this definition of context is not just consolidating key information in a suitable form, but identifying and filling any gaps, and resolving any inconsistencies in what is understood by the management team. As in Chapter 5, the seven Ws framework provides an appropriate generic structure for this definition work. The basic purpose is to provide a starting point for defining and developing understanding of key sources of uncertainty, opportunity and risk.

Focus the process

As discussed in Chapter 6, the focus phase is about adapting a generic uncertainty management process to the specific context of immediate interest. This recognizes that the precise scope and detail of analysis will depend on the context. There is no 'one best approach' for all contexts. Again the seven Ws framework provides a structure to consider the key issues involved. Chapter 14 illustrated what is involved when establishing a project uncertainty management capability, but a similar approach could and should be used when considering or reviewing corporate uncertainty (or risk) management capability.

Essentially the focus phase highlights the importance of considering in scope terms the why, who, what, whichway, where, when, wherewithal aspects of the uncertainty management process, before considering more detailing planning of process applications. Effective operation of the focus phase is predicated on management having a good understanding of the key motives for uncertainty management as discussed in Chapter 3.

A key aspect of focus phase considerations, particularly at a corporate level, is the degree of complexity to employ in analysis. As discussed in Chapter 14, there are good reasons to avoid starting with overly simple risk event based processes.

Most of the people involved in using a PUMP approach do not need to understand the focus phase model and method design issues which flow from this, but if an organization does not have sufficient in-house expertise to manage the focus phase effectively, it will have to acquire it. The authors do not recommend long-term dependence on external consultants, but we also recommend avoiding all variants of a 'not invented here' posture which can limit progress to what those already within the organization can understand easily in their terms. A rich variety of mentoring and benchmarking processes involving external support can be drawn upon, and enlightened governance of such processes is important.

An important corporate objective should be to maintain and continuously develop corporate focus phase capability, even if all the models and processes used seem to be getting simpler because experience is being captured effectively and no big surprises have occurred. However, to deal with new circumstances effectively, the ability to develop new forms of capability may be essential, and there may be scope for holistic development involving operations and strategic concerns as well as project concerns. A particular concern is losing the corporate capability to understand when and where new capabilities would be valuable, to adapt to changing circumstances involving significant opportunities or threats. Losing the capability to capture opportunities is obviously difficult to illustrate, but no less a concern.

Identify *all* the relevant sources of uncertainty, response options and conditions

The problem of identifying *all* the relevant sources of uncertainty, response options and conditions was discussed with a project perspective in Chapter 7. Taking a corporate perspective, this identification problem is more challenging. The scope of relevant sources of uncertainty is much wider. Deciding on an appropriate level of detail is also much more difficult, in conceptual terms and in practice. Different people will have to contribute and share leadership in different areas, so using compatible approaches is a more obvious concern.

An important basic feature of a PUMP approach is getting comfortable with a comprehensive minimum clarity approach – considering *all* uncertainty in simple terms as a top-down starting point, then adding more clarity in an initially simple manner, as illustrated by the Highways Agency example in Chapter 2. This is a significant departure from conventional wisdom ERM approaches to 'risk identification' that are based on bottom-up compilations of lists of 'risk events', prompted via some conceptual framework of risk categories. Such approaches involve a single pass identification process that encourages inefficient generation of all conceivable risk events, lest anything be missed, followed by a focus on prioritized 'top ten' risks for reporting purposes. This is not a very effective or efficient approach compared to an exploratory, iterative approach – in *any* context. It is even more unsuitable at a corporate level than it was in an early safety management context or a related PIG-based project risk management context. All corporate boards need to understand that *all* sources of uncertainty may matter, and constant sense checking by integrating top-down and bottom-up analysis in an iterative manner has to be the basis of a clarity efficient approach to dealing with the uncertainty that underlies risk and opportunity. An inflexible, non-iterative, one-size-fits-all process limited to possible adverse events may do more harm than good. If a board does not understand this kind of basic flaw in common practice, it needs to be enlightened. Competent corporate governance will not be feasible if this is not done.

A further shortcoming of a focus on compiling lists of 'risk events' is that risk identification can become divorced from consideration of related performance objectives, and hence the relative significance of different risk events. In contrast, the PUMP approach adopts an iterative approach to identification of sources of uncertainty, starting with a top-down view of uncertainty related to key performance objectives. In a given context, identification begins with the most important performance objective. It then uses the directly linked Ws to structure sources of uncertainty of immediate interest, typically at a high level of aggregation that involves low clarity. As analysis progresses, other performance criteria, the rest of the seven Ws, and wider aspects of context provide a more insightful structure for all relevant uncertainty.

Perhaps even more so than in project contexts, in a corporate context an appreciation of the way performance at different levels is linked by means-ends chains is particularly important. This can suggest what or whichway perspectives linked to primary and support activities in the corporate value chain (Porter, 1985), or an asset management focus addressing uncertainties associated with key tangible and intangible assets. Tangible, physical assets include buildings, plant, financial assets, material stocks, employees, operating systems, information systems and intellectual property. Intangible assets include customer goodwill, reputation, corporate image, employee commitment, the corporate culture, core competencies and so on. The protection and efficient and effective deployment of assets is a vital aspect of successfully operating and maintaining an organization, and must be an important part of any uncertainty management effort (Ward, 2005, ch. 4).

An alternative corporate performance perspective on sources of uncertainty and risk is provided by taking a systems perspective. This involves appreciating the organization as a coherent and effective system with properties which are distinct from those of its component parts. It is about seeing the wood rather than the trees in organization process terms, and appreciating the cumulative, combined effects of participants, policies, procedures, directives and initiatives on the day-to-day operations of the organization. Viewing an organization as a system that needs to operate successfully in a wider environment leads to the identification of seven basic problems that all organizations need to address: adaptation, resource deployment, coordination, self-integration, tension management, productivity and preservation of identity and integrity (Georgopoulous, 1973). The popular 'balanced score card' approach to performance assessment (Kaplan and Norton, 1992, 1993a, 1993b, 1996) provides a somewhat narrower perspective.

Linked to this systems perspective of organizational effectiveness is the desirability of understanding what causes managerial systems to fail. Relevant issues are discussed at length in Reason's (1990) book on *Human Error*, Turner's (1994) insightful paper 'Causes of disaster: sloppy management', Woods et al. (2010) and Dekker (2011). A key issue here is that failures of managed systems usually arise from the 'unforeseen and usually unforeseen concatenation of several diverse events (or conditions), each one necessary but singly insufficient' (Reason, 1990, p. 197). Turner (1994, p. 216) has argued that these preconditions

stay in place in the organization or in managerial practice, ready to contribute to major failure unless something happens to neutralize them by bringing them out into the open. Until the point at which they combine and react in undesirable ways, the misconceptions about the world which such 'pathogens' embody merely provide elements which are available to contribute to a disaster. They constitute an accident waiting to happen. If they are not uncovered, the preconditions are brought together by some trigger event which sets off a disaster.

This suggests that management needs to watch for signs that preconditions for system failure are building up. *Blowout in the Gulf* (Freudenburg and Gramling, 2010) takes a wide view of these issues in a significant contemporary context.

Given the wide scope for sources of uncertainty that can have a significant (cumulative) effect on corporate performance, there is a particular need for an iterative, efficient process that is intelligent in its search for key sources of uncertainty. An important part of this iterative approach is the desirability of an early proactive identification of responses associated with key sources of uncertainty. The seven points of advice in the conclusion of Chapter 7 are equally applicable to a corporate context for uncertainty identification.

Structure the sources and responses

As discussed in Chapter 8, the objective of the structure phase of the basic PUMP is to improve understanding of the relative importance of different sources of uncertainty given identified response options, to explore relevant interactions, and to test the assumptions implicit or explicit in analysis to date. The structure phase involves testing simplifying assumptions and developing alternative assumptions where appropriate. This may call for more complex structure or simpler structure to improve clarity efficiency.

Failure to address complexity, such as interdependence between sources of uncertainty, can result in seriously misleading conclusions. As noted in Chapter 8 it can be particularly useful to understand chains of causes and effects, even in terms of qualitative influence diagrams, so that virtuous and vicious circle scenarios can be identified and appropriate contingent responses prepared to manage associated threats and opportunities. Such situations are not confined to project contexts. They occur frequently in operations, often with large-scale multi-institution consequences, as in the recent global banking crisis.

A further aspect of the structure phase is the identification of general responses that offer a suitable response to a wide range of sources of uncertainty or future scenarios. The advocacy and pursuit of agility, flexibility or resilience is an example of a corporate general response. However, efficient and effective implementation of agility, flexibility, and resilience generally requires detailed consideration of the forms this can take and an understanding of the specific uncertainties and chain of events that are being addressed (see, for example, Volberda, 1998; Ward et al., 1997; Chapman and Ward, 1996).

Clarify ownership

The need to ensure that every relevant source of uncertainty and all associated responses have an appropriate owner is well understood in all risk management processes. Generally this ownership is associated with managerial responsibility for issues – with responsibility for bearing the consequences typically implicit in documentation. In Chapter 9 discussion of the basic PUMP ownership phase highlighted the importance of making explicit decisions about responsibility for managing sources of uncertainty and responsibility for bearing the consequent effects on performance. Given the project context, the focus in Chapter 9 was on principal–agent relationships involving formal contracts, although the term 'contracts' was used to include both explicit and implicit contracts (as between different parties in the same organization). Contracts between clients and contractors were a central concern, but governance and other intra-organizational relationships were also relevant aspects within the seven-Ws framework. Chapter 15 developed this discussion, highlighting the need to consider the potentially different objectives and incentives operating for different players both external and internal to the project organization. Again the recent banking crisis provides a pertinent example, one where the motivation and incentives of different parties, whether mortgagees, some middle managers in retail banks, or some senior managers in investment banks, played major roles in precipitating the crisis.

Quantify *some* uncertainty

The quantification of uncertainty is an important way of increasing understanding of what matters and how it matters, given assumptions about future conditions – as noted in Chapter 10. However, the reasons for seeking quantification of uncertainty, and some illustrations of how quantification can inform uncertainty and risk management, were also discussed earlier in

Chapters 2 and 3. Such reasons are by no means confined to project management. Two basic reasons for quantification are:

1. to appreciate potential variability in key factors affecting future performance or investment options, and
2. to enable the distinction to be made between targets, expectations which include provisions and commitments which also include contingency allowances.

Organizations that do not quantify uncertainty have no real basis for distinguishing targets, expected values and commitments, let alone making comparisons between uncertain alternatives. Unfortunately, many organizations persist in employing single value performance level measures, often with disastrous results, and often accompanied by seriously dysfunctional organizational behaviour. The ability to manage the gaps between targets, expected values and contingency levels, and the ability to set these values appropriately in the first place, should be a central concern of uncertainty management.

As noted earlier, common practice ERM does not involve quantification of any uncertainty or risk beyond simplistic probability-impact grids. However, in the financial sector the importance of being able to quantify uncertainty and risk associated with key performance criteria is well recognized, for example in terms of aspirations to measure value-at-risk (VAR), via estimated probability distributions of return.

Part of the problem is captured by the Einstein opening quote for this chapter: 'not everything that can be counted counts, and not everything that counts can be counted'. Chapter 10 showed in some detail how quantitative estimates could be arrived at, but equally importantly, Chapter 10 was concerned with clarity efficient quantification in a qualitative framework. In uncertainty management process terms, the quantify phase involves the production of numeric, probability based estimates of *some* uncertainty associated with sources of uncertainty and response options, ultimately in terms of cost, duration, or other *measurable* performance criteria, plus *qualitative* clarification of some uncertainty and criteria when measurement is not helpful or practicable. This implies a process of quantifying uncertainty that is iterative, initially starting with rough, 'sizing' estimates of key sources of uncertainty, and refining or restructuring of these estimates if this helps to increase understanding of uncertainty and informs decision making. It also implies a way of presenting quantitative results that allows effective consideration of non-quantified concerns.

In any context it is important to understand the subjective elements present in all estimating. As noted in Chapter 10, sources of these subjective elements include the quality of information available, and the cognitive processes of different contributors to estimates. The latter can be particularly problematic since estimates may be influenced by both unconscious heuristics resulting in unintended bias, and conscious bias motivated by organizational politics or self preservation. For example, see Flyvbjerg et al. (2003). Such elements pervade all estimates at whatever organizational level, but a common consequence is persistent optimism in performance estimates.

A further significant subjective element arises from choices about the level of detail to model and associated assumptions. For example, see thought-provoking illustrations in Wynne (1992) and Pilkey and Pilkey-Jarvis (2007). The need to note assumptions about resources, choices, and methods of working is well understood, but most of the time the implications of such assumptions are not part of the uncertainty which is quantified or effectively recognized in qualitative terms. For example, most of the time estimates based on measured variability uncertainty ignore the implications of three further areas of uncertainty: 'known unknowns' (identified conditions which are sources of uncertainty because associated assumptions will not hold exactly), 'unknown unknowns' (assumptions or sources of uncertainty which have not been identified), and 'bias' (other bias, associated with assuming perfect positive correlation between sources of uncertainty, or independence, for example). A detailed discussion of a 'cube factor' concept designed to clarify these issues in Chapman and Ward (2002) was summarized in Chapter 10, with several linked suggestions. As a brief reminder, estimators might incorporate a 'provision for other sources of uncertainty', to correct for bias associated with the residual of all sources not explicitly considered in quantitative terms, including unknown and known unknowns. Estimators might also use simple but mildly pessimistic dependence assumptions to correct for other sources of optimistic bias, including the inherent optimism of most subjective probability assessments. However, they need to avoid simplistic but common practice corrections like many of those based on the 'optimism bias' correction factors proposed by HM Treasury (2003a, 2003b), and they need to avoid being distracted by popular notions like 'black swans' (Taleb, 2007) if they do not understand how they fit into a broader 'cube factor' concept.

Evaluate *all* uncertainty

As discussed in Chapter 11, the purpose of the evaluate phase is to combine the results of previous uncertainty quantification, portray the combined effect of different sources, and assess the implications for decision and plans. This assessment needs to bear in mind all sources of uncertainty that are not quantified and all associated relevant conditions or assumptions. Evaluation also involves process decisions like 'do we need to refine earlier quantitative or qualitative analysis, and if so where?' It also addresses planning decisions such as 'is proposal A better than proposal B, and do we need an alternative plan C plus an exit strategy plan D?' Such planning decisions might arise at a corporate strategic level, effectively early in the concept stage of an asset lifecycle, or in various later stages, including the ongoing operational stage of an asset lifecycle.

As with the identification of sources of uncertainty, an iterative approach is necessary to ensure an efficient and effective evaluation process. Extensive probabilistic analysis based on carefully researched data can be very useful, but often such analysis is not appropriate. What is usually essential is an initial rough sizing of uncertainty associated with all the key sources that require management, followed by refinement in some areas where this is worth while. A first pass can be used to portray overall uncertainty and the relative size of all contributing factors. A second pass can be used to explore key issues and the effect of possible alternative response options, obtaining additional data and undertaking more detailed analysis of issues where appropriate. Further passes can further refine and restructure understanding where this is useful. Throughout this process it is vital to understand the relevance of working or framing assumptions, including assumptions about future conditions. Such assumptions might relate to aspects of project activities or to the organizational, economic, technological or environmental context within which a project must be managed. A corporate perspective, as well as a project perspective may be appropriate.

An important early deliverable of uncertainty evaluation might be a prioritized list of sources of uncertainty and associated option choices, while a later deliverable might be a diagnosed potential problem or opportunity associated with a specific aspect of a base plan or contingency plans, plus possible revisions to these plans to resolve a problem or exploit an opportunity. The key deliverable is diagnosis of any and all important opportunities or threats, and comparative evaluation of responses to these opportunities or threats. One key feature of the approach described in Chapter 11 is the use of nested probability distributions like those of Figures 11.5–11.7 to build up a picture of combined sources of uncertainty. A second key feature is the use of cumulative probability curves like those in Figures 11.8–11.10 to represent alternative courses of action. A third key feature is the use of the concept of risk efficiency and associated opportunity efficiency discussed in Chapter 3, to inform the tradeoffs involved in choosing between alternative courses of action.

Assessing or diagnosing the implications of uncertainty in a project context should involve a conscious search for risk efficient courses of action from both a project/asset perspective and a corporate perspective. Chapter 11 characterized this as seeking out opportunities for:

- project risk efficiency;
- corporate risk efficiency;
- risk efficient tradeoffs between various performance constraints;
- corporate relaxation of constraints or conditions initially imposed on projects because this is risk efficient from a corporate perspective.

This characterization of uncertainty assessment recognizes that some opportunities for improving project risk efficiency may require corporate interventions, but also that some option choices may not be risk efficient from a project perspective but could be risk efficient from a corporate perspective. This issue was explored in Chapter 3 using an example involving a North Sea pipe-laying project in relation to the choice between pipe-laying barges, with wave height capabilities specified in metres, 1.6 m and 3 m. Referring to Figure 3.5, the expected cost of the 3 m barge was supposed to be about £5 million more than the expected cost of the 1.6 m barge alternative, but the 3 m barge was supposed to virtually eliminate the 10% chance of pipe laying extending over the winter to the following spring with cost consequences in the order of £100 million. In this hypothetical example, the project manager might argue that it is not worth increasing the expected cost by £5 million by taking the 3 m barge option because risk sharing was in place to cope with £1000 million losses, and persistent over-insurance would not be risk efficient at a corporate level, as suggested in the Chapter 3 discussion. However, if in addition to direct costs portrayed in these terms, the 1.6 m barge ran the risk of botched operations when operating under pressure in autumn storms, leading to a loss of life with linked reputation damage and other non-quantifiable threats, the additional £5 million for the 3 m barge option might be the only sensible choice from a corporate perspective. *In practice, key risk tradeoffs are rarely defined in single criteria measurable terms. They usually involve more than one criteria, some non-measurable. And sound governance from an enlightened corporate perspective has to address all relevant criteria, including criteria which may not be in the forefront of a project manager's mind.* The importance of this observation, the central role of the evaluate phase in the basic PUMP and the central role of the governance aspect of gateways in the PUMP pack approach, is supported by the Einstein quote which opens this chapter. What really matters at a corporate level is rarely reducible to simple metrics, and assuming that it is can be exceedingly misguided.

The evaluate phase does not need to be understood at a deep technical level in order to manage simple forms of uncertainty. However, some very important concepts, like statistical and causal dependence, and risk efficiency, and the importance of criteria that have not been quantified, need to be understood properly at an intuitive level in order to manage *any* uncertainty effectively, including all relevant enlightened governance. An understanding of what is involved when probability distributions are combined is part of this – but by no means the most important part.

Infrastructure for uncertainty management

To be efficient and effective, all uncertainty management processes require an appropriate supporting infrastructure. This infrastructure is in turn influenced, facilitated and supported by the organization's wider administrative infrastructure, which includes physical deployment of resources, processes for coordination and control, associated documentation of policies and procedures, and governance. This is an obvious but important point. How the organization operates will have a major impact on what can be achieved in terms of all formal processes to manage uncertainty, including PUMPs. Organization structure, coordination and control systems, environmental scanning capability, communications and information systems, knowledge management, support for organization learning, and governance, are all key facilitators of uncertainty management. Such factors define the basic resources that uncertainty management processes must work with, and they set the tone for how formal processes will be able (or allowed) to operate. Such factors can enable uncertainty management to flourish, or can present barriers to its development, no matter how capable and determined the champions of uncertainty management effort.

Any infrastructure facilitating the management of uncertainty, opportunity and risk should be driven top-down by a strategic perspective on the possibilities for developing uncertainty management. Such developments will not be confined to the management of projects, but should include strategic initiatives and all aspects of ongoing operations. It follows that the development and provision of infrastructure should not be limited to supporting any one particular aspect of uncertainty management, such as corporate risk management process for corporate governance purposes. If it is, then the opportunity to consider the possibilities for wider uncertainty management development may well be missed or obstructed.

To the extent that uncertainty management activities are formalized, then the supporting infrastructure needs to include:

- Assignment of formal roles for the top-down, systematic development, coordination, and support of uncertainty management activities.
- Guiding principles which relate to the fundamental nature of the organization's business and associated risks.
- A strategy for uncertainty management process application and development which sets out when and why it is to be employed, and how it is to be developed and supported in terms of the seven Ws.
- Policies and guidelines for uncertainty management that indicate how it can and should be undertaken in various contexts and applications.
- The nature of decision support and information systems.

Any strategy for developing this infrastructure also needs to address what will be needed in terms of human resource capability and supporting organizational capabilities.

Roles and responsibilities

In terms of developing uncertainty management throughout the organization, there is a need for top-down systematic development, coordination, and support of related activities. A key part of such an initiative is being clear what the relevant roles and responsibilities of different parties in the organization should be. Relevant parties in this respect include: the chief executive officer (CEO) and the board of directors, the audit committee and internal audit, line management, and specialists in uncertainty management.

Management responsibilities

Generally the board of directors provides guidance and direction to the organization's management. Typically this involves setting strategy, formulating higher level objectives, broad base resource allocation, and responsibility for shaping key infrastructures of the organization, including organization structures and information systems. In particular, the board has ultimate responsibility for managing opportunity, uncertainty and risk in the organization, and for creating the infrastructure for uncertainty management to operate efficiently and effectively. This implies the following responsibilities for:

- maintaining an organizational commitment to the effective operation of uncertainty management, and ongoing development of related capability;
- defining and maintaining policy, methodology, and standards for uncertainty management including clarifying responsibilities for managing and bearing risk;
- assisting management to implement necessary measures across the organization;
- monitoring developments in uncertainty management techniques generally and considering their relevance to the organization;
- providing guidance for management on conducting risk assessments, improving risk control, and monitoring risk on an ongoing basis.

In practice the board may decide to delegate most of the above tasks to a sub-committee. Such a committee may have three basic responsibilities which need to be clearly distinguished: supporting and facilitating uncertainty management; carrying out uncertainty management at a corporate level; and reviewing the effectiveness of uncertainty management activity carried out elsewhere in the organization.

Managers in charge of business units in the organization hierarchy have a cascading responsibility for making uncertainty management operational within units in a manner which is consistent with high-level requirements. The business units also have primary responsibility for managing uncertainty on a day-to-day basis, and for promoting uncertainty awareness within their operations. The AIRMIC, ALARM, IRM Standard (2002) suggests that managers of business units should:

- introduce risk management objectives into their business;
- understand the risks which fall into their area of responsibility, the possible implications of these on other areas, and the consequences other areas may have on them;
- formulate performance indicators which allow them to monitor the key business and financial activities, progress towards objectives, and identify developments which require intervention;

- have systems which communicate variances in budgets and forecasts appropriate frequency to allow action to be taken; ensure that risk management is a regular management meeting item to allow consideration of exposures and to re-prioritize work in the light of effective risk analysis;
- report systematically and promptly to senior management any perceived new risks or failures of existing control measures.

However, all these injunctions need a PUMP-based uncertainty management generalization.

Specialist risk (uncertainty) management functions

The role of the corporate risk manager in uncertainty management terms is discussed in some detail in Ward (2005, 2001). Consider a brief summary here, reflecting our uncertainty management perspective.

Typically, the division of organization tasks and associated specialization lends itself to learned ways of managing opportunity, risk and uncertainty which naturally focus on the scope of relevant tasks. This is particularly pronounced in organization units whose main responsibility is to manage some aspect of risk. Examples of such units include: insurance management, health and safety, legal department, the treasury function, internal audit, quality control, security, public relations, strategic planning. This diversity of separate risk management foci is often critically referred to as a 'risk silos' approach because coordination of risk management activities and cooperation in sharing analyses and information may be quite limited between different silos. From an uncertainty management perspective a further shortcoming of this risk management foci approach is that it may not address uncertainty in sufficiently general terms to embrace all aspects of risk. Further still, it may involve very limited formal treatment of opportunity. The increasing need for more visible, formal risk management has resulted in most large organizations establishing a specific risk management function, typically reporting to top management. However, a broad view of associated uncertainty and opportunity is usually missing. Depending on the size of the organization, the risk management function may range from a single 'risk champion', a part-time 'risk manager', to a substantial risk management department. To build on this basis the 'corporate risk manager' might become the 'corporate uncertainty manager' in spirit, if not in terms of a formal title change, and the role of the uncertainty management function under their direction might be to:

- assist the board in setting policy and strategy for uncertainty management;
- build an uncertainty aware culture within the organization including appropriate education, putting *all* risk and *all* opportunity in context;
- establish associated internal policies and structures for business units;
- design and review formal processes for uncertainty management;
- coordinate the various functional activities which advise on uncertainty management issues within the organization;
- support the development of response generation processes including contingency and business continuity programme formulation;
- prepare reports on significant risk and opportunity issues for the board and stakeholders.

We believe it would be easier to manage the culture change involved if new titles and terminology consistent with uncertainty management were employed. In some organizations such change will be difficult enough without the handicap of common risk management practice terminology. However, a very capable and determined 'corporate risk manager' who fully understood the implications of a PUMP-based approach might get away with an evolutionary approach rather than a revolutionary approach, and in some contexts this approach might be a suitable 'plan A'.

Guiding principles

Guiding principles relate to the fundamental nature of an organization's business and associated uncertainty, opportunity and risk. These principles should be based on the following (Banks and Dunn, 2003, ch. 8):

1. Understanding what business areas the organization will focus on and recognizing the main sources of uncertainty associated with these areas.
2. Deciding what uncertainty is central to the firm's core business strategy and what is not. For example, a manufacturing firm might be prepared to take on commodity price and demand uncertainty as inherent to the core business, but wish to avoid all currency exchange rate uncertainty by appropriate hedging.
3. Understanding shareholder expectations in terms of corporate risk – reward tradeoffs and the firm's strategy.
4. Deciding the organization's tolerance to risk based on:

   - the maximum amount of money the firm is willing to risk losing, preferably conditioned by associated opportunities and other context issues;
   - what resources are available to support potential losses;
   - consideration of whether the firm's return on capital employed is adequate given the risk–return tradeoffs being accepted.

Banks and Dunn (2003) argue that all four of these aspects of guiding principles should be deliberated by the board and then communicated to internal and external stakeholders.

Policies and guidelines for risk (uncertainty) management

As with any formal organizational systems and procedures, formal uncertainty management systems require a clear policy to be formulated. This policy needs to address the following aspects of uncertainty management activity:

- the purpose of uncertainty management;
- what form uncertainty management should take;
- who should do it;
- how uncertainty management should be carried out, supported and monitored;
- when uncertainty management should be undertaken;
- what resources should be applied.

Table 16.1 Possible components of an uncertainty management policy statement

- The level and nature of risk which is acceptable for particular business activities or programmes with context conditions and a risk – reward tradeoffs basis
- Responsibilities for the management of particular sources of uncertainty and associated financing arrangements
- Roles and responsibilities for carrying out various uncertainty management activities
- Mechanisms for monitoring and reviewing uncertainty management activities
- Mechanisms for monitoring and reviewing uncertainty management principles, policies and guidelines
- Rules for reporting significant uncertainty, opportunity and risk higher up the hierarchy
- The nature of PUMPs and other uncertainty management processes in various contexts
- Use of standard documentation for analysis and reporting
- Use of particular sensitivity analysis tools and techniques for ranking and evaluating sources of uncertainty
- Use of particular tools for making decisions between available option choices
- Treatment of interdependencies between sources of uncertainty in a range of ways for different levels of clarity
- Guidance on achieving clarity efficiency and overall opportunity efficiency

Possible components of a risk management policy/guideline are listed in Table 16.1.

Such policies and associated documentation may be set out as formal requirements or as guidance on recommended good practice. Clearly there is scope for varying the level of detail on these aspects. Even rather general statements, endorsed by the board, can have useful symbolic value by flagging top management support for uncertainty management, and by giving designated risk (uncertainty) managers broad authority to operate. Some companies with uncertainty management capability that is well integrated into investment decision making and project management, can have quite extensive documentation which incorporates corporate objectives for uncertainty management, procedures, guidelines, plus general advice on uncertainty management issues and carrying out different forms of analysis. However, it is crucial to clarify what interpretation is put on basic terminology.

There are clear difficulties in deciding on an appropriate level of detail to incorporate in policy statements. To some extent this can be driven by clearly distinguishing practice that is company policy, and therefore mandatory, from recommended guidelines or advice. Even policy statements will warrant some explanation of the underlying rationale and supporting guidance to facilitate effective implementation. Requirements of corporate governance and other regulatory requirements need to be defined as policy, although even here it is always useful to explain the reasons for requirements or policies, and it is always crucial to be clear what the language means.

Given the variety of contexts that risk (uncertainty) management may be applied in, it is not usually practical to specify policy in too much detail, as some degree of flexibility in processes is not just desirable, it is essential for clarity efficiency. Quite apart from being inappropriate in a given context, overspecified policy can stifle initiative and the development of uncertainty management expertise, not to mention motivation. Also, in organizations with a high degree of decentralization, it may be unrealistic to attempt to dictate policy on risk (uncertainty) management processes in too much detail.

A corporate uncertainty management manual

There is a strong argument for supporting uncertainty management with a manual that includes, but goes much further than, setting out corporate policy. The central benefits of an uncertainty management manual are:

- it signals the importance of uncertainty management and illustrates the intended scope of this activity;
- it provides a focal point for communicating an organization's uncertainty management guiding principles, strategy, policies, and guidelines throughout the organization;
- it acts as a one-stop-shop for practical information relevant to effective uncertainty management;
- it can operate as a repository of corporate experience and acquired knowledge.

If 'risk management manual' terminology is used because a real uncertainty management perspective is not fully adopted, some of these benefits are at risk.

If an internal website is established, then information provided can be extensive, but organized in a hierarchical fashion, with appropriate links to external websites and internal data sources to facilitate efficient, effective access to relevant material. Table 16.2 lists possible contents of a corporate uncertainty management manual/website.

Table 16.2 is not definitive in terms of the specific content or the structure employed. For example, the structure could be elaborated to give more prominence to uncertainty management processes in particular specialist functions, or particular contexts (such as crisis management), and more extensive explanations of analytical techniques could be appended. Effective website design enables useful pathways through the material to be defined by a thoughtful use of links. As yet few organizations have manuals or websites as extensive in scope as Table 16.2. However, much more ambitious variants might be useful, even in organizations of very modest size.

Supporting organizational capabilities

Organization culture

In Ward's (2001) study of corporate risk managers, some corporate risk managers observed that the quality of uncertainty management undertaken in business units can be driven by the organizational culture prevailing in business units. This culture can be manifest in a variety of ways, such as attitude to: planning, formal procedures, regulations, criticism, mistakes, uncertainty, and risk. These cultural characteristics can either facilitate or hinder the development of uncertainty management.

Attention to uncertainty may be limited for a variety of reasons. In many operational areas, uncertainty may not be regarded as sufficiently important or significant to warrant attention in systematic uncertainty management terms. Such uncertainty as exists may be considered manageable as part of day-to-day operations. More generally, events may be considered too unpredictable to prepare for, or too unpleasant to contemplate and therefore best ignored in the hope that 'it may never happen'. Such attitudes reflect a perception of uncertainty as something to be avoided, and may encourage decisions and actions that favour 'playing safe' or reducing uncertainty whatever the cost. These perceptions may not be defensible, but to the extent that they exist, they must be managed in any attempts to increase levels of uncertainty management.

Some of the most significant barriers to effective uncertainty management are based on unfavourable features of organizational culture. Sometimes these barriers are induced from outside the organization in the form of convictions, prejudices, biases, and routines of professional groups that can blinker thinking. These may arise from a wish to make decisions efficiently in a particular context according to recognized scientific or professional standards. Such professionally based convictions can strongly influence different groups within the same organization in very different ways, making it very difficult to adopt holistic, enterprise-wide uncertainty management processes. However, many organizations also exhibit a number of more generic culture-based behaviours or conditions inimical to effective uncertainty management. As an illustration, Table 16.3 lists a number of often observed dysfunctional behaviours that reflect inappropriate attitudes to uncertainty, selected and summarized from a more extensive discussion in Chapman and Ward (2002, ch. 12).

Some of the conditions in Table 16.3 may seem mutually exclusive. For example, it might be assumed that an organization cannot simultaneously exhibit both 'po-faced pessimism' and 'El Dorado optimism'. In practice different parts of an organization can exhibit conflicting conditions like these two. However, half a dozen or so complementary cultural conditions seem to be the norm, in terms of a characterization of conditions significant enough to warrant attention and treatment.

Essentially these behaviours seem to evidence the difficulty management has in coping with complexity and uncertainty in decision making. In particular, such behaviours can reflect an inability or unwillingness on the part of managers or groups to recognize the difference between:

- bad management in terms of incompetent clarity management – seriously clarity inefficient choices,
- bad luck with things a manager is responsible for,
- adverse changes in things that are not under a manager's control,
- good management involving managers who apply proactive uncertainty management to reduce problems and enhance performance in a clarity efficient manner,
- good luck with things a manager is responsible for,
- favourable changes in things not under a manager's control.

As noted in Chapter 3, addressing such conditions can be one of the most significant benefits of formal uncertainty management processes. In particular, making 'enlightened caution', 'enlightened gambles' and 'enlightened controls' part of an organization's culture, as discussed in Chapter 3, can be central to killing a risk-averse culture based on a view that 'uncertainty and risk are negative issues, and what you don't know won't hurt you'. This can generate a new 'uncertainty management' culture based on the idea that 'uncertainty is the source of our opportunities, and we need to understand our opportunities to capture them effectively'. Put slightly differently, a very apt Sir Winston Churchill aphorism is 'a pessimist sees the difficulty in every opportunity, an optimist sees the opportunity in every difficulty'. Everyone needs a Churchillian optimism lens plus a Churchillian pessimism lens, using both these lenses as appropriate, along with all other relevant lenses and concepts.

Table 16.2 Corporate uncertainty management manual/intranet site content based on Ward (2005)

Purpose of the uncertainty management manual
Who should use it, why, and for what purposes, how to make best use of this resource.

Corporate philosophy on uncertainty management
A statement of the senior management's fundamental beliefs about the nature of uncertainty management and its potential for contributing to the organization's performance. This might include statements about what management is interested in, in terms of threats, opportunities and underlying uncertainty, and recognition of the linkages between them and their importance to achieving performance in shareholder value terms. It might seek buy-in from all staff by linking shareholder concerns to social concerns and the interests of all employees. For example, the IBM culture change programme discussed earlier empowered all levels of decision makers to take appropriate risk in the company's best interests. This made insurance function staff and safety function staff feel liberated as well as sales people responsible for bids, leading to follow-on developments the authors would never have anticipated, like a synthesis of contradictory fire safety regimes to clarify corporate policy.

Guiding principles
The organization's (senior management's) attitude to opportunity, risk and uncertainty. Clarification of extent of willingness to accept risk. What is not acceptable. Limits on organization's activities. Support for risk taking by management under appropriate conditions. Outline guidance on conditions.

Objectives expected from uncertainty management
How uncertainty management can help deliver performance by identifying long-term aims, benefits in the short term and medium term, and immediate benefits in supporting decision processes and improved control of operations. Some explanation of motives driving the development of uncertainty management would be appropriate. Relationships with corporate strategy, associated objectives and relative priorities. Personal benefits expected for those who undertake uncertainty management.

Uncertainty management strategy
A statement of current capability and practices. Articulation of the organization's intentions for extending uncertainty management practice and building capability. This might outline plans for investment in developing capability, priority areas with the underlying rationale, directions in which existing practice will be developed. Use (if any) of bench-marking.

Regulatory requirements influencing uncertainty management strategy and policies
A statement summarizing the regulatory requirements influencing uncertainty management strategy and policies, their scope, significance and compliance implications.

Uncertainty management policies
Basic rules and procedures within which all uncertainty management activity should operate as a minimum. These might relate to any or all of the seven W's: who, why, what, whichway, wherewithal, when and where. In particular, an outline of compliance procedures for corporate governance and other regulatory requirements could be described (for example, risk reporting and review procedures to the board and audit committee). Policies in respect of uncertainty retention and ownership.

Roles and responsibilities for uncertainty management
A statement of roles and responsibilities in respect of uncertainty management of: the board, Risk Committee equivalent(s), Chief Risk Officer (CRO) equivalent(s), unit uncertainty managers, project managers, unit managers, all employees, specialist functions (legal, treasury, risk financing equivalents, personnel, customer relations, health and safety, maintenance, business continuity, corporate security, etc). The desirability of communication, coordination of uncertainty management efforts, scope of these, existing corporate mechanisms, possible options for *ad hoc* coordination.

Contexts for uncertainty management
Locations and applications of uncertainty management: formulation, evaluation and implementation of strategy; project management; operations management (continuous improvement, operational controls, business continuity, crisis management); environmental assessment; asset recognition, development and utilisation; investment appraisal; improving the quality of decision making, etc.

TABLE 16.2   Continued

Sources of risk, opportunity and uncertainty
Summary descriptions of key areas of uncertainty and related risk and opportunity drivers (sources of uncertainty). For example, senior management's current top ten concerns/issues (regularly updated). These might relate to key assets (tangible and intangible), aspects of corporate culture, strengths or weaknesses in the organization's operations, or developments in respect of: technology, the business environment, global events, competition, markets, government policies, etc.

Uncertainty management processes
General advice on undertaking uncertainty management, recommended process frameworks, sources of information (internal and external). Specific recommendations and general advice about good or best practice in clarity efficient terms in respect of phases in a generic uncertainty management process like the PUMP pack. For example, advice on tools, techniques and issues to address in risk identification (use of frameworks, prompt lists, group processes), structuring (minor/major sources, links between sources), response development (specific/general responses, generic forms of response), uncertainty analysis (estimating, combining sources, importance of recognizing dependency).

Documentation to support uncertainty management processes
Mandatory, recommended, or illustrative pro-forma documents for different phases of uncertainty management process applications. In particular, identification of sources of uncertainty could involve updating a central register and selective downloading for particular contexts and applications. Advice about *ad hoc* modifications to pro-forma documents for particular context applications. Pro-forma documents for self-assessment, and reporting purposes.

Uncertainty ownership and incentives for uncertainty management
Importance of clear decisions about uncertainty allocation (including risk sharing). Implications for effective uncertainty management, especially where multiple parties are involved in cooperative work.

Examples of uncertainty management in action
To promote interest and increase motivation to employ uncertainty management, include examples of uncertainty management in action, both from within and outside the organization. This offers an opportunity to learn from other organizations as well as demonstrating the use of uncertainty management internally. Examples could include recent incidents or decisions in the organization where a more structured approach to uncertainty management could have avoided loss or exploited a missed opportunity. Other examples could include stories of effective uncertainty management applications in the organization, or suggestions of ways in which uncertainty management could contribute operationally and strategically to decision making.

Useful contacts
List of all individuals with responsibility for supporting/facilitating/advising on uncertainty management. Membership of uncertainty (risk) committees, working groups, forums, etc.

Recent developments in uncertainty management
Latest developments internally and externally likely to give rise to changes in uncertainty management practices.

Sources of useful information
Corporate knowledge bases. External websites including government sites, professional bodies, educational institutions, journals, books and other literature.

Uncertainty/risk language issues
Minimal guidance on uncertainty/risk language issues is appropriate for most readers who do not engage with the risk/uncertainty management literature, provided a clear and consistent variant of 'uncertainty speak' is used throughout, and the way it differs from common practice 'risk speak' is explained appropriately. However, those who engage with a variety of external sources of information will need more guidance.

Table 16.3 Some key dysfunctional behaviours in addressing uncertainty

Po-faced pessimism – simplistic, unmitigated pessimism, normally limited to parts of the organization concerned with hazard and safety management.

Eldorado optimism – simplistic unmitigated optimism which may be coupled to a lack of controls, inappropriate contracts, and a willingness to escalate commitment by taking massive gambles against the odds.

Conspiracy of infallibility – the belief that crisis is unlikely, and disaster is not possible.

Conspiracy of optimism – strong corporate pressures to avoid revealing bad news. In many organizations this is associated with a 'can-do' corporate culture, an emphasis on team loyalty, and a Darwinian survival-of-the-fittest struggle between competing projects.

Macho management – a belief that 'real' managers are those who can cope in a crisis. Good 'fire-fighters', managers who face serious problems and sort them out, are recognised and rewarded over managers who appear to have had no problems (and therefore, it is assumed, must have had an easy job). This leads to a vicious circle where macho managers recruit 'in their own image'. Coupled with a 'can-do' corporate culture, this can lead to habitual overloading of managers, and inevitably, more problems to be wrestled with. (Repenning and Sterman, 2001)

A blame culture – a belief that there is no such thing as bad luck, that when something goes wrong or performance targets are not met, someone, or some group, must be at fault and appropriate sanctions should be applied. This can give rise to 'finger-pointing', 'passing the buck' and 'witch-hunts' with knock-on implications for future working relations between different individuals or groups.

Naked emperor phenomenon – no one is prepared to acknowledge a high level of uncertainty which clearly exists. This applies to the all-too-common insistence of senior management on minimal uncertainty in estimates for planning and other purposes. It may be driven by a pathological dislike of uncertainty at the top, encouraged by an authoritarian culture.

Management by mis-direction – constraint setting without appreciation of the consequences for other performance objectives.

Effective use of planning horizons to avoid nugatory detailed planning and other visible reductions in wasted effort and frustration can also be important. This kind of culture change can make an organization more exciting to work for and make going to work more enjoyable. This in turn can lead to higher quality staff wanting to join (and stay with) the organization, with obvious general benefits. Figure 16.1 portrays the spirit of this aspect of the impact of uncertainty management capability.

If this kind of change takes place in an organization, it will be recognized by everyone involved, even if they have never experienced it before. It is another example of the relevance of the opening quote for this chapter – the issues addressed in Figure 16.1 count, even though they cannot be counted.

The human resource capability for uncertainty (risk) management

The effectiveness of uncertainty management is clearly dependent to a substantial degree on the capability and experience of the people undertaking uncertainty management.

Staff selection, retention, education, training and mentoring clearly need careful attention. The requirements for an effective uncertainty management infrastructure imply a mix of skills and level of capability that is well beyond what some people associate with common practice (project or ERM or safety or financial) risk management. Indeed, one of the design criteria for many common practice risk management processes seems to be a simplistic form that can be

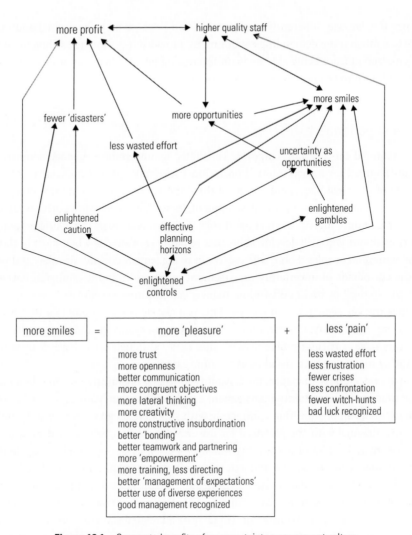

Figure 16.1   Corporate benefits of an uncertainty management culture

applied by staff with limited training and mentoring. More disappointingly, two of the criteria for board level presentations in both private and state sector organizations are frequently held to be 'nothing that will frighten the horses' – because it is too unexpected or challenging, 'delivered in no more than ten minutes'- because of very limited attention spans, euphemistically explained in terms of other pressing concerns. The demands of the PUMP-based approach discussed in this book require a capable coordinator of all the facilitation processes needed plus all the supporting education, training and mentoring of *all* relevant staff plus all the selection and retention of the facilitation, education, training and mentoring staff involved. Leadership and other obvious skills of a very high order are clearly needed.

Inherently weak staff, at all levels, tend to resist change towards a much more demanding environment. The negative effects this can produce need to be neutralized early in the process, to minimize the damage. Inherently strong staff, at all levels, tend to be excited and motivated by change to a much more demanding environment, provided it is more rewarding in all relevant senses – satisfaction from being able to do an interesting job well being at or near the top of the list. Such staff need to be encouraged and supported from the outset.

Skills and experience

The skills required for a strong corporate capability in uncertainty management are similar to the skills required for a good internal operational research/information systems consultancy group. Some of the most successful groups of this kind are used as an elite training ground for future senior executive recruiting and development, as well as a core competitive weapon in the immediate uncertainty management support role. The idea is to attract very bright younger staff as junior consultants who will develop skills that remain very valuable when most of them move on to line management roles. Some will stay on in management consultant roles, and some will become the custodians of uncertainty management processes, training, and staff development. However, the spin-off of very effective line managers and future executives is a central feature. Leadership is the key issue for such groups. This is a classic potential problem that needs to be managed as an opportunity. Organizations which move everyone on to different jobs every two or three years have particular problems with this issue, although some have dealt with it very successfully by modifying their usual rules to some extent.

Developing uncertainty management capability for many organizations should include facilitating and monitoring uncertainty management capability in other 'partner' or 'agent' organizations. For example, an organization contracting with suppliers on an extensive and regular basis ought to be concerned with the potential for uncertainty transfer between the contracting parties. The nature and extent of uncertainty management processes operated by suppliers should have some influence on the nature and extent of uncertainty management undertaken by their business partners. In particular, a client organization might seek to manage uncertainty (risk) by implicitly transferring it to a contractor via a fixed-price contract, but this implicit transfer might be no guarantee that the contractor will identify all related sources of uncertainty, or accept responsibility for managing them. This is one reason why some client organizations require offering contractors to demonstrate uncertainty management capability by requiring them to submit uncertainty management plans along with their fixed-price tenders, recognizing there are important differences between PUMP-based uncertainty management and common practice risk management. Put slightly differently, 'quality matters', in uncertainty management contexts as in other contexts, even if quality is not directly measurable – or 'countable' in Einstein's terms.

Motivation

Motivation is a key factor in the conduct of any organization's participants, and a key management concern is to ensure that all an organization's participants are motivated to work towards appropriate organizational performance objectives.

In respect of uncertainty management, an organization's participants need to be convinced that uncertainty management activity will help them meet their own objectives in a cost effective manner, both directly and indirectly through enhanced organization performance. If not, then participants will be motivated to ignore uncertainty or manage it in their own interests, and they will be less concerned about the impact on organization performance or other participants' objectives. Such considerations apply in all principal–agent relationships whether internal or external to an organization.

For example, consider the relationship between a client and a contractor. For powerful clients putting work out to competitive tender, a requirement that all tenders include an uncertainty management plan is sufficient inducement for offering contractors to comply at some level. However, enlightened client organizations expecting contractors to manage uncertainty in the client's interests will take pains to demonstrate how contractors themselves can benefit directly by improved cost estimation, greater efficiency, improved project control and, ultimately, higher profitability. Such clients will be very aware of the moral hazard of claims-seeking behaviour by contractors who think they are going to lose money on an onerous fixed price contract.

Similar motivation issues arise in persuading different units in the same organization to undertake uncertainty management. Employees or other agents working under aggressive performance targets that are difficult to achieve may be motivated to hide problems from others. For example, Repenning and Sterman (2001) cite the motto of hard-pressed development engineers in one firm, which was 'never reveal you have a problem until you also have the solution'. They also cite another firm where 'engineers called the weekly progress review meetings the Liars Club – each participant overstated the progress of his subsystem and hid known defects from others in the hope that others would be discovered first, giving them time to catch up'.

Motivation is a particularly pertinent consideration if organizations wish to encourage 'whistle blowing'. Unfortunately, employees often hold a belief, sometimes well founded, that 'blowing the whistle' on poor practices or shortcomings in management systems and decision making is unlikely to do them much good personally. Indeed, quite the opposite is the usual perception. Incentives for individuals to 'own up to their own failings' or 'near misses' are usually even more unclear. An obvious effect of staff reluctance to speak out about problems must be that when problems do become obvious, they are bigger than they would otherwise have been. Fear of personal repercussions may be accompanied by self-censoring of doubts as 'defensive avoidance' behaviour. This can happen if the concern is about a single event, and its likelihood of being repeated is uncertain ('the problem might just go away anyway'). It can also arise where the organizational culture encourages team building, camaraderie, and makes strong assumptions of shared common cause/professional integrity. This can cause real 'show-stopper' problems to build up. In any given organization unit, there is a danger that a culture develops which tolerates or condones 'low-level alarms going off'. A potential whistle blower may well have gone along with, or been part of, this culture until things escalate beyond the individual's threshold of acceptability. Self-preservation will motivate them to be concerned about how much they have been part of the situation, and increase the threshold at which they feel impelled to speak out.

Effective uncertainty management should provide a process that has visible, direct benefits to the parties involved. This, however, may be difficult to achieve with conventional 'whistle blowing' or risk management processes. Instead of such conventional processes, organizations concerned about potential failings in their operations probably need to adopt much more proactive systems-focused uncertainty management processes.

Some concluding speculations

The evolution of project uncertainty, opportunity and risk management frameworks has been very rapid in the past decade. For those interested in project uncertainty, opportunity and risk management in general terms, the most productive big issue to address is getting those organizations and institutions that lag well behind the leading edge up to best practice standards defined in clarity efficiency terms. How this is best done is not any easy question to address. A particular difficulty is enabling professional organizations that produce guidelines like those discussed in Chapter 4 to seek excellence which may seem to threaten some of their members. The authors are keen to do what we can in this respect, and we are very hopeful, but our expectations are not overly optimistic. For the past three decades some organizations have maintained project uncertainty management capability at very high levels. But they have been the exception rather than the rule. This is unlikely to change quickly in the short run. This is a major threat for some areas of industry, and a clear opportunity for those who achieve capability that their competitors lack. Similar observations apply to ERM applications.

The relationship between uncertainty management in project, operations and strategic terms needs integration as a corporate issue from a perspective that goes beyond most conventional ERM frameworks, many of which have the same limitations as common practice project risk management approaches.

At a basic level, organizations must have some capability for uncertainty management to continue to survive. Much, if not all, management practice is implicitly about managing opportunity, uncertainty and risk. The basic management tasks of planning, setting objectives, coordination and control procedures are all about clarifying what is to be done, by whom, with what resources and trying to make sure the right things actually happen. Any methodologies, tools, or techniques for understanding and addressing uncertainty and its opportunity and risk implications in one area of management are likely to be transferable to a wide variety of other areas and contexts. Accordingly, the payoffs in terms of improved organization performance of adopting an organization-wide systematic focus on uncertainty management is potentially enormous.

Organizations that have not yet bolstered traditional management concerns of planning, coordination and control with systematic efforts to develop uncertainty management capability are missing a major opportunity. Most organizations are a long way from fully exploiting this opportunity. Consequently, those organizations who seek to develop their uncertainty management capability are likely to gain significant competitive advantage. A starting point is to assess the extent of existing uncertainty management capability. This assessment needs to recognize the importance of facilitating factors such as supporting organizational capabilities, organization culture, and the capability of employees. Current efforts to facilitate this assessment via benchmarking against levels of maturity are in the early stages of development. First, there is a clear need to develop the benchmarking ideas touched on in Chapter 14 into a generally usable operational form in terms of an uncertainty management perspective. The need for sound benchmarking models that are simple when appropriate, without being simplistic, is clear. This chapter should make it clear why they need to be multidimensional to avoid limited characterization.

More efficient, cost effective approaches to developing uncertainty management capability may involve more focused, incremental development that is incorporated into existing decision support systems. Such approaches involve carefully targeting key pulse points in an organization's activities where uncertainty and risk matter most, and where improvements in the quality of decision making will have the greatest impact. However, the success of this approach depends heavily on the knowledge and expertise of uncertainty management possessed by key influencers. For example, if the senior management believes that uncertainty management is merely a formal process for identifying risk events and ranking these events in a rough order of priority for future attention, then most of the reasons for building uncertainty management capability will not be recognized, let alone pursued, and governance will fail.

Building uncertainty management capability needs a strategy, if only because the possible courses of action are so numerous. Plausible strategies for developing uncertainty management capability need to consider the suitability, feasibility, and acceptability of initiatives. Large-scale imposition of formal, 'stand alone' processes may offer the promise of rapid progress (at least initially), but require substantial investment of time, money and effort. Such initiatives often involve the use of proprietary software, simplified processes, and simple forms of analysis on grounds of efficiency and ease of use. However, such approaches can stifle subsequent development of more sophisticated and more effective uncertainty management processes. Also, such initiatives can fail to address significant underlying shortcomings in capability associated with organizational culture, and the capability of employees in respect of uncertainty management.

Understanding the links between concerns about organizational culture and PUMPs plus associated models and concepts used by an organization is the broader 'next frontier' for project uncertainty (risk) management. PUMPs drive culture, and vice versa. A better understanding of how this works, and how to manage it, is *the* big issue for the authors. Some aspects of what is involved are briefly explored in chapter 12 of Chapman and Ward (2002), and are touched on in this book, but these efforts just scratch the surface. Formal contract structures between buyers and suppliers which are different organizations, and buyers and suppliers within the same organization, are the focus of several chapters in Chapman and Ward (2002), with aspects of this work summarized in Chapter 15. Somewhat different issues are addressed in Harwood et al (2009). This is an important part of the 'next frontier' which needs a lot more work in our view.

At the end of the day, most project uncertainty, opportunity and risk are generated by the ways different people perceive issues and react to them, shaped by 'the way we do things around here'. Culture and contracts, including informal contracts, and their interaction with operational PUMPs and background corporate learning processes and infrastructure, take us into territory far removed from the technology uncertainty which drove early project risk management efforts. Culture, incentives and contracts seem to be a favoured natural direction for developments over the next decade.

The real payoffs from uncertainty management come from taking a broad perspective of opportunity, uncertainty and risk, and from appreciating the ways in which uncertainty management can be employed to improve the quality of decision making and organization performance. This book does not provide all the answers, but we hope it will help to point those who read it in the right direction.

This book starts from a project management perspective of the bigger picture. Starting from an operations management, corporate strategic management or fully integrated enterprise management perspective would clearly involve a very different journey. But they should all lead to the same bigger picture.

References

Abrahamson, M. (1973) Contractual risks in tunnelling: how they should be shared. *Tunnels and Tunnelling*, November, 587–598.

Ackermann, F., Eden, C., Williams, T.M. and Howick, S. (2007) Systemic Risk Assessment: a case study. *Journal of the Operational Research Society*, **58**(1), 39–51.

Adams, D. (1979) *The Hitchhiker's Guide to the Galaxy*. London: Pan Books.

Adams, D. (1980) *The Restaurant at the End of the Universe*. London: Pan Books.

Adams, J.R. and Barndt, S.E. (1988) Behavioral implications of the project life cycle, Chapter 10 in Cleland, D.I. and King, W.R. (eds), *Project Management Handbook*. Second edition. New York: Von Nostrand Reinhold.

AIRMIC/ALARM/IRM (2002) *A Risk Management Standard*. London: Association of Insurance and Risk Managers (AIRMIC), Association of Local Authority Risk Managers (ALARM), Institute of Risk Managers (IRM).

AIRMIC Integrated Risk Management Special Interest Group (1999) *A guide to integrated risk management*. London: The Association of Insurance and Risk Managers in Commerce.

Akerlof, G.A. (1970) The market for 'lemons': quality uncertainty and the market mechanism. *Quarterly Journal of Economics*, **84**, 488–500.

Allport, R.J. and Ward, S.C. (2010) Operational risk: the focus for major infrastructure? *Management, Procurement and Law*, **163**, 121–127.

Alpert, M. and Raiffa, H. (1982) A progress report on the training of probability assessors, Chapter 21 in Kahneman, D., Slovic, P. and Tversky, A. (eds), *Judgment Under Uncertainty: Heuristics and Biases*. New York: Cambridge University Press.

Ambrose, S.E. (1988) *Pegasus Bridge, June 6, 1944*. New York: Touchstone.

Ambrose, S.E. (1994) *D-Day, June 6, 1944: The Climatic Battle of World War II*. New York: Touchstone.

Anderson, D.R., Sweeney, D.J., Williams, T.A., Freeman, J. and Shoesmith, E. (2010) *Statistics for Business and Economics*. Second edition. London: Thomson.

Ansoff, H.I. (1984) *Implanting Strategic Management*. Englewood Cliffs, NJ: Prentice-Hall International.

APM (1997) *PRAM Project Risk Analysis and Management Guide*. Norwich: Association for Project Management (APM).

APM (2004) *PRAM Project Risk Analysis and Management Guide*. Second Edition. Norwich: Association for Project Management (APM).

Armstrong, J.S., Denniston, W.B. and Gordon, M.M. (1975) The use of the decomposition principle in making judgments. *Organisation Behaviour and Human Performance*, **14**, 257–263.

AS/NZS 4360 (2004) *Risk Management*. Strathfield: Standards Association of Australia. Available at www.standards.com.au.

Augustine, S. (2005) *Managing Agile Projects*. Prentice Hall: New Jersey.

Baccarini, D. and Archer, R. (2001) The risk ranking of projects: a methodology, *International Journal of Project Management*, **19**(3), 139–145.

Banks, E. and Dunn, R. (2003) *Practical Risk-Management – An Executive Guide to Avoiding Surprises and Losses*. Chichester: John Wiley and Sons Ltd.

Barnes, M. (1984) Effective project organisation. *Building Technology and Management*, December, 21–23.

Baron, D.P. (1972) Incentive contracts and competitive bidding. *American Economic Review*, **62**, 384–394.

Baxter, K. (2010) *Risk Management: FT Fast Track to Success*. Harlow: Pearson Education Limited.

Berny, J. (1989) A new distribution function for risk analysis. *Journal of the Operational Research Society*, **40**(12), 1121–1127.

Bonnai, P., Gourc, D. and Lacosta, G. (2002) The life cycle of technical projects, *Project Management Journal*, **33**(1), 12–19.

British Standard (2000) *BS 6079–3:2000 Project Management – Part 3: Guide to the Management of Business Related Project Risk*. London: British Standards Institution.

British Standard (2001) *IEC 62198:2001 Project Risk Management – Application Guidelines*. London: British Standards Institution.

British Standard (2008) BS 31100:2008 *Risk Management – Code of Practice*. London: British Standards Institution.

Brooks, F.P. (1975) *The Mythical Man-month: Essays on Software Engineering*. Reading, MA: Addison Wesley.

Broome, J. and Perry, J. (2002) How practitioners set share fractions in target cost contracts. *International Journal of Project Management*, **20**, 59–66.

Canes, M.E. (1975) The simple economics of incentive contracting: note. *American Economic Review*, **65**, 478–483.

Chapman, C.B. (1979) Large engineering project risk analysis. *IEEE Transactions on Engineering Management*, EM–26, 78–86.

Chapman, C.B. (1988) Science, engineering and economics: OR at the interface. *Journal of the Operational Research Society*, **39**(1), 1–6.

Chapman, C.B. (1990) A risk engineering approach to project management. *International Journal of Project Management*, **8**(1), 5–16.

Chapman, C.B. (1992a). *Risk Management: Predicting and Dealing with an Uncertain Future*. Exhibit #748, Province of Ontario Environmental Assessment Board Hearings on Ontario Hydro's Demand/Supply Plan, submitted by the Independent Power Producers Society of Ontario, 30 September.

Chapman, C.B. (1992b). My two cents worth on how OR should develop. *Journal of the Operational Research Society*, **43**(7), 647–664.

Chapman, C.B. (2006) Key points of contention in framing assumptions for risk and uncertainty management. *International Journal of Project Management*, **24**, 303–313.

Chapman, C.B. (2008) Sound, practical and fair allowances for uncertainty: a starting position for 'clarity management', in *Tony: An Incredible Man* (Wang, W., Sharples, S. and Martin, H. (eds)). Salford: University of Salford.

Chapman, C.B. and Cooper, D.F. (1983). Parametric discounting. *Omega – International Journal of Management Science*, **11**(3), 303–310.

Chapman, C.B. and Cooper, D.F. (1985) A programmed equity redemption approach to the finance of public projects. *Managerial and Decision Economics*, **6**(2), 112–118.

Chapman, C.B., Cooper, D.F. and Cammaert, A.B. (1984) Model and situation specific OR methods: risk engineering reliability analysis of an L.N.G. facility. *Journal of the Operational Research Society*, **35**, 27–35.

Chapman, C.B., Cooper, D.F., Debelius, C.A. and Pecora, A.G. (1985) Problem solving methodology design on the run. *Journal of the Operational Research Society*, **36**(9), 769–778.

Chapman, C.B., Cooper, D.F. and Page, M.J. (1987) *Management for Engineers*. Chichester: John Wiley & Sons Ltd.

Chapman, C.B. and El Hoyo, J. (1972) Progressive basic decision CPM. *Operational Research Quarterly*, **23**(2), 345–359.

Chapman, C.B. and Harwood, I. (2011) Optimal risk-taking and risk-mitigation, in Cochran, J.J. (ed. in chief) *Wiley Encyclopedia of Operations Research and Management Science*. Chichester: John Wiley & Sons Ltd.

Chapman, C.B. and Howden, M. (1997) Two phase parametric and probabilistic NPV calculations, with possible deferral of disposal of UK Nuclear Waste as an example. *Omega, International Journal of Management Science*, **25**(6), 707–714.

Chapman, C.B., Phillips, E.D., Cooper, D.F. and Lightfoot, L. (1985) Selecting an approach to project time and cost planning. *International Journal of Project Management*, **3**(1), 19–26.

Chapman, C.B. and Ward, S.C. (1994) The efficient allocation of risk in contracts. *Omega—The International Journal of Management Science*, **22**(6), 537–552.

Chapman, C.B. and Ward, S.C. (1996) Valuing the flexibility of alternative sources of power generation. *Energy Policy*, **24**(2), 129–136.

Chapman, C.B. and Ward, S.C. (1997) *Project Risk Management: Processes, Techniques and Insights*. Chichester: John Wiley & Sons Ltd.

Chapman, C.B. and Ward, S.C. (2002) *Managing Project Risk and Uncertainty: A Constructively Simple Approach to Decision Making*. Chichester: John Wiley & Sons Ltd.

Chapman, C.B. and Ward, S.C. (2003) *Project Risk Management: Processes, Techniques and Insights*. Second Edition. Chichester: John Wiley & Sons Ltd.

Chapman, C.B. and Ward, S.C. (2008) Developing and implementing a balanced incentive and risk sharing contracts. *Construction Management and Economics*, **26**(6), 659–669.

Chapman, C.B., Ward, S.C. and Bennell, J.A. (2000) Incorporating uncertainty in competitive bidding. *International Journal of Project Management*, **18**(5), 337–347.

Chapman, C.B., Ward, S.C. and Klein, J.H. (2006) An optimized multiple test framework for project selection in the public sector, with a nuclear waste disposal case-based example. *International Journal of Project Management*, **24**, 373–384.

Charette, R.N. (1993) Essential risk management: note from the front. Second SEI Conference on Risk Management, Pittsburg, Pennsylvania, ITABHI Corporation.

Checkland, P.B. and Scholes, J. (1990) *Soft Systems Methodology in Action*. Chichester: John Wiley & Sons Ltd.

Chevalier, J.M. and Buckles, D. (2007) SAS² 1.0: Instructions for SAS² and Process manager, in Social Analysis Systems² 1.0, http://www.sas-pm.com/ accessed October 2007.

Clark, P. and Chapman, C.B. (1987) The development of computer software for risk analysis: a decision support system development case study. *European Journal of Operational Research*, **29**(3), 252–261.

Cleden, D. (2009) *Managing Project Uncertainty*. Surrey, UK: Gower Publishing.

Cooper, D.F. and Chapman, C.B. (1987) *Risk Analysis for Large Projects – Models, Methods and Cases*. Chichester: John Wiley & Sons Ltd.

Cooper, K.G. (1980) Naval ship production: a claim settled and a framework built. *Interfaces*, **10**(6), 20–36.

Cox, L.A. (2008) What's wrong with risk matrices? *Risk Analysis*, **28**(2), 497–512.

Crosby, A. (1968) *Creativity and Performance in Industrial Organisation*. London: Tavistock Publications.

Cummings, S. (2007) RAAKS internet dossier, scope and brief, http://www.kit.nl/smartsite.shtml?ch=FAB&id=4616&Part=Intro, accessed October 2007.

Curtis, B., Ward, S.C. and Chapman, C.B. (1991) *Roles, Responsibilities and Risks in Management Contracting* (Special Publication 81) London: Construction Industry Research and Information Association (CIRIA).

Dekker, S. (2011) *Drifting into Failure – From Hunting Broken Components to Understanding Complex Systems*. Farnham, UK: Ashgate Publishing Ltd.

DeLoach, J.W. (2000). *Enterprise Wide Risk Management: Strategies for Linking Risk with Opportunity*. London: Financial Times/Prentice Hall.

DeMaere, R., Skulmoski, G., Zaghloul, R. and Hartman, F. (2001) Contracting and the flying trapeze: the trust factor. *Project Management*, **7**(1), 32–35.

Dennison, M. and Morgan, T. (1994) Decision conferencing as a management process – a development programme at Dudley MBC. *OR Insight*, **7**(2), 16–22.

Diffenbach, J. (1982) Influence diagrams for complex strategic issues. *Strategic Management Journal*, **3**, 133–146.

Dixon, N.F. (1987) *Our Own Worst Enemy*. London: Jonathan Cape.

DoE (1994) *Review of Radioactive Waste Management Policy Preliminary Conclusions: A Consultative Document*. Radioactive Substances Division, Department of the Environment.

Doherty, N.A. (2000) *Integrated Risk Management – Techniques and Strategies for Reducing Risk*. New York: McGraw- Hill.

Dowie, J. (1999) Against risk. *Risk Decision and Policy*, **4**(1), 57–73.

Drennan, L.T. and McConnell, A. (2007) *Risk and Crisis Management in the Public Sector*. Abingdon, UK: Routledge.

Eden, C. (1988) Cognitive mapping: a review. *European Journal of Operational Research*, **36**, 1–13.

Eden, C., Williams, T., Ackermann, F. and Howick, S. (2000) The role of feedback dynamics in disruption and delay (D&D) in major projects. *Journal of the Operational Research Society*, **51**, 291–300.

Engineering Council (1993) *Guidelines on Risk Issues*. London.

Fernandez, D. and Fernandez, J. (2008) Agile project management – agilism versus traditional approaches. *The Journal of Computer Information Systems*, **49**(10).

Finlay, P. and Marples, C. (1991) A review of group decision support systems. *OR Insight*, **4**(4), 3–7.

Fischoff, B., Slovic, P. and Lichtenstein, S. (1978) Fault trees: sensitivity of estimated failure probabilistics to problem representation. *Journal of Experimental Psychology: Human Perception and Performance*, **4**, 330–334.

Flyvbjerg, B., Bruzelius, N. and Rothengatter, W. (2003) *Megaprojects and Risk – an Anatomy of Ambition*. Cambridge: Cambridge University Press.

Forrester, J. (1958) Industrial dynamics: a major breakthrough for decision making. *Harvard Business Review*, **36**(4), 37–66.

Forrester, J. (1961) *Industrial Dynamics*. Cambridge, MA: MIT Press.

Freudenburg, W.R. and Gramling, R. (2010) *Blowout in the Gulf: The BP Oil Spill Disaster and the Future of Energy in America*. Cambridge, MA: MIT Press.

Furnham, A. (2000) The brainstorming myth. *Business Strategy Review*, **11**(4), 21–28.

Furnham, A. (2003) *The Incompetent Manager: the Causes, Consequences and Cures of Managerial Failure*. London: Whurr Publishers.

Georgopolous, B.S. (1973) An open system theory model for organizational research. In Negandhi, A.R. (ed.) *Modern Organization Theory*. Kent, Ohio: Kent State University Press, pp. 102–131.

Golenko-Ginzburg, D. (1988) On the distribution of activity time in PERT. *Journal of the Operational Research Society*, **39**(8), 767–771.

Gonik, J. (1978) Tie salemen's bonuses to their forecasts. *Harvard Business Review*, May–June, 116–123.

Gordon, W.J.J. (1956) Operational approach to creativity. *Harvard Business Review*, **34**(6), 41–51.

Gordon, W.J.J. (1968) *Creativity and Performance in Industrial Organisation*. London: Tavistock Publications.

Green, S.D. (1994) Beyond value engineering: SMART value management for building projects. *International Journal of Project Management*, **12**(1), 49–56.

Green, S.D. (2001) Towards an integrated script for risk and value management. *Project Management*, **7** (1), 52–58.

Grenny, J., Maxfield, D. and Shimberg, A (2007) How project leaders can overcome the crisis of silence. *MIT Sloan Management Review*, **48**(4), 46–52.

Grey, S. (1995) *Practical Risk Assessment for Project Management*. Chichester: John Wiley & Sons Ltd.

Hall, W.K. (1975) Why risk analysis isn't working. *Long Range Planning*, December, 25–29.

Hartman, F. and Snelgrove, P. (1996) Risk allocation in lump sum contracts – concept of latent dispute. *Journal of Construction Engineering and Management*. September, 291–296.

Hartman, F., Snelgrove, P. and Ashrafi, R. (1997) Effective wording to improve risk allocation in lump sum contracts. *Journal of Construction Engineering and Management*. December, 379–387.

Harwood, I.A., Ward, S.C. and Chapman, C.B. (2009) A grounded exploration of organisational risk propensity. *Journal of Risk Research*, **12**(5), 563–579.

Hertz, D.B. (1964) Risk analysis in capital investment. *Harvard Business Review*, **42**(1), 95–106.

Hillson, D. (1997) Towards a risk maturity model. *The International Journal of Project and Business Risk Management*. Spring **1**(1), 35–45.

Hillson, D. (2002). Extending the risk process to manage opportunities. *International Journal of Project Management*, **20**(3), 235–240.

HM Treasury (2003a) *The Green Book: Appraisal and Evaluation in Central Government*. London: HM Treasury, 1 Horse Guards Road, London SW1A 2HQ.

HM Treasury (2003b) *The Green Book Supplementary Guidance – Optimism Bias*. www.hm-treasury. gov.uk accessed November 2010.

HMSO (1991) *Economic Appraisal in Central Government: A Technical Guide for Government Departments*. London: HMSO.

Hopkin, P. (2002) *Holistic Risk Management in Practice*, London: Witherby & Co. Ltd.

Hopkinson, M. (2002) Maturity models in practice. *Risk Management Bulletin*, **5**(4).

Hopkinson, M. (2011) *The Project Risk Maturity Model – Measuring and Improving Risk Management Capability*. Abingdon, Oxon: Gower Publishing.

Hopkinson, M., Close, P., Hillson, D. and Ward, S. (eds) (2008) *Prioritising Project Risks – A Short Guide to Useful Techniques*. Princes Risborough, Bucks: Association for Project Management (APM).

Howick, S. (2003) Using systems dynamics to analyze disruption and delay in complex projects for litigation – can modeling purposes be met? *Journal of the Operational Research Society*, **54**, 222–229.

Howick, S., Eden, C., Ackermann, F. and Williams, T.M. (2008) Building confidence in models for multiple audiences: the modelling cascade. *European Journal of Operations Research*, 1068–1087.

Hubbard, D.W. (2009) *The Failure of Risk Management – Why Its Broken and How to Fix It*. Hoboken, New Jersey: John Wiley & Sons Inc.

ICE (1995) *The New Engineering Contract*. Second Edition. Institution of Civil Engineers (ICE). London: Thomas Telford.

ICE and AP (1998) *RAMP Risk Analysis and Management for Projects*. Institution of Civil Engineers (ICE) and the Faculty and Institute of Actuaries (Actuarial Profession or AP). London: Thomas Telford.

ICE and AP (2005) *RAMP Risk Analysis and Management for Projects – A Strategic Framework for Managing Project Risk and its Financial Implications*. Second Edition. Institution of Civil Engineers (ICE) and the Faculty and Institute of Actuaries (AP). London: Thomas Telford.

International Standard (2009) *ISO 31000 Risk Management – Principles and Guidelines*. Switzerland: ISO.

Ishikawa, K. (1986) *Guide to Quality Control*. Second edition. White Plains, NY: Asia Productivity Organization/Quality Resources.

Johnson, G., Scholes, K. and Whittington, R. (2005) *Exploring Corporate Strategy*. Seventh edition. Harlow, Essex: Pearson Education Limited.

Jordanger, I. (1998) Value-oriented management of project uncertainties. *Proceedings of the 14th World Congress on Project Management*, June 10–13, Ljubljana, Volume 2.

Kahneman, D., Slovic, P. and Tversky, A. (eds) (1982) *Judgment Under Uncertainty: Heuristics and Biases*. New York: Cambridge University Press.

Kaplan, R.S. and Norton, D.P. (1992) The balanced scorecard – measures that drive performance. *Harvard Business Review*, **70**(1), 71–79.

Kaplan, R.S. and Norton, D.P. (1993a). Putting the balanced scorecard to work. *Harvard Business Review*, **71**(5), 134–147.

Kaplan, R.S. and Norton, D.P. (1993b). Using the balanced scorecard as a strategic management system. *Harvard Business Review*, **71**(1), 75–85.

Kaplan, R.S. and Norton, D.P. (1996) *The Balanced Scorecard: Translating Strategy into Action*. Boston: Harvard Business School Press.

Keeney, R.L. and Van Winterfeldt, D. (1991) Eliciting probabilities from experts in complex technical problems. *IEEE Transactions on Engineering Management*, **38**(3), 191–201.

Kelly, J. and Male, S. (1993) *Value Management in Design and Construction: The Economic Management of Projects*. UK: E&FN Spon.

Klein, J.H. (1993) Modelling risk trade-off. *Journal of the Operational Research Society*, **44**, 445–460.

Klein, J.H. and Cork, R.B. (1998) An approach to technical risk assessment. *International Journal of Project Management*, **16**(6), 345–351.

Kletz, T.A. (1985) *An Engineer's View of Human Error*. Rugby: The Institution of Chemical Engineers.

Knight, F. (1921) *Risk, Uncertainty and Profit*. Boston: Houghton Mifflin.

Lam, P.T.I. (1999) A sectoral review of risks associated with major infrastructure projects. *International Journal of Project Management*, **17**, 77–87.

Laufer, A., Denker, G.R. and Shenhar, A.J. (1996) Simultaneous management: The key to excellence in capital projects. *International Journal of Project Management*, **14**, 189–199.

Leitch, M. (2008) *Intelligent Internal Control and Risk Management*. Aldershot, Hants: Gower.

Lenfle S. and Loch, C. (2010) Lost roots: how project management came to emphasise control over flexibility and novelty, *California Management Review*, **53**(1), 32–55.

Lewin, K. (1947) Frontiers in group dynamics. *Human Relations*, **1**(1), 5–41.

Lichtenberg, S. (2000) *Proactive Management of Uncertainty using the Successive Principle*. Copenhagen: Polyteknisk Press.

Lichtenstein, S., Fischoff, B. and Phillips, L.D. (1982) Calibration of probabilities: the state of the art to 1980, Chapter 22 in Kahneman, D., Slovic, P. and Tversky, A. (eds), *Judgment Under Uncertainty: Heuristics and Biases*. New York: Cambridge University Press.

Lindquist, E.A. (2001) *Discerning Policy Influence: Framework for a Strategic Evaluation of IDRC-Supported Research*. School of Public Administration, University of Victoria.

Loch, C., De Meyer, A. and Pich, M. (2006) *Managing the Unknown: A New Approach to Managing High Uncertainty and Risks in Projects*. New York: John Wiley & Sons Inc.

Lyles, M.A. (1981) Formulating strategic problems: empirical analysis and model development. *Strategic Management Journal*, **2**, 61–75.

Markowitz, H. (1959) *Portfolio Selection: Efficient Diversification of Investments*. New York: John Wiley & Sons Ltd.

Marples, C. and Riddle, D. (1992) Formulating strategy in the POD—an application of Decision Conferencing with Welwyn Hatfield District Council. *OR Insight*, **5**(2), 12–15.

McCall, J.J. (1970) The simple economics of incentive contracting. *American Economic Review*, **60**, 837–846.

Merkhofer, M.W. (1987) Quantifying judgmental uncertainty: methodology, experiences and insights. *IEEE Transactions on Systems, Man and Cybernetics*, SMC-17, **5**, 741–752.

Miller, R. and Lessard, D. (2001) Understanding and managing risks in large engineering projects. *International Journal of Project Management*, **19**, 437–443.

Miller, K.D. and Waller, H.G. (2003) Scenarios, real options and integrated risk management. *Long Range Planning*, **36**, 93–107.

Mintzberg, H. (1978) Patterns in strategy formation. *Management Science*, **24**(9), 934–948.

Moder, J.J. and Philips, C.R. (1970) *Project Management with CPM and PERT*. New York: Van Nostrand.

Moore, P.G. and Thomas, H. (1976) *Anatomy of Decisions*. London: Penguin Books.

Morgan, M.G. and Herion M. (1990) *Uncertainty—A Guide to Dealing with Uncertainty in Quantitative Risk and Policy Analysis*. New York: Cambridge University Press.

Morris, J. and Imrie, R. (1993) Japanese style subcontracting—its impact on European industries. *Long Range Planning*, **26**(4), 53–58.

Morris, P.W.G. (2009) Implementing strategy through project management; the importance of managing the project front end. Chapter 2 in Williams, T.M., Samset, K. and Suannevag, K.J. (eds) (2009) *Making Essential Choices with Scant Information – Front End Decision Making in Major Projects*. Basingstoke, UK: Palgrave Macmillan.

Network Rail (2007) *The GRIP Process, (v7)* www.networkrail.co.uk/aspx/4171.aspx accessed March 2010.

Newcombe, R. (2003) From client to project stakeholders: a stakeholder mapping approach. *Construction Management and Economics*, **21**(8), 841–848.

Nichols, M. (2007) *Review of Highways Agency's Major Roads Programme: Report to the Secretary of State for Transport*. London: Nichols Group. Available on the Department for Transport (UK) website at www.dft.gov.uk/pgr/roads/nicholsreport/

NUREG (1975) *An Assessment of Accident Risks in US Commercial Nuclear Power Plants*. US Nuclear Regulatory Commission Reactor Safety Study, WASH–1400 (NUREG—75/014).

OGC (2007) *Management of Risk: Guidance for Practitioners*. London: Office of Government Commerce.

Oxford Concise (1995) *The Concise Oxford Dictionary of Current English*. Ninth edition. Thompson, D. (ed.). Oxford: Clarendon Press.

Paulk, M.C., Curtis, W., Chrissis, M. and Weber, C.B. (1993) Capability maturity model, Version 1.1. *IEEE Software* **10**(4), 18–27.

Paulk, M.C., Weber, C.B., Curtis, W. and Chrissis, M. (eds) (1995) *Capability Maturity Model: Guidelines for Improving the Software Process*. Reading, MA: Addison-Wesley.

Perrow, C. (1984) *Normal Accidents: Living with High Risk Systems*. New York: Basic Books.

Perrow, C. (1994) Accidents in high risk systems, *Technology Studies*, **1**(1).

Persig, R.M. (1999) *Zen and the Art of Motorcycle Maintenance: An Enquiry into Values*. 25th Anniversary edition. London: Vintage.

Pidd, M. (1996) *Tools for Thinking: Modelling in Management Science*. Chichester: John Wiley & Sons.

Pilkey, O.H. and Pilkey-Jarvis, L. (2007) *Useless Arithmetic – Why Environmental Scientists Can't Predict the Future*. Columbia University Press, New York.

PMI (1992) Wildeman, M. (ed.). *Project and Program Risk Management: A Guide to Managing Project Risk and Opportunities*. The PMBOK Handbook Series – Volume 6, preliminary edition for trial use and comment, Project Management Institute (PMI), PO Box 43, Drexell Hill PA 19026-0043, USA.

PMI (2008) Project risk management, Chapter 11 in *A guide to the Project Management Body of Knowledge* (PMBOK® Guide), Fourth edition. Newtown Square, Pennsylvania: Project Management Institute (PMI) Inc.

PMI (2009) *Practice Standard for Project Risk Management*. Newtown Square, Pennsylvania: Project Management Institute (PMI) Inc.

Porter, M.E. (1985) *Competitive Advantage: Creating and Sustaining Superior Performance*. New York: Free Press.

Raiffa, H. (1968) *Decision Analysis: Introductory Lectures on Choices Under Uncertainty*. Reading, MA: Addison Wesley.

Reason, J. (1990) *Human Error*. Cambridge: Cambridge University Press.

Reason, J. (1997) *Managing the Risks of Organizational Accidents*. Farnham Surrey, UK: Ashgate.

Reichelstein, S. (1992) Constructing incentive schemes for government contracts: an application of agency theory. *The Accounting Review*, **67**(4), 712–731.

Repenning, J.D. and Sterman, J.D. (2001) Nobody ever gets credit for fixing problems that never happened. *California Management Review*, **43**(4), 64–88.

Rodrigues, A.G. and Williams, T.M. (1998) Systems dynamics in project management: assessing the impacts of client behaviour on project performance, *Journal of the Operational Research Society* **49**, 2–15.

Rosenhead, J. (1989) *Rational Analysis for a Problematic World: Problem Structuring Methods for Complexity, Uncertainty and Conflict*. Chichester: John Wiley & Sons Ltd.

Rosenhead, J. and Mingers, J. (2001) *Rational Analysis for a Problematic World Revisited: Problem Structuring Methods for Complexity, Uncertainty and Conflict*. Chichester: John Wiley & Sons Ltd.

Sabatier, P. and Jenkins-Smith, H.C. (1999) The advocacy coalition framework: an assessment, in Sabatier, P. (ed.), *Theories of the Policy Process*. Boulder: Westview Press, pp. 117–166.

Sadeh, A., Dvir, D. and Shenhar, A. (2000) The role of contract type in the success of R&D defence projects under increasing uncertainty. *Project Management Journal*, **31**(3), 14–22.

Sagan, S.D. (1993) *The Limits of Safety: Organisations, Accidents and Nuclear Weapons*. New Jersey: Princeton University Press.

Samuelson, W. (1986) Bidding for contracts. *Management Science*, **32**(12), 1533–1550.

Scherer, F.M. (1964) The theory of contractual incentives for cost reduction. *Quarterly Journal of Economics*, **78**, 257–280.

Schoemaker, P.J.H. (1995) Scenario planning: a tool for strategic thinking. *Sloan Management Review*, **36**(2), 25–40.

Senge, P.M. (1990) *The Fifth Discipline: The Art and Practice of the Learning Organization*. New York: Doubleday.

Slovic, P., Fischoff, B. and Lichtenstein, S. (1982) Facts versus fears: understanding perceived risk, Chapter 33, in Kahneman, D., Slovic, P. and Tversky, A. (eds), *Judgment Under Uncertainty: Heuristics and Biases*. New York: Cambridge University Press.

Smith, D. and Elliott, D. (eds) (2006) *Key Readings in Crisis Management – Systems and Structure for Prevention and Recovery*. Abingdon, UK: Routledge.

Spetzler, C.S. and Stael von Holstein, C.S. (1975) Probability encoding in decision analysis. *Management Science*, **22**(3), 340–358.

Taleb, N.N. (2007) *The Black Swan – The Impact of the Highly Improbable*. London: Allen Lane, Penguin Books Ltd.

Taylor, A. (1991) Four inch set back for 30 miles of Channel tunnel. *Financial Times*, Tuesday, 9 April.

Thamhain, H.J. and Wileman, D.L. (1975) Conflict management in project life cycles. *Sloan Management Review*, **26**(3), summer.

Thorn, D.G. (1986) *Pricing and Negotiating Defence Contracts*. London: Longman, p. 229.

Trigeorgis, L. (1997) *Real Options: Managerial Flexibility and Strategy in Resource Allocations*. Cambridge MA: MIT Press.

Tummala, V.M.R., Burchett, J.F. (1999) Applying a risk management process (RMP) to manage cost risk for an EHV transmission line project. *International Journal of Project Management*, **17**(4), 223–235.

Turner, B.A. (1994) Causes of disaster: sloppy management. *British Journal of Management* **5**(3), 215–219.

Turner, J.R. (1992) *The Handbook of Project Based Management: Improving Processes for Achieving Your Strategic Objectives*. New York: McGraw-Hill.

Turner, J.R. and Cochrane, R.A. (1993) Goals-and-methods matrix: coping with projects with ill-defined goals and/or methods of achieving them. *International Journal of Project Management*, **11**, 93–102.

Tversky, A. and Kahneman, D. (1974) Judgment under uncertainty: heuristics and biases. *Science*, **185**, 1124–1131; reprinted in Kahneman, D., Slovic, P. and Tversky, A. (eds) (1982) *Judgment Under Uncertainty: Heuristics and Biases*. New York: Cambridge University Press.

van der Heijden, K. (2005) *Scenarios: The Art of Strategic Conversations*. Chichester: John Wiley & Sons Ltd.

Volberda, H.W. (1998) *Building the Flexible Firm – How to Remain Competitive*. Oxford: Oxford University Press.

Walsham, G. (1992) Management science and organizational change: a framework for analysis. *Omega—The International Journal of Management Science*, **20**(1), 1–9.

Ward, S.C. (1989) Arguments for constructively simple models. *Journal of the Operational Research Society*, **40**(2), 141–153.

Ward, S.C. (1999) Assessing and managing important risks. *International Journal of Project Management*, **17**, 331–336.

Ward, S.C. (2001) Exploring the role of the corporate risk manager. *Risk Management: An International Journal*, **3**(1), 7–25.

Ward, S.C. (2005) *Risk Management Organisation and Context*. Institute of Risk Management (IRM) Series. London: Witherby & Co. Ltd.

Ward, S.C. and Chapman, C.B. (1988) Developing competitive bids: a framework for information processing. *Journal of the Operational Research Society*, **39**(2), 123–134.

Ward, S.C. and Chapman, C.B. (1991) Extending the use of risk analysis in project management. *International Journal of Project Management*, **9**(2), 117–123.

Ward, S.C. and Chapman, C.B. (1994) Choosing contractor payment terms. *International Journal of Project Management*, **12**(4), 216–221.

Ward, S.C. and Chapman, C.B. (1995a). Evaluating fixed price incentive contracts. *Omega—The International Journal of Management Science*, **23**(1), 49–62.

Ward, S.C. and Chapman, C.B. (1995b). Risk management and the project life cycle. *International Journal of Project Management*, **13**(3), 145–149.

Ward, S.C. and Chapman, C.B. (2008) Stakeholders and uncertainty management in projects. *Construction Management and Economics*, **26**(6), 563–578.

Ward, S.C., Chapman, C.B. and Curtis, B. (1991) On the allocation of risk in construction projects. *International Journal of Project Management*, **9**(3), 140–147.

Ward, S.C., Klein, J.H., Avison, D., Powell, P. and Keen, J. (1997) Flexibility and the management of uncertainty. *The International Journal of Project and Business Risk Management*, **1**(2), 131–145.

Waring, A. and Glendon, A.I. (1998) *Managing Risk – Critical Issues for Survival and Success into the 21st Century*. London, Thomson Learning.

Wheelwright, S.C. (1978) Reflecting corporate strategy in manufacturing decisions. *Business Horizons*, February, 57–66.

Whiting, C.S. (1958) *Creative Thinking*. New York: Reinhold.

Williams, T.M. (1992) Practical use of distributions in network analysis. *Journal of the Operational Research Society*, **43**(3), 265–270.

Williams, T.M. (2004) Why Monte-Carlo simulation of project networks can mislead, *Project Management Journal*, **35**(3), 53–61.

Williams, T.M. (2005) Assessing and building on project management theory in the light of badly over-run projects. *IEEE Transactions in Engineering Management*, **54**,497–508.

Williams, T.M. (2008) *Management Science in Practice*. Chichester: John Wiley & Sons Ltd.

Williams, T., Eden, C., Ackermann, F. and Tait, A. (1995a). The effects of design changes and delays on project costs. *Journal of the Operational Research Society*, **46**, 809–818.

Williams, T., Eden, C., Ackermann, F. and Tait, A. (1995b). Vicious circles of parallelism. *International Journal of Project Management*, **13**, 151–155.

Woodhouse, J. (1993) *Managing Industrial Risk—Getting Value for Money in Your Business*. London: Chapman and Hall.

Woods, D.D., Dekker, S., Cook, R., Johannesen, L. and Starter, N. (2010) *Beyond Human Error*. Second edition. Farnham, UK: Ashgate Publishing Ltd.

Wynne, B. (1992) Uncertainty and environmental learning – reconceiving science and policy in the preventative paradigm. *Global Environmental Change*, June, 111–127.

Zaghloul, R. and Hartman, F. (2003) Construction contracts: the cost of mistrust. *International Journal of Project Management*, **21**, 419–424.

Glossary of terms as used in this book

Ambiguity uncertainty   Lack of complete/perfect knowledge which could be acquired if plans were made, decisions agreed and other sources of ambiguity in the plain English sense resolved. Uncertainty in the lack of certainty sense as used in this book involves four components: ambiguity uncertainty, inherent variability, event uncertainty and systemic uncertainty. When the meaning is obvious we just use 'ambiguity' instead of 'ambiguity uncertainty'. See Chapter 1.

Balanced incentive and risk sharing (BIARS) contract   Contract using payment scales that incentivize performance on several performance criteria which are balanced so that a client's desired tradeoffs between performance criteria are employed by the contractor and acceptable 'risk sharing' ratios for each performance criterion are used.

Bottom-up   In terms of a model building process, a bottom-up approach starts at a chosen level of decomposition and builds up. For example, a PERT model assumes a level of decomposition defined by the number and nature of the activities chosen, the model building up the uncertainty associated with the duration of each activity via network-based precedence assumptions to define project duration uncertainty.

Clarity   Insight (understanding) which can be shared. Too little clarity is an important decision taking risk. Too much clarity, even if it is obtained in a clarity efficient manner, is an unnecessary drain on resources. What constitutes sufficient understanding and appropriate clarity will depend on the context, and judgements need to be made about how much detail it is worth going into for each aspect of the context under consideration as analysis progresses.

Clarity efficiency   Choosing an approach to analysis that involves the lowest cost in terms of time, effort and other resources to achieve a particular level of clarity – a clarity efficient process.

Clarity efficient process   The lowest cost process of analysis in terms of time and effort and other resources for achieving a particular level of clarity. Tradeoffs between clarity and effort should be considered in terms of clarity efficient processes. An important driver of clarity efficiency is the manner in which qualitative and quantitative analysis is employed in a given context. See Chapter 3.

Composition   In terms of sources of uncertainty, component sources can be composed or aggregated to form a higher level composite. Conversely, a high level composite can be decomposed or disaggregated into lower level composites. A structure is required or implied by the chosen approach to composition or decomposition – a hierarchy which defines the relationships between components.

Constraints, hard and soft   'Hard' constraints are constraints that cannot be relaxed from a particular stakeholder's perspective. 'Soft' constraints are constraints that can be relaxed, albeit at some cost, from a particular stakeholder's perspective. Some constraints may seem 'hard' to those who need to comply, but at a corporate level these constraints may be regarded as 'soft'.

Contingency   The difference between B and E where B is an acceptable commitment level for a performance attribute and E is the expected value of future performance. Performing better than B is usually more likely than performing better than E. Usually B and E are ordered for a positive value. In cost terms contingency = (B − E) > 0.

'Cube' factor   Three-part adjustment factor applied to estimates to adjust for known unknowns, unknown unknowns, and bias (Kuuub adjustment) that can be depicted in a three-dimensional 'cube' format.

Decision diagram   A diagram that portrays the cumulative probability distributions for several alternative courses of action. This facilitates the identification of risk efficient options and clarifies risk–reward tradeoffs. Risk–reward tradeoffs should be considered in terms of choices between risk efficient decisions.

Decomposition   In terms of sources of uncertainty, component sources can be decomposed or disaggregated to form lower level composites. Conversely, a low level composite can be composed or aggregated with other lower level sources to form a higher level composite. A structure is required or implied by the chosen approach to composition or decomposition – a hierarchy which defines the relationships between components.

Hard constraints   'Hard' constraints are constraints that cannot be relaxed from a particular stakeholder's perspective. Conversely, 'soft' constraints are constraints that can be relaxed, albeit at some cost, from a particular stakeholder's perspective. Some constraints may seem 'hard' to those who need to comply, but at a corporate level these constraints may be regarded as 'soft'.

Hierarchy   A structure is required or implied by any chosen approach to composition or decomposition of sources of uncertainty – a hierarchy which defines the relationships between components.

DOT shaping   Label for the lifecycle stage concerned with design, operations and termination strategy development from a design and operations management perspective.

E&D shaping   Label for the lifecycle stage concerned with execution and delivery strategy development from a project management perspective.

Enlightened caution   A willingness to commit resources which may not be needed, because in expected value terms it will be cost effective to commit them.

Enlightened gambles   The selection of a high expected return option from a set of risk efficient options where relatively significant risk that accompanies the high expected returns is considered bearable. Unenlightened gambles are gambles that are not risk efficient, or the risk is not bearable, or both.

Enlightened governance   Governance should operate on a continuous basis as lifecycle stages unfold, not just at lifecycle gateway stages. Enlightened governance involves not just approving plans, but revisiting gateway approvals and replanning where initial planning assumptions no longer hold and reconsidering optimal tradeoffs between project objectives plus optimal tradeoffs between project and broader corporate objectives whenever necessary.

Event uncertainty   Uncertainty associated with events, conditions, circumstances or scenarios that may or may not happen plus associated specific responses.

Fractile methods   A process for estimating cumulative probability distributions by eliciting judgements about the progressive subdivision of ranges into equally likely parts.

Framing assumptions   Fundamental assumptions which shape the conceptual framework and analytical approaches adopted. Starting premises about the nature and scope of risk, opportunity and uncertainty are framing assumptions. The robustness of framing assumptions cannot be tested without using less restrictive framing assumptions.

General responses   Responses that help to manage a number or combination of sources of uncertainty at the same time, including the accumulation of knock-on effects associated with multiple sources which may not have been identified.

Inherent variability   Uncertainty about the future size of a contextual variable, such as inflation rates or weather variations.

Iteration   An essential feature of clarity efficient PUMPs describing the revisiting or looping back to earlier steps within a PUMP phase or to earlier phases or to earlier analysis in any given lifecycle stage or to an earlier lifecycle stage. The purpose of any iteration is to develop, restructure, refine or reconsider aspects of analysis undertaken to date where this is useful. Flexible and effective management of iterations is central to clarity efficient uncertainty management. Not to be confused with recurrent processes carried out at different points in a project lifecycle over time.

Knowledge lens   A conceptual device to indicate a focus on uncertainty as incomplete or imperfect knowledge beyond the direct focus of performance uncertainty management processes. For example, managing uncertainty as incomplete knowledge includes concerns such as: 'What do we need to know to get to the next stage in the project lifecycle beyond what a performance lens perspective will tell us directly?' Addressed over all stages early in a project lifecycle, this can serve a number of useful purposes, including identifying sources of uncertainty which will be resolved before commitments need to be made.

KUMP   Knowledge uncertainty management process. A process based on a knowledge lens perspective. A reminder that uncertainty needs management in a number of ways, a PUMP approach being the focus of this book. KUMPs can support PUMPs.

Lifecycle   The project (asset/change) lifecycle, with 12 notional stages, as set out in the nominal project (asset/change) lifecycle of Table 1.3. The term 'asset lifecycle' is used to emphasize a concern with the whole lifecycle from a client's corporate perspective. Some people may think of a 'project lifecycle' that starts later and ends sooner than the lifecycle in Table 1.3.

Minimalist approach   A histogram-based approach to range estimates using one class defined by a plausible maximum and minimum value approximating P90 and P10 values. See Chapter 2. Usually referred to in this book as a minimum clarity approach.

Minimum clarity approach   An approach to quantifying uncertainty that provides the minimum acceptable level of clarity for the lowest feasible level of effort. More clarity provided in an efficient fashion is always an option, but less clarity than this minimum will be a fundamental problem. The characteristics of a minimum clarity approach are set out in Table 2.1.

O&S   Label for the operation and support stage of the asset lifecycle from an operations management perspective.

Opportunity   Possible favourable outcomes – a nominal definition.

Opportunity efficiency   Risk efficiency for all relevant performance objectives including clarity efficiency plus appropriate risk–reward tradeoffs for all relevant performance objectives and appropriate tradeoffs between all relevant performance objectives. 'Appropriate tradeoffs' include being on an efficient frontier for all objectives, generalizing risk and clarity effeciency. Opportunity efficiency involves a minimum level of risk for any given level of expected outcome for any attribute of interest including non-measurable performance attributes.

Opportunity/risk datum   The point in a range of possible outcomes for a performance attribute of interest that defines the boundary between what are regarded as favourable or unfavourable possible outcomes. For management purposes this datum point might correspond to some designated performance target. This book assumes that the expected value of future performance is the default opportunity/risk datum. Alternatives that may need to be considered include corporate/personal commitment values, corporate/personal stretch target values and, in the case of safety, aspiration values such as zero fatalities or injuries.

Performance lens   A conceptual device to indicate a focus on uncertainty about the achievement of objectives. A performance lens approach to uncertainty is used to directly address questions about likely performance outcomes, decisions involving tradeoffs between all relevant objectives, and optimization of performance by optimizing plans. Opportunity and risk are defined by uncertainty seen through a performance lens.

PIGs   Probability impact grids.

Plans   Plans may be defined in terms of activities, resource plans for activities, relationships and contracts, business cases and so on – see the seven Ws discussion in Chapter 1 and Figure 1.2.

Plans, action   Action plans are the front-end components of tactical plans which involve a commitment to implementation in terms of taking specific actions.

Plans, base   A generic label for 'no-problem, stretch-target plans, what should happen if we capture all relevant opportunities and manage all relevant threats using a clarity efficient PUMP and we are lucky'. Base plans may resemble reference plans after removal of provisions and contingencies and including proactive responses to uncertainty.

Plans, commitment   Commitment plans are plans which it is sensible to commit to, bearing in mind the cost of failing to meet commitments, the cost of adding too much contingency allowance when defining commitment values, the scope for being unlucky and the overall implications of being unlucky.

Plans, contingency   The operational form of recommended reactive responses which include decision rules initiating the reactive responses. Contingency plans reflect anticipated potential departures from base plans.

Plans, reference   Prototype (base or commitment) plans that may also reflect some implicit provisions and contingency. Reference plans reflect the project description at a strategic level captured at the start of the define phase when the PUMP is initiated in the execution and delivery strategy shaping stage of the lifecycle if a PUMP process starts then.

Plans, strategic   Base, contingency and commitment plans developed initially in the strategy shaping stages of the project lifecycle.

Plans, tactical   Base, contingency and commitment plans that provide more detail for implementation than strategic plans.

Project An illustrative definition used in Chapter 1 is:

> *an endeavour in which human, material and financial resources are organized in a novel way, to undertake a unique scope of work of given specification, within constraints of cost and time, so as to achieve unitary, beneficial change, through the delivery of quantified and qualitative objectives.*
>
> —Turner, 1992

The beneficial change may involve the creation of a physical asset or changes in organizational processes. A project may be part of a larger project, or part of a sequence of projects, or may itself be managed as a set of subprojects. Figure 1.1 illustrates three basic interconnected project structures. [In this book the term project is used in inclusive terms, to include 'programmes' and 'portfolios' as sets of lower level projects connected by linked/interrelated objectives and shared resources.]

Provision The difference between E and T, where E is the expected value of a performance attribute and T is any relevant target value. Usually, performing better than T is less likely than performing better than E. Usually, E and T are ordered for a positive value. In cost terms: provision = $(E - T) > 0$.

PUMP Performance uncertainty management process. The basic PUMP described in this book is introduced in Chapter 4 and developed in more detail in Part II. This basic PUMP corresponds to the execution and delivery shaping stage PUMP.

PUMP pack A convenient term for the set of PUMPs appropriately adapted for each of the different lifecycle stages. Taken together this set of PUMPs provides a complete set of related processes for addressing uncertainty over the whole of the asset lifecycle. Part III explains the nature of the PUMP pack.

Responses, general Responses that help to manage a number or combination of sources of uncertainty at the same time, including the accumulation of knock-on effects associated with multiple sources which may not have been identified.

Responses, specific Responses that are specific to particular sources of uncertainty.

Risk Possible unfavourable outcomes – a nominal definition.

Risk efficiency Achieved by making all choices from risk efficient options.

Risk efficient option An option that has the lowest level of risk for a given level of expected performance, or the highest level of expected performance for a given level of risk, with respect to a relevant performance attribute.

Sensitivity diagram A portrayal of a set of cumulative probability distributions that show the combined effect of progressively incorporating additional sources of uncertainty. The result is a visual indication of which sources make the greatest contribution to overall uncertainty about a particular type of outcome or performance attribute. These sensitivity diagrams can be used in a hierarchical structure to portray the implications of all variability associated with sources of uncertainty plus all dependence between all the sources of uncertainty involved as captured by the PUMP, be it simple statistical dependence or more complex dependence. They are an alternative to more common forms of sensitivity analysis which consider one parameter varying at a time, assuming independence.

Seven Ws Key questions relating to who, why, what, whichway, wherewithal, when and where. See Table 1.4 and Figure 1.2.

Shaping   Shaping in the sense of strategy shaping and tactics shaping involves making decisions about how best to proceed in terms of project and process objectives, addressing all aspects of uncertainty. This involves developing all relevant base and contingency plans.

Simple scenario approach   An estimating process for sizing uncertainty in the absence of data based on a rectangular histogram approach. The minimum clarity approach is a special case. More general cases can provide whatever level of clarity may be required without being required to use specific probability distribution function assumptions. The basic simple scenario approach and variants are explained in Chapter 10.

Soft constraints   'Soft' constraints are constraints that can be relaxed from a particular stakeholder's perspective, at a cost. Conversely, 'hard' constraints are constraints that cannot be relaxed from a particular stakeholder's perspective. Some constraints may seem 'hard' to those who need to comply, but at a corporate level these constraints may be regarded as 'soft'.

Sources, primary sources, secondary sources, tertiary sources   Sources of uncertainty associated with base plans are primary sources, leading to primary responses. Primary responses are first-level and other higher order descriptions of responses to identified sources of uncertainty. Sources of uncertainty associated with primary responses are secondary sources, leading to secondary responses. Tertiary and further higher order (deeper) levels of sources and responses may be worth employing in particular circumstances.

Specific responses   Responses that are specific to particular sources of uncertainty.

Systemic uncertainty   Uncertainty involving interdependencies between contextual factors and general or systemic responses. May include uncertainty about the existence and nature of such effects. May be contained within sources of uncertainty used for modelling purposes, or involve important dependences between sources. May be due to underlying common influences such as the level of economic activity, perhaps modelled by simple forms of statistical dependence. May involve knock-on effects which can be very complex.

Top-down   In terms of uncertainty about the achievement of any given objective, a top-down view implies seeing all associated variability in terms of a single source which is a composite that can be decomposed. Clarity efficiency is about choosing the most effective decomposition structure, if one is needed. Maintaining an overall, top-down perspective means considering all relevant objectives, whether or not they are measurable.

Uncertainty   Lack of certainty – a nominal definition.

Unenlightened gambles   Gambles which are not risk efficient, or the risk is not bearable, or both.

Variability uncertainty   A composite of sources of uncertainty which may include inherent variability, ambiguity uncertainty, event uncertainty and systemic uncertainty. Most sources of uncertainty look like variability uncertainty from a top-down perspective at a low level of decomposition. For example, a PERT model of project duration treats all sources of uncertainty for each activity as a single source, independent of all other activities, with no associated response modelling.

Working assumptions   Assumptions of convenience we can and should test for robustness.

Index